Lecture Notes of the Institute for Computer Sciences, Social Informatics and Telecommunications Engineering 201

More information about this series at http://www.springer.com/series/8197

Shangguang Wang · Ao Zhou (Eds.)

Collaborate Computing: Networking, Applications and Worksharing

12th International Conference, CollaborateCom 2016
Beijing, China, November 10–11, 2016
Proceedings

 Springer

Editors
Shangguang Wang
Beijing University of Posts
and Telecommunications
Beijing
China

Ao Zhou
Beijing University of Posts
and Telecommunications
Beijing
China

ISSN 1867-8211 ISSN 1867-822X (electronic)
Lecture Notes of the Institute for Computer Sciences, Social Informatics
and Telecommunications Engineering
ISBN 978-3-319-59287-9 ISBN 978-3-319-59288-6 (eBook)
DOI 10.1007/978-3-319-59288-6

Library of Congress Control Number: 2017942991

Printed on acid-free paper

This Springer imprint is published by Springer Nature
The registered company is Springer International Publishing AG
The registered company address is: Gewerbestrasse 11, 6330 Cham, Switzerland

Preface

Over the past two decades, many organizations and individuals have relied on electronic collaboration between distributed teams of humans, computer applications, and/or autonomous robots to achieve higher productivity and produce joint products that would have been impossible to develop without the contributions of multiple collaborators. Technology has evolved from standalone tools to open systems supporting collaboration in multi-organizational settings, and from general purpose tools to specialized collaboration grids. Future collaboration solutions that fully realize the promises of electronic collaboration require advancements in networking, technology and systems, user interfaces and interaction paradigms, and interoperation with application-specific components and tools.

The CollaborateCom 2016 conference series is a major venue in which to present the successful efforts to address the challenges presented by collaborative networking, technology and systems, and applications. This year's conference continued with several of the changes made for CollaborateCom 2015, and its topics of interest include, but are not limited to: participatory sensing, crowdsourcing, and citizen science; architectures, protocols, and enabling technologies for collaborative computing networks and systems; autonomic computing and quality of services in collaborative networks, systems, and applications; collaboration in pervasive and cloud computing environments; collaboration in data-intensive scientific discovery; collaboration in social media; big data and spatio-temporal data in collaborative environments/systems; collaboration techniques in data-intensive computing and cloud computing.

Overall, CollaborateCom 2016 received a record 116 paper submissions, up slightly from 2015 and continuing the growth compared with other years. All papers were rigorously reviewed, with all papers receiving at least three and many four or more reviews with substantive comments. After an on-line discussion process, we accepted 43 technical track papers and 33 industry track papers, three papers for the Multivariate Big Data Collaborations Workshop and two papers for the Social Network Analysis Workshop. ACM/Springer CollaborateCom 2016 continued the level of technical excellence that recent CollaborateCom conferences have established and upon which we expect future ones to expand.

This level of technical achievement would not be possible without the invaluable efforts of many others. My sincere appreciation is extended first to the area chairs, who made my role easy. I also thank the many Program Committee members, as well as their subreviewers, who contributed many hours for their reviews and discussions, without which we could not have realized our vision of technical excellence. Further, I thank the CollaborateCom 2016 Conference Committee, who provided invaluable assistance in the paper-review process and various other places that a successful conference requires. Finally, and most of all, the entire committee acknowledges the contributions of the authors who submitted their high-quality work, for without community support the conference would not happen.

April 2017

Shangguang Wang
Ao Zhou

Organization

General Chair and Co-chairs

Shangguang Wang   Beijing University of Posts and Telecommunications, Beijing, China
Zibin Zheng   Sun Yat-sen University, China
Xuanzhe Liu   Peking University, China

TPC Co-chairs

Ao Zhou   Beijing University of Posts and Telecommunications, China
Yutao Ma   Wuhan University, China
Mingdong Tang   Hunan University of Science and Technology, China

Workshop Chairs

Shuiguang Deng   Zhejiang University, China
Sherry Xu   CSIRO, China

Local Arrangements Chairs

Ruisheng Shi   Beijing University of Posts and Telecommunications, China
Jialei Liu   Beijing University of Posts and Telecommunications, China

Publication Chairs

Shizhan Chen   Tianjing University, China
Yucong Duan   Hainan University, China
lingyan Zhang   Beijing University of Posts and Telecommunications, China

Social Media Chairs

Xin Xin   Beijing Institute of Technology, China
Jinliang Xu   Beijing University of Posts and Telecommunications, China

Website Chair

Songtai Dai   Beijing University of Posts and Telecommunications, China

Conference Manager

Lenka Laukova   EAI - European Alliance for Innovation, China

Contents

Industry Track Papers

**Security and Privacy in Collaborative System: Workshop
on Multivariate Big Data Collaborations in Meteorology
and Its Interdisciplines**

**Security and Privacy in Collaborative System: Workshop
on Social Network Analysis**

Default Track

Web APIs Recommendation for Mashup Development Based on Hierarchical Dirichlet Process and Factorization Machines

Buqing Cao[1,2(✉)], Bing Li[2], Jianxun Liu[1], Mingdong Tang[1],
and Yizhi Liu[1]

[1] School of Computer Science and Engineering,
Hunan University of Science and Technology, Xiangtan, China
buqingcao@gmail.com, ljx529@gmail.com,
tangmingdong@gmail.com, liuyizhi928@gmail.com
[2] State Key Laboratory of Software Engineering, International School
of Software, Wuhan University, Wuhan, China
bingli@whu.edu.cn

Abstract. Mashup technology, which allows software developers to compose existing Web APIs to create new or value-added composite RESTful Web services, has emerged as a promising software development method in a service-oriented environment. More and more service providers have published tremendous Web APIs on the internet, which makes it becoming a significant challenge to discover the most suitable Web APIs to construct user-desired Mashup application from these tremendous Web APIs. In this paper, we combine hierarchical dirichlet process and factorization machines to recommend Web APIs for Mashup development. This method, firstly use the hierarchical dirichlet process to derive the latent topics from the description document of Mashups and Web APIs. Then, it apply factorization machines train the topics obtained by the HDP for predicting the probability of Web APIs invoked by Mashups and recommending the high-quality Web APIs for Mashup development. Finally, we conduct a comprehensive evaluation to measure performance of our method. Compared with other existing recommendation approaches, experimental results show that our approach achieves a significant improvement in terms of MAE and RMSE.

Keywords: Hierarchical dirichlet process · Factorization machines · Web APIs recommendation · Mashup development

1 Introduction

Currently, Mashup technology has emerged as a promising software development method in a service-oriented environment, which allows software developers to compose existing Web APIs to create new or value-added composite RESTful Web services [1]. More and more service providers have published tremendous Web APIs that enable software developers to easily integrate data and functions by the form of Mashup [2]. For example, until July 2016, there has already been more than 15,400

© ICST Institute for Computer Sciences, Social Informatics and Telecommunications Engineering 2017
S. Wang and A. Zhou (Eds.): CollaborateCom 2016, LNICST 201, pp. 3–15, 2017.
DOI: 10.1007/978-3-319-59288-6_1

Web APIs on ProgrammableWeb, and the number of it is still increasing. Consequently, it becomes a significant challenge to discover most suitable Web APIs to construct user-desired Mashup application from tremendous Web APIs.

To attack the above challenge, some researchers exploit service recommendation to improve Web service discovery [3, 4]. Where, the topic model technique (e.g. Latent Dirichlet Allocation (LDA) [5]) has been exploited to derive latent topics of Mashup and Web APIs for improving the accuracy of recommendation [3, 4]. A limitation of LDA is that it needs to determine the optimal topics number in advance. For each different topic number in model training, there have a new LDA model training process, resulting in time-consuming problem. To solve this problem, Teh et al. [6] proposed a non-parametric Bayesian model—Hierarchical Dirichlet Process (HDP), which automatically obtain the optimal topics number and save the training time. Thus, it can be used to derive the topics of Mashups and Web APIs for achieving more accurate service recommendation.

In recent years, matrix factorization is used to decompose Web APIs invocations in historical Mashups for service recommendations [7, 8]. It decomposes the Mashup-Web API matrix into two lower dimension matrixes. However, matrix factorization based service recommendation relies on rich records of historical Mashup-Web API interactions [8]. Aiming to the problem, some recent research works incorporated additional information, such as users' social relations [9] or location similarity [10], into matrix factorization for more accurate recommendation. Even though matrix factorization relieves the sparsity between Mashup and Web APIs, it is not applicable for general prediction task but work only with special, single input data. When more additional information, such as the co-occurrence and popularity of Web APIs, is incorporated into matrix factorization model, its performance will decrease. FMs, a general predictor working with any real valued feature vector, was proposed by S. Rendle [11, 12], which can be applied for general prediction task and models all interactions between multiple input variables. So, FMs can be used to predict the probability of Web APIs invoked by Mashups.

In this paper, we propose a Web APIs recommendation approach based on HDP and FMs for Mashup development. The contributions of this paper are as follows:

- *We use the HDP to derive the latent topics from the description document of Mashups and Web APIs. Based on these topics, similar Mashups and similar Web APIs will be addressed to support the model training of FMs.*
- *We apply the FMs to train the topics obtained by the HDP for predicting the probability of Web APIs invocated by Mashups and recommending the high-quality Web APIs for Mashup development. In the FMs, multiple useful information is utilized to improve the prediction accuracy of Web APIs recommendation.*
- *We conduct a set of experiments based on a real-world dataset from ProgrammableWeb. Compared with other existing methods, the experimental results show that our method achieves a significant improvement in terms of MAE and RMSE.*

The rest of this paper is organized as follows: Sect. 2 describes the proposed method. Section 3 gives the experimental results. Section 4 presents related works. Finally, we draw conclusions and discuss our future work in Sect. 5.

2 Method Overview

2.1 The Topic Modeling of Mashup and Web APIs Using HDP

The Hierarchical Dirichlet Process (HDP) is a powerful non-parametric Bayesian method [13], and it is a multi-level form of the Dirichlet Process (DP) mixture model. Suppose (Θ, B) be a measurable space, with G_0 a probability measure on the space, and suppose a_0 be a positive real number. A *Dirichlet Process* [14] is defined as a distribution of a random probability measure G over (Θ, B) such that, for any finite measurable partition $(A_1, A_2, \ldots, A_r)$ of Θ, the random vector $(G(A_1), \ldots, G(A_r))$ is distributed as a finite-dimensional Dirichlet distribution with parameters $(a_0 G_0(A_1), \ldots, a_0 G_0(A_r))$:

$$(G(A_1), \ldots, G(A_r)) \sim Dir(a_0 G_0(A_1), \ldots, a_0 G_0(A_r)) \tag{1}$$

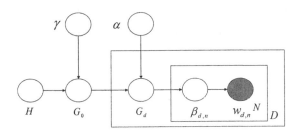

Fig. 1. The probabilistic graph of HDP

In this paper, we use the HDP to model the documents of Mashup and Web APIs. The probabilistic graph of the HDP is shown in Fig. 1, in which the documents of Mashup or Web APIs, their words and latent topics are presented clearly. Here, D represents the whole Mashup documents set which is needed to derive topics, and d represents each Mashup document in D. γ and a_0 are the concentration parameter. H is the base probability measure and G_0 is the global random probability measure. G_d represents a generated topic probability distribution of Mashup document d, $\beta_{d,n}$ represents a generated topic of the nth word in the d from G_d, and $w_{d,n}$ represents a generated word from $\beta_{d,n}$.

The generative process of our HDP model is as below:

(1) *For the D, generate the probability distribution $G_0 \sim DP(\gamma, H)$ by sampling, which is drawn from the Dirichlet Process $DP(\gamma, H)$.*

(2) *For each d in D, generate their topic distributions $G_d \sim DP(a, G_0)$ by sampling, which is drawn from the Dirichlet Process $DP(a, G_0)$.*

(3) *For each word $n \in \{1, 2, \ldots, N\}$ in d, the generative process of them is as below:*

- *Draw a topic of the nth word $\beta_{d,n} \sim G_d$, by sampling from G_d;*
- *Draw a word $w_{d,n} \sim Multi(\beta_{d,n})$ from the generated topic $\beta_{d,n}$.*

To achieve the sampling of HDP, it is necessary to design a construction method to infer the posterior distribution of parameters. Here, Chinese Restaurant Franchise (CRF) is a typical construction method, which has been widely applied in document topic mining. Suppose J restaurants share a common menu $\phi = (\phi)_{k=1}^{K}$, K is the amount foods. The jth restaurant contains m_j tables $(\psi_{jt})_{t=1}^{m_j}$, each table sits N_j customers. Customers are free to choose tables, and each table only provides a kind of food. The first customer in the table is in charge of ordering foods, other customers share these foods. Here, restaurant, customer and food are respectively corresponding to the document, word and topic in our HDP model. Suppose δ is a probability measure, the topic distribution θ_{ji} of word x_{ji} can be regarded as a customer. The customer sits the table ψ_{jt} with a probability $\frac{n_{jt}}{i-1+a_0}$, and shares the food ϕ_k, or sits the new table $\psi_{jt_{new}}$ with a probability $\frac{a_0}{i-1+a_0}$. Where, n_{jt} represents the amount of customers which sit the tth table in the jth restaurant. If the customer selects a new table, he/she can assign the food ϕ_k for the new table with a probability $\frac{m_k}{\sum_k m_k + \gamma}$ according to popularity of selected foods, or new foods $\phi_{k_{new}}$ with a probability $\frac{\gamma}{\sum_k m_k + \gamma}$. Where, m_k represents the amount of tables which provides the food ϕ_k. We have the below conditional distributions:

$$\theta_{ji} | \theta_{ji}, \theta_{ji}, \ldots, \theta_{ji}, a_0, G_0 \sim \sum_{t=1}^{m_j} \frac{n_{jt}}{i-1+a_0} \delta_{\psi_{jt}} + \frac{a_0}{i-1+a_0} G_0 \tag{2}$$

$$\psi_{jt} | \psi_{jt}, \psi_{jt}, \ldots, \psi_{jt}, \gamma, H \sim \sum_{k=1}^{K} \frac{m_k}{\sum_k m_k + \gamma} \delta_{\phi_k} + \frac{\gamma}{\sum_k m_k + \gamma} H \tag{3}$$

Thus, the construction of CRF justly is the process of assigning tables and foods for customers. Actually, the process of assigning tables and foods for customers is respectively corresponding to topic assignment of words and document topic clustering in Mashup documents set. After completing the construction of CRF, we use the Gibbs sampling method to infer the posterior distribution of parameters in the HDP model, and thus obtain topics distribution of whole Mashup documents set.

Similarly, the HDP model construction and topic generation process of Web APIs document set are same to those of Mashup documents set, which are not presented in details.

2.2   Web APIs Recommendation for Mashup Using FMs

2.2.1   Rating Prediction in Recommendation System and FMs

Traditional recommendation system is a user-item two-dimension model. Suppose user set $U = \{u_1, u_2, \ldots\}$, item set $I = \{i_1, i_2, \ldots\}$, the rating prediction function is defined as below:

$$y : U \times I \rightarrow R \tag{4}$$

Here, y represents the rating, i.e. $y(u, i)$ is the rating of user u to item i. The task of rating prediction is to predict the rating of any user-item pairs.

FMs is a general predictor, which can estimate reliable parameters under very high sparsity (like recommender systems) [11, 12]. The FMs combines the advantages of SVMs with factorization models. It not only works with any real valued feature vector like SVMs, but also models all interactions between feature variables using factorized parameters. Thus, it can be used to predict the rating of items for users. Suppose there are an input feature vector $x \in R^{n*p}$ and an output target vector $y = (y_1, y_2, \ldots, y_n)^T$. Where, n represents the amount of input-output pairs, p represents the amount of input features, i.e. the ith row vector $x_i \in R^p$, p means x_i have p input feature values, and y_i is the predicted target value of x_i. Based on the input feature vector x and output target vector y, the 2-order FMs can be defined as below:

$$\hat{y}(x) := w_0 + \sum_{i=1}^{p} w_i x_i + \sum_{i=1}^{p} \sum_{j=i+1}^{p} x_i x_j \sum_{f=1}^{k} v_{i,f} v_{j,f} \tag{5}$$

Here, k is the factorization dimensionality, w_i is the strength of the ith feature vector x_i, and $x_i x_j$ represents all the pairwise variables of the training instances x_i and x_j. The model parameters $\{w_0, w_1, \ldots, w_p, v_{1,1}, \ldots, v_{p,k}\}$ that need to be estimated are:

$$w_0 \in R, w \in R^n, V \in R^{n*k} \tag{6}$$

2.2.2 The Prediction and Recommendation of Web APIs for Mashup Based on FMs

In this paper, the prediction target is a typical classification problem, i.e. $y = \{-1, 1\}$. The Web APIs prediction is defined as a task of ranking Web APIs and recommending adequate relevant Web APIs for the given Mashup. If $y = 1$, then the relevant API will be chosen as a member Web API of the given Mashup. But in practice, we can only obtain a predicted decimal value ranging from 0 to 1 derived from the formula (5) for each input feature vector. We rank these predicted decimal values and then classify them into positive value (+1, the Top-K results) and negative value (−1). Those who have positive values will be recommended to the target Mashup.

As described in Sect. 2.2.1, traditional recommendation system is a two-dimension model of user-item. In our FMs modeling of Web APIs prediction, active Mashup can be regarded as user, and active Web APIs can be regarded as item. Besides the two-dimension features of active Mashup and Web APIs, other multiple dimension features, such as similar Mashups, similar Web APIs, co-occurrence and the popularity of Web APIs, can be exploited as input features vector in FMs modeling. Thus, the two-dimension of prediction model in formula (4) can be expanded to a six-dimension prediction model:

$$y : MA \times WA \times SMA \times SWA \times CO \times POP \rightarrow S \tag{7}$$

Here, MA and WA respectively represent the active Mashup and Web APIs, SMA and SWA respectively represent the similar Mashups and similar Web APIs, CO and POP

respectively represent the co-occurrence and popularity of Web APIs, and S represents the prediction ranking score. Especially, we exploit the latent topics probability of both the documents of similar Mashup and similar Web APIs, to support the model training of FMs, in which these latent topics are derived from our HDP model in the Sect. 2.1.

	Mashup (MA)				Web APIs (WA)				Similar Web APIs (SWA)				Similar Mashup (SMA)				Co-occurrence (CO)				Popularity (POP)		Score (S)	
X_1	0	1	0	...	1	0	0	...	0	0.3	0.7	...	0.3	0	0.7	...	0	0.5	0.5	...	12	0.36 (-1)	y_1
X_2	1	0	0	...	1	0	0	...	0	0.5	0.5	...	0	0.5	0.5	...	0	1	0	...	3	0.92 (+1)	y_2
X_3	0	1	0	...	0	1	0	...	0.7	0	0.3	...	0.5	0	0.5	...	0.5	0	0.5	...	7	0.17 (-1)	y_3
X_4	0	0	1	...	0	1	0	...	0.6	0	0.4	...	0.4	0.6	0	...	0.5	0	0.5	...	21	0.43 (-1)	y_4
X_5	0	0	1	...	0	0	1	...	0.3	0.7	0	...	0.1	0.9	0	...	0.5	0.5	0	...	5	0.69 (+1)	y_5
X_6	1	0	0	...	0	0	1	...	0.4	0.1	0	...	0	0.8	0.2	...	0.5	0.5	0	...	3	0.28 (-1)	y_6
X_7	0	1	0	...	0	1	0	...	0.4	0	0.6	...	0.4	0	0.6	...	0.5	0	0.5	...	8	0.55 (+1)	y_7
X_8	0	0	1	...	1	0	0	...	0	0.8	0.2	...	0.7	0.3	0	...	0	1	0	...	1	0.74 (+1)	y_8
...	...	...	...	...	...	...	...	...	...	...	...	...	...	...	...	...	...	...	...	...	...	... ...	
	M_1	M_2	M_3	...	A_1	A_2	A_3	...	A_1	A_2	A_3	...	M_1	M_2	M_3	...	A_1	A_2	A_3	...	Freq	... ...	
	Box1				Box2				Box3				Box4				Box5				Box6		

Fig. 2. The FMs model of recommending web APIs for mashup

The above Fig. 2 is a FMs model example of recommending Web APIs for Mashup, in which the data includes two parts (i.e. an input feature vector set X and an output target set Y). Each row represents an input feature vector x_i with its corresponding output target y_i. In the Fig. 2, the first binary indicator matrix (Box 1) represents the active Mashup MA. For one example, there is a link between M_2 and A_1 at the first row. The next binary indicator matrix (Box 2) represents the active Web API WA. For another example, the active Web API at the first row is A_1. The third indicator matrix (Box 3) indicates *Top-A* similar Web APIs SWA of the active Web API in Box 2 according to their latent topics distribution similarity derived from HDP described in Sect. 2.2. In Box 3, the similarity between A_1 and A_2 (A_3) is 0.3 (0.7). The forth indicator matrix (Box 4) indicates *Top-M* similar Mashups SMA of the active Mashup in Box 1 according to their latent topics distribution similarity derived from HDP described in Sect. 2.2. In Box 4, the similarity between M_2 and M_1 (M_3) is 0.3 (0.7). The fifth indicator matrix (Box 5) shows all co-occurrence Web APIs CO of the active Web API in Box 2 that are invoked or composed in common historical Mashup. The sixth indicator matrix (Box 6) shows the popularity POP (i.e. invocation frequency or times) of the active Web API in Box 2 in historical Mashup. Target Y is the output result, and the prediction ranking score S are classified into positive value (+1) and negative value (−1) according to a given threshold. Suppose $y_i > 0.5$, then $S = +1$, otherwise $S = -1$. These Web APIs who have positive values will be recommended to the target Mashup. For example, active Mashup M_1 have two active Web APIs member A_1 and A_3, A_1 will be preferred recommended to M_1 since it have the higher prediction value, i.e. $y_2 > 0.92$. Moreover, in the experiment section, we will investigate the effects of *top-A* and *top-M* on Web APIs recommendation performance.

3   Experiments

3.1   Experiment Dataset and Settings

To evaluate the performance of different recommendation methods, we crawled 6673 real Mashups, 9121 Web APIs and 13613 invocations between these Mashups and Web APIs from ProgrammableWeb. For each Mashup or Web APIs, we firstly obtained their descriptive text and then performed a preprocessing process to get their standard description information. To enhance the effectiveness of our experiment, a five-fold cross-validation is performed. All the Mashups in the dataset have been divided into 5 equal subsets, and each fold in the subsets is used as a testing set, the other 4 subsets are combined to a training dataset. The results of each fold are summed up and their averages are reported. For the testing dataset, we vary the number of score values provided by the active Mashups as 10, 20 and 30 by randomly removing some score values in Mashup-Web APIs matrix, and name them as Given 10, Given 20, and Given 30. The removed score values will be used as the expected values to study the prediction performance. For the training dataset, we randomly remove some score values in Mashup-Web APIs matrix to make the matrix sparser with density 10%, 20%, and 30% respectively.

3.2   Evaluation Metrics

Mean Absolute Error (MAE) and Root Mean Squared Error (RMSE) are two frequently-used evaluation metrics [15]. We choose them to evaluate Web APIs recommendation performance. The smaller MAE and RMSE indicate the better recommendation quality.

$$MAE = \frac{1}{N}\sum_{ij}\left|r_{ij} - \hat{r}_{ij}\right| \tag{8}$$

$$RMSE = \sqrt{\frac{1}{N}\sum_{ij}\left(r_{ij} - \hat{r}_{ij}\right)^2} \tag{9}$$

Here, N is the amount of predicted score, r_{ij} represents the true score of Mashup M_i to Web API A_j, and $\hat{r}_{ij}$ represents the predicted score of M_i to A_j.

3.3   Baseline Methods

In this section, we investigate and compare our proposed method with baseline methods. The baseline methods are briefly described as below:

- *WPCC*. Like IPCC [15], Web APIs-based using Pearson Correlation Coefficient method (WPCC), uses PCC to calculate the similarities between Web APIs, and makes recommendation based on similar Web APIs.

- **MPCC.** Like UPCC [15], Mashups-based using Pearson Correlation Coefficient method (MPCC), uses PCC to calculate the similarities between Mashups, and predicts Web APIs invocations based on similar Mashups.
- **PMF.** Probabilistic Matrix Factorization (PMF) is one of the most famous matrix factorization models in collaborative filtering [8]. It supposes Gaussian distribution on the residual noise of observed data and places Gaussian priors on the latent matrices. The historical invocation records between Mashups and Web APIs can be represented by a matrix $R = [r_{ij}]_{n \times k}$, and $r_{ij} = 1$ indicates the Web API is invoked by a Mashup, otherwise $r_{ij} = 0$. Given the factorization results of Mashup M_j and Web API A_i, the probability A_i would be invoked by M_j can be predicted by the equation: $\hat{r}_{ij} = A_i^T M_j$.
- **LDA-FMs.** It firstly derives the topic distribution of document description for Mashup and Web APIs via LDA model, and then use the FMs to train these topic information to predict the probability distribution of Web APIs and recommend Web APIs for target Mashup. Besides, it considers the co-occurrence and popularity of Web APIs.
- **HDP-FMs.** The proposed method in this paper, which combines HDP and FMs to recommend Web APIs. It uses HDP to derive the latent topics probability of both the documents of similar Mashup and similar Web APIs, supporting the model training of FMs. It also considers the co-occurrence and popularity of Web APIs.

3.4   Experimental Results

(1) *Recommendation Performance Comparison*

Table 1 reports the MAE and RMSE comparison of multiple recommendation methods, which show our HDP-FMs greatly outperforms WPCC and MPCC, significantly surpasses to PMF and LDA-FMs consistently. The reason for this is that HDP-FMs firstly uses HDP to derive the topics of Mashups and Web APIs for identifying more similar Mashups and similar Web APIs, then exploits FMs to train more useful information for achieving more accurate Web APIs probability score prediction. Moreover, with the increasing of the given score values from 10 to 30 and training matrix density from 10% to 30%, the MAE and RMSE of our HDP-FMs definitely decrease. It means more score values and higher sparsity in the Mashup-Web APIs matrix achieve better prediction accuracy.

(2) *HDP-FMs Performance vs. LDA-FMs Performance with different topics number*

As we know, HDP can automatically find the optimal topics number, instead of repeatedly model training like LDA. We compare the performance of HDP-FMs to those of LDA-FMs with different topics number. During the experiment, we set different topics number 3, 6, 12, and 24 for LDA-FMs, respectively denoted as LDA-FMs-3/6/12/24. Figures 3 and 4 respectively show the MAE and RMSE of them when training matrix density = 10%. The experimental results in the Figs. 3 and 4 indicate that the performance of HDP-FMs is the best, the MAE and RMSE of LDA-FMs-12 is close to those of HDP-FMs. When the topics number becomes smaller

Table 1. The MAE and RMSE performance comparison of multiple recommendation approaches

Method		Matrix Density = 10%		Matrix Density = 20%		Matrix Density = 30%	
		MAE	RMSE	MAE	RMSE	MAE	RMSE
Given10	WPCC	0.4258	0.5643	0.4005	0.5257	0.3932	0.5036
	MPCC	0.4316	0.5701	0.4108	0.5293	0.4035	0.5113
	PMF	0.2417	0.3835	0.2263	0.3774	0.2014	0.3718
	LDA-FMs	0.2091	0.3225	0.1969	0.3116	0.1832	0.3015
	HDP-FMs	0.1547	0.2874	0.1329	0.2669	0.1283	0.2498
Given20	WPCC	0.4135	0.5541	0.3918	0.5158	0.3890	0.5003
	MPCC	0.4413	0.5712	0.4221	0.5202	0.4151	0.5109
	PMF	0.2398	0.3559	0.2137	0.3427	0.1992	0.3348
	LDA-FMs	0.1989	0.3104	0.1907	0.3018	0.1801	0.2894
	HDP-FMs	0.1486	0.2713	0.1297	0.2513	0.1185	0.2291
Given30	WPCC	0.4016	0.5447	0.3907	0.5107	0.3739	0.5012
	MPCC	0.4518	0.5771	0.4317	0.5159	0.4239	0.5226
	PMF	0.2214	0.3319	0.2091	0.3117	0.1986	0.3052
	LDA-FMs	0.1970	0.3096	0.1865	0.2993	0.1794	0.2758
	HDP-FMs	0.1377	0.2556	0.1109	0.2461	0.1047	0.2057

(LDA-FMs-3, LDA-FMs-6) or larger (LDA-FMs-24), the performance of HDP-FMs constantly decreases. The observations verify that HDP-FMs is better than LDA-FMs due to automatic obtain the optimal topics number.

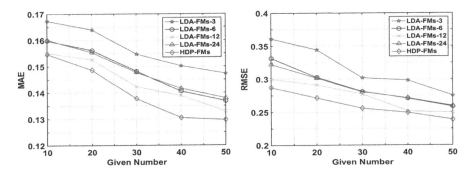

Fig. 3. The MAE of HDP-FMs and LDA-FMs

Fig. 4. The RMSE of HDP-FMs and LDA-FMs

(3) *Impacts of top-A and top-M in HDP-FMs*

As described in Sect. 2.2.2, we use *top-A* similar Web APIs and *top-M* similar Mashups derived from HDP as input variables, to train the FMs for predicting the probability of Web APIs invoked by Mashups. In this section, we investigate the impacts of *top-A* and *top-M* to gain their optimal values. We select the best value of *top-M (top-A)* for all similar *top-A (top-M)* Web APIs (Mashups), *i.e.* $M = 10$ *for all top-A similar Web APIs, $A = 5$ for all top-M similar Mashups.* Figures 5 and 6 show the MAE of HDP-FMs when training matrix density = 10% and given number = 30. Here, the experimental result in the Fig. 5 indicates that the MAE of HDP-FMs is the optimal when $A = 5$. When A increases from 5 to 25, the MAE of HDP-FMs constantly increases. The experimental result in the Fig. 6 shows the MAE of HDP-FMs reaches its peak value when $M = 10$. With the decreasing ($<=10$) or increasing ($>=10$) of M, the MAE of HDP-FMs consistently raises. The observations show that it is important to choose an appropriate values of A and M in HDP-FMs method.

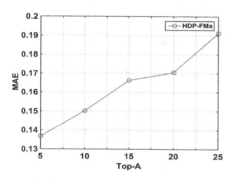   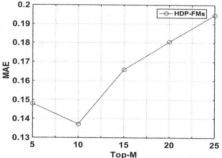

Fig. 5. Impact of top-A in HDP-FMs   **Fig. 6.** Impact of top-M in HDP-FMs

4   Related Work

Service recommendation has become a hot topic in service-oriented computing. Traditional service recommendation addresses the quality of Mashup service to achieve high-quality service recommendation. Where, Picozzi [16] showed that the quality of single services can drive the production of recommendations. Cappiello [17] analyzed the quality properties of Mashup components (APIs), and discussed the information quality in Mashups [18]. Besides, collaborative filtering (CF) technology has been widely used in QoS-based service recommendation [15]. It calculates the similarity of users or services, predicts missing QoS values based on the QoS records of similar users or similar services, and recommends the high-quality service to users.

According to the existing results [19, 20], the data sparsity and long tail problem lead to inaccurate and incomplete search results. To solve this problem, some researchers exploit matrix factorization to decompose historical QoS invocation or Mashup-Web API interactions for service recommendations [21, 22]. Where, Zheng et al. [22] proposed a collaborative QoS prediction approach, in which a neighborhood-integrated matrix factorization model is designed for personalized web service QoS value prediction. Xu et al. [7] presented a novel social-aware service recommendation approach, in which multi-dimensional social relationships among potential users, topics, Mashups, and services are described by a coupled matrix model.

These methods address on converting QoS or Mashup-Web API rating matrix into lower dimension feature space matrixes and predicting the unknown QoS value or the probability of Web APIs invoked by Mashups.

Considering matrix factorization rely on rich records of historical interactions, recent research works incorporated additional information into matrix factorization for more accurate service recommendation [4, 8–10]. Where, Ma et al. [9] combined matrix factorization with geographical and social influence to recommend point of interest. Chen et al. [10] used location information and QoS of Web services to cluster users and services, and made personalized service recommendation. Yao et al. [8] investigated the historical invocation relations between Web APIs and Mashups to infer the implicit functional correlations among Web APIs, and incorporated the correlations into matrix factorization model to improve service recommendation. Liu et al. [4] proposed to use collaborative topic regression which combines both probabilistic matrix factorization and probabilistic topic modeling, for recommending Web APIs.

The above existing matrix factorization based methods definitely boost performance of service recommendation. However, few of them perceive the historical invocation between Mashup and Web APIs to derive the latent topics, and none of them use FMs to train these latent topics to predict the probability of Web APIs invoked by Mashups for more accurate service recommendation. Motivated by above approaches, we integrated HDP and FMs to recommend Web APIs for Mashup development. We use HDP model to derive the latent topics from the description document of Mashups and Web APIs for supporting the model training of FMs. We exploit the FMs to predict the probability of Web APIs invoked by Mashups and recommend high-quality Web APIs for Mashup development.

5 Conclusions and Future Work

This paper proposes a Web APIs recommendation for Mashup development based on HDP and FMs. The historical invocation between Mashup and Web APIs are modeled by HDP model to derive their latent topics. FMs is used to train the latent topics, model multiple input information and their interactions, and predict the probability of Web APIs invoked by Mashups. The comparative experiments performed on ProgrammableWeb dataset demonstrate the effectiveness of the proposed method and show that our method significantly improves accuracy of Web APIs recommendation. In the future work, we will investigate more useful, related latent factors and integrate them into our model for more accurate Web APIs recommendation.

Acknowledgements. This work is supported by the National Natural Science Foundation of China under grant No. 61572371, 61572186, 61572187, 61402167, 61402168, State Key Laboratory of Software Engineering of China (Wuhan University) under grant No. SKLSE2014-10-10, Open Foundation of State Key Laboratory of Networking and Switching Technology (Beijing University of Posts and Telecommunications) under grant No. SKLNST-2016-2-26, Hunan Provincial Natural Science Foundation of China under grant No. 2015JJ2056,2017JJ2098,Hunan Provincial University Innovation Platform Open Fund Project of China under grant No.14K037, Education Science Planning Project of Hunan Province under grant No. XJK013CGD009, and Language Application Research Project of Hunan Province under grant No. XYJ2015GB09.

References

1. Xia, B., Fan, Y., Tan, W., Huang, K., Zhang, J., Wu, C.: Category-aware API clustering and distributed recommendation for automatic mashup creation. IEEE Trans. Serv. Comput. **8** (5), 674–687 (2015)
2. https://en.wikipedia.org/wiki/Mashup_(web_application_hybrid)
3. Chen, L., Wang, Y., Yu, Q., Zheng, Z., Wu, J.: WT-LDA: user tagging augmented LDA for web service clustering. In: Basu, S., Pautasso, C., Zhang, L., Fu, X. (eds.) ICSOC 2013. LNCS, vol. 8274, pp. 162–176. Springer, Heidelberg (2013). doi:10.1007/978-3-642-45005-1_12
4. Liu, X., Fulia, I.: Incorporating user, topic, and service related latent factors into web service recommendation. In: ICWS 2015, pp. 185–192 (2015)
5. Blei, D., Ng, A., Jordan, M.: Latent dirichlet allocation. J. Mach. Learn. Res. **3**, 993–1022 (2003)
6. The, Y., Jordan, M., Beal, M., Blei, D.: Hierarchical dirichlet process. J. Am. Stat. Assoc. **101**(476), 1566–1581 (2004)
7. Xu, W., Cao, J., Hu, L., Wang, J., Li, M.: A social-aware service recommendation approach for mashup creation. In: ICWS 2013, pp. 107–114 (2013)
8. Yao, L., Wang, X., Sheng, Q., Ruan, W., Zhang, W.: Service recommendation for mashup composition with implicit correlation regularization. In: ICWS 2015, pp. 217–224 (2015)
9. Ma, H., Zhou, D., Liu, C., Lyu, M.R., King, I.: Recommender systems with social regularization. In: Proceedings of the Fourth ACM International Conference on Web Search and Data Mining, pp. 287–296. ACM (2011)
10. Chen, X., Zheng, Z., Yu, Q., Lyu, M.: Web service recommendation via exploiting location and QoS information. IEEE Trans. Parallel Distrib. Syst. **25**(7), 1913–1924 (2014)
11. Rendle, S.: Factorization machines. In: ICDM 2010, pp. 995–1000 (2010)
12. Rendle, S.: Factorization machines with libFM. ACM Trans. Intell. Syst. Technol. (TIST) **3** (3), 57–78 (2012)
13. Ma, T., Sato, I., Nakagawa, H.: The hybrid nested/hierarchical dirichlet process and its application to topic modeling with word differentiation. In: AAAI 2015 (2015)
14. Teh, Y., Jordan, M., Beal, M., Blei, D.: Sharing clusters among related groups: hierarchical dirichlet processes. Adv. Neural Inf. Process. Syst. **37**(2), 1385–1392 (2004)
15. Zheng, Z., Ma, H., Lyu, M., King, I.: WSRec: a collaborative filtering based web service recommender system. In: ICWS 2009, Los Angeles, CA, USA, 6–10 July, 2009, pp. 437–444 (2009)
16. Picozzi, M., Rodolfi, M., Cappiello, C., Matera, M.: Quality-based recommendations for mashup composition. In: Daniel, F., Facca, F.M. (eds.) ICWE 2010. LNCS, vol. 6385, pp. 360–371. Springer, Heidelberg (2010). doi:10.1007/978-3-642-16985-4_32
17. Cappiello, C., Daniel, F., Matera, M.: A quality model for mashup components. In: Gaedke, M., Grossniklaus, M., Díaz, O. (eds.) ICWE 2009. LNCS, vol. 5648, pp. 236–250. Springer, Heidelberg (2009). doi:10.1007/978-3-642-02818-2_19
18. Cappiello, C., Daniel, F., Matera, M., Pautasso, C.: Information quality in mashups. IEEE Internet Comput. **14**(4), 14–22 (2010)
19. Huang, K., Fan, Y., Tan, W.: An empirical study of programmable web: a network analysis on a service-mashup system. In: ICWS 2012, 24–29 June, Honolulu, Hawaii, USA (2012)

20. Gao, W., Chen, L., Wu, J., Gao. H.: Manifold-learning based API recommendation for mashup creation. In: ICWS 2015, June 27 - July 2, New York, USA (2015)
21. Koren, Y., Bell, R., Volinsky, C.: Matrix factorization techniques for recommender systems. Computer **42**(8), 30–37 (2009)
22. Zheng, Z., Ma, H., Lyu, M.R., King, I.: Collaborative web service QoS prediction via neighborhood integrated matrix factorization. IEEE Trans. Serv. Comput. **6**(3), 289–299 (2013)

A Novel Hybrid Data Mining Framework
for Credit Evaluation

Yatao Yang[1], Zibin Zheng[1,2], Chunzhen Huang[1], Kunmin Li[1],
and Hong-Ning Dai[3(✉)]

[1] School of Data and Computer Science, Sun Yat-sen University, Guangzhou, China
[2] Collaborative Innovation Center of High Performance Computing,
National University of Defense Technology, Changsha 410073, China
[3] Faculty of Information Technology,
Macau University of Science and Technology, Taipa, Macau SAR
hndai@ieee.org

Abstract. Internet loan business has received extensive attentions recently. How to provide lenders with accurate credit scoring profiles of borrowers becomes a challenge due to the tremendous amount of loan requests and the limited information of borrowers. However, existing approaches are not suitable to Internet loan business due to the unique features of individual credit data. In this paper, we propose a unified data mining framework consisting of feature transformation, feature selection and hybrid model to solve the above challenges. Extensive experiment results on realistic datasets show that our proposed framework is an effective solution.

Keywords: Credit evaluation · Data mining · Internet finance

1 Introduction

Internet finance has been growing rapidly in China recently. A number of online financial services, such as Wechat Payment and Yu'E Bao have receive extensive attentions. In addition to the payment services, Internet loan business has an explosive growth. On such platforms, borrowers request the loans online. The Internet loan service providers then help borrowers find proper loan agencies. However, it is critical for lenders to obtain the *credit worthiness* of borrowers so that they can minimize the loan risk (to avoid the loans to low credit users).

How to evaluate the *credit worthiness* of borrowers is one of challenges in Internet loan services. In conventional loan markets, banks (or other small firms) usually introduce credit scoring system [4] to obtain the credit worthiness of borrowers. During the credit evaluation procedure, the loan officer carefully checked the loan history of a borrower and evaluated the loan risk based on the officer's past experience (i.e., domain knowledge). However, the conventional credit evaluation procedure cannot be applied to the growing Internet loan markets due to the following reasons. First, the loan officers only have the limited information

© ICST Institute for Computer Sciences, Social Informatics and Telecommunications Engineering 2017
S. Wang and A. Zhou (Eds.): CollaborateCom 2016, LNICST 201, pp. 16–26, 2017.
DOI: 10.1007/978-3-319-59288-6_2

of borrowers through Internet loan service platform. Second, there are a tremendous amount of requests for Internet loan business every day, which demands the prompt approval (or disapproval) for customers. Thus, the tedious and complicated procedure of convention credit evaluations is no longer suitable for the fast growth of Internet loan business. Third, the conventional credit evaluation heavily depends on the judgment of loan officers. For example, the credit evaluation is often affected by the knowledge, experience and the emotional state of the loan officer. As a result, there may exist misjudgments of loan officers. It is implied in [8] that computer-assisted credit evaluation approaches can help to solve the above concerns.

In fact, to distinguish the credit borrowers is equivalent to classifying all borrowers into two categories: the "good" borrowers who have good credits and are willing to pay their debts plus interest on time, and the "bad" users who may reject to pay their debts on time. Many researchers employ multiple supervised machine learning algorithms to solve the problem, such as Neural Network, Decision Tree and SVM. In particular, Huang et al. [6] utilize Support Vector Machine (SVM) and Neural Networks to conduct a market comparative analysis. Angelini et al. [1] address the credit risk evaluation based on two correlated Neural Network systems. Pang and Gong [9] also apply the C5.0 classification tree to evaluate the credit risk. Besides, Yap et al. [11] use data mining approach to improve assessment of credit worthiness. Moreover, several different methods have been proposed in [5, 10, 12].

Although previous studies exploit various models, there is no unified hybrid model that can integrate the benefits of various models. Besides, the existing models are not suitable for the growing Internet loan business due the following unique features of individual credit data: (i) *high dimension of features*, which can be as large as 1,000; (ii) *missing values*, which can significantly affect the classification performance; (iii) *imbalanced samples*, in which there are much more positive samples than negative samples. The above features result in the difficulties in analyzing credit data.

In light of the above challenges, we propose a unified analytical framework. The main contributions of this paper can be summarized as follows.

- We propose a novel hybrid data mining framework, which consists of three key phases: feature transformation, feature selection and hybrid model.
- We integrate various feature engineering methods, feature transformation procedures and supervised learning algorithms in our framework to maximize their advantages.
- We conduct extensive experiments on realistic data sets to evaluate the performance of our proposed model. The comparative results show that our proposed model has the better performance in terms of classification accuracy than other existing methods.

The remaining paper is organized as follows. We describe our proposed framework in Sect. 2. Section 3 shows experimental results. Finally, we conclude this paper in Sect. 4.

2   Our Framework

In order to address the aforementioned concerns, we propose a hybrid data mining framework for credit scoring. As shown in Fig. 1, our framework consists of three key phases: feature transformation, feature selection, hybrid model. We then describe the three phases in detail in the following sections.

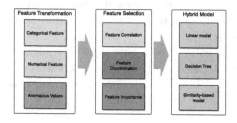

Fig. 1. Our proposed hybrid data mining framework consists of three phases

2.1   Feature Transformation

We categorize the features into two types: (i) *numerical* features are continuous real numbers, representing borrower's age, height, deposit, income, *etc.*; (ii) *categorical* features are discrete integers, indicating borrower's sex, educational background, race, *etc.* Since the two kinds of features cannot be treated as the same, we conduct a conversion so that they can be fit into an unified model.

Categorical Feature Transformation. Regarding to categorical features, we exploit a simple *one-hot encoding*. For example, we use a four-bit one-hot binary to represent four seasons in a year. Specifically, '1000', '0100', '0010' and '0000' denote spring, summer, autumn and winter, respectively. The one-hot encoding conversion is intuitive and easy to be implemented. It converts a categorical feature with the unknown range into multiple binary features with value 0 or 1.

Numerical Feature Transformation. The range of numerical features may differ vastly. For instance, the age is normally ranging from 1 to 100 while the deposit may vary from several hundred to several millions. We utilize the following mapping functions on original features and replace them with the mapped values so that we can reduce the differences between features.

$$Normalize(x_k) = \frac{x_k - mean}{std}, \tag{1}$$

$$Sigmoid(x_k) = \frac{1}{1 + e^{-x_k}}, \tag{2}$$

$$Tanh(x_k) = \frac{e^{x_k} - e^{-x_k}}{e^{x_k} + e^{-x_k}}, \tag{3}$$

$$Maxmin(x_k) = \frac{x_k - \min}{\max - \min}, \tag{4}$$

$$LogAll(x_k) = \log(x_k - \min + 1), \tag{5}$$

where $x_k = \{x_k^{(1)}, x_k^{(2)}, \ldots, x_k^{(n)}\}$ is a set of feature values indicating the kth dimension of the dataset, $x_k^{(i)}$ indicates its value for the ith sample, *mean* denotes the mean value, *std* represents the standard deviation of x_k, max denotes the maximum and min denotes the minimum value. Note that the above basic mapping functions can be nested. For example, a feature can be first transformed by *LogAll* function and can then be mapped into range $(0, 1)$ by *Sigmoid* function.

Anomalous Values Handling. Data sets may contain some values deviated from normal values (i.e., outliers) and some missing values. Specifically, we distinguish outliers by Eq. (6) according to the "3 sigma rules" in classical statistics:

$$Outlier(x_k^{(i)}) = \begin{cases} True, & \text{if } |x_k^{(i)} - mean| \geq 4 \times std \\ False, & \text{otherwise} \end{cases}. \tag{6}$$

Depending on the fraction of anomalous values in feature x_k, we first define the anomalous factor $f = \frac{N_{missing} + N_{outlier}}{N_{sample}}$, where $N_{missing}$ represents the number of missing values, $N_{outlier}$ denotes the number of outliers, and N_{sample} is the number of samples. We then propose three different methods to handle the outliers and the missing values: *replace*, *delete*, and *convert* based on different values of anomalous factor f,

$$Anomalous(x_k) = \begin{cases} Replace, & \text{if } f \leq \alpha \\ Delete, & \text{if } f \geq \beta \\ Convert, & \text{otherwise} \end{cases}. \tag{7}$$

Extra Feature Extraction. We also apply statistical methods to extract extra features. Specifically, we construct ranking features from numerical features and percentage features from categorical features. If the value of the kth numerical feature for the ith sample is $x_k^{(i)}$, the value of ranking feature for it is $a_k^{(i)} = r_k^{(i)}$, where $r_k^{(i)}$ represents $x_k^{(i)}$'s ranking in x_k. However, this simple extension of numerical features significantly increases the dimension, which leads to the extra computational cost. To solve the problem, we use percentiles of the expanded features to represent them in a more concise way. If the extra features are $A = \{a_1, a_2, \ldots, a_n\}$, we use 0th, 20th, 40th, 60th, 80th and 100th percentiles of A as final numerical extra features, which can be represented as $e^{num} = \{a_{0\%}, a_{20\%}, a_{40\%}, a_{60\%}, a_{80\%}, a_{100\%}\}$.

We use a similar method to obtain extra features from categorical features. Suppose $x_k^{(i)}$ represent the kth categorical feature for the ith sample, the value of extra feature for it is $b_k^{(i)} = p_k^{(i)}$, where $p_k^{(i)}$ represents the percentage of category $b_k^{(i)}$ in x_k. If the extra categorical features are $B = \{b_1, b_2, \ldots, b_m\}$, we use 0th,

20th, 40th, 60th, 80th and 100th percentiles of B as final categorical features as $e^{cat} = \{b_{0\%}, b_{20\%}, b_{40\%}, b_{60\%}, b_{80\%}, b_{100\%}\}$.

After feature conversion, each $x_k^{(i)}$ is within the same range, we then use statistics to describe them to capture a high level information $e^{sat} = \{mean, std, perc\}$, where $mean, std$ and $perc$ represent the mean value, the standard deviation of $x^{(i)}$ and the percentage of missing values in $x^{(i)}$, respectively.

2.2 Feature Selection

After the feature transformation, the dimension of features can be significantly increased (e.g., 3,000 in our testing datasets), which lead to the high computational complexity. Thus, it is crucial for us to select the most important and informative features to train a good model. In this paper, we combine three different feature selection techniques to extract the most useful features.

Feature Correlation. If two features are correlated to each other, it implies that they convey the same information. Therefore, we can safely remove one of them. Consider an example that a person who has the higher income will pay the more tax. So, we can remove the tax feature and only keep the income feature during model training. There are many methods to measure the correlation (or similarity) between features. In this paper, we use the Pearson Correlation Coefficient (PCC), which is calculated by Eq. (8).

$$r_{xy} = \frac{\sum_{i=1}^{n}(x_i - \overline{x})(y_i - \overline{y})}{\sqrt{\sum_{i=1}^{n}(x_i - \overline{x})^2}\sqrt{\sum_{i=1}^{n}(y_i - \overline{y})^2}}, \tag{8}$$

where $x = x_1, x_2, \ldots, x_n$ and $y = y_1, y_2, \ldots, y_n$ represent two features, x_i and y_i denote the corresponding values for features x and y in the ith sample, and $\overline{x}$ and $\overline{y}$ denote the means for x and y, respectively. In practice, for the feature pairs whose r_{xy} is higher than 0.95, we arbitrarily remove one of them.

Feature Discrimination. In model training, our goal is to discriminate different categories based on feature information. If a feature itself can distinguish positive and negative samples, implying that it has a strong correlation with the label, we shall include it in model training since it is an informative feature. For instance, F-score [3] is a simple technique to measure the discrimination of two sets of real numbers. Specifically, F-score is calculated by Eq. (9) as follows,

$$\frac{\left(\overline{x}^{+} - \overline{x}\right)^2 + \left(\overline{x}^{-} - \overline{x}\right)^2}{\frac{1}{n^{+}-1}\sum_{k=1}^{n^{+}}\left(x_k^{+} - \overline{x}^{+}\right)^2 + \frac{1}{n^{-}-1}\sum_{k=1}^{n^{-}}\left(x_k^{+} - \overline{x}^{-}\right)^2}, \tag{9}$$

where $\overline{x}$, $\overline{x}^{+}$, $\overline{x}^{-}$ are the average values of the whole sets, the positive and negative data sets, respectively, x_k^{+} is the kth positive instance and x_k^{-} is the kth negative instance. The larger F-score is, the more likely feature x is more discriminative.

Feature Importance. Before applying hybrid model training in Sect. 2.3, we need to evaluate the importance of every feature in training set. Specifically, we choose the features that contribute the most to our model. After each training, we assign a certain importance value v_k to each feature x_k. Taking all information into consideration, we use Eq. (10) to calculate Feature Importance index (FI),

$$FI_k = 0.6 \times v_k^{gbdt} + 0.2 \times v_k^{rf} + 0.2 \times f_k, \tag{10}$$

where v_k^{gbdt} and v_k^{rf} represent importance values given by Gradient Boosting Decision Tree (GBDT) and Random Forest (RF), respectively and f_k denotes F-score of x_k. Since v_k^{gbdt}, v_k^{rf} and f_k may not be within the same range, we use function $Maxmin$ defined in Eq. (4) to normalize them first.

Summary. We illustrate the whole feature selection procedure in Algorithm 1. In particular, after conducting feature transformation, we first remove features with large number of anomalous values. Then, we remove the highly correlated feature. Finally, we calculate Feature Importance Index and select the top K features based on the trained RF and GBDT values.

Algorithm 1. Feature Selection

Require: a set of features $X = \{x_1, x_2, \ldots, x_n\}$, selection threshold K
Ensure: a subset of X
1: **for** each x_k in X **do**
2:     conduct feature transformation
3:     **if** $Anomalous(x_k) == Delete$ **then**
4:         delete x_k from X
5:     **end if**
6: **end for**
7: **for** each feature pairs (x_i, x_j) in X **do**
8:     calculate correlation r_{ij}
9:     **if** $r_{ij} \geq 0.95$ **then**
10:        delete x_i or x_j from x
11:    **end if**
12: **end for**
13: train a RF and a GBDT with X
14: **for** each x_k in X **do**
15:     obtain feature importance v_k^{rf} and v_k^{gbdt}
16:     calculate F-score f_k
17: **end for**
18: $v_k^{rf} \leftarrow Maxmin(v_k^{rf})$
19: $v_k^{gbdt} \leftarrow Maxmin(v_k^{gbdt})$
20: $f_k \leftarrow Maxmin(f_k)$
21: $FI_k \leftarrow 0.6 \times v_k^{gbdt} + 0.2 \times v_k^{rf} + 0.2 \times f_k$
22: $X' \leftarrow K$ feature x_k in X with largest FI_k
23: **return** X'

2.3   Hybrid Model

We first present the models that we use as follows:

– **Linear model.** To reduce the generalization error, we train 10 different Logistic Regression (LR) models with various parameters and blend their results.

Table 1. Performance of AUROC on different methods during different phases

Factor		Classifier		
Data	Dimension	LR	RF	AdaBoost
Original	1138	0.6442 + 0.0170	0.6540 ± 0.0313	0.6625 ± 0.0335
Extended	1984	0.6566 ± 0.0235	0.6558 ± 0.0314	0.6624 ± 0.0319
Refilled	1984	0.6755 ± 0.0198	0.6573 ± 0.0356	0.6649 ± 0.0329
Selected	200	0.7025 ± 0.0257	0.6635 ± 0.0362	0.6772 ± 0.0291
Data	Dimension	GBDT	XGBoost	LR+XGBoost
Original	1138	0.6574 ± 0.0350	0.6988 ± 0.0058	0.7048 ± 0.0065
Extended	1984	0.6539 ± 0.0431	0.7000 ± 0.0060	0.7103 ± 0.0058
Refilled	1984	0.6548 ± 0.0432	0.7025 ± 0.0059	0.7127 ± 0.0027
Selected	200	0.6722 ± 0.0362	0.7200 ± 0.0049	0.7248 ± 0.0053

– **Decision Tree model.** Gradient Boosting Decision Tree (XGBoost)[2] is a popular scalable Gradient Boosting approach. Like LR, we train 20 different XGBoost models and blend their prediction results.
– **Similarity-based model.** We use Pearson Correlation Coefficient (PCC) to evaluate the similarity between samples. Due the imbalance of samples, we identify the negative samples as many as possible. Therefore, we compare each sample in the test set with each negative sample in the training set and label those with high similarity as negative.

We then describe our proposed hybrid model. In particular, our model exploits one of ensemble classification algorithms - "bagging" [5,7]. More specifically, we average the predictions from various models. With regard to a single model (e.g., LR), we average predictions of the same model with different parameters. We then average results from LR and XGBoost. The bagging method often reduces overfit and smooths the separation board-line between classes. Besides, we also use PCC to identify the samples that are most likely to be negative.

Our hybrid model has a better performance than traditional single model due to the following reasons. Firstly, we exploit a diversity of models and the "bagging" method combines their results together so that their advantages are maximized and their generalization errors are minimized. Secondly, we utilize XGBoost library, which is an excellent implementation of Gradient Boosting algorithm, which is highly efficient and can prevent model from over-fitting.

3   Experiment

We use the sample dataset from CashBus[1], a micro credit company in China, which offers the online loaning service to individuals. The dataset contains 15,000

---
[1] http://www.cashbus.com/.

samples. Since all the samples are anonymous in order to protect user privacy, we cannot use any domain knowledge in problem analysis. The dataset has the following features: (1) **High Dimension**. The dataset contains 1,138 features, including 1,045 numerical features and 93 categorical features. (2) **Missing values**. There are a total of 1,333,597 missing values in our dataset, making the missing rate 7.81%. The number of missing values for each feature is ranging from 19 to 14,517 and the number of missing values for each sample is ranging from 10 to 1,050. (3) **Imbalanced samples**. There are 13,458 positive samples while only 1,532 negative samples in the dataset.

3.1 Experimental Setup and Evaluation Metrics

We predict the probability that a user has a good credit and evaluate the prediction results by Area under the Receiver Operating Characteristic curve (AUROC), i.e., $AUROC = \frac{\sum_i S_i}{|P| \times |N|}$, where P and N represent the positive samples and the negative samples in test set, respectively, and S_i is the score for the ith pairs between each positive sample and each negative sample, defined by

$$S_i = \begin{cases} 1, & score_{i-p} > score_{i-n} \\ 0.5, & score_{i-p} = score_{i-n} \\ 0, & score_{i-p} < score_{i-n}, \end{cases} \tag{11}$$

where $score_{i-p}$ and $score_{i-n}$ represent the scores for the positive and the negative sample, respectively. A higher value of AUROC means that the prediction result is more precise.

3.2 Performance Comparison

To investigate the prediction performance, we compare our proposed hybrid model (LR+XGBoost) with other five approaches (each with single model): Logistic Regression (LR), Random Forest (RF), AdaBoost, Gradient Boosting Decision Tree (GBDT) and XGBoost. Table 1 presents the comparative results of different models in different phases in terms of AUROC. Origin represents the raw data set. Extended represents feature transformation. Refilled represents the anomalous values handling process, where we set $\alpha = 0.1$ to choose feature to refill them. Selected represents feature selection process, where we select the top $K = 200$ features. We have the following observations: (1) in all four phases, our proposed hybrid model obtains a better AUROC score than any other methods; (2) our proposed model has a relatively small variation compared with other models, implying the stable performance; (3) LR + XGBoost outperform others, indicating that they are the right choices for constructing the hybrid model.

3.3 Impact of Feature Transformation

We then investigate the impact of feature transformation. Figure 2 shows the impact of *LogAll* function on one numerical feature. After the feature transformation, the distribution of the features becomes more smooth and the extremely large values are minimized.

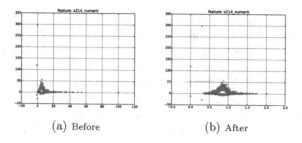

(a) Before   (b) After

Fig. 2. Impact of LogAll Transformation, where green points and red points represent positive and negative samples, respectively. (Color figure online)

3.4   Impact of Refilling Anomalous Values

To deal with the large amount of missing values and outliers, we propose a method to refill the anomalous values based on anomalous value rate under α. We set α to be 0.02 to 0.6 to investigate the impact of α. Table 2 presents the results, where Fill Features represent the number of features that are affected during this process. It is shown in Table 2 that AUROC values for both LR and XGBoost models first increase and then slowly decrease. This can be explained by the fact that filling the anomalous values can bring more information while too many extra filled values also cause noise. In fact, the best performance is obtained when $\alpha = 0.1$.

Table 2. Performance of AUROC on LR and XGBoost under different fill criterion

Factor		Classifier	
Criterion α	Fill features	LR	XGBoost
0.02	661	0.6560 ± 0.0243	0.6991 ± 0.0063
0.05	883	0.6563 ± 0.0240	0.7001 ± 0.0062
0.1	881	0.6755 ± 0.0198	0.7025 ± 0.0059
0.2	885	0.6567 ± 0.0234	0.7021 ± 0.0053
0.3	905	0.6567 ± 0.0227	0.7008 ± 0.0054
0.4	1018	0.6561 ± 0.0231	0.7016 ± 0.0052
0.5	1024	0.6562 ± 0.0238	0.7015 ± 0.0053
0.6	1026	0.6558 ± 0.0239	0.7013 ± 0.0072

3.5   Impact of Feature Selection

After feature transformation, the dimension of features is significantly increased due to the introduction of extra features. We then exploit the feature selection algorithm to reduce the dimension of features. Specifically, we investigate the impact of the feature importance values given by different models and we set

Table 3. Performance of different models under different feature selection methods

Factor		Classifier		
Importance calculation	Dimensions	LR	RF	AdaBoost
RF	200	0.6818 ± 0.0168	0.6626 ± 0.0372	0.6656 ± 0.0359
XGBoost	200	0.6995 ± 0.0263	0.6732 ± 0.0267	0.6695 ± 0.0367
FSore	200	0.6716 ± 0.0193	0.6586 ± 0.0373	0.6608 ± 0.0367
Ensemble	200	0.7025 ± 0.0257	0.6635 ± 0.0362	0.6772 ± 0.0291
Importance calculation	Dimensions	GBDT	XGBoost	LR+XGBoost
RF	200	0.6602 ± 0.0350	0.6888 ± 0.0073	0.6927 ± 0.0423
XGBoost	200	0.6641 ± 0.0333	0.7195 ± 0.0051	0.7214 ± 0.0031
FSore	200	0.6572 ± 0.0454	0.6701 ± 0.0133	0.6843 ± 0.0245
Ensemble	200	0.6722 ± 0.0362	0.7200 ± 0.0049	0.7248 ± 0.0053

the feature selection threshold to be Top $K = 200$. It is shown in Table 3 that our proposed LR+XGBoost achieve the best performance.

3.6   Impact of Selection Threshold

In addition to the feature importance, the threshold top K also contributes to the final quality of the selected features. To investigate the impact of K, we set K to be 100 to 1500 and conduct experiments based on LR and XGBoost models. It is shown in Table 4 that AUROC values first increase and then slowly decrease as K increases. The best performance is obtained when $K = 200$.

Table 4. Performance of LR and XGBoost under different thresholds

Factor	Classifier	
Threshold	LR	XGBoost
100	0.7019 ± 0.0235	0.7156 ± 0.0035
200	0.7025 ± 0.0257	0.7200 ± 0.0049
300	0.6996 ± 0.0184	0.7176 ± 0.0048
400	0.6912 ± 0.0217	0.7129 ± 0.0031
500	0.6853 ± 0.0186	0.7092 ± 0.0038
600	0.6810 ± 0.0157	0.7043 ± 0.0062
800	0.6775 ± 0.0174	0.7032 ± 0.0061
1200	0.6748 ± 0.0237	0.7003 ± 0.0051
1500	0.6721 ± 0.0246	0.7020 ± 0.0060

4   Conclusion and Future Work

In this paper, we propose a novel hybrid data mining framework for individual credit evaluation. To address the challenging issues in individual credit data, such as the high dimension, the outliers and imbalanced samples, we exploit various feature engineering methods and supervised learning models to establish a unified framework. The extensive experimental results show that our proposed framework has a better classification accuracy than other existing methods. There are several future directions in this promising area. For example, we can apply the unsupervised algorithms to utilize the unlabeled data. Besides, we shall use the domain knowledge in finance to further improve the feature transformation and the feature selection procedure.

Acknowledgment. The work described in this paper was supported by the National Key Research and Development Program (2016YFB1000101), the National Natural Science Foundation of China under (61472338), the Fundamental Research Funds for the Central Universities, and Macao Science and Technology Development Fund under Grant No. 096/2013/A3.

References

1. Angelini, E., di Tollo, G., Roli, A.: A neural network approach for credit risk evaluation. Q. Rev. Econ. Finan. **48**(4), 733–755 (2008)
2. Chen, T., Guestrin, C.: Xgboost: A scalable tree boosting system. arXiv preprint arXiv:1603.02754 (2016)
3. Chen, Y.W., Lin, C.J.: Combining svms with various feature selection strategies. In: Guyon, I., Nikravesh, M., Gunn, S., Zadeh, L.A. (eds.) Feature Extraction, pp. 315–324. Springer, Heidelberg (2006)
4. Gray, J.B., Fan, G.: Classification tree analysis using TARGET. Comput. Stat. Data Anal. **52**(3), 1362–1372 (2008)
5. Hsieh, N.C., Hung, L.P.: A data driven ensemble classifier for credit scoring analysis. Expert Syst. Appl. **37**(1), 534–545 (2010)
6. Huang, Z., Chen, H., Hsu, C.J., Chen, W.H., Wu, S.: Credit rating analysis with support vector machines and neural networks: a market comparative study. Decis. Support Syst. **37**(4), 543–558 (2004)
7. Koutanaei, F.N., Sajedi, H., Khanbabaei, M.: A hybrid data mining model of feature selection algorithms and ensemble learning classifiers for credit scoring. J. Retail. Consum. Serv. **27**, 11–23 (2015)
8. Lessmann, S., Baesens, B., Seow, H.V., Thomas, L.C.: Benchmarking state-of-the-art classification algorithms for credit scoring: an update of research. Eur. J. Oper. Res. **247**(1), 124–136 (2015)
9. Pang, S.L., Gong, J.Z.: C5. 0 classification algorithm and application on individual credit evaluation of banks. Syst. Eng. Theory Pract. **29**(12), 94–104 (2009)
10. Wang, Y., Wang, S., Lai, K.K.: A new fuzzy support vector machine to evaluate credit risk. IEEE Trans. Fuzzy Syst. **13**(6), 820–831 (2005)
11. Yap, B.W., Ong, S.H., Husain, N.H.M.: Using data mining to improve assessment of credit worthiness via credit scoring models. Expert Syst. Appl. **38**(10), 13274–13283 (2011)
12. Yu, L., Wang, S., Lai, K.K.: Credit risk assessment with a multistage neural network ensemble learning approach. Expert Syst. Appl. **34**(2), 1434–1444 (2008)

Parallel Seed Selection for Influence Maximization Based on *k-shell* Decomposition

Hong Wu[1,2], Kun Yue[1(✉)], Xiaodong Fu[3], Yujie Wang[1], and Weiyi Liu[1]

[1] School of Information Science and Engineering,
Yunnan University, Kunming, China
kyue@ynu.edu.cn
[2] School of Information Engineering, Qujing Normal University, Qujing, China
[3] Faculty of Information Engineering and Automation,
Kunming University of Science and Technology, Kunming, China

Abstract. Influence maximization is the problem of selecting a set of seeds in a social network to maximize the influence under certain diffusion model. Prior solutions, the greedy and its improvements are time-consuming. In this paper, we propose candidate shells influence maximization (*CSIM*) algorithm under heat diffusion model to select seeds in parallel. We employ *CSIM* algorithm (a modified algorithm of greedy) to coarsely estimate the influence spread to avoid massive estimation of heat diffusion process, thus can effectively improve the speed of selecting seeds. Moreover, we can select seeds from candidate shells in parallel. Specifically, First, we employ the *k-shell* decomposition method to divide a social network and generate the candidate shells. Further, we use the heat diffusion model to model the influence spread. Finally, we select seeds of candidate shells in parallel by using the *CSIM* algorithm. Experimental results show the effectiveness and feasibility of the proposed algorithm.

Keywords: Parallel · Social networks · Influence maximization · *K-shell* decomposition

1 Introduction

With the rising popularity of online social works (OSNs) such as Facebook, Twitter and WeChat and etc., OSNs play a critical role range from the dissemination of information to the adoption of political opinions and technologies [1, 2]. OSNs can be ubiquitously used to various applications, e.g., viral marketing, popular topic detection, and virus prevention [3]. A problem that received considerable attention in this context is that of influence maximization, first proposed by Domingos et al. [4, 5] and formulated by Kempe et al. [6].

Formally, given a social network $G = (V, E)$, budget k and a stochastic model, the problem of influence maximization is to find a k-node set of maximizing the influence spread under certain stochastic model. Kempe et al. [6] proposed two classic diffusion models: linear threshold model (LTM) and independent cascade model (ICM), and they proved the influence maximization problem under these two diffusion models is

© ICST Institute for Computer Sciences, Social Informatics and Telecommunications Engineering 2017
S. Wang and A. Zhou (Eds.): CollaborateCom 2016, LNICST 201, pp. 27–36, 2017.
DOI: 10.1007/978-3-319-59288-6_3

NP-hard. Further, it was proved that the objective function of influence spread under these two diffusion models is monotone and submodular, and thus the greedy algorithm can be used to approximately select the optimal seed set based on the theory of [7]. However, the greedy algorithm is time consuming. Consequently, extensive follow-up studies along with the above work were launched [7–13] and mainly focus on improving the greedy algorithm or proposing new heuristic algorithm.

Despite the immense progress has been made in the past decades, parallel seed selection is also challenging. Actually, we can obtain the seed set timely by selecting seeds in parallel. We consider the following scenario of viral marketing. A company develops a new product and wants to advertise this new product via viral marketing within a social network. If the advertiser takes weeks to select some initial user as seeds to provide them free sample or discount to promote products, then they may lose their superiority because of non-timeliness [14].

It is known that the *k-shell* decomposition method partitions a network into sub-structures, and this process assigns an integer index k_s to each node, where the index k_s represents its location according to successive layers (i.e., shells) in the network [18]. The *k-shell* decomposition can depict the structure feature of social network and discover the layer feature [19]. We can further obtain multiple candidate shells, which are independent with each other. We further select seeds of multiple candidate shells in parallel. In this paper, we mainly discuss the problem of parallel seed selection for influence maximization based on *k-shell* decomposition. For this purpose, we need consider the following questions:

(1) How to model the influence spread (i.e., diffusion model)?
(2) How to obtain the *k-shell* structure of social network?
(3) How to select seeds in parallel for influence maximization?

For the question (1), we adopt the heat diffusion model presented by Ma et al. [15] due to its time-dependent property, which can simulate the product adoptions step by step and help companies divide their marketing strategies in to several phases. For example, a company may want to know the production adoption incurred by the initial user (i.e., seeds) in two days, five days or a week, etc.

For the question (2), we first borrow the idea from [16–18] and divide the social network by employing the method of *k-shell* decomposition. We further obtain the candidate shells and the number of their seeds based on the number of nodes in shell and the value of k_s (i.e., a k shell with index k_s).

For the question (3), we propose candidate shells influence maximization (*CSIM*) algorithm to select seeds in parallel based on the GraphX framework on Spark [20]. The influence maximization problem based on heat diffusion model is NP-hard, and the greedy algorithm can approximate the optimal result with $1-1/e$ [15]. In this paper, we employ the *CSIM* algorithm (a modified algorithm of greedy) to coarsely estimate the influence spread based on the seed set, the active set and non-seed nodes, which can avoid massive estimation of heat diffusion process, thus can effectively improve the speed of selecting seeds. Specifically, we first select the max-degree nodes of candidate shells in parallel as the first seed. For any shell, if its $n(k_s = i) = j > 1$, here, n $(k_s = i)$ denotes the number of seeds with index of shell $k_s = i$, then we compute the mean of shortest distance (MSD) from seed set to its active set. Further we compute the number of neighbors of v in MSD range. Here, v excludes from the seed set. Finally, we compute the value that the number of neighbors of v in MSD range subtracts the number of intersection of the neighbors of v in MSD range and the active set, and select node v_j with the maximum value added into the seed set as the jth seed node.

Experimental results on real-world social networks show the effectiveness and feasibility of the method proposed in this paper.

2 Related Work

With the popularity of online social networks, diffusion models have received considerable attention. In addition to the heat diffusion model adopted in this paper, there are some classic diffusion models. Kempe et al. [6] proposed two diffusion models: linear threshold (LT) model and independent cascade (IC) model. In the LT model, if the total weight from active in-neighbors reaches the threshold of a node, then this node is activated. In the IC model, an active node tires to active its inactive out-neighbors with a given probability, and this activation process is independent with other activations. Comparing to the LT model and IC model, the heat diffusion model adopted in this paper is a realistic model, which can predict the future behavior of the social network (e.g., Amazon networks) since it includes the time factor.

Kempe et al. [6] proved that the objective function under the LT model and IC model is NP-hard, and they further prove the monotonicity and submodularity of this objective function, thus the greedy algorithm can be used to approximately select seeds based on the theory of Nemhauser et al. [7]. However, the greedy algorithm is time consuming. Aimed at addressing this issue, many follow-up studies tried to improve the greedy algorithm or propose new heuristics [8–14, 21–23]. In terms of greedy selection, our *CSIM* algorithm is similar to the Core Covering Algorithm of [21], which is assigned a covering distance, but our *CSIM* algorithm estimates the influence spread based on the active set of seed set and converge area of non-seed set, and the computation of our converge area by using the MSD not assigning the covering distance. Moreover, in the aspect of selecting seeds, we select seeds from the candidate shells in parallel.

The approaches of graph analysis have high computation complexity in large-scale graphs [24]. In order to solve this problem, some frameworks have appeared including Hama [25], Giraph [26], GraphLab [27], GraphX [28] and etc. In terms of parallel framework, we adopt the GraphX, which combines the advantages of both data-parallel and graph-parallel systems by efficiently expressing graph computation within the Spark data-parallel framework and extends Spark's Resilient Distributed Dataset (RDD) abstraction to introduce the Resilient Distributed Graph (RDG) and leverage advances in data-flow systems to exploit in-memory computation and fault-tolerance.

3 Heat Diffusion Model

A social network is modeled as an undirected graph $G = (V, E)$, where V is the set of nodes representing individuals, and E is the set of edges representing the relationships between the individuals. The heat diffusion model can be formulated as follows [15]

$$f(t) = (I + \frac{\alpha t H}{P})^P \times f(0) \tag{1}$$

where I, α, H, P and $f(0)$ is the identity matrix, thermal conductivity-heat diffusion coefficient, matrix, positive integer and initial distribution of heat respectively.

Here, H is denoted as

$$H = \begin{cases} 1, & (v_i, v_j) \in E \quad or \quad (v_j, v_i) \in E \\ -d(v_i), & i = j \\ 0, & otherwise \end{cases} \tag{2}$$

where $d(v_i)$ is the degree of node v_i.

Given the activation threshold θ at time t, if the amount heat of node v_i exceeds θ, then node v_i is active.

4   Generating Candidate Shells and Selecting Seeds Based on Candidate Shells in Parallel

In this section, we first give the approach of k-shell decomposition. Further, we generate the candidate shells based on the value of shell and the number of nodes in shell. Finally, we select the seeds of candidate shells in parallel.

4.1   Generating Candidate Shells

We first introduce the basic idea of *k-shell* decomposition [18]. We first remove the nodes with degree $k = 1$. After removing the nodes with degree $k = 1$, some nodes may be left with degree $k = 1$, so we continue pruning the system iteratively until there is no node with degree $k = 1$ left. The removed nodes along with the corresponding links for a *k shell* with index $k_s = 1$. Similarly, we continue removing higher-k shells until all nodes are removed.

We then generate the candidate shells based on the value of k_s and the number of nodes in shell. Given the number of seeds (i.e., k), we select $k_1 = ck$ seeds based on the number of nodes in shell, and select $k_2 = k-ck$ seeds based on the index of k_s. We employ Eq. (3) to compute the number of seeds based on the number of nodes in each shell as follows

$$k_1(k_s = i) = k_1 \times \frac{n(k_s = i)}{n(G)} \tag{3}$$

where $k_1(k_s = i)$, $n(k_s = i)$ and $n(G)$ denote the number of seeds with $k_s = i$, the number of nodes with $k_s = i$ and the number of nodes with social network $G = (V, E)$. If $k_1(k_s = i)$ is equal to 0, then we will not select the seeds based on the number of nodes.

We further compute the number of seeds in each shell by using Eq. (4) based on the value of k_s. The maximum of k_s is *max*, then we only consider these shells range from *max* to *max-m*. Here, the number of seeds of $k_s = max\text{-}i$ is $\beta_{max\text{-}i} \times k_2$.

$$k_2 = (\beta_{max} + \ldots + \beta_{max\text{-}i} \cdots + \beta_{max\text{-}m}) \times k_2 \tag{4}$$

Here, $\beta_{max} + \ldots + \beta_{max\text{-}i} \ldots + \beta_{max\text{-}m} = 1$ and $\beta_{max} > \ldots > \beta_{max\text{-}i} \ldots > \beta_{max\text{-}m}$. Then, we can filter some shells with $k_1(k_s = i) = 0$ and $k_s \leq max\text{-}i\text{-}1$, and there are n' candidate shells left.

4.2 Selecting Seeds of Candidate Shells

We first select the nodes of candidate shells with maximum degree as the first seed in parallel, i.e.,

$$S^1_{k_s=i} = argmax(d(v_j)) \quad v_j \in G_{k_s=i} \tag{5}$$

where $S^1_{k_s=i}$ denotes the first seed with index $k_s = i$.

For any shell, if $k_1(k_s = i) > 1$ or $k_2(k_s = i) > 1$, to obtain the *jth* seed, we first compute the *MSD* from $S^{j-1}_{k_s=i}$ to its active set $A_S(S^{j-1}_{k_s=i})$ by Eqs. (6) and (7).

$$SP(v_j \rightarrow A_s(v_j)) = \frac{\sum_{u \in A_s(v_j)} SP(v_j \rightarrow u)}{|A_s(v_j)|} \tag{6}$$

$$MSD = \frac{\sum_{v_j \in S^{j-1}_{k_s=i}} SP(v_j \rightarrow A_s(v_j))}{\left|S^{j-1}_{k_s=i}\right|} \tag{7}$$

We further compute the number of neighbors of $v_k \in G_{k_s=i} \backslash S^{j-1}_{k_s=i}$ with *MSD* steps, i.e., $|N_{msd}(v_k)|$ and the number of intersection between $N_{msd}(v_k)$ and $A_s(S^{j-1}_{k_s=i})$, i.e., $|N_{msd}(v_k) \cap A_s(S^{j-1}_{k_s=i})|$. Finally, we select the following v_k by computing Eq. (8) as the *jth* seed with index $k_s = i$.

$$v_k = argmax(|N_{msd}(v_k)| - \left|N_{msd}(v_k) \cap A_t(S^{j-1}_{k_s=i})\right|) \tag{8}$$

4.3 Parallel Algorithm for Seed Selection Based on Candidate Shells

Based on the above descriptions of selecting seeds of candidate shells, the algorithm for the candidate shells influence maximization (*CSIM*) is given in Algorithm 1. Ma et al. proved the greedy algorithm approximate the optimal result with $1 - 1/e$ [15]. However, the greedy algorithm is time consuming due to the massive matrix computation, and thus we propose the *CSIM* algorithm (a modified algorithm of greedy) to coarsely estimate the influence spread based on the seed set, the active set and non-seed nodes, which can avoid massive estimation of heat diffusion process. At the same time, we obtain the candidate shells by the *k-shell* decomposition, and these candidate shells are independent of each other, thus we can further efficiently select seeds of candidate shells in parallel. Specifically, the *CSIM* algorithm can be described as follows. First, we employ the *k-shell* decomposition approach to divide the social network $G = (V, E)$ (lines 1–3). For each shell, we compute its number of seeds based on its index k_s and prune these shells with $k_1(k_s = i) = 0$ and $k_2(k_s = i) \leq max\text{-}m\text{-}1$ to generate the candidate shells (lines 4–8). Finally, we select the seeds from candidate shells in parallel (lines 9–18).

Algorithm 1. *CSIM* (G, k)

Input: Graph of social network $G=(V, E)$; Number of seeds k; Parameters α, t, P, θ
Output: S: seed set

  // *k-shell* decomposition of social network $G=(V, E)$
1: for each $v \in V$ do
2: construct v's shell by *k-shell* decomposition in parallel
3: end for // candidate shells generation
4: $k_1 \leftarrow ck$
5: $k_2 \leftarrow k\text{-}k_1$
6: if $k_1(k_s{=}i){=}0$ and $k_2(k_s{=}i){=}max{-}m{-}1$ then
7: prune these shells with $k_1(k_s{=}i){=}0$ and $k_2(k_s{=}i){\leq}max{-}m{-}1$
8: candidate shells $CS = \{ks_1', ks_2', \ldots, ks_n'\}$
    // selecting seeds of candidate shells in parallel
9: for each ks_1' in CS do
10: $n(k_{s_i}') \leftarrow k_1(k_s = i) + k_2(k_s = i)$
11: parallel for $ks_i' \in CS$ do
12:    $S_{k_s=i}^1 \leftarrow argmax(d(v_j))$ $v_j \in G_{k_s=i}$
13:    execute the heat diffusion process on $G_{k_s=i}$ with seed set $S_{k_s=i}^{j-1}$
14:    if $n(k_{s_i}') > 1$ then
15:      for $n(k_{s_i}') = 2$ to m do
16:      compute $MSD \leftarrow \dfrac{\sum_{v_j \in S_{k_s=i}^{j-1}} SP(v_j \to A_t(v_j))}{\left| S_{k_s=i}^{j-1} \right|}$
17:      select v_k with $v_k = argmax(|N_{msd}(v_k)| - |N_{msd}(v_k) \cap A_t(S_{k_s=i}^{j-1})|)$ as the jth
      seed in $k_s{=}i$
18:    end for
19: end for
20:return S

---

5   Experimental Results

5.1   Experiment Setup

Datasets: We choose ca-GrQc, ca-HepPh and com-DBLP for our experiments [6, 29]. The ca_Hepth and Ca-GrQc are collaboration networks extracted from the e-print arXiv (http://www.arXiv.org). The former is extracted from the "High Energy Physics-Theory" and the latter is extracted from the General Relativity. The com-DBLP is a much larger collaboration network extracted from the DBLP (http://dblp.uni-trier.de/db/), which is Computer Science Bibliography Database. The nodes in these two networks are authors and an edge between two nodes means the two coauthored at least one paper.

Running environment: All algorithms were implemented in Scala. All experiments were conducted on a machine (i.e., master node) with 3.3GHZ 32-Core CPUs and 32 GB memory, and 10 machines (i.e., worker nodes) with 3.3GHZ 8-Core CPUs and 16 GB memory.

5.2   Performance Studies

We measured the following metrics: (1) the influence spread of *CSIM* algorithm, max-degree algorithm and random algorithm under heat diffusion model with 30 seeds; (2) the influence spread of *CSIM* algorithm with different activation threshold θ; (3) the influence spread with different flow duration t; (4) the Speed-up of *CSIM* algorithm; (5) the parallel efficiency of *CSIM* algorithm.

All the experiments presented in this paper use the heat diffusion model, where we specified two parameters the initial heat of each heat source and P. Here, we choose N/k as the amount of heat for each heat source, where N is the number of nodes in social network, k the number of seeds and $P = 30$.

(1)   *Influence spread of three algorithms.* Table 1 shows the influence spread of three algorithms with the following parameters on $\alpha = 1, t = 0.1, \theta = 0.01$ and $|k| = 30$. From Table 1, we can observe that the number of active nodes with *CSIM* algorithm is larger the max-degree and random algorithms. This is because max-degree algorithm does not consider the overlap between seeds and the random algorithm as baseline algorithm, some selected seeds cannot spread the influence effectively.

Table 1. The influence spread of different algorithms

Data	*CSIM*	Max-degree	Random
ca-GrQc	329	311	278
ca-HepPh	741	606	374

(2)   *Activation threshold θ.* Given $\alpha = 1$ and $t = 0.1$, Fig. 1 shows the influence spread of *CSIM* algorithm of 30 seeds with different activation threshold θ from

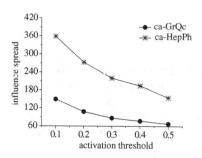

Fig. 1. Influence spread with different activation threshold

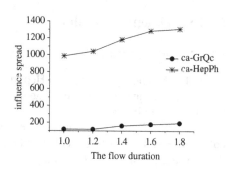

Fig. 2. Influence spread with different flow duration

0.1 to 0.5 with a span of 0.1, respectively. The x-axis indicates the activation threshold, and y-axis indicates the influence spread. From Fig. 1, we can see that the influence spread of *CSIM* algorithm will decrease with the increase of activation threshold θ. The reason is that the nodes are hard to be influenced when the activation threshold is larger.

(3) **Flow duration t.** Given $\alpha = 1$ and $\theta = 0.5$, Fig. 2 shows the influence spread of *CSIM* algorithm of 30 seeds with different flow duration t from 1 to 1.8 with a span of 0.2, respectively. The x-axis indicates the flow duration, and the y-axis indicates the influence spread. From Fig. 2, we can obtain that the influence spread of *CSIM* will increase with the increase of flow duration t. This is because the larger flow duration t will lead to more nodes influenced.

(4) **Speed-up.** Speed-up of a parallel algorithm is a ration of the processing time between of singer worker and multiple workers. Figure 3 shows the speed-up trends for parallel *CSIM* algorithm. In all datasets, the speed-up will increase as the number the workers increase.

(5) **Parallel efficiency.** Figure 4 shows the trends for parallel *CSIM* with different datasets. To the same dataset, the parallel efficiency will decrease as the number of workers increase.

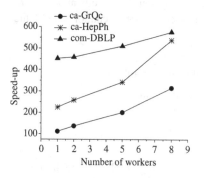

Fig. 3. Speed-up

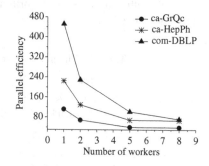

Fig. 4. Parallel efficiency

6   Conclusions and Future Work

To select seeds timely, we propose *CSIM* algorithm for parallel seed selection for influence maximization based on *k-shell* decomposition. First, we employ the *k-shell* decomposition method to divide a social network and generate the candidate shells. Further, we use the heat diffusion model to model the influence spread. Finally, we select seeds of candidate shells in parallel by using the *CSIM* algorithm. In a candidate shell, if the number of seeds is larger than 1, then we adopt the *CSIM* algorithm (a modified algorithm of greedy) to select seeds in parallel.

In this paper, we employ the value of index *k*-shell and the number of nodes to generate candidate shells based on experience. For our future work, we are to adopt modified algorithm to generate candidate shells. Moreover, the heat diffusion model in this paper only includes one kind of information spread, while there exist competitive influence spread in reality. Meanwhile, we are to analyze the competitive influence spread of heat diffusion model.

Acknowledgement. This work was supported by the National Natural Science Foundation of China (Nos. 61472345, 61462056, 61402398), Natural Science Foundation of Yunnan Province (Nos. 2014FA023, 2014FA028), Program for Excellent Young Talents of Yunnan University (No. XT412003), Research Foundation of the Education Department of Yunnan Province (Nos. 2014C134Y, 2016YJS005, 2016ZZX013).

References

1. Granovetter, M.: Threshold models of collective behavior. Am. J. Soc. **83**, 1420–1443 (1978)
2. Watts, D.J., Strogatz, S.H.: Collective dynamics of 'small-world' networks. Nature **393** (6684), 440–442 (1998)
3. Chen, W., Wang, C., Wang, Y.: Scalable influence maximization for prevalent viral marketing in large-scale social networks. In: SIGKDD, pp. 1029–1038 (2010)
4. Domingos, P., Richardson, M.: Mining the network value of customers. In: KDD, pp. 57–66 (2001)
5. Richardson, M., Domingos, P.: Mining knowledge-sharing sites for viral marketing. In: KDD, pp. 61–70 (2002)
6. Kempe, D., Kleinberg, J., Tardos É.: Maximizing the spread of influence through a social network. In: KDD, pp. 137–146 (2003)
7. Nemhauser, G.L., Wolsey, L.A., Fisher, M.L.: An analysis of approximations for maximizing submodular set functions—I. Math. Program. **14**(1), 265–294 (1978)
8. Leskovec, J., Krause, A., Guestrin, C., et al.: Cost-effective outbreak detection in networks. In: KDD, pp. 420–429 (2007)
9. Wang, C., Chen, W., Wang, Y.: Scalable influence maximization for independent cascade model in large-scale social networks. Data Min. Knowl. Disc. **25**(3), 545–576 (2012)
10. Cheng, S., Shen, H., Huang, J., Zhang, G., Cheng, X.: Staticgreedy: solving the scalability-accuracy dilemma in influence maximization. In CIKM, pp. 509–518 (2013)
11. Chen, W., Wang, Y., Yang, S.: Efficient influence maximization in social networks. In: KDD, pp. 199–208 (2009)

12. Chen, Y.C., Zhu, W.Y., Peng, W.C., Lee, W.C., Lee, S.Y.: CIM: community-based influence maximization in social networks. ACM Trans. Intell. Syst. Technol. **5**(2), 25 (2014)
13. Horel, T., Singer, Y.: Scalable methods for adaptively seeding a social network. In: WWW, pp. 441–451 (2015)
14. Chen, Y.C., Peng, W.C., Lee, S.Y.: Efficient algorithms for influence maximization in social networks. Knowl. Inf. Syst. **33**(3), 577–601 (2012)
15. Ma, H., Yang, H., Lyu, M.R., King, I.: Mining social networks using heat diffusion processes for marketing candidates selection. In: CIKM, pp. 233–242 (2008)
16. Bollobás, B.: Graph theory and combinatorics. In: Proceedings of the Cambridge Combinatorial Conference in honor of Paul Erdös, Academic, p. 35 (1984)
17. Carmi, S., Havlin, S., Kirkpatrick, S., Shavitt, Y., Shir, E.: A model of Internet topology using k-shell decomposition. In: PNAS, pp. 11150–11154 (2007)
18. Kitsak, M., Gallos, L.K., Havlin, S., Liljeros, F., Muchnik, L., Stanley, H.E., Makse, H.A.: Identification of influential spreaders in complex networks. Nat. Phys. **6**(11), 888–893 (2010)
19. Ren, Z.M., Liu, J.G., Shao, F., Hu, Z.L.: Guo, Q: Analysis of the spreading influence of the nodes with minimum K-shell value in complex networks. Acta. Phys. Sin **62**(10), 108902-1–108902-6 (2013)
20. https://spark.apache.org/docs/latest/graphx-programming-guide.html
21. Cao, J.X., Dong, D., Xu, S., Zheng, X., Liu, B., Luo, J.Z.: A *k*-core based algorithm for influence maximization in social networks. Chin. J. Comput. **38**(2), 238–248 (2015)
22. Song, G., Zhou, X., Wang, Y., Xie, K.: Influence maximization on large-scale mobile social network: a divide-and-conquer method. IEEE Trans. Parallel Distrib. Syst. **26**(5), 1379–1392 (2015)
23. Kim, J., Kim, S.K., Yu, H.: Scalable and parallelizable processing of influence maximization for large-scale social networks. In: ICDE, pp. 266–277 (2013)
24. Bello-Orgaz, G., Jung, J.J., Camacho, D.: Social big data: recent achievements and new challenges. Inf. Fusion **28**, 45–59 (2016)
25. Seo, S., Yoon, E.J., Kim, J., Jin, S., Kim, J.S., Maeng, S.: Hama: an efficient matrix computation with the mapreduce framework. In: CloudCom, pp. 721–726 (2010)
26. Avery, C.: Giraph: Large-scale graph processing infrastructure on hadoop. In: Hadoop Summit (2011)
27. Low, Y., Gonzalez, J.E., Kyrola, A., Bickson, D., Guestrin, C.E., Hellerstein, J.: Graphlab: a new framework for parallel machine learning. In: UAI, p. 10, (2014)
28. Xin, R.S., Gonzalez, J.E., Franklin, M.J., Stoica, I.: GraphX: a resilient distributed graph system on spark. In: GRADES, pp. 2:1–2:6 (2013)
29. Yang, J., Leskovec, J.: Defining and evaluating network communities based on ground-truth. In: ICDM, pp. 745–754 (2012)

The Service Recommendation Problem: An Overview of Traditional and Recent Approaches

Yali Zhao[(⊠)] and Shangguang Wang

State Key Laboratory of Networking and Switching Technology, Beijing
University of Posts and Telecommunications, Beijing, China
{zhaoyali2015, sgwang}@bupt.edu.cn

Abstract. Service recommendation has become a hot fundamental research topic in service computing. With the increasing number of services, QoS is becoming more and more important for describing non-functional characteristics of services. The most popular technique is the Collaborative Filtering (CF) based on QoS values. Existing few approaches for service recommendation based on CF have been studied, so we are going to do a survey of these techniques in depth. In this paper, some of the main known results relative to the Service Recommendation Problem both traditional and recent approaches are surveyed. The paper is organized as follows: (1) definition; (2) traditional approaches; (3) recent approaches; (4) conclusion.

Keywords: Service recommendation problem · Survey · Collaborative filtering

1 Problem Definition

The Service Recommendation Problem (SRP) can be described as the problem of recommending service which provides both the required functionalities and has optimal QoS performance from many candidate services with equivalent function to the target user [1], subject to side constraints. The SRP plays an important role in the fields of service computing and cloud computing. There exists a wide variety of SRPs and a broad works on this class of problems recently, for example, the surveys of Pranjali M. Patil and R.B. Wagh [2], Ruchita V. Tatiya et al. [3], M. Subha and M. Uthaya Banu [4], and the recent survey proposed by Ashwini Puri and Mansi Bhonsle [5] and other works [6, 7]. However, these works lack in comparison with other classical works. Inspired by this, our paper surveys the main traditional and recent approaches based on Collaborative Filtering proposed by Z. Zheng et al. [8, 9] developed for the SRP.

Z. Zheng et al. [8, 9] proposed an approach for predicting QoS values of services by combining the traditional user-based and item-based collaborative filtering methods, then based on QoS values, they recommended the optimal service to an active service user.

In this section, we present the SRP definition and introduce the approach's main steps for service recommendation based on Z. Zheng's papers [8, 9].

Given a recommender system consisting of M service users and N service items, the relationship between service users and service items is denoted by an $M \times N$ matrix,

© ICST Institute for Computer Sciences, Social Informatics and Telecommunications Engineering 2017
S. Wang and A. Zhou (Eds.): CollaborateCom 2016, LNICST 201, pp. 37–47, 2017.
DOI: 10.1007/978-3-319-59288-6_4

called the user-item matrix. To simplify the description of our paper, we formalize the Service Recommendation Problem as follows:

$U = \{u_1, u_2, ..., u_m\}$ is a set of service users, where m is total number of service users registered in the recommendation system.

$S = \{s_1, s_2, ..., s_n\}$ is a set of services, where n is total number of services collected by the recommendation system.

$M = \{r_{i,j} | 1 \leq i \leq m, 1 \leq j \leq n\}$ is the user-service matrix, where $r_{i,j}$ is a vector of QoS attribute values (e.g., response-time, failure-rate, etc.) acquired from service user u_i invoking service item s_j. If service user u_i did not invoke the service item s_j before, then $r_{i,j} = 0$.

Next, we take user-based approach as an example to introduce main steps of the approach as follows:

Step 1: Compute the similarity of different service users as well as service items.

$$sim(a, u) = \frac{\sum_{i \in I} (r_{a,i} - \bar{r}_a)(r_{u,i} - \bar{r}_u)}{\sqrt{\sum_{i \in I} (r_{a,i} - \bar{r}_a)^2} \sqrt{\sum_{i \in I} (r_{u,i} - \bar{r}_u)^2}} \tag{1}$$

where $sim(a, u)$ denotes degree of similarity between user a and user u, I is the set of service items that are invoked by user a and user u. $\bar{r}_a$ and $\bar{r}_u$ represent an average QoS value for user a and user u respectively.

Employ a significance weight to reduce the influence of a small number similar common invoked items

$$sim'(a, u) = \frac{2 \times |I_a \cap I_u|}{|I_a| + |I_u|} sim(a, u) \tag{2}$$

where $|I_a \cap I_u|$ is the number of service items that are employed by both two users, and $|I_a|, |I_u|$ are the number of services invoked by user a and user u, respectively.

Step 2: Find top k similar neighbors for the active user, where neighbors with similarities smaller or equal to 0 will be excluded.

Predict the missing values as follows:

$$P(r_{u,i}) = \bar{u} + \frac{\sum_{u_a \in S(u)} sim'(u_a, u)(r_{u_{a,i}} - \overline{u_a})}{\sum_{u_a \in S(u)} sim'(u_a, u)} \tag{3}$$

where $P(r_{u,i})$ is the predicted QoS values for the active user u and $S(u)$ is a set of similar users for service user u.

Employ two confidence weights to balance the results from these two prediction methods.

$$con_u = \sum_{u_a \in S(u)} \frac{sim'(u_a, u)}{\sum_{u_a \in S(u)} sim'(u_a, u)} \times sim'(u_a, u) \tag{4}$$

where con_u is the prediction confidence of the user-based method.

$$w_u = \frac{con_u \times \lambda}{con_u \times \lambda + con_i \times (1 - \lambda)} \tag{5}$$

$$w_i = \frac{con_i \times \lambda}{con_u \times \lambda + con_i \times (1 - \lambda)} \tag{6}$$

where both w_u and w_i are the combinations of the confidence weights (con_u and con_i) and the parameter λ.

Step 3: Prediction for active users. The formula was defined as

$$P(r_{a,i}) = w_u \times \overline{r_a} + w_i \times \overline{r_i} \tag{7}$$

Based on the service recommendation problem proposed by Z. Zheng et al. [8, 9], our paper surveys approaches for the SRP which can be classified into traditional and recent approaches.

2 Traditional Approaches

Based on the service recommendation problem approached by Z. Zheng et al. [8, 9], traditional approaches for the SRP can be classified into three categories: (1) personalized collaborative filtering; (2) time-aware approach; (3) location-aware approach and other traditional approaches, like trust-aware approach. Because the number of proposed approaches is very large, we provide one representative example for every category.

2.1 The Region-Sensitive Personalized Collaborative Filtering Approach

The following approach due to Xi Chen et al. [10] presented an effective region-sensitive collaborative filtering method for the SRP. The method recognized the characteristics of QoS and employed it by building an efficient region model. They clustered users into several regions based on their physical locations and historical QoS similarities.

According to their observation, QoS, highly relates to users' physical locations. For instance, as Fig. 1 [10] depicts, Bob and Alice check the same public service registry located in America. From the recorded QoS values, they find that service A provided by an American provider outperforms others. After trying it, however, Alice finds that the response time of service A is much higher than her expectation, while Bob thinks A is what he wants. Then Alice recognizes that some QoS properties, like response time and availability, highly relate to the network environment of the region where she locates. She returns to her colleagues and they suggest service B provided by a local company based on their past experiences.

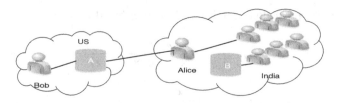

Fig. 1. Alice is working in India with a low bandwidth and Bob is in America with a higher one. Both of them need an email filtering service with low response time.

In this method, they took RTT (round-trip time) as an example to describe their approach and define the notations as follows: $T_u = \{R_u(s_1), R_u(s_2), \ldots, R_u(s_m)\}$ is an RTT vector or a user's RTT profile associated with each other, where $R_u(s_i)(1 \leq i \leq m)$ denotes the RTT of service s_i provided by user u. $\overline{R_u}$ denotes the average RTT provided by user u.

They defined a *region* as a group of users who were closely located with each other and had similar RTT profiles. Firstly, they detected the region-sensitive services. The set of RTTs $\{R_1(s), R_2(s), \ldots, R_k(s)\}(1 \leq k \leq n)$ collected from all users of service s is a sample from population R. They used media and media absolute deviation (MAD) to estimate the μ and the standard deviation σ of R.

$$MAD = median_i\left(\left|R_i(s) - median_j(R_j(s))\right|\right)(i = 1, \ldots, k, j = 1, \ldots, k) \qquad (8)$$

The two estimators are

$$\widehat{\mu} = median_i(R_i(s)) \qquad (9)$$

$$\widehat{\sigma} = 1.4862 MAD_i(R_i(s)) \qquad (10)$$

Then, the similarity of two regions M and N was measured by the similarity of their region centers which were defined as the median vector of all the RTT vectors. The similarity of the two region centers m and n was formally defined as:

$$sim(m, n) = \frac{\sum\limits_{s \in S(n) \cap S(m)} (R_m(s) - \overline{R_m})(R_n(s) - \overline{R_n})}{\sqrt{\sum\limits_{s \in S(n) \cap S(m)} (R_m(s) - \overline{R_m})^2}\sqrt{\sum\limits_{s \in S(n) \cap S(m)} (R_n(s) - \overline{R_n})^2}} \qquad (11)$$

where $S(m)$ and $S(n)$ is the set of services invoked by users in region M, N respectively.

Based on the region similarity, they used the region aggregation algorithm for regions and generate QoS prediction and recommendation. The method significantly improves the prediction accuracy regardless of the sparsity of the training matrix and its scalability advantage over traditional approaches.

There are many other works considering the personalization. For example, YeChun Jiang et al. [11] proposed a personalized QoS-Aware service recommendation approach; Lingshuang Shao et al. [12] and Jinliang Xu et al. [13] also proposed similar methods as before.

2.2   The Time-Aware Approach

Yan Hu et al. [1] proposed a novel time-aware approach for SRPs, which integrated time information into both the similarity measurement and the final QoS prediction, and a hybrid personalized random walk algorithm to infer more indirect user similarities and service similarities. They redefine the user-service matrix with adding the time information for service users as follows:

$M = \{(r_{i,j}, t_{ij}) | 1 \leq i \leq m, 1 \leq j \leq n\}$ is the user-service matrix, each entry of M is a 2-tuple $(r_{i,j}, t_{ij})$, where $r_{i,j}$ is a vector of QoS attribute values acquired from service user u_i invoking service item s_j, and t_{ij} is the timestamp when u_i invoked s_j.

They found that a longer timespan indicated a higher probability that a QoS value deviated from its original value. Based on it, there are two intuitive principles behind the user similarity measurement. (1) More temporally close QoS experience from two users on a same service contributes more to the user similarity measurement. (2) More recent QoS experience from two users on a same service contributes more to the user similarity measurement.

As Fig. 2 [1] depicts, if Δt_1 is long, even though u_i and u_j have very similarity QoS experience on s_k, it does not really mean high similarity between u_i and u_j, since u_i's QoS experience in s_k may change violently over Δt_1. Therefore, a shorter Δt_1 generally indicates a greater contribution of s_k to the similarity measurement between u_i and u_j. So the contribution of s_k can be approximately weighted by an exponential decay function of Δt_1, which is defined as:

$$f_1(t_{ik}, t_{jk}) = e^{-\partial |t_{ik} - t_{jk}|} \tag{12}$$

where α is a non-negative decay constant, with a large α making the value of f_1 vanish more rapidly with increase of the timespan $|t_{ik} - t_{jk}|$.

They utilized $\Delta t_4 = (\Delta t_2 + \Delta t_3)/2$ to denote the second time factor. A shorter Δt_4 generally indicates a greater contribution of s_k to the service user similarity measurement. Thus, the contribution of s_k decays exponentially with the increase of Δt_4. The exponential decay function is defined as:

$$f_2(t_{ik}, t_{jk}) = e^{-\beta |t_{current} - (t_{ik} - t_{jk})/2|} \tag{13}$$

where β is a non-negative decay constant, with a larger β making f_2 vanish much more rapidly with the increase of the timespan $|t_{current} - (t_{ik} - t_{jk})/2|$.

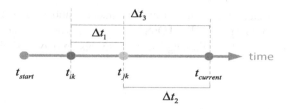

Fig. 2. Suppose that the service recommender system starts at t_{start}. A service user u_i invoked service s_k at t_{ik}, and another user u_j invoked the same service s_k at t_{jk}. The timespan between t_{ik} and t_{jk} is denoted by Δt_1, Δt_2 is the timespan between u_j's invocation on service s_k and the current moment, and Δt_3 is the timespan between u_i's invocation on s_k and the current moment.

Based on the definition of f_1 and f_2, the time-aware PCC-based similarity measurement between u_i and u_j, can be defined as:

$$sim(u_i, u_j) = \frac{\sum\limits_{s_k \in S} (r_{i,k} - \overline{r_i})(r_{j,k} - \overline{r_j}) f_1(t_{ik}, t_{jk}) f_2(t_{ik}, t_{jk})}{\sqrt{\sum\limits_{s_k \in S} (q_{ik} - \overline{q_i})} \sqrt{\sum\limits_{s_k \in S} (q_{jk} - \overline{q_j})}} \tag{14}$$

2.3   The Random Walk Method

Mingdong Tang et al. [14] proposed a method considering the service users' locations to solve the data sparsity issue for improving the precision of service recommendation.

Typically, a user invokes only a small number of services, thus the matrix M is likely very sparse, i.e., $r_{u,i}$ is missing for most u and i. The random walk method is inspired by the service selection process in real life.

To imitate the process, they built a user network defined as NU_u, which connected user u with its nearest Top-K neighbors. Based on the motivate that QoS information provided by near neighbors of the source user on the target or similar services are more reliable than QoS information provided by far neighbors, they combined the location-based and item-based method to make QoS prediction and propose a random walk model called *WSWalker*.

Firstly, they proposed a method to measure distance between users of the user network. The location of a user is represented by its latitude and longitude, so the distance between users is calculated as follows:

$$d_{u,v} = \sqrt{(\varphi_u - \varphi_v)^2 + (\lambda_u - \lambda_v)^2 * \cos^2\left(\frac{\varphi_u + \varphi_v}{2}\right)} \tag{15}$$

where φ_u is the latitude of u, λ_u is the longitude of u and φ_v, λ_v is the latitude and longitude of v respectively. They also proposed a method to measure the weight of edges in the user network.

$$t_{u,v} = \frac{1}{1 + d_{u,v}} * sim''(u,v) \tag{16}$$

where $t_{u,v}$ represents the weight of edge(u,v) in the user network, which can be viewed as a trust value between u and v and $sim''(u,v)$ represents the similarity between u and v based on a modified PCC, i.e. Based on the Formula (1), The modified PCC measured as follows:

$$sim'(u,v) = \frac{1}{1 + e^{\frac{|IC_{u,v}|}{2}}} sim(u,v) \tag{17}$$

where $|IC_{u,v}|$ is the number of services co-invoked by u and v. Both values of $sim(u,v)$ and $sim'(u,v)$ are in the range $[-1, 1]$. However, it is meaningless for $t_{u,v}$ taking negative values. They converted the similarity value into range $[0, 1]$ as follow:

$$sim''(u,v) = \frac{(1 + sim'(u,v))}{2} \tag{18}$$

$$P(S_u = v) = \frac{t_{u,v}}{\sum_{w \in NU_u} t_{u,w}} \tag{19}$$

where $P(S_u = v)$ denotes the probability of the condition that when a user walk at the node u and select the user v to go on walking.

$$P(X_{u_0,i,k+1} = v | X_{u_0,i,k} = u, \widetilde{R_{u,i}}) = (1 - \phi_{u,i,k}) \times \frac{t_{u,v}}{\sum_{w \in NU_u} t_{u,w}} \tag{20}$$

where $P(X_{u_0,i,k+1} = v | X_{u_0,i,k} = u, \widetilde{R_{u,i}})$ is the probability of the condition that a user at node u in step k and select the user v in step $k + 1$ for source user u_0 and $\widetilde{R_{u,i}}$ denotes the condition that the user u in step $k - 1$ does not have QoS experience for target service i.

$$\phi_{u,i,k} = \max_{j \in I_u} sim'(i,j) \times \frac{1}{1 + e^{-\frac{k}{2}}} \tag{21}$$

$$sim'(i,j) = \frac{1}{1 + e^{-\frac{|UC_{i,j}|}{2}}} sim(i,j) \tag{22}$$

where $|UC_{i,j}|$ is the number of users who have invoked both service i and j.

For each random walk, there are three *cases* to stop it:

Case 1. Arriving at a user who has QoS experience on the target service i.

Case 2. At some user node u, we decide to stay at the node and randomly select one of the services invoked by u which is similar to i and returns its QoS values as the result of random walk.

Case 3. When a single random walk continues forever, they limit the maximum depth ($k >$ *max-depth*). According to the idea of "six-degrees of separation" in social networks, we set *max-depth* to 6.

The proposed random walk method could achieve significantly better tradeoffs between coverage and precision than the other CF methods and also showed that more confident recommendations are of greater quality.

3   Recent Approaches

Existing many approaches for solving the SRP different from the method proposed by Z. Zheng et al. [8, 9] are classified into the category called recent approach in our paper. The recent approaches have a large number of categories, including the approach for solving code-start SRPs, considering multi-dimensional algorithm for SRPs and applying in mobile internet and so on. In this section, we describe three recent approaches specifically developed for the SRP.

3.1   The Multi-dimensional QoS Prediction Approach

In SRP, most contemporary QoS prediction methods exploit the QoS characteristics for one specific dimension, e.g., time or location, and do not exploit the structural relationships among the multi-dimensional QoS data. Shangguang Wang et al. [7] proposed an integrated QoS prediction approach which unifies the modeling of multi-dimensional QoS data via multi-linear-algebra based concepts of tensor and enables efficient Web service recommendation for mobile clients via tensor decomposition and reconstruction optimization algorithms. A possible implementation of the method is following.

Step 1. Adopt the multi-linear-algebra concept of tensor to model multi-dimensional QoS data. The QoS data can be modeled as a tensor $x \in \mathbb{R}^{m \times n \times k \times l \times p}$, which has five dimensions: m users, n services, k time periods, l locations and p QoS properties. $x_{i_1 i_2 i_3 i_4 i_5}$ is an entry of x, denoting the value of i_5-th QoS property for the i_1-th user invoking the i_2-th service and the invocation must occur in the i_3-th time period and at the i_4-th location.

Step 2. Use the concept of rank one tensor to decompose a tensor. A tensor $x \in \mathbb{R}^{I_1 \times I_2 \times \ldots \times I_N}$ can be decomposed as:

$$x = \sum_{r=1}^{R} a_r^{(1)} \circ a_r^{(2)} \ldots \circ a_r^{(N)} \tag{23}$$

where $a_r^{(j)}$ denotes the j-th vector whose length is $I_j (1 \leq j \leq N)$ and the subscript r indicates that $a_r^{(j)}$ is x_r specific, the superscript (j) indicates that $a_r^{(j)}$ is the j-th vector.

Let every $a_r^{(j)}$ in Formulate (23) be a column vector, then for a given j, the R columns $a_1^{(j)}, a_2^{(j)}, \ldots, a_R^{(j)}$ constitute an $I_j \times R$ matrix denoted as A^j. Then Formulate (24) is equivalent to:

$$x = \sum_{r=1}^{R} A_r^{(1)} \circ A_r^{(2)} \circ \ldots \circ A_r^{(N)} \tag{24}$$

Finally all the values of x including the unknown values can be estimated from Formulate (25) as:

$$x_{i_1 i_2 \ldots i_N} \approx \widehat{x}_{i_1 i_2 \ldots i_N} = \sum_{r=1}^{R} A_{i_1 r}^{(1)} \cdot A_{i_2 r}^{(2)} \cdot \ldots \cdot A_{i_N r}^{(N)} \tag{25}$$

Step 3. Use the QoS tensor established in Step 2 and compute the component matrices, then we can predict the unknown QoS values by reconstructing the QoS tensor as Formulate (25).

This procedure can be executed in $O(S \cdot C \cdot R)$, where C is number of known values of χ and S is the number of iterations required. The core of this approach is one of the fastest optimization mechanisms and the performance can result in much better accuracy in recommending service.

3.2   The MF and Decision Tree Integration Approach

This approach was proposed by Qi Yu [15] to solve cold-start SRPs which integrated Matrix Factorization (MF) with decision tree learning to service recommendation systems.

Step 1. Matrix Factorization discovers the hidden user group structure from a set of incomplete QoS data. It computes two low-rank matrices $F \in R_+^{m \times k}$ and $G \in R_+^{n \times k}$ to approximate the original QoS matrix $M_{m \times n}$, i.e., $M \approx FG'$

Step 2. The tree learning algorithm constructs a decision tree to partition the users to fit the group structure discovered by MF. Firstly, discover user groups that contain users sharing similar QoS experience. Then, estimate the unobserved entries in the QoS matrix M.

Step 3. Cold-start service recommendation. The new user is expected to share similar QoS experience with other users in the same group. Therefore, the new user should not deviate much from the group mean, which makes the group mean a good estimate for the new user's QoS experience.

The cold-start performance of this approach outperforms the warm-start performance of other approaches. Compared to the ternary tree approach, which is not suitable for the initial interview of service recommendation, this approach contributes to the good performance for the cold-start issue.

3.3   The Context-Aware Role Mining Approach

Jian Wang et al. [16] proposed the approach to group users automatically to their interests and habits for mobile service recommendation of SRPs. Then, popular mobile services can be recommended to other members in the same group in a context dependent manner. This approach can be implemented as follow steps.

Step 1. Mine the minimal set of roles from the user-context-behavior matrix, and output the user-role assignment matrix and the role-context-behavior assignment matrix.

Step 2. Create a role tree based on FCA (Formal Concept Analysis) approach [17] and a formal context can be represented as a matrix, where rows represent objects and columns represent attributes.

This approach was successfully applied to recommend service on mobile devices and evaluated as an efficient and scalable for mobile service recommendation.

4   Conclusion

The Service Recommendation Problem lies at the heart of commercial systems (i.e., Amazon, Ebay and so on), service computing [18, 19], cloud computing [20] and mobile computing [21] and so on. There exist several versions of the problem, and a wide variety of traditional and recent approaches have been proposed for its solution. Traditional approaches can only solve relatively small problems, but a number of recent approaches have proved very satisfactory.

Acknowledgments. The work was supported by the National Natural Science Foundation of China (61472047); and the Fundamental Research Funds for the Central Universities (2016RC19).

References

1. Hu, Y., Peng, Q., Hu, X.: A time-aware and data sparsity tolerant approach for web service recommendation. In: Proceeding of IEEE International Conference on Web Services, pp. 33–40. IEEE (2014)
2. Patil, P.M., Wagh, R.B., Patil, P.M., Wagh, R.B.: Survey on different ranking and prediction for quality of service, pp. 6–8 (2014)
3. Tatiya, R.V., Vaidya, A.S.: A survey of recommendation algorithms. IOSR J. Comput. Eng. **1**, 16–19 (2014)
4. Subha, M., Banu, M.U.: A survey on QoS ranking in cloud computing. Int. J. Emerg. Technol. Adv. Eng. **4**, 482–488 (2014)
5. Puri, A., Bhonsle, M.: A survey of web service recommendation techniques based on QoS values
6. Ma, Y., Wang, S., Hung, P.C., Hsu, C.-H., Sun, Q., Yang, F.: A highly accurate prediction algorithm for unknown web service QoS values (2015)

7. Ma, Y., Wang, S., Yang, F., Chang, R.N.: Predicting QoS values via multi-dimensional QoS data for web service recommendations. In: Proceeding of IEEE International Conference on Web Services, pp. 249–256. IEEE (2015)
8. Zheng, Z., Ma, H., Lyu, M.R., King, I.: Wsrec: a collaborative filtering based web service recommender system. In: Proceeding of IEEE International Conference on Web Services, pp. 437–444. IEEE (2009)
9. Zheng, Z., Ma, H., Lyu, M.R., King, I.: QoS-Aware web service recommendation by collaborative filtering. IEEE Trans. Serv. Comput. **4**, 140–152 (2011)
10. Chen, X., Liu, X., Huang, Z., Sun, H.: Regionknn: a scalable hybrid collaborative filtering algorithm for personalized web service recommendation. In: Proceeding of IEEE International Conference on Web Services, pp. 9–16. IEEE (2010)
11. Jiang, Y., Liu, J., Tang, M., Liu, X.: An effective web service recommendation method based on personalized collaborative filtering. In: Proceeding of IEEE International Conference on Web Services, pp. 211–218. IEEE (2011)
12. Shao, L., Zhang, J., Wei, Y., Zhao, J., Xie, B., Mei, H.: Personalized QoS prediction for web services via collaborative filtering. In: Proceeding of IEEE International Conference on Web Services, pp. 439–446. IEEE (2007)
13. Xu, J., Wang, S., Su, S., Kumar, A.P., Wu, C.: Latent interest and topic mining on user-item bipartite networks. In: IEEE International Conference on Services Computing, pp. 778–781. IEEE (2016)
14. Tang, M., Dai, X., Cao, B., Liu, J.: WSWalker: a random walk method for QoS-aware web service recommendation. In: Proceeding of IEEE International Conference on Web Services, pp. 591–598. IEEE (2015)
15. Yu, Q.: Decision tree learning from incomplete QoS to bootstrap service recommendation. In: Proceeding of IEEE International Conference on Web Services, pp. 194–201. IEEE (2012)
16. Wang, J., Zeng, C., He, C., Hong, L., Zhou, L., Wong, R.K., Tian, J.: Context-aware role mining for mobile service recommendation. In: Proceedings of the 27th Annual ACM Symposium on Applied Computing, pp. 173–178. ACM (2012)
17. Priss, U.: Formal concept analysis in information science. Arist **40**, 521–543 (2006)
18. Wang, S., Zhou, A., Lei, W., Yu, Z., Hsu, C.-H., Yang, F.: Enhanced user context-aware reputation measurement of multimedia service (2010)
19. Wang, S., Zheng, Z., Wu, Z., Lyu, M.R., Yang, F.: Reputation measurement and malicious feedback rating prevention in web service recommendation systems. IEEE Trans. Serv. Comput. **8**, 755–767 (2015)
20. Zhou, A., Wang, S., Li, J., Sun, Q., Yang, F.: Optimal mobile device selection for mobile cloud service providing. J. Supercomput. 1–14 (2016)
21. Wang, S., Sun, L., Sun, Q., Li, X., Yang, F.: Efficient service selection in mobile information systems. Mobile Information Systems (2015)

Gaussian LDA and Word Embedding for Semantic Sparse Web Service Discovery

Gang Tian[1,2], Jian Wang[1(✉)], Ziqi Zhao[2], and Junju Liu[3]

[1] State Key Lab of Software Engineering, Wuhan University, Wuhan, China
{tiangang,jianwang}@whu.edu.cn
[2] College of Information Science and Engineering,
Shandong University of Science and Technology, Qingdao, China
1362190630@qq.com
[3] Zhixing College, Hubei University, Wuhan, China
orange_wh@qq.com

Abstract. In recent years, more and more Web services are published in API marketplaces founded by cloud service providers or third party registries. In this situation, users rely heavily on the search engine model to retrieve their expected Web services. However, due to the fact that Web services registered in API marketplaces are described in short texts, the search engine based discovery method suffers from the semantic sparsity problem, which in turn leads to a poor recall during service discovery. To address this issue, in this paper, we propose a novel Web service discovery approach that uses Gaussian Latent Dirichlet Allocation (Gaussian LDA) and word embedding. More specifically, instead of clustering Web services like most existing service discovery approaches, we use word embedding to map the words as continuous word embeddings to extend and enrich the semantics of service descriptions. We also leverage the Gaussian LDA in service discovery, which takes continuous word distribution as the input and interprets the Web service description as a hierarchical model by its two distributions. Based on the Gaussian LDA and word embedding, we propose a Web service query and ranking approach. Experiments conducted on a real-world Web service dataset demonstrate the effectiveness of the proposed approach.

Keywords: Word embedding · Gaussian LDA · Semantic sparsity · Web service discovery

1 Introduction

Benefited by well-constructed Internet infrastructure and the advantages of service-oriented computing, more and more enterprises are driven to develop or transform their business applications into distributed Web services. These Web services that are usually deployed on the providers' servers are scattered over the Internet. Many enterprises tend to build their own Web service marketplaces on which the registered Web services are mainly built by using the platform owner's

© ICST Institute for Computer Sciences, Social Informatics and Telecommunications Engineering 2017
S. Wang and A. Zhou (Eds.): CollaborateCom 2016, LNICST 201, pp. 48–59, 2017.
DOI: 10.1007/978-3-319-59288-6_5

cloud services or closely related to the platform owner's business. Google Apps Marketplace, Amazon Web service marketplace and Microsoft Azure Web service marketplace are the well known representatives. In this trend, the search engine based approach is widely used to help users in discovering Web services. However, Web service search engines that mainly focus on keyword-based matching may result in the poor recall problem due to the scattered registration, the lack of keywords in Web service descriptions, the use of synonyms, or variations of keywords [5]. To enhance the capability of search engines by clustering services into functionally similar groups is a useful method to handle this problem. However, some new issues are emerging in recent years. One typical problem is the semantic sparsity, which results from short text descriptions of Web services provided by most marketplaces. That is, there is no sufficient information to express the full semantics of Web services. Towards this issue, many works on how to transfer external information to enrich the semantic representation of short text documents have been proposed. For example, Jin et al. [7] present a transfer learning approach, which can facilitate short texts clustering by using auxiliary long texts. Hu et al. [6] introduce a short text clustering method by using world knowledge. These works generally make an implicit assumption that the auxiliary information is semantically related to the short texts. However, it is not trivial to find such kind of auxiliary information, which makes the assumption not always true in real data.

To address this issue, we introduce the word embeddings which have been shown to capture lexico-semantic regularities in language. In the embedding space, words with similar syntactic and semantic properties are found to be close to each other [11]. Thus, this feature is particularly suitable to solve the problems of using synonyms/variations of keywords in the query. Furthermore, the context information such as the co-occurrence information in the word embeddings can be effectively used to enrich the semantics of a document. Inspired by this, we leverage word embeddings to handle the semantic sparsity problem in Web service discovery. Our main contributions are listed as follows:

- We leverage pre-trained word embeddings to enrich the semantics of Web service descriptions.
- We use Gaussian LDA to model the user query and Web service descriptions based on the continuous word embeddings, aiming to improve the quality of Web service discovery.
- We conduct experiments to illustrate the feasibility of the proposed approach.

The rest of the paper is organized as follows. Section 2 discusses related works in the area of Web service discovery. Section 3 introduces the proposed model in detail. Section 4 reports our empirical experiments. Section 5 concludes the paper.

2 Related Work

Web service discovery is viewed as a significant part of service computing and cloud computing, and many progresses have been made in this area. Because

Web services are often described in different description languages, the non-semantic based discovery approaches are fairly different. For example, Liu et al. [10] extract four features including service content, context, host name, and service name from WSDL documents to cluster Web services by text mining techniques. Similarly, Elgazzar et al. [5] also extract content, types, messages, ports, and service name from WSDL documents as features of their information retrieval model to cluster Web services. In these works, the features in the information retrieval models come from the content extracted WSDL documents. If Web services are described in other description languages, these WSDL based methods may not be efficient enough or even fail to work. In this paper, we focus on the discovery of Web services which contain even less features. Therefore, the above methods may fail to work since they lack ways to handle the semantic sparsity problem.

Several studies have revealed that it is helpful to integrate external information to improve the performance of Web service discovery. Chen et al. [3] propose an augment LDA model to integrate WSDL and tags, which can improve the performance of Web service clustering. It has been shown that leveraging external information can enhance the discovery method to a certain extent. In the research field of Information Retrieval (IR), there are also some works to handle the semantic sparsity problem. For example, Hu et al. [6] aim to improve the performance of clustering short text by using world knowledge. Jin et al. [7] introduce a transfer learning based approach which clusters short texts by using auxiliary long texts. These methods can partially handle the semantic sparsity problem. However, they also have some limitations. For example, the work in [6] make the implicit assumption that the auxiliary data are semantically related to the short texts, which may have difficulties in practice. Similarly, the work [7] assumes that the topical structures of two domains are completely identical, which would be also unreasonable in the practice. Faced with these problems, we integrate external context information using word embeddings which can boost the performance in information retrieval tasks such as computing the short text similarity [8].

Probabilistic models such as Probabilistic Latent Semantic Analysis (PLSA), LDA and extensions of these models have been identified as efficient methods for boosting the performance of Web services discovery [2,3]. However, the basic assumption of these probabilistic models is that the words are discrete multinomial distribution, these models can not benefit from the word embeddings whose vectors are continuous. In contrast, we use Gaussian LDA [4] to leverage the advantages of both word embeddings and probabilistic models.

To the best of our knowledge, there is still no reported approach on leveraging word embedding techniques combined with Gaussian LDA for the semantic sparsity Web service discovery.

3   The Proposed Approach

We first describe the discovery process of the proposed approach in Sect. 3.1. In Sect. 3.2, we illustrate the service modelling method based on Gaussian LDA.

Finally, we introduce the query modelling method that integrates the word embedding in Sect. 3.3.

3.1   The Discovery Process of the Proposed Approach

Figure 1 illustrates the discovery process of the proposed approach, which consists of three major parts: service modeling, query modeling and service ranking.

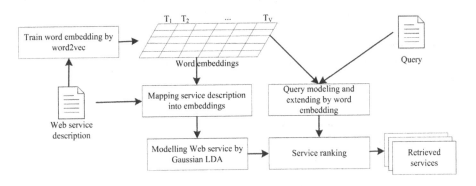

Fig. 1. Overall discovery process.

As shown in Fig. 1, service descriptions distributed on the Internet are firstly crawled and preprocessed. Then these service descriptions are taken as the input of the word2vec model[1] to create word embeddings. In this step, we can also introduce the pre-trained word embeddings directly, such as the word embeddings trained by using Wikipedia. After getting the word embeddings, we map the words in service descriptions into word embeddings to generate the input of Gaussian LDA. The Gaussian LDA plays the role of modeling each Web service as hierarchies of latent factors.

In the query modeling phase, the words in a given query are firstly mapped into embeddings by using the word embedding set produced in the service modeling step. Afterwards, in order to integrate more contextual information to enrich the semantics of the query, we use a query extension algorithm which finds similar neighbors of each word in a query by using the word embedding set to extend the query. After that, an extended query is obtained.

In the service ranking step, based on the hierarchies and the extended query, a probabilistic service ranking model is proposed to retrieve relevant services for the user.

Please note that the steps of training word embeddings and service modeling are conducted offline, only the query modeling and service ranking steps are performed online. Hence, the focus of the paper is placed more on the accuracy of discovery, not the efficiency.

---

[1] https://code.google.com/archive/p/word2vec/.

3.2 Web Service Modelling Using Gaussian LDA

In Gaussian LDA [4], the word embedding of each term w or v_{di} in a document d at position i is written as $v(w) \in R^M$, and M is the length of the word embedding. Thus, the words in a document are no longer discrete values but are mapped into continuous vectors in an M dimensional space. As a result, each topic k is characterized as a multivariate Gaussian distribution with mean μ_k and covariance Σ_k. The parameterization for the Gaussian is justified by both analytic convenience and the semantic similarity of embeddings [4]. To govern the mean and variance of each Gaussian, the Gaussian distribution centered at zero and an inverse Wishart distribution for the covariance are placed as the conjugate priors.

Using Gaussian LDA, each word w represented by its embedding e in a Web service description is associated with the latent variable topic z, and each topic z is associated with the service description d. With these two relations, a service can be viewed as two layers: the Service-Topic layer and the Topic-Embedding layer. First, each word w (e.g., "API" and "access") is represented as a vector of a fixed length after running the word2vec model. For example, the word 'academic' is represented as $[0.26\ -0.30\ -0.14\ \dots\ -0.05]$ with size of 50. Before using Gaussian LDA, each word in a Web service description is represented by the vector trained by word2vec. Thus, a Web service is mapped into a matrix with fixed columns of 50 in this paper. Secondly, the matrices representing the Web services are fed into the Gaussian LDA to produce that two layer represented by two distributions: Web service-topic distribution and topic-embedding distribution. The Web service-topic distribution is derived from the parameter θ ($\theta \in |services| \times |topics|$) as the traditional LDA model. In another side, the multivariate gaussian distributions are achieved by calculating the Cholesky triangular matrices. Finally, we established the hierarchies of Gaussian LDA by above mentioned two distributions.

To infer the posterior distribution of services over the topics and the topic assignments of individual words, a collapsed Gibbs sampler is derived to re-sample topic assignments to individual word vectors.

3.3 Retrieving Web Services

We define the process of retrieving Web services as three main steps: query modelling, query extension and service ranking.

Query Modelling. The first step is query modelling, which maps the user query into the word embedding feature space. A user query is defined as a set of words in the query: $Q = \{w_1, w_2, ..., w_{|Q|}\}$. We look up each word in the word embeddings.

Query Extension. Combining implicit or explicit semantics are helpful to enhance the performance of Web service matching and ranking by alleviating the problems due to service author/user heterogeneity [12]. Distributed word

---

Algorithm 1. Query Extension

Input: query Q, similarity weight τ, the embedding set E
Output: the extended query Q_e .
$Q_e \leftarrow \varnothing$;
for *word* $w \in Q$ **do**
    for *word* $e_w \in E.most\_similar(w)$ **do**
        $\Xi_w \leftarrow \varnothing$;
        if *similarity(e_w,w)* $\geq \tau$ **then**
            $\Xi_w \leftarrow \Xi_w \cup e_w$;
        end
        $Q_e \leftarrow Q_e \cup \Xi_w$;
    end
end
return Q_e

---

representations, such as word embeddings which map every word into a dimensional continuous space, are assumed to represent semantic and syntactic information of words [9]. In the continuous representation space, words with similar meanings have similar vectors, which means that synonym, near-synonym and semantic related words of a word have high probability to appear in the similar neighbors. For example, the top 3 most similar words to 'month' trained on our dataset by the word2vec model are 'minute', 'hour' and 'day'. According to this characteristic, we can simply extended the query by integrating the similar words based on the word embedding model to convey more context information since the query is often short and semantic sparse. As shown in Algorithm 1, we extend the query by using the close neighbors in the embedding space. In Algorithm 1, we take query Q, similarity weight τ and the embedding set E trained by word2vec as input and the extended query Q_e as output. According to the word2vec model, we add neighbors whose similarity weights are greater than parameter τ for each word in a query Q into the extended query Q_e.

Services Ranking. To rank the retrieved Web service for a query, we need to create the base criteria to calculate the similarity between the user queries and the retrieved Web services. Similar to the work in [1], we use the generated probabilities to calculate the similarity. To this end, we model the service retrieval as a probabilistic query to the topic model. We note this as $P(Q|s_i)$ where Q is the set of words contained in the query. s_i is the i-th Web service. Thus, using the assumptions of the Gaussian LDA, $P(Q|s_i)$ can be calculated by Eq. 1.

$$P(Q|s_i) = \prod_{e \in Q_e} P(e|s_i) = \prod_{e \in Q_e} \sum_{z=1}^{K} P(e|z)P(z|s_i) \qquad (1)$$

Here, Q_e is obtained from Algorithm 1 which is the extended query of Q. $P(e|z)$ and $P(z|s)$ are the posterior probabilities which can be computed and the matrix θ, respectively.

The most relevant services are the ones that maximize the conditional probability of the query $P(Q|s_i)$. Consequently, relevant services are ranked according to their similarity scores to the query. In this way, we can obtain a ranking of the retrieved services towards a query.

4   Experiments

4.1   Experimental Preparation

To evaluate the performance of the proposed approach, we conducted several experiments on a real-world Web service discovery dataset called SAWSDL-TC3. We used a Python package named Gensim to train the word embeddings. As for Gaussian LDA, we directly used the Java implementation in Github[2].

Since different corpus conveys different context information for the word embeddings, we trained two word embedding sets using the corpus of Wikipedia and SAWSDL-TC3, respectively. We set the size of the word embedding as 50. In order to train Wikipedia, we use the default configuration of Gensim where the *size* is set to 50, *windowsize* is 5 and *min_count* equals 5. For SAWSDL-TC3 (TC3, for short), we pre-process them by parsing the WSDL documents, removing stop words and lemmatizing the remaining words. Note that, we adopt TC3 to verify the proposed approach, albeit it is still a WSDL service set, not a short text based service set. There are two reasons for doing this. On one hand, as far as we know, there are no standard test dataset for short text based Web service discovery, while TC3 is a widely used dataset in the field of Web service discovery. On the other hand, we apply word embeddings to extend the query, which can solve the semantic sparsity issue. That is, the main purpose of the experiments is to validate the query extension performance of the proposed approach. Thus, a WSDL based test set plays the similar role as a short text based test set.

In our experiments, we used precision p, recall r and F-Measure f as the evaluation criterion for the proposed approach. The larger the F-Measure is, the better the performance of the discovery is. The TC3 dataset contains different queries (i.e., 42 requests), which are also represented in WSDL documents. Furthermore, a binary and graded relevance set for each query is provided which is viewed as the grounding truth in computing the precision or recall.

4.2   Performance of the Proposed Approach

To demonstrate the performance of our method, we compare the proposed method with four Web service discovery approaches. These approaches are illustrated as follows:

1. TF-IDF: We represent each description of the Web service with TF-IDF, and calculate the similarity with Cosine similarity.

---

[2] https://github.com/rajarshd/Gaussian_LDA.

Table 1. Performance of the proposed approach

Query	TF-IDF			PLSA			LDA			GLDA			GLDA+QE		
	p	r	f	p	r	f	p	r	f	p	r	f	p	r	f
@10	0.67	0.30	0.41	0.73	0.34	0.46	0.64	0.30	0.40	0.76	0.37	0.50	0.81	0.42	0.55
@15	0.57	0.35	0.43	0.66	0.41	0.50	0.57	0.35	0.43	0.69	0.43	0.53	0.74	0.49	0.59
@20	0.50	0.38	0.44	0.59	0.46	0.52	0.50	0.38	0.44	0.61	0.47	0.53	0.67	0.53	0.60
@25	0.46	0.45	0.44	0.56	0.51	0.53	0.45	0.31	0.43	0.58	0.51	0.54	0.64	0.57	0.60
@30	0.37	0.46	0.42	0.53	0.56	0.54	0.41	0.44	0.43	0.55	0.54	0.54	0.61	0.62	0.62
@35	0.34	0.48	0.40	0.49	0.60	0.53	0.38	0.46	0.42	0.51	0.59	0.55	0.57	0.66	0.61
@40	0.30	0.52	0.38	0.46	0.62	0.51	0.36	0.49	0.42	0.49	0.61	0.54	0.54	0.68	0.60
Average	0.459	0.42	0.439	0.574	0.50	0.534	0.472	0.39	0.427	0.599	0.503	0.547	0.654	0.567	0.61

Notes: GLDA denotes Gaussian LDA; GLDA+QE denotes Gaussian LDA + Query Extension.

2. PLSA: In this approach, Web services are clustered according to the latent factors learned from the Web service descriptions [2].
3. LDA: LDA is another commonly used latent factor based model for service clustering. Services are also grouped according to their latent factors [2].
4. Gaussian LDA: For Gaussian LDA, we first train the word embeddings by Word2vec from the prepared corpus such as Wikipedia. Then we change the words in each Web service into embedding vectors and take the word embeddings in the service description as the input of the Gaussian-LDA. Finally, we take it as the discovery model according to the methods in Sect. 3 except for extending the query.

For the PLSA and LDA models, we learned the topics from the descriptions of the Web services following the procedures described in the work [2], and we tune each algorithm to its best parameter setting by cross validation and the parameters influence will be discussed in Sect. 4.5.

According to these experiments, we have several observations. Firstly, the F-Measure performance of the proposed approach (Gaussian LDA + Query Extension) outperforms other approaches as shown in Table 1, which demonstrates the effectiveness of the proposed approach.

Secondly, the Gaussian LDA based approach without query extension has better performance than LDA based approach. The results show that Gaussian LDA which takes continuous embeddings as input may capture more semantically coherent topics compared to the LDA based approach.

Thirdly, extending the queries by using word embeddings contributes to the performance improvement of the Web service discovery. As shown in Table 1, the approach of Gaussian LDA + Query Extension which uses Algorithm 1 to extend the query has a better performance in all conditions compared with the Gaussian LDA approach. A possible explanation for this may be that more contextual information of the query is introduced to enrich the semantics of the query.

4.3   Validation of Embedding

In the proposed approach, the embedding set plays two important roles: one is to change the Bag of Words model into continuous embedding space, and the other is to extend the query by providing additional contextual information. Figure 2 shows the F-Measure performance of the proposed approach with different word embeddings trained by word2vec model using two different corpus TC3 and Wikipedia, as described in Sect. 4.1.

According to these results, we can see that the proposed method using TC3 has a better performance than using Wikipedia. However, the improvement of the performance is not very significant. There are several possible explanations for this result: the word embeddings trained from TC3 may be more domain specific than that of Wikipedia, that is, the domain that the words in a Web service description belong to may have different word distribution compared with Wikipedia. Another possible reason may be that some words, which are parsed from the WSDL files but do not have enough occurrence time in the Wikipedia corpus, are removed when training the embeddings though they are very informative. For example, the term 'lendingduration' composed of words 'lending' and 'duration' is informative in many descriptions, but it is dismissed in the embeddings as it is not parsed into individual words.

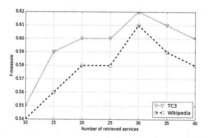

Fig. 2. Influence of different embedding sets.

4.4   Validation of Query Extension and Semantic Sparsity

Query extension illustrated in Sect. 3.3 is introduced to enrich the contextual information for the query. Figure 3(a) shows the F-Measure performance of two approaches using Gaussian LDA: one with query extension and the other one without extending the query. According to these results, we can discover that the performances of Gaussian LDA with query extension outperforms the approach without query extension in all conditions of different size of retrieved Web services. The results of this study indicate that integrating more contextual information will contribute to the performance improvement of the proposed approach. However, in our approach, we did not distinguish the relation between the added words and the original one, which will be further investigated in our future work.

An experiment on validating the sparsity problem is also conducted and the result is shown in Fig. 3(b). We truncated each WSDL file by randomly choosing feature words according to a certain scale to simulate the sparsity context. For example, we choose 10% words of a WSDL to create a new semantic sparsity file to stand for the original one when the number of retrieved services is 30. Based on the new file, we conducted the similar retrieval task to check the performance of the proposed approach in dealing with the semantic sparsity problem by following the process discussed in above sections. As shown in Fig. 3(b), the retrieval performances of both approaches are getting better with the increase of the percentage of WSDL involved in the experiments, which shows that the semantic sparsity problem does affect the performance of the retrieval model. Moreover, the more percentage of the WSDL files are involved in, the better performance is achieved, which validates that the proposed model can handle the semantic sparsity problem. The results also show the F-Measure under all settings of the proposed model are better than that of Guassian LDA without query extension, which further indicates that query extension contributes to retrieval task.

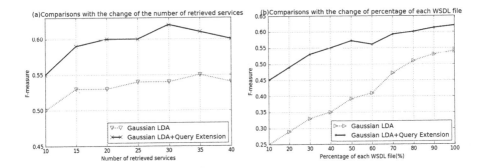

Fig. 3. Validation of semantic sparsity

4.5   Influence of Parameters

Hyperparameters: In Gaussian-LDA, the parameter α denotes the weight of language model contribution while μ and Σ control the document contribution.

In our work, some parameters are set as $\alpha = 1/K$, μ = zero mean and $\Sigma = 3 * I$ as defined in the work [4]. Here K is the number of topics and I is the identity matrix.

Topic Numbers: We computed an estimate of $P(e|k)$ for different K values. For all values of k, we ran the Gaussian LDA model until it converges. In that case, the log-likelihood values stabilized within a few hundred iterations, as shown in Fig. 4(a). The results suggest that the data are best accounted for by a model incorporating 6 topics.

Similarity Weight τ: As illustrated in Algorithm 1, the value τ is used to control the similar neighbors of each word to extend a query. A higher value results in less words to be chosen. On the other hand, a small value may bring more irrelevant contextual information into the queries. Thus we tune the parameter according to the performance of the proposed approach by cross validation.

Figure 4(b) shows the influence for discovery performance under different settings of similarity weight τ. As shown in Fig. 4(b), an F-measure performance is achieved when τ is 0.96.

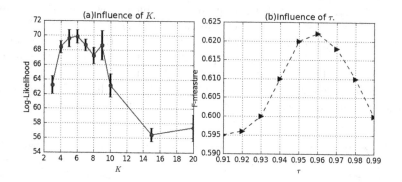

Fig. 4. Influence of parameters.

5   Conclusion

In this paper, we proposed a Web service discovery approach that combines Gaussian LDA with word embeddings to deal with the poor recall problem in searching semantic sparse Web services. We used word embeddings to model the word as continuous embedding, which can extend and enrich the semantics of Web service descriptions. We also introduced the Gaussian LDA which models the Web services as three layers by its two distributions. Based on the Gaussian LDA and word embedding, we proposed a service query and ranking approach.

We validated the proposed approach by using a real-world Web service dataset. Several experiments were conducted to assess the effectiveness of the proposed approach. Experimental results suggested that the proposed approach is feasible, and in particular the inclusion of meaningful word embeddings in the discovery process leads to enhanced performance.

In the future, we plan to further investigate the usefulness of various sources of word embeddings in Web service discovery. We also try to incorporate more linguistic features to provide goal oriented Web service discovery.

Acknowledgment. The work is supported by the National Basic Research Program of China under grant No. 2014CB340404, the National Natural Science Foundation of China under grant Nos. 61672387 and 61373037, the State Key Laboratory of Software Engineering Foundation under the grant No.SKLSE 2014-10-07, University Science and Technology Program of Shandong Province under the grant No.J16LN08, Scientific Research Foundation of Shandong University of Science and Technology for Recruited Talents under the grant No.2016RCJJ045. Jian Wang is the corresponding author.

References

1. Aznag, M., Quafafou, M., Jarir, Z.: Leveraging formal concept analysis with topic correlation for service clustering and discovery. In: Proceedings of the 2014 IEEE International Conference on Web Services (ICWS), pp. 153–160. IEEE (2014)
2. Cassar, G., Barnaghi, P., Moessner, K.: Probabilistic methods for service clustering. In: Proceeding of the 4th International Workshop on Semantic Web Service Matchmaking and Resource Retrieval, Organised in Conjonction the ISWC. Citeseer (2010)
3. Chen, L., Wang, Y., Yu, Q., Zheng, Z., Wu, J.: WT-LDA: user tagging augmented LDA for web service clustering. In: Basu, S., Pautasso, C., Zhang, L., Fu, X. (eds.) ICSOC 2013. LNCS, vol. 8274, pp. 162–176. Springer, Heidelberg (2013). doi:10. 1007/978-3-642-45005-1_12
4. Das, R., Zaheer, M., Dyer, C.: Gaussian LDA for topic models with word embeddings. In: ACL 2015 July 26–31, 2015, Beijing, China, vol. 1, Long Papers, pp. 795–804 (2015)
5. Elgazzar, K., Hassan, A.E., Martin, P.: Clustering wsdl documents to bootstrap the discovery of web services. In: Proceedings of the 2010 IEEE International Conference on Web Services (ICWS), pp. 147–154. IEEE (2010)
6. Hu, X., Sun, N., Zhang, C., Chua, T.S.: Exploiting internal and external semantics for the clustering of short texts using world knowledge. In: Proceedings of the 18th ACM Conference on Information and Knowledge Management, pp. 919–928. ACM (2009)
7. Jin, O., Liu, N.N., Zhao, K., Yu, Y., Yang, Q.: Transferring topical knowledge from auxiliary long texts for short text clustering. In: Proceedings of the 20th ACM International Conference on Information and Knowledge Management, pp. 775–784. ACM (2011)
8. Kenter, T., de Rijke, M.: Short text similarity with word embeddings. In: Proceedings of the 24th ACM International on Conference on Information and Knowledge Management, pp. 1411–1420. ACM (2015)
9. Li, Y., Xu, L., Tian, F., Jiang, L., Zhong, X., Chen, E.: Word embedding revisited: a new representation learning and explicit matrix factorization perspective (2015)
10. Liu, W., Wong, W.: Web service clustering using text mining techniques. Int. J. Agent Oriented Softw. Eng. **3**(1), 6–26 (2009)
11. Mikolov, T., Yih, W.t., Zweig, G.: Linguistic regularities in continuous space word representations. In: HLT-NAACL, pp. 746–751 (2013)
12. Tekli, J.: An overview on xml semantic disambiguation from unstructured text to semi-structured data: background, applications, and ongoing challenges. IEEE Trans. Knowl. Data Eng. **28**, 1383–1407 (2016)

Quality-Assure and Budget-Aware Task Assignment for Spatial Crowdsourcing

Qing Wang[1], Wei He[1(✉)], Xinjun Wang[1,2], and Lizhen Cui[1]

[1] School of Computer Science and Technology, Shandong University, Jinan, China
wang_qing@mail.sdu.edu.cn, {hewei,wxj,clz}@sdu.edu.cn
[2] Dareway Software Co., Ltd, Jinan, China

Abstract. With the increasingly ubiquity of mobile devices and the rapid development of communication technologies, spatial crowdsourcing has become a hot topic research among academic and industry community. As participants may possess different capabilities and reliabilities, as well as the changeable locations and available time slots of both tasks and potential workers, a major challenge is how to assign spatial tasks to appropriate workers from lots of potential applicants, which should assure the result quality of the crowdsourcing task. Also, as different workers may receive variable rewards for the same task, the crowdsourcing budget renders task assignment more complicated. This paper focuses on the issue of quality assurance for task assignment in spatial crowdsourcing while considering budget limitation. The problem is first modeled as Quality-assure and Budget-aware Task Assignment (QBTA) problem. Then two two-phase greedy algorithms are proposed. Finally, experiments are conducted to show the effectiveness and efficiency of the algorithms.

Keywords: Spatial crowdsourcing · Task assignment · Quality assurance

1 Introduction

With the increasingly ubiquity of mobile devices [1] and the rapid development of ultra-broadband wireless networks (e.g., 4G) [2], spatial crowdsourcing has attracted more and more attention in both the academic and industry community. It aims to allocate each spatial task (i.e., the task related to its location and time) to a set of workers, whom are required to reach the predetermined physical position to perform the task (e.g., taking a picture or checking in a spot) before the expiration time. In order to attract more participants, each worker who has been assigned and performed the task is probably rewarded in any form of incentive such as monetary payment or diverse coupons which can be exchanged for goods or services [3].

As the potential workers may possess different capabilities and reliabilities, a major impediment to the success of any spatial crowdsourcing [1] is how to guarantee the quality of results (e.g., the accuracy of the collected results) obtained from the workers [3]. An intuitive idea of quality assurance for spatial crowdsourcing is assigning tasks to workers with high reputations and abilities. Kazemi et al. defined a confidence level for every spatial task and stated that each assignment is accepted only if the confidence of candidate workers is higher than a certain threshold [1]. In their approach, a parameter "maxT" is introduced for each worker to limit the maximum number of tasks assigned to him/her in order to avoid global imbalance of task assignment. As a result, each task will be assigned to as few workers as possible which satisfies the confidence level of the task. However, it is not always reasonable because the task publisher may expect a large number of different workers to perform the same task, rather than a small set of skilled workers. For example, in order to check the condition of the billboards at different locations, an advertising agent expects to collect a great many photos of the billboards to assure a right decision could be made on whether the billboards need to be repaired/ replaced or not. Note that the photos with diverse directions and different time of photography always show different conditions. Therefore, to obtain the full view of the billboards, a straightforward method is to employ a large number of workers to perform the task, which provides a high probability to get more satisfied and diverse results. But it is usually impractical because the task publisher will provide a personal reward for every worker who performs the task, which may be resulted in an expensive cost on workers' rewards for the task publisher. Han Yu et al. aim to figure out a set of workers for each spatial task with the maximum expected quality of results and the total rewards within a pre-specified budget [3]. However, it is not reasonable for the assumption that every worker will perform the assigned task correctly. As the potential workers may locate at various positions to perform the task, which probably leads to different traffic costs (i.e., time, distance and money), the expensive traffic costs may discourage the workers to reach the task location and perform the task correctly before expiration time in case that the traffic costs exceed their expectations.

In this paper, we focus on the issue of quality assurance (i.e., at least a given number of workers could reach the task location and perform the task correctly before the expiration time) for task assignment in spatial crowdsourcing while considering a total the budget limitation. For one specific spatial task, the objective is to figure out a set of workers from large numbers of potential applicants to perform the task, which satisfies both the pre-specified confidence requirement and budget limitation. The problem is first modeled as Quality-assure and Budget-aware Task Assignment (QBTA) problem. A confidence score (CS) is proposed for each individual worker to indicate the probability that he/she will reach the task location and correctly perform the specific spatial task before the expiration time. Based on the confidence score of individual workers, the Aggregate Confidence Score (ACS) is computed for a worker set to indicate the total confidence for the specific spatial task, which is the probability that at least a given number of workers in the worker set will reach the task location and perform the task correctly before the expiration time. Then, we propose a two-phase greedy algorithm (Quality_Sensitive) to figure out a worker set with higher quality for QBTA problem. Additionally, based on the Quality_Sensitive, another greedy algorithm (Cost_Sensitive) is developed to find out a worker set with less total rewards for QBTA problem. Finally, experiments on the real-world dataset are conducted to show the effectiveness and efficiency of our algorithms.

The rest of the paper is organized as follows. In Sect. 2, we review the related work and then define our problem formally in Sect. 3. We present our approaches namely

Quality_Sensitive and Cost_Sensitive in Sect. 4. Section 5 reports the results of our experiments. Finally, we conclude the paper in Sect. 6.

2   Related Work

With the ubiquity of mobile devices, spatial crowdsourcing is emerging as a new platform, enabling spatial tasks assigned to and performed by human workers [4]. Based on the motivation of the workers, spatial crowdsourcing has been classified into two classes: reward-based and self-incentivised [4]. With reward-based spatial crowdsourcing [6], every spatial task has a price and workers will receive a certain reward for every spatial task they perform correctly. The self-incentivised spatial crowdsourcing is for workers who are self-incentivised to perform tasks voluntarily [4]. We focus on the former class of spatial crowdsourcing.

As the fact that multiple available workers may compete for the same spatial task, the research on finding efficient solutions of task assignment in spatial crowdsourcing has attracted significant interest. Shahabi et al. focus on how to assign every worker his/her nearby tasks with the objective of maximizing the overall number of assigned tasks [4]. Deng et al. aim to find a task schedule for a worker that maximizes the number of performed tasks [2]. In [7], Yu Li et al. recommend an optimal route for a crowdsourcing worker with the maximum rewards of tasks along the route. Note that the workers with different levels of competence [3] may provide the results with different qualities and may receive different rewards for the same task. A major challenge for the reward-based spatial crowdsourcing is how to find an efficient solution of task assignment satisfying both the quality requirement and budget limitation of the task. Han Yu et al. determine the reward of a worker based on his/her past performance [8–10] and propose a *Budget-TASC* algorithm to find a task allocation plan to maximize the expected quality of the result while satisfying the budget limitations [3]. Yuko Sakurai et al. also propose a method for constructing an appropriate set of reward plans under a requester's constraints on budget and required accuracy [9]. In [1], a *HGR* algorithm is proposed to assign the task whose result is in the form of data modality, such as a binary value (0/1) to a set of workers. In reality, spatial tasks are required to support different other modalities of results (e.g., text, photos). Therefore, the algorithms aim to assign the task whose result is in more complex form of modality are needed.

3   Problem Definitions and Formulation

In this paper, we focus on how to find an efficient solution of task assignment in spatial crowdsourcing. As the fact that the spatial task always needs to be performed correctly by multiple workers in order to assure the quality of task result and the task publisher always offers variable rewards for different workers based on their track records and ratings, the objective of task assignment is to figure out a set of workers from large numbers of potential workers for each spatial task, which assures: (i) at least a given number of workers could reach the task location and correctly perform the task before expiration time, and (ii) the total rewards of the selected workers would not exceed the budget. In this section, we first formally define the QBTA problem and then give an example to illustrate the problem. Last, we discuss the confidence evaluation model.

3.1 Problem Definitions

Definition 1 (Worker). A worker w is represented as a 4-tuple $<r, rk, l_w, t_w>$, which denotes that the worker w with a reputation r and a rank rk locates in the location l_w at time t_w. The reputation r indicates the worker's credibility and computed based on his/her historical ratings and track records, which is used to measure the probability that he/she will perform the task and submit a satisfied result if he/she has been assigned the task. For simplicity of discussions, workers are classified as having *high* (*H*), *medium* (*M*) or *low* (*L*) ranks based on their reputations [3], i.e., rk = H/M/L.

In many crowdsourcing applications, such as *Uber* [11], the worker will receive a rating from the task publisher to evaluate the result quality after he/she has performed the task. Many approaches [12–15] can be used to calculate the worker's reputation based on his/her historical ratings and track records. In this paper, the reputation $r(w)$ of worker w is calculated as follows:

$$r(w) = \frac{EX(R)}{M} \text{ and } EX(R) = \frac{1}{n}\sum_{i=1}^{n} R_i. \tag{1}$$

Where n is the total number of tasks assigned to w, $R_i(1 \le i \le n)$ is the rating of task t_i the worker w received, M is the maximum rating the task publisher could give.

Definition 2 (Spatial Task). A spatial task t is represented as a 5-tuple $<l_t, et, minW,$ $rew, B>$, which denotes that the task t should be performed in the location l_t before the expiration time et by at least $minW$ number of workers correctly. rew is a 2-tuple $<p_H,$ $p_M>$ to state the rewards for workers with *high* and *medium* ranks, respectively. Similar to [3], we assume that a task publisher would not to engage a *low-rank* worker. $B(t)$ is the budget limitation of the task t, which means that t should be assigned to a set of workers which the total rewards are less than $B(t)$.

Definition 3 (Confidence Score CS). Confidence Score $CS(t, w)$ is a probability that the worker w will reach the task location and correctly perform the task t before the expiration time, which indicates the confidence level of the worker w for task t.

Definition 4 (Aggregate Confidence Score ACS). Aggregate Confidence Score $ACS(t, W)$ is the probability that at least $minW_t$ number of workers in a worker set W will reach the task location and perform the task t correctly before the expiration time, which indicates the confidence level of the worker set W for the task t.

Definition 5 (Confidence Requirement CR). The Confidence Requirement of task t is represented as $CR_t(conf_t, minW_t)$, which states that t should be assigned to a set of workers W, which satisfies that $ACS(t, W) \ge conf_t$ and $|W| \ge minW_t$.

Based on the definitions above, the issue of task assignment for a spatial crowd-sourcing task is formalized as the QBTA problem, which described as follows:

Given a spatial tasks t and a set of workers W, the objective is to figure out a subset $W*(t)$ of W which satisfies $CR_t(conf_t, minW_t)$ and $B(t)$ of the task t. The QBTA problem can be expressed as follows:

$$subject\ to:\ ACS(t, W*(t)) \geq conf_t, |W*(t)| \geq minW_t$$
$$\sum_{w \in W*(t)} rew(w) \leq B(t),\ W*(t)\ is\ the\ subset\ of\ W. \tag{2}$$

3.2   An Example of QBTA Problem

An example of QBTA problem is shown in Fig. 1, where there is one spatial task and ten potential workers. The task t is located in position (5, 5), which will expire after 10 time units and is expected to be performed by at least 3 workers correctly. The task publisher would offer 6-cent and 4-cent rewards for each worker with a high rank and medium rank, respectively and spend at most 25 cents on workers' rewards totally (i.e., $B(t) = 25$). Also, the task publisher requires that the probability of at least 3 workers correctly perform the task is more than 0.6 (i.e., $CR_t(0.6, 3)$). Based on the track records and ratings of each worker w_i, $r(w_i)$ is computed using Eq. (1) and then his/her rank $rk(w_i)$ and reward $rew(w_i)$ are determined. Then, the $CS(t, w_i)$ will be computed by the following confidence evaluation model in the next subsection. Thereafter, our objective is to figure out a set of workers $W*(t)$ from the ten workers for task t which satisfies $CR_t(0.6, 3)$ and $B(t)$. In this example, task t could be assigned to a worker set $\{w_3, w_4, w_6, w_8\}$ or $\{w_3, w_4, w_6, w_9\}$ which satisfies $CR_t(0.6, 3)$ and $B(t)$.

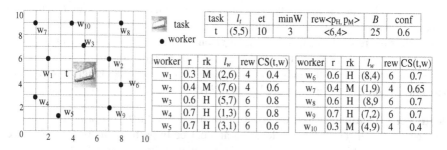

task	l_t	et	minW	rew<p_H, p_M>	B	conf
t	(5,5)	10	3	<6,4>	25	0.6

worker	r	rk	l_w	rew	CS(t,w)	worker	r	rk	l_w	rew	CS(t,w)
w_1	0.3	M	(2,6)	4	0.4	w_6	0.6	H	(8,4)	6	0.7
w_2	0.4	M	(7,6)	4	0.6	w_7	0.4	M	(1,9)	4	0.65
w_3	0.6	H	(5,7)	6	0.8	w_8	0.6	H	(8,9	6	0.7
w_4	0.7	H	(1,3)	6	0.8	w_9	0.7	H	(7,2)	6	0.7
w_5	0.7	H	(3,1)	6	0.6	w_{10}	0.3	M	(4,9)	4	0.4

Fig. 1. An example of QBTA problem

3.3   Confidence Evaluation Model

We propose a confidence evaluation model to calculate the confidence score of an individual worker and the aggregate confidence score of a worker set.

Given the spatial task $t(l_t, et, minW, B)$ and a set of workers $W\{w_1, w_2 ..., w_m\}$, for $1 \leq i \leq m$, $CS(t, w_i)$ depends on three main factors: (1) worker's reputation $r(w_i)$, a worker with a higher reputation generally provides more reliable results than workers with lower reputations [3]. (2) Worker's traffic distance to the task location $dis(w, t)$. A further traffic distance always leads to an expensive traffic cost, which renders the worker unwilling to reach the task location. (3) Worker's available time $\Delta t(t, w_i)$ to perform the task after reaching the task location, which is calculated by Eq. (3). The abundant $\Delta t(t, w_i)$ always promotes the worker w_i to offer a more satisfied result.

$$\Delta t(t, w_i) = et(t) - t_{w_i} - \tau(w_i, t) \ and \ \tau(w_i, t) = \frac{dis(w_i, t)}{speed_{w_i}}. \tag{3}$$

Where $\tau(w, t)$ and $dis(w, t)$ denote the traffic time and distance from l_w to l_t, respectively $speed_w$ is the (constant) traffic speed of worker w. Note that any distance function can be used to calculate $dis(w, t)$ only if it satisfies the triangle inequality, such as Euclidean distance, Manhattan distance and road network distance [7].

In a word, $CS(t, w_i)$ is calculated as follows:

$$CS(t, w_i) = r(w_i) * \delta(l_{w_i}, l_t) * f(w_i, t). \tag{4}$$

Where $\delta(l_{w_i}, l_t)$ is a function calculating the discount to the worker's reputation as a result of his/her location proximity to the task location [3]. It is defined as:

$$\delta(l_{w_i}, l_t) = 1 - \max[0, \ \min[\log_D(d(l_{w_i}, l_t)), \ 1]]$$
$$where \ d(l_{w_i}, l_t) \ is \ the \ Euclidean \ dis\tan ce \ and \ D \ is \ the \ diameter \ of \ a \ given \ area \tag{5}$$

$f(w_i, t)$ is a function to calculate the discount to the worker's reputation and location proximity as a result of his/her available time $\Delta t(t, w_i)$. It is defined as:

$$f(w_i, t) = \frac{\Delta t(t, w_i)}{\max_{w_i \in W}\{\Delta t(t, w_i)\}} \ where \ W \ is \ a \ worker \ set. \tag{6}$$

Thereafter, based on the $CS(t, w_i)$ of worker $w_i (1 \leq i \leq m)$ from W with size m, the $ACS(t, W)$ could be calculated as follows:

$$ACS(t, W) = \sum_{k=\min w_i}^{|W|} \sum_{A \subset F_k} \prod_{w \in A} CS(t, w) \prod_{w \notin A} (1 - CS(t, w))$$
$$where \ F_k \ is \ all \ the \ subsets \ of \ W \ with \ size \ k \tag{7}$$

4   Assignment Protocol

In this section, we propose two two-phase greedy algorithms for QBTA problem. The first algorithm (Quality_Sensitive) is proposed to find out a worker set with higher quality, while another algorithm (Cost_Sensitive) is developed to find out a worker set with less total rewards.

4.1 The Quality_Sensitive Algorithm

The two-phase greedy algorithm namely Quality_Sensitive is proposed for QBTA problem, which is shown in Algorithm 1.

In the first phase (lines 1–4), it traverses the worker set W to select the workers who satisfy both $\Delta t(t, w) \geq 0$ and $r(w) = H/M$, and then inserts them to $W'(t)$ in the descending order of $CS(t, w)$. In the second phase (lines 5–20), it first selects the top-K workers of $W'(t)$ to constitute the original W^* and the other workers constitute W_{re}. Then it needs to decide whether W^* satisfies the $CR_t(conf_t, minW_t)$ and $B(t)$ or not. There may incur three different conditions to be solved: (i) W^* does not satisfy the $CR_t(conf_t, minW_t)$. It will start the next loop. (ii) W^* satisfies $CR_t(conf_t, minW_t)$ and $B(t)$, it will return W^*. (iii) W^* only satisfies $CR_t (conf_t, minW_t)$. It will first find out the high-rank worker w_a with lowest CS in W^* and the medium-rank worker w_b with highest CS in W_{re}, then exchange them to generate the new W^* and W_{re}, finally, it returns to execute the eighth step in the current loop.

Algorithm1 Quality_Sensitive (t, W)

Input: a spatial task t, a worker set W
Output: $W^*(t)$

1: for each worker $w \in W$ do
2:   if w satisfies that $\Delta t(t,w) \geq 0$ and $rk(w)$=H or M
3:      compute $CS(t,w)$ based on the Eq. (4)
4:      insert w into $W'(t)$ in the descending order of the $CS(t,w)$
5: $W^* = \Phi$; $W_{re} = \Phi$
6: for $K=minW_t$ to $|W'(t)|$
7:   $W^*=\{w_1,w_2,\ldots,w_K\}$ and $W_{re}=\{w_{K+1},w_{K+2},\ldots,w_{|W'(t)|}\}$
8:   if W^* does not satisfy the $CR_t(conf_t, minW_t)$
9:      continue;/*stop the current loop and start the next loop*/
10: else if W^* satisfies the $B(t)$
11:     return W^*;
12: else
13:     $w_a \leftarrow$ the high-rank worker with lowest CS in W^*
14:     $w_b \leftarrow$ the medium-rank worker with highest CS in W_{re}
15:     if w_a and w_b are both exist
16:        $W^* \leftarrow W^* \cup \{w_b\}-\{w_a\}$
17:        $W_{re} \leftarrow W_{re} \cup \{w_a\}-\{w_b\}$
18:        continue to execute start from the eighth step
19:     else
20:     $W^* = \Phi$
21: end

Let us consider the example of Fig. 1. It first realigns the workers in the descending order of $CS(t, w)$ and then choose the top-3 workers w_3, w_4, w_6 to constitute W^*. However, $\{w_3, w_4, w_6\}$ does not satisfy the CR(0.6, 3), thus $K = 4$, $\{w_3, w_4, w_6, w_8\}$ satisfies the CR(0.6,3) and B(t). Therefore, $W^* = \{w_3, w_4, w_6, w_8\}$.

For the task t, the algorithm needs to traverse the worker set W for one time to generate the ordered $W'(t)$. Thereafter, for min W K $\leq$ |W'(t)|, it greedily chooses the top-K workers to constitute the W* and then decides W* whether satisfies $CR_t(conf_t, minW_t)$ and $B(t)$ or not. Therefore, the time complexity is $O(|W|)$.

4.2 The Cost_Sensitive Algorithm

Considering the task publisher always prefers to spend less cost for workers' rewards. Based on the Quality_Sensitive algorithm, another two-phase greedy algorithm namely Cost_Sensitive is proposed to return a worker set with less total rewards.

Given a spatial task t and a worker set W, it first inserts the workers who satisfy both $\Delta t(t, w) \leq 0$ and $r(w) = H/M$ to $W'(t)$ in the ascending order of the reward. Then it gives higher priority to the workers with higher CS among those with equal rewards. In the second phase, it will decide whether W* satisfies both $CR_t(conf_t, minW_t)$ and B_t or not. There may incur three different conditions to be solved: (i) W* does not satisfy $B(t)$, the algorithm must stop. (ii) W* satisfies $CR_t(conf_t, minW_t)$ and $B(t)$, so it will return W*. (iii) W* only satisfies $B(t)$, it will first find out the worker w_a with lowest CS in W* and the worker w_b with highest CS in W_{re} whose $CS(t, w_b) > CS(t, w_a)$, then exchange them to generate the new W* and W_{re}, finally, it will continue to execute the thirteenth step in the current loop. The time complexity is $O(|W|)$.

5 Performance Evaluation

In this section, we first discuss the experimental setting and then present the experimental results.

5.1 Experimental Setting

The real check-in dataset are obtained from Gowalla [16], a location-based social network, where users check in at different hotels in their vicinities. We collect the check-in records over one week from Oct/9/2010 to Oct/15/2010 with 38,940 records, 2,226 users and 30,242 hotels. Then we partition it into 56 sub-datasets with a three-hour time range, based on the necessary of constructing the experimental data. Each check-in record indicates the location and time that user have entered the hotel.

For each sub-dataset, spatial taskset is generated based on the check-in records with the same hotel. The end of the time range is used as the expiration time of the task. The other attributes including $minW$, B and $conf$ are randomly selected in the range [4, 7], [25, 75], [0.5, 0.7], respectively. The corresponding worker set is constituted by the earliest check-in record of each user, and the location is used as the worker's current location. We measure the travel time as the Euclidean distance divided by the average travel speed (i.e., 30 miles/h). Additionally, each worker has a reputation parameter which is randomly selected in the range [0, 1].

To save the space, we only list the number of spatial tasks (T), workers (W), high-rank workers (HW), medium-rank workers (MW) in total for six sub-datasets in Table 1 and show their experimental results in the next subsection.

Table 1. The details for six sub-datasets

Sub_dataset	t1	t2	t3	t4	t5	t6
T	653	2498	2116	981	1242	2338
W	766	533	451	450	432	376
HW	102	61	66	170	179	149
MW	200	121	101	150	124	113

5.2 Experimental Results

Budget-TASC [3] is an algorithm which figures out a worker set with the maximum expected quality of the result and the total rewards within a pre-specified budget. We compare it with our two algorithms in terms of the runtime, the total ACS (*total_ACS*) and the total costs on workers' rewards (*total_rew*).

Runtime: This metric is used to measure how efficient of an algorithm. Figure 2 (left) shows the runtime of the three algorithms on six sub-datasets. Cost_Sensitive performs better than Quality_Sensitive because Quality_Sensitive always calculates the ACS first, which is time-consuming. Budget_TASC performs best on three sub-datasets (i.e., t4, t5 and t6) because there are more high-rank workers than medium-rank workers, which will effectively reduce the number of worker combinations and thus decrease the runtime.

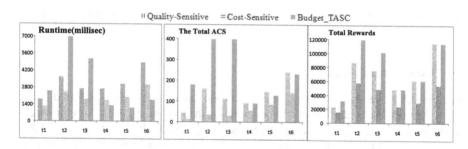

Fig. 2. The runtime, total ACS and total rewards for six sub-datasets

total_ACS: This metric is used to measure how effective of an algorithm, which is calculated in Eq. (8). Figure 2(middle) shows the *total_ACS* for three algorithms. Quality_Sensitive performs better than Cost_Sensitive, because it will find out the worker set for each task with least size and a higher ACS than others with same size for QBTA problem. But it may do not find the worker set with highest ACS. Thus, Budget_TASC performs better than Quality_Sensitive on t1, t2 and t3.

$$total\_ACS(T) = \sum_{t \in T} ACS(t, W * (t)) \text{ where } T \text{ is a spatial taskset.} \tag{8}$$

total_rew: This metric is used to measure how effective of an algorithm, which is calculated in Eq. (9). Figure 2(right) shows the *total_rew* of three algorithms on six sub-datasets. Cost_Sensitive performs better because it will find out the worker set for QBTA problem with least size and a lower *total_rew* than others with same size.

$$total\_rew(T) = \sum_{t \in T} \sum_{w \in W*(t)} rew(w) \text{ where } T \text{ is a spatial taskset.} \tag{9}$$

6 Conclusions

With the rapid development of communication technologies, spatial crowdsourcing has become more and more popular. As workers may possess different capabilities, a major challenge is how to assure the quality of results while considering the limit budget. This paper focuses on the issue of quality assurance for task assignment while considering budget limitation and then proposes two two-phase greedy algorithms. Finally, experimental results show that Quality_Sensitive gets the worker set with higher quality and Cost_Sensitive gets a worker set with less cost. Also, their less runtime makes them interactive and suitable for running on mobile platform.

Acknowledgments. This work is supported by National Natural Science Foundation of China under Grant No. 61572295; Innovation Method Fund of China No. 2015IM010200; Natural Science Foundation of Shandong Province under Grant No. ZR2014FM031; Science and Technology Development Plan Project of Shandong Province No. 2014GGX101047, No. 2015GGX101007, No. 2015GGX101015; Shandong Province Independent Innovation Major Special Project No. 2015ZDJQ01002, No. 2015ZDXX0201B03.

References

1. Kazemi, L., Shahabi, C., Chen, L.: GeoTruCrowd: trustworthy query answering with spatial crowdsourcing. In: ACM SIGSPATIAL, Orlando, FL, USA, pp. 304–313 (2013)
2. Deng, D., Shahabi, C., Demiryurek, U.: Maximizing the number of worker's self-selected tasks in spatial crowdsourcing. In: ACM SIGSPATIAL, Orlando, FL, USA, pp. 314–323 (2013)
3. Yu, H., Miao, C., Shen, Z., Leung, C.: Quality and budget aware task allocation for spatial crowdsourcing. In: AAMAS, pp. 1689–1690 (2015)
4. Kazemi, L., Shahabi, C.: GeoCrowd: enabling query answering with spatial crowdsourcing. In: ACM SIGSPATIAL, Redondo Beach, CA, USA, pp. 189–198 (2012)
5. Gao, D., Tong, Y., She, J., Song, T., Chen, L., Xu, K.: Top-k team recommendation in spatial crowdsourcing. In: WAIM, pp. 191–204 (2016)
6. Xie, X., Chen, H., Wu, H.: Bargain-based stimulation mechanism for selfish mobile nodes in participatory sensing network. In: SMAHCN, pp. 72–80 (2009)
7. Li, Y., Yiu, M.L., Xu, W.: Orient online route recommendation for spatial crowdsourcing task workers. In: SSTD, pp. 137–156 (2015)

8. Kittur, A., Nickerson, J.V., Bernstein, M., Gerber, E., Shaw, A., Zimmerman, J., Lease, M., Horton, J.: The future of crowd work. In: CSCW, pp. 1301–1318 (2013)
9. Sakurai, Y., Okimoto, T., Oka, M., Shinoda, M., Yokoo, M.: Ability grouping of crowd workers via reward discrimination. In: HCOMP, pp. 147–155 (2013)
10. Liu, Y., Zhang, J., Yu, H., Miao, C.: Reputation-aware continuous double auction. In: AAAI, pp. 3126–3127 (2014)
11. http://www.uber.com
12. Khosravifar, B., Bentahar, J., Gomrokchi, M., Alam, R.: CRM: an efficient trust and reputation model for agent computing. In: KBS, pp. 1–16 (2012)
13. Yu, H., Shen, Z., Miao, C., An, B., Leung, C.: Filtering trust opinions through reinforcement learning. In: Decision Support Systems, pp. 102–113 (2014)
14. Fang, H., Guo, G., Zhang, J.: Multi-faceted trust and distrust prediction for recommender systems. In: Decision Support Systems, pp. 37–47 (2015)
15. Wahab, O.A., Bentahar, J., Otrok, H., Mourad, A: A survey on trust and reputation models for web services: single, composite, and communities. In: Decision Support Systems, pp. 121–134 (2015)
16. http://snap.stanford.edu/data/loc-gowalla.html

Collaborative Prediction Model of Disease Risk by Mining Electronic Health Records

Shuai Zhang, Lei Liu, Hui Li, and Lizhen Cui$^{(\boxtimes)}$

School of Computer Science and Technology,
Shandong University, Jinan, China
zhangshuai01@mail.sdu.edu.cn,
{l.liu,lih,clz}@sdu.edu.cn

Abstract. Patient Electronic Health Records (EHR) is one of the major carriers for conducting preventative medicine research. However, the heterogeneous and longitudinal properties make EHRs analysis an inherently challenge. To address this issue, this paper proposes CAPM, a Collaborative Assessment Prediction Model based on patient temporal graph representation, which relies only on a patient EHRs using ICD-10 codes to predict future disease risks. Firstly, we develop a temporal graph for each patient EHRs. Secondly, CAPM uses hybrid collaborative filtering approach to predict each patient's greatest disease risks based on their own medical history and that of similar patients. Moreover, we also calculate the onset risk with the corresponding diseases in order to take action at the earliest signs. Finally, we present experimental results on a real world EHR dataset, demonstrating that CAPM performs well at capturing future disease and its onset risks.

Keywords: Electronic Health Records · Temporal graph · Collaborative prediction · Disease risk profile

1 Introduction

Healthcare is increasingly becoming an important research field that is closely related to everyone's daily life. A huge amount of money is wasted every year due to the high degree of complexity in medical area. This crisis has motivated the drive towards preventative medicine, where the main concern is identifying the onset risk of diseases and taking preventive measures at the earliest signs [1]. Patient EHRs are systematic collections of patients' longitudinal clinical information generated from different healthcare industry institutions. Effective utilization of EHR data is the key to many medical informatics research problems [2]. Working directly with raw EHRs is very challenging due to its sparsity, noise and the existence of heterogeneity. To address this challenge, we should first do consistent representation for each patient before going into the stage of detailed disease risk prediction applications, which is a basic step to transform the raw EHRs into clinically relevant information.

Based on the EHR data, care providers typically want to assess the risk scores of a patient developing different diseases. Once the risk of a patient is predicted, proper intervention and care plan can be designed accordingly. A lot of diseases have

© ICST Institute for Computer Sciences, Social Informatics and Telecommunications Engineering 2017
S. Wang and A. Zhou (Eds.): CollaborateCom 2016, LNICST 201, pp. 71–82, 2017.
DOI: 10.1007/978-3-319-59288-6_7

preventable risk factors or at least indicators of disease onset risk. Adequately describing the characteristics of these diseases may assist in preventative medicine, and help reduce the burden of disease [3]. However, it is impossible for an individual medical doctor to give a sufficient real-time analysis in the process of patient interaction, due to the complexity of risk factors' possible combination. Thus, we need a computational analysis model to take effective measures in preventive medicine. For instance, we can integrate and utilize the medical data of patients, discover deep knowledge about patient similarity relationship, and provide personalized disease risk profiles for each individual patient. The data above derived from not only the EHRs of patient, but also from similarities of the patient to thousands of other patients [4].

To deal with the aforementioned problems, this paper proposes an integrative temporal graph representation based collaborative assessment prediction model called CAPM which mainly consists of two parts: *Patient Temporal Graph* and *Disease Risk Profile*. The first part transforms temporal clinical events that extracted from raw EHRs of each patient into medical temporal graph. In open literatures, studies [2, 7, 8] proposed how to represent patient EHRs, which represents the patient historical records in sequence [2], matrix [7] and graph [8] respectively. The works above did not consider the temporal relationship between different clinical events. Thus, an approach is developed to construct the temporal graph for each patient EHRs.

The second part *Disease Risk Profile* is to predict the most probable diseases that a patient will develop in the future. Our work is inspired by learning from the work on collaborative filtering methodology [9–11] used in other settings and motivated by patient-centric model that creates a personalized healthcare [3, 4, 12]. The difference with these studies is that we utilized a *hybrid collaborative filtering approach* based on temporal graph representation to calculate the disease risk of individual patient. We calculate the similarity between a patient's record and other patients' records, and then derived the risk of a certain disease. More importantly, our CAPM also calculates the onset of the corresponding certain disease. The output is a ranked list of diseases and corresponding disease's onset risk for a patient. Thus, the patient's *disease risk profile* obtained by our method not only includes the list of diseases, but also contains the onset risk of each disease.

The main contributions of this paper are summarized as follows:

(1) The CAPM provides a unified representation (i.e., temporal graph) to express each patient's raw EHR data, and can conveniently extract ICD-10 codes in chronological order from graph to predict future disease risk.
(2) A hybrid collaborative prediction approach is developed, combining three kinds of similarity calculation methods and proposing an approach to calculate the onset risk of disease.
(3) Extensive experiments on a real-world EHR dataset are implemented to prove the predictive effectiveness of our model.

The remainder of this paper is organized as follows. Section 2 reviews related work. In Sect. 3 we describe an outline of our proposed model. The details of temporal graph based collaborative prediction model CAPM are presented in Sect. 4. Section 5 studies the performance of the proposed model through real world experiments. Section 6 concludes this paper.

2 Related Work

Patient EHR data is collected over time on patients' clinical information and is becoming section of big data revolution [3]. Furthermore, EHRs contain heterogeneous data such as diagnoses, medications lab results, and etc. Diverse modeling techniques are needed to meet the heterogeneity of EHR data, which offers many options for their combination [13]. There are a number of related works on how to represent patient EHR data [2, 7, 8]. However, these works did not consider the temporal relationships among different clinical events, which are the crucial information on the impending disease conditions.

It is a hot research topic to predict disease risks and rank diseases by their risks for individuals in data mining techniques. Some researches have been done along this line of thought. Davis *et al.* [12] proposed CARE, which is the first well-known system using collaborative filter technique to predict the disease risk of one patient. Hussein *et al.* [14] proposed Integrated Collaborative Filtering framework to develop recommender system to suggest medical advice to patients. However, all these works did not consider the onset time risk of patient's each ranked list disease.

On the one hand, this paper develops a temporal graph based representation for patient raw EHR data. Not only the temporal relationships are considered, but also the close degree of clinical events connection is computed. Thus, we can conveniently extract the required information based on the temporal graph, which make the results more interpretative. While, the existing researches are based on the raw data to conduct similarity study. On the other hand, we develop a hybrid collaborative filtering approach, which combing three kinds of similarity calculation methods. It is different from the traditional calculation using one way to compute similarity. In addition, this paper proposes an approach to calculate the onset risk of each predicted disease, so that take action at the earliest signs.

3 Overview of Collaborative Prediction Model

The preliminary of CAPM is illustrated in Fig. 1. Our model mainly contains two parts: the construction of the temporal graph from patient's raw EHR data, and the diagnoses extracted from temporal graph in time order, which are used to construct the disease risk profile of patient. The following is a brief summary of two parts.

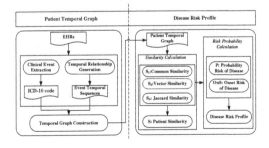

Fig. 1. The overview of CAPM

3.1   Patient Temporal Graph

This part provides a unified view for each patient by summarizing the longitudinal EHR data and from this view we can capture holistic temporal information for collaborative prediction analysis task. First, this component extracts clinical events, and generates the temporal sequences among these events based on the timestamp. Then, the obtained event sequences are transformed into the temporal graphs. This representation can use a more compact way to capture temporal structures hidden in the event sequences. Moreover, the repeated pairwise events with the same ordering in patient sequence will only appear once in patient temporal graph, which means this representation is resistant to sparse and irregular observations. Details of the temporal graph construction are described in Sect. 4.1.

3.2   Disease Risk Profile

The *Disease Risk Profile* part provides a hybrid collaborative filtering algorithm to obtain the individual patient's risk profile based on the temporal graph. The detailed EHR data documents the clinical events in time, which typically includes diagnosis, medication, and lab test. The diagnosis events are among the most structured and informative events, for which they are regarded as the prime candidates for constructing features for risk prediction. In the temporal graph, the diagnosis events are often in the form of International Classification of Diseases 10 (ICD-10) codes. Each disease is given a unique code, and can be up to 6 characters long. For example, code *I10* represents *Essential Hypertension*, *I10.X02* and *I10.X08* indicates the *Benign Hypertension* and *Hypertension* respectively. We can obtain the ICD-10 codes in time sequence based on the each patient temporal graph. Then, combine three methods to calculate the patient's similarity. Moreover, use our proposed approach to calculate the onset risk of corresponding disease. The output of this part is the disease risk profile for each patient, consisting of two aspects which are ranked list of diseases and corresponding disease's onset risk.

4   Collaborative Assessment Prediction Model

This section presents the details of the collaborative assessment prediction model to predict a ranked list of potential diseases and corresponding onset risk for a patient. In the first step, patients' medical histories are represented in the form of temporal graphs, which are constructed from the raw EHR data. After data cleaning and expressing, the patients' diagnoses are fed into the hybrid collaborative filtering approach, training it to predict comorbidities and onset risk of the disease. When the model is applied to a new patient's record, the collaborative filtering computes and selects the neighborhood of patients who are most similar to the specific patient. Finally, the likelihood of each possible disease is calculated, and a ranked list of possible diseases and its onset risk based on the likelihood is built for this patient.

4.1 Temporal Graph Representation

Inspired by Liu *et al.* [5], we construct the following temporal graph for each patient's sequence s_n:

Definition 1 *(Temporal Graph)*. Let temporal graph G_n of sequence s_n be a directed and weighted graph $G = (V, E)$ with vertex set V and directed edge set E. The weight of the edge from node i to node j is defined as the averaged temporal closeness between any ij-th of each input event sequence s_n:

$$W_{ij}^n = \sum_{1 \le p \le q \le L_m} [e_p^n = i \wedge e_q^n = j] \frac{1}{L_m} \delta_\mu(t_q^n - t_p^n). \tag{1}$$

Here, the $\delta_\mu(\cdot)$ is a non-increasing function parameterized by μ, vertex set $V = e_l^n \in M$, M is the medical events set. The event sequence is denoted by $s_n = ((e_l^n, t_l^n) : l = 1, \ldots, L_M)$, L_M is the length of s_n and $t_p^n < t_q^n$ for all $p < q$, that is to say, at time t_l^n we can observe event e_l^n in the sequence s_n.

As $\delta_\mu(\cdot)$ is a non-increasing function, so the more often and closer events i and j appear to each other in s_n, the higher W_{ij}^n is in graph G_n. We use the exceedance of the Exponential distribution $\delta_\mu(d) = \exp(-d/\mu)$ to construct the temporal graph, where d is the time interval between two events. In other words, we calculate a stronger edge weight for a smaller time interval d, when $d \le \Delta$, Otherwise, if a time interval d is larger than the threshold Δ, this event pairs will be ignored. Obviously, the weight of edge is controlled by parameters μ, Δ that can be selected according to the specific applications. That is to say, if the correlation is very small between events pairs, such as the time interval larger than 2 months, then we can set $\Delta = 2$ months, and the value of μ can be empirically set according to the average time interval between successive events.

4.2 Hybrid Collaborative Prediction Approach

We can conveniently obtain the diagnosed ICD-10 codes in time order based on the patient temporal graph representation. Thus, each patient is expressed as a vector of diagnosed diseases in time sequence. Because the diseases are not a patient choice, so the value of patient vector in medical domain is binary: a patient either has a disease (value is 1) or does not have a disease (value is 0). Using hybrid collaborative filtering algorithm that we developed to generate predictions based on a series of other similar patients with their diseases. An example of collaborative prediction model is given in Fig. 2.

Patients and diseases are represented as a matrix $\Re = I \times J$, where I refers to *all patients* and J indicts *all the possible diseases*. $J_i = (D_1, D_2, \ldots, D_z)$ represents all the diseases extracted from temporal graph of patient i and ordered by diagnosis date, as

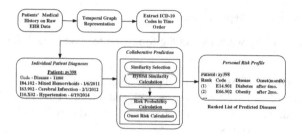

Fig. 2. Example of collaborative prediction model

shown *Patient zy398* in Fig. 2. We can see that $J = (J_1 \cup J_2 \cdots \cup J_i \mid i \in I)$. To predict future diseases for a new patient a, given $J_a = (D_1, D_2, ..., D_z)$ and $H_a = (D_1, D_2, ..., D_k)$ where $k \leq z$. The J_a is the existing diseases of patient a and H_a represent a head sequence of diseases that will be used as an input for the hybrid collaborative filtering algorithm. We define $R_a \subseteq J - H_a$ as a set of diseases to be predicted for the patient a. The goal of the collaborative prediction algorithm is to predict the probability and onset risk, then rank each disease in R_a.

Our hybrid collaborative filtering technique is derived from the similarity algorithm presented by [6], vector similarity algorithm [12] and Jaccard similarity. $S_1(a, i)$ is the first calculation measure of the similarity between testing patient a and training patients i ($i \in I$). It is defined as the proportion of patient i's diseases to the patient a's diseases in head set:

$$S_1(a, i) = \frac{|\{D|D \in H_a \wedge D \in J_i\}|}{|H_a|}. \tag{2}$$

The second measure $S_2(a, i)$ uses vector similarity to calculate. Formally the vector similarity of patient a and i is defined in the following equation:

$$S_2(a, i) = \frac{\sum_{j \in J} v_{a,j} \cdot v_{i,j}}{\sqrt{\sum_{d \in J_a} v_{a,d}^2} \cdot \sqrt{\sum_{d \in J_i} v_{i,d}^2}}, \tag{3}$$

where $v_{a,j}$ is the value of patient a with the disease j, the possible value of v is 1 or 0.

Then, we give the third calculation method $S_3(a, i)$, which inspired by the applications of Jaccard similarity coefficient. It is suitable for all dimensions to be 0 or 1, for example, the background of this article, whether or not suffering from a certain disease. Formally the Jaccard similarity of patient a and patient i is defined in the following equation:

$$S_3(a, i) = \frac{g(|v_{a,j} = 1 \wedge v_{i,j} = 1|)}{g(|v_{a,j} = 1 \wedge v_{i,j} = 1|) + q(|v_{a,j} = 1 \wedge v_{i,j} = 0|) + r(|v_{a,j} = 0 \wedge v_{i,j} = 1|)}, \tag{4}$$

where $j \in J$, g represents the number of dimensions of patient a and i suffer from disease d, similarly, q represents the number of dimensions of only patient a have disease d, the meaning of r is opposite to q.

Thus, the ultimate similarity calculation formula is given in the following:

$$S(a, i) = \frac{1}{L} \sum_{1 \leq k \leq 3} S_k(a, i). \tag{5}$$

here, the value of L is 3, that is, this equation is the average of three similarity calculation measures.

For each disease d in R_a, the $N_d = \{i \mid i \in I \wedge d \in J_i\}$ represents all other patients with disease d that are similar to patient a. The probability of patient a having disease d in the future is calculated by the following equation:

$$P(a, d) = \bar{v}_d + \mu (1 - \bar{v}_d) \sum_{i \in N_d} S(a, i), \tag{6}$$

where $\bar{v}_d$ is the random expectation of disease d, i.e., $\bar{v}_d = |N_d|/|I|$, μ is a normalizing constant $\mu = 1/\sum_{i \in I} S(a, i)$. That is, the equation treats random expectation $\bar{v}_d$ as the baseline probability of each patient having disease d and adds additional risk based on similarity to other patients with disease d.

In the end, we design a formula $T(a, d)$ to calculate the approximate onset time for patient a having disease d in the future, which is shown below:

$$T(a, d) = \frac{1}{|N_d|} \sum_{i \in N_d} (t_{i,d} - t_{i,x}), \tag{7}$$

here, the x is a disease that occurs d's the previous one, thus $t_{i,d} - t_{i,x}$ indicts the time interval between two adjacent disease (i.e., d and x) of patient a.

4.3   Hybrid Collaborative Prediction Example

Table 1 gives an example of patient dataset in order to illustrate our hybrid collaborative prediction approach. The diseases and time interval of each patient are obtained based on the temporal graph. Thus, these diseases are ordered by the diagnosis date. For example, patient i_3 was first diagnosis as d_1, then diagnosed as d_3, the last diagnosed as d_4, and the time interval between diseases is 4 month and 3 month respectively. From Table 1, we can see the set of all patients is $I = \{i_1, i_2, i_3, i_4, i_5\}$, and the set of all possible diseases is $J = \{d_1, d_2, d_3, d_4, d_5, d_6\}$, each disease corresponds to a unique ICD-10 code. Thus, each patient can be represented a binary vector, the dimensions of this vector is six. A new patient a with diagnosed diseases d_1, d_3 and d_4 inputs the hybrid collaborative prediction measure, that is, the $H_a = \{d_1, d_3, d_4\}$, thus the target diseases to be predicted $R_a \subseteq J - H_a = \{d_2, d_5, d_6\}$.

Consider the first disease d_2 in R_a, the similar patients that have this disease d_2 are selected $N_{d2} = \{i_2, i_4, i_5\}$. We can obtain the similarity between patients (i.e., a and N_{d2}) according to the Eq. (5), so $S(a, i_2) \approx 0.26$, $S(a, i_4) \approx 0.71$, and $S(a, i_5) \approx 0.26$. Then based on the Eq. (6) to calculate the disease probability $P(a, d_2) = 0.79$. Finally, we need to compute the onset risk of disease according to the Eq. (7), $T(a, d_2) = 2$ month. Similarly, the probability of patient a developing diseases (i.e., d_5 and d_6) and onset risk corresponding to disease are as follows: d_5: $P(a, d_5) = 0.6$, $T(a, d_5) = 5$ month, d_6: $P(a, d_6) = 0.92$, $T(a, d_6) = 2$ month. Therefore the ranked list of predicted diseases for patient a is $(d6, d2, d5)$, as shown in Table 2.

Table 1. An example of patient dataset

Patient	Diagnosis
i_1	$d_4 \xrightarrow{2mo} d_6$
i_2	$d_2 \xrightarrow{3mo} d_4 \xrightarrow{2mo} d_6 \xrightarrow{4mo} d_5$
i_3	$d_1 \xrightarrow{4mo} d_3 \xrightarrow{3mo} d_4$
i_4	$d_1 \xrightarrow{2mo} d_2 \xrightarrow{1mo} d_3 \xrightarrow{5mo} d_4 \xrightarrow{3mo} d_6$
i_5	$d_3 \xrightarrow{4mo} d_2 \xrightarrow{5mo} d_5 \xrightarrow{1mo} d_6$

Table 2. Disease risk profile of new patient a

Rank	Code (ICD-10)	Disease	Onset (month)
(1)	code1	d_6	after 2 mo
(2)	code2	d_2	after 2 mo
(3)	code3	d_5	after 5 mo

5 Experiments

This section presents the experimental results to evaluate the performance of the proposed CAPM model. We apply developed approach on real world Electronic Health Records to demonstrate the improvement on predictive effectiveness.

5.1 Data Preparation

We validate the effectiveness of our presented model on a real world clinical data including the records of 92652 patients over 5 years (2011-2015). These data is collected from the medical system of a certain city in North China. The head of patient i is H_i and the head size $|H_i|$ is a parameter in our experiments. Only the patients that have $|H_i| + 1$ diseases are used for validation. In our experiments, we select patients that have at least five different diseases (i.e., $|J_i| \geq 5$) in our database so that there could be sufficient medical history for both training and evaluation. As a result, 7372 patients are selected in the final who meet the condition.

This paper use the inpatient diagnosis information of International Classification of Disease 10 (ICD-10) codes and the medication information according to drug action and corresponding timestamps to construct the temporal sequences. Then the patient temporal graphs are constructed from those sequences in terms of *Definition 1*. Figure 3 gives an example of one patient's temporal graph, which contains five diseases that are uniquely encoded by ICD-10. Then, we extract these codes in time order based on temporal graph representation, which is used to be the input of the hybrid collaborative prediction approach.

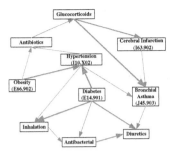

Fig. 3. Example of one patient's temporal graph

To evaluate the hybrid collaborative prediction measure, we use a leave-one-patient-out validation strategy similar to [11]. One active patient i is taken out and the other patients are used for training every time. Then the $|H_i|$ diseases of patients i are fed into the trained hybrid collaborative prediction model. The remaining $|J_i|-|H_i|$ diseases are considered as future diseases and used for evaluation. The top-K diseases in the ranked list of predicted conditions are considered. Above process is repeated for each patient.

5.2 Validation of the Developed Approach

Baselines. In order to evaluate our model introduced in Sect. 4, the following baseline methods for comparison purpose will be considered:

(1) *Baseline-1 (BL$_1$)*, this method implements the similarity calculation algorithm proposed in [12], which only uses vector similarity (i.e., Eq. (3)) to calculate the similarity among patients.
(2) *Baseline-2 (BL$_2$)*, this way implements the similarity calculation approach proposed in [6], which only uses Eq. (2) to compute the similarity between patients.
(3) *Baseline-3 (BL$_3$)*, this method only uses the Eq. (4) that we designed to calculate the similarity of different patients.

Metrics. We use *Coverage* and *Average rank* to assess the prediction performance for each patient. The content of the two metrics are as follows statement:

(1) *Coverage*. It is defined as the percentage of diseases for which a prediction is ranked. That is to say, coverage is the proportion of correct future diseases in the top-K ranked list to the total number of correct future diseases, as shown in the Eq. (8). Apparently, we desire to capture as many future diseases as possible, so the higher coverage, the better prediction performance of approach.

$$Coverage = \frac{\#Predicted\ target\ diseases}{\#Total\ target\ diseases}. \tag{8}$$

(2) *Average rank*. It is satisfactory for future diseases to have the low rank positions. Thus, we use the average rank of all correct future diseases in the ranked list for this patient as an evaluation metric. As shown in the Eq. (9). Ideally, if a patient actually has the diseases, which should be near the top of ranked list, so that they are most probably to be noticed and used.

$$Average\ rank = \frac{\#Total\ target\ number}{\#Total\ target\ diseases}. \tag{9}$$

Results. Table 3 displays the prediction performance of CAPM compared with the baselines ranking, where the head size is 3. Results on the top 20 and top 100 ranks are more significant, because the medical experts or other users are impossible to consider a large portion of the list. The hybrid collaborative assessment prediction model achieves a coverage value of 49% and 76% for top-20 and top-100 ranked lists respectively. From the top-20 we can observe that our developed approach CAPM significantly improve the predictive performance compared to the baseline BL_3 method, the coverage obtained by BL_3 is only 32% (a gain of 8%). Similarly, from top-100, we also can observe that the CAPM outperforms other three methods, compared to the basic BL_1 method that achieves 60% (a gain of 16%). Table 4 shows the specific examples of predictions using our developed model. Because this paper sets the parameter of $|H_i| = 3$, the number of Diagnosed Diseases is three in the Table 4. As a summary, the experimental results have demonstrated the effectiveness of our developed model on a real EHR data, which can achieve better prediction performance compared to the baseline methods.

Table 3. Prediction performance of CAPM compared with the baseline ranking

Comparison of methods				
	BL_1	BL_2	BL_3	CAPM
Top 20				
Coverage	43%	47%	41%	49%
Average rank	7.81	7.22	6.80	5.76
Top 100				
Coverage	60%	70%	68%	76%
Average rank	26.63	21.32	22.04	20.19
All				
Coverage	94%	96%	89%	99%
Average rank	170.39	122.19	91.19	90.37

Table 4. Example of future predictions for individual patients

Patient ID	Diagnosed diseases	Top 2 predicted diseases
zy398	Mixed Hemorrhoids(I84.102), Cerebral Infarction (I63.902), Hypertension(I10.X02)	Diabetes(E14.901), Obesity(E66.902)
zyl5177	Esophagus Cancer(Z98.850), Liver Cancer (C22.902), Hypertension(I10.X02)	Pneumonia(J12.901), Lung Cancer(C34.904)
zyl1138	Heart Disease(I11.901), Obesity(E66.902), Esophagitis(K22.103)	Diabetes(E14.901), Hypertension(I10.X02)

6 Conclusion

This paper has proposed a Collaborative Assessment Prediction Model (CAPM) based on patient temporal graph to predict future disease risks. The CAMP provided a unified temporal graph representation by summarizing each patient's longitudinal raw EHRs, which is informative for a variety of challenging analytic tasks because it can capture temporal relationships between clinical events. Moreover, this paper developed a hybrid collaborative prediction approach to calculate the similarity among patients, which only use ICD-10 codes extracted from patient temporal graph. In addition, we have proposed an approach to calculate the onset risk of each predicted disease. The patient's disease risk profile obtained by our model not only includes the ranked list of diseases, but also contains the onset risk of each disease. The experimental results have shown that the proposed model could improve the effectiveness compared to the basic prediction methods in our real world EHR dataset.

Acknowledgement. This work is partially supported by NSFC No. 61303005, 61572295; the Innovation Method Fund of China No. 2015IM010200; SDNSFC No. ZR2014FM031; the Science and Technology Development Plan Project of Shandong Province No. 2014GGX101019, 2015GGX101007, 2015GGX 101015; the Shandong Province Independent Innovation Major Special Project No. 2015ZDJQ010 02, 2015ZDXX0201B03; the Fundamental Research Funds of Shandong University No. 2014JC025, 2015JC031.

References

1. Laura, B.M.: Data-Driven Healthcare: How Analytics and BI are Transforming the Industry. Wiley (2014)
2. Gotz, D., Wang, F., Perer, A.: A methodology for interactive mining and visual analysis of clinical event patterns using electronic health record data. Biomed. Inform. **48**, 148–159 (2014)
3. Davis, D.A., Chawla, N.V.: Predicting individual disease risk based on medical history. In: Information and Knowledge Management, pp. 769–778 (2008)
4. Dentino, B., Davis, D., Chawla, N.V.: HealthCareND: leveraging EHR and ARE for prospective healthcare. In: Health Informatics Symposium, pp. 841–844 (2010)

5. Liu, C., Zhang, K., Xiong, H., Jiang, G., Yang, Q.: Temporal skeletonization on sequential data: patterns, categorization, and visualization. In: KDD, pp. 211–223 (2014)
6. Ji, X., Chun, S.A., Geller, Z., Oria, V.: Collaborative and trajectory prediction models of medical conditions by mining patients' Social Data. In: BIBM, pp. 695–700 (2015)
7. Zhou, J.Y., Wang, F., Hu, J.Y., Ye, J.P.: From micro to macro: Data driven phenotyping by densification of longitudinal electronic medical records. In: SIGKDD, pp. 135–144 (2014)
8. Ooi, B.C., Tan, K.-L., Tran, Q. T., Yip, J.W.L., Chen, G., Ling,Z.J., Nguyen, T., Tung, A.K. H., Zhang, M.: Contextual crowd intelligence. In: SIGKDD, pp. 39–46 (2014)
9. Linden, G., Smith, B., York, J.: Amazon.com recommendations: item-to-item collaborative filtering. IEEE Internet Comput. 7, 76–80 (2003)
10. Hofmann, T.: Latent semantic models for collaborative filtering. Trans. Inf. Syst. 22, 89–115 (2003)
11. Xia, P., Liu, B., Sun, Y., Chen, C.: Reciprocal recommendation system for online dating. Soc. Netw. Anal. Mining. 9, 234–241 (2015)
12. Davis, D.A., Chawla, N.V., Christakis, N.A., Barabási, A.L.: Time to CARE: a collaborative engine for practical disease prediction. Data Min. Knowl. Disc. 20, 388–415 (2010)
13. Sun, J., Wang, F., Hu, J., Edabollahi, S.: Supervised patient similarity measure of heterogeneous patient records. In: SIGKDD, pp. 16–24 (2012)
14. Hussein, A.S., Omar, W.M., Li, X., Hatem, M.A.: Smart collaboration framework for managing chronic disease using recommender system. Health Syst. 3, 12–17 (2014)

An Adaptive Multiple Order Context Huffman Compression Algorithm Based on Markov Model

Yonghua Huo[1(✉)], Zhihao Wang[1], Junfang Wang[1], Kaiyang Qu[2], and Yang Yang[2]

[1] Science and Technology on Information Transmission and Dissemination in Communication Networks Laboratory, 54th Research Institute of China Electronics Technology Group Corporation, Shijiazhuang, China
tsdhyh2005@163.com, {cetc540016,jfwang2015}@sina.com
[2] State Key Laboratory of Networking and Switching Technology, Beijing University of Posts and Telecommunications, Beijing, China
1445154975@qq.com, echo_lzjf@163.com

Abstract. In this paper, an adaptive multiple order context Huffman compression algorithm based on Markov chain is proposed. Firstly, the data to be compressed is traversed, and the character space of the data and the times that one character transfers to its neighboring character are figured out. According to the statistical results, we can calculate the one-step transition probability matrix and the multi-step transition probability matrix. When the conditional probability between two adjacent characters is greater than the set threshold value, the adjacent characters are merged and compressed as an independent encoding unit. Improve the compression efficiency by increasing the length of the compression characters. The experimental results show that the algorithm achieves good compression efficiency.

Keywords: Data compression · Multiple order contexts · Markov chain · Huffman compression

1 Introduction

With the rapid development of information technology, the increasing amount of data in time and space brings great challenges to the storage of information. In this case, the data compression is particularly important, and is also a long-term concern in the field of data management.

Huffman algorithm [1] is a kind of compression algorithm with a fine effect. Huffman algorithm calculates the probability of each character to give the corresponding weight to each character, and constructs a Huffman tree, in which shorter higher probability

This work was supported by Open Subject Funds of Science and Technology on Information Transmission and Dissemination in Communication Networks Laboratory (ITD-U15002/KX152600011). NSFC (61401033, 61372108, 61272515). National Science and Technology Pillar Program Project (2015BAI11B01).

distribution of characters with high probability occurring are assigned short code, and encoding, of characters with low probability occurring are assigned longer code. The Huffman algorithm achieves good compression effect by reducing average code length of single character.

There is a certain relation between characters in the actual text environment. For example, a character sequence as 'abcabdefgabg', it is observed that the 'b' character is always behind the 'a' character, just like the 'man' always behind the 'Huff'. Therefore, this paper proposes a compression algorithm based on Markov chain and Huffman algorithm. Each character is regarded as a state in the Markov chain, and according to the jump numbers between characters calculates one step transition probability matrix and multi-step transition probability matrix.

Different threshold for different characters, when the transition probability between characters is greater than the threshold value, characters should be combined, otherwise, they are compressed separately as independent characters. When the N order context does not meet the conditions of the combined compression, it is automatically adjusted to the N-1 order context compression, and the worst case is the 0-order context compression, that is, Huffman compression algorithm.

In the paper, we briefly discuss related work in Sect. 2. An adaptive Huffman compression model is proposed in Sect. 3, and Sect. 4 is the experimental results and comparative analysis. Section 5 concludes the paper.

2 Related Works

There are related works including Huffman compression algorithm [1], arithmetic coding [2], dictionary coding [3] and other compression algorithms popular at present. Arithmetic coding is a compression scheme which recodes based on the statistical results of the occurrence probability of characters. Arithmetic coding bypasses the idea of replacing an input symbol with specific code. It replaces the sequences of symbols in the input file with single arithmetic (float) number. More longer input messages, more bits are needed in the arithmetic number [4]. Output from an arithmetic coding process is a single number less than 1 and greater than or equal to 0. This single number can be uniquely decoded to create the exact stream of symbols. To construct the output number, the symbols are assigned a set of probabilities.

Dictionary coding is similar to the way of looking up the dictionary. Its basic principle is considering long strings or combination of characters with high probability occurring as notes in the dictionary, and using short number or symbols to represent these notes [3]. Dictionary-based code compression is commonly used in embedded systems [5], because it can achieve an efficient CR, possess a relatively simple decoding hardware, and provide a higher decompression bandwidth than the code compression by applying lossless data compression methods. The compression of dictionary coding is determined on the reoccurring data.

Huffman algorithm [4] has been proven the best fixed-length coding method available [6], which reduces average code length for a single character. If the probability of a symbol's appearance in a message is known, Huffman techniques can encode that symbol using a minimal number of bits. A Huffman code is an optimal prefix code that guarantees unique decidability of a file compressed [7]. The code was devised by Huffman as part of a course assignment. It uses a code tree and has uniquely decodable code that is a proper prefix of any other code word.

But Huffman code does not consider the relationship between the characters [7]. In [8], a multiple subgroup data compression technique based on Huffman coding is proposed. This technique extends the work on Entropy calculation by reducing the codeword length of the characters. In [9], a quasi-lossless compression algorithm was proposed based on the analysis and comparison of performance between Huffman coding and arithmetic coding. Predictive coding and Huffman coding were organically combined. Furthermore, this algorithm removed redundant information through compression preprocessing and secondary quantization.

3 Adaptive Multiple Order Context Huffman Compression Algorithm Based on Markov Model

3.1 Definition and Symbol

In a sequence of characters, for example "abcdefg......z", the distance between character 'a' and 'b' is one step, so we call "ab" one-order context. Similarly, the distance between 'a' and 'c' 'a' and 'd' and 'a' and 'z' are two steps, three steps and n steps, thus the relationship between them are two-order context, three-order context and n-order context respectively. If the number of steps is greater than two, we call it multiple order.

Suppose that the text to be compressed is T, and V is the character space of T. $V = \{v_1, v_2, v_3, \ldots \ldots v_n\}$, v_i is i-th character of V. C, a two-order matrix, C_i represents the appearing times of v_i and C_{ij} represents the appearing times of v_j behind v_i. According to the C_{ij}, the one-step transition probability $P^{(1)}$ can be calculated. Further, we can get multiple transition probability matrix $P^{(n)}$.

Based on the n-step transition probability matrix, we define a set of Statistics $p = \{p_1, p_2, \ldots \ldots p_{2n-1}\}$ to stand for the relationship between $n + 1$ states. For example, if the n is three, the $p = \{p_1, p2, p3, p4, p5\}$. For four characters (states), $T_0, T1, T2$ and T_3, $p_1 (p_1 = p(X_{n+1} = T_1 \mid X_n = T_0))$ represents the one-step transition probability from T_0 to T_1, that is the conditional probability of T_1 appearing when the T_0 appears. p_2 represents the one-step transition probability from T_1 to T_2, p_3 represents the one-step transition probability from T_2 to T_3; $p_4 (p_4 = p(X_{n+2} = T_2 \mid X_n = T_0))$ represents the two-step transition probability from T_0 to T_2, that is the probability of the situation that T_2 is the second character after T_0; $p_5 (p_5 = p(X_{n+3} = T_3 \mid X_n = T_0))$ represents the three-step transition probability from T_0 to T_3. The state transition is as following (Fig. 1):

If p_1 is greater than the threshold $TEMP$, we consider the T_0 and T_1 are relevant. If p_2 is greater than $TEMP$, then the T_1 and T_2 are also relevant. T_0 and T_1 are relevant, T_1 and T_2 are relevant don't stand for the relation between T_0 and T_2. Only when p_3 is greater than the $TEMP$, the T_0, T_1 and T_2 are relevant. The value of $TEMP$ will be discussed later. Equally, the T_0, T_1, T_2 and T_3 are relevant if all the p_1, p_2, p_3, p_4 and p_5 meet the condition.

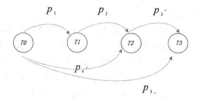

Fig. 1. State transition

3.2 Steps of Algorithm

In this paper, we set the number of context order to three. The method of n-order context is also same. How the number of context order influences the compression results will be discussed.

(1) First go through the text T, get character collection of T, $V = \{v_1, v_2, v_3 \cdots v_n\}$. Compute the occurring times of $v_i (1 \leq i \leq n)$ as C_i, and C_{ij} is the times that v_j is behind v_i. A two-order matrix C made up with C_{ij} is as follow:

$$C = \begin{bmatrix} c_{11} & c_{12} & \cdots & c_{1n} \\ c_{21} & c_{22} & \cdots & c_{2n} \\ \vdots & \vdots & c_{ij} & \vdots \\ c_{n1} & c_{n2} & \cdots & c_{nn} \end{bmatrix} \tag{1}$$

(2) According to the model of Markov chain, we consider $v_i (1 \leq i \leq n)$ as a state, and the one-step transition probability matrix $P^{(1)}$ can be got from (1):

$$P^{(1)} = \begin{bmatrix} p_{11} & p_{12} & \cdots & p_{1n} \\ p_{21} & p_{22} & \cdots & p_{2n} \\ \vdots & \vdots & p_{ij} & \vdots \\ p_{n1} & p_{n2} & \cdots & p_{nn} \end{bmatrix} \tag{2}$$

and

$$P_{ij} = P(X_{n+1} = v_j \mid X_n = v_i) = c_{ij} / \sum_{k=1}^{n} c_{ik} \tag{3}$$

P_{ij} is the appearing probability of j, when i occurs. According the one-step transition probability matrix, two-step transition probability matrix:

$$P^{(2)} = P^{(1)} * P^{(1)} \tag{4}$$

Three-step transition probability matrix:

$$P^{(3)} = P^{(2)} * P^{(1)} \tag{5}$$

Four-step transition probability matrix:

$$P^{(4)} = P^{(3)} * P^{(1)} \tag{6}$$

(3) Read the four character T_0, $T1$, $T2$ and T_3 in T, according to the step (2), we can get a five tuples $p = \{p_1, p_2, p_3, p_4, p_5\}$ about T_0, $T1$, $T2$ and T_3 to show the relationship among them. The detail of judging the relevance of these four characters is described by the following Algorithm 1.

Algorithm 1: The Algorithm for relation

Input: The sequence of four characters, T_0, T_1, T_2 and T_3 and the $p = \{p_1, p2, p3, p4, p5\}$

Output: The Independent coding unit that to be compressed.

1   if(p_1>=*TEMP*) {
2   there is a relationship between T_0 and T_1;
3   if(p_2>=*TEMP*){
4   there is a relationship between T_1 and T_2;
5   if(p_3>=*TEMP*){
6   there is a relationship between T_2 and T_3;
7   if(p_4>=*TEMP* && p_5>=*TEMP*){
8   T_0, T_1, T_2 and T_3 can be merged and compressed.
9   else if(p4>=TEMP) {
10   T_0, T_1, T_2 can be merged and compressed.
11   else{
12   (*T0* and *T1*) or (*T1* and *T2*) or (*T2*, *T3*) are merged and
13   compressed.
14   } else{
15   (*T0* and *T1*) or (*T1* and *T2*) are merged and compressed. }
16   } else{
17   *T0* and *T1* are merged and compressed. }
18   }else{
19   The *T0* compressed separately, and read the following four
20   characters in *T*, repeat the process above.
21   }

TEMP is the threshold which will influence the compression results. When one-step transition probability from character T0 to T1 p_1 >= *TEMP*, we think that there is relationship between T_0 and T_1, which should be merged and compressed. What's more, if p_2 >= *TEMP* and p_3 >= *TEMP*, T_0, T_1 and T_2 are relevant and should be merged. If all the probabilities p_1, p_2, p_3, p_4 and p_5 satisfy the condition, then the T_0, T_1, T_2 and T_3 are relevant. Otherwise, the max related string is "$T_0 T_1 T_2$", which doesn't include "$T3$". If the n-order context doesn't contain the max related string, we will try to find the max related string in the $(n-1)$-order until we find the max related string. At last, the max related string is output as an independent coding unit.

(4) The occurring frequency of each individual coding unit is calculated as their weight, e.g. $\{W_1, W_2, \ldots W_i, \ldots W_n\}$ create n binary trees, and the set of these binary trees is $F = \{T_1, T_2, \ldots T_i, \ldots T_n\}$. each binary tree T_i in the set only has a root node with weight value w_i and its left and right subtrees are empty (In order to facilitate the implementation of algorithm in computer, T_i are also required to be in ascending order as the value of W_i).

(5) select two trees with the least weight of root node as the left and right subtree of a new binary tree, whose weight of root node is the sum of the subtrees' weights.

(6) Delete the two trees with the least weight, and the new tree should be inserted in the set F in ascending order.

(7) Repeat the two steps (5) and (6), until there is only one tree in the set F.

Construct the Markov chain model based on the statistical results of text T in step (1) and (2), and then get the n-step transition probability matrix; The step (3) is the main part of this algorithm, which search for independent compression units according to the transition probability matrix, in order to increase the length of independent encoding units and realize the automatic adjustment between the multiple order context; calculate the occurrence probability of independent encoding units according to their occurrence times and give them corresponding weights. Construct the Huffman tree and output compression code according to the Huffman algorithm.

3.3 The Confirmation of Threshold

The value of *TEMP* will influence the results of the compression. So, a proper value is very important.

According to the statistics of the text, the transfer one-step transfer distribution of the text (based on letter a, b, c, d) is as following.

Two-step and three-step transfer distribution are same as above. Ordinate represents the occurrence times of one-step transition, horizontal ordinate represents the adjacent characters, and each number is a corresponding character. Corresponding relationship is shown in Table 1 as following.

Table 1. Corresponding relationship

Integer value	Corresponding character
0–25	a–z
26–51	A–Z
52–61	0–9
62	space
63	.

As Fig. 2-1, the circumstance that letter 'a' behind 'a' occurs 0 times, the circumstance that 'b' behind 'a' occurs 6 times, and the letter 'c' is 5 times, 'd' is 14 times. As shown in the Fig. 2-1, the first 25 characters are more active, occurring times of the rest are almost 1. In order to increase the length of the compression coding and also improve the compression speed, we define the n-order *TEMP* of character 'a' as following:

$$TEMP = \frac{p_{i0}^{(n)} + p_{i1}^{(n)} + p_{i2}^{(n)} + \cdots + P_{i25}^{(n)}}{25} \tag{7}$$

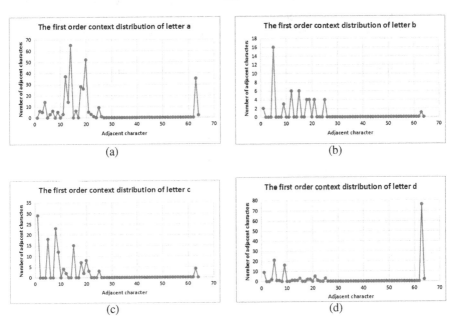

(a)   (b)

(c)   (d)

Fig. 2. 1. The first order context distribution of the letter a. 2. The first order context distribution of the letter b. 3. The first order context distribution of the letter c. 4. The first order context distribution of the letter d

4   Experimental Results and Analysis

4.1   The Experimental Environment

Intel(R) Core(TM) i3-4010U 4 CPU 1.70 GHz, memory 4 GB,cache L1:128 KB,cache L2:512 KB, cache L3:3.0 MB. Operating system is Windows 8,the development environment is DEV-C++. We realize the multiple order context Huffman compression algorithm based on Markov chain model by C language, and compare this algorithm with Huffman compression algorithm [12] and adaptive Huffman [13] compression algorithm.

The compression test is carried out on (20 KB, 200 KB, 500 KB, 1000 KB) four kinds of text data of different sizes.

4.2 Experimental Results and Analysis

This paper compares the compression algorithm Huffman compression algorithm, adaptive Huffman compression algorithm and the multiple order context Huffman compression algorithm based on Markov model, from two aspects:

Comparison of Compression ratio: Comparison of different amount of data on the same type of data (the string type). (Note: compression ratio = amount of data after compression/amount of data before compression)

Figures 3, 4, 5 and 6 are the comparison result of one-order, two-order, three-order and four-order Markcov chain compression algorithm with the other two compression algorithm respectively. Figure 7 is the comparison result of different order.

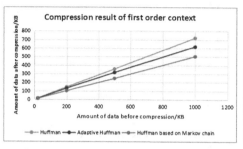

Fig. 3. Compression result of one-order context

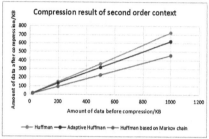

Fig. 4. Compression result of two-order context

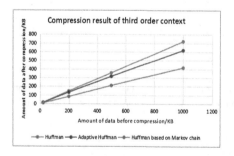

Fig. 5. Compression result of three-order context

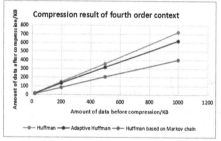

Fig. 6. Compression result of four-order context

As shown in Fig. 3, the compression effect of the Huffman algorithm based on Markov chain is better than the other two algorithms in the case of using one-order context compression. The compression effect using two-order context compression is shown in Fig. 4. We can see the advantage of Huffman algorithm based on Markov chain is more obvious. When the amount of data reaches 1000 KB, compression ratio of the Huffman algorithm based on Markov chain is 45%, the other algorithm are 72% and 62% respectively.

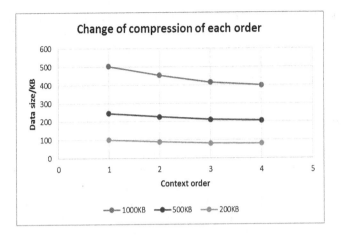

Fig. 7. Change of compression of each order

The three-order case is shown in Fig. 5, and the compression algorithm proposed in this paper has a good compression effect. The compression rate can reach 42%. We can see that compared to the other two algorithms, the advantage of Huffman algorithm based on Markov chain is more and more obvious in the four-order case.

As shown in above, multiple order context compression algorithm based on Markov chain is better than the other two compression algorithms. This is because the Huffman compression algorithm and the adaptive Huffman compression algorithm only take each character as an independent coding unit without taking into account the link between characters. The algorithm proposed in this paper considers the link between the characters, and makes the letters merged and compressed. But with the increase of the compression order, the compression rate is stable. Comparison of the compression ratio in different order of context is shown in Fig. 8 for the algorithm proposed in this paper.

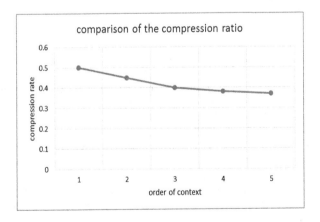

Fig. 8. Comparison of the compression ratio

As can be seen in Fig. 8, with the increase of the order of context, the compression ratio is gradually reduced, and the compression effect becomes better. But when the order is more than three, the compression rate becomes stable. This is because with the increase of the context order, the relation between characters becomes weak. So the optimal context compression order should be three or four.

5   Conclusion

Through the analysis of Sect. 4, we can see Huffman compression algorithm based on Markov chain is superior to the traditional Huffman compression algorithm and the adaptive Huffman compression algorithm. By constructing the Markov model and calculating the transfer probability matrix, characters are merged and compressed, which gets fine effect. The performance of the compression algorithm proposed in this paper is good, but we use threshold (e.g. *TEMP*), the value of which is also an important factor affecting the results of the experiment. These thresholds need to be further tested to achieve better compression results.

References

1. Kuruvila, M., Gopinath, D.P.: Entropy of Malayalam language and text compression using Huffman coding. In: First International Conference on Computational Systems and Communications. IEEE, pp. 150–155 (2014)
2. Wu, J., Dai, W., Xiong, H.: Regional context model and dynamic Huffman binarization for adaptive entropy coding of multimedia. In: IEEE International Symposium on Broadband Multimedia Systems and Broadcasting, pp. 1–6. IEEE (2014)
3. Wang, Z., Le, J.J., Wang, M., et al.: The column storage district level data compression mode and compression strategy selection method. In: ndbc2010 National Database Conference of China, pp. 523–1530 (2010)
4. Darwiyanto, E., Pratama, H.A., Septiana, G.: Text data compression for mobile phone using burrows-wheeler transform, move-to-front code and arithmetic coding (Case Study: Sunan Ibnu Majah Bahasa Translation). In: International Conference on Information and Communication Technology, pp. 178–183. IEEE (2015)
5. Wang, W.J., Lin, C.H.: Code compression for embedded systems using separated dictionaries. IEEE Trans. Very Large Scale Integr. Syst. **24**, 1 (2015)
6. Yokoo, H.: An adaptive data compression method based on context sorting. In: Data Compression Conference, pp. 160–169. IEEE (1996)
7. Ziv, J., Lempel, A.: A universal algorithm for sequential data compression. IEEE Trans. Inform. Theory **23**(3), 337–343 (1977)
8. Ren, W., Wang, H., Xu, L., et al.: Research on a quasi-lossless compression algorithm based on huffman coding. In: 2011 International Conference on Transportation, Mechanical, and Electrical Engineering (TMEE), pp. 1729–1732. IEEE (2011)
9. Ong, G.H., Ng, J.P.: Dynamic Markov compression using a crossbar-like tree initial structure for chinese texts. In: International Conference on Information Technology and Applications, pp. 407–410. IEEE (2005)

10. Wei, J., Wang, S., Zhang, L., et al.: Minimizing data transmission latency by bipartite graph in MapReduce. In: IEEE International Conference on CLUSTER Computing, pp. 521–522. IEEE (2015)
11. Papamichalis, P.E.: Markov-Huffman coding of LPC parameters. IEEE Trans. Acoust. Speech Signal Proc. **33**(2), 451–453 (1985)
12. Nandi, U., Mandal, J.K.: Adaptive region based huffman compression technique with selective code interchanging. In: Advances in Computing and Information Technology, pp. 739–748 (2012)
13. Singh, S., Singh, H.: Improved adaptive huffman compression algorithm. Int. J. Comput. Technol. **1**(1), 1–6 (2011)

Course Relatedness Based
on Concept Graph Modeling

Pang Jingwen[1], Cao Qinghua[1], and Sun Qing[1,2(✉)]

[1] School of Computer Science and Engineering,
Beihang University, Beijing 100191, China
{pangjingwen,caoqinghua,sunqing}@buaa.edu.cn
[2] School of Economics and Management, Beihang University,
Beijing 100191, China

Abstract. Analyzing the relatedness between courses can help students
plan their own curricula more efficiently, especially for the learning on
MOOC platforms. However, there are few researchers that concentrate
on mining the relationship between courses. In this paper, we propose a
method to compare relatedness between courses based on representing
courses as concept graphs. The concept graph comprises not only the
semantic relationship between concepts but also the importance of concepts in the course. Moreover, we take a cluster analysis to find relevant
concepts between two courses and take advantage of Similar Concept
Groups to compute the degree of course relatedness. We experimented
with a collection of English syllabi from Beihang University and experiments show better performance than the state-of-the-art.

Keywords: Course relatedness · Concept graph · DBpedia · Clustering

1 Introduction

Understanding the relatedness among curricula is important for students to
make curriculum planning. As the quantity of online educational resources grows
rapidly, it becomes necessary to obtain the course relatedness automatically. If a
student already learnt *Data Mining* at school and wants to learn more about it on
a MOOC platform, how does he choose an appropriate course from the ones with
similar titles, such as *Data Mining Capstone, Pattern Discovery in Data Mining,
Cluster Analysis in Data Mining* and so on? It is hard to solve these problems without an accurate representation of overlapped course contents. In addition, more
and more students take part in international exchange student programs in universities. There is not a detailed criterion to compare contents between courses in
different universities and complete credit transfer. Hence, many students have to
waste time to retake similar courses. Additionally, curriculum design and evaluation requires a deep insight into the difference and relatedness between courses
and abundant domain knowledge. It will take much more time to finish the task
manually as the quantity of courses grows. Therefore, it is significant to give an

© ICST Institute for Computer Sciences, Social Informatics and Telecommunications Engineering 2017
S. Wang and A. Zhou (Eds.): CollaborateCom 2016, LNICST 201, pp. 94–103, 2017.
DOI: 10.1007/978-3-319-59288-6_9

accurate measure of course relatedness automatically in order to help students and teachers improve their efficiency of study or work.

Some methods have been proposed to automate the process to measure course relatedness. Since course data is usually text, most work will involve methods of computing text similarity. Yang et al. [14] learn a directed universal concept graph and use it to explain the course content overlap and detect prerequisite relations among courses. They use four different schemes to represent the course content. Two of schemes use human-readable words or Wikipedia categories as the concept space and the others map course contents into latent features. Although this method has a good performance on inducing prerequisite relations, there is no single concept graph to describe contents of a course and no specific evaluation of course relatedness. Jean et al. [10] analyze conceptual overlap between courses with Latent Dirichlet allocation (LDA) [1]. This method transforms every course into a topic vector and calculates the distance between vectors. However, latent topics are not explicit course concepts and cannot represent the course content directly. Sheng-syun et al. [12] compute similarity between lectures in different online courses retrieved from a query and structure related lectures into a learning map. They utilize words and grammatical features of lecture titles to evaluate the similarity. In terms of a course, concepts are its basic components. All methods described above do not combine various semantic relationships and the importance of concepts to analyze the course relatedness.

In this paper, we propose a new method to measure the course relatedness. We first link terms in syllabi to concepts from a knowledge base and regard these concepts as nodes to build a concept graph for each course. Then, we assign weights to edges in the concept graph to measure the association between each pair of concepts. Since the relationship between terms in syllabi is usually implicit, we leverage abundant semantic resources in a knowledge base such as internal links in Wikipedia to obtain explicit relations between concepts. Based on the degree of association between concepts in the graph, we can measure the node strength to represent the concept importance in the course. Finally, after mapping each concept into a continuous vector, we cluster all concepts from any pair of courses to filter irrelevant ones between two courses, and compute course relatedness by leveraging picked concepts and their weights in concept graphs. In this way, we can reduce the impact of irrelevant concepts on the precision of similarity computation.

Our contributions are as follows.

- We propose a new method to assess the course relatedness. The method represents the course content as a concept graph and compare the similarity between concept graphs. We combine two types of semantic relationship of concepts in the knowledge base to construct concept graphs for courses.
- We integrate clustering with similarity computation between concept graphs. By clustering, we classify related concepts from a pair of courses into groups and remove irrelevant concepts between two courses, which reduces the impact of irrelevant concepts on the accuracy of similarity computation.
- In the process of measuring the course relatedness, we take the pairwise similarity of concepts into consideration as well as the importance of concepts in each course to achieve better performance.

2   Concept Graph Construction

Given a course syllabus, our aim is to build a graph in which nodes are detected concepts from DBpedia by a mention detection tool. We connect any pair of concepts if their associative degree is non-zero. In terms of associative degree, co-occurrence relationship and category relationship are taken into consideration. Finally, we regard associative degree between concepts as edge weights and compute node strength for nodes in the graph.

2.1   DBpedia

Knowledge base such as Wikipedia provides a large wide-coverage repository of encyclopedic knowledge [6]. It also includes massive concepts in curricula. In this paper, we leverage concept information in DBpedia to find the association between concepts. DBpedia [4] extracts structured data from Wikipedia and maps these data into ontology. Each Wikipedia article title is regarded as a concept in DBpedia. DBpedia can be cast as a knowledge graph containing disambiguated entities and explicit semantic relations [11]. Besides, DBpedia also extracts internal links between Wikipedia articles and the category information, which we utilize to compute the associative degree between concepts.

2.2   Co-occurrence Relationship

Wikipedia articles that contain both concepts indicate relatedness, while articles with only one of the concepts suggest the opposite [13]. Thus, we use the shared incoming links of both concepts in Wikipedia to compute the degree of co-occurrence relatedness between concepts. The shared incoming links are Wikipedia pages where both concepts appear as internal links. Inspired by [13], the metric to measure the co-occurrence relatedness is:

$$CoDegree(A,B) = 1 - \frac{\log(\max(|L_a|,|L_b|)) - \log(|L_a \cap L_b|)}{\log|W| - \log(\min(|L_a|,|L_b|))} \tag{1}$$

where A and B are two concepts, L_a and L_b are sets of incoming links to A and B, and W is the set of Wikipedia articles. The degree of co-occurrence relatedness increases as more common incoming links of both concepts exist.

2.3   Category Relationship

Every concept in DBpedia belongs to one or more categories. Each category may have subcategories. For example, *Category: Statistics* has subcategories such as *Category: Statisticians, Category: Applied statistics* and so on. Thus categories can be organized into tree-like structures and form a category hierarchy. Concepts which belong to similar categories are related to similar subjects. Analyzing the category relationship between two concepts can measure their level of subject association. When we get two concepts A and B, $C_a = \{a_1, a_2, ..., a_m\}$

and $C_b = \{b_1, b_2, ..., b_n\}$ are category sets that A and B belong to respectively. We first measure the similarity of each pair of category (a_i, b_i) and then compute the relatedness between two category sets C_a and C_b. The similarity of two categories mainly depends on the extent to which they share information in common [8]. Thus, we can measure the similarity based on their information content (IC) in the category hierarchy. Categories in lower levels of the hierarchy contain more information content. For example, *Category: Machine learning* has a subcategory *Category: Artificial neural networks*, the subcategory refers to a more specific algorithm and thus its level of IC is higher. There are several metrics to quantify IC as described in [7]. According to the experiment result of [7], the depth of concepts in the hierarchy is more fit for the measurement of IC. Formally,

$$IC(c) = \frac{\log(max\_depth(c))}{\log(max\_depth(H))} \tag{2}$$

where c is a concept, H is the category hierarchy, $max\_depth(x)$ denotes the maximum depth of x.

Then, we compute similarity between each pair of categories (a_i, b_i) as below:

$$CatSim(a_i, b_j) = \frac{IC(MSCA(a_i, b_j))}{IC(a_i) + IC(b_j)} \tag{3}$$

where $MSCA(a_i, b_i)$ denotes the common ancestor of a_i, b_i with the highest information content.

With pairwise similarity of categories, the category relatedness between two concepts A and B can be obtained as follows.

$$CatDegree(A, B) = \frac{1}{2}*(\frac{1}{m}*\sum_{i=1}^{m} maxCatSim(a_i) + \frac{1}{n}*\sum_{j=1}^{n} maxCatSim(b_j)) \tag{4}$$

where $a_i \in C_a$, $b_j \in C_b$, C_a and C_b are category sets for concepts A and B respectively. The $maxCatSim(a_i)$ denotes the similarity between a_i and a category b_j which is most similar to a_i among categories in C_b.

2.4 Importance of Concepts

In terms of the concept graph of a course, the centrality of a node represents the importance of a concept in the course. We measure the centrality of a node on basis of its associativity with other nodes in the concept graph:

$$Centrality(t) = \frac{1}{N} * \sum_{i=1}^{n} Association(t, t_i) \tag{5}$$

where N is the number of nodes in the concept graph.

Co-occurrence relationship reflects contextual similarity of two concepts and category relationship reflects the subject association. Thus we can define the associativity degree of pairwise concepts as a linear combination of co-occurrence relatedness and category relatedness:

$$Association(A, B) = CoDegree(A, B) + \alpha * CatDegree(A, B) \qquad (6)$$

where α is the parameter to balance the contribution of two parts. The associativity degree between two concepts will be regarded as the edge weight between them in the graph.

3   Course Relatedness Model

In Sect. 2, we describe the approach to construct a concept graph. Our aim is to measure the relatedness between courses based on their concept graph representation. Therefore, the basic issue is how to assess the concept similarity between two concept graphs. We first map each concept into a continuous vector and then propose a clustering-based method to compute course relatedness.

3.1   Concept Vector

In order to assess the concept similarity, we represent each concept as a vector based on the Word2Vec framework. Word2Vec[1] takes a large corpus of text as input and output a high-dimensional vector for each word. The vector representation of words captures semantic and syntactic patterns of words [5]. Thus, we can utilize word vectors to compute the similarity among words on a fine-grained level. Inspired by Word2Vec, we train a model to represent concepts in courses as vectors. Every internal link in the Wikipedia page refers to a Wikipedia article, which has a corresponding concept in DBpedia. Therefore, we can replace the link text with DBpedia concepts and get a corpus for training concept vectors. We preprocess the Wikipedia dump with Wiki2Vec[2]. It adds referred DBpedia concepts into Wikipedia text, i.e., the raw text "Among other categories of machine learning problems, [[Meta learning (computer science) | learning to learn]] learns its own [[inductive bias]] based on previous experience." is transformed into "Among other categories of machine learning problems, DBPEDIA_ID/Meta_learning_(computer_science) learning to learn learns its own DBPEDIA_ID/inductive_bias based on previous experience." The text in brackets is the referred DBpedia concept and the link text.

The similarity between two concepts, A and B, is measured by cosine similarity:

$$ConceptSim(A, B) = \frac{\overrightarrow{a} * \overrightarrow{b}}{\| \overrightarrow{a} \| * \| \overrightarrow{b} \|} \qquad (7)$$

where $\overrightarrow{a}$ and $\overrightarrow{b}$ are concept vectors for A and B respectively, and $\| \overrightarrow{a} \|$ and $\| \overrightarrow{b} \|$ are the magnitude of vectors. The closer that the value of $ConceptSim(A, B)$ is to 1, the higher that the degree of similarity between two concepts is.

---

[1] https://code.google.com/p/word2vec.
[2] https://github.com/idio/wiki2vec.

3.2   Similar Concept Group

For course A and course B, let $S_a = \{c_{a1}, c_{a2}, \ldots, c_{am}\}$ and $S_b = \{c_{b1}, c_{b2}, \ldots, c_{bn}\}$ denote concept sets of them respectively, where c_{ij} is the $j-th$ concept of course i. The most intuitive approach to compute the degree of course relatedness is to compare pairs of concepts c_{ai} and c_{bi} and then accumulate these similarities. However, there are many pairs of concepts are irrelevant. If we use them to compute the course relatedness, the rating accuracy of course relatedness will be affected. Therefore, we adopt a clustering-based method to classify concepts in $S_{ab} = \{S_a, S_b\}$ into several groups and select Similar Concept Groups which contain both concepts from course A and course B. Concepts in each of Similar Concept Groups are related to each other. Each selected group represents a part of associative content between two courses.

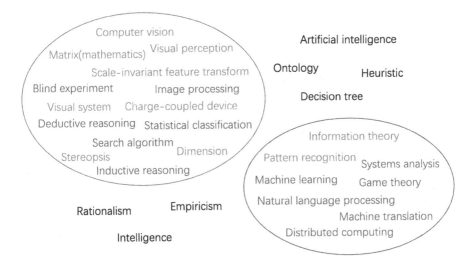

Fig. 1. The clustering result of course A and course B: the green concepts are from A and the blue ones are from B. Most concepts are classified into two groups. Concepts outside circles are sparse and cannot reflect associative knowledge between two courses. (Color figure online)

Figure 1 depicts the clustering result for two courses. Course A is *Computer Vision and Computation* and course B is *Artificial Intelligence*. Concepts belong to the same group are related to each other to some extent. We can find that most of concepts in the left group are about computer vision knowledge and reasoning, while concepts in the right group are mainly related to artificial intelligence.

We use the clustering algorithm [9] based on finding high-density and large-distance cluster centers. Compared with other clustering algorithms, this approach is independent with data distribution and only take the distance between data points into consideration. Besides, the dimensionality of the data space will not affect clustering performance. Our concept vector space is uncertain and high-dimensional. Hence, this clustering algorithm is fit for our concept data.

The algorithm decides a cluster center from two aspects. The first one is the local density of a data point. If its local density is higher than its surrounding neighbors, it is likely to be a cluster center. We denote the local density ρ_i of data point i as below:

$$\rho_i = \sum_j \chi(d_{ij} - d_c) \tag{8}$$

where $\chi(x) = 1$ if the distance between point i and point j is shorter than d_c, otherwise $\chi(x) = 0$. d_c is a cutoff distance. We can compute d_{ij} by Euclidean Distance, Manhattan Distance, etc. In this paper, we use Euclidean Distance to measure the distance between two points.

The second aspect is the distance δ_i from a data point i to any other point j with a higher local density:

$$\delta_i = \min_{j:\rho_i > \rho_j} (d_{ij}) \tag{9}$$

In conclusion, cluster centers are data points with high local density and its ρ_i is extremely large. After finding cluster centers, each remaining point is classified into the group of which the group centre has higher density and is nearest to the point.

3.3 The Degree of Course Relatedness

With Similar Concept Groups, we can compute the degree of course relatedness. First, we measure similarity between concepts inside each group, which is defined as group similarity. Then, the course relatedness can be assessed based on the combination of each group similarity.

Given two courses A and B, we suppose the number of Similar Concept Groups is n. Let set $S_i = \{c_{a1}, \ldots, c_{ap}, c_{b1}, \ldots, c_{bq}\} (i = 1 \ldots n)$ denotes concepts in group i, p and q are the number of concepts belong to course A and course B in S_i respectively. The group similarity is defined as:

$$GroupSim_i = \frac{1}{2}\left(\frac{\sum_{e=1}^{p} w_{ae} * (\frac{1}{q} * \sum_{f=1}^{q} ConceptSim(c_{ae}, c_{bf}))}{\sum_{e=1}^{p} w_{ae}} + \frac{\sum_{f=1}^{q} w_{bf} * (\frac{1}{p} * \sum_{e=1}^{p} ConceptSim(c_{ae}, c_{bf}))}{\sum_{f=1}^{q} w_{bf}}\right) \tag{10}$$

where $\{w_{a1}, \ldots, w_{ap}\}$ and $\{w_{b1}, \ldots, w_{bf}\}$ denotes node strength in concept graph A and concept graph B respectively. Therefore, we define the relatedness between course A and B as:

$$CourseRelatedness(A, B) = \frac{1}{m} \sum_{i=1}^{n} num_i * GroupSim_i \tag{11}$$

where m is the total number of concepts contained in course A and B, and num_i is the quantity of concepts in group i.

This method assesses course relatedness based on Similar Concept Groups, which represents the associative content between courses. In this way, we filter irrelevant concepts between two courses and reduce their impact on the precision of relatedness computation.

4 Experiments

4.1 Dataset and Experimental Setting

We collected 100 English syllabi of Computer Science courses from Beihang University. The syllabus includes the course name, course aims and tasks and the content description for each chapter. We invited 20 students major in Computer Science to annotate pairwise course relatedness with the rating on a scale from 1 (highly unrelated) to 5 (highly related). Students have a wide knowledge about these courses, hence their judgements can be considered as the gold standard. The final pairwise relatedness score is the average of ratings from all annotators for a pair of courses. Following the similar work [7], we evaluate the performance of our algorithm with Pearsons linear correlation coefficient.

We took advantage of TagMe [2] to extract concepts from syllabi. TagMe is a mention detection tool. It assigns an attribute to each annotation, called ρ, which estimates the "goodness" of the annotation with respect to the other entities of the input text. We set ρ as 0.1 to discard extracted concepts which cannot reflect the course content. Every course has 40 discriminant concepts on average. After preprocessing the Wikipedia dump as Sect. 3.1, we trained a model to generate concept vectors. Training parameters were set as follows, sub-sampling=1e-3, min-count=5, window=10, sg=1.

4.2 Compare Related Methods

Course data is usually text, hence some methods of computing text similarity are usually used to measure course relatedness. We compare our method with Bag-of-words (BOW), Latent Dirichlet allocation (LDA) [1], Explicit Semantic Analysis (ESA) [3] and ConceptGraphSim (CGS) [7], which can compute text similarity. CGS generates a concept graph for a document. Nodes in the graph are concepts and edges between nodes are inferred based on knowledge in DBpedia. CGS makes a comparison between concept graphs to obtain text similarity. The results in Table 1 show that our work has better performance than the other methods. Both ESA and CGS use weighted concepts to represent the document. However, weights of concepts in ESA ignore relations between concepts. Our method combines co-occurrence and category semantic relations to measure the importance of concepts in the graph. Besides, compared with CGS we use Similar Concepts Groups to compute the relatedness between two courses, which eliminates the impact of irrelevant concepts between two courses. Therefore, our method outperforms ESA and CGS with respect to analyzing course relatedness.

In order to verify the effect of each step of our method, we use weighted and unweighted concepts with intuitive (without clustering), K-Means and our

Table 1. Comparison with methods of text similarity on course syllabi dataset

Method	Pearson correlation
BOW	0.45
LDA [1]	0.52
ESA [3]	0.63
CGS [7]	0.68
Ours	0.71

clustering strategy respectively to calculate Pearson Correlation. The results are shown in Table 2. We can see that the Pearson correlation of the intuitive method is just 0.62. Our clustering method achieves a correlation of 0.71, which is better than the correlation of 0.69 by K-Means. K-Means chooses initial cluster centers randomly, while our clustering strategy can determine the number of cluster centers automatically and is robust to data distribution. With respect to concept weights, we see that methods which assign weights to concepts are better than the ones without weights.

Table 2. Comparison among different clustering strategies with weighted and unweighted concepts

Pearson correlation	Unweighted	Weighted
Intuitive	0.54	0.62
K-Means	0.64	0.69
Ours	0.65	0.71

5   Conclusions

In this paper, we propose a method to measure the course relatedness. Our method represents course content as a concept graph by leveraging knowledge in DBpedia and each concept in the graph is weighted to denote its significance in the course. During the process of comparing concept graphs, concepts in a pair of courses are classified into Similar Concept Groups. We utilize Similar Concept Groups to compute the degree of relatedness between courses. The experiments show that the proposed approach has good performance in measuring the course relatedness. For future work, we intend to collect more data about course to enrich our concept graphs, such as the annotation of concept importance by teachers, and improve the accuracy of concepts extracted from DBpedia.

References

1. Blei, D.M., Ng, A.Y., Jordan, M.I.: Latent dirichlet allocation. J. Mach. Learn. Res. **3**, 993–1022 (2003)
2. Ferragina, P., Scaiella, U.: Fast and accurate annotation of short texts with wikipedia pages. arXiv preprint arXiv:1006.3498 (2010)
3. Gabrilovich, E., Markovitch, S.: Computing semantic relatedness using wikipedia-based explicit semantic analysis. IJcAI **7**, 1606–1611 (2007)
4. Lehmann, J., Isele, R., Jakob, M., Jentzsch, A., Kontokostas, D., Mendes, P.N., Hellmann, S., Morsey, M., van Kleef, P., Auer, S., et al.: Dbpedia-a large-scale, multilingual knowledge base extracted from wikipedia. Seman. Web **6**(2), 167–195 (2015)
5. Mikolov, T., Yih, W., Zweig, G.: Linguistic regularities in continuous space word representations. HLT-NAACL **13**, 746–751 (2013)
6. Navigli, R., Ponzetto, S.P.: Babelnet: the automatic construction, evaluation and application of a wide-coverage multilingual semantic network. Artif. Intell. **193**, 217–250 (2012)
7. Ni, Y., Xu, Q.K., Cao, F., Mass, Y., Sheinwald, D., Zhu, H.J., Cao, S.S.: Semantic documents relatedness using concept graph representation. In: Proceedings of the Ninth ACM International Conference on Web Search and Data Mining, pp. 635–644. ACM (2016)
8. Resnik, P.: Using information content to evaluate semantic similarity in a taxonomy. arXiv preprint cmp-lg/9511007 (1995)
9. Rodriguez, A., Laio, A.: Clustering by fast search and find of density peaks. Science **344**(6191), 1492–1496 (2014)
10. Rouly, J.M., Rangwala, H., Johri, A.: What are we teaching? Automated evaluation of cs curricula content using topic modeling. In: Proceedings of the Eleventh Annual International Conference on International Computing Education Research, pp. 189–197. ACM (2015)
11. Schuhmacher, M., Ponzetto, S.P.: Knowledge-based graph document modeling. In: Proceedings of the 7th ACM International Conference on Web Search and Data Mining, pp. 543–552. ACM (2014)
12. Shen, S., Lee, H., Li, S., Zue, V., Lee, L.: Structuring lectures in massive open online courses (moocs) for efficient learning by linking similar sections and predicting prerequisites. In: Sixteenth Annual Conference of the International Speech Communication Association (2015)
13. Witten, I., Milne, D.: An effective, low-cost measure of semantic relatedness obtained from wikipedia links. In: Proceeding of AAAI Workshop on Wikipedia and Artificial Intelligence: An Evolving Synergy, pp. 25–30. AAAI Press, Chicago (2008)
14. Yang, Y., Liu, H., Carbonell, J., Ma, W.: Concept graph learning from educational data. In: Proceedings of the Eighth ACM International Conference on Web Search and Data Mining, pp. 159–168. ACM (2015)

Rating Personalization Improves Accuracy: A Proportion-Based Baseline Estimate Model for Collaborative Recommendation

Zhenhua Tan[✉], Liangliang He, Hong Li, and Xingwei Wang

Software College of Northeastern University, Shenyang 110819, China
{tanzh, wangxw}@mail.neu.edu.cn,
{1501666, 1501667}@stu.neu.cn

Abstract. Baseline estimate is an important latent factor for recommendations. The current baseline estimate model is widely used by characterizing both items and users. However, it doesn't consider different users' rating criterions and results in predictions may be out of recommendation's rating range. In this paper, we propose a novel baseline estimate model to improve the current performance, named PBEModel (Proportion-based Baseline Estimate Model), which uses rating proportions to compute the rating personalization. The PBEModel is modeled as a piecewise function according to different rating personalization. In order to verify this new baseline estimate, we apply it into SVD++, and propose a novel SVD++ model named PBESVD++. Experiments based on six real datasets show that the proposed PBEModel is rational and more accurate than current baseline estimate model, and the PBESVD++ has relatively higher prediction accuracy than SVD++.

Keywords: Recommender system · Latent factor model · Baseline estimate model · PBEModel · PBESVD++

1 Introduction

Recommender systems, which are important information filtering mechanisms to predict item rating or user preference, have been applied in variety internet-based systems, such as videos, music, news, and some social networks. Recommender systems learn user preference pattern to items from user-item transactions based on Collaborative Filtering (CF) [1], to predict users' possible interesting items from unknowns.

In order to establish recommendations, CF needs to compare items against users, which are quite different two objects. Usually, the neighborhood approach [2] and latent factor models [3] are two main disciplines to do the comparison in CF. In terms of latent factor models, there are several approaches, such as Singular Value Decomposition (SVD) model [4], pLSA [5], Latent Dirichlet Allocation [6] and SVD++ [7], to uncover latent features that explain observed ratings by historical feedbacks. In these models, the SVD++ model proposed by Yehuda Koren [7] has relatively high recommendation accuracy, and many researchers proposed related models based on it, such as TimeSVD++ [8], SocialSVD++ [9], and TrustSVD [10].

© ICST Institute for Computer Sciences, Social Informatics and Telecommunications Engineering 2017
S. Wang and A. Zhou (Eds.): CollaborateCom 2016, LNICST 201, pp. 104–114, 2017.
DOI: 10.1007/978-3-319-59288-6_10

To improve the prediction accuracy, most of researchers focus on the key challenges underlying the recommender systems and collaborative filtering are data sparseness and personalized data sparseness, such as [7–10]. Some researchers focused on properties of recommendations to propose more accurate prediction method, such as integrated QoS prediction approach HDOP [11], prediction method of unknown QoS properties [12], and reputation measurement based on malicious rating detection [13]. In this paper, we focus on the improvement of baseline estimate model.

Observed from current models, such as [7–10], we can find that almost all recommender models have a same baseline estimate model, as:

$$\hat{r}_{ui} = b_u + b_i + \mu \tag{1}$$

Where $\hat{r}_{ui}$ denotes the baseline prediction for unknown item i by user u; μ denotes the overall average rating; b_u and b_i denote the observed deviations of user u and item i from the average respectively.

By analyzed the baseline estimate model in the above Eq. (1), we find the prediction of $\hat{r}_{ui}$ for unknown items may be out of recommender range. The main reason is that the current baseline estimate model doesn't consider different users' rating criterions.

Thus, we propose a proportion-based baseline estimate model, named PBEModel (Proportion-based Baseline Estimate Model). The improved PBEModel consider users' rating personalization via a proportional baseline estimate method. To our knowledge, it is the first time to improve the baseline estimate model based on proportion concept. In order to prove the rightness, we also proposed a PBESVD++ model to improve the prediction accuracy of SVD++ based on PBEModel.

This paper has the following innovative features:

(1) We uncover the shortcoming and reason of the current baseline estimate model, and propose a novel Proportion-based Baseline Estimate Model (PBEModel) to get better prediction ability.
(2) We propose an improved SVD++ model based on PBEModel, named PBESVD++, and get more prediction accuracy based on different recommendation datasets.
(3) The proposed method in this paper may bring a novel approach to improve prediction accuracy of recommender system.

In the remainder of this paper, we introduce the related work in the next section. PBEModel is proposed in Sect. 3, and PBESVD++ is proposed in Sect. 4. The experiments and analysis follow in Sect. 5, with conclusion afterwards in the last section.

2 Related Work About SVD++

Collaborative filtering (CF) methods are usually used in recommender systems, based on collecting and analyzing a large amount of users' behaviors and predicting what users will like based on their similarity to other users. One of the primary areas of CF is latent factor model which try to explain the ratings by characterizing both items and users.

As one of the main methods of latent factor models, SVD is a commonly used matrix decomposition technique. SVD++ is an improved model based on SVD and had more remarkable improvement of recommendation accuracy than SVD model. The detailed improvement is that a free user-factor vector p_u is complemented by $|I_u|^{-\frac{1}{2}} \cdot \left(\sum_{j \in I_u} y_j \right)$, and a user u is modeled as $\left(p_u + |I_u|^{-\frac{1}{2}} \cdot \left(\sum_{j \in I_u} y_j \right) \right)$. The equation of SVD++ is as:

$$\hat{r}_{ui} = b_u + b_i + \mu + q_i^T \left(p_u + |I_u|^{-\frac{1}{2}} \cdot \left(\sum_{j \in I_u} y_j \right) \right) \tag{2}$$

where $\hat{r}_{ui}$ denotes the prediction of unknown item i by user u; μ is the overall average rating; b_u and b_i represent the observed deviations of user u and item i, respectively, from μ; I_u represents the set of items rating by user u; p_u and q_i^T represent a d-dimensional latent feature vector of user u and item i, respectively; y_j represents the implicit influence of items rated by user u in the past on the ratings of unknown items in the future. Kumar et al. [9] merged the user's social factors into the SVD++ and proposed SocialSVD++ model to get better prediction performance with equation as:

$$\hat{r}_{ui} = b_u + b_i + \mu + q_i^T \left(p_u + |I_u|^{-\frac{1}{2}} \cdot \left(\sum_{j \in I_u} y_j \right) + |p_i|^{-\frac{1}{2}} \cdot \left(\sum_{i \in p_i} x_i \right) \right) \tag{3}$$

where p_i denotes the set of implicit feedback (the set of item that are rated by most users) in SocialSVD++. Guo et al. [10] took social trust information into account in the SVD++ and proposed TrustSVD model, which merged trust factor and get better accuracy, the equation is as:

$$\hat{r}_{ui} = b_u + b_i + \mu + q_i^T \left(p_u + |I_u|^{-\frac{1}{2}} \cdot \left(\sum_{j \in I_u} y_j \right) + |T_u|^{-\frac{1}{2}} \cdot \left(\sum_{v \in T_u} w_v \right) \right) \tag{4}$$

where w_v denotes the user-specific latent feature vector of users (trustees) trusted by user u. Yehuda Koren [8] proposed a Time Changing Baseline Predictors to improve the baseline estimate model by allowed the baseline ratings to be changed over time as $\hat{b}_{ui} = b_u(t_{ui}) + b_i(t_{ui}) + \mu$, where $b_u(\cdot)$ and $b_i(\cdot)$ are real valued functions that change over time; t_{ui} denotes time of rating in term of individual days. Finally, they proposed TimeSVD++ based on their SVD++.

All of these models have a relatively same baseline estimate model as Eq. (1). As it is known for many recommender systems, the baseline estimate model is a key factor. And, these similar considerations were mentioned in the Pearson method, which considers the differences of user ratings [14], and this concept also inspires us to improve the current baseline estimate.

3 Proposed PBEModel

As we can see from Sect. 2, related latent factor models for recommender systems are based on the current baseline estimate model described in Eq. (1) as $\hat{r}_{ui} = b_u + b_i + \mu$, where b_u represents the deviation of user u from the overall average rating, that is the difference between the average rating $\bar{r}_u$ of user u and the overall average rating $\bar{r}$. And b_i represents the deviation of item i from the overall average rating that is the difference between the average rating $\bar{r}_i$ of item i and the overall average rating $\bar{r}$. So, $b_u = \bar{r}_u - \bar{r}$ and $b_i = \bar{r}_i - \bar{r}$, where $\bar{r} = \mu$. Thus,

$$\hat{r}_{ui} = \bar{r}_u + \bar{r}_i - \bar{r} \tag{5}$$

Let $\Delta r = \bar{r}_u - \bar{r}$, then

$$\hat{r}_{ui} = \bar{r}_i + \Delta r \tag{6}$$

where Δr denotes the difference between the average rating of user u and the overall average rating $(\bar{r})$, which reflects the difference between the users rating habits and the public habits.

Obviously, Eq. (1) is equal to Eqs. (5) and (6). Based on the equivalent equations, we can easily find the current baseline estimate model does not consider different users' rating criterions. In real recommender systems, users have different rating preferences. Some are used to relatively higher ratings for items than others, while some have very strict rating criterion for a same item. This problem result in that predictions based on current baseline estimate model would be out of rating range. Let's take some examples, and assume the rating range is $[1, 5]$.

Example (1): for user Alice.
Assume $\bar{r}_u = 4.2, \bar{r}_i = 4, \bar{r}_i = 3.1$, then $\hat{r}_{ui} = 4.2 + 4 - 3.1 = 5.1 > 5$.

Example (2): for user Bob.
Assume $\bar{r}_u = 4.2, \bar{r}_i = 4, \bar{r}_i = 4.2$, then $\hat{r}_{ui} = 4.2 + 4 - 4.2 = 4 = \bar{r}_i$.

Example (3): for user Carl.
Assume $\bar{r}_u = 1.5, = 2, = 4.2$, then $\hat{r}_{ui} = 1.5 + 2 - 4.2 = (-1.7) < 0$.

In Example (1), Alice's average rating $\bar{r}_u > \bar{r}$ and $\Delta r > 0$, which means Alice has relatively slack rating criterion than most of other users, while Carl has stricter rating criterion in Example (3) where $\bar{r}_u < \bar{r}$ and $\Delta r < 0$. In Example (2), Bob has a relatively average rating criterion with $\bar{r}_u = \bar{r}$ and $\Delta r = 0$, and his prediction $\hat{r}_{ui}$ is equal to $\bar{r}_i$. Obviously, the predictions in Examples (1) and (3) are unreasonable because of they out of range $[1, 5]$, and it proves that the baseline estimate model needs improvement. We consider the personalization of users' rating criterions to improve the baseline estimate model in this paper.

Definition 1. Rating Strict Level represents a user's personalization during rating items. Let **L1** denote user's relatively average criterion to make a rating between given range; let **L2** denote relatively strict criterion that means users in this level will make a relatively lower rating than others. And let **L3** denote relatively slack criterion and users in this level will make relatively higher ratings for items. Usually, a L1 user's average rating $\bar{r}_u = \bar{r}$, while a L2 user's $\bar{r}_u < \bar{r}$ and a L3 user's $\bar{r}_u > \bar{r}$. Figure 1 shows these users in different personalized rating.

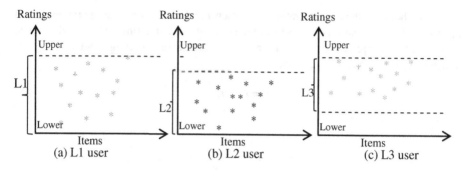

Fig. 1. Personalized rating levels

For users of L1, just like Bob in Example (2), their ratings ranged between the given data area [m, n] of recommender systems. But users of L2, whose rating criterion is stricter, usually have a personal upper limit for ratings, which is less than the given range upper limit n. For example, in a recommender system with rating range [1, 5], a L2 user would think number 4 is the best rating in his mind, while a L1 user would think number 5 is the best level. In this paper, this difference between users' rating criterion is the personalization. Therefore, in real systems, these three kinds of users have different personalized rating ranges, just as shown in Fig. 2.

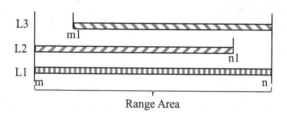

Fig. 2. Personalized compressed rating ranges

Ratings of L1 users ranges between given [m, n], and L2 between [m, n1] while L3 between [m1, n]. Based on the analysis above, we improve the baseline estimate model according to the three kinds of personalization. We compute users' rating personalization by rating proportion to improve the current baseline estimate model.

Firstly, assume the range area is [0, n].

(1) When $\bar{r}_u = \bar{r}$, according to Eq. (6), we can get

$$\hat{r}_{ui} = \bar{r}_i \tag{7}$$

(2) When $\bar{r}_u < \bar{r}$, then

$$(\hat{r}_{ui} - \bar{r}_u)/\bar{r}_u = (\bar{r}_i < \bar{r})/\bar{r} \tag{8}$$

(3) When $\bar{r}_u > \bar{r}$, then

$$(\hat{r}_{ui} - \bar{r}_u)/(n - \bar{r}_u) = (\bar{r}_i - \bar{r})/(n - \bar{r}) \tag{9}$$

Based on the above Eqs. (7)–(9), we can get the new baseline estimate equation for system with rating range [0, n], as

$$\hat{r}_{ui} = \begin{cases} (\bar{r}_u/\bar{r}) \cdot (\bar{r}_u/\bar{r}) + \bar{r}_u & \text{when } \bar{r}_u \leq \bar{r} \\ ((n - \bar{r}_u)/(n - \bar{r})) \cdot (\bar{r}_i - \bar{r}) + \bar{r}_u & \text{when } \bar{r}_u > \bar{r} \end{cases} \tag{10}$$

Obviously, if $\bar{r}_u = \bar{r}$, Eq. (10) is same with Eq. (5). Generally, if the rating range of recommender system is between [m, n], the baseline estimate equation could be:

$$\hat{r}_{ui} = \begin{cases} ((\bar{r}_u - m)/(\bar{r} - m)) \cdot (\bar{r}_i - \bar{r}) + \bar{r}_u & \text{when } \bar{r}_u \leq \bar{r} \\ ((n - \bar{r}_u)/(n - \bar{r})) \cdot (\bar{r}_i - \bar{r}) + \bar{r}_u & \text{when } \bar{r}_u > \bar{r} \end{cases} \tag{11}$$

In Eq. (11), because $\bar{r}_u$, $\bar{r}_i$ and $\bar{r}$ belong to [m, n], it is easy to prove that $\hat{r}_{ui}$ also belong to [m, n]. Finally, the current baseline estimate model $\hat{r}_{ui} = b_u + b_i + \mu$ can be improved as:

$$\hat{r}_{ui} = \begin{cases} \frac{b_u + \mu - m}{\mu - m} \cdot b_i + b_u + \mu, & \text{when } b_u \leq 0 \\ \frac{n - b_u - \mu}{n - \mu} \cdot b_i + b_u + \mu, & \text{when } b_u > 0 \end{cases} \tag{12}$$

Related elements, such as $\hat{r}_{ui}$, b_u, b_i and μ, have same meanings as Eq. (1), and rating area is [m, n] where n $\geq$ m $\geq$ 0. We named this novel baseline estimate model with Eq. (12) as **PBEModel**.

4 PBESVD++: An Improved SVD++ Based on PBEModel

In order to verify the recommendation performance of PBEModel, we apply it into SVD++, and proposed an improved SVD++ named PBESVD++. The SVD++ model is described as Eq. (2). Firstly, we replace the baseline estimate part in Eq. (2) with Eq. (12), and get the following new equation, as:

$$\hat{r}_{ui} = \begin{cases} \frac{b_u + \mu - m}{\mu - m} \cdot b_i + b_u + \mu + q_i^T \cdot \left(p_u + |I_u|^{-\frac{1}{2}} \cdot \left(\sum_{j \in I_u} y_j\right)\right) & \text{when } b_u \leq 0 \\ \frac{n - b_u - \mu}{n - \mu} \cdot b_i + b_u + \mu + q_i^T \cdot \left(p_u + |I_u|^{-\frac{1}{2}} \cdot \left(\sum_{j \in I_u} y_j\right)\right) & \text{when } b_u > 0 \end{cases} \tag{13}$$

where I_u represents the set of items rating by user u; p_u and q_i^T represent a d-dimensional latent feature vector of user u and item i, respectively; y_j represents the implicit influence of items rated by user u in the past on the ratings of unknown items in the future. All of these parameters have same meanings as in SVD++. We named the new SVD++ model with Eq. (13) as **PBESVD++**.

Model Learning. Involved parameters in PBESVD++ could be learned by minimizing the regularized squared error function associated. The regularized squared error function is:

$$L = \frac{1}{2}\sum_u \sum_{i \in I_u} (\hat{r}_{ui} - r_{ui})^2 + \frac{\lambda}{2}\left(\sum_u b_u^2 + \sum_i b_i^2 + \sum_u \|p_u\|_F^2 + \sum_i \|q_i\|_F^2 + \sum_j \|y_j\|_F^2 \right) \quad (14)$$

where $\|\cdot\|$ denotes the Frobenius norm, and λ is to alleviate operation complexity and avoid over-fitting. We use same strategy proposed by Guo et al. [10] to do model learning. Therefore the new loss function can be obtained as:

$$L = \frac{1}{2}\sum_u \sum_{i \in I_u} (\hat{r}_{ui} - r_{ui})^2 + \frac{\lambda}{2}\left(\sum_u |I_u|^{-\frac{1}{2}}\left(b_u^2 + \|p_u\|_F^2 \right) \right) + \sum_i |U_i|^{-\frac{1}{2}}\left(b_i^2 + \|q_i\|_F^2 \right) + \sum_j |U_j|^{-\frac{1}{2}}\|y_j\|_F^2 \quad (15)$$

Instead of least square solvers, we employ the gradient descent solver to faster solve this convex problem to obtain a local minimization of the objection function. We perform the following gradient descents on b_u, b_i, p_u, q_i and y_j for all the users and items. In addition, the PBEModel is a piecewise function, so the gradient descent processes are divided into two parts in PBESVD++.

(1) When $b_u \leq 0$,

$$\frac{\partial L}{\partial b_u} = \sum_{i \in I_u}\left(\left(1 + \frac{b_i}{\mu - m} \right) \cdot e_{ui} \right) + \lambda \cdot |I_u|^{-\frac{1}{2}} \cdot b_u$$

$$\frac{\partial L}{\partial b_i} = \sum_{u \in U_i}\left(\frac{b_u + \mu - m}{\mu - m} \cdot e_{ui} \right) + \lambda \cdot |U_i|^{-\frac{1}{2}} \cdot b_i$$

$$\frac{\partial L}{\partial p_u} = \sum_{i \in I_u}(q_i \cdot e_{ui}) + \lambda \cdot |I_u|^{-\frac{1}{2}} \cdot p_u$$

$$\frac{\partial L}{\partial q_i} = \sum_{u \in U_i}\left(\left(p_u + |I_u|^{-\frac{1}{2}} \cdot \left(\sum_{j \in I_u} y_j \right) \right) \cdot e_{ui} \right) + \lambda \cdot |U_i|^{-\frac{1}{2}} \cdot q_i$$

$$\forall_{j \in I_u}\left(\frac{\partial L}{\partial y_j} = \sum_{i \in I_u}\left(e_{ui} \cdot \lambda \cdot |I_u|^{-\frac{1}{2}} \cdot q_i \right) + \lambda \cdot |U_j|^{-\frac{1}{2}} \cdot y_j \right)$$

(2) When $b_u > 0$, we only need replace the first two steps,

$$\frac{\partial L}{\partial b_u} = \sum_{i \in I_u}\left(\left(1 - \frac{b_i}{n - \mu} \right) \cdot e_{ui} \right) + \lambda \cdot |I_u|^{-\frac{1}{2}} \cdot b_u$$

$$\frac{\partial L}{\partial b_i} = \sum_{u \in U_i} \left(\frac{n - b_u - \mu}{n - \mu} \cdot e_{ui} \right) + \lambda \cdot |U_i|^{-\frac{1}{2}} \cdot b_i$$

where $e_{ui} = \hat{r}_{ui} - r_{ui}$, and represents the prediction error the predicted rating from the real rating for user u on item i.

Complexity Analysis. In terms of space complexity, it is obvious that the growth on PBESVD++ almost can be ignored compared with SVD++. Due to the consideration of PBESVD++ is more detailed, the time space complexity cannot be completely ignored. Nevertheless, the range area limit m and n are constants, so the magnitude of time complexity is not changed, just a linear growth. The time complexity of the PBESVD++ model is mainly from the loss function L (Eq. (15)) and its gradients. In terms of L, the time complexity is $O(d \cdot |R|)$, where d represents the matrix dimensionality, and $|R|$ represents the number of the observed ratings. And in terms of the gradients, the time complexities of $\frac{\partial L}{\partial b_u}, \frac{\partial L}{\partial b_i}, \frac{\partial L}{\partial p_u}$, and $\frac{\partial L}{\partial q_i}$ are $O(d \cdot |R|)$, and the time complexity of $\frac{\partial L}{\partial y_j}$ is $O(k \cdot d \cdot |R|)$, where k represents the average of the number a user marks or an item receives, respectively.

5 Experiments and Analysis

In order to verify the rightness and efficiency of proposed PBEModel and PBESVD++, we deploy the experiment platform based on LibRec [15]. Table 1 shows the details of experimental datasets.

Table 1. Details of datasets for experiments

Data sets	Users	Movies	Ratings	Density	Rating ranges
ml-latest-small	700	10000	100000	1.43%	[0.5,5]
FilmTrust	1508	2071	35497	1.14%	[0.5,4]
Flixster	53213	18197	409803	0.04%	[0.5,5]
Minifilm	55	334	1000	5.44%	[0.5,4]
Epinions	40163	139738	664824	0.05%	[1, 5]
Ciao	7375	99746	280391	0.03%	[1, 5]

We perform a series of experiments based on six datasets FilmTrust, Movielens Latest (ml-latest-small), Flixster, Minifilm, Ciao and Epinions. We test three important evaluation metrics in experiments, there are **MAE** (Mean Absolute Error), **RMSE** (Root Mean Square Error) and **RE** (Relative Error). Assumed $\tau = \{(u, i) | \exists_r ((u, i, r) \in R)\}$, and N is the number of observed ratings.

There are $MAE = \dfrac{\sum\limits_{(u,i) \in \tau} |r_{ui} - \hat{r}_{ui}|}{N}$, $RMSE = \sqrt{\dfrac{\sum\limits_{(u,i) \in \tau} (r_{ui} - \hat{r}_{ui})^2}{N}}$, and $RE = \sqrt{\dfrac{\sum\limits_{(u,i) \in \tau} (r_{ui} - \hat{r}_{ui})^2}{\sum\limits_{(u,i) \in \tau} (r_{ui}^2)}}$.

Experiment (1). Baseline estimation performance of PBEModel.

In order to verify the rightness and efficiency of PBEModel, we do experiments on the six data sets respectively. Each data set is divided into two parts, the first part (80%) is used for training, the other one (20%) for testing. We compare performances of PBEModel with other three models. The first one is current baseline estimate model according to Eq. (1), we name it as **BE** in experiments; the second one is part of PBEModel with $b_u \leq 0$, we name it as **PBE_1**; the last one is another part of PBE-Model with $b_u > 0$, and we name it as **PBE_2** during experiments. Table 2 shows the detailed results.

Table 2. Performance of PBEModel

Data Sets	Metrics	BE	PBEModel PBE_1	PBEModel PBE_2	PBEModel Both	Improved (vs BE)
ml-latest-small	RMSE	0.9262	0.9226	0.9136	0.9100*	1.75%
	RE	0.2525	0.2515	0.2490	0.2480*	1.75%
	MAE	0.7072	0.7051	0.6985	0.6964*	1.54%
Film-Trust	RMSE	0.8406	0.8367	0.8308	0.8262*	1.71%
	RE	0.2674	0.2662	0.2643	0.2628*	1.71%
	MAE	0.6389	0.6379	0.6300	0.6289*	1.56%
Minifilm	RMSE	0.9694	0.9571	0.9556	0.9430*	2.72%
	RE	0.3099	0.3059	0.3054	0.3014*	2.72%
	MAE	0.7307	0.7225	0.7221	0.7140*	2.29%
Filxster	RMSE	0.9080	0.9072	0.9029	0.9021*	0.65%
	RE	0.2406	0.2404	0.2392	0.2390*	0.65%
	MAE	0.6809	0.6799	0.6738	0.6729*	1.18%
Epinions	RMSE	1.1126	1.1062	1.1038	1.0972*	1.39%
	RE	0.2667	0.2652	0.2646	0.2630*	1.39%
	MAE	0.8423	0.8413	0.8234	0.8224*	2.37%
Ciao	RMSE	1.0542	1.0451	1.0375	1.0283*	2.46%
	RE	0.2506	0.2485	0.2467	0.2445*	2.46%
	MAE	0.7872	0.7827	0.7487	0.7442*	5.46%

Note: * is the best value.

We can see that the proposed baseline estimate model PBEModel gets wonderful higher performances of RMSE, MAE and RE, compared with current baseline estimate model. It also proves that the two parts of PBEModel are efficient, and has better baseline estimate accuracy. The improvement is up to 1.7% both in Movielens and FilmTrust, and up to 2.7% in Minifilm. Especially, the improvement exceeds 5.46% in Ciao, and 2.37% in Epinions.

Experiment (2). Performance of PBESVD++

We test the performance of PBESVD++ comparing with SVD++ on data sets Film-Trust, Flixster, and Minifilm. Each dataset is computed with d = 5 and d = 10. Table 3 discloses the data details.

Table 3. Performance of PBESVD++

Dataset	Metrics	SVD++	PBESVD++	Improved (vs SVD++)
FilmTrust (d = 5)	RMSE	0.8158	0.8117*	0.50%
	RE	0.2595	0.2582*	0.50%
	MAE	0.6250	0.6220*	0.47%
FilmTrust (d = 10)	RMSE	0.8119	0.8078*	0.51%
	RE	0.2583	0.2570*	0.51%
	MAE	0.6226	0.6196*	0.49%
Flixster (d = 5)	RMSE	0.9873	0.9762*	1.12%
	RE	0.2492	0.2464*	1.12%
	MAE	0.7406	0.7246*	2.16%
Flixster (d = 10)	RMSE	0.9857	0.9745*	1.14%
	RE	0.2488	0.2460*	1.14%
	MAE	0.7403	0.7238*	2.22%
Minifilm (d = 5)	RMSE	0.9485	0.9272*	2.25%
	RE	0.3032	0.2964*	2.25%
	MAE	0.7182	0.7062*	1.68%
Minifilm (d = 10)	RMSE	0.9450	0.9269*	1.92%
	RE	0.3021	0.2963*	1.92%
	MAE	0.7235	0.7051*	2.55%

Note: * is the best value.

As you can see, results show that PBESVD++ has relatively higher prediction accuracy than SVD++ during all the experimental datasets. Based on data set FilmTrust, the performance of RMSE, RE and MAE are improved 0.5% or so by PBESVD++. And the improved rate exceeds 1.12% during other experimental datasets. Especially in dataset Flixster and Minifilm, the performances are improved more than 2.22%.

6   Conclusion

In this paper, we analyze the current baseline estimate model, and find some interesting issues need to be improved. For example, the predictions may out of recommendation range. The main reason for this phenomenon is that the current baseline estimate doesn't consider different users' rating criterions. We call these criterions' differences as rating personalization. Thus, we proposed a novel baseline estimate model named PBEModel, which uses rating proportions to compute the rating personalization. In order to verify this new baseline estimate, we apply it into SVD++, and proposed a novel SVD++ model named PBESVD++. We disclose the mathematics modeling of PBEModel and PBESVD++ in this paper. We make a series of experiments with six real datasets, and results show that the PBEModel has more accuracy than current baseline estimate model, and the PBESVD++ have higher prediction performance than SVD++.

Acknowledgements. This work is supported by the National Natural Science Foundation of China under Grant No. 61402097, No. 61572123 and No. 61502092; the National Science Foundation for Distinguished Young Scholars of China under Grant No. 61225012 and No. 71325002; the Natural Science Foundation of Liaoning Province of China under Grant No. 201602261; the Fundamental Research Funds for the Central Universities under Grant No. N151708005, and No. N151604001.

References

1. Goldberg, D., Nichols, D., Oki, B.M., et al.: Using collaborative filtering to weave an information tapestry. Commun. ACM **35**(12), 61–70 (1992)
2. Takács, G., Pilászy, I., Németh, B., et al.: Major components of the gravity recommendation system. ACM SIGKDD Explor. Newsl. **9**(2), 80–83 (2007)
3. Sarwar, B.M., Konstan, J.A., Borchers, A., et al.: Applying knowledge from KDD to recommender systems. Univ. Minnesota, Minneapolis **1**(612), 625–4002 (1999)
4. Deerwester, S., Dumais, S.T., Furnas, G.W., et al.: Indexing by latent semantic analysis. J. Am. Soc. Inform. Sci. **41**(6), 391 (1990)
5. Hofmann, T.: Latent semantic models for collaborative filtering. ACM Trans. Inform. Syst. (TOIS) **22**(1), 89–115 (2004)
6. Blei, D.M., Ng, A.Y., Jordan, M.I.: Latent dirichlet allocation. J. Mach. Learn. Res. **3**, 993–1022 (2003)
7. Koren, Y.: Factorization meets the neighborhood: a multifaceted collaborative filtering model. In: Proceedings of the 14th ACM SIGKDD International Conference on Knowledge Discovery and Data Mining, pp. 426–434. ACM (2008)
8. Koren, Y.: Collaborative filtering with temporal dynamics. Commun. ACM **53**(4), 89–97 (2010)
9. Kumar, R., Verma, B.K., Rastogi, S.S.: Social popularity based SVD++ recommender system. Int. J. Comput. Appl. **87**(14) (2014)
10. Guo, G., Zhang, J., Yorke-Smith, N.: TrustSVD: collaborative filtering with both the explicit and implicit influence of user trust and of item ratings. In: AAAI, pp. 123–129 (2015)
11. Wang, S., Ma, Y., Cheng, B., Yang, F.M.: Multi-dimensional QoS prediction for service recommendations. IEEE Trans. Serv. Comput., 12 (2016). doi:10.1109/TSC.2016.2584058
12. Ma, Y., Xin, X., Wang, S., Li, J., Sun, Q., Yang, F.: QoS evaluation for web service recommendation. China Commun. **12**(4), 151–160 (2015)
13. Wang, S., Zheng, Z., Wu, Z., Micheal, R.L., Yang, F.: Reputation measurement and malicious feedback rating prevention in web service recommendation system. IEEE Trans. Serv. Comput. **8**(5), 755–767 (2015)
14. Jannach, D., Zanker, M., Felfernig, A., et al.: Recommender Systems: an Introduction. Cambridge University Press (2010)
15. Guo, G.: LibRec: A Java Library for Rcommender Systems[EB/OL] (2016). http://www.librec.net

A MapReduce-Based Distributed SVM for Scalable Data Type Classification

Chong Jiang[1], Ting Wu[1], Jian Xu[1], Ning Zheng[1], Ming Xu[1], and Tao Yang[2(✉)]

[1] Internet and Network Security Laboratory, School of Computer Science and Technology,
Hangzhou Dianzi University, Hangzhou, China
{141050032,jian.xu,nzheng,mxu}@hdu.edu.cn,
peterwuting@hotmail.com
[2] The Third Research Institute of Ministry of Public Security, Hangzhou, China
yangtao@stars.org.cn

Abstract. Data type classification is a significant problem in digital forensics and information security field. Methods based on support vector machine have proven the most successful across varying classification approaches in the previous work. However, the training process of SVM is notably computationally intensive with the number of training vectors increased rapidly. In this study, we proposed parallel distributed SVM (PDSVM) based on Hadoop MapReduce for scalable data type classification. First the map phase determines support vectors (SVs) in the splits of dataset by running the sequential minimal optimization. Then the reduce phase merges SVs and computes the degree of global convergence. Finally, PDSVM utilizes the global convergence SVs to get SVM model. The experimental results demonstrate that PDSVM can not only process large scale training dataset, but also perform well in the term of classification accuracy.

Keywords: Data type classification · Digital forensics · Support vector machine · Distributed · MapReduce

1 Introduction

The capacity of digital equipment storage is increased rapidly with the development of the computer technology. The quantity of electronic data that stored in the hard drive is in exponential growth from KB, MB to GB, TB, PB, simultaneously. Data deluge has become a severe problem should be solved in digital forensics domain. The classification of data or file fragments is an important problem in digital forensics, particularly for the purpose of carving fragmented files [1]. Unfortunately, the substantial research efforts focused on the accuracy of classification over a decade, seldom investigators take the efficiency of classification into account.

The classification of data or file fragment means there are two work to be resolved: data type classification and file type classification [2, 3]. For each concept, Erbacher and Mulholland's [4] made a clear definition:

"Data type: Indicative of the type of data embedded in a file." (p. 56)

© ICST Institute for Computer Sciences, Social Informatics and Telecommunications Engineering 2017
S. Wang and A. Zhou (Eds.): CollaborateCom 2016, LNICST 201, pp. 115–126, 2017.
DOI: 10.1007/978-3-319-59288-6_11

"File type: The overall type of file. This is often indicated by the application used to create or access the file." (p. 56)

From the above statements, we can find a problem as Vassil et al. [1] said file types can have very loose, ambiguous, and extensible set of rules, especially for complex file types. A compound file ".docx" can have different data type content, which may embedded JPG images, OLE objects, Excel spreadsheet, etc. Besides, fragments which come from varieties of file types may belong to one data types. The result of file type classification may produce effectively meaningless classification rates and confusion matrices. Therefore Vassil et al. introduced data encoding classification instead of file type classification. Motivation by the Vassil et al's work, we use data type classification instead of data and file fragment classification. We use data type to indicate both file type and data type. For convenience, we put the data or file fragment referred to as data fragment in the remainder of this article.

Support vector machine (SVM) as one of machine learning techniques have gained popularity in terms of their application for data type classification problem. Numerous researchers have engaged in the development of sequences-based SVM for data type classification [1–3, 7]. Their evaluation results show sequences-based SVM perform better than other machine learning techniques in term of accuracy. However the training dataset (MB) of evaluation is far less than storage capacity (GB, TB) of digital devices in the real world [6]. Among them, one of the excellent works is a multithread-based SVM developed by Beebe et al. [3]. Modern digital drives involve millions or billions of data fragments, classifying such huge amount of data by one computer requires much more time. SVM's compute and storage requirements increase rapidly with the number of training vectors, putting big data classification task out of its reach [7]. Efficient parallel distributed algorithms and implementation techniques are essential to meeting the scalability and performance requirements for classification task.

MapReduce is a well-known parallel distributed frame work for processing big data first introduced by Google [29]. It has currently become a major enabling technology in support of large-scale data intensive applications [10]. In this article, we present a novel MapReduce-based parallel distributed SVM (PDSVM) model for large scale classifying data fragment using the information of byte frequency distribution and statistical measurements. From Google's Hadoop MapReduce perspective [28], training data be split over a cloud computing system's data nodes. Each Map task will process the associated data chunk to obtain a respective set of Support Vectors (SVs). The Reducer will aggregate the SVs to find out global support vectors. The global support vectors of the final SVM are used to evaluate a global convergence is whether or not reached. If not, then the whole process will be repeated until the global optimum is reached. The basic idea behind this approach is to filter out non-support vectors, and then merge local support vectors to save as global support vectors.

The remainder of the paper is structured as follows. In Sect. 2, we briefly describe related work to support our hypothesis. In Sect. 3, we fully represent the design and implementation of the parallelized distributed SVM algorithm for data type classification. In Sect. 4, we introduce our experimental setup to facilitate replication and comparative evaluation. In Sect. 5, we discuss the results of experiments. In Sect. 6, we conclude the paper and point out some limitations and contributions of this study.

2   Related Work

Data fragment type classification problem has been conducted in the past many years, especially in the digital forensics domain [1–3, 6, 14–18]. Previous work that explores the application of a combination of machine learning techniques and statistical analysis to solve the problem of data fragment classification. And SVM achieved the best data type classification accuracy on the most machine learning techniques in related literature.

Li et al. (2010) [16] made use of the histogram of the byte values as feature vectors to classify high entropy file fragments. They used a private dataset of 14080 KB and file type including jpg, mp3, pdf and dll. For the classification prediction accuracy, they achieved 81.5%. However, the number of file type is too small and other significant high entropy file type (specially, rar or zip) don't be take into account. Fitzgerald et al. (2011) [6] used unigrams, bigrams, and several complexity measures as feature vectors and 4800 KB as the maximum experimental setting. They achieved 48% classification accuracy across 24 file types. Beebe et al. used several statistical measures similar as Fitzgerald, moreover, a combination of unigram and bigram frequencies and other byte frequency-based measures as feature vectors. They achieve 73.4% classification accuracy across 38 files and data types.

As we can see, the size of dataset used to build SVM classifier is quite small in previous work. All of them used a single computer with SVM for file type classification, except Beebe et al., none of them consider scalable problem. SVM training is a computationally intensive process when the size of training dataset is very large. Besides, SVM classifier's compute and storage requirements increase rapidly with the number of training vectors, putting classification problem of digital forensics research out of their reach. Although Beebe et al. produces the Sceadan tool, they achieved sector-level data processing capacity by multithread and optimized code. However, the key to meeting the scalability and performance requirements is efficient parallel and distributed techniques.

Distributed SVM techniques [6–10] partition the large training dataset into small data chunks and process each chunk in parallel by utilizing the resources of a cluster of computers [17–21]. The approaches based on message passing interface (MPI) [18] have been proposed for distributed implementation of SVM based on a decomposition technique that splits the problem into smaller quadratic programming sub-problems and combine the outcomes of each sub problems. However, MPI is realized in homogeneous computing environments and has limited support for fault tolerance. Graf et al. [22] have been proposed a SVM algorithm that the training data is partitioned and a SVM is solved for each partition. The support vectors from each pair of classifiers are subsequently combined into a new training dataset for which an SVM is solved. The process carries on until a single final classifier is left, namely Cascade SVM.

It is to be noted that several distributed SVM algorithms are implemented on MapReduce frameworks [7, 8, 10]. Mapreduce is a distributed framework and programming model for processing large scale data in a parallel and distributed manner. Mapreduce manages data by its Distributed File System and organizes data process into three phases: map, shuffle and reduce. All data is treated as a key-value pair from a distributed file system, produces a set of intermediate key-value pairs by the application of a map function, then group all intermediate value by key, finally reduce function process each group with different keys. A typical MapReduce workflow is described pictorially in Fig. 1.

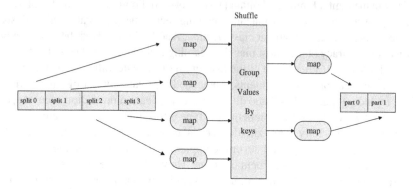

Fig. 1. Illustration of the MapReduce workflow

Sun and Fox [23] implemented a parallel SVM based Twister MapReduce framework. In this model, the training dataset is split into smaller subsets. Each subset is trained, in a distributed note, with a SVM model. The support vectors of each note are taken as the input of next layer SVMs. The global SVM model is obtained through such iteration. Catak and Balaban [24] implemented a parallel SVM based on the Hadoop MapReduce framework early. To the practical application of distributed SVM, Ku et al. [7] took advantage of a distributed SVM for email classification. Alham et al. [9, 21] implemented a parallel SVM based hadoop MapReduce for large scale image classifications and annotation. However, to the best of our knowledge, there is no parallel distributed SVM solution available for data type classification.

3   The Proposed Solution: PDSVM

In this section, we describe how to parallelize the SVM algorithm based on MapReduce in detail. The basic principle of the design of our parallel implementation is similar to Kun et al. [27]. The parallel distributed SVM (PDSVM) architecture is illustrated in Fig. 2 and the program is presented as follows.

At the first, we partition the entire training dataset into several smaller subsets (TD1 … TD4) by balanced random sampling and each of the subset is allocated to a Map worker machine. Each map task is then run Sequential Minimal Optimization (SMO) algorithm to compute the associated training subset in corresponding Map worker machine. SMO was developed by Platt [25] as one of the fastest quadratic programming (QP) optimization algorithm. To solving this QP problem, SMO breaks this problem into series of smallest possible QP problem, using Osuna's theorem to ensure convergence. Every time SMO selects two Lagrange multipliers α_i and α_j parameters to optimize by a heuristic method of choice. So the output of each Map task is support vectors (SV1…SV4) which corresponds to Lagrange multipliers $\alpha > 0$ in local

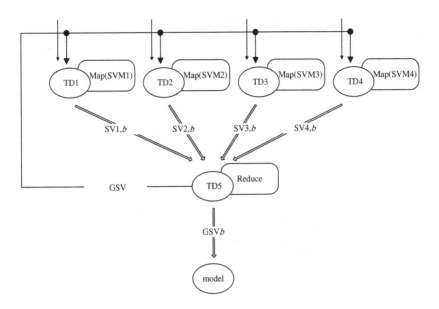

Fig. 2. The architecture of PDSVM.

partition and bias threshold b. Which then combined as input is forwarded to the reduce task, reducer joins the partial support vectors to produce the global support vectors (GSV) which will be tested for global convergence restriction. Here we use parameter λ (λ = the current iteration's number of GSV/the previous iteration's number of GSV) to determine the level of convergence, which used to observe the change of the total number of GSV. If $\lambda > 0.95$, means the number of GSV has changed little, global convergence is achieved, and vice versa. Owing to in normal conditions, the number of GSV has little change and the convergence for global optimum is very near after two times of iteration. Our experiment also proved this. So the time of iteration is rarely.

In addition, the reducer has to deal with the bias threshold b, as this value is different for each partition. If the global convergence is not achieved, then return the GSV of reducer into Map worker machines and make the next iteration computation. Otherwise the reducer calculates the weighted average of b for all partitions to obtain global b. Then the output of reduce is GSV and bias threshold b, which are used to training SVM model will be used in the classification.

Hence PDSVM algorithm can guarantee that each iteration takes full advantage of Hadoop cluster's parallel computation ability providing excellent scalability. Furthermore, the parameter λ can reduce the number of unnecessary iterative calculation, ensure the ultimate SVM in term of accuracy can be guaranteed at the same time. The simple description of PDSVM algorithm is represented in the form of pseudo code showing Algorithm 1.

Algorithm 1. Implement of PDSVM

Input: training dataset x;
Output: global support vectors (GSV) and weighted average of bias value b;
Preparation: data partition and allocate to the computation node;
1   Map$_i$,(i is equal to the number of sub-dataset)
2   input: training sub-dataset x_i;
3   running SMO algorithm to train allocated sub-dataset x_i;
4   output: support vectors and bias threshold b;
5   Reduce
6   input: the result (SVs and b) from each map node;
7   calculate parameter λ. if $\lambda \leq 0.95$, broadcast support vectors to each map node and go to step 2, otherwise proceed to the next step;
8   calculate GSV and weighted average of b;
9   use global SVs and b to get SVM classification model

---

4   Experimental Setup

4.1   Data Collection and Preprocess

In our experiments, the data is derived from open available corpus of dataset—Govdocs dataset and synthesized dataset. Fourteen well-known kinds of data types are chose for our experiment evaluation. The smallest available sector size on currently magnetic media is 512-bytes, so we select 512-bytes as the fragment size. We used a random sampling without replacement technique to collect files for each file type from Govdocs dataset. Besides, we downloaded some not copyright files and create some synthesized files to augment dataset for the ground truth.

For each of the fourteen data types, we would have at least 10000 files composed of at least 9000000 512-bytes fragments (see Table 1). And we removed the header and tail segments of each file to avoid potential data signature bias in the SVM training phase. Since the header segments frequently contains an information of data type identifier and the tail segments might not be 512-bytes in length. The aforementioned processing enables us to generate a 120 GB dataset of file fragments.

The classification problem of data type classification usually involve more than two classes. Researchers have proposed various approaches to solve multiclass problems with SVMs such as One Against Rest (OAR), One Against One. In this study, we used LIBLINEAR [26] which implement multiclass classification with SVMs by OAR approach.

Table 1. Specification of the datasets.

Data type	Number of 512-bytes fragments
CSV	18244684
BASE64	16312485
TXT	15364415
XML	16644902
LOG	18947086
JAVA	16368603
MP3	17144629
GIF	18349146
BMP	20511396
AVI	18774634
WMV	21929567
PDF	20166485
FLV	16957853
DOC	19052705

4.2 Feature Vectors Selection

In order to apply SVMs to data type classification, we need vectors of features to represent each data fragment and to discriminate different data types from each other. N-gram bytes have been found highly classification performance in previous work hence we follow the same choice of features. We selected 256 and 256^2 features which are the histogram of the byte values (i.e. the unigram and bigram) for the file fragment.

We also used several statistical measurements of data fragments as feature vectors as outlined in the here. The Shannon entropy of the unigram and bigram, as the entropy is a measure of randomness of the data. Low, medium and high ASCII frequency with range 0x00-0x1F, 0x20-0x7F and 0x80-0xFF in the block respectively. The Hamming weight, mean byte value and standard deviation of byte values are taken into account.

4.3 Environment Configuration

We have implemented PDSVM for our distributed data type classification which is developed using the Weka package. The Hadoop cluster for the set of experiments consists of ten machines each having a 4-core 2.4 GHz Xeon CPU and 12GBs of RAM. Ubuntu Linux12.04.5 and Apache Hadoop 1.2.1 were installed on the all machines.

The main goal of our experiment was to compare the accuracy and scalability of data type classification. For this purpose, the set of data fragments was partitioned into a training set and a testing set in a, roughly 5-to-1 ratio. The experiment made decisions on each data fragment in dataset belongs to which group with respect to a specific type, can be divided into four groups: True Position (TP), True Negative (TN), False Position (FP) and False Negative (FN). The scalability and accuracy measurements are defined as follows:

$$\text{Accuracy} = \frac{TP + TN}{TP + FP + TN + FN} \tag{1}$$

$$\text{Speedup} = \frac{\text{computing time on one machine}}{\text{computer time on cluster}} \tag{2}$$

5 Experiment Results

Experimental results showed that our approach produced very good performance. The performance evaluation of the proposed PDSVM with respect to accuracy and scalability is presented in Fig. 3, 4 and 5. Our classifier not only achieved the similar classification accuracy, but also spent much less time comparing with the previous work. The promoted method's average classified accuracy achieved 80.92% that is significantly better than random chance (1/14).

	CSV	BASE64	TXT	XML	LOG	JAVA	MP3	JPG	BMP	AVI	WMV	PNG	FLV	DOC
CSV	100%													
BASE64		100%												
TXT			99%											
XML			2%	98%										
LOG			1%		98%	1%								
JAVA			1%			97%							1%	
MP3							94%	3%						
JPG							8%	84%				3%	4%	
BMP									82%	10%	2%			5%
AVI							7%			77%	6%	3%	2%	3%
WMV							6%	1%		1%	74%	5%	3%	
PNG							2%	8%	4%	6%		61%	5%	7%
FLV							7%			6%	10%	7%	54%	7%
DOC							9%	9%	6%	3%		14%	3%	53%

Fig. 3. Confusion matrix of experiment result

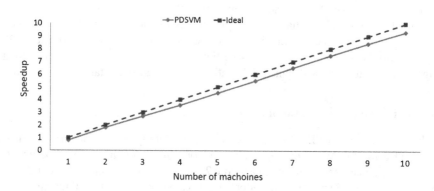

Fig. 4. The performance of speedup

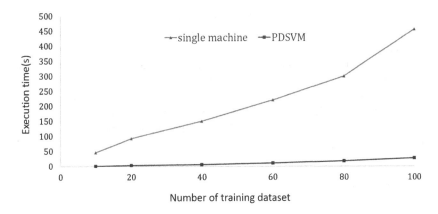

Fig. 5. The computation efficiency of PDSVM

Table 2 shows the accuracy of the experimental result achieved for 120 G data fragment processed by PDSVM with ten machine Hadoop cluster. Figure 3 shows the confusion matrix for the experimental result in detail. The classification on low entropy data types (e.g. CSV, BASE64, TXT, etc.) achieved the best performance and the worst on the high entropy data types (e.g. PDF, FLV, etc.). Therefore one of the future investigative work in data type classification is to improve the classification performance on the high entropy data types.

Table 2. Data fragment classification accuracy of experiment

Type	Accuracy
CSV	100%
BASE64	100%
TXT	99%
XML	98%
LOG	98%
JAVA	97%
MP3	94%
GIF	84%
BMP	82%
AVI	77%
WMV	74%
PDF	61%
FLV	54%
DOC	53%

To determine the scalability performance, we maintained the number of training dataset constant and increased the number of machines in the Hadoop cluster. We used formula 2 to calculate the speed of PDSVM with work machines increased. We executed PDSVM using only one machine and then we added additional machine. Figure 4 shows the speedup values along with the number of machines increases. PDSVM shows nearly linear speedup as the number of machines increases and the slope approximating the ideal slope.

We also maintained the number of machines constant and enhanced the number of training dataset. We set the number of machines to one and ten respectively, then we used LIBLINEAR running SVM on single machine and PDSVM running on ten machines. With the number of training dataset increased, the running time overhead is described in the Fig. 5. The experimental shows that the running time of distributed SVM outperformance the sequential SVM with an increasing number of training dataset.

6 Conclusion

Data fragment classification is a well-known critical problem in digital forensics and network security, such as data recovery, reverse engineering and intrusion detection and so on. For this paper, we explored the application of distributed frame work to this problem. We generated a large dataset of data fragment for 14 kinds of file type, which is difficult for classical SVM model to process large scale dataset in a short time. We proposed a parallel distributed SVM (PDSVM) algorithm based on iterative Hadoop MapReduce, which can improve the computation speed greatly. We performed several experiments to evaluate the accuracy and scalability of PDSVM for the data type classification. Our experiments show that PDSVM not only can tackle large scale training dataset, but also performs well in the term of classification accuracy.

As part of the future work, we are planning to deeply analyze more data types and to infer the relationship of each data type, for more clearly discriminate data fragment with different data type. We also are planning to consider load balancing schemes to optimize the performance of PDSVM in a dynamic heterogeneous environment.

Acknowledgments. This work is support by Natural Science Foundation of China under Grant No. 61070212 and 61572165, the State Key Program of Zhejiang Province Natural Science Foundation of China under Grant No. LZ15F020003 and Key Lab of Information Network Security of Ministry of Public Security.

References

1. Foster, I., Kesselman, C., Nick, J., Tuecke, S.: The physiology of the grid: an open gridservices architecture for distributed systems integration. Technical report, Global Grid
2. Zheng, N., Wang, J., Wu, T., et al.: A fragment classification method depending on data type. In: IEEE International Conference on Computer and Information Technology; Ubiquitous Computing and Communications; Dependable, Autonomic and Secure Computing; Pervasive Intelligence and Computing. IEEE (2015)
3. Beebe, N.L., Maddox, L.A., Liu, L., et al.: Sceadan: using concatenated n-gram vectors for improved file and data type classification. IEEE Trans. Inf. Forensics Secur. **8**(9), 1519–1530 (2013)

4. Erbacher, R.F., Mulholland J.: Identification and localization of data types within large-scale file systems. In: International Workshop on Systematic Approaches to Digital Forensic Engineering, pp. 55–70. IEEE Computer Society (2007)
5. Beek, H.M.A.V., Eijk, E.J.V., Baar, R.B.V., et al.: Digital forensics as a service: game on. Digital Invest. **15**, 20–38 (2015)
6. Fitzgerald, S., Mathews, G., Morris, C., et al.: Using NLP techniques for file fragment classification. Digital Invest. **9**(15), S44–S49 (2012)
7. Xu, K., Wen, C., Yuan, Q., et al.: A MapReduce based parallel SVM for email classification. J. Networks, **9**(6) (2014)
8. Ke, X., Jin, H., Xie, X., et al.: A distributed SVM method based on the iterative MapReduce. In: IEEE International Conference on Semantic Computing (ICSC), pp. 116–119. IEEE Computer Society (2015)
9. Çatak, F.Ö.: Polarization measurement of high dimensional social media messages with support vector machine algorithm using MapReduce (2015)
10. Guo, W., Alham, N.K., Liu, Y., et al.: A resource aware MapReduce based parallel SVM for large scale image classifications. Neural Process. Lett., 1–24 (2015)
11. Na, G., Shim, K., Moon, K., Kong, S., Kim, E., Lee, J.: Frame-based recovery of corrupted video files using codec specifications. IEEE Trans. Image Process. **23**(2), 517–526 (2014)
12. Moody, S.J., Erbacher, R.F.: SÁDI - statistical analysis for data type identification. In: International Workshop on Systematic Approaches to Digital Forensic Engineering, SADFE 2008, Berkeley, California, USA, May, pp. 41–54 (2008)
13. Zhang, L., White, G.B.: An approach to detect executable content for anomaly based network intrusion detection. In: 21th International Parallel and Distributed Processing Symposium (IPDPS 2007), Proceedings, 26–30 March 2007, Long Beach, California, USA, pp. 1–8 (2007)
14. Amirani, M.C., Toorani, M., Mihandoost, S.: Feature-based type identification of file fragments. Secur. Commun. Networks **6**(1), 115–128 (2013)
15. Amirani, M.C, Toorani, M., Beheshti, A.: A new approach to content-based file type detection. In: Computer Science, pp. 1103–1108 (2008)
16. Li, Q., Ong, A., Suganthan, P., et al.: A novel support vector machine approach to high entropy data fragment classification (2010)
17. Hazan, T., Man, A., Shashua, A.: A parallel decomposition solver for SVM: distributed dual ascend using fenchel duality, pp. 1–8 (2008)
18. Do, T.N., Poulet, F.: Classifying one billion data with a new distributed SVM algorithm. In: International Conference on Research, Innovation and Vision for the Future, pp. 59–66 (2006)
19. Chang, E.Y., Zhu, K., Wang, H., Bai, H., Li, J., Qiu, Z.: PSVM: parallelizing support vectormachines on distributed computers. In: Proceedings of Advances in Neural Information Processing Systems, pp. 257–264 (2007)
20. Zhu-Hong, Y., Jian-Zhong, Y., Lin, Z., Shuai, L., Zhen-Kun, W.: A MapReduce based parallel SVM for large-scale predicting protein-protein interactions. Neurocomputing **145**, 37–43 (2014)
21. Guo, W., Alham, N.K., Liu, Y., et al.: A resource aware MapReduce based parallel SVM for large scale image classifications. Neural Process. Lett., 1–24 (2005)
22. Graf, H., Cosatto, E., Bottou, L., Durdanovic, I., Vapnik, V.: Parallel support vectormachines: the cascade SVM. In: Proceedings of Advances in Neural Information Processing Systems (NIPS) (2004)
23. Sun, Z., Fox, G.: Study on Parallel SVM Based on MapReduce (2013)
24. Çatak, F.O., Balaban, M.E.: CloudSVM: training an SVM classifier in cloud computing systems. In: Proceedings of the Pervasive Computing and the Networked World—Joint International Conference (ICPCA/SWS), pp. 57–68 (2012)

25. Platt, J.: Sequential minimal optimization: a fast algorithm for training support vector machines. Technical report, MSR-TR-98-14, Microsoft Research (1998)
26. Fan, R.E., Chang, K.W., Hsieh, C.J., et al.: LIBLINEAR: a library for large linear classification. J. Mach. Learn. Res. 9(9), 1871–1874 (2008)
27. Kun, D., Yih, L., Perera, A.: Parallel SMO for training support vector machines, SMA 5505, project final report (2003)
28. Apache Hadoop. http://hadoop.apache.org
29. Ghemawat, S., Gobioff, H., Leung, S.: The Google file system. In: Proceedings of the 19th ACM Symposium on Operating Systems Principles (SOSP), pp. 29–43 (2003)

A Method of Recovering HBase Records from HDFS Based on Checksum File

Lin Zeng[1], Ming Xu[1], Jian Xu[1], Ning Zheng[1], and Tao Yang[2(✉)]

[1] Internet and Network Security Laboratory,
School of Computer Science and Technology,
Hangzhou Dianzi University, Hangzhou, China
{141050046,mxu,jian.xu,nzheng}@hdu.edu.cn
[2] Key Lab of Information Network Security of Ministry of Public Security,
Hangzhou, China
yangtao@stars.org.cn

Abstract. Data recovery is a key problem in disaster recovery and digital forensics fields. The HDFS (Hadoop Distributed File System) is widely used for storing high-volume, velocity and variety dataset. However, previous work about data recovery mainly focuses on personal computers or mobile phones, and few attentions have been taken to HFDS. This paper analyzes the feature of HDFS and proposes a recovery method based on checksum file in order to address the records recovery problem of HBase, which is a common application on HDFS. We first carve out the Data blocks of HFile (HBase data file) using the corresponding checksum file, then analyze the format of HBase table records to extract them from the carved Data blocks. The experiments demonstrate that our method can restore HBase records effectively. The recovery rate is nearly 100% when the cluster size is 4 KB and 2 KB.

Keywords: HBase · HDFS · Records recovery · File carving · HFile

1 Introduction

HDFS is the file system primarily used by Hadoop which is currently the commonly used open-source software framework for big data. It is an abstracted file system layer that stores data in its own format to enable cross-platform functionality. Data in HDFS may be lost due to human error, device malfunction, or deliberate deletion, which highlights the need for recovering it.

File carving is an effective technology to solve the recovery problem. It does not rely on the file system meta-data and just recovers data from unstructured binary data stream (i.e. the original copy of a digital device) by analyzing the raw data contents or structures. It overcomes the disadvantages existing in traditional data recovery methods when the file system meta-data information is corrupted or lost [17].

When a file is deleted, its contents are often not actually erased but only the file system meta-data that points to file contents is altered or disabled. The actual storage of HDFS resides in the host operating system's file system, such as NTFS and ExtX.

© ICST Institute for Computer Sciences, Social Informatics and Telecommunications Engineering 2017
S. Wang and A. Zhou (Eds.): CollaborateCom 2016, LNICST 201, pp. 127–139, 2017.
DOI: 10.1007/978-3-319-59288-6_12

Therefore, even if a file in HDFS is deleted, there is the possibility to recover it from the storage devices.

This work mainly aims at HBase which is a commonly used application of HDFS. We use file carving technology for recovering the Data blocks of HFile (HBase data file). Because HFile in HDFS may split into a number of blocks stored across multiple machines. Piecing all blocks together into a complete file is difficult. But we can carve out the Data blocks of HFile from a single node and recover records from them. The main challenge of file carving is the fact that file data stored within a file system may not in a linear or continuous way [11]. So the most important issue is that identifying the clusters that belong to the same file and reassembling them into a correct order.

Existing file carving technology is aimed at the typical file type (i.e. JPEG, ZIP, PNG, WORD, PDF, MPEG etc.) on personal computers and mobile phones. Current work often identifies the clusters by specific file structure or the feature of file content. But the only feature can be used in HFile Data block is the header signature and the length embedded in the header. In addition, the content is just key-value pair which has no specific format. And using file structure is very suited for the situation that a file is unfragmented. Existing methods are not suited for the recovery problem of HFile Data block. Given this, we analyze the HDFS feature and propose a carving method using checksum file which can identify and reassemble the file clusters easily. Our checksum file based method works well for HDFS files even under the highly fragmented situation.

The remainder of the paper is organized as follows. First, we position the related work in Sect. 2, and analyzing the checksum file in HDFS and the format of HFile in Sect. 3, then we outline our methodology and evaluate our empirical results in Sects. 4 and 5 respectively. In Sect. 6, we draw some conclusion and discuss the limitations and the potential options for future work.

2   Related Work

The earliest research of file carving began from the signature-based restoration technique [1]. This method simply searches for a known header signature and the corresponding footer signature, then try to merge all clusters in-between them. Some forensic tools provide this type of recovery, e.g. EnCase [4], X-Ways Forensics [8], Autopsy [7], etc. Unfortunately, this simple header-footer carving method is only applied to the files which are unfragmented.

Garfinkel [2] extended the signature-based method by using additional information stored in the file header. For some files, file header may contain file size or length. If the file footer can't be found, the information can be utilized to extract a file. The author also utilized the fast object validation for recovery of bifragmented files (the file that is broken into two fragments). The method places a gap between the header and footer, and repeats the process by growing the gap until a validation is found. But the approach is limited to the file which has two fragments and the gap is not large.

In [3], the authors proposed a method to carve image files based on graph theory. They redefined the reassembly of files into a path optimizing problem. Every cluster is considered as a vertex, and the edge between vertexes is weighted based on the weighting function which is determined by the likelihood that one cluster follows another. The goal of reassembly problem is to find k-vertex disjoint paths but that is too costly and complex.

Cohen [13] considered the problem of carving fragmented files as being the procedure of estimating a mapping function between the file bytes and the image bytes. The core idea is based on the reason that the clusters of storage media can only belong to one file. File recovery procedure consists of generating all possible mapping functions and they are evaluated by the corresponding validator. Cohen used this approach to carve the PDF and ZIP files.

Gi-Hyun Na et al. [10] proposed the frame-based recovery of corrupted video files using the specifications of video codec. It addressed the recovery problem of a video file which was severely fragmented or even partly overwritten. Johan et al. [11] presented an advanced tool JPGcarve for automated recovery of fragmented JPEG files. JPGcarve contains four main methods: cluster size estimation, single-fragment carving, space reduction and multi-fragmented carving.

The literatures on file recovery only reported the algorithms for the typical file type on personal computers and mobile phones. These approaches cannot extend to HDFS common files directly. In this paper, we analyze the feature of HDFS and try to recover Data blocks of HFile based on the checksum file and extract records from them.

3 Background

3.1 The Checksum File in HDFS

HDFS has its own architecture to store data in a distributed way. It is so called master/slave architecture. A HDFS cluster primarily consists of two types of nodes: NameNode and DataNode. The NameNode as a master server manages the file system metadata and the DataNode stores the actual data. A file stored in HDFS is split into one or more blocks and stored across multiple DataNodes. By default, the block size is 64 M or 128 M.

In order to ensure the data integrity, the HDFS implements checksum checking on the contents of HDFS files. When a client requests to create a HDFS file, the file data being written to a DataNode is split into a number of packets. Each packet is 64 bytes and consists of multiple chunks with corresponding checksums. Each chunk is 512 bytes by default. The checksums are stored in a separate file with the meta extension in the same HDFS namespace. Figure 1 shows an example of the block files and

blk_1857886797832904623	blk_-575142751576769158
blk_1857886797832904623_1631.meta	blk_-575142751576769158_1630.meta
blk_-2001094327894351771	blk_-6899707740992334183
blk_-2001094327894351771_1859.meta	blk_-6899707740992334183_1637.meta
blk_2864080511916640498	blk_8026835587436878571
blk_2864080511916640498_1633.meta	blk_8026835587436878571_1638.meta

Fig. 1. Block files and checksum files on DataNode.

corresponding checksum files on a DataNode. The files named after "blk_" plus a block id are HDFS block files and the files with a meta extension are checksum files. When a deletion operation is executed, both two are deleted at the same time. The checksum algorithm used by HDFS is CRC32, so each checksum is stored with 4 bytes. It means every 4 bytes in the checksum file checks 512 bytes section in the block file. Part of the content of a checksum file is shown in Fig. 2. The first 7 bytes is file header that contains the file version, checksum type and the number of bytes for which a checksum is computed. From the offset at 0x07, it stores each checksum in sequence. The "checksum1" and "checksum2" in Fig. 2 denote the checksum of the first and second 512 bytes section in the corresponding block file.

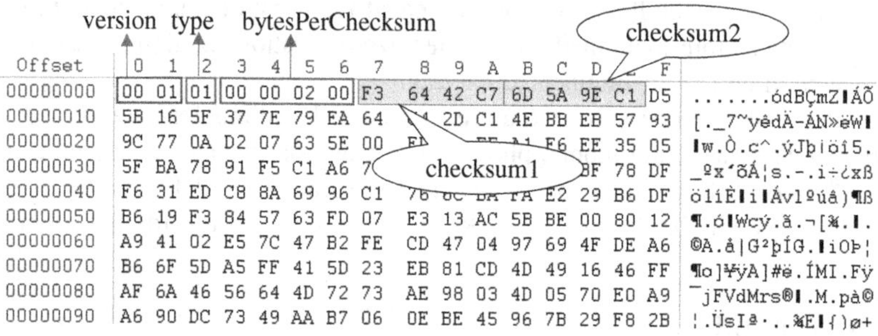

Fig. 2. The format of checksum file.

3.2 Format of HFile

HBase is an open source, non-relational, column-oriented, distributed database and runs on the top of HDFS. HBase table records are stored as "HFile" on HDFS and they are column-oriented. One HFile stores the data for one column family. In this section, we analyzed the structure of its data file in order to recover the deleted files and extract records.

The overview structure of HFile is shown as Fig. 3. HFile consists of four sections: Scanned block section, Non-scanned block section, Load-on-open section and Trailer. Every section contains one or more blocks. The Trailer block is a fixed file trailer, which contains some basic information of HFile and the offsets of other blocks. Data in Load-on-open section will be loaded into memory when HBase region server starts. It contains FileInfo, Bloom filter block, Root index block and Meta index block. Scanned block section means that it will be read when the HFile be sequential scanned. It contains Data block and Leaf index block. Root index block, Intermediate Data index block and Leaf index block are organized in a tree structure and they store the index point to the blocks in the next lever. The table records are stored on the Data block. In this paper, we aim at carving out the Data block from a raw image and extracting corresponding records. The functions of other blocks is not introduced because it is out of the main work.

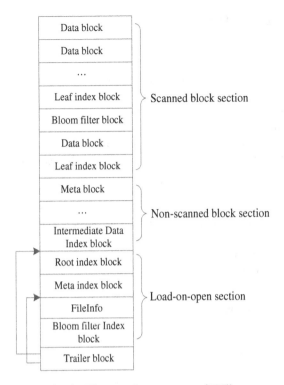

Fig. 3. The overview structure of HFile.

The physical format of the Data block is shown in Fig. 4. The first 8 bytes denotes the header signature whose value is "0x44415441424C4B2A". It can be used to identify the start position of Data block. The 4 bytes at offset 0x08 is the size of the data in the block. The following 8 bytes at offset 0x10 is the offset of the previous block on disk. Then the rest part stores records in key-value pair format.

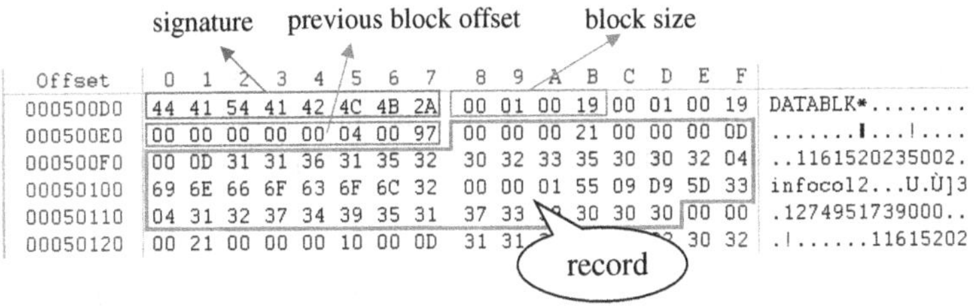

```
              signature   previous block offset      block size
  Offset      0  1  2  3  4  5  6  7   8  9  A  B  C  D  E  F
000500D0    44 41 54 41 42 4C 4B 2A  00 01 00 19 00 01 00 19  DATABLK*........
000500E0    00 00 00 00 00 04 00 97  00 00 00 21 00 00 00 0D  .......!...!....
000500F0    00 0D 31 31 36 31 35 32  30 32 33 35 30 30 32 04  ..1161520235002.
00050100    69 6E 66 6F 63 6F 6C 32  00 00 01 55 09 D9 5D 33  infocol2...U.Û]3
00050110    04 31 32 37 34 39 35 31  37 33   30 30 30 00 00  .1274951739000..
00050120    00 21 00 00 00 10 00 0D  31 31        30 32  .!......11615202
                                      record
```

Fig. 4. The format of HFile Data block.

4   The Proposed Method

4.1   Collecting Disk Image

In order to recover data, a raw image of storage media is first required. The raw image means a bit-by-bit copy of the target media. The technique includes software based copy and hardware based copy. Some tools like Winhex, Autopsy can be used to get the disk image under Windows operate system. Under Linux operate system, DD command is a simple way which often used for generating a back-up file for the target media. When the file system is corrupted or the disk is damaged, the hardware based method will be considered.

In this paper, we use DD command to acquire a raw image of the certain disk partition. Firstly, the disk partition in which HDFS files are stored can be identified by the HDFS configuration file. If we know which partition contains the data we should recover in advance, we can just copy the certain partition instead of the whole disk. The following DD command "dd if = /dev/sda1 of = /data.img" is an example which makes a raw image of the partition "sda1" into a DD format file "data.img" in the root directory.

4.2   Recovering Data Blocks of HFile

HDFS is an abstracted file system layer and the actual storage of the file block is based on the host operating system's file system (e.g. NTFS/ExtX). This is so called the local file system. An important property of the most common file systems is that a file is allocated in equally sized unit, which is called "cluster" in NTFS and is called "block" in ExtX. In order to distinguish it from HDFS block, we only call the unit as "cluster".

Fragmentation in file system can only occur on cluster boundaries. It means data in one cluster only belongs to one file. Based on this fragmentation rule, the recovery problem of HFile Data blocks can be split into two subproblems, i.e.: 1. recovering of single-fragmented Data block; 2. recovering of multi-fragmented Data block.

Assuming that there are in total N blocks in a HFile, let B_i denotes the i'th block in it and the first fragment of B_i is denoted as $b_f(i)$. As described in Fig. 5(a), the Data block is stored continuously, that is there is only one fragment. To check whether it is a single fragment or not, we first find the start position $p_{head}(i)$ of $b_f(i)$ by the magic bytes, followed by acquiring the block size d_l and finding the start position $p_{head}(i + 1)$ of $b_f(i + 1)$.

If $p_{head}(i + 1)-p_{head}(i)-24$ equals to d_l, then B_i is single-fragmented. It means we can extract the bytes between $p_{head}(i)$ and $p_{head}(i + 1)$ directly. If the Data block is split into multiple fragments, as shown in Fig. 5(b), the recovery problem can be divided into three subproblems, i.e.:

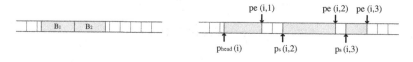

(a) Single-framented Data block.   (b) Multi-framented Data block.

Fig. 5. Simplified example of the Data block fragmentation.

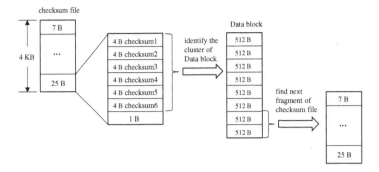

Fig. 6. Example of cross-find method under 4096-byte sized cluster.

1. Finding the start position $p_{head}(i)$ of the first fragment of B_i;
2. Determining the ending position $p_e(i, j)$ of the each fragment j of B_i;
3. Finding the start position $p_s(i, j)$ of each fragment($j > 1$);

In order to find each fragment of both block file and checksum file, we propose a "cross-find" method. It means we use the checksum file to identify the corresponding cluster of the Data block and use the identified cluster to find the next fragment of the checksum file at the same time. The method is based on the fragmentation rule. A S-byte sized cluster stores $(S-7)/(4*S/512)$ checksums of the block file, so the last b_l bytes can be used to find the next cluster of the Data block. Once found, we can use the rest non-matching section in the identified cluster to find the next fragment of the checksum file. The b_l can be calculated through Eq. (1), where S is the cluster size and b_l is the last non-matched bytes.

$$b_l = (S - 7)mod(4 * S/512). \tag{1}$$

To detail this, an example using the proposed method under 4096-byte sized disk cluster is described in Fig. 6. The first 7 bytes is the header bytes and (4096-7) mod (4*4096/512) is 25, so the last 25 bytes can be used to determine the position of the Data block cluster. When the block file cluster is determined, we can use the last two 512-byte section to find the next fragment of the checksum file. According to this method, the Data block and the checksum file can be reconstructed easily.

The algorithm of recovering HFile Data block in pseudo-code is presented in Algorithms 1 and 2. In which DATABLKsig means the Data block header signature (0x44415441424C4B2A) and BLKsig means other block header signature. Algorithm 1 describes the single-fragmented recovery method. It is described at first in this section. The process of mutil-fragmented recovery is: from the cluster that DATABLKsig belongs to, match the checksum of each 512-byte section in the cluster with the bytes in data dump D. Once a mismatch appears, match the b_l bytes of the checksum hexadecimal string. If the match is failed, it means the Data blocks is fragmented, else the checksum file is fragmented. Then we use the above method (cross-find) to identify the next fragment of each other. Do these repeatedly until the Data block being totally reconstructed or can't find any fragments.

Algorithm 1. single-fragmented recovery

---

input   : data dump D, cluster size S
output   : the recovered file R,offset list(p)

1   **for** all data in D **do**
2   p ← find next DATABLKsig's offset;
3   l ← read block size;
4   locate at p+l in D;
5   m ← read 8 bytes;
6   **if** m == DATABLKsig or m == BLKsig **then**
7   add the data between p and p+l into file R;
8   **else**
9   lsit(p) ← add p to a list;
10   **end if**
11   **end for**
11   **return** list(p);

Algorithm 2. multi-fragmented recovery

---

input   : data dump D, cluster size S, offset list(p)
output   : the recovered file R

1   **for** each item p in list(p) **do**
2   C ← calculate the cluster that p belongs to;
3   calculate checksums of each 512-byte section in C;
4   cksum   ← combines checksums into a hexadecimal string;
5   **for** all data in D **do**
6   match cksum with data in D;
7   **if** not match **then**
8   break;
9   **else**
10   ckpos ← record the matched offset;
11   **end for**
12   **for** all data in D **do**
13   match the cluster from C continuously with the data from ckpos;
14   add the matched data into file R;
15   **if** not match **then**
16   match the first b_i (see Eq. (1)) bytes;
17   **if** not match **then**
18   find the next fragment of Data block;
19   **if** not found **then return**;
20   **else**
21   find the next fragment of checksum file;
22   **if** not found **then return**;
23   **end if**
24   **end if**
25   **end for**
26   **end for**

4.3 Extracting Records from the Carved Data Block

Unlike traditional relational database (RDBMS), each record in HBase table is a key-value pair. The record header contains key length and value length and the rest portion stores the content of key and value. The value format is just byte array which has no specific type. Key format is more complex, which comprises rowKey, column family, column, timestamp and keyType. The record structure is illustrated in Fig. 7.

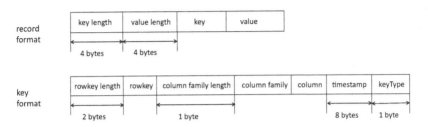

Fig. 7. The format of HBase table record.

Each column belongs to a column family, and a column name is prefixed by a column family (e.g. info: title, info: name). A record may have many versions, using timestamp to distinguish. The timestamp is a 64-bit Integer. RowKey, column and timestamp identify a record uniquely. The keyType represents the type of a record (like "put", "delete", "deleteColumn", "deleteFamily"). For example, if the keyType is 0x00, it means this is a deleted record and if it is 0x04, the type is put. According to the record structure we can extract it easily. Firstly read Data block header and then locate to the first record start position, and then read key, value content based on the key length and value length. Note that, the column size can by calculated by key length minus other fields length.

5 Experiment and Evaluation

To evaluate the performance of our method, we conducted a series of experiments, which mainly consist of two scenarios. Scenario one verifies the effectiveness of the proposed method under 4096-byte clustered disk because it is the default cluster size in Ext4 file system which is commonly used in Linux. Scenario two compares the performance of the method under different cluster sized disk.

5.1 Scenario One

In this scenario, we set up four virtual machines. One is NameNode and the other three are DataNodes. Each machine is under Linux operate system (CentOS 6.7). The Hadoop version we used is hadoop1.1.2 and the HBase version is 0.94.27. We download data in CSV format from the internet and then create corresponding table in HBase using command "create 'testtable' , 'info'", where "testtable" denotes table name and "info" denotes column family. After this, the data is loaded into HBase database using the following command:

```
[root@NameNode /]# hadoop jar /usr/local/hbase/hbase-0.94.27.jar importtsv -importtsv.columns=
HBASE_ROW_KEY,info:col1,info:col2 -Dimporttsv.separator=, testtable /data.csv
```

Then the corresponding HFile is generated in disk. The structure of this file follows the file structure described in Sect. 4. Finally we delete this file using the HDFS shell command and using DD command to get the disk image.

Table 1. Experiment results of recovering HBase records on three DataNodes.

	Total records	Recovered records	Recovery rate (%)
DataNode1	141968	141968	100
DataNode2	141977	141857	99.91
DataNode3	55590	55500	99.83
Total	339535	339325	99.93

The experiment result of recovering HBase table records from HDFS is shown in Table 1. The HFile we deleted is split into three blocks stored across three DataNodes respectively. Each of the DataNodes contains 141968, 141977 and 55590 records respectively. As is shown in Table 1, we recovered most of the HBase table records.

5.2   Scenario Two

In order to evaluate our method under different cluster sized disk, we set up three Hadoop clusters. The cluster size of the local file system of each Hadoop cluster is 1024 bytes, 2048 bytes and 4096 bytes respectively. The experiments result is shown in Table 2. Under 2048-byte and 4096-byte cluster sized disk, the recovery rate is nearly 100%. It means the most records can be recovered effectively. Note that, the effectiveness under 1024-byte cluster sized disk is a little poorer than the other two situations. Because the information in one cluster of the checksum file can verify total 127 clusters of the block file, and the rest one byte is too small to determine the next cluster of the block file. Once the checksum file is fragmented, we should find the header signature of next Data block again.

Table 2. Experiment results under different cluster size

	Total records	1024-byte		2048-byte		4096-byte	
		Recovered records	Recovery rate (%)	Recovered records	Recovery rate (%)	Recovered records	Recovery rate (%)
DataNode1	141968	141386	99.59	141968	100	141968	100
DataNode2	141977	140415	98.89	141857	99.91	141857	99.91
DataNode3	55590	46481	83.61	55500	99.83	55500	99.83
Total	339535	328282	96.68	339325	99.93	339325	99.93

5.3   Comparing Research

In order to verify the effectiveness of the proposed approach, it is compared with the traditional head-length carving method [2] which just search the header signature and extract data continuously until the size equals to the length recorded in the header.

Two criterions that precision rate (define as Eq. (2)) and recall rate (defined as Eq. (3)) have been adopted to evaluate the proposed method, and F-value (defined as Eq. (4)) is used to evaluate the quality of the recovery method. In these equations, A is used to denote the number of recovered records belong to HFile; B is used to denote the number of recovered records do not belong to HFile while C denotes the number of records which belong to HFile but do not be recovered from the data dump D.

$$Precision(P) = \frac{A}{A+B}. \tag{2}$$

$$Recall(R) = \frac{A}{A+C}. \tag{3}$$

$$F - value = \frac{2 * P * R}{P+R}. \tag{4}$$

The comparing experiment is based on 1024-byte cluster sized disk. The comparing result is shown as Fig. 8. There is no false positive in our test because we extract the records based on their structure described in Sect. 4. It can be seen that the proposed method gets higher scores of precision, recall, and F-value than the traditional approaches. The traditional head-length carving method is suited for recovering continuous files. The recovery effectiveness depends on the data set. The less fragments the files contain, the better the recovery result is. Our method which is based on checksum file not only applies to continuous files but works very effective when the files are split into many fragments.

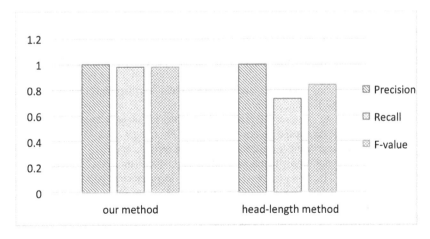

Fig. 8. The comparing result of the two methods.

6 Discussion and Conclusion

In this work, we talk about the data recovery problem in HDFS and provide an effective method of recovery HBase records. The HDFS is a distributed file system and recovery of a complete file is more difficult. However, partly recovery of data is valuable as well. We analyze the HDFS structure and HFile format in detail, and recover the Data blocks of HFile using the corresponding checksum file and extract records from them.

Our carving technique utilizes the information in checksum files which can piece the file fragments together in a correct order conveniently. So it can effectively address the problem of recovering highly fragmented files. We test the method on the disk whose cluster size is 1 KB, 2 KB and 4 KB respectively. It behaves well in 4 KB and 2 KB cluster sized disk, where the effectiveness is a little poorer on 1 KB cluster sized disk. But all the recovery rates are more than 83.61%.

Another important aspect is the computational efficiency of the proposed recovery method. To determine this, the average computation time for recovering the data from different cluster sized disk image has been measured. Our methods are implemented by JAVA and performed on a PC with Intel 3.2 GHz i5-3407 CPU and 8 GB RAM and the size of the each disk image in our experiments is 20 GB. The average computation times under 1 KB, 2 KB and 4 KB cluster sized disk image is, respectively 75, 35 and 27 min. Note that, the computational time depends on the size of dataset. We will compare the computational time of different sized disk image in our future work. In addition, data in HDFS may be stored across several machines. How to choose the most correlated machine for recovery is of great importance. This will also be considered in our future work.

Acknowledgments. This work is supported by the Natural Science Foundation of China under Grant Nos. 61070212 and 61572165, the State Key Program of Zhejiang Province Natural Science Foundation of China under Grant No. LZ15F020003 and Key Lab of Information Network Security, Ministry of Public Security.

References

1. Richard III, G.G., Roussev, V.: Scalpel: a frugal, high performance file carver. In: DFRWS (2005)
2. Garfinkel, S.L.: Carving contiguous and fragmented files with fast object validation. Digital Invest. **4**, 2–12 (2007)
3. Memon, N., Pal, A.: Automated reassembly of file fragmented images using greedy algorithms. IEEE Trans. Image Process. **15**(2), 385–393 (2006)
4. EnCase Forensic. http://guidancesoftware.com/encase-forensic.htm
5. Adroit Photo Forensics. http://digital-assembly.com/products/adroit-photo-forensics/
6. Pal, A., Sencar, H.T., Memon, N.: Detecting file fragmentation point using sequential hypothesis testing. Digital Investigation. **5**, 2–13 (2008)
7. Autopsy/The Sleuth Kit. http://sleuthkit.org
8. X-Ways Forensics. http://x-ways.net/forensics

9. Cohen, M.: Advanced jpeg carving. In: Proceedings of the 1st International Conference on Forensic Applications and Techniques in Telecommunications. Information, and Multimedia and Workshop, pp. 16:1–16:6 (2008)
10. Na, G., Shim, K., Moon, K., Kong, S., Kim, E.: Lee, J: Frame-based recovery of corrupted video files using codec specifications. IEEE Trans. Image Process. 23(2), 517–526 (2014)
11. Bock, J., Smet, P.: JPGarve: An advanced tool for automated recovery of fragmented JPEG files. IEEE Trans. Inf. Forensics Secur. 11(1), 19–24 (2016)
12. Uzun, E., Sencar, H.T.: Carving orphaned JPEG file fragments. IEEE Trans. Inf. Forensics Secur. 10(8), 1549–1563 (2015)
13. Cohen, M.: Advanced carving techniques. Digital Invest. 4, 119–128 (2007)
14. Shvachko, K., Kuang, H., Radia, S., Chansler, R.: The hadoop distributed file system. In IEEE Symposium on Mass Storage Systems (2010)
15. Martini, B., Choo, K.R.: Distributed filesystem forensics: XtreemFS as a case study. Digital Invest. 11, 295–313 (2014)
16. Yoon, J., Jeong, D., Kang, C., Lee, S.: Forensic investigation framework for the document store NoSQL DBMS: MongoDB as a case study. Digital Invest. 17, 53–65 (2016)
17. Pal, A., Memon, N.: The Evolution of File Carving. IEEE Signal Process. Mag. 3, 59–71 (2009)
18. Karresand, M., Shahmehri, N.: Fileprints: identifying file type by n-gram analysis. In: Proceedings of 7th IEEE Systems, Man and Cybernetics Information Assurance Workshop, pp. 64–71. IEEE (2006)
19. Veenman, C.J.: Statistical disk cluster classification for file carving. In: Proceedings of 3rd International Symposium on Information Assurance and Security, pp. 393–398. IEEE Computer Society (2007)
20. Jeon, S., Bang, J., Byun, K., Lee, S.: A recovery method of deleted record for SQLite database. Pers. Ubiquit. Comput. 16(6), 707–715 (2012)
21. Xu, M., Yang, X., Wu, B., Yao, J., Zhang, H.P., Xu, J., Zheng, N.: A metadata-based method for recovering files and file traces from YAFFS2. Digital Invest. 10, 62–72 (2013)
22. Sencar, H.T., Memon, N.: Identification and recovery of JPEG files with missing fragments. Digital Invest. 6, 88–98 (2009)
23. Yoo, B., Park, J., Lim, S., Bang, J., Lee, S.: A study on multimedia file carving method. Multimedia Tools Appl. 61(1), 243–261 (2012)

A Continuous Segmentation Algorithm for Streaming Time Series

Yupeng Hu[1,2], Cun Ji[1], Ming Jing[1], Yiming Ding[1], Shuo Kuai[1], and Xueqing Li[1(✉)]

[1] School of Computer Science and Technology,
Shandong University, Jinan, China
{huyupeng,jicun,jingming,xqli}@sdu.edu.cn,
dingyiming@mail.sdu.edu.cn, kuaishuo_sdu@163.com
[2] State Key Laboratory for Novel Software Technology,
Nanjing University, Nanjing, China

Abstract. Along with the arrival of Industry 4.0 era, massive numbers of detecting instruments in various fields are continuously producing a plenty number of time series stream data. In order to efficiently and effectively analyze and mine the high-dimensional streaming time series, the segmentation which provides more accurate representation to the raw time series data, should be done as the first step. In this paper, we propose a novel online segmentation approach based on the turning points to partition the time series into some continuous subsequences and maintain a high similarity between the processed subsequences and the raw data. It achieves the best overall performance on the segmentation results compared with other baseline methods. Extensive experiments on all kinds of typical time series datasets have been conducted to demonstrate the advantages of our method.

Keywords: Data mining · Time series · Online segmentation · Algorithms

1 Introduction

Along with the arrival of Industry 4.0 era, the evolving of IoT (Internet of Things) has stimulated the deployment of massive numbers of detecting instruments in various fields including business, finance, medicine, astronomy, aviation and so on, which are continuously producing a plenty number of time series stream data [1–3]. Time series stream data can be described as an ordered collection of elements, where the elements are continuously generated in a high speed and potentially forever [4, 5]. Due to the large amount, high-dimensional, continuous and other related properties, it is not capable to do in-depth researches for the streaming time series.

In consideration of the above situation, the segmentation of the streaming time series should be done as the first step to reduce both the space and the computational cost of storing and transmitting such data. In this paper, we are concerned with the online linear segmentation approach for the streaming time series, which is aimed for not only producing approximate representation conformed the temporal features, but also being effective in continuous segmentation. An efficient online segmentation

© ICST Institute for Computer Sciences, Social Informatics and Telecommunications Engineering 2017
S. Wang and A. Zhou (Eds.): CollaborateCom 2016, LNICST 201, pp. 140–151, 2017.
DOI: 10.1007/978-3-319-59288-6_13

algorithm for streaming time series would be a useful tool for other data mining tasks, for instance:

1. The similarity search and pattern recognition in time series first need several "primitive shapes" [6] and "frequent patterns" [7] subsequences, which can be used for the next similarity measure steps.
2. In time series **classification** tasks, the typical prototypes should be created for the predefined classes, which could be generated by the segmentation approach as a preprocessing step.
3. In time series **clustering** tasks, some renowned heuristic methods such as K-means need to use several meaningful temporal feature sequences rather than random points to improve its convergence ability [8].

At present, most existing representation-based segmentation approaches do not work well for our problems. Some methods [9, 10] process segmentation on static data sets, and may incur a high cost if applied directly to streaming data. There do exist works that address the segmentation problem for data streams [11], which is called Sliding Windows (SW) but the accuracy of the segmentation is in low level, due to the lack of a more holistic view of segmentation. To solve this problem, Keogh et al. [12] consider combining the online nature of Sliding Windows and the superiority of Bottom-Up, which is called Sliding Window and Bottom-up (SWAB). However, this algorithm treats every point of the time series equally and exists some computation redundancy. In order to speed up the efficiency of the online segmentation algorithm, Liu et al. [13] propose the Feasible Space Window (FSW) method, which introduces the concept of feasible space to find the farthest segmenting point of each segment. This method greatly enhances the efficiency of the segmentation, but the partitioned subsequences are unable to make more accurate representation than SWAB.

In this paper, we propose a novel segmentation approach based on the turning points to piecewise linear representation (PLR) for streaming time series, and our method can provide a more accurate segmentation than all of the baseline methods previously used. In summary, we have achieved the following contributions in this paper.

1. We propose an online time series segmentation algorithm called the continuous segmentation algorithm based on turning points (CS_TP) which partitions the time series by a set of temporal feature points and maintains a high similarity between the processed subsequences and the raw data.
2. We adopt two segmentation criteria to refine the FSW-based segmentation results by standing on a more holistic view with the temporal features, and propose an optimal merging algorithm to reduce computation redundancy.
3. We compare the CS_TP with other baseline methods on both real open source data sets and some kinds of the typical industry time series datasets to demonstrate the superiority of our approach.

The remainder of the paper is organized as follows. In Sect. 2 we present the related work. Section 3 describes some preliminaries. The online segmentation approach is described in detail in Sect. 4. Section 5 presents the experiment results and analyses. Finally, we conclude this paper in Sect. 6.

2   Related Work

Segmentation which supplies more accurate and compact representations of time series can be considered as a discretization problem. Piecewise Linear Representation (PLR) [14] has been one of the most widely used segmentation methods for many practical applications [15, 16], which divides a time series into segments and uses a linear function to approximate each segment.

Compared with other methods, PLR is more consistent with human visual experience. In addition, PLR has some advantages of low index dimension for storing, fast speed for calculating and similarity searching. For this, PLR method is more fit for segmenting and detecting, so we use PLR to divide time series data into linear segments, which can be subdivided into three main segmentation strategies: Top-Down (TD), Bottom-Up (BU) and Sliding Windows (SW).

1. The PLR based on Top-Down algorithm

The PLR based on Top Down (PLR_TD) algorithm, which starts with an unsegmented sequence and introduces one cutting point at a time, repeating this process until some stopping criteria are met, in that case, the raw time series data would be partitioned into some straight lines. According to the temporal features of time series data, Zhou et al. [17] propose a novel time series segmentation based on series importance point (PLR_SIP). However, the algorithm is mainly designed to investigate the error of segments, the error of single point is not considered in this algorithm. To solve this problem, Ji et al. [18] propose a new piecewise linear representation based on importance data point (PLR_IDP) for time series, which finds the important points by calculating the fitting error of single point and piecewise segments. As a consequence of this, the fitting error of PLR_IDP is much smaller than any other PLR_TD methods.

2. The PLR based on Bottom-Up algorithm

The PLR based on Bottom-Up (PLR_BU) algorithm, starting with the n-1 segments, and then, two adjacent segments are greedily merged into one by choosing the lowest cost of merging pairs, iterating this process until some stopping criteria are met. Keogh et al. [19] present an improved method, which not only produces segments, but also predetermines the number of segments represented the time series.

3. The PLR based on Sliding Windows algorithm

The PLR based on Sliding Window (PLR_SW) algorithm, initializing the first data point of time series as the left endpoint of a segment and then trying to find the right endpoint of a segment by sequential scanning time series data. Keogh et al. [12] consider combining the online nature of sliding window and the superiority of bottom-up, which is called Sliding Window and Bottom-up (SWAB). However, this algorithm treats every point of the time series equally and exists some computation redundancy. In order to speed up the efficiency of the online segmentation algorithm, Liu et al. [13] propose the Feasible Space Window (FSW) and Stepwise FSW (SFSW) method, which introduce the concept of feasible space to find the farthest segmenting point of each segment. FSW method greatly enhances the efficiency of the segmentation, but the partitioned subsequences are unable to make more accurate representation, due to the lack of a more holistic view of segmentation.

According to the different requirements, the PLR segmentation can also be categorized into two classes: online and offline. The offline methods segment the whole data sequence, and the online methods can continuously partition these streaming data as long as the data is continuously producing (potentially forever). We can see that the PLR_TD methods (e.g., PLR_SIP, PLR_IDP et al.) and the PLR_BU methods should be grouped into the offline segmentation approaches, the PLR_SW methods including SWAB, FSW, SFSW and so on should be grouped into the online segmentation approaches.

Through the comparative analysis of the above algorithms, the major advantage of the PLR_SW methods is their ability to continuous segmentation, which meets our requirement for streaming time series segmentation. The main problem of the PLR_SW is the accuracy of representation which can not be guaranteed, compared with its offline counterparts. The PLR_TD and PLR_BU methods can produce more accurate approximation, but the entire data set should be scanned first, which is impossible for the streaming time series segmentation.

3   Preliminaries

3.1   The Turning Points Definition

When we plan on dividing the streaming time series into some continuous subsequences, it is advisable for us to segment the stream according to their temporal features. The temporal feature is constructed by a sequence of data points and each point actually has the different influence on the variation trend. In our paper, we focus on some data points indicating the change trend of time series, which can be called as the Turning Points (TPs).

Judging from the intuition, these local maximum and minimum points seemingly can be defined as the TPs since they indicate the change in the trend of the time series which has been proposed by Yin et al. [20] on the financial time series. According to the analysis on the different types of time series data sets, we draw the conclusion: The TPs are not only composed by the local extreme points (e.g., inflection points, step points etc.) and not all local extreme points should be defined as TPs in consideration of the noise and disturbance. For such reason, we provide our definition of TPs as follow:

1. For a time series $T = (. . ., a_i, . . ., a_j, ...)$ where $a_i = (x_i, y_i)$ is a raw data point in time series. If a_i meets one of the following two inequations, it can be defined as the **Level 1 TP**:

$$y_{i-1} < y_i < y_{i+1} \ or \ y_{i-1} < y_i = y_{i+1} \ or \ y_{i-1} = y_i < y_{i+1} \tag{1}$$

$$y_{i-1} > y_i > y_{i+1} \ or \ y_{i-1} > y_i = y_{i+1} \ or \ y_{i-1} = y_i > y_{i+1} \tag{2}$$

2. For a time series $T = (. ., a_i . ., a_j, ...)$ where $a_i = (x_i, y_i)$ and $a_j = (x_j, y_j)$ are **TPs** in the **level 1**. If a_j meets the following condition, it can be defined as the **Level 2 TP**:

$$x_j - x_i \geq \mu \; and \; \frac{|y_j - y_i|}{(|y_j| + |y_i|)/2} \geq \rho \qquad (3)$$

The intuitive idea of the **Level 2** is to discard unimportant fluctuations and keep major peaks and valleys with parameter μ and ρ, which can be specified by users. In order to make our intention clearer, we select one subset of data from the Fig. 1(a) to magnify in the Fig. 1(b). As shown in Fig. 1(b), if the value $\mu = 3$ and $\rho = 1$, two TPs in the **Level 1** (i, j) can be defined as the TPs in the **Level 2** and two TPs (k, m) can be smoothed. In other words, we can directly draw a straight line from the point i to point j so as to discard unimportant fluctuations in the streaming time series.

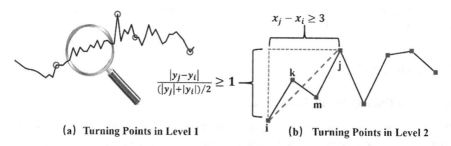

(a) Turning Points in Level 1   (b) Turning Points in Level 2

Fig. 1. The definitions of turning points

3.2   The Segmentation Criteria

To ensure the accuracy and the efficiency of the segmentation algorithm, we need to introduce two segmentation criteria for a potential segment.

1. The maximum error for single point (**ME_SP**)

The ME_SP is used to evaluate the fitting error of the single data in a segment. In the classic PLR_SW method, a segment continues to grow until the maximum vertical distance (MVD) for certain data point exceeds the ME_SP. The FSW method greatly simplifies the calculation of the MVD by the slope calculation (SC) [13], and therefore, we will adopt this SC measure instead of the direct MVD calculation and combine with the discovery of the TPs for our online segmentation. In order to make this concept clearly, we will provide some definitions and instructions of the SC measure (more details in reference 13) in Table 1: for a time series $T = (a_i, ...a_j, ...a_k)$ and the σ (the ME_SP specified by users) >0, if $sline(a_i, a_k)$ satisfies the inequation: $slow(a_i, a_j)$

Table 1. The definitions of the slope calculation

Definitions	Instructions
$line(a_i, a_j)$	The straight line from point a_i to a_j
$sline(a_i, a_j)$	The slope of the straight line from point a_i to a_j
$slow(a_i, a_j)$	The slope of the straight line from point a_i to $a_i - \sigma$
$sup(a_i, a_j)$	The slope of the straight line from point a_i to $a_i + \sigma$

$\leq sline(a_i, a_k) \leq sup(a_i, a_j)$, the MVD between a_j and $line(a_i, a_k)$ will not exceed the σ(ME_SP). Along with the growth of a segment, the values of $slow()$ and $sup()$ are constantly changing, and we define the $maxslow_{(i:j)}$ and $minsup_{(i:j)}$ to find the maximum value of $slow()$ and the minimum value of $sup()$. The definition is as follow:

$$maxslow_{(i:j)} = max_{i<t<j}slow(a_i, a_t) \tag{4}$$

$$minsup_{(i:j)} = min_{i<t<j}sup(a_i, a_t) \tag{5}$$

When such condition: $maxslow_{(i:j)} > minsup_{(i:j)}$ is satisfied, the current segmentation will be ended and then to repeat the above operation until the entire stream data has been processed.

2. The maximum error for entire segment (**ME_ES**)

The ME_ES is used to evaluate the fitting error for the entire segment, and we use this segmentation criterion to eliminate the insufficiency of only relying on the ME_SP to segment the streaming time series, in other words, the segmentation criterion ME_SP only guarantees the fitting error of each point under certain threshold, but fails to control the fitting error of the entire segment in a reasonable range.

For this reason, we will introduce an additional reference condition ME_ES to guarantee the accurate representation for online segmentation.

4   Algorithm Description

In this section, we first describe our online segmentation algorithm CS_TP, and then, we will provide the time complexity analysis of our algorithm. The CS_TP algorithm can be divided into three major steps, as follow:

1. Initial segmentation by the ME_SP and SC

The initial segmentation can divide the streaming time series into several segments by the **SC** measure (proposed in Sect. 3) and ensure the fitting error of each point is under the ME_SP. More importantly, the initial segmentation will find all of the TPs in segment by the definition of the **TPs (in Level 2)**, which is prepared for optimizing the results of segmentations. Figure 2(a) and (b) describe this process. The red rhombus points denote the segmenting points of three segments and the blue dots between two rhombus points denote the TPs in a segment.

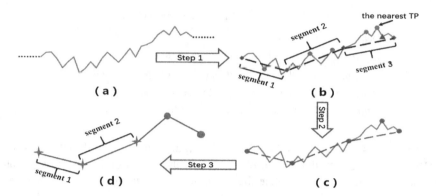

Fig. 2. The major steps of the segmentation

2. Segmentation error evaluation by the ME_ES and TPs in Level 2

After the above process, we will use the ME_ES to evaluate the fitting error of the segments by accumulating the fitting error of the single point until the last point of segment has been accumulated or the accumulative value exceeds the ME_ES. We will record the position of the current point and find the nearest TP, Fig. 2(b) and (c) describes this process. In these pictures, it is obvious that, in Fig. 2(b), the accumulation of the segment 1 and segment 2 do not exceed the MP_ES, however when the accumulative calculation of the segment 3 at the red triangular point, the value of the accumulation has exceeded the MP_ES, in that case, we will select the nearest TP in Fig. 2(b). The accumulative calculation will restart at the new selected point. As shown in Fig. 2(c), When the evaluation of the segmentation error is complete, we can get all of the original segmenting points and the nearest TPs (violet dots in Fig. 2(c)).

3. Merging the subsequences by standing on holistic view

After the above two steps, we can make use of the segmenting points to refine the FSW-based segmentation results by iteratively merging the lowest cost of the consecutive pairs of the sequences. The process of our method is similar with the SWAB methods, however we optimize the process from two aspects:

On one hand, the merging process begins with the consecutive sequences instead of connecting two adjacent points, in other words, the merging process can retain the segmentation results in the first two steps and keep the number of the segments as low as possible. On the other hand, not only the leftmost segment would be removed from the buffer, the consecutive segments behind the leftmost one can also be removed as long as the segmenting points are exactly the initial segmenting points defined in the first step. With the above optimization, the efficiency of our approach can be significantly improved compared with the SWAB. As shown in Fig. 2(d), the segment 1 and the segment 2 can be removed from the buffer immediately, and segment 3 which has been divided into two subsequences, will be merged along with the next arriving segments. The summary of notations and the pseudo code is described as follows (Table 2):

Table 2. The summary of notations

Definitions	Instructions
nsp_qu	The queue for storing the segmentation points which are process by step 1 and step 2
m_cost	The merging cost of the consecutive pair of segments
cost_priqu	The priority queue for storing the cost of the merge
calc_merg()	The calculation of the cost of the merge
rsp_qu	The queue for storing the segmentation points of segments which have been considered to complete the segmentation

---

Function merge_seg()

```
Input: nsp_qu, ME_ES
Output: rsp_qu
Begin
    for i=1 :2 : nsp_qu.length
        m_cost = calc_merg();
        cost_priqu.enqueue(m_cost);
    end for
        m_cost = cost_priqu.dequeue();
    while m_cost < ME_ES
        merge the two adjacent sequences;
        m_cost = calc_merg();   // update the merging cost
        cost_priqu.enqueue(m_cost);
    end while
    while nsp_qu.top() is the original segmenting point
        rsp_qu.enqueue(nsp_qu.dequeue());
    end while
    remove the segments whose segmenting points are stored in the rsp_qu queue
    return rsp_qu
End
```

According to the above description of the algorithm, in the first step, the slope calculation and the TPs discovery can be done by scanning the whole sequence in linear time, so the time cost of this operation is $O(n)$. In the second step, the evaluation of the fitting error of the entire segments should consider the number of the segmenting points and the number of the TPs. In our method the buffer can store about 6 segments (7 segmenting points), and the number of TPs (k) in one segment is far less than the number of points (n) in the segment, which can be represented by $k \ll n$, the time complexity of the second step is $O(7*k*n)$. In the third step, the operation is similar with the PLR_BU, but our method optimizes the process from two aspects, which has been described above. So the time complexity of the third step is no worse than $O(Ln)$, (L is the average segment length). So the total time complexity of our method is $O(O(n) + O(kn) + O(Ln))$, that is $O(Ln)$. Finally, we summarize the time complexities for all of the online segmentation methods mentioned in the Table 3.

Table 3. The time complexities of online segmentation methods

Algorithm	Complexity
CS_TP	$O(Ln)$ L is the average segment length
SWAB	$O(Ln)$ L is the average segment length
FSW	$O(Mn)$ M is the number of segmenting points
SFSW	$O(Mn^2)$ M is the number of segmenting points

5 Experiment and Analysis

In this section, we evaluate the performance of our online segmentation algorithm: CS_TP by compared with the SWAB, FSW and SFSW, which are nearly the most highly cited online segmentation algorithm based on the PLR up to date. We are concerned not only the representation accuracy of these techniques, but also the efficiency by using different datasets.

5.1 Dataset and Evaluation Metrics

In order to accomplish the experiment, we select some kinds of typical time series datasets which contain an average of 10,000 records from different fields, including medicine, finance, industry provided by the UCR homepage [21], and we also choose some representative industrial streaming time series including the monitoring data of Jinan municipal steam heating system (JMSHSD) from December 2013 to March 2016 (i.e.,100,532 data points), the monitoring data of Dong Fang Hong satellite (DFHSD) from January 2015 to June 2015 (i.e.,320,675 data points), which is the Chinese satellite dataset provided by China Academy of Space Technology.

In our experiment, the goal of our segmentation is to minimize the holistic representation error and obtain as few segments as possible in a more efficient manner. Therefore, in order to evaluate the segmentation for a given streaming time series, we consider the representation error, as well as the number of segments by two parameters: the ME_SP and ME_ES.

5.2 Comparison with Existing Methods

We compare our methods with the three baseline methods (FSW, SFSW, SWAB) by varying the ME_SP and ME_ES.

The SWAB [12] combines the main features of the PLR_SW and PLR_BU, which segments the streaming time series by iteratively using the BU merging method to the new sliding window and removing the leftmost segment as a finished one. The FSW and SFSW [13] belong to the PLR_SW, the former adopts the slope calculation instead of the direct MVD calculation to segment streaming time series, the latter is carried out corresponding optimization on the basis of the former. When two consecutive segments have been segmented, the SFSW would adopt backward segmenting strategy to refine the previously segmenting result.

Finally, we provide the overall performances of segmentation methods on all of the above-mentioned datasets. Before the experiments, considering the variety and complexity of the datasets, some conditions need to be defined in advance.

First of all, we adopt the Maximum Error Percentage for Single Point (MEP_SP) to substitute the absolute ME_SP, which is proposed by Liu et al. [10] and MEP_SP can eliminate the influences on different data sets by specifying the percentage of the value range on different data sets. What's more, with the change of the MEP_SP, the ME_ES in CS_TP should also be changed simultaneously to avoid that the ME_SP exceeds the ME_ES, so we will adopt the Maximum Error Percentage for Entire Segment (MEP_ES) to substitute ME_ES, and the MEP_ES is set as an integral multiple of N which is an integer greater than 2. Last but not least, we consider the result of the SWAB with MEP_SP whose value is 10% as the benchmark (set as 1), and we can normalize the results of other methods with the benchmark.

When we vary the MEP_SP from 10% to 50% in the Fig. 3(a), we can see that the CS_TP has the lowest the normalized representation error, which means this method can provide more accurate representation than other methods, and the error of all methods gradually increase with the rising of MEP_SP. However, the error of CS_TP grows more slowly than the other three methods because of the restriction of the MEP_ES, in other words, the CS_TP can guarantee a relative accurate representation even though the single point fitting error is constantly increased. In the Fig. 3(b), we can also find that the normalized number of segments of all methods gradually decrease with the rising of MEP_SP, and when the value of MEP_SP is up to 40%, the number of CS_TP is less than the SWAB because of the optimal merging step in our method.

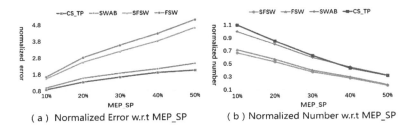

(a) Normalized Error w.r.t MEP_SP   (b) Normalized Number w.r.t MEP_SP

Fig. 3. The MEP_SP analysis

When we vary the MEP_ES from 2*MEP_SP to 5*MEP_SP in the Fig. 4(a), the three baseline methods are shown as three straight lines parallel to the X axis, because these methods do not use MEP_ES to segment the time series. However, the CS_TP relies on the MEP_ES to refine the result of initial segmentation. We can see that the normalized representation error of CS_TP constantly increases with the gradually loosened restriction of the MEP_SP and the error of CS_TP is close unlimitedly to the FSW. In the Fig. 4(b), the normalized number of segments of CS_TP continues to decrease with the change of the MEP_SP, finally the number of segments of CS_TP is nearly the same as the FSW, which means that the segmentation effect of CS_TP is no lower than the FSW in the worst case.

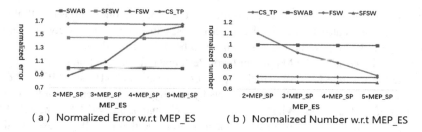

(a) Normalized Error w.r.t MEP_ES   (b) Normalized Number w.r.t MEP_ES

Fig. 4. The MEP_EP analysis

At last, we provide the representation error for all methods on the above-mentioned datasets, the result of the SWAB is set as the benchmark. The results are listed in the Table 4. We can find that the CS_TP can provide more accurate segmentation than the FSW, SFSW and SWAB.

Table 4. Normalized representation error of different methods

Normalized representation error of different methods				
Data sets	Method			
	SWAB	CS_TP	FSW	SFSW
DFHSD	1	0.79	2.43	2.39
JMSHSD	1	0.89	2.21	2.17
ECG	1	0.97	1.97	2.03
Phone1	1	1.01	1.98	1.73
Powerplant	1	0.91	2.15	1.83
Wind	1	0.95	1.24	1.01
Average	1	0.92	2.00	1.86

6   Conclusion

In this paper, we propose a new segmentation algorithm (CS_TP) which performs well on segmenting the streaming time series, and holds the main characteristic of time series by refining he FSW-based segmentation result and reducing computation redundancy. The extensive numeric experiments demonstrate the advantages of our algorithm. The CS_TP can produce lower representation error to guarantee more accurate representation for online segmentation. In future, we plan to use this algorithm as a useful tool for time series classification, clustering and anomaly detection.

Acknowledgment. The authors would like to acknowledge the support provided by the Novel Software Technology Project(KFKT2015B02) and the Science & Technology Development Project of Shandong Province (2015GGX101009).

References

1. Lin, J., Keogh, E., Lonardi, S.: A symbolic representation of time series, with implications for streaming algorithms. In: Proceedings of ACM SIGMOD (2003)
2. Chandra, R.: Competition and collaboration in cooperative coevolution of Elman recurrent neural networks for time-series prediction. IEEE Trans. Neural Netw. Learn. Syst. **26**(12), 3123–3136 (2015)
3. Jamali, S., Jönsson, P., Eklundh, L., Ardö, J., Seaquist, J.: Detecting changes in vegetation trends using time series segmentation. Remote Sens. Environ. **156**, 182–195 (2015)
4. Palpanas, T., Vlachos, M., Keogh, E.: Online amnesic approximation of streaming time series. In: Proceedings of IEEE ICDE 2004 (2004)
5. Luo, G., Yi, K., Cheng, S.W., Li, Z., Fan, W., He, C., Mu, Y.: Piecewise linear approximation of streaming time series data with max-error guarantees. In Proceedings of IEEE ICDE 2015(2015)
6. Chiu, B., Keogh, E., Lonardi, S.: Probabilistic discovery of time series motifs proceedings. In: Proceedings of ACM SIGKDD 2003 (2003)
7. Lin, J., Keogh, E., Patel, P., Lonardi, S.: Finding motifs in time series. In: Proceedings of ACM SIGKDD 2002 (2002)
8. Fayyad, U., Reina, C., Bradley, P.: Initialization of iterative refinement clustering algorithms. In: Proceedings of ACM SIGKDD 1998 (1998)
9. Yi, B., Faloutsos, B.: Fast time sequence indexing for arbitrary Lp-norms. In: Proceedings of VLDB International Conference 2000 (2000)
10. Lazaridis, I., Mehrotra, S.: Capturing sensor-generated time series with quality guarantees. In: Proceedings of IEEE ICDE 2003 (2003)
11. Wang, C., Wang, S.: Supporting content-based searches on time Series via approximation. In: Proceedings of IEEE SSDBM 2000 (2000)
12. Keogh, E., Chu, S., Hart, D., Pazzani, M.: An online algorithm for segmenting time series. In: Proceedings of IEEE ICDM 2001 (2001)
13. Liu, X., Lin, X., Wang, H.: Novel online methods for time series segmentation. TKDE **20**(12), 1616–1626 (2008)
14. Shatkay, H., Zdonik, S.B.: Approximate queries and representations for large data sequences. In: Proceedings of IEEE ICDE 1996 (1996)
15. Chen, Y., Nascimento, M.A., Ooi, B.C., Tung, A.K.H.: SpADe: on shape-based pattern detection in streaming time series. In: Proceedings of IEEE ICDE 2007 (2007)
16. Li, Q., Lopez, I.F.V., Moon, B.: Skyline index for time series data. IEEE Trans. Knowl. Data Eng. **16**(6), 669–684 (2004)
17. Zhou, D.: Time Series Segmentation Based on Series Importance Point. Computer Engineering, 2008(34) (2008)
18. Ji, C., Liu, S., et al.: A piecewise linear representation method based on importance data points for time series data. In: Proceedings of IEEE CSCWD 2016 (2016)
19. Keogh, E., et al.: Fast similarity search in the presence of longitudinal scaling in time series databases. In: Proceedings of IEEE ICTAI 1997 (1997)
20. Yin, J., Si, Y., Gong, Z.: Financial time series segmentation based on turning points. In: IEEE ICSSE 2011 (2011)
21. Keogh, E., Folias, T.: The UCR Time Series Data Mining Archive, Computer Science and Engineering Department, University of California (2002). www.cs.ucr.edu/~eamonn/TSDMA/index.html

Geospatial Streams Publish with Differential Privacy

Yiwen Nie[✉], Liusheng Huang, Zongfeng Li, Shaowei Wang,
Zhenhua Zhao, Wei Yang, and Xiaorong Lu

University of Science and Technology of China, Hefei, China
{nyw2016,lzf01,wangsw,hzq,ldayy}@mail.ustc.edu.cn,
{lshuang,qubit}@ustc.edu.cn

Abstract. Continuous releasing geospatial data is benefiting numerous areas, such as information push service, traffic scheduling and task assignment in crowdsourcing, etc. This kind of data is generated by people using positioning service in daily life, from which much sensitive information can be derived. Differential privacy is a strong theoretical and practical tool to provide protection; it has already been used on streams composing by datasets with fixed attributes. However, there is limited work on geospatial stream releasing with dynamic *scopes* for the requirement of accurate query. In this paper, aiming at achieving privacy protection of real-time geospatial synopsis with high utility, we introduce a method, called *Realtime Geospatial Publish* (*RGP*), which adopts differential privacy to geospatial stream with a new structure *k-memo*. We prove the privacy and utility of *RGP* theoretically and show the improvement of utility by experimental comparison with existing approaches on real datasets.

Keywords: Differential privacy · Geospatial partition · Streams · Location

1 Introduction

Personal data have been increasingly collected and analyzed. With the development of mobile device positioning technologies, such as GPS, WiFi or cellular network based positioning, there are plenty of ways to pinpoint individual's location. The collection of location data is useful for analysis, so as for providing customized services for mobile users. For instance, advertisers can benefit from these geospatial datasets, by understanding the market deeply and making more profits with less cost through delivering ads to target group at specific places; crowdsourcing server may schedule the tasks to executors with better acceptance, for most of the users choose tasks based on the distance from current location to target; police can be arranged in time in case of emergency relying on people flow.

Though geospatial data analysis facilitates enormous applications in daily life, the privacy breach issue should not be ignored when these data are directly

© ICST Institute for Computer Sciences, Social Informatics and Telecommunications Engineering 2017
S. Wang and A. Zhou (Eds.): CollaborateCom 2016, LNICST 201, pp. 152–164, 2017.
DOI: 10.1007/978-3-319-59288-6_14

released. Location stream, which is an important component to geospatial datasets, is severely vulnerable to privacy breach due to the time correlation between neighboring timestamps. [15] shows that approximate 6 locations with timestamps would be able to uniquely identify a trajectory and further locate the individual, though the sensitive information, such as name, gender and address, has been deleted. The malicious third-party can further abstract users' daily schedule, activity range and social relations by analyzing trajectories. Hence, releasing geospatial datasets privately has received more and more attention.

Some of the previous works focusing on static geospatial datasets indeed guarantee location privacy and utility for query, but only reflect empirical information from the past and cannot catch up with the trend in time. Some other proposed several definitions and privacy preserving methods for dynamics streams, but their topologies of locations are under fix structure, which, to some extent, ensure the total utility in one-way publish, but ignore the accuracy of query based on publishes in user-interaction model. In that case, how to overcome the limitations of two aspects above is the key to make geospatial synopsis practical without compromise of privacy. To this end, in this paper, we propose a method to release geospatial streams privately and accurately with adaptive region structure in interactive model.

Our contributions are as follow:

(i) We observe a newly common scenario of geospatial data releasing, which is realtime publish in interactive model, and show some limitations of existing works in this scenario.

(ii) We propose a new method, *Realtime Geospatial Publish (RGP)*, to mitigate limitation of previous works in dynamic geospatial data publish by combining the adaptive region partition with the strategy of privacy budget allocation. What's more, a new data structure *k-memo* is used to optimize privacy strategy.

(iii) Theoretically, we prove the process of *RGP* over streams can satisfy differential privacy requirement. Then we further analyze the utility of algorithm and the effect *k-memo* has on the accuracy of result.

(iv) Through the experiments on real world datasets, we demonstrate utility improvements of *RGP* with comparison to existing methods. We also experimentally study the effects of the size of *k-memo* on the utility of synopsis.

2   Background

In this section we present some necessary background knowledge for our method. Differential privacy provides rigorous information-theoretical guarantee for data privacy, which conceals the small change of the original datasets in the output.

Definition 1 (Neighboring datasets). *Let D and D' be the two neighboring datasets, if D' is obtained from D by adding or deleting one tuple.*

Based on the neighboring datasets, *differential privacy* is defined as follow,

Definition 2 (ϵ-differential privacy [6]). *Let D and D' be the two neighboring datasets. $\mathcal{A}$ is a randomized mechanism over these datasets and o be the possible output of $\mathcal{A}$. $\mathcal{A}$ is said to satisfy ϵ-differential privacy, where $\epsilon \geqslant 0$, if $Pr[\mathcal{A}(D) = o] \leqslant e^\epsilon Pr[\mathcal{A}(D') = o]$.*

According to the definition, for two neighboring datasets, the multiplicative difference between the two probabilities of final outputs should not be more than e^ϵ or less than $e^{-\epsilon}$. Hence, parameter ϵ (namely, privacy budget) is important to control the leakage of privacy. Besides ϵ, the design of randomized mechanism which achieves ϵ-differential privacy also has much impact on the utility of data.

Definition 3 (Global sensitivity). *The global sensitivity of a query $q : D \to R^d$, denoted as Δq, is defined as the largest $L1$ norm of the difference between the answers of querying two neighboring datasets D, D', written as $max_{D,D':\|D-D'\|=1}\|q(D) - q(D')\|_1$.*

Through global sensitivity, randomized mechanisms can be adaptive to various queries and provide appropriate noisy outputs to achieve *differential privacy*. There are mainly two mechanisms, *Laplace Mechanism* for numerics, and *Exponential Mechanism* for non-numerics.

Theorem 1 (Laplace Mechanism [7,8]). *A query $q : D \to R^d$ with the global sensitivity Δq. A randomized mechanism $\mathcal{A}$ outputs $o = q(D)+ < Lap(\frac{\Delta q}{\epsilon}) >^d$, by adding noise derived from the Laplace distribution with scale $\lambda = \frac{\Delta q}{\epsilon}$ to $q(D)$, where ϵ is the privacy budget for $\mathcal{A}$.*

Theorem 2 (Exponential Mechanism (EM) [13]). *A utility function $u(D,o)$ measures the quality of an output o, given the dataset is D. A randomized mechanism $\mathcal{A}$ satisfying ϵ-differential privacy, outputs o with probability proportional to $exp(-\frac{\epsilon u(D,o)}{2\Delta u})$, where Δu refers to the sensitivity of u.*

In practice, there are two rules for exploiting these mechanisms sequentially or respectively.

Theorem 3 (Composition Theorem [14]). *Let $\mathcal{M}_1$, $\mathcal{M}_2$, $\mathcal{M}_3$, ..., $\mathcal{M}_n$ be a series of mechanisms, where $\mathcal{M}_i$ provides ϵ_i-differential privacy. The $\mathcal{M}$ is said to satisfy $(\sum_{i=1}^n \epsilon_i)$-differential privacy, if it executes $\mathcal{M}_1(D), \mathcal{M}_2(D), \mathcal{M}_3(D)...,$ $\mathcal{M}_n(D)$ with randomness independently and outputs a vector of these mechanisms.*

Theorem 4 (Parallel Theorem [14]). *If db_i is one of disjoint subsets of original dataset D, and $\mathcal{M}_i$ is a set of mechanism which provides ϵ_i-differential privacy, applying on db_i. Then the overall $\mathcal{M}_i$ assures $max(\epsilon_i)$-differential privacy for D.*

3   Problem Model and Proposed Method

3.1   Model Description

Publish Model. The publish model considered here is a two-way interactive model. One of the interacting parties is users or any third-parties, malicious or not, who query on the sanitized geospatial synopses; the other is the published sanitized synopses provider. Some trusty location data collectors can be the provider, e.g. *Cellular Service Provider* (*CSP*). Every user of mobile phone has ratified an accord that allows *CSP* to access their locations. As a consequence, *CSP*s are capable to integrate the coordinates from various moving objects and publish the processed synopses. The query type discussed in this paper is the count of moving object in any area of any size.

Data Model. The type of dataset we consider is the coordinate data of moving objects collected periodically. The original collected dataset exploits user identification as data collecting unit, without consistent counting structure. By mapping user location into relevant subdomain, attributes of the transferred dataset D_i are a set of non-overlapped subdomains over the whole region; every tuple records the location of an user at time i. The released geospatial synopses are the count of each subdomain.

However, the releases will bring potential privacy threaten, if they are not handled carefully. Through the continuously observation of synopses and relevant background knowledge, adversaries can guess a certain user's trace with high probability. This attack mode is *time correlation attack* (*TCA*).

In Fig. 1, we give a concrete example, in which user u is the target. Suppose that points can only move among adjacent grids. The synopsis is collected from 11 p.m to 12 p.m, which indicates that most of people have already slept and few users hang around. Attacker *Alice* has known that u is in the region c_{31} at time i. From time i to $i+1$, only the neighboring grids c_{22} and c_{31} have changed, and the trajectory of u is $c_{31} \rightarrow c_{22}$. In time interval $[i-1, i]$, one user leaves from c_{11} and c_{21}; one enters to c_{12} and c_{31} respectively. Based on the movement rules, user u only can be in grid c_{21} at $i-1$. Therefore, *Alice* infers that the trace of u is $c_{21} \rightarrow c_{31} \rightarrow c_{22}$ with certainty.

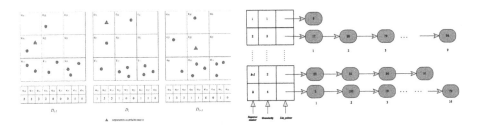

Fig. 1. *TCA*   **Fig. 2.** *k-memo*

Privacy Model. Motivated by the privacy threaten mentioned above, we synthesize sliding window strategy [12] with adaptive domain partition [16] to defend against *TCAs*. Here are some relevant concepts which need to be redeclared on streams.

Definition 4 (stream prefix). *Let stream F be a series of sequential geospatial datasets* $F = (D_1, D_2, D_3, ...)$ *and* $F[i] = D_i$. *The stream prefix at time t is* $F_t = (D_1, D_2, ..., D_t)$.

In analogy to the *neighboring datasets* for static datasets, the similar concept over streams is defined below.

Definition 5 (ω-neighboring [12]). *Two prefixes F_t and F_t' are said to be ω-neighboring, if one of these conditions is satisfied: (1) there is only one timestamp $i \leq t$, $F_t[i] \neq F_t'[i]$ or (2) there are two timestamps i, i', with $i < i'$ and $i' - i + 1 \leq \omega$, $F_t[i] \neq F_t'[i]$ and $F_t[i'] \neq F_t'[i']$.*

The definition of differential privacy based on ω-neighboring merges the privacy gap between *user-level* [9] (hiding any single user over finite streams) and *event-level* [3,4,12] (hiding any single event over infinite streams).

Definition 6 ((ω, ϵ)-differential privacy [12]). *A randomized mechanism $\mathcal{A}$ takes a stream prefix as input, and can be decomposed into sub-mechanisms $\mathcal{A}_1, ..., \mathcal{A}_m$, with each $\mathcal{A}_i$ providing independent ϵ_i-differential privacy. The $\mathcal{O}$ is defined as the set of all possible outputs of $\mathcal{A}$, such that $\mathcal{A}_i(F_t[i]) = o_i$ and $o_i \in \mathcal{O}$. $\mathcal{A}$ is said to satisfy (ω, ϵ)-differential privacy, if for arbitrary t and ω-neighboring stream prefix F_t, F_t', formula $Pr[\mathcal{A}(F_t) \in \mathcal{O}] \leq e^\epsilon Pr[\mathcal{A}(F_t') \in \mathcal{O}]$ is held, with $\forall t, \sum_{i=t-\omega+1}^{t} \epsilon_i \leq \epsilon$.*

Main Idea. The granularity of 1_{st}-level partition is calculated by $\sqrt{\frac{N\epsilon}{c}}$, where N is initialized total count of moving objects. It is fixed during subsequent processing. Then the 1_{st}-level grid is split into 2_{nd}-level with the same formula, and keeps a *k-memo*, as shown in Fig. 2, to save previous results.

According to Theorem 4, the privacy budget is independent among grids of the same level. ϵ is total budget that every 1_{st}-level grid has over stream, and is split into two parts. One is for 1_{st}-level counts, denoted as ϵ', uniformly distributed inside the ω-sliding window; the other ϵ^*, is for the count of 2_{nd}-level grids.

ϵ^* is also divided into two sections with ratio $\frac{1}{4}$. The first uniformly allocated in window is used to protect *dissimilarity estimation*. The second part $\frac{3\epsilon_*}{4}$ works for disturbing the 2_{nd}-level count with the distribution strategy *BD* [12].

Figure 3 shows a snapshot of the process of *RGP*. The size of sliding window ω and *k-memo* is set to 5 and 3 respectively; the total budget for the 2_{nd}-level count is $E = \frac{3\epsilon_*}{4}$. The table above shows the consumption of privacy budget over time. When $t = 5$, the *k-memo* of grid *ld*, shown in blue, has already recorded 2 different versions of synopses. The count of *ld* decreases obviously, resulting in a new partition. *RGP* uses half of remaining budget ($\frac{(E - \frac{E}{4})}{2} = \frac{3E}{8}$) to protect

ld's count privacy, and inserts it to k-$memo$. At time $t = 7$, based on the result of *dissimilarity estimation*, k-$memo[2]$ can be the substitute without consuming budget. Next, the distribution of points inside ld is totally different and cannot be replaced, but the k-$memo$ is full. Therefore, RGP removes the oldest record and insert the new version.

3.2   Algorithm

Initialization for Geospatial Data. This algorithm mainly works for setting parameters and fixing the basic 1_{st}-level grid structure. Line 1–3 is parameter initialization. E_0 will be explained in detail in the next algorithm. The calculation of the granularity of 1_{st}-level m_1 (line 4) uses all the possible budget can be used to assure the accuracy of structure and lower down the uniform error, including budget $\epsilon^\#$ for 1_{st}-level count, half of residue $\frac{3\epsilon^*}{8}$ for 2_{nd}-level count and $\frac{\epsilon^*}{4\omega}$ for protecting dissimilarity.

Algorithm 1. Initialization

Require: D_0, ϵ
Ensure: $Publish_i$.
1: $c_1 = 10$, $\epsilon' = \frac{\epsilon}{4}$
2: $\epsilon^* = 1 - \epsilon'$
3: $\epsilon^\# = \frac{\epsilon'}{\omega}$, $\epsilon_0 = \epsilon^\# + (\frac{3}{8} + \frac{1}{4\omega})\epsilon^*$
4: $m_1 = max(10, \frac{1}{4}\sqrt{\frac{|D_0|\epsilon_0}{c_1}})$
5: $E_0[1...m_1^2] = \frac{3\epsilon^*}{4}$
6: Partition the region into $m_1 \times m_1$, recorded in $Grid\_1$
7: $Publish_0 = RGP(D_0, Grid\_1, kmemo, m_1, E_0)$

Real-time releasing. Algorithm 2 shows the process of RGP. It publishes every 1_{st}-level grid independently. $E_i[t]$ (line 2) records the available privacy budget for 2_{nd}-*level count calculation* of 1_{st}-level grid t at time i, called *budget residue*. The renewed granularity $temp$ (line 4) is grounded on the newest noisy count N' calculated from actual point number in t with fixed budget $\epsilon^\#$ (line 3). Then, if the number of POI in grid t has non-neglectable change (line 5), leading to a new granularity which cannot be found in k different publishes before, RGP exploits UA (line 6) to update the structure inside t and recompute the 2_{nd}-level. Otherwise, k-$memo$ is valid (line 13–30). For every 1_{st}-level grid, the average dissimilarity between actual $count_i^t$ and versions having the same 2_{nd}-level division recorded in k-$memo$ is calculated by *mean absolute error* (MAE) (line 16). $Kmemo_t[h].syn$ shows the noisy counts of 2_{nd}-level, and $Kmemo_t[h].gra$ is the corresponding granularity.

Algorithm 2. Real-time Geospatial Partition (RGP)

Require: D_i, $region$, $Kmemo$, m_1, E_i
Ensure: E_{i+1}, $Kmemo$, $Publish_i$.

    /*$Basic module$*/
1: **for** $t = 1$ to m_1^2 **do**
2:    $\lambda' = \frac{1}{\frac{E_i[t]}{2} + \frac{\epsilon^*}{4\omega}}$
3:    $N' = $ the count of grid t with noise $Lap(\frac{1}{\epsilon\#})$
    /*$Submodule$*/
4:    $temp = \sqrt{\frac{N'\frac{1}{\lambda'}}{\sqrt{2}}}$
    /*$Futile\ k\text{-}memo$*/
5:    **if** ($\nexists h \in [1, k]$, s.t. $temp = Kmemo_t[h].gra$) **then**
6:       $Publish_i[t] = UA\ (N', \frac{1}{\lambda'}, region[t], D_i)$
7:       $E_{i+1}[t] = \frac{E_i[t]}{2} + Expire_{i-\omega+1}[t]$
8:       **if** $Kmemo_t$ is full **then**
9:          Delete the record having the oldest timestamps.
10:      **end if**
11:      Insert $Publish_i[t]$ into $Kmemo_t$
    /*$Valid\ k\text{-}memo$*/
12:    **else**
13:      $\lambda = \frac{2}{E_i[t]}$
14:      Calculate the real number of point $count_i^t$ in grid t with granularity $temp$
15:      **for** (all $h \in [1, k]$, s.t. $temp = Kmemo_t[h].gra$) **do**
16:        $var = \{\frac{1}{temp^2} \sum_{j=1}^{temp^2} |Kmemo_t[h].syn[j] - count_i^t[j]|\}$
17:        Choose the var by $EM(-var\frac{\epsilon^* temp^2}{32\omega})$, and memorize h
18:        $dis = var + Lap(\frac{16\omega}{3\epsilon^* temp^2})$
19:      **end for**
20:      **if** $dis > (\lambda + \frac{16\omega}{3\epsilon^* temp^2})$ **then**
21:        $Publish_i[t] = count_i^t + Lap(\lambda)$
22:        $E_{i+1}[t] = \frac{E_i[t]}{2} + Expire_{i-\omega+1}[t]$
23:        **if** $Kmemo[t]$ is full **then**
24:           Delete the record with the oldest timestamps.
25:        **end if**
26:        Insert $Publish_i[t]$ into $Kmemo[t]$
27:      **else**
28:        $Publish_i[t] = Kmemo_t[h].syn$
29:        $E_{i+1}[t] = E_i[t] + Expire_{i-\omega+1}[t]$
30:      **end if**
31:    **end if**
32: **end for**

RGP uses MAE as a score function for EM to choose substitute for current synopsis (line 17) with a quarter of the budget; the rest is for Laplace Mechanism to protect the chosen var (line 18). Relying on Definitions 1 and 3, it is easy to infer that the sensitivity of count query $count_i^t$ is $\Delta count_i^t = 1$. In that case, the sensitivity of MAE is $\Delta var = \frac{1}{temp^2}$.

Next, if the variation of point distribution in grid t is so obvious (line 20) that the accuracy of the estimation by a previous publish is worse than generating new version with noise, RGP releases a new one (line 21). In the two situations mentioned above, there is a new release needed to be saved in k-memo (line 11, 26). If the size of k-memo is larger than k, it discards the oldest version in k-memo (line 8–10, 23–25). The $budget\ residue$ for next timestamp is the sum of current remain and the budget $Expire_{i-w+1}[t]$ used at $i - w + 1$ which will be outside of w-windows (line 7, 22). When the estimation in k-memo is acceptable, RGP replaces the current one (line 28), so as to save the budget (line 29). As there is no new version generated, the k-memo remains.

Uniform Partition. Algorithm 3 generates the new partition for 1_{st}-level grids. The value of parameter c_2 is optimized, which has been proved in [17].

Algorithm 3. The UA Partition

Require: N, ϵ, region, D_i
Ensure: $Publish_i$.
1: $c_2 = \sqrt{2}$
2: $m_2 = \sqrt{\frac{N\epsilon}{c_2}}$
3: Partition the region into $m_2 \times m_2$
4: **for** $t = 1$ to m_2^2 **do**
5:    $Grid\_2_i[t]$ record the region of grid t
6:    $Num\_2_i[t]$ record the count of points in grid t
7:    $Publish_i[t] = Num2\_i[t] + Lap(\frac{1}{\epsilon})$
8: **end for**

3.3 Utility Analysis

The error of RGP comes from three parts — $uniform\ error$ due to the partition, $noise\ error$ and $replacement\ error$ which is from k-memo. $Uniform\ error$ and $noise\ error$ are treated as an integral to be analyzed. Assume that the region is partitioned into $b \times b$ grids, and the query covers r portion of the whole area. Apparently, the uniform error is coming from the grids intersected with query edge, which is $\sqrt{r}b$; the noise error is proportional to the number of grids the query contains which is $\frac{\sqrt{2r}b}{\epsilon}$. Total error for a query is $\sqrt{r}b + \frac{\sqrt{2r}b}{\epsilon}$. When $b = \sqrt{\frac{n\epsilon}{\sqrt{2}}}$, the sum is minimized, where $\sqrt{2}$ can be replaced by other constants to accommodate different datasets. The more detailed proof can be seen in [16].

The distribution strategy is the source of $replacement\ error$. When $k = 1$, the $replacement\ error$ per timestamp is $4\frac{2^m-1}{m\epsilon} + \frac{16w}{3\epsilon^* temp^2}$, if m new publications occur in a window [12]. With the increase of the size of k-memo, m decreases, as well as the $replacement\ error$, for there is more chance to find a appropriate substitute in k-memo. The lower bound is $\frac{4}{\epsilon} + \frac{16w}{3\epsilon^* temp^2}$. In Fig. 4, we show the limitation of RGP, by randomly selecting several timestamps to set the used budget to zero imitating replacement. λ fluctuating with time, reflects the usage of budget at every timestamp; more importantly, it leads to the non-stable quality of chosen substitute.

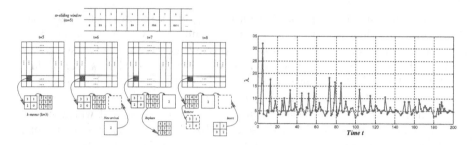

Fig. 3. A snapshot of RGP **Fig. 4.** The change of λ ($\omega = 10$)

3.4 Privacy Analysis

The process of RGP is on two levels, 1_{st}-level as *Basicmodule* and 2_{nd}-level as *Submodule*. Depending on privacy budget distribution, RGP in *Submodule* can be split into *dissimilarity estimation* and 2_{nd}-level count calculation; it can also be divided into *futile k-memo* and *valid k-memo*. We prove that *valid k-memo* satisfies (ω, ϵ^*)-differential privacy at first.

Lemma 1. *2_{nd}-level count calculation satisfies $(\omega\text{-}\frac{3\epsilon^*}{4})$-differential privacy.*

Proof. According to the Algorithm 1, $\frac{3\epsilon^*}{4}$ is total privacy budget over ω-window on 2_{nd}-level count calculation, for which half of the *privacy residue* $E_i[t]$ within window until current timestamp i is allowed to be used.

Therefore, no matter what the timestamp is, the budget consumption in window is no more than $\frac{3\epsilon^*}{4}$, written as $\sum_{j=i-\omega+1}^{i} \epsilon_j \leqslant \frac{3\epsilon^*}{4}$. Based on Definition 6, we have the conclusion that 2_{nd}-level count calculation satisfies $(\omega\text{-}\frac{3\epsilon^*}{4})$-differential privacy.

Lemma 2. *dissimilarity estimation satisfies $(\omega\text{-}\frac{\epsilon^*}{4})$-differential privacy.*

Proof. When current granularity of 1_{st}-level grid t can be found in *k-memo*, $-var\frac{\epsilon^* temp^2}{32\omega}$ is taken as an argument for EM to choose estimation result privately. Since the sensitivity of MAE is $\Delta var = \frac{1}{temp^2}$, according to Definition 3, substitute selection is ϵ_1^*-differentially private at one timestamp, where $\epsilon_1^* = -\frac{2(\Delta var)\epsilon^* temp^2}{32\omega} = \frac{\epsilon^*}{16\omega}$. The noise abstract from Laplace distribution for dissimilarity protecting follows the scale of $\lambda_{dis} = \frac{16\omega}{3\epsilon^* temp^2}$, so the dissimilarity protection holds ϵ_2^*-differential privacy, where $\epsilon_2^* = \frac{\Delta var}{\lambda_{dis}} = \frac{3\epsilon^*}{16\omega}$. In terms of Theorem 3 and Definition 6, *dissimilarity estimation* meets the requirement of $(\omega\text{-}\frac{\epsilon^*}{4})$-differential privacy.

Theorem 5. *vaild k-memo satisfies $(\omega\text{-}\epsilon^*)$-differential privacy.*

Proof. From Lemmas 1 and 2, we deduce that $(\omega\text{-}\epsilon^*)$-differential privacy is hold for *vaild k-memo*.

Theorem 6. *Submodule satisfies $(\omega\text{-}\epsilon^*)$-differential privacy.*

Proof. In *futile k-memo*, the granularity is new to *k-memo*, but the budget usage is similar to *valid k-memo* with replacement. Additionally, these two parts are non-overlapped over stream. In that case, *Submodule* integrating *futile k-memo* with *valid k-memo* satisfies $(\omega$-$\epsilon^*)$-differential privacy.

Theorem 7. *RGP satisfies $(\omega$-$\epsilon)$-differential privacy.*

Proof. For grid t, the newest noisy count N' is necessary at every timestamp for which the budget $\epsilon^\# = \frac{\epsilon'}{\omega}$ is needed, to make a judgement for internal structure. The process on 1_{st}-level *Basicmodule* is $(\omega$-$\sum_{j=i-\omega+1}^{i} \epsilon^\#)$-differentially private. With Theorems 3 and 6, *RGP* satisfies $(\omega$-$\epsilon)$-differential privacy for whole geographical region, where $\epsilon = \epsilon^* + \epsilon'$.

3.5 Efficiency Analysis

The efficiency of *RGP* is analyzed from two aspects, time complexity and space complexity.

Time Complexity. *RGP* only scan the data twice to form the final sanitized synopsis. The first scan is for determining the structure inside every 1_{st}-level grid; the second is to compute the private count of the 2_{nd}-level grid. In that case, the time consumption of *RGP* is proportional to the number of moving objects N, denoted as $O(N)$.

Space Complexity. The space occupation of 1_{st}-level is related to the number of grids which is computed by $\frac{N\epsilon_1}{16c_1}$. ϵ_1 represents the privacy budget used in 1_{st}-level partition. Every 1_{st}-level grid needs extra memory to store *k-memo*. Assuming the average size of the version recorded in *k-memo* is s. The average count of 1_{st}-level grid is $\frac{16c_1}{\epsilon_1}$. According to the same dividing formula, we figure out $s = \frac{16c_1\epsilon_2}{c_2\epsilon_1}$. In that case, the total space consumption from the structure *k-memo* is $\frac{kN\epsilon_2}{c_2}$. The space complexity of *RGP* is $O(N)$.

4 Performance Evaluation

4.1 Experiment Settings

Two datasets we used here for experiments are T-drive and Rome. T-drive (*T-BJ*) records the *GPS* trajectories of almost 10 thousand taxies in Beijing [19] over a week within the range of $(39.6°N, 116.1°E)$ and $(40.1°N, 116.612°E)$. The trajectory dataset of Rome (*T-R*) [1] contains about 3 hundred taxies in the bounding box $(41.6°N, 12.1°E)$ and $(42.1°N, 12.6°E)$. We reorder these trajectories by time and set the sampling interval to $10\,min$. In order to make comprehensive contrast with fixed structure, the control groups used here are of three different division granularity $d_1 = 0.005°$, $d_1 = 0.01°$ and $d_3 = 0.05°$ with the same strategy of distribution BD. The query are of 4 different sizes, $q_1 = 0.005° \times 0.01°$, $q_2 = 0.01° \times 0.02°$, $q_3 = 0.02° \times 0.04°$ and $q_4 = 0.04° \times 0.08°$. For each size, we randomly choose query location and test 200 times. The experimental result is measured by Mean Relative Error (*MRE*) of different query sizes.

4.2 Experiment Result

Effect of *k-memo*. The total privacy ϵ is set to 1 in this experiment. As shown in Fig. 5, the relative error is decreasing with the incremental size of *k-memo* as a whole; when k has covered the period of data, the query error would be stable. There is a drop-off in the range $[0, 20]$, which means for most 1_{st}-level grids, the irreplaceable 2_{nd}-level count is more than 20. In Fig. 5(a) and (b), we see that *MRE* approximately stable when k reaches 110 and 140 respectively for *T-BJ* and *T-R*, inferring that the period of location records in datasets are possibly 18 hours and 23 hours which conforms to people daily routine.

Performance Comparison. The performance of fixed uniform shows various trends with the granularity. Under fine partition, the total error goes up following the incremental query size, shown by blue and green lines in Fig. 6; yet goes down under coarse partition, like red lines. We believe that with the increased query size, the main error for answer is changed from uniform error to noise error, because the ratio between area and perimeter is increased as query range enlarges, lowering the uniform error percentage. For the large size, more grids are contained on refined resolution than on coarse one, causing that more noise is added declining the utility. On the contrary, noise is limited for the small size due to only few covered grids, but uniform error is much larger on coarse-grained domain. These two reason lead to the trend in Fig. 6. On the whole, the *MRE* of *RGP* remains low and outperforms fixed structure methods, no matter what granularity the partition is.

From the two performance analysis and comparison, we conclude that *RGP* outperforms methods with the fixed partition without *k-memo* over streams.

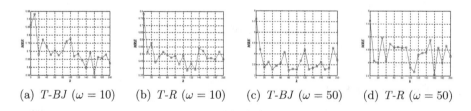

(a) *T-BJ* ($\omega = 10$)   (b) *T-R* ($\omega = 10$)   (c) *T-BJ* ($\omega = 50$)   (d) *T-R* ($\omega = 50$)

Fig. 5. *MRE* vs k.

5 Related Work

Numerous work study releasing static geospatial data with region partition to improve publish utility without privacy compromise. Most of them used *differential privacy* [6] as theoretical support and corresponding mechanisms [7,8,11,13] to balance the utility and privacy. Cormode used non-uniform noise with post-processing [5] to generate spatial decomposition satisfying privacy requirement.

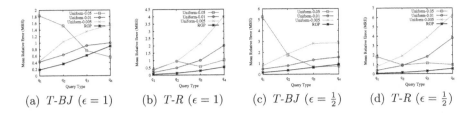

(a) $T\text{-}BJ$ ($\epsilon = 1$)   (b) $T\text{-}R$ ($\epsilon = 1$)   (c) $T\text{-}BJ$ ($\epsilon = \frac{1}{2}$)   (d) $T\text{-}R$ ($\epsilon = \frac{1}{2}$)

Fig. 6. Performance Comparison.

Qardaji proposed an adaptive uniform partition on space [16] to improve the accuracy of query aiming at static geospatial dataset.

Some researchers work on differentially private releasing over infinite streams (*event-level* privacy) [3,4,12] and finite streams [9](*user-level* privacy). Fan [10] proposed a filtering and sampling-based method *FAST* for real-time publish. Kellaris [12] proposed *ω-event privacy*, to merge the gap between these two levels over streams. Further, Andrés proposed a generalized differential privacy, *geo-indistinguishablity* [2], for location based systems. Xiao optimized the sensitivity set of differential privacy [18] to deal with the temporal correlations.

6   Conclusion

In this paper, we propose an approach *RGP* with new structure *k-memo* for geospatial streams release. This approach avoids individual privacy breach on real-time geospatial data under the *time correlation attack*. Meanwhile, *RGP* makes these synopses available on user-interaction model with improved accuracy for count query, which is favourable for various practical scenarios. In theoretical aspect, we prove privacy property of *RGP*, and illustrate its improvement of utility. Also, from a practical standpoint, we study the effectiveness of *RGP* with *k-memo* and show its significant error reduction achieved by *RGP* through experimental comparison with existing methods on real stream datasets. For the future work, we will investigate more sophisticated schemes to allocate privacy budget more appropriately over stream and try to answer broader types of query privately without much utility loss.

References

1. Amici, R., Bonola, M., Bracciale, L., Rabuffi, A., Loreti, P., Bianchi, G.: Performance assessment of an epidemic protocol in vanet using real traces. Procedia Comput. Sci. **40**, 92–99 (2014)
2. Andrés, M.E., Bordenabe, N.E., Chatzikokolakis, K., Palamidessi, C.: Geo-indistinguishability: Differential privacy for location-based systems. In: Proceedings of the 2013 ACM SIGSAC Conference on Computer & Communications Security, pp. 901–914. ACM (2013)

3. Bolot, J., Fawaz, N., Muthukrishnan, S., Nikolov, A., Taft, N.: Private decayed predicate sums on streams. In: ICDT, pp. 284–295. ACM (2013)
4. Chan, T.-H.H., Li, M., Shi, E., Xu, W.: Differentially private continual monitoring of heavy hitters from distributed streams. In: Fischer-Hübner, S., Wright, M. (eds.) PETS 2012. LNCS, vol. 7384, pp. 140–159. Springer, Heidelberg (2012). doi:10.1007/978-3-642-31680-7_8
5. Cormode, G., Procopiuc, C., Srivastava, D., Shen, E., Yu, T.: Differentially private spatial decompositions. In: ICDE, pp. 20–31. IEEE (2012)
6. Dwork, C.: Differential privacy. In: Bugliesi, M., Preneel, B., Sassone, V., Wegener, I. (eds.) ICALP 2006. LNCS, vol. 4052, pp. 1–12. Springer, Heidelberg (2006). doi:10.1007/11787006_1
7. Dwork, C.: A firm foundation for private data analysis. Commun. ACM **54**(1), 86–95 (2011)
8. Dwork, C., McSherry, F., Nissim, K., Smith, A.: Calibrating noise to sensitivity in private data analysis. In: Halevi, S., Rabin, T. (eds.) TCC 2006. LNCS, vol. 3876, pp. 265–284. Springer, Heidelberg (2006). doi:10.1007/11681878_14
9. Fan, L., Xiong, L.: Real-time aggregate monitoring with differential privacy. In: CIKM, pp. 2169–2173. ACM (2012)
10. Fan, L., Xiong, L., Sunderam, V.: Fast: differentially private real-time aggregate monitor with filtering and adaptive sampling. In: SIGMOD, pp. 1065–1068. ACM (2013)
11. Inan, A., Kantarcioglu, M., Ghinita, G., Bertino, E.: Private record matching using differential privacy. In: EDBT, pp. 123–134. ACM (2010)
12. Kellaris, G., Papadopoulos, S., Xiao, X., Papadias, D.: Differentially private event sequences over infinite streams. VLDB **7**(12), 1155–1166 (2014)
13. McSherry, F., Talwar, K.: Mechanism design via differential privacy. In: FOCS, pp. 94–103. IEEE (2007)
14. McSherry, F.D.: Privacy integrated queries: an extensible platform for privacy-preserving data analysis. In: SIGMOD, pp. 19–30. ACM (2009)
15. de Montjoye, Y.A., Hidalgo, C.A., Verleysen, M., Blondel, V.D.: Unique in the crowd: the privacy bounds of human mobility. Scientific reports 3 (2013)
16. Qardaji, W., Yang, W., Li, N.: Differentially private grids for geospatial data. In: ICDE, pp. 757–768. IEEE (2013)
17. To, H., Ghinita, G., Shahabi, C.: A framework for protecting worker location privacy in spatial crowdsourcing. VLDB **7**(10), 919–930 (2014)
18. Xiao, Y., Xiong, L.: Protecting locations with differential privacy under temporal correlations. In: Proceedings of the 22nd ACM SIGSAC Conference on Computer and Communications Security, pp. 1298–1309. ACM (2015)
19. Yuan, J., Zheng, Y., Zhang, C., Xie, W., Xie, X., Sun, G., Huang, Y.: T-drive: driving directions based on taxi trajectories. In: SIGSPATIAL, pp. 99–108. ACM (2010)

A More Flexible SDN Architecture Supporting Distributed Applications

Wen Wang[1], Cong Liu[2(✉)], and Jun Wang[2]

[1] National University of Defense Technology, Changsha, China
[2] PLA Logistic Information Center, Beijing, China
congliu2005@163.com

Abstract. Software Defined Networking (SDN) abstracts network control logic from switches to a logically centralized controller with software implemented applications. Unfortunately, not all the applications fit the centralized control architecture, and the centralization may even degrade the performance of these applications. Moreover, even though SDN articulates a vision for programmable networks, the OpenFlow instructions with simple match-action fields restrict the flexibility of switches, and the programmability of switches has rarely been actually touched. To strike a balance between programmability and pragmatism of SDN, we propose a more flexible and powerful SDN control architecture to support distributed applications besides simple OpenFlow instructions. The distributed applications run independently in switches, and the controller is responsible for the installation and configuration of these applications. The evaluation shows the proposed architecture is able to access more local details efficiently with the centralized SDN control.

Keywords: SDN · Distributed applications

1 Introduction

Software Defined Networking (SDN) has attracted a lot of attentions in recent years with the separation of network functions, moving network control logic from switches to software applications on the controller, which results in increasing flexibility. Unfortunately, flexibility and efficiency rarely go hand in hand, as there is always a trade-off between programmability and performance. Even though switches do not need to implement protocol details, the centralized control logic may be a critical performance bottleneck. A lot of applications compete for computation and storage resources of the control plane. Moreover, applications communicate remotely with switches through control messages to manipulate flow tables, which adds to the communication overhead between the control plane and data plane. To relieve the bottleneck, a logically centralized control plane with multiple distributed controllers has been proposed, however, because of the management complexity among multiple control nodes, the scalability of SDN is still restricted.

© ICST Institute for Computer Sciences, Social Informatics and Telecommunications Engineering 2017
S. Wang and A. Zhou (Eds.): CollaborateCom 2016, LNICST 201, pp. 165–174, 2017.
DOI: 10.1007/978-3-319-59288-6_15

While network functions in SDN have been abstracted to the centralized controller, a lot of network functions require to access distributed information from switches in real time, e.g., network monitoring, intrusion detection. Therefore, the centralized node has to collect distributed information from switches frequently. Considering the transmission overhead and limited storage space on the centralized node, fine-grained distributed information collection is prohibitive. Only coarse-grained sampling is acceptable, which usually results in relatively · low accuracy.

In order to make SDN more flexible and effective, a huge number of extensions to OpenFlow have been proposed in recent years, however, the OpenFlow control messages are still limited to simple match-action instructions. The match-action instructions oversimplify the flow tables in switches, as the action field is simply forwarding, dropping or modifying packets. However, supporting a wide range of network services would require much more sophisticated functions to analyze and manipulate traffic, e.g., deep packet inspection (DPI), compression and encryption [7]. Therefore, there is no means to deploy complicated services on switches with the simple match-action instructions, so that the flexibility of SDN is still limited. Meanwhile, these simple actions underutilize the switches hardware potentiality, which equip with powerful hardware, e.g., memory, processor, and storage. Even though SDN claims a programmable network with easily deployed applications and configurable flow tables, the programmability of switches has rarely been touched actually.

To make switches more powerful to utilize the underlying hardware while maintaining the flexibility of SDN, switches should support more complicated actions besides current simple OpenFlow actions. In this paper, we extend switches in SDN to support distributed applications, so that switches are able to provide more complicated functions. The controller installs and configures these distributed applications in switches with extended application control messages. Thus, a part of previously tightly centralized control logic is released to switches. We present two types of distributed applications based on their implementations in this paper: administrator-developed applications which are executable programs developed by the administrators, and module-constructed applications which are constructed with Click [9] elements and run as lightweight VMs. The evaluation shows that distributed applications could access more local details than centralized approaches with a little overhead, and the controller is able to manage these applications efficiently.

The rest of the paper is organized as follows. Section 2 looks at the related work. Section 3 proposes the architecture supporting distributed applications. Section 4 describes implementation details, and Sect. 5 evaluates the basic performance of the architecture. Finally, Sect. 6 concludes the paper.

2   Related Work

A lot of existing researches have been aware of the insufficiency of current SDN to support complicated actions. [3,7] note that current SDN produces insufficient abstractions with simple instructions to cover a wide range of sophisticated networking services. [5,6] indicate that the programmability and flexibility of SDN should be extended to the data plane to allow network owners to add their custom network functions. Therefore, a lot of efforts have been made to create programmable network infrastructures. [3] uses the Click modular router language to orchestrate Linux networking tools. NetOpen [8] supports configurable networking with programmable networking switch nodes. [4,13] suggest switches should support flexible mechanisms for parsing packets and matching header fields with protocol-independent packet processors. [11] proposes an extended application-aware SDN architecture with stateful actions in switches to use L4-L7 information. [12] extends SDN to control the scheduling and queueing behavior of a switch by adding a small FPGA in switches. However, these approaches either require extra modifications in switches or are little controlled by the control plane, which lose the flexibility and manageability of SDN.

3   A Switch Supporting Distributed Applications

3.1   SDN Architecture Supporting Distributed Applications

The complexity and overhead of implementing and executing all these software applications in the centralized controller motivate it to release parts of control logic to switches, especially for the applications which need to access distributed information frequently. Therefore, these software applications should be distributed into multiple locations for advanced performance, while being managed by a logically centralized controller.

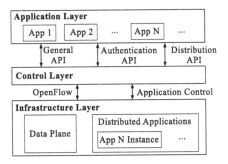

Fig. 1. System architecture

To support these distributed applications, the infrastructure layer not only acts as a data plane, but also runs instances of distributed applications in switches. These distributed instances could be programs transferred and installed by the controller, and run in switches with local fine-grained information. A distributed application instance is able to execute independently and usually does not need to communicate with instances in other switches, but may require to contact with the controller when necessary. Hence, in spite of OpenFlow to manipulate flow tables in switches, extended application control messages are used between the control layer and the infrastructure layer to install, configure and communicate with distributed application instances in switches as Fig. 1 shows. These messages enable distribution applications to be dynamically programmed in network infrastructures so as to enhance the scalability and flexibility of SDN. Therefore, administrators are able to develop their own distributed applications and then dynamically install them in switches.

Even though there is no standard northbound API currently, we consider that SDN deploys centralized applications on the controller with general APIs, and we only focus on the distributed applications in this paper. The distributed applications need to define the distribution features such as concerned flows, executable programs, initial parameters with a distribution API, which is unnecessary for centralized applications. With distributed instances running in switches, more switch details are exposed to these distributed applications. However, as applications are able to manipulate flow tables in switches to control network behaviors, poorly implemented, misconfigured or malicious applications may modify flow tables deliberately. Therefore, the controller has to ensure the legitimacy of distributed applications to prevent abnormal activities. Unfortunately, the absence of the northbound API fails to limit the access authorities granted to applications. Thus, an authentication API is added to verify the access permissions of distributed applications between the application layer and control layer. To ensure the legitimacy of distributed applications, the controller has a white list record of legal distributed applications. Distributed application control requests should be issued by authenticated applications, otherwise, requests to manipulate distributed applications in switches will be rejected by the controller.

3.2 Distributed Applications in SDN Switches

A lot of SDN applications running in the controller require to communicate with switches frequently for fine-grained information collection or data plane control. These applications obviously need to deal with distributed information in distributed architectures, e.g., network monitoring, intrusion detection, while the current SDN manages all the applications as centralized. To distinguish distributed applications from centralized ones, we define the criteria of a distributed application which is appropriate to be deployed distributedly in switches:

- Access local fine-grained information such as traffic statistics or packet payload frequently, and do not need to wait for other remote data or control messages.
- There are few control message exchanges with the controller. The controller just needs to set up the distributed application in switches at the beginning, and then a switch is able to execute the distributed instance independently.
- Require configurations or updates occasionally, so that the controller manages a distributed instance with extended application control messages instead of proprietary application implementations on switches.

– Execute complicated functions instead of simple OpenFlow actions, and the complicated functions could be triggered by sophisticated conditions other than the simple match field of the flow table.

Due to the remote installation and configuration, distributed applications should be carefully designed to ensure the correctness and effectiveness during execution. Considering the construction and implementation of applications, in this paper, we present two types of distributed applications: administrator-developed applications and module-constructed applications.

Administrator-Developed Applications. These applications are executable programs developed by the administrators and then deployed in switches with control messages. For the application management, the controller transfers the executable programs to the switch with control messages and installs a corresponding entry for each application in the application table. The executable programs are recorded in the disk of the switch, so that distributed applications will not be lost when switches reboot. Application table records the application entries and related programs. When packets matching the application entry arrive, the corresponding programs are executed in the execution engine. The execution engine uses memory and processor of the host switch, so that the hardware is highly utilized with various distributed applications. When an application is being executed, it may need to access information in the flow table or capture packet payload, e.g., DPI. Therefore, we also design interfaces between the execution engine and flow tables.

Module-Constructed Applications. These applications are running in ClickOS [10] VMs assembled with modules in switches. ClickOS is a Xen-based tiny virtual machine that runs Click [9], and it can be quickly instantiated in 30 ms with a compressed 5 MB image. As Click equips with over 300 stock elements, which make it possible to construct applications with minimal efforts. Therefore, module-constructed applications could be assembled with these elements in virtual machines to be ClickOS VMs. Moreover, we can easily extend this framework and develop new elements with the administrators-developed to support more applications. To set up a module-constructed application in ClickOS VM, the controller dispatches a Click configuration to related switches, which is essentially a text file specifying elements. Once receiving the configuration file, the switch instantiates a VM for the application based on the defined configuration. As applications are isolated into multiple fast booted VMs, they do not interfere with each other during processing.

As distributed applications run locally in switches, these applications are able to execute in real time with detailed local data, which is impossible for the centralized controller to perform such fine-grained controls. As the application table is separated from the flow table, it does not affect the flow table lookup efficiency. Moreover, the distributed applications are restricted with isolated hardware resource (e.g., CPU, memory) for the both types of applications, so that the extended lightweight functions do not affect the basic packet processing of the data plane, which means the extended programmability does not decrease the packet processing efficiency.

4   Implementation

In this section, we design and implement control messages and execution engines for the two types of distributed applications with Open vSwitch [1].

4.1   Distributed Application Control

We implement two kinds of control messages for distributed applications to communicate between the controller and switches APP_MOD and APP_REP. APP_MOD is used to set up or update distributed application in switches. For the administrator-developed applications, despite the distributed programs, the control message also transfers the initial parameters for the programs together. For the module-constructed application, the controller sends the Click configuration to a switch, so that the configuration is used to instantiate a ClickOS VM. When an application instance becomes expired or loses effectiveness, the controller could remove it by deleting the corresponding application entry and removing related programs or shutting down VMs in the switch using APP_MOD messages. During the execution of an application, if it would like to communicate with the controller, it sends APP_REP messages to the controller.

4.2   Execution Engine

Administrator-Developed Application Execution. As the administrator-developed applications are executable programs running in execution engine, we implement an execution engine supporting programs developed in C, JAVA and MATLAB. The programmed functions could be triggered by the arrival of packets or run periodically every a short interval, which is decided by the programs developed by the administrators. Thus, these applications can capture finer-grained details than centralized schemes. The local information on switches utilized by administrator-developed applications could be divided into three categories: traffic statistics (e.g., packet count, flow duration), packet sampling which capture and analyze packet header or payload, and other local information of switches (e.g., CPU and memory utilization).

Module-Constructed Application Execution. The module-constructed applications are constructed with various Click elements, e.g., IPRateMonitor, TCPCollector, Classifier. The variety of Click elements allows applications in VMs to perform diverse complicated functions in addition to simple OpenFlow actions in the flow table. The module-constructed applications are isolated into VMs with restricted memory and CPU resources, and ClickOS accesses packets with a direct pipe between NIC and VMs [10]. Therefore, applications in VMs do not affect the basic efficiency of data plane packet processing, while OpenFlow handles regular requests to manipulate the flow table as usual.

5   Evaluation

The distributed applications not only reduce communication overheads between the controller and switches, but also relieve administrators from heavy labour configuring work by deploying and controlling these distributed applications with the centralized controller. To show the efficiency of the proposed architecture, we evaluate the execution and management performance of the two types of distributed applications. As the application performance greatly depends on the design and implementation of each application, we mainly focus on information collection performance, throughput and management overhead of these distributed applications.

5.1   Distributed Information Collection Performance

As distributed applications usually utilize local information for network monitoring or anomaly analysis, we evaluate the collection efficiency of the three kinds of local information in distributed applications and compare them with centralized approaches.

(a) Traffic Statistics: As OpenFlow provides control messages to poll traffic statistics from switches, the centralized controller usually uses periodical polling which collects traffic statistics every several seconds. With the remote polling, the fetching delay of port statistics using OFPMP_PORT_STATS messages is almost 400 µs, while the distributed application is able to access the statistics locally within 13 µs in Table 1. Moreover, the periodical interval is difficult to decide for different statistics granularity, and the communication overhead also depends on the polling interval and grows linearly with the polling frequency. On one hand, the smaller the collecting interval is, the larger the overhead is. On the other hand, if the collecting interval is quite large, it may miss a lot of short abnormal details because of the coarse monitoring granularity. Hence, it is hard to strike a balance between the statistic overhead and accuracy in centralized approaches, which is not a problem in distributed schemes.

(b) Packet Payloads: Due to the large network traffic volume, network monitoring applications which analyze packet payload (e.g., DPI) usually capture packets with sampling. Compared with the centralized packet capturing approaches, the distributed applications in switches do not need to transfer packets to a centralized node which saves a lot of transmission delay for real-time analysis. We compare our distributed packet payload capturing with sFlow [2], and the result shows that the centralized approach takes over 7×10^5 µs which is almost 9000 times larger than 86 µs locally in switches to fetch packet payloads. Furthermore, the communication overhead and limited memory space in a centralized node also restrict the performance of centralized packet payload capturing and inspection. Similar to the traffic statistic, the collected packet payload size also grows proportional to the sampling rate, which brings a great overhead for centralized fine-grained packet capturing.

(c) CPU/Memory Information: With distributed instances running in switches, these instances are able to access more local information with assigned permissions, such as CPU and memory utilization. The latency to access CPU and memory statistics with system files /proc/stat and /proc/meminfo in Ubuntu is about 14 µs while it is unavailable for centralized approaches.

Table 1. Information collection latency (µs)

	Distributed	Centralized
Traffic statistics	13.14 ± 1.96	405.11 ± 93.24
Packet payloads	86.41 ± 12.17	$7.535 \times 10^5 \pm 1.204 \times 10^5$
CPU/Mem info	14.12 ± 0.91	NA

In spite of the shorter latency of information collection in distributed applications, they also transfer less control messages between the controller and switches than centralized schemes. The controller just needs to transfer programs or configurations at the setup of distributed applications, and distributed instances could then execute independently.

5.2   Throughput of Distributed Applications

As the performance of distributed application strongly depends on the design and implementation of programs, we only evaluate the throughput of these applications by injecting related packets. The switch is equipped with a 1Gb/s connection. We use an administrator-developed application to get statistics from the flow table. The throughput is almost closed to line rate in Fig. 2, as the statistics collection between the execution engine and the flow table does not affect the basic packet processing. For the module-constructed applications, we evaluate an application constructed with element *Counter*, and the throughput achieves at least 80% injection rate. The optimized I/O pipe of ClickOS helps to improve the throughput [10], which means simple ClickOS configurations add little overhead.

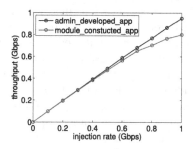

Fig. 2. Throughput of distributed applications

5.3   Distributed Application Management Overhead

To show the efficiency of distributed application management, we evaluate the application transmission and configuration latency with the increasing of the program/configuration file size and the network size respectively. As switches are connected directly to the controller, the application management is independent from the network topology. We test a 2-D mesh network with Mininet, and each switch in the network connects to the controller with a 1 Gb/s link.

To execute multiple applications in switches efficiently, the administrator-developed applications are usually small-sized lightweight programs. Meanwhile, as the configuration file of module-constructed applications only needs to define the element names and rules with integrated elements in ClickOS, the size of configuration file is also quite small at the level of kilobytes. In Fig. 3, when the size of transferred program/configuration file grows, the distribution latency also increases, and it takes over 20 ms to send a 10 Mb program/configuration file to a switch. Nevertheless, it is still acceptable for the overall lifetime of a distributed application, as the controller only transfers programs or configuration files at the beginning. In the proposed SDN architecture supporting distributed applications, when a switch sets up a distributed instance, it inserts a corresponding entry in the application table and records the programs/configuration file on the disk. The application table latency is quite short as the result shows. The administrator-developed application executes the corresponding programs, while a module-constructed application boots a ClickOS VM. We notice that the ClickOS VM booting takes about 30 ms and does not increase a lot when the configuration file size grows. The overall setting up time of a module-constructed application is less than 100 ms for a 10 Mb configuration file. Thus, the setting up latency is quite acceptable to relieve the centralized controller from frequent information fetching.

Meanwhile, when the network size scales, the number of switches running distributed applications is expected to increase to relieve control logic overhead. The overhead of distributing and managing distributed instances in switches also grows as Fig. 4 shows. It takes about 250 ms to distribute a 100 Kb program/configuration file to 100 switches at once. The latency is still much shorter than the collecting and sampling interval in centralized approaches, which usually perform at the level of several seconds. Therefore, the distribution and management overheads of distributed applications are reasonably acceptable.

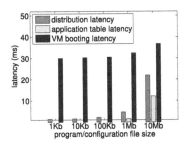

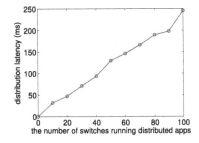

Fig. 3. Scalability with app size   Fig. 4. Scalability with network size

6   Conclusion

Considering the dumbness of switches and the simpleness of OpenFlow actions in current SDN, we propose an extended OpenFlow-enabled switch architecture to support distributed applications in addition to simple match-action Open-Flow instructions. Therefore, a lot of previously centralized applications could be deployed as distributed instances in switches, e.g., network monitoring, intrusion detection, etc. The distributed applications do not mean distributed control logic, as the controller is still controlling these distributed instances with application control messages. The evaluation shows that distributed applications could access more local information efficiently than centralized schemes, while the controller manages these distributed applications with low overheads.

References

1. Open vswitch. http://openvswitch.org/
2. sflow. http://www.sflow.org/
3. Bhatia, S., Bavier, A., Peterson, L.: Wanted: systems abstractions for SDN. In: HotOS (2013)
4. Bosshart, P., Daly, D., Gibb, G., et al.: P4: Programming protocol-independent packet processors. In: SIGCOMM (2014)
5. Farhad, H., Lee, H., Nakao, A.: Data plane programmability in SDN. In: ICNP (2014)
6. Farhadi, H., Du, P., Nakao, A.: User-defined actions for SDn. In: CFI (2014)
7. Feamster, N., Rexford, J., Zegura, E.: The road to SDN: an intellectual history of programmable networks. In: SIGCOMM (2014)
8. Kim, N., Yoo, J.-Y., Kim, N.L., Kim, J.: A programmable networking switch node with in-network processing support. In: ICC (2012)
9. Kohler, E., Morris, R., Chen, B., Jannotti, J., Kaashoek, M.F.: The click modular router. ACM Trans. Comput. Syst. **18**, 263–297 (2000)
10. Martins, J., Ahmed, M., Raiciu, C., et al.: Clickos and the art of network function virtualization. In: NSDI (2014)
11. Mekky, H., Hao, F., Mukherjee, S., Zhang, Z.-L., Lakshman, T.: Application-aware data plane processing in SDN. In: HotSDN (2014)
12. Sivaraman, A., Winstein, K., Subramanian, S., Balakrishnan, H.: No silver bullet: extending SDN to the data plane. In: HotNets (2013)
13. Song, H.: Protocol-oblivious forwarding: unleash the power of sdn through a future-proof forwarding plane. In: HotSDN (2013)

Real-Time Scheduling for Periodic Tasks in Homogeneous Multi-core System with Minimum Execution Time

Ying Li[1(✉)], Jianwei Niu[1], Jiong Zhang[1], Mohammed Atiquzzaman[2], and Xiang Long[1]

[1] State Key Laboratory of Software Development Environment,
School of Computer Science and Engineering,
Beihang University, Beijing 100191, China
liying@buaa.edu.cn
[2] School of Computer Science,
University of Oklahoma, Norman, OK 73019, USA

Abstract. Scheduling of tasks in multicore parallel architectures is challenging due to the execution time being a nondeterministic value. We propose a task-affinity real-time scheduling heuristics algorithm (TARTSH) for periodic and independent tasks in a homogeneous multicore system based on a Parallel Execution Time Graph (PETG) to minimize the execution time. The main contributions of the paper include: construction of a Task Affinity Sequence through real experiment, finding the best parallel execution pairs and scheduling sequence based on task affinity, providing an efficient method to distinguish memory-intensive and memory-unintensive task. For experimental evaluation of our algorithm, a homogeneous multicore platform called NewBeehive with private L1 Cache and sharable L2 Cache has been designed. Theoretical and experimental analysis indicates that it is better to allocate the memory-intensive task and memory-unintensive task for execution in parallel. The experimental results demonstrate that our algorithm can find the optimal solution among all the possible combinations. The Maximum improvement of our algorithm is 15.6%).

Keywords: Task affinity · Real-time scheduling · Periodic tasks · Homogeneous multicore system · Beehive

1 Introduction

With the changes of application, real time demands are being developed, e.g. scientific computing, industrial control and especially mobile clients. The popularity of mobile clients provided a broad space for the internet industry and presented higher demands on the performance of hardware. The traditional way to improve the processing speed relied on accelerating the clock speed, which resulted in a bottleneck due to a large amount of energy consumption. It forced companies to use multi-core technology [1–5]. But all of the traditional calculation models belong to Turing Machine which can only be used for serial instructions. If we wrote some parallel programmes on a single-core processor, they cannot be executed in parallel, essentially [6–9]. Therefore,

© ICST Institute for Computer Sciences, Social Informatics and Telecommunications Engineering 2017
S. Wang and A. Zhou (Eds.): CollaborateCom 2016, LNICST 201, pp. 175–187, 2017.
DOI: 10.1007/978-3-319-59288-6_16

the single-core calculation models cannot be simply transplanted to multi-core. Parallel computing brings great challenges both to hardware structure and software design.

The *objective* of this paper is to find an efficient scheduling strategy which allows a set of real-time periodic and independent tasks to be executed in a **Homogeneous Multi-Core system** (HMC) with as little time as possible. In a multi-core system, the execution time of tasks is not a deterministic value and it is very difficult to find a sufficient condition for scheduling a set of periodic tasks. We solved this problem based on **task affinity** (defined in Sect. 3). First, we obtain the affinity between each task according to the actual measurement data. Second, we applied a scheduling heuristics algorithm to find an optimal parallel scheme and a reasonable execution sequence. This work will be useful to researchers for scheduling real-time tasks in a multicore processor system.

Real-time task scheduling for single-core processor was proposed in 1960 and the most representative algorithms are EDF and RM. Liu et al. [9–12] presented the scheduling policy and quantitative analysis of EDF and RM. In 1974, Horn proposed the necessary conditions for scheduling a set of periodic tasks. [13]. In 2005, Jiwei Lu [14] proposed a thread named Helper can be used to increase the percentage of Cache hits. But the time complexity of [14] algorithm is $O(N!)$ which had no practical significance. Kim, Chandra and Solihin studied the relationship between the fairness of sharing L2 Cache and the throughput of processor under the architecture of chip multiprocessors (CMP) and introduced some methods for measuring the fairness of sharing Cache [15]. Fedorova studied the causes of the unfairness of sharing Cache between tasks based on the SPEC CPU2000 [16]. Zhou et al. proposed a dynamic Cache allocation algorithm which can re-assign Cache resource by recording the parallel tasks' behaviors of using Cache [17]. Shao et al. [18] and Stigge et al. [19] divided the tasks into delay-sensitive ones and memory-intensive ones according to the characteristics of their memory access behaviors.

Although these works for multicore tasks scheduling have made some progress, most of them still used the same scheduling algorithms and analytic methods used in single-core processers, which indicated the execution time of a task is a deterministic value. But in multi-core system, the execution time is a nondeterministic value due to sharing of resources between tasks. Moreover, their experimental data is mostly obtained from simulation models which lack real data.

This paper is *different from previous work* in terms of using a nondeterministic scheduling algorithm for multicore processor and a real experimental environment.

In this paper, we *focus* on the scheduling strategy for a set of periodic and real-time tasks which can be executed on a multicore computing platform. We proposed a Task-Affinity Real-Time Scheduling Heuristics algorithm (TARTSH) for periodic tasks in multicore system based on a Parallel Execution Time Graph (PETG) which was obtained by accurately measuring the tasks' number of memory access and quantitatively analysing their delays due to resource competition. This algorithm focused on avoiding the execution of memory-intensive tasks in parallel, which can improve the real-time performance of the multi-core processor system.

The main *contributions* of this paper include:

- We proposed a quantitative method to measure the affinity between each task and obtained an affinity sequence according to the order of execution time which is affected by resource sharing.
- We designed a scheduling heuristic algorithm to find the best parallel execution pairs according to the task affinity and obtained an optimal tasks assignment method and scheduling strategy to minimize the sum of each core's execution time.

The rest of the paper is organized as follows. The Task Affinity model and related theorems are presented in Sect. 2. A motivational example is presented in Sect. 3 to illustrate the basic ideas of TARTSH algorithm. The multicore scheduling model is described in Sect. 4. The task-affinity real-time scheduling heuristics algorithm is presented in Sect. 5. The experimental results are presented in Sect. 6. Section 7 concludes the paper.

2 Basic Model

In this section, we introduce the Homogeneous Multi-Core system (HMC) architecture, followed by the Parallel Execution Time Graph (PETG) and definitions.

2.1 Hardware Model

In view of the research aim in this paper, we hope to find a multicore computing platform which can support a complete tool chains for writing a programme in advanced language and understanding the hardware program language for modifying hardware structure. Our investigation shows that Microsoft Research Beehive, which provides a multi-core prototype system, can meet our requirements. We modified the interconnection structure and storage architecture of Beehive by adding L2 Cache, clock interrupt, etc., to design a new multi-core processor, NewBeehive, as shown in Fig. 1.

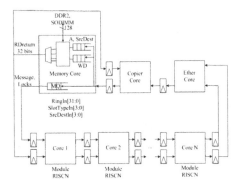

Fig. 1. The structure of NewBeehive.

NewBeehive is a RISC multi-core processor with bus architecture which can be implemented on FPGA. At present, NewBeehive can support up to 16 cores and each of them can be regarded as an independent computing entity. In Fig. 1, MemoryCore, CopierCore and EtherCore belong to service cores which are mainly designed to provide service for computing. MasterCore and Core1-Core4 belong to computing cores which are mainly used to execute tasks. In NewBeehive, Core1-Core4 are homogeneous and they share L2 cache and have their own private L1 Instruction Cache and L1 Data Cache. Core1-Core4 can access data from memory through L2 Cache, bus and MemoryCore. In order to meet the requirements of research, we incorporated some new functions in NewBeehive, including cache-coherent protocol, statistical analysis for Cache, clock interrupt and exclusive access to sharing resource, etc.

2.2   Definitions

In this paper, we use a *Parallel Execution Time Graph* (*PETG*) to model the tasks. The PETG is defined as follows:

Definition 2.1 *Parallel Execution Time Graph* **(PETG).** A *PETG* $G = < V, E >$ is an undirected strongly connected graph where nodes $V = \{v_1, v_2, \ldots, v_i, \ldots, v_n\}$ represents a set of tasks and edges $E = \{e_{12}, \ldots, e_{ij}, \ldots, e_{nn}\}$ represents a set of execution time for which e_{ij} is the sum of the execution time of task v_i and the execution time of task v_j when they are executed in parallel, $e_{ij} = e_{ji}$, $i \neq j$. $e_{ij} = t_j^i + t_i^j$ where t_i^j is the parallel execution time of task v_i when it is executed in parallel with task v_j.

Each task's parallel execution time is recorded in the Task Parallel Execution Time Table which is used to calculate task affinity.

Definition 2.2 *Task Parallel Execution Time Table* **(TPET).** A *TPET* A is a table for which t_i^j represents the average parallel execution time of task v_i when it is executed in parallel with task v_j under different combinations of tasks and $t_i^j \neq t_i^j . t_i^j = \frac{\sum_{k=1}^{N} t_{i_k}^j}{N}$, where $N = C_m^n(v_i, v_j)$ indicates the number of different combinations of tasks including task v_i and v_j, N is the number of cores and m is the number of the tasks.

Task affinity which indicates the parallel appropriateness between tasks is recorded in the Task Affinity Sequence.

Definition 2.3 *Task Affinity Sequence* **(TAS).** A *TAS* S is an ordered sequence for which s_i represents the influence degree of task v_i affected by other tasks, $s_i = \{s_i^1, s_i^2, \ldots s_i^j, \ldots, s_i^n\}$, where $s_i^{j-1} \cdot \bar{s} < s_i^j \cdot \bar{s}$ and $i \neq j$. s_i^j is a tuple, $s_i^j = < v_j, \bar{s} >$, $s_i^j \cdot \bar{s}$ is the difference ratio between the independent execution time and the parallel execution time of task v_i. $s_i^j \cdot \bar{s} = \frac{t_i^j - t_i}{t_i}$, where t_i represents the independent execution time of task v_i when it works on a single core and t_i^j represents the parallel execution time of task v_i when it is executed in parallel with task v_j.

Given a PETG G, TPET A and TAS S, the goal is to obtain a parallel execution set and a scheduling sequence on the target multicore computing platform *NewBeehive* to make the sum of each core's execution time as little as possible. To achieve this, our proposed methods need to solve the following problems:

- Task Affinity Sequence: Task affinity sequence is obtained by actually testing the independent execution time and the parallel execution time for each task on the multicore computing platform NewBeehive.
- Task Scheduling Sequence: Task scheduling sequence is composed of a tasks assignment which represents the best match of tasks work on different cores and an execution sequence which indicates the serial sequence of tasks work on one core.

3 Motivational Example

To illustrate the main techniques proposed in this paper, we give a motivational example.

3.1 Construct Task Affinity Sequence Table

In this paper, we assume all the real-time periodic tasks are independent so that and the execution time cannot be affected by the different combinations of tasks. The independent tasks we used in this paper are shown in Table 1. Tasks 1, 2, 3, 4, 5 and 6 are Matrix Multiplication, Heap Sort, Travelling Salesman Problem, Prime Solution, Read or Write Cache and 0-1 Knapsack Problem, respectively.

Table 1. Task list

Num	Tasks
v_1	Matrix
v_2	Sorter
v_3	Tsp
v_4	Prime
v_5	Cachebench
v_6	Pack

Table 2. Independent Execution Time (1000 clocks)

Num	Execution time on a single core				Average time
	Core1	Core2	Core3	Core4	
v_1	71619	72013	**72029**	71972	72015
v_2	74542	76712	74566	74510	75083
v_3	75317	78973	75317	75317	76231
v_4	75654	75654	75654	75654	75654
v_5	100641	100641	100637	100637	100639
v_6	72817	72816	72817	72816	72816

In order to calculate the delay between each task due to their sharing L2 Cache, we need to test the independent execution time TSi and parallel execution time TPi for each task, respectively. To make it easier to understand, we use two cores, Core3 and Core4 to execute the tasks in parallel.

First, we obtained the independent execution time TSi by executing task v_i on a single core which indicates task v_i can exclusively use all the resources and not be affected by other tasks. Table 2 is constructed by separately executing the target tasks on a single core of NewBeehive. For the better result, we take the average of four tests. Table 2 shows one task's respective execution times on different cores are basically the same, which indicates Core1 $\sim$ Core4 are homogeneous. And it accords well with the design of NewBeehive in Sect. 2.

Second, we test the parallel execution time Tpi by executing task v_i on one core and other tasks on the left cores. These tasks will be affected by each other due to sharing L2 Cache. The value $t_{v1}^{v2} = 76062$, which represents the parallel execution time of task v_1 when it works on Core3 and v_2 works on Core4 at the same time. And $t_{v2}^{v1} = 83811$ represents the parallel execution time of task v_2. They are different because they belong to different tasks' parallel execution time.

According to Table 2, we find each task's parallel execution time is longer than its independent execution time. Furthermore, if a task belongs to the memory-intensive application, it will significantly increase the other task's execution time. For example, task 5 is a Cachebench, which accesses data from memory frequently and all the other tasks will have a great delay when they are executed in parallel. In Table 2, task 1's independent execution time on core3 is 72029, but its parallel execution time on core3 is 90644 when task 5 works on core4.

Third, we calculated the influence ratio between each task based on its independent execution time and parallel execution time, as shown in Table 3. E.g., $= \frac{t_{v2}^{v1}-t_{v2}}{t_{v2}} = \frac{83811-74542}{74542} = 12.4\%$.

By analyzing the task affinity sequence s_i in Table 3, we conclude the following two results:

(1) In a row, if the task affinity grows very little, it indicates the task in this row belongs to memory-unintensive application. The reason is the task's parallel execution time is less influenced by other tasks when it rarely accesses memory, e.g. task 4.
(2) In a column, if the task has a significant impact on other tasks, it indicates the task in this column belongs to memory-intensive application. The reason is the task will severely impact the execution time of others when it frequently updates L2 Cache and uses Bus, e.g. task 5.

Table 3. Influence Ratio of Two Cores (Unit: %)

Cores	Core4					
Core3	v_1	v_2	v_3	v_4	v_5	v_6
1	–	5.6	0.8	0.3	25.9	4.0
2	**12.4**	–	2.7	1.7	65.4	8.3
3	2.5	2	–	0.01	21.3	0.2
4	0.24	0.22	0.11	–	0.6	0.12
5	27.4	26.3	8.3	3.6	–	21.7
6	14.6	11.2	0.3	0.01	55.7	–

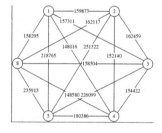

Fig. 2. Parallel execution time graph.

3.2 Find an Optimal Tasks Scheduling

In order to find an optimal Task Scheduling Sequence, we apply a task-affinity real-time scheduling heuristics algorithm (TARTSH) based on graph theory to assign tasks. According to the conclusions in Sect. 3, it is better to allocate the memory-intensive task and memory-unintensive task to be executed in parallel, which can reduce the competition for resources and improve the real-time performance.

First, we draw a Parallel Execution Time Graph (PETG) based on Table 2, as shown in Fig. 2. Each edge in graph G is the sum of the parallel execution times of two nodes, e.g. $e_{12} = t_1^2 + t_2^1 = 76062 + 83811 = 159873$.

Second, we find the best parallel execution pairs based on the TARTSH algorithm. We obtained a global task affinity sequence by ordering each task's parallel influence. The parallel influence of task v_i indicates the total influence of task v_i to all the other tasks when they are executed in parallel, which is calculated by adding all the $s_j^i.\bar{s}$, where i = 1,2,...,n and i $\neq$ j. For example, according to Table 3, the parallel influence of task $v_5 = 25.9 + 65.4 + 21.3 + 0.6 + 55.7 = 168.9$ and the global task affinity sequence (GTAS) is $\{v_5, v_1, v_2, v_6, v_3, v_4\}$. And the best parallel execution pairs are obtained by finding their best match task which has the strongest affinity according to the order the global task affinity sequence. E.g., $\{ <v_5, v_4> , <v_1, v_3> , <v_2, v_6> \}$.

Third, we find the optimal task scheduling sequence by allocating the tasks in each sub-sequence in the global task affinity sequence to their appropriate cores based on the task affinity sequence of the most influence task. In this paper, the most influence task is task v_5 which indicates it has the largest influence on the other tasks. And the task affinity sequence of task v_5 is $\{v_4, v_3, v_6, v_2, v_1\}$. Therefore, the optimal task scheduling sequence is composed of the task execution sequence on each core. $P(c_i)$ is the set of tasks assigned to core c_i. E.g., $P(c_3) = \{v_5, v_1, v_2\}$ and $P(c_4) = \{v_4, v_3, v_6\}$. If two tasks have the same index in the different cores, they will be executed in parallel, e.g. v_1 is executed with v_3.

4 Multicore Scheduling Model

In this section, we propose a multicore scheduling model to achieve an optimal tasks assignment method and scheduling strategy in *HMC* system that makes the sum of each core's execution time as little as possible. First, the notations and assumptions used to construct the multicore scheduling model are presented in Table 4. Then, the theorems are introduced.

The aim of multicore scheduling model is to minimize the total execution time on the condition that the set of periodic and independent tasks can be scheduled. The total execution time is defined as:

$$T_{opt}(V) = \min(\sum_{c_i \in C} T(c_i))$$
$$= \min(\sum_{v_i \in V} TP(v_i) + \sum_{v_i \in V} TD(v_i)) \tag{1}$$

Table 4. Notations of TARTSH Algorithm

V	A set of periodic and independent tasks	V	A set of periodic and independent tasks
$T_{opt}(P)$	The optimal tasks scheduling with the minimum execution time	$\beta(v_i)$	The parallel influence of task v_i to all the other tasks
$TA_{opt}(S)$	The optimal tasks assignment with the minimum sum of task affinity	$\theta(v_i)$	The parallel influence of the best match tasks $M(v_i)$ to task v_i
$M(v_i)$	the best match tasks of task v_i	$T(c_i)$	the execution time of core c_i
$\bar{V}_i$	The set of tasks in $M(v_i)$	$TS(v_i)$	The independent execution time of task v_i
$P(c_i)$	The task execution sequence assigned to core c_i	$TP(v_i)$	The parallel execution time of task v_i
$\varepsilon(v_i)$	The parallel influence of all the other tasks to task v_i	$TD(v_i)$	The delay when task v_i is executed in parallel

Where $TD(v_i)$ is defined as:

$$TP(v_i) = TS(v_i) \times (1 + \theta(v_i)) \tag{2}$$

$$TD(v_i) = TS(v_i) \times (1 + \varepsilon(v_i)) \tag{3}$$

Then, according to Eqs. (1)–(3), it holds that

$$T_{opt}(V) = \min\{\sum\nolimits_{v_i \in V} [TS(v_i) \times (2 + \theta(v_i) + \varepsilon(v_i))]\} \tag{4}$$

Theorem 4.1. If a set of periodic and independent tasks are executed in parallel, the optimal tasks assignment TA_{opt} composed of $M(v_i)$ can be obtained by sorting its $\beta(v_i)$ in ascending order.

Proof: According to the definition,

$$TA_{opt}(S) = \{S_1, \ldots, S_m, \ldots, S_n\}$$
$$= \sum\nolimits_{m=1}^{N} S_m \cdot s$$

where, $S_m = M(v_i)$, $S_m \cdot s = \sum_{v_i, v_j \in S_m} (s_i^j \cdot \bar{s} + s_i^j \cdot \bar{s})$ (defined in Sect. 3), and N is the number of the cores. Then,

$TA_{opt}(S) = M^1(v_l), \ldots, M^m(v_i), \ldots, M^n(v_j)$,   where $\bar{V}_l \cup \ldots \bar{V}_i \cup \ldots \cup \bar{V}_j = V$, $\bar{V}_i \cap \bar{V}_j = \emptyset$ and $\beta(M^{m-1}(v_k)) > \beta(M^m(v_i))$.

Assume $\beta(M^{m-1}(v_k)) < \beta(M^m(v_i))$, then there is a new the optimal tasks assignment TA'_{opt} whose total task affinity is smaller than TA_{opt}'s. It holds that

$$TA'_{opt}(S') = \{S'_1, \ldots, S'_m, \ldots, S'_n\}$$

$$= \sum\nolimits_{m=1}^{N} S'_m \cdot s$$

where $S'_m \cdot s = \sum_{v_k, v_l \in S'_m} (s'^l_k \cdot \bar{s} + s'^k_l \cdot \bar{s})$

If $\beta(M^{m-1}(v_k)) < \beta(M^m(v_i))$, then

$\sum_{v_k, v_l \in S'_m} (s'^l_k \cdot \bar{s} + s'^k_l \cdot \bar{s}) > \sum_{v_i, v_j \in S_m} (s^j_i \cdot \bar{s} + s^j_i \cdot \bar{s})$ which indicates $\sum_{m=1}^{N} S'_m \cdot s >$
$\sum_{m=1}^{N} S'_m \cdot s$

And it is different from assuming which indicates $M(v_i)$ in $TA_{opt}(S)$ is ordered by
its $\beta(v_i)$.

Theorem 4.2. Based on $TA_{opt}(P)$, the optimal tasks scheduling T_{opt} can be obtained by
making the tasks executed with their strong affinity tasks.

Proof: Assume the most influence task with the largest $\beta(v_i)$ is v_{max}, and its task
affinity sequence $s_i(v_{max}) = \{s^1_{max}, \ldots s^j_{max}, \ldots, s^n_{max}\}$ (defined in Sect. 3). Then,

$$TA_{opt}(P) = \{P(c_1), \ldots, P(c_m), \ldots, P(c_N)\} \quad \text{and} \quad P(c_m) = <v^1_m, \ldots, v^k_m, \ldots, v^n_m>,$$

where the tasks in $P(c_m)$ are the same with those in S_m but ordered according to the task
affinity of v_{max} from small to large.

Assume a task v' is assigned to core c_m to replace the task v^k_m and
$\theta(v_{max}, v') > \theta(v_{max}, v^k_m)$. Then, a new optimal tasks scheduling $TA'_{opt}(P')$ is obtained.

$$TA'_{opt}(P') = \{P'(c_1), \ldots, P'(c_m), \ldots, P'(c_N)\} \quad \text{and} \quad P'(c_m) = <v^1_m, \ldots, v^k_i, \ldots, v^n_m>.$$
According to the Eqs. (2), we have that

$$TP(v_{max}, v') = TS(v_i) \times (1 + \theta(v_{max}, v'))$$

Therefore, $TP(v_{max}, v') > TP(v_{max}, v^k_m)$ which indicate

$$TA'_{opt}(P') > TA'_{opt}(P)$$

And it is different from assuming.

5 TARTSH Algorithm

In this section, we propose a task-affinity real-time scheduling heuristics algorithm
(*TARTSH*) to find the T_{opt} which has the minimum total execution time on the condition
that the set of periodic and independent tasks can be scheduled in a given HMC
according to task affinity.

Algorithm 5.1 shows the *TARTSH* algorithm. Initially, we build a matrix
$TA[V_n][V_n]$ to record task affinity between tasks and $TA[v_i][v_j]$ represents the $s^j_i \cdot \bar{S}$
(defined in Sect. 3). The variables $S(v_i)$, $C_i(S)$ and PS are used to record the parallel
influence of task v_i, the already assigned tasks on the core c_i and the global priority of
all the tasks based on the task affinity, respectively. And $U(C_i)$ is a function to calculate

the resource utilization rate of core Ci and $Li(n)$ is the least upper bound of the utilization ratio of core c_i.

The *TARTSH* algorithm tries to find the best parallel execution sequence according to the task affinity and obtained an optimal tasks assignment method and scheduling strategy to make the sum of each core's execution time as little as possible. From line 4 to line 16, the algorithm construct the priority of each task, $PS[V_n][V_n]$, which satisfies the condition $PS[v_i][v_x] > PS[v_i][v_y]$, where $x < y$, $PS[v_i][v_x]$ is the task affinity between v_i and v_x. Then, we sort $PS[V_n][V_n]$ based on $PS[V_n][0]$ in line 17. From line 19 to line 23, the task pairs with the highest tasks affinity will be assigned to the empty cores. PS' is obtained in line 24 by deleting the assigned tasks from PS. From line 25 to line 38, the tasks assignment on each core is obtained by finding the best match task for the core's latest task based on task affinity.

Algorithm 5.1. Task-Affinity Real-Time Scheduling Heuristics Algorithm (TARTSH)
Input: (1) An Independent Execution Time A; (2) A Parallel Execution Time B; (3) A graph model PETG G =<V, E> (4) A Homogeneous multi-core system Pm; **Output**: The optimal tasks scheduling with the minimum total execution time
1:Initialize a $N \times N$ matrix TA$[V_n][V_n] \leftarrow 0$;
2:Initialize $S(V) \leftarrow 0$, $C(S) \leftarrow 0$, $PS[V_n][V_n] \leftarrow 0$, $k = 0$;
3: Initialize $CoreNum = M$;
4:**for** $v_i \in V$ **do**// construct $PS[N][N]$
5:    $k = N$
6:    **while** $k > 0$ **do**
7:       $ta = 0$
8:       v_j = the task of TA$[V_i][k]$
9:       **for** $v_j \in V$ **do**
10:          **if** TA $[v_i][v_j] > ta$ **then**
11:             $ta = $ TA $[v_i][v_j]$
12:             $PS[v_i] \leftarrow v_j$//find the largest task affinity of v_i
13:          $k = k - 1$
14:       **end for**
15:    **end while**
16:**end for**

17:$PS = $ Sort$(PS[v_i])$
18:$m = 0$
19:**while** $m < CoreNum$ **do** // assign tasks to the empty cores
20:    v_m = the task of $PS[m]$, v_n = the task of $PS[v_m][0]$
21:    $Ci(S) \leftarrow <v_m, v_n>$
22:    $m = m + 1$
23:**end while**
24: $PS' = PS = \sum_{i=0}^{N} Ci(S)$
25:**for** Ci in Pm **do**
26:    v_c = find the latest task in $Ci(S)$
27:    $PS''[v_c] = PS'[v_c]$
28:    **while** True **do**
29:       $v_p = \max(PS''[v_c][\ v])$
30:       $U(Ci) \equiv U(Ci) + U(v_p)$
31:       **if** $U(Ci) \leqslant Li(n)$ **then**
32:          $Ci(S) \leftarrow v_p$
14:       **end for**
15:    **end while**
16:**end for**
33:       $PS''[v_c] = PS''[v_c] - v_p$
34:       $PS'[v_c] = PS''[v_c]$
35:       **break**
36:    **else**:
37:       $PS''[v_c] = PS''[v_c] - v_p$
38:**end for**

6   Experiments

Experimental results are presented in this section. To demonstrate the effect of the *TARTSH* algorithm across different cores, we complete our experiment in a homogenous multi-core system with 2 cores, 4 cores and 8 cores, respectively. Our main method is to generate all the periodic tasks sets consisted of real-time tasks defined in Table 1 based on random algorithm and record their execution time, cache read failure times and hit rate, respectively. Then, the effectiveness of the *TARTSH* algorithm is proved according to the statistical data.

6.1   Periodic Tasks Set

We design different sizes of periodic tasks set consisted of different real-time tasks defined in Table 1 by making them executed randomly for many times, as shown in Table 5. In our experiment, the number of periodic tasks set is limited between 100 and 1500 for very small number of tasks will lead to inaccurate, but a large number of tasks will increase the difficulty of collecting data. The execution sequence of tasks is also generated randomly. E.g., Set1 just includes two tasks and they will be {T1, T2} or {T1, T3} or {T1, T4} or other combinations of two tasks. And we execute them for 50 times to obtain a periodic tasks set with 100 tasks, e.g., {{T1, T2}, {T1, T2},..., {T1, T2}}.

Table 5. Periodic tasks set table

Set No.	Number of tasks	Size of set	Number of cores
Set1	2	100	{1,2}
Set2	4	500	{1,2,3,4}
Set3	6	1000	{1,2,3,4,5,6}
Set4	8	1500	{1,2,3,4,5,6,7,8}

6.2   Task Affinity

In this paper, our purpose is to schedule a set of real-time periodic and independent tasks with as little time as possible based on the task affinity. Task affinity can be measured qualitatively based on the parameters of cache read-failure times, task execution time, etc., which are obtained by executing the periodic tasks sets in different size of homogenous multi-core systems, as shown in Table 6.

In advance, we know T1, T3 and T5 access memory frequently and T2 and T4 rarely access memory. Table 6 shows a part of the statistical data of set1 and it indicates T1 and T5 have the strongest affinity for they share data. But T1 and T3 will cause the failure of reading cache for their data is stored on different lines of cache.

Table 6. A part of statistical data of set1

No.	Tasks	Cache performance parameters on one core			Cache performance parameters on two core		
		Read times	Read-failure times	Hit Rate	Read times	Read-failure times	Hit Rate
1	T1, T2	725301	54397	92.5	401631	34942	91.3
2	T1, T5	638120	15953	97.5	309162	9893	96.8
3	T2, T4	65390	6931	89.4	39125	3717	90.5
4	T2, T5	640145	60174	90.6	392174	41178	89.5
5	T1, T3	1025471	255342	75.1	8946756	1261493	85.9
6	T2, T3	825301	179090	78.3	579834	92–93	83.6

7 Conclusion

In this paper, we propose a task-affinity real-time scheduling heuristics algorithm (TARTSH) for periodic and independent tasks in a homogeneous multicore system based on a Parallel Execution Time Graph (PETG) to minimize the execution time. We build multicore scheduling model to obtain the best parallel execution pairs and scheduling sequence based on task affinity. The experimental results show that TARTSH algorithm spends less time than any other combination which is implemented in a real homogeneous multicore platform.

Acknowledgments. This work was supported by the National Natural Science Foundation of China (61572060, 61190125, 61472024), 973 Program (2013CB035503), and CERNET Innovation Project 2015 (NGII20151004).

References

1. Bastoni, A., Brandenburg, B.B., Anderson, J.H.: An empirical comparison of global, partitioned, and clustered multiprocessor EDF schedulers. In: Proceedings of the 31st IEEE Real-Time Systems Symposium (RTSS), pp. 14–24 (2010)
2. Liu, J.W.S.: Real-Time System. Pearson Education (2002)
3. Liu, C.L., Layland, J.W.: Scheduling algorithms for multiprogramming in a hard real time environment. J. ACM **20**(1), 46–61 (1973)
4. Davari, S., Dhall, S.K.: An online algorithm for real-time tasks allocation. In: IEEE Real-time Systems Symposium, pp. 194–200 (1 986)
5. Baruah, S.K., Li, H., Stougie, L.: Towards the design of certifiable mixed-criticality systems. In: The Real-Time and Embedded Technology and Applications Symposium (RTAS), pp. 13–22 (2010)
6. Lauzac, S., Melhem, R., Mosse, D.: Comparison of global and partitioning schemes for scheduling rate monotonic tasks on a multiprocessor. In: 10th Euromicro Workshop on Real Time Systems, pp. 188–195, June 1998
7. Davis, R.I., Burns, A.: A survey of hard real-time scheduling for multiprocessor systems. ACM Comput. Surv. **4**, 1–44 (2011)

8. Mok, A.K.: Fundamental design problems of distributed systems for the hard real-time environment. Ph.D. Dissertation, MIT (1983)

9. Lakshmanan, K., de Niz, D., Rajkumar, R., Moreno, G.: Resource allocation in distributed mixed-criticality cyber-physical systems. In: The 30th International Conference on Distributed Computing Systems (ICDCS), pp. 169–178 (2010)

10. De Niz, D., Lakshmanan, K., Rajkumar, R.: On the scheduling of mixed-criticality real-time task sets. In: The 30th Real-Time Systems Symposium (RTSS), pp. 291–300 (2009)

11. Guan, N., Ekberg, P., Stigge, M., Yi, W.: Effective and efficient scheduling of certifiable mixed-criticality sporadic task systems. In: The 32rd Real-Time Systems Symposium (RTSS), pp. 13–23 (2011)

12. Burchard, A., Liebeherr, J., Oh, Y.F., Son, S.H.: New strategies for assigning real-time tasks to multiprocessor systems. IEEE Trans. on Comput. **44**(12), 1429–1442 (1995)

13. Han, C.C., Tyan, H.: A better polynomial-time schedulability test for real-time fixed-priority scheduling algorithms. In: The 18th IEEE Real-Time Systems Symposium, San Francisco, pp. 36–45 (1997)

14. Lu, J., Das, A., et al.: Dynamic helper threaded prefetching on the sun ultra SPARC CMP processor. In: The 38th Microarchitecture, pp. 93–104, October 2005

15. Kim, S., Chandra, D., Solihin, Y.: Fair cache sharing and partitioning in a chip multiprocessor architecture. In: 13th International Conference on Parallel Architecture and Compilation Techniques, Los Alamitos, CA, pp. 111–122 (2004)

16. Fedorova, A.: Operating System Scheduling for Chip Multithreaded Processors. Ph.D. thesis, Harvard University (2006)

17. Benhai, Z., Jianzhong, Q., Shukuan, L.: Dynamic shared cache allocation algorithm for multicore professor. J. Northeast. Univ. **32**(1), 44–47 (2011)

18. Shao, J., Davis, T.: A burst scheduling access reordering mechanism. In: 13th International Symposium on High Performance Computer Architecture, pp. 285–294 (2007)

19. Stigge, M., Ekberg, P., Guan, N., et al.: On the tractability of digraph-based task models. In: 23rd Euromicro Conference on Real-Time Systems (ECRTS), Porto, Portugal, pp. 162–171 (2011)

Sweets: A Decentralized Social Networking Service Application Using Data Synchronization on Mobile Devices

Rongchang Lai[(⊠)] and Yasushi Shinjo

Department of Computer Science, University of Tsukuba,
Tsukuba, Ibaraki 305-8573, Japan
yas@cs.tsukuba.ac.jp
http://www.softlab.cs.tsukuba.ac.jp/~yas/

Abstract. Conventional Social Networking Services (SNSs) or Online Social Networks (OSNs) are implemented based on a centralized architecture, and this centralization causes privacy problems. This paper describes Sweets, a decentralized SNS application that synchronizes tweets among users' own mobile devices and enables users to retain ownership of their data. Sweets provides user authentication and access control without centralized servers. Sweets improves the data availability using an indirect replication scheme. Experimental results show that Sweets has a feasible performance over a 4G cellular network.

Keywords: Decentralized Social Networking Services (DSNSs) · Decentralized Online Social Networks (DOSNs) · Data synchronization · Decentralized user authentication · High data availability · Access control

1 Introduction

Most current popular Social Networking Services (SNSs) or Online Social Networks (OSNs) are constructed based on a centralized architecture and all of the user data are hosted on centralized servers. Service providers can easily access user data to improve the user experience and commercial benefits through targeted advertising. Obviously, from the user's perspective, such centralized architecture causes a violation of privacy. People lose control of their own data and are tracked by SNS providers. Some recent events have proved the existence of such concerns [10]. Finally, if service providers shut down their services, users may lose their data and can no longer retrieve them.

Due to these drawbacks of current centralized SNSs, a number of decentralized SNS approaches [1,5,6,8] have been proposed. However, these approaches suffer from multiple problems, such as permanently available data storage required, lack of revocation support, and high overheads. In addition, to the best of our knowledge, no existing decentralized SNS approach is compatible with mobile devices, which is the major mode by which people use SNS applications.

© ICST Institute for Computer Sciences, Social Informatics and Telecommunications Engineering 2017
S. Wang and A. Zhou (Eds.): CollaborateCom 2016, LNICST 201, pp. 188–198, 2017.
DOI: 10.1007/978-3-319-59288-6_17

To address these problems, we are implementing a decentralized SNS application using data synchronization. We call our application Sweets, which stands for Sync Tweets. The goal of Sweets is to realize a decentralized SNS application that runs on mobile devices.

Sweets achieves basic SNS functionality with data synchronization using Couchbase Lite [3] and supports revocation of tweets. Users can also define and enforce a fine-grained access control policy to restrict the dissemination of their data. We implement decentralized user authentication in Sweets using OpenID Connect [14].

Since we implement an indirect replication scheme, the application provides high data availability regardless of whether users are online or offline. For the indirect replication, we implement access control with Attribute Based Encryption (ABE) [9].

2   Related Work

Twister [8] is a decentralized microblogging application over a Distributed Hash Table (DHT). However, the DHT network is unsuitable for mobile devices. Since a device must serve all the other devices in the DHT network, this quickly depletes battery life and data volumes can become very large. Furthermore, Twister does not support revocation. Unlike Twister, we implement a decentralized SNS application without DHTs, and enable users to delete or update their posted tweets.

Vegas [6] accomplishes decentralization using a federated server architecture. In this research, data synchronization is achieved through a component called datastores. A datastore represents the abstract concept of a public user-writable storage space with world-readable access. Datastores can be deployed on a cloud storage service like Google Drive or Dropbox. Compared with Vegas, our research realizes this component on users' mobile devices.

Persona [1] is a privacy-enhanced decentralized SNS application that provides flexible, user-defined access control with ABE. Similar to Vegas, Persona's design requires permanently available data storage. The data hosted on data storage systems are encrypted by ABE. Sweets differs from Persona in respect to data storage, as it stores user data on their own devices instead of permanently available data storage. Sweets combines data synchronization and ABE, so that encrypted data can be transferred among mobile devices and relayed by friends who have no permission to access the data.

3   Implementing Basic SNS Functionality on Mobile Devices

We implement our SNS application, Sweets on Android mobile devices. Figure 1 shows a screenshot of Sweets. The user interface of the application is similar to current popular SNS applications and gives users a similar user experience.

A user can post tweets with texts and photos from an album or camera. Users can pull the latest tweets from their friends by pulling the main view down. Each tweet item has a number of buttons that allow users to comment on a tweet or give it a thumbs-up. If their friends pull these changes back, they can retrieve these comments and thumbs-up updates. When a user deletes a posted tweet, Sweets forces other friends who have previously pulled this tweet to delete it from their devices immediately.

3.1   Basic SNS Functionality by Data Synchronization

We implement Sweets based on data synchronization among mobile devices. Figure 1 shows the high level architecture of Sweets. Each user runs Sweets on a mobile device. Sweets consists of the user interface, the identity provider, and an embedded database. When a user posts tweets and photos, they are first stored on the local database. Next, Sweets synchronizes the local database with other users' databases using peer-to-peer TCP connections over Social Virtual Private Networks (VPNs) [7]. During the synchronization process, Sweets pulls new or modified data from remote databases and stores them on the local database. Finally, Sweets shows the user tweets, photos, and friends' comments in the local database.

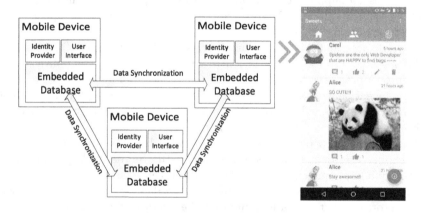

Fig. 1. Overview of sweets

Data synchronization is executed asynchronously as a background task. Users are unaware of the time consumption during data synchronization and the user interface avoids becoming frozen due to data synchronization.

3.2   Couchbase Lite

We use Couchbase Lite for data synchronization among mobile devices. Couchbase Lite is an embedded document-oriented database management system

(DBMS). It uses a technique called Multiversion Concurrency Control (MVCC) to manage data replication in a distributed environment, and documents in Couchbase Lite are automatically versioned. With the MMVC technique, Couchbase Lite enables developers to process the revision history of a document.

We integrate Couchbase Lite into Sweets. With Couchbase Lite, any data element that should be replicated is versioned, and any data update is tracked. Sweets only replicates missing updates during data synchronization. Most of the time, Sweets pulls updates rather than pushing them. By this means, data updates are only synchronized if some other users are willing to retrieve them. As a result, Sweets minimizes data synchronization traffic and confines the resource consumption, which is sensitive for mobile devices.

Data synchronization among mobile devices comes with some inherent problems, including data conflict and deletion synchronization. The following sections describe how we resolved these problems.

3.3   Conflict Resolution

In Sweets, posted tweets are replicated to remote databases, and friends can comment on them. A tweet can be updated on multiple databases. We want to gather all comments and resolve this conflict; namely, we need to merge these branches. Unfortunately, Couchbase Lite provides a simple conflict detection and resolution mechanism, selecting a winner revision; this requires us to drop a number of comments.

To avoid this, we solve the conflict by other means. Every time the conflict occurs during synchronization, we aggregate all conflicting revisions of a tweet document in the device on which the user has posted the tweet. Next, we merge all these contents, and create a new revision for the conflicting tweet document that incorporates all the comments obtained from other friends. Next, we set the new revision as the current revision of the document. Finally, we delete all obsolete conflicting revisions. Once someone pulls this tweet again, the latest revision will be pulled and the obsolete revision in her/his database will be updated. By this way, she or he can also retrieve the latest comments from other users.

3.4   Implementing Revocation

Revocation is another problem we need to solve. We want to ensure that deleted tweet documents are deleted from other databases as soon as possible.

To realize such rapid tweet message revocation, we use a special revision object called *tombstone revision* and a different replication scheme. When a user deletes a tweet from her/his own device, a tombstone revision object, which indicates that the deleted document will be created for this document. We use a push rather than a pull scheme to synchronize the tombstone revision. Once the tombstone revision is set as the current revision, the corresponding document will be deleted from other remote databases.

4   User Authentication and Access Control in Data Synchronization

One of the fundamental features of SNSs is their ability to share selected pieces of information with selected friends or groups. To accomplish this fundamental feature, we implement access control in our decentralized SNS without central authority.

4.1   Implementation of Decentralized User Authentication with OpenID Connect

OpenID Connect is the third generation of OpenID technology [13]. It is an authentication layer on top of OAuth2.0. OpenID Connect utilizes the OAuth 2.0 semantics and flows to allow applications to access the user's identity, which is encoded in a JSON Web Token (JWT) called *ID token*. The design of OpenID Connect protocol is flexible. The Identity Provider (IDP) can not only comprise central Internet services such as Google and Yahoo but also many other types of IDP, including IDPs that run on users' own mobile devices. The latter are called *self-issued OpenID providers*.

Based on OpenID Connect, we implement decentralized user authentication for Sweets. We run self-issued OpenID providers on users' devices, and provide users with ID tokens as their identity. While a typical centralized application uses a user name and password to log in, our SNS application uses this ID token. When a user opens the Sweets, the IDP running on the same mobile device is called automatically. Following user authentication, the IDP sends back her/his ID token to the SNS application. This ID token will be sent to a remote device in data synchronization. The remote node will verify the received ID token thought the OpenID Connect procedure, and perform access control using the user ID in the ID token.

When two users establish the social relationship, they exchange their user identities with ID tokens in a face-to-face way rather than over untrusted servers. Due to the features of mobile devices, users can exchange their identities conveniently using Quick Response (QR) codes and cameras, Bluetooth, and Near Field Communication (NFC) networks.

4.2   Access Control Model for Direct Replication

The access control model used in direct data synchronization is similar to that for files in the Microsoft Windows operating system [12]. In this access control model, any user data have a corresponding access control list (ACL) that identifies the users and groups with allowed or denied access to the data element. When a user tries to pull a data element, the application steps through the ACL for each document and checks Access Control Entry (ACE) until it obtains the permission defined by the user.

We integrate our access control model with filtered replication in Couchbase Lite. *Filtered replication* examines documents through a filter function [3]. A filter function is executed when a remote user tries to synchronize data with the local database. Once the remote user tries to pull data from the local database with her/his ID token, the filter function steps through documents and determines whether the document can be pulled based on the ACL.

5   Indirect Replication

To improve data availability, we enable users to pull the data of offline friends indirectly from mutual friends. For this indirect replication, we realize another access control scheme based on Attribute Based Encryption (ABE).

5.1   Access Control for Indirect Replication

With the aim of providing access control during indirect replication without an access control list, we integrate Attribute-Based Encryption (ABE) into Sweets and implement a novel access control scheme using ABE.

In an ABE cryptosystem, ciphertexts are labeled with sets of attributes and secret keys (SK) are associated with access structures that control which ciphertexts a user can decrypt. In particular, we utilize Ciphertext-Policy Attribute Encryption (CP-ABE) [2] in our application. In this cryptosystem, a user's secret key is associated with an arbitrary number of attributes expressed as strings. With ABE, we implement a hybrid encryption scheme for access control in indirect replication.

In indirect replication, we use two types of documents: tweet documents and encrypted tweet documents. An encrypted tweet document comprises the encrypted content of a tweet, which is encrypted using Advanced Encryption Standard (AES) [4] with a random key. We encrypt the AES key with the given access policy using ABE and store the encrypted AES key within the encrypted tweet document.

At initialization time, when two users establish a social relationship, they determine each other's attributes within their social network (e.g., family, friend, etc.), and exchange public keys (PK) and secret keys of ABE.

In Fig. 2, Bob is the mutual friend of Alice and Carol. Alice publishes a tweet and Sweets creates a tweet document and the corresponding encrypted tweet document. In direct replication, Sweets checks the ACL. If Bob is given permission to access the tweet, he can pull both documents. However, since Alice forbids Bob from accessing the tweet, Bob pulls only the encrypted tweet document. Finally, Alice goes offline.

When Carol tries to pull the tweet from Alice directly, Sweets is aware that Alice has been offline; thus, Sweets pulls the encrypted tweet document from Bob. After replicating the encrypted tweet document, Sweets decrypts the AES key within the document using the ABE secret key. If Alice allows Carol to

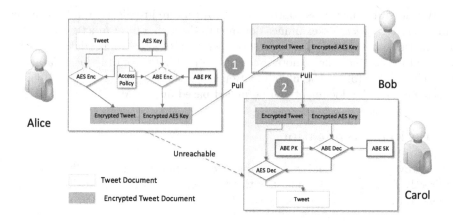

Fig. 2. Access control implementation with ABE

access the tweet, then she can decrypt it and obtain the AES key successfully. With the AES key, Carol can decrypt the tweet content.

As a result, Sweets achieves high data availability with this access control scheme. Furthermore, our implementation comes with some other merits. First, the access control is executed on the receiver side. Relaying friends cannot be aware who has the permission. Sweets allows users to grant fine-grained access to their data without replicating the access control list to other users. Second, with the hybrid encryption scheme, users can encrypt the tweet content with its key again after update, e.g., making comments and thumbing-up. Obviously, the new revision is also access limited under the same access policy. The author of the tweet can receive the comment indirectly.

5.2   Mirror Selection

As described in Sect. 3.2, Couchbase keeps the revision history of a document, and increases the sequence number of a database for each update. Our implementation uses this sequence number for mirror selection in indirect replication. In particular, Sweets selects the most eligible mutual friend as the mirror by comparing their sequence numbers when they pull encrypted tweet documents from offline friends. Our mirror selection scheme enables users to obtain almost the latest tweet documents of offline friends. Moreover, we can rank mirrors in terms of objective reputation scores which are calculated by reputation measurement [11]. The reputation score of a mirror represents the overall performance, and it can be determined not only by the sequence number, but also the response time, availability, etc.

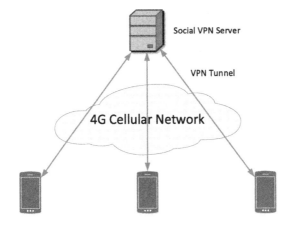

Fig. 3. Performance evaluation experiment configuration

6   Evaluation

In this section, we evaluate Sweets. Sweets is operational using the Social Soft-Ether VPN over a 4G cellular network. Social SoftEther VPN [15] is an implementation of Social VPN based on SoftEther VPN [16]. SoftEther VPN is our open-source VPN software. In our experiment, we established the connection between several Android devices over the cellular network using Social Soft-Ether VPN. Social SoftEther VPN allows Sweets to identify friends and connect their devices with domain names that include friends' identifiers.

6.1   Qualitative Aspect

So far, we have achieved the following goals. First, compared with current centralized SNS applications, Sweets preserves user privacy by discarding centralized storage servers and enabling users to store their data on their own devices. Second, Sweets runs on mobile devices, which is the major mode by which people participate in SNSs. Third, Sweets provide strong access control schemes in both direct and indirect replication.

The current implementation has some limitations. First, Sweets depends on a social VPN. We use SoftEther VPN to realize the social VPN, and users must trust VPN servers and their owners. If the VPN server is cracked, Sweets can leak private information. Second, due to the features of the distributed network, Sweets does not support certain functionality, e.g., search.

6.2   Performance

We measured the performance of Sweets. The experiment configuration and experiment environment is as follows (Fig. 3):

- Mobile device: Nexus 5X (Android 6.0, 1.8 GHz Snapdragon 808 CPU, 2 GB RAM)
- Mobile network operator: Softbank (4G)
- Average latency over VPN: 101 ms
- Bandwidth over VPN: 1.73 Mbps

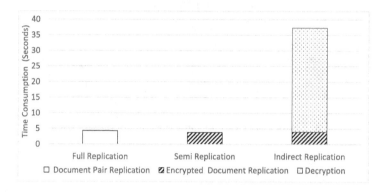

Fig. 4. Execution time of replicating 50 tweets

For the comparison, we have measured the performance in a LAN. However, due to the implementation of an Android Wi-Fi module, which limits the Wi-Fi connection performance, we obtained a worse performance on a LAN than on the 4G cellular network. Hence, we omitted the LAN performance results.

We measured the time consumption to transfer 50 tweets in direct and indirect replication. Figure 4 shows the results. Full replication means direct replication when the receiver has the permission for the tweets. In this case, both tweet documents and encrypted tweet documents are replicated. Semi replication means direct replication, which replicates only encrypted tweet documents. The indirect replication consists of two phases. The first phase entails pulling encrypted tweet documents. After the first phase, Sweets decrypts these encrypted tweet documents.

Sweets took approximately 4 s to pull 50 tweets in direct replication and approximately 35 s in indirect replication. These execution times are adequate for exchanging short tweets among a small number of friends over the 4G network. If a user has 100 friends, and they post 10 tweets per day, Sweets handles 2,000 tweets per day. Sweets can handle these messages within a few minutes per day in direct replication and 20 min per day in indirect replication. Obviously, tweet document decryption is the bottleneck in the indirect replication. We noticed that AES decryption only took 30 ms for 50 tweet documents, and the replication time can be substantially shorten by reusing AES keys [1].

Data synchronization is conducted as a background task asynchronously after as soon as Sweets is launched. When users refresh the time line through the user interface, the application simply retrieves the data from the local database and shows them to users. Hence, we believe that Sweets is feasible for mobile device users and can provide almost the same user experience as that provided by current popular centralized SNS applications.

7   Conclusions and Future Work

This paper has described a decentralized SNS application, Sweets. We implemented Sweets using data synchronization among mobile devices. Sweets also provides user authentication and access control without centralized servers. Furthermore, we improved the data availability of Sweets using an indirect replication scheme. We realized basic social networking functionality on Android devices. Finally, we have shown that Sweets has a feasible performance over a 4G cellular network.

As future work, we plan to realize a better mirror selection scheme in indirect replication and achieve higher data availability.

References

1. Baden, R., Bender, A., Spring, N., Bhattacharjee, B., Starin, D.: Persona: an online social network with user-defined privacy. In: The ACM SIGCOMM 2009 Conference on Data Communication, pp. 135–146 (2009)
2. Bethencourt, J., Sahai, A., Waters, B.: Ciphertext-policy attribute-based encryption. In: IEEE Symposium on Security and Privacy, pp. 321–334 (2007)
3. Couchbase Lite. http://www.couchbase.com/nosql-databases/couchbase-mobile
4. Daemen, J., Rijmen, V.: The Design of Rijndael: AES-The Advanced Encryption Standard. Springer Science & Business Media, Heidelberg (2013)
5. Datta, A., Buchegger, S., Vu, L.H., Strufe, T., Rzadca, K.: Decentralized online social networks. In: Furht, B. (ed.) Handbook of Social Network Technologies and Applications, pp. 349–378. Springer, Heidelberg (2010)
6. Durr, M., Maier, M., Dorfmeister, F.: Vegas-a secure and privacy-preserving peer-to-peer online social network. In: 2012 International Conference on Privacy, Security, Risk and Trust (PASSAT), pp. 868–874. IEEE (2012)
7. Figueiredo, R.J., Boykin, P.O., Juste, P.S., Wolinsky, D.: Integrating overlay and social networks for seamless P2P networking. In: Workshop on Enabling Technologies: Infrastructure for Collaborative Enterprises, pp. 93–98. IEEE (2008)
8. Freitas, M.: Twister-a P2P microblogging platform. arXiv preprint (2013). arXiv:1312.7152
9. Goyal, V., Pandey, O., Sahai, A., Waters, B.: Attribute-based encryption for fine-grained access control of encrypted data. In: Proceedings of the 13th ACM Conference on Computer and Communications Security, pp. 89–98. ACM (2006)
10. Greenwald, G.: No Place to Hide. Metropolitan Books, New York (2014)
11. Huang, L., Wang, S., Hsu, C.H., Zhang, J., Yang, F.: Using reputation measurement to defend mobile social networks against malicious feedback ratings. J. Supercomput. **71**(6), 2190–2203 (2015)
12. Microsoft Windows access control. https://msdn.microsoft.com/en-us/library/windows/desktop/aa374860(v=vs.85).aspx
13. OpenID. http://openid.net/

14. OpenID Connect. http://openid.net/connect/
15. Shinjo, Y., Kunyao, X., Kainuma, N., Nobori, D., Sato, A.: Friend news system: a modern implementation of Usenet over social VPNs. In: 7th IEEE International Conference on Social Computing and Networking, pp. 432–440 (2014)
16. Softether VPN Project. http://www.softether.org/

LBDAG-DNE: Locality Balanced Subspace Learning for Image Recognition

Chuntao Ding[✉] and Qibo Sun

State Key Laboratory of Networking and Switching Technology,
Beijing University of Posts and Telecommunications, Beijing 100876, China
ctding@bupt.edu.cn

Abstract. The cloud-computing environment makes it possible to select the best features when tuning parameters. Various dimensionality reduction algorithms can achieve the best features with the tuning of parameters. Double adjacency graphs-based discriminant neighborhood embedding (DAG-DNE) is a typical graph-based dimensionality reduction method, and has been successfully applied to image recognition. It involves the construction of two adjacency graphs, with the goal of learning the intrinsic structure of the data. However, it may impair the different degrees of importance of the intra-class information and inter-class information of the given data. In this paper, we develop an extension of DAG-DNE, called locality balanced double adjacency graphs-based discriminant neighborhood embedding (LBDAG-DNE) by considering the intra-class information and inter-class information of the given data differently. LBDAG-DNE can find a good projection matrix, which allows neighbors belonging to the same class to be compact while neighbors belonging to different classes become separable in the subspace. Experiments on two image databases illustrate the effectiveness of the proposed approach.

Keywords: DAG-DNE · Intrinsic structure · Image recognition · Dimensionality reduction

1 Introduction

Dimensionality reduction is one of the most useful tools for data analysis in data mining. Many dimensionality reduction algorithms can achieve the best features when tuning parameters. However, tuning parameters in the process of dimensionality reduction significantly increases the time cost. Cloud computing [6, 7], which has supercomputing power, can extract features more efficiently when tuning parameters.

The most popular dimensionality reduction algorithms include locally linear embedding (LLE) [1], ISOMAP [2], and Laplacian eigenmap (LE) [3]. These algorithms only provide the embedding results for training samples. There are many extensions that attempt to solve the out-of-sample problem, such as locality preserving projections (LPP) [4, 5]. These algorithms could preserve the local information by constructing an adjacency graph, but they cannot work well in classification because they are unsupervised.

© ICST Institute for Computer Sciences, Social Informatics and Telecommunications Engineering 2017
S. Wang and A. Zhou (Eds.): CollaborateCom 2016, LNICST 201, pp. 199–210, 2017.
DOI: 10.1007/978-3-319-59288-6_18

Many supervised algorithms have been proposed to overcome the aforementioned drawbacks. Linear discriminant analysis (LDA) was proposed in [8–10], Yan et al. proposed marginal Fisher analysis (MFA) [11]; Zhang et al. proposed discriminant neighborhood embedding (DNE) [12]; Ding et al. proposed similarity-balanced discriminant neighborhood embedding (SBDNE) [14] and double adjacency graph-based discriminant neighborhood embedding (DAG-DNE) [13], and so on. However, these algorithms may not consider the different degrees of intra-class information and inter-class information, which is important to learn the projection matrix.

Inspired by recent progress, in this study, we propose a novel supervised discriminant subspace learning algorithm called locality balanced double adjacency graphs-based discriminant neighbor embedding (LBDAG-DNE). In LBDAG-DNE, we employ DAG-DNE to construct two adjacency graphs to preserve the intra-class information and inter-class information, which link every sample to its homogeneous and heterogeneous neighbors, respectively. In LBDAG-DNE, we introduce a parameter that can balance the intra-class information and inter-class information depending on the situational requirements. Thus, LBDAG-DNE could maintain the balance between intra-class information and inter-class information and find an optimal projection matrix. Experimental results validate the effectiveness of LBDAG-DNE in comparison with several related state-of-the-art methods.

The rest of this paper is structured as follows. In Sect. 2, we provide a summary of the classic algorithms. Our LBDAG-DNE algorithm is introduced in Sect. 3. The experimental results are presented in Sect. 4. Finally, we provide the concluding remarks in Sect. 5.

2   Related Work

Over the past few years, dimensionality reduction techniques have received much attention, and correspondingly, many algorithms have been proposed [11–13, 15]. We will briefly introduce some of the classic algorithms in this section.

Yan et al. [11] proposed MFA in 2005, which finds an optimal projection matrix by simultaneously minimizing the intra-class scatter and maximizing the inter-class scatter by constructing two adjacency graphs. However, it cannot determine the optimal discriminant subspace.

Soon after this, Zhang et al. [12] proposed DNE. It maintains the local structure and distinguishes homogeneous and heterogeneous neighbors by constructing an adjacency graph, which can determine the optimal discriminant subspace. However, DNE does not construct a link between each point and its heterogeneous neighbors when constructing the adjacency graph.

Recently, Ding et al. [13] proposed DAG-DNE, which can effectively solve the problem of DNE and LDNE, with each sample respectively linked to its homogeneous and heterogeneous neighbors by constructing double adjacency graphs. However, DAG-DNE simply considers intra-class information and inter-class information to have the same degree of importance. In actuality, they play different roles in the classification task.

The above algorithms may simply consider intra-class information and inter-class information to have the same degree of importance. However, they play different roles in the classification task. Thus, when projected into a low-dimensional space, some more important discriminative information may be missed.

3   Our Proposed LBDAG-DNE

3.1   LBDAG-DNE

Let $\{(\mathbf{x}_i, y_i)\}_{i=1}^{N}$ be a set of training samples, where $\mathbf{x}_i \in R^d$ and $y_i \in \{1, 2, \dots, C\}$. LBDAG-DNE aims to find a projection matrix $\mathbf{P}$, with the ability to project the data from a high-dimensional space into a low-dimensional space $\mathbf{V}_i = \mathbf{P}^T \mathbf{x}_i$, which allows neighbors belonging to the same class to be compact while neighbors belonging to different classes become separable.

Similar to DAG-DNE, LBDAG-DNE requires the construction of two adjacency graphs. Let $\mathbf{F}^w$ and $\mathbf{F}^b$ be the intra-class and inter-class adjacency matrices, respectively. For a sample $\mathbf{x}_i$, $NH_k^w(\mathbf{x}_i)$ and $NH_k^b(\mathbf{x}_i)$ denote its K homogeneous and heterogeneous neighbors, respectively.

The intra-class adjacency matrix $\mathbf{F}^w$ is defined as

$$F_{ij}^w = \begin{cases} +1, & \mathbf{x}_i \in NH_k^w(\mathbf{x}_j) \text{ or } \mathbf{x}_j \in NH_k^w(\mathbf{x}_i) \\ 0, & otherwise \end{cases} \tag{1}$$

and the inter-class adjacency matrix $\mathbf{F}^b$ is

$$F_{ij}^b = \begin{cases} +1, & \mathbf{x}_i \in NH_k^b(\mathbf{x}_j) \text{ or } \mathbf{x}_j \in NH_k^b(\mathbf{x}_i) \\ 0, & otherwise \end{cases} \tag{2}$$

The intra-class scatter is defined as follows:

$$\begin{aligned} \Phi(\mathbf{P}) &= \sum_{i,j} ||\mathbf{P}^T \mathbf{x}_i - \mathbf{P}^T \mathbf{x}_j||^2 F_{ij}^w \\ &= 2tr\{\mathbf{P}^T \mathbf{X}(\mathbf{D}^w - \mathbf{F}^w)\mathbf{X}^T \mathbf{P}\} \end{aligned} \tag{3}$$

where $\mathbf{D}^w$ is a diagonal matrix, and its entries are the column sums of $\mathbf{F}^w$.

The inter-class scatter is as follows:

$$\begin{aligned} \Psi(\mathbf{P}) &= \sum_{i,j} ||\mathbf{P}^T \mathbf{x}_i - \mathbf{P}^T \mathbf{x}_j||^2 F_{ij}^b \\ &= 2tr\{\mathbf{P}^T \mathbf{X}(\mathbf{D}^b - \mathbf{F}^b)\mathbf{X}^T \mathbf{P}\} \end{aligned} \tag{4}$$

where $\mathbf{D}^b$ is a diagonal matrix, and its entries are the column sums of $\mathbf{F}^b$.

The goal is to allow neighbors belonging to the same class be compact, while neighbors belonging to different classes become separable in the subspace. We need to maximize the margin of total inter-class scatter and total intra-class scatter, i.e.,

$$\Theta(\mathbf{P}) = \Psi(\mathbf{P}) - \beta\Phi(\mathbf{P}) \tag{5}$$

where $\beta \in [0, 10]$ is a tuning parameter that controls the tradeoff between intra-class information and inter-class information.

LBDAG-DNE seeks to find a projection matrix $\mathbf{P}$ by solving the following objective function. The complete derivation and theoretical justifications are similar to those of DAG-DNE. Therefore, the details of the derivation and theoretical justification can be found in [13].

$$\begin{cases} \max_{\mathbf{P}} \ \mathrm{tr}\{\mathbf{P}^T\mathbf{XSX}^T\mathbf{P}\} \\ s.t. \quad \mathbf{P}^T\mathbf{P} = \mathbf{I} \end{cases} \tag{6}$$

where $S = \mathbf{D}^b - \mathbf{F}^b - \beta * \mathbf{D}^w + \beta * \mathbf{F}^w$.

The projection matrix $\mathbf{P}$ can be found by solving the generalized eigenvalue problem as follows:

$$\mathbf{XSX}^T\mathbf{P} = \lambda\mathbf{P} \tag{7}$$

Thus, $\mathbf{P}$ is composed of the optimal r projection vectors corresponding to the r largest eigenvalues.

The details for LBDAG-DNE are given in Algorithm 1.

Algorithm 1. Locality balanced double adjacency graphs-based discriminant neighborhood embedding (LBDAG-DNE)

Input: A training set $\{(\mathbf{x}_i, y_i)\}_{i=1}^N$ and the dimensionality of discriminant subspace r.

Output: Projection matrix $\mathbf{P}$.

Step 1. Compute the intra-class scatter matrix $\mathbf{F}^w$ and inter-class scatter matrix $\mathbf{F}^b$ according to (1) and (2), respectively.

Step 2. Eigendecompose the matrix, where $\mathbf{XSX}^T$. Let the eigenvalues be $\lambda_i, i = 1,...,d$, and their corresponding eigenvectors be $\mathbf{p}_i (i = 1,...,d)$, with $\lambda_1 \geq \lambda_2 \geq ... \geq \lambda_d$.

Step 3. Choose the first r largest eigenvalues so that return $\mathbf{P} = [\mathbf{p}_i,...,\mathbf{p}_r]$.

3.2 Connection to LBDAG-DNE and DAG-DNE

By constructing two adjacency graphs, DAG-DNE can maintain the local intrinsic structure for the original data in the subspace, allowing it to effectively find optimal discriminant directions. However, DAG-DNE simply considers the intra-class information and inter-class information to have the same degree of importance. In actuality, they play different roles in the classification task. Thus, when projected into the low-dimensional space, some more important discriminative information may be missed. LBDAG-DNE regulates the different levels of the intra-class information and inter-class information by introducing a balance factor. As a result, LBDAG-DNE can adjust the balance factor according to the actual situation to achieve a good performance.

4   Experiments and Analysis

4.1   Data Sets

We conducted experiments on three data sets that are publicly available: MNIST[1], UMIST[2]. Brief descriptions of these data sets are given below (see Table 1 for some important statistics):

Table 1.   Data sets used in our experiments

Data set	#of instances	#of features	#of classes
MNIST	70000	784	10
UMIST	564	10304	20

MNIST is a data set of handwritten digits. Each image is represented as a 784-dimensional vector.

UMIST is a data set that takes into account race, sex, and appearance, which we downsampled to a size of 32×32 for computational efficiency.

4.2   Experimental Setup

All of the algorithms were implemented in MATLAB 2012b, and executed on an Intel (R) i5 Core CPU 2.50 GHz machine with 4 GB of RAM. Our experiment required the nearest neighbor parameter K to construct adjacency graphs. For simplicity, the nearest neighbor (NN) classifier was used for classifying test images in the projected spaces.

---

[1] http://yann.lecun.com/exdb/mnist/.
[2] web.mit.edu/emeyers/www/face_databases.html#umist.

4.3 Comparison Algorithms

To demonstrate the effectiveness and efficiency of our proposed LBDAG-DNE, we compared it with three other state-of-the-art algorithms. The following is a list of information concerning the experimental settings of each method:

(1) DNE: discriminant neighborhood embedding proposed in [12].
(2) MFA: marginal Fisher analysis proposed in [11].
(3) DAG-DNE: double adjacency graphs-based discriminant neighborhood embedding proposed in [13].

4.4 Performance Metric

The classification result was evaluated by comparing the obtained label of each sample with the label provided by the data set. We used the accuracy [11, 12] to measure the classification performance. Given a data point $\mathbf{x}_i$, let $c(\mathbf{x}_i)$ and $c'(\mathbf{x}_i)$ be the obtained classification label and the label provided by the corpus, respectively. The accuracy is defined as follows:

$$Accuracy = \frac{\sum_{i=1}^{N} \delta(c(\mathbf{x}_i), c'(\mathbf{x}_i))}{N} \tag{9}$$

where N is the total number of samples, and $\delta(a, b)$ is the delta function that equals one if $a = b$ and equals zero otherwise.

4.5 Experimental Results

To evaluate the effectiveness and correctness of the proposed algorithm, experiments were carried out on the MNIST, UMIST, and ORL databases, and the results were compared with those of DNE, MFA, and DAG-DNE.

In the parameter selection step, we randomly selected 60% of the images from the 60% training set as the training set, and the remaining 40% of the images from the 60% training set as the test set to selection parameters and then used the result to choose β.

4.5.1 Results with Handwritten Dataset

For the MNIST data set, we considered five classes, including the digits 1, 3, 5, 7, and 9. For each class, we randomly selected 50 samples from the original training set as our training samples, and 50 samples from the original test set as our test samples. Figure 1 shows some image samples from the MNIST dataset. The performances of the four methods are reported in Fig. 2. We used $K = 1, 3, 5$, and 7 to construct the adjacency graphs for all the methods.

Here, we mainly focus on the effect of the dimensionality of the discriminant subspace on the classification accuracy under different choices for the nearest neighbor parameter K. Without prior knowledge, K was set to be 1, 3, 5, and 7. PCA was utilized to reduce the dimensionality from 784 to 80. We repeated 30 trials and report the average results. Figure 2(a), (c), (e), and (g) shows the accuracy of the four methods with different dimensions and different values of K. Figure 2(a), (c), (e), and (g) shows that the classification accuracies of all four methods increase rapidly, and then almost become stable. More importantly, we can obviously see that LBDAG-DNE performs better than DNE, MFA, and DAG-DNE across a wide dimensionality range on the MNIST dataset, and the increase for LBDAG-DNE is the most rapid.

From Fig. 2(b), (d), (f), and (h), we can observe that LBDAG-DNE can obtain a good performance at a relatively low discriminant subspace, and can reduce the computational complexity and improve the classification performance.

Thus, the experimental results on the MNIST dataset illustrate that LBDAG-DNE outperforms the other algorithms. In spite of the variation in K, LBDAG-DNE has the highest recognition accuracy among these methods.

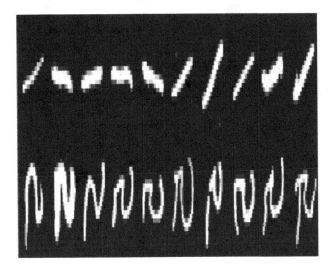

Fig. 1. Sample face images from MNIST database

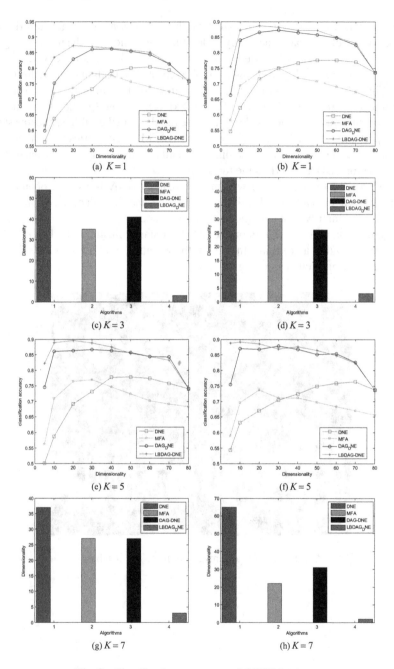

Fig. 2. Classification accuracy on MNIST database

4.5.2 Results with UMIST Dataset

For UMIST datasets, we randomly selected 20% of the images from the database as training samples, with the remaining 80% used as test samples. Figure 3 shows some image samples from the UMIST dataset. We repeated 20 runs and report the average results and corresponding parameters in Table 2.

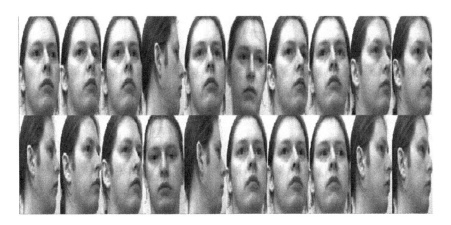

Fig. 3. Sample face images from UMIST database.

Table 2. Best average recognition rates of all methods on UMIST dataset.

Method	$K = 1$	$K = 3$
PCA	$85.37 \pm 0.71(80)$	$85.37 \pm 0.71(80)$
LPP	$75.57 \pm 0.96(80)$	$74.72 \pm 1.59(80)$
MFA	$83.55 \pm 0.33(36)$	$81.95 \pm 1.79(31)$
DNE	$85.90 \pm 1.74(76)$	$84.26 \pm 1.64(77)$
DAG-DNE	$87.72 \pm 0.52(47)$	$87.23 \pm 0.82(32)$
LBDAG_DNE	$89.53 \pm 0.18(16)$	$89.76 \pm 0.46(19)$

First, we consider the parameter selection. The nearest neighbor parameter K is selected from the set $\{1, 3\}$. Figure 4 illustrates the relationship between the accuracy and the value of β. From Fig. 4, we know that the accuracy is not the highest when $\beta = 1$, where β is a tuning parameter that balances the tradeoff between intra-class information and inter-class information. The intra-class information and inter-class information play different roles in the classification task.

Figure 5(a) and (c) shows the accuracies of the four methods vs. the dimensionality of the subspace with different K. Figure 5(b) and (d) shows the relationship for the subspace dimension with the best accuracy. As seen in Fig. 5(a) and (c), the classification accuracies of all four algorithms increase rapidly. However, LBDAG-DNE has the fastest increase. From Fig. 5(b) and (d), we can see that LBDAG-DNE has the lowest discriminant subspace, which provides a good performance.

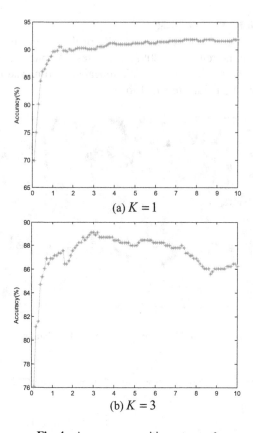

(a) $K = 1$

(b) $K = 3$

Fig. 4. Average recognition rates vs.β

Furthermore, Table 2 reports the best average recognition rates on the test sets for all of the methods, along with the corresponding dimension of the reduced subspace under different values of K. In spite of the variation in K, LBDAG-DNE has the highest recognition rate among these algorithms.

Based on the results of the handwriting and face recognition experiments, we can see that the classification performance of LBDAG-DNE is the best compared to DNE, MFA, and DAG-DNE. This suggests that the intra-class information and inter-class information have different degrees of importance for classification. In other words, they play different roles in the classification task. Moreover, the superiority of LBDAG-DNE was effectively demonstrated in all of the experiments. We could reduce the computational complexity and improve the classification using LBDAG-DNE to extract the effective features.

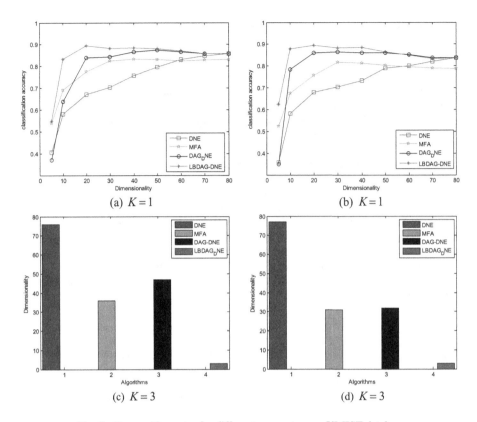

Fig. 5. Recognition rates for different parameters on UMIST database

5 Conclusion

The superior computing power of cloud computing makes it possible to utilize tuning parameters to select the best features. In this paper, we proposed a novel supervised discriminant subspace learning algorithm, called LBDAG-DNE, with the goal of learning a good embedded subspace from the original high-dimensional space for classification. LBDAG-DNE maintains the intra-class and inter-class structure by constructing adjacency graphs and balances them by introducing a balance parameter. More importantly, by introducing a balance parameter, it can also regulate the different levels of the intra-class information and inter-class information. Thus, LBDAG-DNE could find an optimal projection matrix. Experimental results show that LBDAG-DNE could achieve the best classification performance in comparison with several related state-of-the-art methods.

Acknowledgement. This work is supported by the National Science of Foundation of China, under grant No. 61571066 and grant No. 61472047.

References

1. Roweis, S.T., Saul, L.K.: Nonlinear dimensionality reduction by locally linear embedding. Science **290**(5500), 2323–2326 (2000)
2. Tenenbaum, J., Silva, V.D., Langford, J.C.: A global geometric framework for nonlinear dimensionality reduction. Science **290**(5500), 2319–2323 (2000)
3. He, X.F., Yan, S.C., Hu, Y.C., Niyogi, P.: Face recognition using laplacianfaces. IEEE Trans. Pattern Anal. Mach. Intell. **27**(3), 328–340 (2001)
4. He, X.F., Niyogi, P.: Locality preserving projections. In: Proceedings of Advances in Neural Information Processing Systems, pp. 153–160 (2003)
5. Xu, Y., Zhong, A.N., Yang, J., Zhang, D.: LPP solution schemes for use with face recognition. Pattern Recogn. **43**(12), 4165–4176 (2010)
6. Wang, S.G., Zhou, A., Hsu, C.H., Xiao, X.Y., Yang, F.C.: Provision of data-intensive services through energy-and QoS-aware virtual machine placement in national cloud data centers. IEEE Trans. Emerg. Top. Comput. **4**(2), 290–300 (2016)
7. Wang, S.G., Fan, C.Q., Hsu, C.H., Sun, Q.B., Yang, F.C.: A vertical handoff method via self-selection decision tree for internet of vehicles. IEEE Syst. J. **10**(3), 1183–1192 (2016)
8. Fukunaga, K.: Introduction to Statistical Pattern Recognition. 2nd edn. Academic Press (2013)
9. Martinez, A.M., Kak, A.C.: PCA versus LDA. IEEE Trans. Pattern Analysis Mach. Intell. **23**(2), 228–233 (2001)
10. Yu, H., Yang, J.: A direct LDA algorithm for high-dimensional data with application to face recognition. Pattern Recogn. **34**(10), 2067–2070 (2001)
11. Yan, S.C., Xu, D., Zhang, B.Y., Zhang, H.J., Yang, Q., Lin, S.: Graph embedding and extensions: a general framework for dimensionality reduction. IEEE Trans. Pattern Analysis Mach. Intell. **29**(1), 40–51 (2007)
12. Zhang, W., Xue, X.Y., Guo, Y.F.: Discriminant neighborhood embedding for classification. Pattern Recogn. **39**(11), 2240–2243 (2006)
13. Ding, C.T., Zhang, L.: Double adjacency graphs-based discriminant neighborhood embedding. Pattern Recogn. **48**(5), 1734–1742 (2015)
14. Ding, C.T., Zhang, L., Lu, Y,P., He, S.P.: Similarity-balanced discriminant neighborhood embedding. In: Proceedings of 2014 International Joint Conference on Neural Networks, pp. 1213–1220 (2014)
15. Xu, J.L., Wang, S.G., Zhou, A., Yang, F.C.: Machine status prediction for dynamic and heterogeneous cloud environment. In: Proceedings of 2016 IEEE International Conference on Cluster Computing, pp. 136–137 (2016)

Collaborative Communication in Multi-robot Surveillance Based on Indoor Radio Mapping

Yunlong Wu, Bo Zhang$^{(\boxtimes)}$, Xiaodong Yi, and Yuhua Tang

State Key Laboratory of High Performance Computing, College of Computer,
National University of Defense Technology, Changsha, China
zhangbo10@nudt.edu.cn

Abstract. This paper considers a scenario where multiple sensing robots are deployed to monitor the indoor environments, and transmit the monitored data to the base station. In order to ensure favorable surveillance quality, we aim at achieving a high throughput for the multi-robot system. We firstly establish the stochastic wireless channel model and derive the expression of the throughput. Then, we propose the non-collaborative and collaborative communication strategies, both adopting the joint frequency-rate adaptation based on the stochastic channel model. The experimental results have shown that the throughput can be largely improved with the collaboration between robots. Furthermore, considering our surveillance scenario is approximate time-invariant (ATI), we propose the joint frequency-rate communication strategies based on proactive channel measurements, and the effectiveness of the strategies is validated by experimental results.

Keywords: Multi-robot collaboration · Joint frequency-rate communication strategies · Relays · Wireless channel modeling

1 Introduction

A multi-robot system aims at achieving challenging tasks or significantly improving mission performance compared with a single robot, which demands consensus and cooperation among robots [1]. In this paper, we consider a scenario where a team of sensing robots are deployed to monitor an indoor area, and transmit the monitored data (e.g., videos) to a base station through wireless communications. In the base station, the data will be analyzed for identifying abnormalities (e.g., an intruder) in the area.

For this multi-robot surveillance scenario, communication planning is demanded for maintaining reliable and high-throughput communications between each sensing robot and the base station. In [2], a rate-configurable robot was deployed to collect the generated data from several points of interest (POIs). A multi-robot communication planning strategy was considered in [3], where the authors aimed at maximizing the connectivity probabilities of the multi-robot

© ICST Institute for Computer Sciences, Social Informatics and Telecommunications Engineering 2017
S. Wang and A. Zhou (Eds.): CollaborateCom 2016, LNICST 201, pp. 211–220, 2017.
DOI: 10.1007/978-3-319-59288-6_19

network by optimizing the routing variables. However, the communication strategies above just consider the case that the robots adopt the fixed communication frequency-allocation.

Against this background, in this paper we propose the joint frequency-rate communication planning and a series of strategies for multi-robot systems. The contributions of this paper are as follows:

In Sect. 2, in order to support the joint frequency-rate communication planning, we firstly establish the multi-frequency wireless channel model which reflects the received signal quality (RSQ) of each communication frequency at each spatial location. Then, the channel model is used to evaluate the communication performance metric (e.g., throughput) and the packet error rate (PER). The distribution of RSQ may be depicted as a stochastic model with three main parts: path loss, shadowing and multipath fading [4]. The multi-robot system can select the optimal frequency-rate setting to maximize the throughput according to the RSQ-location mappings.

In Sect. 3, we propose two joint frequency-rate communication strategies based on the stochastic channel model. The *non-collaborative communication* strategy considers that each sensing robot communicates with the base station, and there is no information exchange among the sensing robots. The *collaborative communication* strategy allows the sensing robots to assist each other by relaying. For example, if a sensing robot is experiencing deep fading, relaying by other robots may greatly improve the throughput for supporting the monitored data transmission [5,6].

In Sect. 4, we pinpoint the fact that the stochastic channel model may capture the distribution of RSQ, however cannot exploit the exact RSQ at different locations for improving the throughput. Therefore, we propose to construct the RSQ-location mapping with proactive channel measurements, which may capture the RSQ more precisely than the stochastic model. Especially, when the RSQ changes rapidly in spatial domain variation, while changing slowly over the time domain. The experimental results have proved that the actual indoor measurements can identify the approximate time-invariant (ATI) scenarios and a higher throughput may be achieved in comparison with the stochastic model-based strategies.

In Sect. 5, the experimental results prove the effectiveness of joint frequency-rate communication planning, the collaboration strategy as well as the proactive channel measurements in improving the throughput of multi-robot systems.

2   Problem Formulation

We assume a N-sensing-robot system is deployed to monitor an area, where the surveillance route of each sensing robot is predefined and periodic. That is to say, when the sensing robot returns to the initial location, it may continue another loop. The sensors equipped on robots are responsible for collecting the environment information, and we may require the monitored data should be transmitted to the base station in real-time. Considering the high data sampling rates of the sensors on the robots (e.g., 4 Mbps per channel for a 1080P camera), we need to reasonably configure the communication settings, in the context of this paper, the frequency or the modulation and coding patterns, for the sake of maximizing the throughput of the multi-robot network based on the channel quality of the current location.

In order to avoid the interference between sensing robots, we adopt the frequency division multiple access (FDMA) mechanism, where the sensing robots are allocated orthogonal frequency channels for communications. However, we also allow dynamic frequency re-allocation during the operations. In an indoor environment, the geometric structure is often complicated which leads to the high complexity of the wireless communication channel. In order to get an optimal communication setting, we need to predict the received signal power at each spatial location and of multiple frequency bands.

2.1   Wireless Channel Modeling

The wireless communication channel can be modeled as a system affected by path loss, shadowing and multipath fading [7]. Let $G(q, f)$ denote the channel gain for the receiver node at location $q \in \mathcal{W}$ in frequency $f \in \mathcal{F}$, where $\mathcal{W} \subset \mathbb{R}^2$ is the workspace and $\mathcal{F}$ is the set of all candidate frequencies. Therefore, $G(q, f)$ can be expressed as $G(q, f) = G_{\mathrm{PL}}(q, f) G_{\mathrm{SH}}(f) G_{\mathrm{MP}}$, where $G_{\mathrm{PL}}(q, f)$ is the distance-dependent path loss. $G_{\mathrm{SH}}(f)$ and G_{MP} represent the impacts of shadowing and multipath fading respectively. G_{MP} can be regarded as a random variable having a mean value of 1. Let $P_{\mathrm{RX}}(q, f)$ denote the received signal power at $q \in \mathcal{W}$ in frequency $f \in \mathcal{F}$. We have $P_{\mathrm{RX}}(q, f) = P_{\mathrm{TX}} G(q, f)$, where P_{TX} is the transmit power from a fixed transmitter at $q_{\mathrm{TX}} \in \mathcal{W}$ and can be treated as a constant. Let $P_{\mathrm{RX,dB}}(q, f) = 10\log_{10}(P_{\mathrm{RX}}(q, f))$ represent the received signal power in dB. We have

$$P_{\mathrm{RX,dB}}(q, f) = K_{\mathrm{PL,dB}}(f) + 10 n_{\mathrm{PL}}(f) \log_{10} \|q - q_{\mathrm{TX}}\| \\ + K_{\mathrm{SH,dB}}(f) + \omega_{\mathrm{MP,dB}}. \tag{1}$$

In Eq. (1), $K_{\mathrm{PL,dB}}(f)$ and $n_{\mathrm{PL}}(f)$ are the path loss parameters respectively. $\|q - q_{\mathrm{TX}}\|$ represents the distance between the transmitter and the receiver at $q \in \mathcal{W}$. $K_{\mathrm{SH,dB}}(f)$ is set according to if there existing shadowing. When there is no line-of-sight (LOS) communication channel, $K_{\mathrm{SH,dB}}(f)$ is non-zero. If a LOS channel exists, $K_{\mathrm{SH,dB}}(f) = 0$. $\omega_{\mathrm{MP,dB}}$ is a zero-mean random variable which represents the multipath fading effect in dB.

2.2   Parameters Estimation

The parameters of Eq. (1) contains $K_{\mathrm{PL,dB}}(f)$, $n_{\mathrm{PL}}(f)$, $K_{\mathrm{SH,dB}}(f)$ and $\omega_{\mathrm{MP,dB}}$. In order to estimate the parameters, we designed a radio-mapping robot by mounting a universal soft-defined radio peripheral (USRP) device on a TurtleBot robot. We scheduled the robot to move along a trajectory in the LOS and non-ling-of-sight (NLOS) areas respectively, while recording the signal power along the route. Figure 1a and b, for instance, show the received power in dB along a LOS route and a NLOS route in our laboratory with three frequencies: 900 Hz, 1.8 GHz and 2.6 GHz. We may fit the measured data with a linear function based on least-square estimation. The fitting parameters are shown in Fig. 1a and b, where n_{PL} denotes the slope of the linear functions. In the LOS case, the intercept is $K_{PL,dB}(f)$. While, in the NLOS case, the intercept is $K_{PL,dB}(f) + K_{SH,dB}(f)$. It is shown that the path loss parameters of different frequencies are also different. As the frequency increases, the path loss parameters are more significant. In the LOS or NLOS area, the parameters are also different.

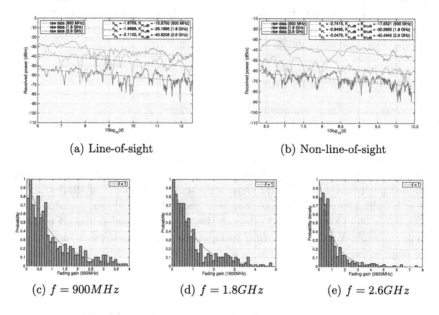

(a) Line-of-sight

(b) Non-line-of-sight

(c) $f = 900MHz$

(d) $f = 1.8GHz$

(e) $f = 2.6GHz$

Fig. 1. Line-of-sight (a) and non-line-of-sight (b) path loss parameter estimation in 900 MHz, 1.8 GHz and 2.6 GHz. Rayleigh distribution fitting in 900 MHz (c), 1.8 GHz (d) and 2.6 GHz (e).

The distribution of the fading effect is often based on specific environments. In the literatures, the variable ω_{MP} ($\omega_{MP} = 10^{\omega_{MP,dB}/10}$) follows some classical distribution models, such as Nakagami, Rayleigh or Rician [8]. For estimating the random variable ω_{MP}, we may extract samples in a NLOS area and ensure the distance from the sampling location to the base station does not change significantly and there is constant shadowing. In Fig. 1c to e, for instance, we collect about 500 samples for 900 MHz, 1.8 GHz and 2.6 GHz respectively, and draw the normalized histogram for each case. The results show that the ideal Rayleigh distribution (the line with $\delta = 1$) may fit the measurements well. Therefore, in this paper, we assume ω_{MP} follows the ideal Rayleigh distribution.

2.3 Rate Adaptation

Transmission rates may be adapted by selecting different combinations of channel coding and modulations. In this subsection, we may use the received signal-to-noise ratio (SNR) to derive the expression of the optimal transmission rate. We adopt the adaptive modulation and coding (AMC) scheme in 802.11n protocols, where SNR-triggered rate-selection allows adaptively choosing from a set of 6 transmission rates [9]. According to [9], the per-hop PER model is given by: $\text{PER}_n(\gamma) = a_n \exp(-g_n\gamma)$ if $\gamma \geq \gamma_{pn}$ and $\text{PER}_n(\gamma) = 1$ if $0 < \gamma < \gamma_{pn}$, where γ is the instantaneous received SNR, γ_{pn} is the switch threshold, and a_n, g_n are relative to the transmission mode index n, which represents the specific modulation and transmission rate as shown in Table II of [9]. We assume the wireless fading channel is quasi-static and Rayleigh distributed [7], then the resulted per-hop PER is

$$
\begin{aligned}
\text{PER}_n(\overline{\gamma}) &= \int_0^{+\infty} \text{PER}_n(\gamma) \frac{1}{\overline{\gamma}} \exp\left(-\frac{\gamma}{\overline{\gamma}}\right) d\gamma \\
&= 1 - \exp\left(-\frac{\gamma_{pn}}{\overline{\gamma}}\right) + \frac{a_n}{\overline{\gamma}g_n + 1} \exp\left(-g_n\gamma_{pn}\right) \exp\left(-\frac{\gamma_{pn}}{\overline{\gamma}}\right),
\end{aligned}
\tag{2}
$$

where $\overline{\gamma}$ is the average received SNR. In order to guarantee the communication quality, the PER of each sensing robot to the base station should be below a predefined threshold p_{ub}. In other words, when given p_{ub}, we may obtain the SNR thresholds for each mode. However, deriving the inverse function of Eq. (2) directly may be difficult. As an alternative, we may calculate $\text{PER}_n(\overline{\gamma})$ by enumerating all possible values of $\overline{\gamma}$ for each mode. When given p_{ub}, we may look up the most similar SNR threshold $\overline{\gamma}_{n,ub}$ for each mode n. Therefore, according to the average received SNR $\overline{\gamma}$, we may derive the optimal transmission mode n^* and transmission rate R^* as: $n^* = \arg\min_{n}(\overline{\gamma} - \overline{\gamma}_{n,ub}), \forall \overline{\gamma}_{n,ub} \leq \overline{\gamma}$, $R^* = R(n^*)$.

2.4 Throughput Modeling

The metric of throughput is often used to measure the data transmission capability of a communication network. For the sake of numerical analysis, we discretize the surveillance route (with length of L) into M steps, and the length of each step is $\Delta l = L/M$. We assume every sensing robot surveys the indoor environment with the constant speed v. Therefore, the time consumption by the sensing robot moving a distance of Δl is $\Delta t = \Delta l/v$. In surveillance applications, each sensing robot should achieve a favorable throughput. Therefore, the throughput $\mathcal{T}$ of the system can be modeled as a minimum-rate expression

$$
\mathcal{T} = \frac{\sum_{i=1}^{M}\left(\min\left(R_1^i, R_2^i, ..., R_N^i\right)\Delta t\right)}{M\Delta t},
\tag{3}
$$

where R_j^i represents the transmission rate of the j-th sensing robot in the i-th step. In each step, R_j^i is assumed fixed. Equation (3) shows that the communication performance of the system is dominated by the sensing robot with the minimum transmission rate.

3   Joint Frequency-Rate Communication Based on Stochastic Fading Modeling

3.1   Non-collaborative Communication Strategy

According to the analysis and experimental results, we may adjust the per-robot throughput by jointing frequency allocation and rate adaptation. According to Eq. (1), we may derive the average received power at each spatial location $q \in \mathcal{W}$ and frequency $f \in \mathcal{F}$. Figure 2a to c, for instance, show the distribution of the average received power in a rectangle indoor area for three different frequencies, where the base station is located in the southwest corner. Due to the effects of shadowing and path loss, the average received signal quality in the northeast corner of the map may be the worst. Given the same transmit power, the average received power of a lower frequency may be higher than that of a higher frequency. Therefore, we may propose a strategy that, in the worse channel-quality area based on the prediction results, a reliable frequency and modulation pattern may be adopted. We also assume the average noise power at each robot is identical. Let $\overline{\gamma}_i$ denote the predicted average SNR of the i-th robot, and further assume $\overline{\gamma}_1 > \overline{\gamma}_2 > \cdots > \overline{\gamma}_N$. We have the frequency allocation as $f_1 > f_2 > \cdots > f_N$, where f_i is the communication frequency of the i-th robot. When the frequency allocation is finished, each sensing robot can select the optimal transmission rate with the method in Subsect. 2.3.

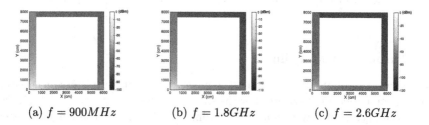

(a) $f = 900MHz$ (b) $f = 1.8GHz$ (c) $f = 2.6GHz$

Fig. 2. Received signal power prediction for different frequencies.

3.2   Collaborative Communication Strategy

The non-collaborative strategy does not exploit the inter-robot channels, which may provide additional degree-of-freedom for improving the throughput. Therefore, we propose the collaborative communication strategy, where a sensing robot can also provide communication relaying for other sensing robots. However, as the half-duplex wireless device is considered, the robot acting as a relay may sacrifice its own transmission resources for the sake of assisting other robots. Against this interesting trade-off, we will formulate the optimization problem of the collaborative strategy and evaluate its throughput performance. Let R_i denote the allowed transmission rate of the i-th node ($i = 0$ represents the base station and $i \neq 0$ represents the sensing robot), which can be expressed as the difference between the outgoing and incoming rates

$$R_i\left(\boldsymbol{F}, \boldsymbol{\lambda}\right) = \begin{cases} \underbrace{\sum\limits_{j=0,j\neq i}^{N} \lambda_{i,j} R_{i,j}}_{\text{outgoing}} - \underbrace{\sum\limits_{j=1,j\neq i}^{N} \lambda_{j,i} R_{j,i}}_{\text{incoming}}, \forall i \neq 0, \\ \infty - \sum\limits_{j=1,j\neq i}^{N} \lambda_{j,i} R_{j,i}, i = 0, \end{cases} \tag{4}$$

where $\lambda_{i,j}$ is the fraction of time from the i-th node to the j-th node, and $R_{i,j}$ is the corresponding transmission rate. We further define vectors $\boldsymbol{F} = (f_1, f_2, ..., f_N), f_i \in \mathcal{F}$, $\boldsymbol{R} = (R_{1,0}, ..., R_{N,N-1}) \in \mathbb{R}^{N^2}$ and $\boldsymbol{\lambda} = (\lambda_{1,0}, ..., \lambda_{N,N-1}) \in \mathbb{R}^{N^2}$. The base station ($i = 0$) is the destination of all information flows. To guarantee that we can find the optimal communication strategy, we set its outgoing rate an infinity. Equation (3) indicates that maximizing the thoughput $\mathcal{T}$ is equivalent to maximizing the minimum transmission rate of the multi-robot system in each step, which can be formulated as an optimization problem shown by Eq. (5).

$$\begin{aligned} \max_{\boldsymbol{F}, \boldsymbol{\lambda}} \quad & \mathcal{J} = \min\left\{R_0\left(\boldsymbol{F}, \boldsymbol{\lambda}\right), R_1\left(\boldsymbol{F}, \boldsymbol{\lambda}\right), ..., R_N\left(\boldsymbol{F}, \boldsymbol{\lambda}\right)\right\} \\ s.\,t. \quad & 1 \geq \lambda_{i,j} \geq 0, \forall i, j, \\ & \sum_{j=1}^{N} \lambda_{i,j} \leq 1, \forall i \neq 0, \\ & R_i\left(\boldsymbol{F}, \boldsymbol{\lambda}\right) \geq 0, \forall i, \\ & f_i \neq f_j, \forall i \neq j, i \neq 0, j \neq 0. \end{aligned} \tag{5}$$

Considering the variable f_i can only be assigned several discrete values, we may separate the variable f_i from the Eq. (5) and get the optimization problem with a specific $\boldsymbol{F}$, as shown in Eq. (6). To find the optimal communication strategy, we may compare the optimized results of Eq. (6) for different frequency settings $\boldsymbol{F}$, and get the optimal one.

$$\begin{aligned} \min_{\boldsymbol{\lambda}} \quad & \mathcal{J}_{\boldsymbol{F}} = \max\left\{-R_0\left(\boldsymbol{\lambda}\right), -R_1\left(\boldsymbol{\lambda}\right), ..., -R_N\left(\boldsymbol{\lambda}\right)\right\} \\ s.\,t. \quad & 1 \geq \lambda_{i,j} \geq 0, \forall i, j, \\ & \sum_{j=1}^{N} \lambda_{i,j} \leq 1, \forall i \neq 0, \\ & R_i\left(\boldsymbol{\lambda}\right) \geq 0, \forall i. \end{aligned} \tag{6}$$

$-R_i\left(\boldsymbol{\lambda}\right)$ is a linear function of $\boldsymbol{\lambda}$, which is also convex. We may set a variable θ that satisfies $0 \leq \theta \leq 1$ and $\boldsymbol{\lambda}_1, \boldsymbol{\lambda}_2 \in \mathbf{dom}\ \mathcal{J}_{\boldsymbol{F}}$, and prove the function $\mathcal{J}_{\boldsymbol{F}}$

is convex by definitions: $\mathcal{J}_F \left(\theta \lambda_1 + (1 - \theta) \lambda_2 \right) \leq \theta \mathcal{J}_F \left(\lambda_1 \right) + (1 - \theta) \mathcal{J}_F \left(\lambda_2 \right)$. Therefore, Eq. (6) is a convex optimization problem, which can be solved optimally by numerical optimization methods, for example the interior point method.

4 Joint Frequency-Rate Communication Based on Channel Measurements

According to the analysis and experiments in Sect. 2 as well as widely acknowledged in the literature [8], the complex interactions between the environments and the electro-magnetic waves make the exact channel quality of a given location/frequency hard to predict. For example, as shown in Fig. 1a and b, there exists some deep fading locations that cannot be effectively predicted. By assuming the fading effect is a random process, the stochastic model in Sect. 2 aims at finding the fading distribution rather than predicting the actual channel quality of each location/frequency.

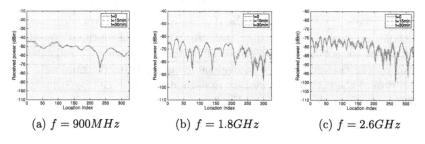

(a) $f = 900MHz$ (b) $f = 1.8GHz$ (c) $f = 2.6GHz$

Fig. 3. Received signal power of different frequencies in the same area every 15 min.

In this paper, we propose another way to circumvent the problem by proactive channel measurements and radio mapping. We may take samples in the whole area densely and construct a realistic RSQ-location mapping based on channel measurements. The mapping can be updated by the sensing robot every few minutes. In a quasi-static environment, such as our indoor scenario, the mapping remains static during a period of time, which is verified by our experimental measurements. Specifically, we measure the received signal power of different frequencies when time $t = 0, 15, 30$ min in the same area, and the results are shown in Fig. 3. The figure demonstrates that the received signal power changes rapidly as the robot moves along a trajectory because of fading. However, the fading pattern changes slowly over time, which allows the measurements of a robot to be effectively utilized by other robots. Therefore, designing communication strategies based on such a measurement-based RSQ-location mapping may benefit a lot than the model-based prediction, as shown in Sect. 5.

5   Experimental Results

In this section, we may compare the effectiveness of different communication strategies. The workspace for experimentation is a 60 m × 80 m rectangle region, and three sensing robots are deployed to survey the corridors of an indoor environment. The surveillance route is divided into 520 discrete segments (steps). In each step, we assume the communication settings may not change. The base station is located at the southwest corner of the workspace. The experiments test all five strategies proposed in this paper, as shown in Table 1. Figure 4a demonstrates the optimized minimum transmission rate of a complete surveillance period of the five communication strategies. With the fixed frequency allocation, the communication of the multi-robot system is interrupted ($\mathcal{J} = 0$) in most of time. When incurring dynamic reconfiguration of frequency and transmission mode, the performance gain is apparent. However, this strategy just considers the data transmission between the sensing robot and the base station, and ignores the collaboration between sensing robots. In the third strategy, we explore the performance gain based on collaborative communications, and the communication interrupts are improved significantly. Moreover, when taking the realistic channel measurements into consideration, the number of communication interrupts is greatly reduced, which is shown in Fig. 4a. The detailed number of interrupts and the throughput for the five strategies are shown in Table 1.

Table 1. Experiment design and results

Strategy index	Description	Interrupts	Throughput
1	Fixed frequency allocation	411	0.1995
2	Model-based non-collaboration	216	0.5995
3	Model-based collaboration	160	0.6995
4	Measurement-based non-collaboration	147	0.7476
5	Measurement-based collaboration	38	1.1459

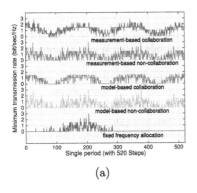

(a)

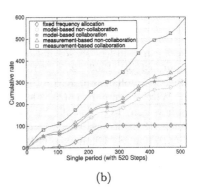

(b)

Fig. 4. Minimum transmission rate (a) and cumulative minimum transmission rate (b) in each step of a complete surveillance period, which contains 520 steps.

We also record the cumulative minimum transmission rate of a complete surveillance period, as shown in Fig. 4b. We may conclude that, compared with the model-based and fixed frequency allocation strategies, the performance gain of the collaborative strategies with realistic channel measurements is evident.

6   Conclusion

In this paper, we considered a multi-robot surveillance scenario and explored the communication performance gain with and without collaboration between robots. In order to achieve this objective, we modeled the wireless channel and throughput of the multi-robot system, and proposed the communication strategies based on the priori channel model and realistic measurements respectively. Furthermore, we proposed the concepts of non-collaborative communication and collaborative communication. The simulations compared the communication performance of different strategies and showed that the measurement-based collaborative communication may obtain a higher throughput and a smaller number of communication interrupts.

References

1. Olfati-Saber, R., Fax, J.A., Murray, R.M.: Consensus and cooperation in networked multi-agent systems. Proc. IEEE **95**(1), 215–233 (2007)
2. Yan, Y., Mostofi, Y.: To go or not to go: on energy-aware and communication-aware robotic operation. IEEE Trans. Control Netw. Syst. **1**(3), 218–231 (2014)
3. Fink, J., Ribeiro, A., Kumar, V.: Robust control for mobility and wireless communication in cyber-physical systems with application to robot teams. Proc. IEEE **100**(1), 164–178 (2012)
4. Yan, Y., Mostofi, Y.: Co-optimization of communication and motion planning of a robotic operation under resource constraints and in fading environments. IEEE Trans. Wirel. Commun. **12**(4), 1562–1572 (2013)
5. Han, B., Li, J., Su, J., Cao, J.: Self-supported cooperative networking for emergency services in multi-hop wireless networks. IEEE J. Sel. Areas Commun. **30**(2), 450–457 (2012)
6. Liang, W., Luo, J., Xu, X.: Network lifetime maximization for time-sensitive data gathering in wireless sensor networks with a mobile sink. Wirel. Commun. Mob. Comput. **13**(14), 1263–1280 (2013)
7. Lindhé, M., Johansson, K.H.: Using robot mobility to exploit multipath fading. IEEE Wirel. Commun. **16**(1), 30–37 (2009)
8. Malmirchegini, M., Mostofi, Y.: On the spatial predictability of communication channels. IEEE Trans. Wirel. Commun. **11**(3), 964–978 (2012)
9. Liu, Q., Zhou, S., Giannakis, G.B.: Cross-layer combining of adaptive modulation and coding with truncated ARQ over wireless links. IEEE Trans. Wirel. Commun. **3**(5), 1746–1755 (2004)

How to Win Elections

Abdallah Sobehy$^{(\boxtimes)}$, Walid Ben-Ameur, Hossam Afifi, and Amira Bradai

Samovar, CNRS, Télécom SudParis, University Paris-Saclay,
9 Rue Charles Fourier, 91000 Évry, France
a.sobehy@gmail.com, walid.benameur@telecom-sudparis.eu

Abstract. Consider an election with two competing candidates and a set of voters whose opinions change over time. We study the best strategies that can be used by each candidate to influence voters. We also evaluate the knowledge advantage when one of the candidates knows in advance the adversary's strategy. We prove that an economy of up to 50% of the budget can be saved in such a scenario.

Keywords: Opinion dynamics · Reputation systems · Trust management · Social networks · Random graphs · Mixed integer programming

1 Introduction

Consider a social network where members interact within their social neighborhood leading to some opinion dynamics. Opinions can change when some kind of influence is applied on the members. Assume that two candidates are competing to win an election. The aim of this paper is to compare strategies that can be used to win an election given a limited budget to influence voters.

Elections should be understood in a broad sense since we might be interested in the propagation of two opposite pieces of information through a social network. In a distributed system, we might need to evaluate the authenticity of some information [2], the popularity of some contents [3–5] based on the contribution and collaboration of distributed agents. In network security context [6], a node whose neighbors are attacked becomes vulnerable leading to vulnerability propagation. Countermeasures are implemented to stop this propagation.

Another example of opinion dynamics is related to reputation of agents. As per the taxonomy defined in [1], reputation systems are divided into two main categories: implicit and explicit. Explicit reputation systems have an underlying implementation to assist members in assessing the trustworthiness of some entities. Examples of such systems are: Stackoverflow [7] where members who ask/answer good quality questions/answers are given reputation points; EigenTrust [8] which is used in P2P networks to choose trusted members to download files from; or more robust approaches as proposed in [9]. While in implicit reputation systems, there is no structured implementation for managing reputation. However, members use available reputation related information in decision making. Voting systems and social networks such as Twitter [10], and

© ICST Institute for Computer Sciences, Social Informatics and Telecommunications Engineering 2017
S. Wang and A. Zhou (Eds.): CollaborateCom 2016, LNICST 201, pp. 221–230, 2017.
DOI: 10.1007/978-3-319-59288-6_20

Facebook [11] are examples of implicit reputation systems. Modeling such systems can help predict reputable members and the effect of their publications on others. Furthermore, it can be used to enhance explicit reputation systems as in SocialLink [12].

Regardless of the problem we are evaluating (popularity, reputation, authenticity, etc.), results depend on the underlying structure of the distributed system along with how agents update their opinions/beliefs. One general approach is based on imitation where each agent adopts the behavior or the opinion of some neighbors with some probability. An example of imitation is the DeGroot model [13] where each agent is updating his opinion using a weighted convex combination of neighbors' opinions. More sophisticated models are proposed in [9,14] allowing an agent to pay more attention to beliefs that do not differ too much form his/her own current opinion. Several other models are reviewed in [15].

For simplicity, we will only consider the DeGroot model in this paper. As previously mentioned, we assume that two candidates are competing to win an election. The set of voters will be modeled by a graph. Three types of graphs are considered in this paper and several strategies to influence voters are compared. We will also consider the case where one of the candidates knows exactly what will be done by the other candidate and tries to exploit this knowledge.

The organization of the paper is as follows: in Sect. 2 we introduce a Gossip-based model with stubborn agents. In Sect. 3 we consider this model in the context of elections where stubborn agents are the two candidates. Several strategies are then compared. A strategy based on prior knowledge of opponent's connections in order to win with a minimum budget is presented in Sect. 4. Conclusion and further research directions follow in Sect. 5.

2 A Gossip Model with Stubborn Agents

2.1 Overview

We propose an abstract solution to suit diverse contexts. Members of a network are represented as nodes of a graph. Each member has an opinion which describes his/her evaluation of a position. The value of the opinion is simulated as a continuous range, in our case from −1 to 1. This range can be a notion of trust towards a member where −1 means completely not trusted and 1 means completely trusted and 0 is neutral. Opinions disseminate through the network via edges with positive weight simulating the effect connected nodes have on one another; larger weight yields higher effect. Biased opinions are introduced by two forceful peers with unchanging opinions 1 and −1. Other peers are called normal peers with initial opinion of 0 that change over time. Forceful peers have been called stubborn agents in [16,17]. Each forceful peer tries to connect through the network in an efficient manner to have the majority of followers. A normal peer is considered as a follower of the positive opinion forceful peer if its opinion is greater than zero and vice versa. Peers whose final opinions are very close to 0 are considered neutral. Let us now describe the system model in details.

2.2   System Model

As previously mentioned, the network is represented by a graph; we will consider three types of graphs: Erdos-Renyi [18], Geometric [19], and Scale-free [20]. The graph is made up of N normal nodes and 2 forceful peers with different strategies which will be discussed later in details. The main target of our problem is to compute the opinions of nodes given the initial state of the graph topology and forceful peers. Let's assume the opinion of nodes are stored in an N+2 vector R where the first N elements R_N are the opinions of normal peers and the last two elements R_F are 1 and -1 respectively (opinions of forceful peers). Let R^i denote the final opinion of ith node while O^i represents its initial opinion. Let $w_{i,j}$ be the edge weight between i^{th} and j^{th} nodes. The list of neighbors of the ith node is noted neigh(i) while $w(i)$ denotes the sum of weights of incident edges $\sum_{j \in neigh(i)} w_{ij}$. We also use α to represent the weight given to the initial self opinion. *conv_thresh* is a convergence threshold used to decide whether convergence is reached. A small positive number *neut_thresh* is also used to define neutrality (if the opinion of an agent is between $- neut\_thresh$ and $neut\_thresh$, the agent is considered to be neutral). We assume that each normal peer is updating his opinion according to

$$R^i \leftarrow \alpha.O^i + \frac{1-\alpha}{w(i)} \sum_{j \in neigh(i)} R^j.w_{i,j}. \tag{1}$$

Put differently, each normal peer is combining his own initial opinion with the current opinion of the neighborhood. Writing this in matrix form, we get

$$R_N \leftarrow W_N R_N + W_F R_F + \alpha O_N. \tag{2}$$

where W_N is a $N \times N$ weight matrix, W_F is a $N \times 2$ matrix and O_N is a vector of size N representing the initial opinion of all normal peers. Matrix W_N is defined by $W_{Nij} = (1 - \alpha)\frac{w_{i,j}}{w(i)}$ if $j \in neigh(i)$ and 0 otherwise. Observe that W_N is a substochastic matrix where the sum of elements of each row is strictly less than 1. This obviously implies that its spectral radius is strictly less than 1. Consequently, the sum $I + W_N + W_N^2 + W_N^3 + ...$ is an invertible matrix and its inverse is $I - W_N$, where I is the identity matrix. Observe also that by applying (2) k times, the obtained vector R_N is given by $W_N^k O_N + (W_N^{k-1} + ... + W_N + I)$ $(W_F R_F + \alpha O_N)$. This immediately proves that by repetition of (2), the vector R_N will converge and the limit is given by

$$R_N \rightarrow (I - W_N)^{-1}(W_F R_F + \alpha O_N). \tag{3}$$

Notice that the system does not generally reach a consensus. The limit depends on the internal structure of the graph (W_N), the initial opinion (O_N), the opinion of forceful peers (R_F), and how they are influencing the normal peers (W_F).

To compute the final opinions, we can either compute the inverse of $(I - W_N)$ or repeatedly apply (2). The latter way is illustrated in Algorithm 1. As stated above *conv_threshold* acts as the stopping condition for the algorithm.

Algorithm 1. R_N iterative update

1: $R^i = O^i$ **for** each $i \in N$
2: **do**
3:     $c\_op = R^i$ **for** each $i \in N$
4:     **for** each node $i \in N$ **do**
5:         $R^i = \alpha.O^i + \frac{1-\alpha}{w(i)} \sum_{j \in neigh(i)} c\_op^j.w_{i,j}$
6:     **end for**
7:     Update max_diff from R and c_op
8: **while** $\max_{i \in N} |R^i - c\_op| > conv\_threshold$

---

3   Strategies to Win an Election

We introduce 4 strategies by which forceful peers establish edges with normal peers given a bounded budget of connections (total edge weights for each forceful peer). Then we run Algorithm 1 to compute the final opinion for each normal peer. The forceful peer with the majority of followers is the winner. The simulation is run for different graph topologies and different budget values. We conclude this section with ordering strategies' efficiency for different graph configurations and formulating the relationship between followers' and winning percentages. For each strategy, forceful peers probabilistically choose their neighbors. 4 strategies are considered depending on how a forceful peer chooses the peers to connect with. In strategy D (resp. D^2, $1/D$), a node is chosen with a probability proportional to its degree (resp. the square of the degree, the inverse of the degree), while the choice is made uniformly in Strategy U. It is worth mentioning that when a normal node is chosen to be a neighbor, an edge is established with $weight = 1$. While if a neighbor is chosen again, the $weight$ of the edge is incremented by 1. Moreover, to facilitate the interpretation of results, we assume that the weights of edges between normal peers are equal to 1 and the initial opinion of normal peers (the vector O_N) are set to 0. In other words, normal peers are initially neutral.

To examine the strategies mentioned above, we assign two different strategies to the opposing forceful peers (we will refer to forceful peers by their adopted strategies). Then we run a simulation of opinion dissemination as mentioned in Algorithm 1. The winning strategy is the one which has the majority of followers, with $neut\_thresh = 0.001$. For a fair judgment of the efficiency of strategies, we repeat the simulation 15,000 times for each strategy pair match. The value of α in Algorithm 1 is 0.3.

The matches are realized for all possible combinations of strategy pairs: U vs D, U vs D^2, U vs $1/D$, D vs D^2, D vs $1/D$, D^2 vs $1/D$. Matches between pairs are examined on different graph types maintaining a density ≈ 0.1 (excluding forceful peers). The number of Nodes is equal to 100. For illustration, we present results in a tabular form for matches between one pair of strategies (U against D) where Followers column is the average percentage of followers, and Wins column is the percentage of simulations won over the 15,000 simulations. To avoid confusion, the sum of wins of both opposing strategies can be less than 100% due to the matches where the followers of both strategies are equal. Then we present a figure that summarizes the results of the six matches combined by showing the average winning percentage each strategy had against all other strategies.

3.1   Geometric Graph

We first consider random geometric graphs, also known as disc graphs where nodes are uniformly distributed in a square. Each node is connected to all nodes within a circular vicinity centered at the node with a specified radius parameter. As mentioned above, the number of normal nodes is 100 and the density of the graph is around 0.1.

Table 1 details the outcome of strategies U vs D clash. The left part of Fig. 1 summarizes the results obtained for differents strategies by showing the order of dominance of strategies at each budget value. As shown in Fig. 1 for a small budget of 10, focusing on connecting to highly connected nodes proves to be the favored strategy. This can be seen as D and D^2 strategies have approximately the same effect. By Increasing the budget to 50, we can notice that the negative effect of over focusing on highly connected nodes is beginning to appear as D^2 loses its winning percentage to U. Not long after, D strategy follows D^2 at a budget of

Table 1. Geometric graph: U vs D

Budget	U followers	D followers	U wins	D wins
10	45.17%	47.61%	41.71%	55.37%
50	48.88%	49.50%	44.93%	50.31%
100	49.56%	49.48%	47.16%	46.83%
200	49.88%	49.43%	48.61%	44.18%
500	50.13%	49.30%	51.19%	40.80%

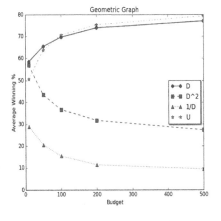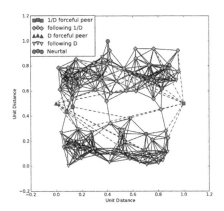

Fig. 1. Geometric graph: order of dominance and community structure

100 to leave U as the most effective strategy. Increasing the budget to 200 and 500, the negative effect of over focusing is mostly evident. An explanation of the effect of budget increase on strategies' efficiency can be related to the community structure exhibited by the geometric graph. The right part of Fig. 1 depicts a match between D and $1/D$ strategies, each with *budget* = 10. Noticeably, the graph can be divided into two major communities of nodes each condensed in a region and connected to the other communities by smaller number of nodes. Generally in geometric graphs, the number of communities is small and central nodes are highly connected, so D or D^2 strategies achieve good balance between spreading and connecting to highly connected nodes with small budget. As the budget increases, the focus on highly connected nodes becomes less and less efficient giving the advantage to strategy U.

3.2   Erdos-Renyi Graph

In contrast to the geometric graph, the Erdos-Renyi graph does not exhibit the community structure as it is more uniform. That is why it can be noticed that the negative effect of focusing on highly connected nodes appears in later stages. D^2 proves to be the most efficient with budget 10 exploiting all the available edges to connect to highly connected nodes. As shown by the left part of Fig. 2, at budget 50, D overcomes D^2 which implies that it achieves better balance between spreading in the network and connecting to high degree nodes. U strategy begins to exploit its spreading property at budgets of 100 and 200 until it overtakes the D strategy at a budget of 500.

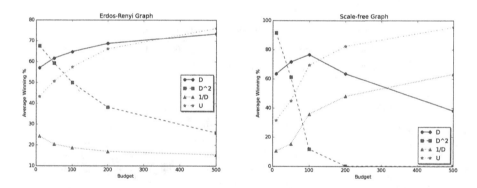

Fig. 2. Erdos-Renyi and sacle-free graphs: order of dominance of strategies

3.3   Scale-Free Graph

We have chosen barabasi-Albert as a model of scale-free graphs for our experiment. The Barabasi-Albert graph shows scale-free property with a power law degree distribution. Very few but very highly connected nodes are present due to the preferential attachment property that is acquired during the growth of the graph. The extremely high degrees for few nodes have a drastic effect on strategies and some results are quite unexpected (right part of Fig. 2).

Firstly, the $1/D$ which occupied the least position in all matches in previous graphs moves up the ranking with budget change. Moreover, unexpectedly the D^2 strategy which is the most effective for a budget of 10 turns to have a zero average winning percentage when the budget increases to 200. Similar to what happened in geometric graph but with a larger magnitude D^2 leverages on its few resources (budget) to target the most important nodes in the graph, followed by D, U then $1/D$. The increase of budget in this case shows more rapidly the negative effect of over-focusing on high degree nodes, letting the D^2 be the worst strategy for a budget of 100 surpassed by the $1/D$. The unanticipated improvement in $1/D$ can be explained also by the spreading of opinion factor. Since very few nodes are highly connected, the majority of nodes chosen by the $1/D$ strategy are efficiently balanced. At the budget of 200, D begins to suffer and U takes the first place. Finally, with a 500 budget D^2 is totally paralyzed and even D is surpassed by $1/D$.

3.4 Followers' and Winning Percentages

Winning percentage can be seen as the probability of winning against the opponent. Intuitively, the probability of winning increases as the difference in the followers' percentages increases. We only point out the main observation: even if the difference between two strategies in terms of number of followers is small, the difference between wining probabilities can be large. This is of course easy to understand since having just one more follower than his opponent is enough to win.

4 Knowledge Advantage

In this section we introduce the smart peer who has prior knowledge of connections established by the opposing peer. This knowledge is used by the smart peer to formulate a mixed integer linear program (MILP) in order to acquire the majority of followers with the least possible budget.

The strategy adopted by the other forceful peer is supposed to be known. Let λ^i be the number of connections from (non-smart) forceful peer to i^{th} node $\forall i \in N$. Let d^i be the total weight from i^{th} node to normal nodes only. Both d^i and λ^i are known. Let us now introduce the problem variables. Let x^i be the number of connections from smart peer to i^{th} node and let y^i be the final opinion of ith node. A binary variable p^i is equal to 0 if the ith node follows the smart peers, and 1 otherwise. We also use z^i_j binary variabes to represent x^i (see, (4b)). Some intermediate variables t^i_j are used to denote the products $(y^i z^i_j)$. The problem can then be formulated using the following MILP.

$$\min \sum_{i \in N} x^i \tag{4a}$$

$$x^i = \sum_{j=0}^{b} z_j^i 2^j \tag{4b}$$

$$y^i \left(\lambda^i + d^i \right) + \sum_{j=0}^{b} t_j^i 2^j = (1 - \alpha) \left(x^i - \lambda^i + \sum_{k \in neigh(i)} y^k \right) \tag{4c}$$

$$-z_j^i \le t_j^i \le z_j^i \tag{4d}$$

$$y^i - 1 + z_j^i \le t_j^i \le 1 + y^i - z_j^i \tag{4e}$$

$$y^i \ge -1 + p^i (1 + neut\_thresh) \tag{4f}$$

$$\sum_{i \in N} p^i \ge \lceil \frac{N+1}{2} \rceil \tag{4g}$$

$$z_j^i, p^i \in \{0, 1\} \tag{4h}$$

The objective function (4a) aims to minimize the total budget used by the smart peer to win. The first constraint (4b) is a binary representation of the edge weights of the smart peer which will be used to conserve linearity of the problem. The b upper limit of the summation is the number of binary digits representing weight; it limits the maximum edge weight the smart peer can assign to a normal peer. The second constraint (4c) is derived from the opinion update equation mentioned in Algorithm 1 with the introduction of variables t_j^i to avoid variable multiplication $(y^i x^i)$. t_j^i represents the product $(y^i z_j^i)$ as ensured by (4d) and (4e). In constraint (4c), we used the fact that the initial opinion O_N is 0 and the weights of links between normal peers are equal to 1. p^i is defined in (4f), and used in (4g) to guarantee that more than half of the normal nodes follow the smart peer. Gurobi solver [21] is used. For all matches we set a time limit of one hour for the optimization problem computation after which the reached solution is returned by the solver.

Smart Peer Vs Other Strategies

From the four strategies mentioned above we run a simulation match between the smart peer against the most dominant strategy in each graph/budget configuration. Figure 3 shows the budget needed by the smart peer to win against the most dominant strategy in each graph configuration.

To quantify the budget needed by the smart peer to beat an existing forceful peer, we draw a best fit line. The best fit line shown as a solid line in Fig. 3 has the following equation: $f(x) = 0.5x + 4.85$, where x is the budget of the dominant strategy (non-smart) and $f(x)$ is the budget needed by the smart peer to win. The main conclusion is that with prior knowledge of opponent's connections, it is possible to win with nearly half of his/her budget.

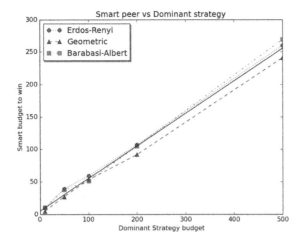

Fig. 3. Smart Peer against dominant strategies

5   Conclusion

We have shown that the best strategy to strongly influence the members of a social network depends on the underlying graph structure and the budget. Thus, for each budget/graph pair configuration, the proposed strategies can be ranked from worst to best. We also observed that knowing the opponent's strategy is a decisive advantage; the budget can be reduced by 50%!

This work can be extended in several ways. Strategies have been compared given the same budget. It might be interesting to study the robustness of the ranking of strategies by assuming that one strategy has slightly more budget than another. Other opinion propagation models can also be studied. One can for example consider the majority model where each node has a binary opinion following the opinion of the majority of his neighbors. Another worth-studying problem is the competition between more than two candidates. Finally, one can also consider antagonistic interactions inside the network represented by negative link weight.

References

1. Hendrikx, F., Bubendorfer, K., Chard, R.: Reputation systems: a survey and taxonomy. J. Parallel Distrib. Comput. **75**, 184–197 (2015)
2. Block Chain Principle. http://blockchain.info
3. Altman, E., Kumar, P., Venkatramanan, S., Kumar, A.: Competition over timeline in social networks. In: 2013 IEEE/ACM International Conference on Advances in Social Networks Analysis and Mining (ASONAM), pp. 1352–1357. IEEE (2013)
4. Neglia, G., Ye, X., Gabielkov, M., Legout, A.: How to network in online social networks. In: 2014 IEEE Conference on Computer Communications Workshops (INFO-COM WKSHPS), pp. 819–824. IEEE (2014)

5. Borodin, A., Filmus, Y., Oren, J.: Threshold models for competitive influence in social networks. In: Saberi, A. (ed.) WINE 2010. LNCS, vol. 6484, pp. 539–550. Springer, Heidelberg (2010). doi:10.1007/978-3-642-17572-5_48

6. Chen, L., Leneutre, J.: Fight jamming with jamming-a game theoretic analysis of jamming attack in wireless networks and defense strategy. Comput. Netw. **55**(9), 2259–2270 (2011)

7. Stackoverflow. http://stackoverflow.com/

8. Kamvar, S.D., Schlosser, M.T., Garcia-Molina, H.: The eigentrust algorithm for reputation management in p2p networks. In: Proceedings of the 12th International Conference on World Wide Web, pp. 640–651. ACM (2003)

9. Bradai, A., Ben-Ameur, W., Afifi, H.: Byzantine resistant reputation-based trust management. In: 2013 9th International Conference Conference on Collaborative Computing: Networking, Applications and Worksharing (Collaboratecom), pp. 269–278. IEEE (2013)

10. Twitter. http://twitter.com

11. Facebook. http://www.facebook.com

12. Chen, K., Liu, G., Shen, H., Qi, F.: Sociallink: utilizing social network and transaction links for effective trust management in P2P file sharing systems. In: 2015 IEEE International Conference on Peer-to-Peer Computing (P2P), pp. 1–10. IEEE (2015)

13. DeGroot, M.H.: Reaching a consensus. J. Am. Stat. Assoc. **69**(345), 118–121 (1974)

14. Krause, U.: A discrete nonlinear and non-autonomous model of consensus formation. In: Communications in Difference Equations, pp. 227–236 (2000)

15. Acemoglu, D., Ozdaglar, A.: Opinion dynamics and learning in social networks. Dyn. Games Appl. **1**(1), 3–49 (2011)

16. Ben-Ameur, W., Bianchi, P., Jakubowicz, J.: Robust distributed consensus using total variation. IEEE Trans. Autom. Control **61**(6), 1550–1564 (2016)

17. Ben-Ameur, W., Bianchi, P., Jakubowicz, J.: Robust average consensus using total variation gossip algorithm. In: 2012 6th International Conference on Performance Evaluation Methodologies and Tools (VALUETOOLS), pp. 99–106. IEEE (2012)

18. Erdos, P., Renyi, A.: On random graphs I. Publ. Math. Debrecen **6**, 290–297 (1959)

19. Penrose, M.: Random Geometric Graphs (No. 5). Oxford University Press (2003)

20. Barabási, A.L., Albert, R.: Emergence of scaling in random networks. Science **286**(5439), 509–512 (1999)

21. Gurobi optimizer reference manual. http://www.gurobi.com

Research on Short-Term Prediction of Power Grid Status Data Based on SVM

Jianjun Su[1], Yi Yang[1], Danfeng Yan[2], Ye Tang[2(✉)], and Zongqi Mu[2]

[1] State Grid ShanDong Electric Power Research Institute, Jinan 250001, China
13953187960@163.com, yangyi814@gmail.com
[2] Beijing University of Posts and Telecommunications, Beijing 100876, China
{yandf,2015213126}@bupt.edu.cn,
tangye_bupt@foxmail.com

Abstract. EMS (Energy management system) is a collection of computer hardware and software, which collects, monitors, controls and optimizes data provided by power control system, and provide trading scheme, security services and service analysis for power market. The prediction of status data is a basic function module of advanced application software systems. Therefore it is meaningful to do research on new method and new technology of predicting power grid status data. In this paper, support vector machine is used to do regression prediction for active power of EMS. In training process, the training set and kernel function of SVM are selected, and parameters are optimized, also, the performance of SVM is evaluated. Experiments show that SVM can get higher accuracy in short term active power prediction although the data set is small. This paper provides a new idea for related research works in electric power industry system.

Keywords: EMS · SVM · Regression prediction · Parameter optimization · Machine learning

1 Introduction

Electric power industry is one of the most important basic national industries, and is the lifeblood of the national economy, engine of economic development. It plays a crucial role for our national security, economic development, social stability, life quality. In modern society everywhere is inseparable from the power supply.

With the rapid development of power industry, research of the high precision prediction technology and application system on power state data is becoming more important and has direct and significant economic benefits and social benefits.

Active power value, usually expressed with letter P, is one of the most important statistic records in power grid. Active power is the power of electric energy that transfer into other forms of energy (mechanical energy, light energy, thermal energy) power, therefore the active power could reflect the usage of the whole power grid. Through active power we could have a better understanding of the power grid energy

Funded by the national high technology research and development program (863 Program) (No. 2015AA050204)

consumption, moreover we could better monitoring the operational state of the power grid. Therefore, it is very necessary to seek the way to predict the active power value in the EMS of power grid network.

The main research of this paper is to predict the active power in power condition monitoring data. We try use the existing EMS (energy management system) monitoring data, comprehensively consider meteorological factors, historical data to design and construct the input training set using support vector machine (referred to as SVM) algorithm for active power index regression prediction.

2 Research Status of Related Works

The prediction of state monitoring data of power grid is an important basic project. The improvement of the mechanism of power market will accelerate research on the new method and new technology of state power grid monitoring data prediction.

At present, there is plenty of the domestic and foreign research on the prediction of the state data of the power grid. Elke Lorenz offers a way to predict regional PV power output based on weather forecasts information up to three days ahead [1]. In order to predict the risk of failures for components and systems, Cynthia Rudin gives a general process which transforms historical electrical grid data into models by machine learning [2]. Louka P predicts wind speed of speed using Kalman filtering to give a prediction of wind power [3]. M. Carolin Mabel and E. Fernandez discuss a neural network model to predict the energy from wind farms in their paper [4].

As for using support vector machines for regression prediction, Vladimir Cherkassky and Yunqian Ma did a research on selection of parameters of support vector machines regression, and their experiments indicate under sparse sample settings, SVM regression has an excellent generalization performance for different types of additive noise [5]. Existing theory, methods, and recent developments as well as research range of SVR is discussed in Debasish Basak, Srimanta Pal and Dipak Chandra Patranabis's paper [6]. Chih-Chung Chang and CHIH-JEN LIN from offer a library for Support Vector Machines that has been developed since 2000, the library is called LIBSVM and now is widely used in machine learning and many other areas [7], which is also used in this paper.

3 The Introduction of SVM

Frequently used prediction technology includes Artificial Neural Networks [8], Times Series Analysis Method [9], Kalman Filter Analysis Method [10], Grey Models [11], Multi-output Support Vector Regression [12]. These methods have different characteristics, and they are already used in power systems. However, there are various defects, which makes practice effect not ideal. In this paper, the Support Vector Machine is applied to electric load prediction to achieve a better effect on active power prediction in the power system.

Support vector machine, namely SVM, is a new machine learning method based on Statistical Learning theory proposed by Vapnik et al. SVM is a supervised learning model used for pattern recognition, classification and regression analysis. SVM solves the problem of the linear inseparable problems by the probability of soft-margin, and introduces the kernel function to make the solution plane expand from the linear to the nonlinear [13].

To deal with linearly inseparable problems, SVM uses kernel functions. Kernel function, in essence, is a kind of mapping function, which maps the low dimensional space nonlinear problem to the high dimension space programming linear problem and then solve it.

So the basic function of a kernel function is to accept two lower dimensional space vectors, and calculate the vectors' inner-product in high dimension space after a transformation. In the nonlinear case, determine mapping function $\phi(x_i)$ is the kernel function that satisfy the Mercer conditions:

$$\phi(x_i) \cdot \phi(x_j) = K(x_i, x_j) \tag{1}$$

All functions can be used as the kernel function, as long as it satisfies the Mercer condition function. Common kernel functions include:

1. Linear Kernel Function

$$K(x_i, x_j) = x_i \cdot x_j \tag{2}$$

2. Polynomial Kernel Function

$$K(x_i, x_j) = [\gamma(x_i \cdot x_j) + c]^d \tag{3}$$

3. Radical Basis Kernel Function, which also called Gauss Kernel Function, the expression is:

$$K(x_i, x_j) = exp[-\frac{|x_i - x_j|^2}{\sigma^2}] \tag{4}$$

Where σ is the Radial Basis Radius, take $g = \frac{1}{\sigma^2}$ into formula (4) is another common expression of Gauss's function:

$$K(x_i, x_j) = exp(-g|x_i - x_j|^2) \tag{5}$$

4. Sigmoid Kernel Function

$$K(x_i, x_j) = tanh(\gamma(x_i, x_j) + c) \tag{6}$$

4 Scenario Description and Definition of the Research Problem

4.1 Data Preprocessing and Scenario Description

Main source of data for the research is from the history EMS state information of an electricity substation of the Shandong province power grid in June 2015, including meteorological temperature information. Table 1 are examples of the contents of the meteorological table of the EMS records.

Table 1. Examples of meteorological data in the EMS

ID	Device	Time	Temperature	Humility
1	StationA	2015-07-15 00:00:00	23.2	099
2	StationA	2015-07-15 00:10:00	23.5	098

Table 2 shows the records of transformer equipment state data in the EMS. It can be seen in the table recording the record ID, equipment ID, the site code, as well as the record time, active power value orderly.

Table 2. Examples of equipment state data in the EMS

ID	dev_id	dev_name	Time	P
1	1800002459	Station C	2015-07-15 00:00:00	147.7919
2	1800002459	Station C	2015-07-15 00:05:00	150.3291
3	1800002459	Station C	2015-07-15 00:10:00	145.8889

Data pre-processing can be divided into two steps, data cleaning, and data association to integrate into the SVM training data set. After remove redundant, abnormal and wrong information, there are 4018 records of temperature data, also 4018 records of EMS's active power value data.

By simple statistics, we can see the temperature in three days shown in Fig. 1.

The active power of the corresponding time range is shown in Fig. 2.

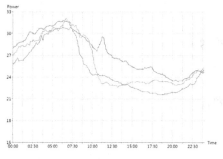 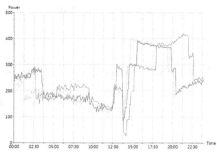

Fig. 1. Range of temperature within 3 days   **Fig. 2.** Range of active power within 3 days

It can be clearly seen from the two pictures, the temperature and active power show a relatively fixed variation law. This rule can be used as a reference for the design and construction of the training set of data in the following chapters.

In this scenario, we hope to develop a good regression prediction model, making grid equipment meteorological data, environment data, state information as input to predict the specific value of active power(referred to as P) in the future time. The prediction can be a reference to the assessment of whole grid operation state, avoiding major accidents, making decisions of power grid operation and so on. Due to the short term prediction's characteristics such as efficient and agile, as well as to be able to get accurate results using less sample data, short term prediction is very suitable for the support vector machine learning methods for regression prediction which has a small demand on data size.

4.2   Problem Definition

There is n set of records of active power (P) in future time corresponding to input samples are abstracted as n dependent variables, and are denoted by a vector:

$$Y_n = (y_1, y_2, \ldots, y_n) \tag{7}$$

In formula (7), n is the number of samples, and y_i indicates the active power (P) of the predicted time of the ith input sample P. Independent variable is:

$$X_n = (x_1, x_2, \ldots, x_n) \tag{8}$$

And x_n is a $n*N$ matrix. The ith row of the matrix x_i is a vector that comprises N dimensional variables corresponding to y_i where N dimension representing N kinds of grid environment factors (temperature, historical data, etc.), and N can be one or more of these factors. Moreover n is the number of samples, a total of n samples is independent variables. For the specific selection and design of training data set x_n will be discussed in the following chapters.

Do regression training using model M, which takes x_n as input vector, and y_n as SVM's label.

In regression prediction, using the trained model M to predict data vector x_s:

$$X_s = (x_1, x_2, \ldots, x_s) \tag{9}$$

As input, X_s is a $n*S$ matrix that has the same structure with input vector X_n. The output is Y_s:

$$Y_s = (y_1, y_2, \ldots, y_s) \tag{10}$$

Each value y_i in Y_s represents the corresponding input vector in X_s, which is the active power value corresponding to the ith row x_i.

Moreover, to measure the error and analyze the result, in this paper, the mean relative error e_{MRE} and root mean square error e_{RMSE} are used as the basis for judging the effect of various prediction methods. Their calculation methods are as follows:

$$e_{MRE} = \frac{1}{N}\sum_{i=1}^{N} \left| \frac{L(i) - L'(i)}{L(i)} \right| \times 100\% \tag{11}$$

$$e_{RMRE} = \sqrt{\frac{1}{N}\sum_{i=1}^{N} (\frac{L(i) - L'(i)}{L(i)})^2} \times 100\% \tag{12}$$

In the formulas, $L(i)$ representing the actual active power value at a certain time and $L'(i)$ representing the predicted active power value.

At the same time for every moment of the actual active power value and prediction active power value, we make the e_{single} as a single moment prediction results of the error percentage, the formula is as follows:

$$e_{single} = \left| \frac{L(i) - L'(i)}{L(i)} \right| \times 100\% \tag{13}$$

In this paper, we make 5% as the judging criterion, if a result having $e_{single} > 5\%$, we consider this prediction result fails. We define the qualified rate of r for active power prediction of algorithm result:

$$r = \frac{p'}{p} \times 100\% \tag{14}$$

Where P' is the number of results satisfy $e_{single} < = 5\%$, that is the number of qualified prediction results. P is the total number of prediction results.

In summary, we select the prediction results pass rate r, the mean relative error e_{MRE} and the root mean square error e_{RMSE} as the gauge of prediction accuracy rate.

5 Experiment Process and Result of the Algorithm

5.1 Brief Introduction of the Algorithm

The algorithm of this paper is divided into four parts, the first part carries on the construction of the training set data in different ways, and compares the results to select the optimal design, the second part is the selection of the kernel function, the third part is the adjustment of penalty factor and kernel function under the condition of the selected kernel function, the fourth part is the analysis of experimental results.

5.2   The Selection of Training Set

The randomness of the power measurement index is very strong and has many influ-ence factors, so the short-term active power prediction is a multi-variable regression prediction problem.

As described in the previous chapter, the active power y_i of the predicted time point is the output value of the function. And the factors that affect the y_i, such as: historical data, temperature and meteorological information, as the input vector x_i of function. So we take multiple designs on input vector x_i checking the effect of prediction based on SVM regression, specific designs are as follows.

Scheme 1 is designed as follows:

$$x_i = \{b_1, b_2, b_3, b_4\} \tag{15}$$

In the formula b_1, b_2, b_3, b_4 represent the active power values of the 4 records before the target prediction time.

Scheme 2 is designed as follows:

$$x_i = \{t_1, b_1, b_2, b_3, b_4\} \tag{16}$$

In the formula b_1, b_2, b_3, b_4 represent the active power values of the 4 records before the target prediction time. And t_1 represents the temperature data of the pre-diction time most recently

Scheme 3 is designed as follows:

$$x_i = \{h_1, h_2, b_1, b_2, b_3, b_4\} \tag{17}$$

In the formula b_1, b_2, b_3, b_4 represent the active power values of the 4 records before the target prediction time. And h_1 represents the active power value of yesterday at the same time with the prediction time, h_2 represents the active power value of last week at the same time with the prediction time.

Scheme 4 is designed as follows:

$$x_i = \{t_1, h_1, h_2, b_1, b_2, b_3, b_4\} \tag{18}$$

In the formula b_1, b_2, b_3, b_4 represent the active power values of the 4 records before the target prediction time. And t_1 represents the temperature data of the pre-diction time most recently. And h_1 represents the active power value of yesterday at the same time with the prediction time,. h_2 represents the active power value of last week at the same time with the prediction time.

For the four design schemes of the input vector, we select 5 consecutive days that have more than 1440 records to structure training data set. And the default Gauss kernel function and the unmodified standard parameters are used as the configuration of the algorithm model. Predict the active power value of 288 time points in the next 1 day.

The assessment of the results is as described in the previous. The results are shown in the following table (Table 3):

Table 3. Experimental results of different training set

Design scheme	r	e_{MRE}	e_{RMSE}
Scheme 1	66.315%	8.079%	16.055%
Scheme 2	68.571%	6.422%	12.158%
Scheme 3	68.214%	6.386%	12.066%
Scheme 4	68.571%	6.439%	12.062%

Through the experimental results on the table, the difference between the results of the four designs is small. Comparing the results of four designs, we choose scheme 4 as the training set design.

5.3   The Selection of Kernel Function

As the formula (1) mentioned in the third chapter, the SVM kernel function is required to meet the Mercer condition. Four commonly used kernel functions introduced before have different characteristics:

Linear kernel function is mainly used in the case of linear separable. Less parameters, faster speed, for the common data, the classification effect can achieve an ideal result.

Polynomial kernel function in SVM is not commonly used, much more used for the NLP Natural Language Processing.

Radical Basis Kernel Function. Also known as the Gauss kernel function, which is mainly used in the case of linear non separable. The number of parameters is relatively more, and the classification results are very dependent on the parameters.

Sigmoid kernel function. When choose sigmoid function as kernel function, support vector machine is a multilayer perceptron neural network.

In practical application, we can choose the reasonable kernel function according to the scope of the application of the four kinds of kernel functions. In this paper, four kinds of kernel functions are compared with the standard parameters, and the results are shown in Table 4:

Table 4. Experimental results of different kernel function

Kernel function	r	e_{MRE}	e_{RMSE}
Linear kernel function	58.947%	9.251%	17.601%
Polynomial kernel function	6.667%	26.846%	32.199%
Radical basis kernel function	68.214%	6.386%	12.066%
Sigmoid kernel function	13.684%	14.148%	17.247%

According to the experimental results, the performance of the radial basis kernel function is better. So it is more appropriate to select the radial basis kernel function (i.e. Gauss's function) as the kernel function the SVM model.

5.4   Adjustment of Penalty Factor and Parameters of Kernel Function

For the parameter adjustment of Gauss kernel function, we mainly adjust the parameters of the Gauss kernel function C and gamma.

In summary, gamma is the balance factor between the sparse degree of result expression and the density of data points. Penalty factor C is to prevent the model from giving up some important data in the learning process and to avoid loss of data.

We implement the optimization and adjustment to parameter of the kernel function, the specific steps are as follows:

1. Set range of parameter gamma, parameter C, set the search step size.
2. For each pair of gamma, C, calculate SVM's pass rate of r for the test data;
3. Form each pair C, gamma, choose the optimal C, gamma value by the rate r.
4. If pass rate r cannot achieve the requirements, select a smaller search range based on current results, reduce the search step distance for search.

In this paper, the initial selection of C search range is $[2^{-8}, 2^8]$, step distance is 0.5; Gamma search range is $[2-10, 23]$, step distance is 0.5. The algorithm is trained by libSVM. Training data is 48 consecutive hours of the historical data from a substation in Shandong province since June 9, 2015, including weather condition. The total number of the training data is 573. And 141 pieces of test data of the next 12 h of data is used for regression prediction.

The results of some parameters are shown in the following Table 5.

Table 5. Partial results of some parameters of Gauss kernel function

C	gamma	r
1	1	25.532%
1	0.1	25.532%
1	0.01	25.532%
1	0.0001	22.695%
16	0.1	25.532%
16	0.01	25.532%
16	0.0001	29.087%
32	0.1	19.149%
32	0.01	24.531%
32	0.0001	46.099%
32	0.000001	80.142%
64	0.0001	60.284%
64	0.00001	72.340%
64	0.000001	80.851%
100	0.00001	71.631%
100	0.000001	82.269%
128	0.0001	58.156%
128	0.000001	80.851%

Through the results of the test, the pass rate r achieved the highest value of 82.269% when $C = 100$, Gamma = 0.000001. So in this paper, we choose $C = 100$, Gamma = 0.000001 as the optimal parameter of the algorithm model.

Compared with the Sect. 5.3 default SVM regression prediction model using the Gauss kernel function, the prediction results are shown to the following Table 6.

Table 6. The comparison of results before and after adjust the parameters of kernel function

SVM model	r	e_{MRE}	e_{RMSE}
Default Gauss kernel function	68.214%	6.386%	12.066%
After parameter optimization	82.269%	3.451%	6.419%

We can see through parameter optimization, algorithm model's pass rate r, mean relative error e_{MRE} and root mean square relative error e_{RMSE} gained a substantial increase, and we get better the regression prediction results.

5.5   Analysis of Experiment Result

The experimental process of the whole algorithm is the design and implementation of the algorithm, the selection of the training set, the selection of kernel function and the optimization of the parameters, which greatly improves the accuracy of prediction.

According to the results of the previous experimental process, we select 48 h substation EMS data since June 9, 2015 as training data, and according to Sect. 5.2 we choose scheme 4 as the structure of the training set, and as the comparison result of Sect. 5.3 we use Gaussian kernel function. Meanwhile we set the parameters at Sect. 5.4. Then we predict the active power value of the next 12 h using the algorithm we developed. The comparison between the predicted data and the real data of the active power value is as follows (Fig. 3):

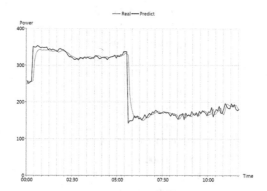

Fig. 3. Comparison between the predicted value and the real value

We can see through the selection of kernel function and parameters optimization, algorithm performs well in the prediction, the rate of accuracy is relatively high.

6 Summary

Short-term prediction of the power system's state data based on SVM algorithm model can achieve a high level of regression prediction accuracy. To a certain extent, in the case of fewer samples, SVM is a relatively good regression prediction algorithm model. Through the selection of kernel function and kernel function parameter optimization, SVM's performance is more excellent, which proved the necessity and importance of SVM parameter optimization. This paper provides guide for the practice of prediction of power grid status data.

References

1. Lorenz, E., Hurka, J., Heinemann, D., et al.: Irradiance forecasting for the power prediction of grid-connected photovoltaic systems. IEEE J. Sel. Topics Appl. Earth Observations Remote Sens. **2**(1), 2–10 (2009)
2. Rudin, C., Waltz, D., Anderson, R.N., et al.: Machine learning for the New York City power grid. IEEE Trans. Pattern Anal. Mach. Intell. **34**(2), 328–345 (2012)
3. Louka, P., Galanis, G., Siebert, N., et al.: Improvements in wind speed forecasts for wind power prediction purposes using Kalman filtering. J. Wind Eng. Ind. Aerodyn. **96**(12), 2348–2362 (2008)
4. Mabel, M.C., Fernandez, E.: Analysis of wind power generation and prediction using ANN: A case study. Renew. Energy **33**(5), 986–992 (2008)
5. Cherkassky, V., Ma, Y.: Practical selection of SVM parameters and noise estimation for SVM regression. Neural Netw. **17**(1), 113–126 (2004)
6. Basak, D., Pal, S., Patranabis, D.C.: Support vector regression. Neural Inf. Process. Lett. Rev. **11**(10), 203–224 (2007)
7. Chang, C.C., Lin, C.J.: LIBSVM: A library for support vector machines. ACM Trans. Intell. Syst. Technol. (TIST) **2**(3), 27 (2011)
8. Kara, Y., Boyacioglu, M.A., Baykan, Ö.K.: Predicting direction of stock price index movement using artificial neural networks and support vector machines: The sample of the Istanbul stock exchange. Expert Syst. Appl. **38**(5), 5311–5319 (2011)
9. Box, G.E.P., Jenkins, G.M., Reinsel, G.C., et al.: Time Series Analysis: Forecasting and Control. Wiley, New York (2015)
10. Wei, G., Ling, Y., Guo, B., et al.: Prediction-based data aggregation in wireless sensor networks: Combining grey model and Kalman filter. Comput. Commun. **34**(6), 793–802 (2011)
11. Hamzacebi, C., Es, H.A.: Forecasting the annual electricity consumption of Turkey using an optimized grey model. Energy **70**, 165–171 (2014)
12. Wang, S., Hsu, C.H., Liang, Z., et al.: Multi-user web service selection based on multi-QoS prediction. Inf. Syst. Front. **16**(1), 143–152 (2014)
13. Maji, S., Berg, A.C., Malik, J.: Efficient classification for additive kernel SVMs. IEEE Trans. Pattern Anal. Mach. Intell. **35**(1), 66–77 (2013)

An Effective Buffer Management Policy for Opportunistic Networks

Yin Chen[1], Wenbin Yao[1(✉)], Ming Zong[2], and Dongbin Wang[3]

[1] Beijing Key Laboratory of Intelligent Telecommunications Software and Multimedia, School of Computer Science, Beijing University of Posts and Telecommunications, NO. 10, Xitucheng Road, Beijing 100876, China
chenyin0629@163.com, yaowenbin_cdc@163.com
[2] Yingcai Honors College, University of Electronic Science and Technology of China, Chengdu 610054, China
[3] National Engineering Laboratory for Mobile Network Security, Beijing University of Posts and Telecommunications, NO. 10, Xitucheng Road, Beijing 100876, China

Abstract. Opportunistic networks are wireless networks where disruptions may occur frequently due to the challenging environments. Multiple message replicas have to be propagated to improve delivery probability; combining long-term storage with replication gives rise to a high storage overhead. Many forward/drop policies have been proposed to achieve high delivery ratio, low latencies and low overheads. These policies have improved the performance of opportunistic networks to some extent. However, they all have their own disadvantages. Therefore, an efficient buffer management policy based on the average encounter frequency and the average encounter duration of nodes is proposed in this paper. Simulation results show that our buffer management policy has better performance than the existing DO, DF, MDC-SR and the ACF-based policy.

Keywords: Opportunistic networks · Forward policy · Drop policy · Average encounter frequency · Average encounter duration

1 Introduction

Opportunistic Networks [1] are networks that utilize opportunistic connectivity and node mobility to relay and carry messages around, respectively. This approach is applied in sparse sensor networks for wildlife tracking and habitat monitoring [2], deep-space interplanetary networks [3], vehicle ad hoc networks [4] and military networks [5], where assume that a complete end-to-end path between any pair of nodes may not exist all the time due to sparse coverage, malicious attacks, etc.. In order to increase the probability of delivery, the existing routing mechanisms often replicate the bundles many times as designed in Epidemic routing [6], where two nodes will always exchange all their non-common messages when encounters with each other. At the same time, long-term storage combining with the message replication imposes a high storage overhead on nodes [7]. A large amount of effort has been invested in the design of efficient

© ICST Institute for Computer Sciences, Social Informatics and Telecommunications Engineering 2017
S. Wang and A. Zhou (Eds.): CollaborateCom 2016, LNICST 201, pp. 242–251, 2017.
DOI: 10.1007/978-3-319-59288-6_22

routing algorithms for opportunistic networks till now. However, there has not been equivalent focus on message scheduling and dropping policies. It has been proved in [8, 9] that the buffer constraints and management policies have severe influence upon the relative and absolute performance of opportunistic networks routing.

In this paper, we propose a novel buffer management policy based on data transmission probability, which is derived from the average encounter frequency and the average encounter duration. Particularly, we also take the size and the time to live of bundles into consideration when determining which bundles to forward and which ones to drop.

The rest of this paper is organized as follows: Sect. 2 describes the current state of the art of drop/forward policies. In Sect. 3, we present the forwarding and dropping policy proposed in this paper. Then, we evaluate our method in epidemic routing by Opportunistic Network Environment (ONE) simulator. Finally, a conclusion about our work is made in Sect. 5.

2 Related Work

In this section, we describe various drop/forward policies introduced lately, most of which are mainly applied in delay tolerant networks or opportunistic networks. Up to now, a sequence of simple drop schemes have been proposed, such as Drop Random (DR), Drop Oldest (DO), Drop Youngest (DY), Drop Front (DF) and Drop Last (DL). In DR, a node simply drops a bundle at random. DO and DY discard bundles based on time-to-live (TTL). DO drops the bundle with shortest TTL; it assumes that a short TTL indicates the bundle has been in the network for a long time, and therefore, is more likely to have been delivered. In contrast, DY drops the bundle with longest remaining life time in the first place. DF considers the arrival time of a bundle and handles the queue in FIFO order; the bundle first entered into the queue will be dropped when the buffer is full. Similar to DF, Drop Last (a.k.a. Drop Tail) simply removes the newly received bundle. In [8], Zhang et al. present an analysis of the impacts of buffer constraints and short contact duration when using epidemic routing protocol and evaluated some of the said buffer management policies. The conclusion is that DF outperforms DL in terms of both delivery rate and delivery delay of bundles. But these simple buffer management policies previously described just take a single factor into account or even provide no mechanism for preferential forwarding and dropping, which are actually affected by several factors. Thereby they are not appropriate and exact for the optimal selection of bundle from buffer overflow.

In [10], Lindgren and Phanse evaluate the following dropping and scheduling policies under the Prophet routing protocol: first-in-first-out (FIFO), most forwarded first (MOFO), most favorably forwarded first (MOPR), shortest life time first (SHLI) and least probable first (LEPR). It demonstrates that MOFO policy presents the best performance among all these diverse drop policies in terms of all different buffer sizes. However, MOFO policy does not consider the lifetime of bundles; in this case, a bundle with insufficient lifetime for delivery but has not been forwarded most will not be dropped. Besides, a large number of dropped bundles may be forwarded again to the same node in the future due to the mobility mode, which is quite a waste of network resource. A buffer management policy called Message Drop Control Source Relay (MDC-SR) [11] that controls the number of dropped bundles is proposed as a variant of MOFO.

Several drop policies with respect to the size of the stored bundles are proposed in [12–14]. In [12], they drop bundles which have a size equal to or greater than that of the incoming bundle. Similarly, Rashid et al. in [13] propose a drop policy that drops the buffered bundle whose size is no less than the mean value. In another work [14], a bundle with the largest size will be dropped simply when congestion occurs. Ayub and Rashid [15] propose a policy, T-drop, where a bundle is dropped if its size is within a certain threshold range. Synthetically, the common problem of the above-mentioned drop policies is that they all ignore how bundle scheduling priorities influence the performance of opportunistic networks. In [16], a novel buffer scheduling and dropping scheme called ACF-based policy is proposed, which considers the average contact frequency among nodes. Yet, the impacts of short contact duration and limited bandwidth on delivery ratio and average delay are disregarded.

In a word, the opportunistic networks are the environment where the partitioned networks and dynamic topologies problems make it difficult to get network-wide information. So local knowledge-based policies have more advantages than the global knowledge-based ones [11]. The DTP-based policy proposed in this paper is based on local knowledge, and has been proved to be an effective solution to the said problem, since it uses the average encounter frequency and the average encounter duration collectively to decide which bundle to forward and which one to drop.

3   Approach

N nodes with finite buffer are assumed to be in the network; each of them has a unique identity number ranging from 1 to N. Nodes move independently of each other at different speed. Source nodes periodically generate random-size bundles, which must be delivered to their destinations within a given TTL. Moreover, each node records its encounter times and duration with other nodes. Nodes update these records when they meet each other. Obviously, if a node has met other nodes many times in the past, it is more likely to encounter with any of them again in the near future. With the contact frequency between two nodes, each node can estimate the possibility for a bundle to reach the destination. However, the times of nodes' encounter cannot reflect the real ability of communication anymore. In addition, contact duration is one of the determining factors of data transmission capability. Therefore, basing on average encounter duration and average encounter frequency, we propose a data transmission probability function, which is used to determine the forwarding priority of a bundle at each contact, and to determine which bundles to drop when congestion occurs. Formally, we define the average encounter frequency and average encounter duration time as follows:

The average encounter frequency (AEF) is defined as the number of encounters between two nodes in the unit time. And the average encounter duration (AED) is defined as the average duration time of several encounters between two nodes in constant time. Let $c_t(m, n)$ describe whether node m and node n encounter at time t. If node m encounters with node n, $c_t(m, n) = 1$; if not, $c_t(m, n) = 0$. Thus, $n_T(m, n)$, the total number of encounters between node m and node n in the given time interval T, can be calculated as follows:

$$n_T(m, n) = n_{t_0+T}(m, n) - n_{t_0}(m, n) = \sum_{t_0}^{t_0+T} c_t(m, n), \tag{1}$$

$$AEF_n^m = f_T(m, n) = \frac{n_T(m, n)}{T} = \frac{\sum\limits_{t_0}^{t_0+T} c_t(m, n)}{T}. \tag{2}$$

Specifically, in Eq. (1), t_0 is an initial time of the networks. According to Eq. (1), the variable AEF, which represents a node's encounter frequency with others, can be computed with Eq. (2). If node m and node n encounter each other at time t, let $d_t(m, n)$ be the duration time of this encounter. Consequently, the variable $s_T(m, n)$ which denotes the total duration time of encounters between node m and node n in the given time interval T can be computed as follows:

$$s_T(m, n) = s_{t_0+T}(m, n) - s_{t_0}(m, n) = \sum_{t_0}^{t_0+T} d_t(m, n), \tag{3}$$

$$AED_n^m = t_T(m, n) = \frac{s_T(m, n)}{n_T(m, n)} = \frac{\sum\limits_{t_0}^{t_0+T} d_t(m, n)}{\sum\limits_{t_0}^{t_0+T} c_t(m, n)}. \tag{4}$$

The meaning of t_0 is same as that in Eq. (1). Combining Eq. (2) with Eq. (3), we can derive approximate calculation of the variable AED, which denotes the average duration time of encounters in the interval T as shown in Eq. (4). Then, for each interval T, data transmission probability (DTP), which indicates the capability to deliver bundles to their destinations through encounters, is decided by average encounter frequency and average encounter duration. Specifically,

$$DTP_n^m = p_T(m, n) = \alpha f_T(m, n) + \beta t_T(m, n), \tag{5}$$

where α and β are normalized parameters of $f_T(m, n)$ and $t_T(m, n)$ respectively.

3.1   Forward Policy

In addition to DTP described above, the size and the time to live (TTL) of the bundles also have effects on whether bundles can be transferred to destination successfully. With a limited bandwidth and short contact duration, nodes are not able to forward all bundles in their buffer to other nodes. In general, bundles with small size are more likely to be delivered successfully. A long TTL implies that a bundle still has a long time to propagate in the network, which may be helpful to deliver the bundle to its destination.

In order to introduce forward strategy, we will first consider a contact between node a and b. Assume that node a plays a role as a sender, whilst node b is a receiver. We will show the details of forward policy based on DTP in Algorithm 1.

Algorithm 1. forward policy

---

while connection between node a and b is up
  do SVs are exchanged between node a and b
    node a pushes bundles not in b's buffer into *forwardSelection*
    for every bundle i in *forwardSelection*
      do if $d_i = $ b
        then push bundle i into *directForwardQueue*
          if $S_m = S_n$
            then *sort(TTL, directForwardQueue, desc)*
          else *sort(Si, directForwardQueue, asc)*
          end if
        else if $DTP^b_{d_i} > DTP^a_{d_i}$
          then push bundle i into *forwardQueue*
            if $DTP^b_{d_m} = DTP^b_{d_n}$ and $S_m = S_n$
              then *sort(TTL, forwardQueue, desc)*
            else if $DTP^b_{d_m} = DTP^b_{d_n}$ and $S_m \neq S_n$
              then *sort(Si, forwardQueue, asc)*
            else *sort(DTP^b_{di}, forwardQueue, desc)*
            end if
        end if
    end for
    forward(directForwardQueue, b)
    forward(forwardQueue, b)
end while

In Algorithm 1, SV is a summary vector of bundles at a node. While a connection between node a and b is up, SVs are exchanged each other. Then node a pushes bundles not in b's buffer into *forwardSelection* which is a set of bundles to be forwarded. d_i and S_i denote the destination and the size of the ith bundle at node a, respectively. Similarly, both *directForwardQueue* and *forwardQueue* are queues of bundles to be forwarded. If bundle i in *forwardSelection* is destined to node b, it will be pushed into *directForwardQueue* directly. Otherwise, if $DTP^b\ di > DTP^a\ di$, it will be pushed into *forwardQueue*. *sort(x, y, z)* is a custom ranking function which sorts bundles in the specified way. For example, *sort(TTL, directForwardQueue, desc)* means that the bundles in *directForwardQueue* will be sorted in *desc* order of their TTLs. As described in Algorithm 1, the bundles will be sorted by various kinds of methods according to different conditions that they satisfy. Finally, the function *forward (directForwardQueue, b)* and *forward (forwardQueue, b)* are to replicate bundles stored in *directForwardQueue* and *forwardQueue* to node b respectively.

3.2 Drop Policy

A drop policy defines which bundle to drop if the buffer of a node is full and a new bundle is to be accommodated. Due to the essential impacts of the average encounter frequency and the average encounter duration on data transmission capability, we should take DTP into account when determining which bundle to drop. Besides, the size and TTL of bundles are also auxiliary determinants of drop policy. This is because dropping bundles with large size can result in less bundle drop. In addition, a bundle with a short TTL implies it has been in the network for a long time and thus is more likely to have been delivered. The details of drop policy based on DTP are shown in Algorithm 2.

Algorithm 2. drop policy

bundle M is forwarded to node a
node a is congested
   for every bundle i in a's buffer
      do if $DTP^a_{dM} > DTP^a_{di}$
         then push bundle i into $dropQueue$
      end if
   end for
   while $dropQueue \neq NULL$ and $FS_a < S_M$
      do for bundle m and n in $dropQueue$
         do if $DTP^a_{dm} = DTP^a_{dn}$ and $S_m = S_n$
            then $sort(TTL, dropQueue, asc)$
         else if $DTP^a_{dm} = DTP^a_{dn}$ and $S_m \neq S_n$
            then $sort(S_i, dropQueue, desc)$
         else $sort(DTP^a_{di}, dropQueue, asc)$
         end if
      end for
      $drop(dropQueue)$
   end while
   if $FS_a \geq S_M$
      then store bundle M
   else refuse to store bundle M
   end if

When a new bundle M is forwarded to node a, it becomes congested and runs Algorithm 2. If $DTPa\ dM > DTPa\ di$, bundle i will be pushed into $dropQueue$ which is a queue of bundles to be dropped. The meaning of d_i, S_i, $sort(x, y, z)$ are same as those of Algorithm 1. Additionally, FS_a denotes the free space of node a's buffer. The bundles will be arranged according to the TTL, S_i or DTP values of bundles. Then $drop\ (dropQueue)$ is to drop the bundles in $dropQueue$ sequentially until $dropQueue$ becomes empty or node a has enough space for bundle M. If $FS_a \geq S_M$, node a will store bundle M in its buffer; otherwise, it refuses to store bundle M.

4 Simulation and Results

In this section, we will evaluate the DTP-based policy proposed in this paper against the following local knowledge policies: DO, DF, MDC-SR and the ACF-based policy in Epidemic routing with ONE simulator [17]. The main simulation parameters used in the experiment are listed in Table 1.

Table 1. Simulation parameters.

Simulation area	4500*3400 m²
Number of nodes	100
Movement model	Random Way Point
Speed of nodes	Randomly selected in (0,15)m/s
Size of messages	Randomly selected in [50 KB,100 KB]
Message generation interval	25 s,35 s
Transmission range	10 m
Transmission speed	250KBps
Simulation duration	12 h

The definitions of the main performance metrics are defined as follows:

(1) Delivery ratio: the ratio of the number of bundles received by destination nodes to the number of bundles created by source nodes, shown in Eq. (6).

$$delivery\_ratio = \frac{N_d}{N_c} \times 100\%. \tag{6}$$

The terms N_d and N_c respectively represent the number of bundles delivered to destination nodes and the number of bundles created by source nodes.

(2) Average delay: the average latency of all bundles received by destination nodes, shown in Eq. (7).

$$average\_delay = \frac{\sum_{i=1}^{N_d} D_i}{N_d}. \tag{7}$$

D_i denotes the delay of the *ith* bundle received by destination nodes.

(3) Overhead: the ratio of the number of bundles received by destination nodes to the number of bundles carried by them, shown in Eq. (8).

$$overhead = \frac{N_d}{N_{ca}} \times 100\%. \tag{8}$$

N_{ca} is the number of bundles carried by destination nodes.

Firstly, Fig. 1 reveals the comparison of DO, DF, MDC-SR, the ACF-Based and the DTP-Based policy proposed in this paper with respect to delivery ratio. As a whole, the delivery ratio of all policies increase rapidly at early stage and then attain a stable state. The impact of buffer size on delivery ratio decreases gradually with the increment of buffer size. When the buffer of node is enough to accommodate all bundles, buffer size is no longer regarded as the bottleneck of delivery ratio increase. The DTP-Based policy has up to 7.4% improvement as compared with DO and up to 23.2% improvement as compared with the ACF-Based policy. As shown in this graph, the ACF-Based policy

and MDC-SR show lower delivery ratio comparing with others. This is because they just consider delivery probability of bundles based on the encounter frequency of nodes, which is inexact in random way point mobility model. However, the DTP-Based policy also takes the encounter duration, the size and the time to live of nodes into account when estimating how likely a bundle will be delivered.

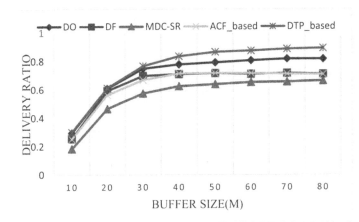

Fig. 1. Delivery ratio under random way point model with different node buffer sizes.

Figure 2 shows the average delay of DO, DF, MDC-SR, the ACF-Based and the DTP-Based policy. The average delay of MDC-SR and the ACF-Based policy are larger than that of DO and DF. In random way point mobility model, it may be inaccurate to use nodes' encounter frequency to estimate delivery delay of bundles. But the DTP-Based policy also takes advantage of node's encounter duration, bundle lifetime and bundle size to address the said issue. Consequently, comparing with MDC-SR and the ACF-Based policy, it has up to 40.6% and 22.6% reduction in average delay, respectively. Furthermore, the average delay of the DTP-Based policy keeps more stable than others with the increasing of buffer size.

Finally, it can be seen that the overhead of the DTP-based policy is much lower than that of others, especially than that of MDC-SR, when they are in the same scenario. The bundles are delivered to the nodes with a higher DTP value, which indicates the probability of meeting the destination nodes. Comparing with MDC-SR and the ACF-based policy, the DTP-based policy takes both the average encounter frequency and the average encounter duration into consideration. Apart from this, the size and the time to live of bundles are also auxiliary determinants of the DTP-based policy. Therefore, our policy has achieved a much better and more stable performance (Fig. 3).

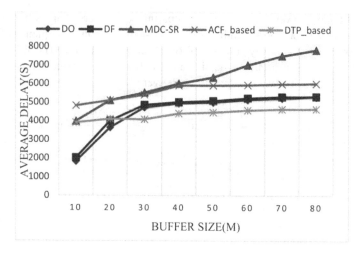

Fig. 2. Average delay under random way point model with different node buffer sizes.

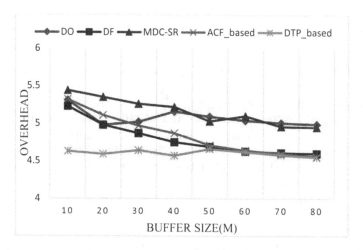

Fig. 3. Overhead under random way point model with different node buffer sizes.

5   Conclusion

In this paper, we investigate the problems of buffer management policies in the opportunistic networks. We propose a new metric derived by the average encounter frequency and the average encounter duration, called as data transmission probability, indicates the capability of node to deliver bundle to its destination through encounter.

Then an effective scheduling and dropping policy based on the DTP, TTL value and the size of bundles is proposed to decide which bundle to forward and which bundle to drop. The simulation results show that our strategy outperforms DO, DF, MDC-SR and the ACF-based policy in terms of delivery ratio, average delay and overhead.

Acknowledgments. This work was partly supported by the NSFC-Guangdong Joint Found (U1501254) and the Co-construction Program with the Beijing Municipal Commission of Education and the Ministry of Science and Technology of China(2012BAH45B01) and the Fundamental Research Funds for the Central Universities (BUPT2011RCZJ16, 2014ZD03-03) and China Information Security Special Fund (NDRC).

References

1. Xiong, Y.P., Sun, L.M., Niu, J.W., et al.: Opportunistic networks. J. Softw. **20**, 124–137 (2009)
2. Tekdas, O., Bhadauria, D., Isler, V.: Efficient data collection from wireless nodes under the two-ring communication model. Int. J. Robot. Res. **31**, 774–784 (2012)
3. Wang C., Wang W., Sohraby K., et al.: QoS optimized and energy efficient power control for deep space multimedia communications in InterPlaNetary networks. In: International Conference on Wireless for Space and Extreme Environments, pp. 1–3. IEEE (2013)
4. Burgess, J., Gallagher, B., Jensen, D., et al.: MaxProp: Routing for vehicle-based disruption-tolerant networks. In: Proceedings - IEEE INFOCOM, pp. 1–11 (2006)
5. Krishnan, R., Basu, P., Mikkelson, J.M., et al.: The SPINDLE disruption-tolerant networking system. In: Military Communications Conference, pp. 1017–1023. IEEE (2007)
6. Rashid, S., Ayub, Q., Zahid, M.S.M., et al.: Impact of mobility models on DLA (Drop Largest) optimized DTN epidemic routing protocol. Int. J. Comput. Appl. **18**, 35–39 (2011)
7. Jain, S., Chawla, M.: Survey of buffer management policies for delay tolerant networks. J. Eng. (2014)
8. Zhang, X., Neglia, G., Kurose, J., et al.: Performance modeling of epidemic routing. Comput. Netw. **51**, 827–839 (2006)
9. Krifa, A., Barakat, C., Spyropoulos, T.: An optimal joint scheduling and drop policy for delay tolerant networks. In: World of Wireless, Mobile and Multimedia Networks, pp. 1–6. IEEE, California (2008)
10. Lindgren, A., Phanse, K.S.: Evaluation of queueing policies and forwarding strategies for routing in intermittently connected networks. In: International Conference on Communication System Software and Middleware, pp. 1–10. IEEE (2006)
11. Rashid, S., Ayub, Q., Zahid, M.S.M., et al.: Message drop control buffer management policy for DTN routing protocols. Wireless Pers. Commun. **72**, 653–669 (2013)
12. Rashid, S., Ayub, Q., Soperi, M.Z.M., et al.: E DROP an effective drop buffer management policy for DTN routing protocols. Int. J. Comput. Appl. **13**, 8–13 (2010)
13. Rashid, S., Abdullah, A.H., Soperi, M., et al.: Mean drop an effectual buffer management policy for delay tolerant network (2012)
14. Ayub, Q., Rashid, S., Zahid, M.S.M.: Buffer scheduling policy for opportunitic networks (2013)
15. Ayub, Q., Rashid, S.: T-Drop: An optimal buffer management policy to improve QOS in DTN routing protocols. J. Comput. **2**, 46–50 (2010)
16. Tang, L., Chai, Y., Li, Y., et al.: Buffer management policies in opportunistic networks. J. Comput. Inf. Syst. **8**, 5149–5159 (2012)
17. Keränen, A., Ott, J., et al.: The ONE simulator for DTN protocol evaluation. In: International Conference on Simulation TOOLS and Techniques for Communications, Networks and Systems, Simutools, Rome, Italy (2009)

Runtime Exceptions Handling for Collaborative SOA Applications

Bin Wen$^{(\boxtimes)}$, Ziqiang Luo, and Song Lin

School of Information Science and Technology, Hainan Normal University,
Haikou 571158, China
binwen@hainnu.edu.cn

Abstract. For all kinds of computing infrastructure, services have become the important channel to enlarge theirs resource utilization performance. Services computing achieves resource sharing value. Because of the lack of runtime exception handling consideration, collaborative service-based software system often encounters unexplained interrupt and collapse. This paper focuses on the collaborative ability of service-based system, especially in the adjustment mechanism for runtime exception handling. Main contributions: (1) Self-adaptive exception handling architecture for services resource has been built. (2) Runtime collaborative adjustment mechanism has been designed to deal with requirements and context changes. Experiment and empirical analysis for Hainan agricultural E-business platform have been acquired so as to support collaborative SOA with above-mentioned approaches. Combination of theoretical research and empirical validation, the paper tries to provide a technical operational and cost-effective solution with collaborative mechanism and promoting SOA runtime adaptive ability for runtime requirements evolution and exception handling. The solution will provide systematical support to build collaborative SOA.

Keywords: Collaborative SOA · Exception handling · Runtime

1 Introduction

Software and resource usage have entered into the cloud infrastructure for consumer use in the form of services. Service has been become the basic way to access and enlarge the capability of all kinds of computing infrastructure. Services computing achieves resource sharing value. In the study of Bigdata, Analytics as a service (AaaS), and Software as a service (SaaS), Platform as a service (PaaS), Infrastructure as a service for Cloud computing, the core is services provisioning. Services computing related researches in recent years also more involved in resource sharing and application integration based on infrastructure. "Software as a service", "Big service: resource as a service". Making full use of the available online software resource to meet the requirements of diversified and distributed stakeholders, we are going to the service-oriented software engineering (SOSE) era [1–3].

© ICST Institute for Computer Sciences, Social Informatics and Telecommunications Engineering 2017
S. Wang and A. Zhou (Eds.): CollaborateCom 2016, LNICST 201, pp. 252–261, 2017.
DOI: 10.1007/978-3-319-59288-6_23

IOSOC2013 is the famous conference for services computing held on Nov. 3, 2013. Carlo Ghezzi, Fellow of ACM and IEEE, published keynote titled "Surviving in a world of change: forward evolvable and self-adaptive service-oriented systems" [4] and also aimed to focus on the adaptability and collaborative capability of service-oriented system. He pointed out that runtime adaptability is a major challenge to promote the development of software technology. The preface on the proceeding of IOSOC2014 [5] also emphasized that "In addition to traditional topics such as service-oriented architecture, service design, service description, and service composition, service change management is a key topic that reflects the need for services to adapt to dynamic environments."

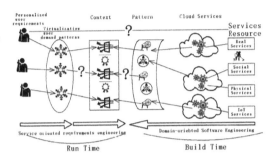

Fig. 1. Software Production Methods and Problems Based on the Services

General process for service-based software (SBS) production is as follow: producing services resource→publishing services→selecting services→services aggregation (services binding and combination). It is similar to the waterfall model or mixed alignment mode between top-down and bottom-top approach (Fig. 1). But the process lacks of runtime exception handling without starting from the requirements to overcome the exceptions, services resource insufficiency and context changes (Fig. 1: "?").

Therefore, establishing the direct feedback channel from user requirements to services aggregation, and implementing SOA runtime adjustable exception handling to build collaborative SOA are the motivations of the studying and significance.

Services resource provisioning has become the consensus of SBS development for industrialization. Now knowledge body of services computing mainly includes lifecycle planning, resource production, publishing, billing and management of SBS. Industry and academic community generally focus on the services discovery and services composition, the starting point of research is to assume that services resource is rich enough. Actually, services resource for meeting the users' needs often does not exist or cannot get in runtime at present stage. As mentioned in the literature [6], "If no services are available for some parts, the application developer can register them in the service broker's directory and wait until the needed services are available." Thus these problems lead to the difficulty, high complexity and low availability of services composition.

At the same time, due to the dynamic nature of web services and error-prone supply environment of services resource, all kind of provisioning exceptions may occur during the process of composition [7,8]. Exception refers to the services failure (fault), network error or abnormal events caused by resource or requirements changes. Lack of exception handling mechanism, it will lead to these problems such as poor performance, resource waste, poor optimized services and even failure. So services resource provisioning must be able to actively produce. They should have adaptive runtime exception capability.

The main SBS development platform in industry, such as IBM RSA[1], ActiveBPEL[2], Websphere Integration Developer[3], are also lack of considerations for active provisioning and runtime exception handling.

The main problem of the existing SOA mainly lies in:

1. Traditional SOA does not have runtime adaptive regulating mechanism and ability to meet the runtime context changes.
2. Lack of effective runtime exception handling solutions for SBS.

The current services resource is produced in advance by services provider. The process is lack of runtime exception handling consideration. Therefore, adjusting the runtime architecture to deal with context changes and resolving interrupt and collapse with runtime exception handling have become the urgently solved problems.

How to build self-adaptive exception handling architecture for services resource? How to design the runtime collaborative adjustment mechanism to deal with requirements and context changes? This is what our motivations focus on the runtime exceptions handling for collaborative SOA applications.

This paper aims at study the runtime exception handling for Collaborative SOA. We will mainly investigate the applicable SOA runtime exception handling mechanism. The rest of the article is organized as follows. Section 2 introduces the runtime exception handling. Section 3 presents runtime adjustment mechanism to deal with context changes. Section 4 shows the experiment and empirical analysis with the approach. Conclusions with main contributions of proposed approach and further work plans are also touched upon in Sect. 5.

2   Runtime Exception Handling

Due to lack of considering time changes and integrating method between requirements and architecture, we propose a adaptive approach with predictive control to put the requirements of problem space adaptively mapped to the runtime architecture of solution space. The approach can learn the model based on wavelet transform to predict the performance of services component, and induce requirements evolution or model transformation of architecture to achieve

---

[1] http://www.ibm.com/developerworks/rational/products/rsa/.

[2] http://www.activebpel.org/samples/samples-4/samples.php.

[3] http://www-01.ibm.com/software/integration/wid/.

runtime adaptive ability. And dynamic self-adaptive production based on customized services resource and legacy software servicilization will be choose for runtime adaptive exception handling according to users' requirements.

Service virtualization is designed to shield the heterogeneous properties of IT resource. Software abstraction expression will be decoupled with concrete IT resource to realize semantic equivalence mapping between web service of IT level and business functional requirements [9].

With the aid of service virtualization, active customization of personalized services resource is explored to complete instant and on-demand production for unmatched services resource in runtime. These efforts should compensate the lack of on-demand adaptive services customization for research community.

Services requester-centric collaborative SOA is different from triangle equal traditional SOA. Service requesters (consumers) lie in active status. Services consumers not only launch services requirements to select match and combine among the provided services, but also they can dominate the customized process. Predictive control can monitor requirements changes so as to map requirements and requirements evolution into the elements of architecture at run time.

As the project experimental carrier, we choose a software system based on Internet focusing on Hainan agricultural E-business services. Because the service-oriented Hainan agricultural platform is faced with rich stakeholders, more services resource, diversified individuation needs and SOA style to lead to the variety of customized requirements. Also, legacy software components for agricultural products processing are numerous. These situations conform to the demand for empirical carrier.

3 Runtime Adjustment Mechanism to Deal with Context Changes

Here in this section, runtime exception handling mechanism for collaborative SOA will be discussed based on context and requirements changes.

Services actively satisfy the consumers' needs to produce. It can change passive services selection shortcoming that is unable to satisfy users' needs. Unmatched and unqualified services in runtime will be appended into the queue of customization that will be processed to notify providers for on-demand production using Atom subscribe/inform style by customization manager. For customized and matched services, they will rerun to the aggregation flow to continue to complete the business process.

3.1 Self-adaptive Custom Service Resources Optimization

The main core algorithms includes the services customer preferred selection, services aggregation with customization, self-adaptive optimization, services evaluation algorithm, customization management process, customization information feedback and services re-aggregation with joined custom services and application effectiveness analysis for services resource customized production.

Self-adaptive optimization algorithm partly adopts the early results of ours effort, namely SSOA (Space Search Optimization Algorithm) (see Algorithm 1). In custom resource provisioning, selection and search efficiency will be improved. Space search algorithm uses search operation to realize optimization object. Algorithm starts from the known solution, and also produces new subspace and searches this subspace.

```
1 INPUT:solution set (population)
2 OUTPUT:optimization space
   1:  Begin
   2:    Initialization:
   3:      1) Initialize a solution set (population) at random.
   4:      2) Opposition-based space search.
   5:    While (the termination conditions are not met)
   6:      IF (rand(0, 1) < C_r) // C_r is a fixed given number
   7:        Local space search:
   8:          1) Generate a new space: Generate a new space based on three given solutions.
   9:          2) Search the new space: Reflection, Expansion, and Contraction.
  10:        Global space search: Cauchy search (Cauchy mutation).
  11:      Else
  12:        Opposition-based space search.
  13:    End While
  14:  End
```

Algorithm 1. SSOA Algorithm pseudo code.

The algorithm consists of three types of space search operations.

1. Local space search:
   The operation has been improved based on the Simplex algorithm (plus the search with constraint conditions)
2. Global space search:
   Essentially, the operation is Cauchy mutation.
3. Reverse operation:
   To accelerate the convergence speed of the algorithm, the operation referred the "reverse number". The result has proved better than pure random search.
4. Algorithm characteristics:
   SSOA has stronger local search ability. For example, compared with most of the DE algorithm, SSOA algorithm has relatively stronger global search ability, this is because it includes Cauchy mutation. SSOA algorithm has faster convergence speed.
5. Algorithm advantages:
   The experimental results have showed that SSOA has faster convergence speed, and has more possibility to obtain the approximate solution or more precise value compared some famous DE algorithm. Especially in the high dimensional optimization problem, these advantages perform more outstanding.

3.2 Custom Service Resources Management Monitoring Mechanism

On-demand customization of services resource needs runtime abnormal monitoring to trigger the customization process. So services quality evaluation metrics should be explored. Monitoring mechanism needs to define the boundary conditions of abnormal action, and it is also a real-time system that must meet the demand of real-time triggering, releasing and feedback.

When an exception occurs, the process of services aggregation will be interrupted. Services aggregation should be restarted and worked again with the recovery of unavailable services. Implementation method is drawn lessons from the scientific workflow's transaction in that the process either completed or terminated. At the same time, related process operation data should be retained. For the terminated process aggregation again, resumed process does not affect the services resource providers. So related data tables of system database are required to design. These data records will support the aggregation restart again.

The main operation points of services resource custom management method are as follows.

1. We propose a personalized active custom approach driven by requirements fragments for services requester-centric SOA with adaptive mechanism. It will reinforce current status for customized services resource without runtime on-demand customization.
2. We have designed a full set of architecture and implementation including self-adaptive custom, services aggregation restart and exception handling monitor for abnormal case of user services. Also, feasibility and simplicity will be focused.
3. Through some mathematical methods such as custom optimization algorithm of services resource, exception handling ability with adaptability will be built to optimize and quantity services resource production in runtime.

3.3 Runtime Adaptive Adjustment Mechanism with the Changes

By real-time adjusting the runtime software architecture to adapt to the requirements and context changes, software system can guarantee its performance under dynamic load. Due to lack of general method, how to adaptive map the requirements of problem space into architecture evolution of solution space, it will become a key issue. This section presents an adaptive control method based on predictive control, combining with the requirements model and software architecture to drive the adaptive SOA. This approach adopts learning model based on wavelet transform in order to accurate/flexible predict the evolution of services resource. Through real-time predictive control induced requirements model changes to realize the evolution of software architecture in runtime, the runtime adaptive adjustment of SOA should be finished.

Now runtime adaptive adjustment is still a difficult problem for Internet-intensive software system. It needs to solve how to map requirements changes into architecture units at runtime. Driven by predictive control for SaaS components to induce requirements evolution, runtime architecture change will be realized, and the validity of predictive control can be proved in the aspect of requirements/architecture evolution [10]. But this method is not extended to SOA level with requirements change-driven architecture evolution.

As shown in Fig. 2, we propose the runtime adaptive adjustment scheme combined with effective predictive control method [10] and MAPE-K control circuit model [11]. The proposed adjustment system divided into real-time monitor, analysis engine, software architecture adjustment manager, requirements evolution manager and Aspect execution engine. First of all, the real-time monitor acquires QoS values of services resource and saves into the log records. Then the QoS value will be transferred to the analysis engine that uses analysis model based wavelet transformation to predict next QoS value according to the logs. Software architecture adjustment manager seeks the best runtime design decision under the requirements constraints according to the predicted QoS value and the current QoS values. If the feasible runtime model can be found, the Aspect script will be automatically generated. Execution engine runs the script to complete the model transformation at runtime. Otherwise, design decision manager should identify the specific improvement points of requirements evolution to induce these changes.

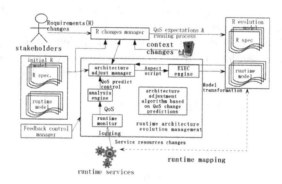

Fig. 2. Runtime adaptability to deal with the changes of requirements and scenario

The core points of the scheme are as follows.

(1) How to select the predictive QoS value for runtime services resource? Wavelet transformation is the best choice.
(2) How to build software architecture adjustment mechanism based on QoS changes to predict in advance? The runtime adaptive adjustment algorithm is designed (Algorithm 2) for solving the above concerned points.

```
1 INPUT: QoS value of service resources for SBS in time t and t+1; QoS value of
  the expected output.
2 OUTPUT:control operation vector in t+1 moment
   1: Begin
   2:    Initialization: training classification prediction model; the points of tags to improve
         training requirements model;
   3:    IF Classification prediction (QoS value of services resource in run time
         t and t+1, expected output of QoS value) = requirements
   4:    THEN
   5:        control operation vector in t+1 moment=tag improvement point
         (QoS value of services resource in t and t+1 moment at runtime, the expected output
         of QoS value)
   6:    ELSE
   7:        control operation vector in t+1 moment = architecture evolution (AOP style)
         (QoS value service resources in t and t+1 moment at runtime, the expected
         output of QoS value)
   8:    END IF
   9:    RETURN control operation vector in t + 1 moment
  10: End
```

Algorithm 2. Runtime adaptive adjustment algorithm.

4   Experiment and Empirical Analysis

Hainan agricultural e-commerce platform-NongBo Mall[4] should be chosen as experimental carrier which integrated the Internet of things, cloud and big data technology to build a service-oriented Internet based application software system. NongBo Mall is a service-oriented platform faced with richness stakeholders, diversity personalized requirements, thus leading to a variety of personalized customization requirements. Meanwhile, the platform adopts SOA development style and a large number of service resources (including Microsoft Asmx or Java Axis) have developed. The above characteristics conform to exploring empirical collaborative SOA carrier requirements. The author's team is the technical support of online/offline design for NongBo Mall. Close cooperation can help research achievements timely and effective application for Hainan agricultural electric business platform. Through continuous iteration, we can get a comprehensive CASE tool needs to support collaborative SOA.

A large number of services have been developed for the platform. For example, only for agricultural products traceability information service, the WCF interface service address is as follows:

http://218.77.186.198:8000/TracesDataService.svc

Web service interface address is:

http://218.77.186.198:8000/TracesDataWebService.asmx

Its identification code is 2C516EF7-CBD8-4C1C-9EE0-00EB34AFBCB5.

---

[4] http://www.963110.net.

The test data:

PID(Product ID): A003121910013001
PRID(Planting ID): XH03020130401

For example, production history batch No. is
ProductionHistoryGetProductionHistoryByPID(string PID, string IDs)
Parameters:

PID: 16 digits batch no.
IDs: identification codereturns a ProductionHistory object.

The main data structures, such as ProductionHistory (production record) class structure is as follows:

⟨*summary*⟩ Batch no. ⟨*/summary*⟩
publicstringPID{get; set; }
⟨*summary*⟩ Planting number ⟨*/summary*⟩
publicstringPRID{get; set; }
⟨*summary*⟩ Planting time ⟨*/summary*⟩
publicDateTimePlantTM{get; set; }
⟨*summary*⟩ Picking time ⟨*/summary*⟩
publicDateTimePickTM{get; set; }
⟨*summary*⟩ Pesticide recordset ⟨*/summary*⟩
publicList⟨PesticideHistory⟩PesticideHistoryList{get; set; }
⟨*summary*⟩ Fertilization recordset ⟨*/summary*⟩
publicList⟨FertilizerHistory⟩FertilizerHistoryList{get; set; }

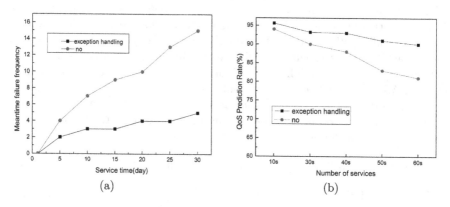

Fig. 3. Effect comparison for E-business platform using exception handling mechanism

In addition to platform-developed services, system also has called a large number of external services, such as map services, weather services and other physical services etc., which are typical SBS applications. In the early stage, platform operation is extremely unstable. No corresponding runtime exception handling mechanism is the main reason. Figure 3(a) is the comparison result for the two sets of same system platform running at the same time. One of platforms is running under the part of the designed exception handling mechanism in this paper. Comparison results (Fig. 3) show that the embedded runtime exception handling mechanism obviously improved the platform's ability (including the rate of QoS prediction) to deal with all kinds of uncertainty.

5   Conclusions

The main contributions of this paper are summarized as follows: (1) Self-adaptive exception handling architecture for active services resource provisioning has been built. (2) Runtime adaptive adjustment mechanism has been designed to deal with requirements and context changes. This paper gives a general solution framework, but the details are still to be further in-depth study.

The paper aims at explore the collaborative SOA with runtime exception handling to enhance the operation reliability. We mainly focus on collaborative SOA runtime exception handling mechanism. The results and progresses of the study will provide systematical solutions to perfect the collaborative SOA.

Acknowledgements. This research has been supported by the Natural Science Foundation of China (No. 61562024, No. 61463012) and Natural Science Foundation of Hainan Province (No. 20156236).

References

1. Liu, L.: Editorial: services computing in 2016. IEEE Trans. Serv. Comput. **9**(1), 1 (2016)
2. Zhang, L.J.: Big services era: global trends of cloud computing and big data. IEEE Trans. Serv. Comput. **5**(4), 467–468 (2012)
3. Bin, W.: On-demand Service Software Engineering for Cloud Computing. National Defence Industry Press, Beijing (2014)
4. Ghezzi, C.: Surviving in a world of change: towards evolvable and self-adaptive service-oriented systems. In: Keynote Speech at Proceedings of the 11th International Conference on Service Oriented Computing, ICSOC 2013. Springer, Heidelberg (2013)
5. Kappel, G., Maamar, Z., Motahari-Nezhad, H.R. (eds.): ICSOC 2011. LNCS, vol. 7084. Springer, Heidelberg (2011)
6. Yau, S.S., An, H.G.: Software engineering meets services and cloud computing. Computer **44**(10), 46–52 (2011)
7. Allier, S., et al.: Multitier diversification in web-based software applications. IEEE Softw. **32**(1), 83–90 (2015)
8. Lemos, A.L., Daniel, F., Benatallah, B.: Web service composition: a survey of techniques and tools. ACM Comput. Surv. **48**(3), 1–41 (2015)
9. Chouiref, Z., Belkhir, A., Benouaret, K., Hadjali, A.: A fuzzy framework for efficient user-centric web service selection. Appl. Soft Comput. **41**, 51–65 (2016). Elsevier
10. Xiong, W., et al.: A self-adaptation approach based on predictive control for SaaS. Chin. J. Comput. **39**(2), 364–376 (2016)
11. Kephart, J.O., Chess, D.M.: The vision of autonomic computing. Computer **36**(1), 41–45 (2003)

Data-Intensive Workflow Scheduling in Cloud on Budget and Deadline Constraints

Zhang Xin, Changze Wu$^{(\boxtimes)}$, and Kaigui Wu

College of Computer Science, Chongqing University, Chongqing 400044, China
zx06063068@163.com, {wuchangze,kaiguiwu}@cqu.edu.cn

Abstract. With the development of Cloud Computing, large-scale applications expressed as scientific workflows are often executed in cloud. The problems of workflow scheduling are vital for achieving high efficient and meeting the needs of users in clouds. In order to obtain more cost reduction as well as maintain the quality of service by meeting the deadlines, this paper proposed a novel heuristic, PWHEFT (Path-task Weight Heterogeneous Earliest Finish Time), based on Heterogeneous Earliest Finish Time (HEFT). The criticality of tasks in a workflow and data transmission between resources are considered in PWHEFT while ignored in some other algorithms. The heuristic is evaluated using simulation with five different real world workflow applications. The simulation results show that our proposed scheduling heuristic can significantly improve planning success rate.

Keywords: Workflow · HEFT · Bi-criteria · Data-intensive workflow scheduling

1 Introduction

Large-scale businesses and scientific applications which are usually comprised of big-data, multitasking and multidisciplinary sciences, have required more computing power beyond single machine capability [1]. An easy and popular way is to execute these applications which include scientific workflows, multi-tier web service workflows, and big data processing workflows on the cloud. In order to execute these workflows in reasonable amount of time and acceptable cost, the workflow scheduling problem has been studied extensively over past years.

Workflow scheduling is a process of mapping inter-dependent tasks on the available resources such that workflow application is able to complete its execution within the user's specified Quality of Service (QoS) constraints such as deadline and budget [2]. Workflow scheduling in the cloud faces some challenges. Typically, the non-dedicated nature of resources imposes more difficulties as the contention for shared resources on the cloud needs to be considered during planning. These suggest that the planner may have to somehow query resources for their runtime information (e.g., the existing load) to make informed decisions. And planning should be performed in short time, because users may require a real-time response, and the runtime information, on which a planning decision has been made, varies over time and, thus, a planning decision made using out of date information may not be valid. Moreover, a user may

© ICST Institute for Computer Sciences, Social Informatics and Telecommunications Engineering 2017
S. Wang and A. Zhou (Eds.): CollaborateCom 2016, LNICST 201, pp. 262–272, 2017.
DOI: 10.1007/978-3-319-59288-6_24

require his/her workflow application to complete within a certain deadline and budget. However, minimizing makespan and minimizing execution cost are two conflicting objectives. There have been a few bi-criteria DAG planning heuristics in the literature [3–5], some of them have sophisticated designs, such as guided random research or local search, which usually require considerably high planning costs. Moreover, most of these heuristics do not take the data transmission between resources into account, which may lead to an invalid plan in Data-intensive workflow scheduling. Taking computation costs of scheduling into consideration, an efficient algorithm tries to compromise these values (makespan and execution cost) and still obtain approximate optimal solution. In this paper, we aim for bi-criteria scheduling of workflow with the cloud. We address a new heuristic aiming at seeking out a beneficial trade-off between execution time and execution cost under Budget and Deadline constraints. The proposed heuristic, namely, PWHEFT, is based on HEFT [6] algorithm, which maximizes efforts to reduce the overall execution time of a workflow. The HEFT algorithm selects the task with the highest upwards rank value at each step and assigns the selected task to the resource, which minimizes its earliest finish time with an insertion-based approach. While being effective at optimizing makespan, the HEFT algorithm does not consider the monetary cost and budget constraint when making scheduling decisions. Compared with HEFT, PWHEFT figures out appropriate schedule plan after considering Budget, Deadline, criticality of tasks and data transfer rates between processors.

The remaining paper is organized as follows: Sect. 2 presents the related work in the area of workflow scheduling. The problem description is presented in Sect. 3. The proposed heuristic, PWHEFT, is discussed with the help of an example in Sect. 4. The proposed PWHEFT algorithm is evaluated in Sect. 5 and Sect. 6 concludes the paper.

2 Related Work

Due to the NP-complete nature of the parallel task scheduling problem in general cases [7], many heuristics have been proposed in recent researches [8] to deal with this problem, and most of them achieve good performance in polynomial time. In the previous works, the heuristic-based algorithms can be classified into a variety of categories, such as list scheduling algorithms, clustering heuristics, and duplication-based algorithms.

Among them, the list scheduling algorithms are generally more practical, and their performances are better at a lower time complexity. There are different list based heuristic algorithms in literature like Dynamic Critical Path(DCP) [9], Dynamic Level Scheduling (DLS) [10], Critical Path on Processor (CPOP) [6], Heterogeneous Earliest Finish Time (HEFT) [6] etc. From all of these, HEFT outperforms in terms of makespan.

Only few works in the past considered bi-objective (time and cost mainly) criteria to schedule workflow tasks in cloud environment. Recently, Amandeep Verma and Sakshi Kaushal [11] proposed Cost-Time Efficient Scheduling Plan, BDHEFT, which is the extension of HEFT algorithm that schedule workflow tasks over the available cloud resources under Budget and Deadline Constrained. However, this heuristic generates a schedule plan only by considering the spare deadline along with spare budget which are calculated by simple average while selecting the suitable resource for each workflow task without taking criticality of tasks and parallelism of executing workflow into consideration. To address all these gaps, we introduced in this paper, a novel heuristic that gains a Budget and Deadline Constrained tasks and resources mapper by considering high weights of critical task and the parallelism time efficiency.

3   Models

3.1   Workflow Application Model

A Directed Acyclic Graph (DAG), $G = (T, E)$, is used to model the aforementioned workflow application, where T is the set of n tasks and E is the set of e edges between the tasks. Each edge $(i, j) \in E$ denotes a dependency between two dependent tasks such that the execution of $t_j \in T$ cannot be started before $t_i \in T$ finishes its execution. A task with no parent represents an entry task and a task with no children represents exit task. If there is more than one exit (entry) task, they are connected to a zero-cost pseudo exit (entry) task with zero-cost edges. The task size ($amount_i$) is expressed in Million of Instructions (MI). Data is a n × n matrix of communication data, where $data_{i,j}$ is the amount of data required to be transmitted from task t_i to task t_j.

3.2   Cloud Resources Model

A cloud service provider which offers m computational resources, $R = (r_1 r_2 \cdots r_m)$ at different processing power and different prices, provides information which is needed to make planning decisions. Each r_i is represented by $r_i = (Msr_i, Psr_i)$, where Msr_i denotes Million of Instruction per Second (MIPS) which refers to processing power of a resource r_i and Psr_i denotes the price unit of using resource r_i for each time interval. The data transfer rates between resources are stored in matrix B with size p × p. The communication time between task t_i (scheduled on r_m) and t_j (scheduled on r_k) is defined as:

$$Tran_{(i,j)} = \frac{data_{(i,k)}}{B_{(m,k)}} \tag{1}$$

Before scheduling, average communication time is used to label the edges. The average communication time between task t_i and t_j is defined as

$$\overline{Tran_{(i,j)}} = \frac{data_{(i,k)}}{\bar{B}} \tag{2}$$

where B is the average transfer rate among the resources. Due to each task can be executed on different resources, the execution time, $ET_{(i,j)}$ of a task t_i on a resource r_j, is estimated by the following equation:

$$ET_{(i,j)} = \frac{amount_i}{Msr_j} * (1 + \alpha), \alpha \in [0, 1] \tag{3}$$

where α is random number ranging from 0 to 1, and the execution cost $EC_{(i,j)}$ is given by:

$$EC_{(i,j)} = Psr_i * ET_{(i,j)} \tag{4}$$

Therefore, the average execution time of a task t_i which is defined as

$$\overline{ET_i} = \sum_{j=1}^{m} ET_{(i,j)} \tag{5}$$

and the average execution cost $\overline{EC_i}$ is given by:

$$\overline{EC_i} = \sum_{j=1}^{m} EC_{(i,j)} \tag{6}$$

Although most of the commercial clouds (like Amazon) transfer the internal data at free of cost, the data transfer time cannot be ignored while a large amount of data is needed to be transferred between tasks.

3.3   Scheduling Model

There are three entities in our workflow scheduling model: User, Planner and Cloud Service Provider (CSP). A CSP has a set of computational resources with different capabilities which include processing power and prices and responds to the queries from the planner about the availability of requested resources. The user submits a workflow application along with budget, B and deadline, D to the planner. The planner decides how to execute workflow tasks over available resources.

4   Time and Cost Efficient Scheduling Algorithm

4.1   The PWHEFT

The proposed heuristic, Path-task Weight Heterogeneous Earliest Finish Time (PWHEFT), is based on HEFT, which is a well-known DAG scheduling heuristic. It is an extension of HEFT and considers budget and deadline constraints while scheduling tasks over available resources. PWHEFT has two major phases: task attributes calculation and resource schedule.

First Phase: task attributes calculation
First phase in PWHEFT, the attributes of each task are calculated and all tasks are sorted by priority. The priorities of all tasks are computed using upward ranking. The upward rank of a task t_i is recursively defined by

$$rank_u(t_i) = \overline{ET_i} + \max_{t_j \epsilon succ(t_i)} \left\{ Tran_{(i,j)} + rank_u(t_j) \right\}. \tag{7}$$

where $succ(t_i)$ represents the set of all the children tasks of t_i. Taking into account the criticality level of the task, downward rank is also calculated by:

$$rank_d(t_i) = \max_{t_j \epsilon pred(t_i)}\{Tran_{(j,i)} + rank_d(t_j) + \overline{ET_j}\} \tag{8}$$

where $pred(t_i)$ represents the set of immediate predecessor of t_i. Thus, the criticality level of a task t_i is given by:

$$\text{Clvl}(t_i) = \frac{(rank_u(t_i) + rank_d(t_i)) * 2}{\min_{t_i \in T}\{rank_u(t_i) + rank_d(t_i)\} + \max_{t_i \in T}\{rank_u(t_i) + rank_d(t_i)\}} \tag{9}$$

In order to facilitate the calculation, $EST_{(t_i,r_j)}$ and $EFT_{(t_i,r_j)}$ are used to denote the earliest start time and the earliest finish time of task t_i which been scheduled on processor r_j respectively. For the entry task t_{entry}, the EST can be calculated as:

$$EST_{(t_{entry},r_j)} = 0 \tag{10}$$

For the other tasks in the graph, starting from the entry task, the EST and EFT values can be calculated as:

$$EST_{(t_i,r_j)} = \max\{avail[j], \max_{t_m \in pred(t_i)}\{AFT(t_m) + Tran_{(m,i)}\}\} \tag{11}$$

$$EFT_{(t_i,r_j)} = EST_{(t_i,r_j)} + EC_{(i,j)} \tag{12}$$

where $pred(t_i)$ is the set of immediate predecessor tasks of task t_i, $avail[j]$ is the time when the resource r_j is ready for task execution, and $AFT(t_m)$ represents the actual finish time of task t_i. Analogously, $LFT(t_i)$ which denotes latest finish time of task t_i is calculated by:

$$\text{LFT}(t_i) = \begin{cases} D, \text{when } t_i = t_{exit} \\ \min_{t_j \in succ(t_i)}\{\text{LFT}(t_j) - \overline{ET_j} - \overline{Tran_{(i,j)}}\}, \text{others} \end{cases} \tag{13}$$

where D is given deadline. The schedule length also called makespan is equal to the maximum of actual finish time of the exit task t_{exit}.

$$\text{makespan} = AFT(t_{exit}) \tag{14}$$

Second Phase: resource schedule
In the resource schedule phase, candidate resources are generated and the best resource is selected. For each task which is ordered by $rank_u$, the set of candidate resources is constructed using the six variables: Workflow Prediction Budget (WPB), Prediction Task Budget (PTB), Prediction Budget Factor (PBF), Weight Deadline Factor (WDF), Prediction Deadline Factor (PDF) and Prediction Task Deadline (PTD). For a task t_i, the value of these variables is given by (15) to (20), as follows:

$$\text{WPB} = B - \sum_{t_i \in allocatedTasks} EC_{(i)} - \sum_{t_i \in unallocatedTasks} \text{Clvl}(t_j) * \overline{EC_j} \qquad (15)$$

$$\text{PBF}(t_i) = \begin{cases} 0, when\ WPB < 0 \\ \text{Clvl}(t_i) * \overline{EC_i} / \sum_{t_j \in unallocatedTasks} \text{Clvl}(t_j) * \overline{EC_j}, others \end{cases} \qquad (16)$$

$$\text{PTB}(t_i) = \text{Clvl}(t_i) * \overline{EC_i} + \text{PBF}(t_i) * \text{WPB} \qquad (17)$$

$$\text{WDF}(t_i) = \begin{cases} 1, when\ t_i = t_{exit} \\ \left(\text{Clvl}(t_i) * \max_{t_k \in succ(t_i)}\{Tran_{(i,k)}\}\right)^{-1} * \overline{EC_i}, others \end{cases} \qquad (18)$$

$$\text{PDF}(t_i) = \frac{\text{WDF}(t_i)}{\sum_{t_k \in unallocatedTasks} \text{WDF}(t_k)} \qquad (19)$$

$$\text{PTD}(t_i) = \begin{cases} 0, when\ LFT(t_i) - \min_{r_j \in R}\left\{EFT_{(t_i,r_j)}\right\} < 0 \\ \min_{r_j \in R}\left\{EFT_{(t_i,r_j)}\right\} + \text{PDF}(t_i) * \left(LFT(t_i) - \min_{r_j \in R}\left\{EFT_{(t_i,r_j)}\right\}\right), others \end{cases} \qquad (20)$$

where B is given budget, $EC_{(i)}$ is the execution cost of allocated task t_i, $\overline{EC_j}$ and $\overline{ET_j}$ are average execution cost and average execution time of un-allocated task t_j. PBF or PDF is a value intended to act as a weight that tunes the impact on PTB or PTD Such prediction function is designed to determine which resources the task t_j PBF or PDF is a value intended to act as a weight that tunes the impact on PTB or PTD Such prediction function is designed to determine which resources the task t_i is predicted to finish on.

Based on the allocated deadline and budget to a task t_i, a candidate set CS_i is calculated by considering possible resources for a task t_i, by:

$$CS_i = \left\{ S_{(i,j)} | \exists S_{(i,j)}, EC_{(i,j)} \leq \text{PTB}(t_i), EFT_{(t_i,r_j)} \leq \text{PTD}(t_i) \right\} \qquad (21)$$

where $S_{(i,j)}$ represents the possible resource, from the given R, which satisfies the inequality .Then the best possible resource is selected by the selection rules as follows:

- I. If $CS_i \neq \emptyset$ then the best resource is selected from this set that minimizes the following expression: $\theta * EFT_{(t_i,r_j)} + (1 - \theta) * EC_{(i,j)}$ for all $j \in CS_i$ where $EFT_{(t_i,r_j)}$ is the earliest finish time and $EC_{(i,j)}$ is the execution cost of a task t_i over all possible j resources in CS_i respectively and θ is the cost-time balance factor in a range of [0,1] which represents the user preference for execution time and execution cost.
- II.If $CS_i = \emptyset$ and WPB ≥ 0, then the resource from all the available resources that minimize the above equation is chosen.

Input: DAG G with Budget B and Deadline D
Output: Schedule Plan

1.	Compute the $rank_u$, $rank_d$, Clvl and LFT using equation (7), (8), (9) and (13) for all the tasks.
2.	Sort all the tasks in an unallocated list in descending order of upward rank.
3.	While there are tasks in unallocated list do
4.	Select the first tasks t_i, from the unallocated list.
5.	Compute WPB, PTB and PTD for a task t_i using equation (15) to (20).
6.	Calculate the candidate set CS_i using equation(21)
7.	Select a resource for a task t_i using the defined selection rules.
8.	End while

Fig. 1. The PWHEFT heuristic

- III.If $CS_i = \emptyset$ and WPB < 0, the cheapest resource is selected from all the available resources.

The algorithm terminates when all tasks ordered by their rank are considered. The proposed heuristic, PWHEFT is shown in Fig. 1.

4.2   Time Complexity Analysis

To find out the time complexity of PWHEFT algorithm, suppose that the scheduler receives a Workflow, $G(T, E)$ as an input with n tasks and e dependencies. As G is directed graph, so maximum number of dependencies is $(n-1)(n-1)/2 \approx O(n^2)$. The first step of the algorithm is to find two type ranks of all the tasks which requires processing of all workflow tasks and edges, so its time complexity equals $O(n+e) \approx O(n^2)$. Similarly, the step 3, consists of two nested loops. The outer loop is for n tasks and inner loop which refer to calculating the candidate set CS_i is for all the possible m resources. Therefore time complexity of scheduling all tasks is $O(n \cdot m)$. The overall time complexity of PWHEFT algorithm equals $\max(O(n^2), O(n \cdot m))$.

5   Experiments and Analysis

5.1   Experimental Settings

To evaluate the heuristic, the core framework of CloudSim simulator [12] was extended by adding those variables and the heuristic, PWHEFT. And five types of DAGs based on realistic workflows from diverse scientific applications were considered in the experiments, which are:

- LIGO: Gravitational physics
- SIPHT: Biology
- Epigenomics: Biology
- Montage: Astronomy
- CyberShake: Earthquake

The detailed characterization for each workflow including their structure, data and computational requirements can be found in [13]. The Directed Acyclic Graph in XML (DAX) format for all these workflows are available at website (https://confluence. pegasus.isi.edu/display/pegasus/WorkflowGenerator). The cloud environment consisting of a resource provider, which offers 20 different computation resources with different processing speed and hence with different prices, was assumed for the simulation.

The communication computation ratio CCR, which is the ratio of the average of $\overline{Tran_{(i,j)}}$ to the average of $\overline{ET_i}$, is about 2. And the data amount transmitted between tasks is randomly generated according to the CCR. Accordingly, the DAG can be considered as a data-intensive workflow. Given a DAG, constraints for reasonable values for deadline and budget are generated as follows:

$$Deadline\ D = Dbound_d + k_1 * (Dbound_u - Dbound_l),$$

where $Dbound_l = M_{HEFT}$ (makespan of HEFT), $Dbound_u = 3 * M_{HEFT}$ and k_1. is a deadline ratio in range from 0 to 1.

$Budget B = Bbound_d + k_2 * (Bbound_u - Bbound_l)$, where $Bbound_l$ is the lowest cost obtained by mapping each task to the cheapest service and $Bbound_u$ is the highest cost obtained conversely and k_2 is a budget ratio in range from 0 to 1.

After the heuristic was run, if the schedule length and cost of a plan were in conformance with Deadline and Budget, the planning succeeded. To analyze the performance of a heuristic, the experiment was repeated multiple times and the metric Planning Success Rate (PSR), Normalized Schedule Cost (NSC) and Normalized Schedule Length (NSL) were used, as defined below:

$$PSR = \frac{number\ of\ successful\ plan}{number\ of\ total\ repeated\ times\ of\ experiment} \tag{22}$$

$$NSC = \frac{total\ cost}{\sum_{t_i \in T} \min_{r_j \in R} \left\{ EC_{(i,j)} \right\}} \tag{23}$$

$$NSL = \frac{Total\ Execution\ Time}{\sum_{t_i \in T} \overline{ET_i}} \tag{24}$$

5.2 Results and Analysis

For comparison purpose, the BDHEFT which is aforementioned and the PWHEFT have been compared on the basis of PSR, makespan and monetary cost. An average value of PSR was captured through 1500 runs of simulations by selecting different values of cost-time balance factor θ, i.e., $\theta = 0.3, 0.5,$ and 0.7, each consisting of 500 simulations. Figure 2 shows the PSR, respectively, of scheduling different workflows with BDHEFT and PWHEFT for three different values of deadline ration k_1., i.e., $k_1 = 0.2, 0.4,$ and 0.8 and three different values of budget ration k_2, i.e., $k_2 = 0.2, 0.4,$

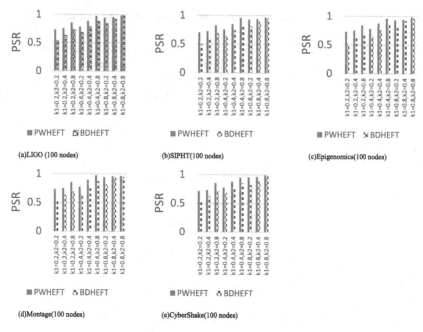

Fig. 2. Average PSR of different workflows

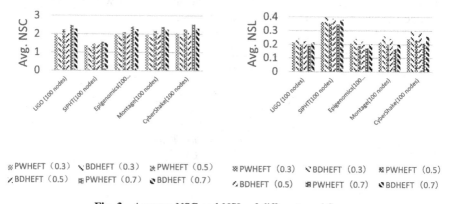

Fig. 3. Average NSC and NSL of different workflows

and 0.8, in total 9 combinations. Even in harsh situations where deadline ration $k_1 = 0.2$ and budget ration $k_2 = 0.2$ as shown in Fig. 2, the average PSR of PWHEFT is significantly higher than BDHEFT.

Figure 3 shows the comparison of execution cost and makespan of schedule plan created by PWHEFT (0.3), PWHEFT (0.5) and PWHEFT (0.7) over schedule plan created by BDHEFT (0.3), BDHEFT (0.5) and BDHEFT (0.7) under the same deadline ratio and budget ratio. The results shows that PWHEFT outperform BDHEFT

Table 1. Comparative results of PWHEFT vs. BDHEFT

Average of PWHEFT over BDHEFT			
Workflow Structure	Cost	Makespan	PSR
LIGO (100 nodes)	+9.08%	−11.39%	+12.95%
SIPHT(100 nodes)	+3.69%	−9.04%	+14.65%
Epigenomics(100 nodes)	+6.29%	−14.65%	+14.07%
Montage(100 nodes)	+6.69%	−17.12%	+15.33%
CyberShake(100 nodes)	+9.71%	−19.56%	+14.24%

algorithm significantly by reducing the makespan while increasing execution cost of schedule slightly under the same cost-time balance factor.

Table 1 shows the overall comparison of execution cost, makespan and PSR of schedule plan created by PWHEFT over schedule plan created by BDHEFT. The overall results shows that PWHEFT algorithm is able to achieve a significant improvement on PSR. Furthermore, PWHEFT has a lower Makespan, while making the execution cost as good as given by BDHEFT under the same deadline and budget constraint and using same pricing model in all cases.

6 Conclusion and Future Works

This paper proposed PWHEFT, a new workflow scheduling algorithm for cloud environment, which is an extension of HEFT algorithm. The proposed heuristic is evaluated with synthetic workflows that are based on real world workflows with different structures and different sizes. The comparison of proposed algorithm is done with BDHEFT heuristic, under same deadline and budget constraint and pricing. The simulation results show that our proposed algorithm outperforms BDHEFT algorithm in terms of PSR and makespan while producing the monetary cost as good as produced by BDHEFT algorithm. Based on the work in this paper, further work could try to examine the performance of PWHEFT using different settings such as diverse CCRs, storage and file transfer model such as a global storage model.

References

1. Juve, G., Chervenak, A., Deelman, E., Bharathi, S., Mehta, G., Vahi, K.: Characterizing and profiling scientific workflows. Futur. Gener. Comput. Syst. **29**(3), 682–692 (2013)
2. Juve, G., Deelman, E., Berriman, G.B., Berman, B.P., Maechling, P.: An evaluation of the cost and performance of scientific workflows on amazon ec2. J. Grid Comput. **10**(1), 5–21 (2012)
3. Prodan, R., Wieczorek, M.: Bi-criteria scheduling of scientific Grid workflows. IEEE Trans. Autom. Sci. Eng. **7**, 364–376 (2010)
4. Talukder, A.K.M., Kirley, M., Buyya, R.: Multiobjective differential evolution for scheduling workflow applications on global Grids. Concurr. Comput. Pract. Exp. **21**(13), 1742–1756 (2009)

5. Yu, J., Buyya, R.: Multi-objective planning for workflow execution on Grids. In: Proceedings of the 8th IEEE/ACM International Conference on Grid Computing, pp. 10–17 (2007)
6. Topcuoglu, H., Hariri, S., Wu, M.: Performance-effective and low-complexity task scheduling for heterogeneous computing. IEEE Trans. Parallel Distrib. Syst. 13(3), 260–274 (2002)
7. Garey, M.R., Johnson, D.S.: Computers and Intractability: A Guide to the Theory of NP-Completeness. W.H. Freeman and Company, New York (1979)
8. Wu, F., Wu, Q., Tan, Y.: Workflow scheduling in cloud: a survey. J. Supercomput., 71(9), 3373–3418
9. Kwok, Y.K., Ahmad, I.: Dynamic critical-path scheduling: an effective technique for allocating task graphs to multiprocessors. IEEE Trans. Parallel Distrib. Syst. 7(5), 506–521 (1996)
10. Sih, G.C., Lee, E.A.: A compile-time scheduling heuristic for interconnection-constrained heterogeneous processor architectures. IEEE Trans. Parallel Distrib. Syst. 4(2), 175–187 (1993)
11. Verma, A., Kaushal, S.: Cost-Time efficient scheduling plan for executing workflows in the cloud. J. Grid Comput. 13(4), 1–12 (2015)
12. Rodrigo, N.C., Ranjan, R., Anton, B., Cesar, A.F.D.R., Buyya, R.: Cloudsim: a toolkit for modeling and simulation of cloud computing environments and evaluation of resource provisioning algorithms. J. Softw. Pract. Exp. (SPE) 41(1), 23–50 (2011)
13. Bharathi, S., Lanitchi, A., Deelman, E., Mehta, G., Su, M.H., Vahi, K.: Characterization of scientific workflows. In: Workshop on Workflows in Support of Large Scale Science, CA, USA, pp. 1–10 (2008)

PANP-GM: A Periodic Adaptive Neighbor Workload Prediction Model Based on Grey Forecasting for Cloud Resource Provisioning

Yazhou Hu[1(✉)], Bo Deng[1], Fuyang Peng[1], Dongxia Wang[2], and Yu Yang[1]

[1] Beijing Institute of System Engineering, Beijing 100101, China
huyazhou@mail.ustc.edu.cn,
{deng_bo0, fy_peng0, yu_yang0}@sina.com
[2] National Key Laboratory of Science and Technology
on Information System Security, Beijing 100101, China
dx_wang0@sina.com

Abstract. Cloud computing platforms provide on-demand service to meet users' need by adding or removing cloud resources dynamically. The cloud resource provisioning is often based on the feedback model, which causes time delay and resource wasters. Workload prediction methods can make the resource provisioning more instantaneous and reduce resource and power consumption, to meet service level objectives (SLOs) and improve quality of service (QoS) of cloud platform. In this paper, we propose a periodic adaptive neighbor workload prediction model based on grey forecasting (PANP-GM) for cloud resource provisioning. Firstly, the model analyzes the growth rate and evaluates the periodicity of workload. Secondly, this model uses the growth rate of previous neighbor periodicity to predicate the trend of upcoming workload. To adapt to dynamic changes and emergencies, the grey forecasting model is applied for automatic error correction and improving prediction accuracy. Experimental results demonstrate that PANP-GM can achieve better resource prediction accuracy than basic and general approaches. Furthermore, this model can effectively improve the QoS of cloud platform and reduce SLO violations.

Keywords: Workload prediction · Periodicity · Grey forecasting model · Resource provisioning

1 Introduction

Cloud computing platform supports tenants to add or remove cloud resource dynamically based on the on-demand service. The on-demand service model provisions or removes resource depending on feedback of resource utilization. However, this method often causes over-provisioning and under-provisioning resource. Under-provisioning can't meet demands of sudden surge workload, which causes SLO violations. Over-provisioning causes resource wasters. Meanwhile, the feedback method will result in significant delays.

© ICST Institute for Computer Sciences, Social Informatics and Telecommunications Engineering 2017
S. Wang and A. Zhou (Eds.): CollaborateCom 2016, LNICST 201, pp. 273–285, 2017.
DOI: 10.1007/978-3-319-59288-6_25

To reduce the provisioning delay and improve QoS of cloud platform, researchers propose some different workload prediction models. Based on the evaluation results, cloud platforms can provision resource to meet and match tenants' need. Although workload prediction methods have lots of advantages in resource provisioning, these methods still have many challenges such as:

(a) Complexities of workload: Cloud platform provides the variety of services and applications, which can vary different kinds and patterns of workload. Further more, the highly dynamic workload also improves the difficulty of prediction.
(b) Emergencies: Sometimes, there are certain emergencies in cloud platforms. Due to the sudden and randomness, prediction algorithms are extremely hard to predict upcoming workload based on history information.
(c) Tenants' behaviors: Different tenants have different behaviors of using cloud resource. Meanwhile, when and how to use cloud resource are preconditions of the prediction. Thus, the variety of tenants' behaviors is another challenge for workload prediction.

To counter these above prediction challenges, we propose a periodic adaptive neighbor workload prediction model based on grey forecasting for cloud resource provisioning. This model analyzes historical workload to find periodicities and characters of tenants' behaviors. Based on the periodicity of workload, this model uses the growth rate of previous neighbor periodicity to predicate the upcoming workload. Meantime, to adapt to the dynamic change and certain emergency, grey forecasting model is applied as the supplement of the prediction model. The main contributions of this paper are summarized as follows:

(a) The periodic adaptive neighbor workload prediction model based on grey forecasting is proposed in this paper. This model has high adaptability, which is suitable for periodic and dynamic workload;
(b) In addition to prediction accuracy, this paper presents QoS evaluation metrics, including lead time, under-provisioning and over-provisioning resource; Meanwhile, the relationship of time and resource is analyzed in our work;
(c) Experimental results demonstrate that PANP-GM can achieve better resource prediction accuracy than basic and general approaches and reduce SLO violations.

The rest of this paper is organized as follows. Section 2 reviews related works. Section 3 presents the problem description and background knowledge. Section 4 introduces the predicting model, PANP-GM. Section 5 describes the experiments and evaluation results. Section 6 concludes the paper along with suggestions for future research.

2 Related Work

Researchers have proposed many different prediction models for cloud resource provisioning, to meet and match tenants' need. These models can broadly divided into three categories: time series methods, machine learning methods and queuing theory methods. These methods are summarized as follows.

Time series methods are most common methods in workload prediction. Jiang et al. [1] presented an online temporal data mining system called ASAP, which was used to model and predict the cloud virtual machine demand by using moving average (MA) model et al. Khan et al. Hoffmann et al. [2] proposed a practice guide for building empirical models, such as auto regression (AR) model, to predict Apache web server workload. Morais et al. [3] proposed a framework for the implementation of auto-scaling services that followed both reactive and proactive approaches, and also proposed some predicted models, including auto correlation (AC), linear regression (LR), auto regression, auto regression integrated moving average (ARIMA) et al. [4] searched for repeatable workload patterns by exploring virtual machines, and then introduced an approach based on Hidden Markov Modeling to characterize and predict workload patterns. Roy et al. [5] developed a model-predictive algorithm for workload predicting based on auto regression moving average (ARMA). Time series approaches, such as moving average and auto regression, were also used in [6, 7].

Machine learning methods are also widely used in workload prediction. Bankole [8] developed a cloud client prediction model using three machine learning models: support vector regression, neural networks and linear regression. Imam et al. [9] presented time delay neural network and regression methods to predict the grid and cloud platform workload. Islam et al. [10] developed resource measurement and provisioning strategies using neural network and linear regression to predict upcoming resource demands.

Queuing theory methods are popular methods in workload prediction and resource provisioning. Calheiros et al. [11] presented a predicting model based on queueing network system model and QoS.

Apart from these above three main kinds of prediction methods, there some novel prediction methods are proposed. Such as, Jheng et al. [12] presented fuzzy model to prediction workload in cloud data center. Saripalli et al. [13] proposed hot spot detection for autonomic cloud computing.

Although these above methods can predict upcoming workload based on historical workload, they still have some limitations. Time series methods are easy to deploy, but the prediction accuracy is not high. Machine learning methods have better prediction accuracy, but training parameter is difficult and time-consuming. Queuing theory methods require that workload is completely random, which is difficult to achieve.

3 Preliminary

In this section, we first introduce the workload prediction problem, including prediction framework and prediction steps. Then we show cloud resource provisioning. The grey forecasting model is presented at the end of this section.

3.1 Workload Prediction

Nowadays, cloud platform, such as Amazon and Aliyun, provides elasticity mechanism which supports adding or removing cloud resource to adapt to workload changes. The elastic scaling is often based on the feedback model, which causes time delay and resource wasters. Workload prediction methods can make the resource provisioning more instantaneous and reduce resource the power consumption, to meet service level objectives (SLOs) and improve quality of service (QoS) of cloud platform. Figure 1 shows workload prediction and resource provisioning process. As shown in Fig. 1, the cloud resource provisioning mainly includes three steps, including workload analyzing, workload prediction and elastic scaling.

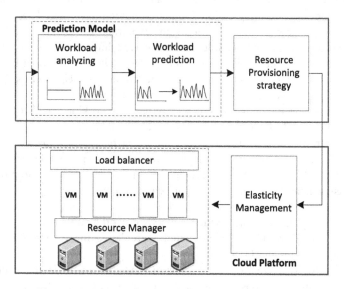

Fig. 1. Overview of cloud resource provisioning process

The prediction model is often based on historical workload data to predict trends of upcoming workload. Historical workload data include different metrics, such as CPU utilization, memory utilization, IO requests, etc. Cloud platform monitors these historical metrics and calculates tenants' resource need. Then, cloud platform scales up or scales down to provision cloud resource.

3.2   Resource Provisioning

To reduce the latency of resource allocation and meet SLOs, cloud platform should deploy resource ahead of time. Calheiros et al. [11] introduced that cloud provisioning consists of three key steps: virtual machine provisioning, resource provisioning and application provisioning. Virtual machine provisioning involves instantiation of virtual machines to coordinate hardware and software. Resource provisioning is the managing and scheduling of virtual machines on physical servers. Application provisioning is deployment of predictions to meet the SLOs. In commercial cloud platform, cloud resource provisioning is often based on virtual machines.

3.3 Grey System Theory

Grey forecasting model is based on the grey system theory [14] and fuzzy model. Deng J. L. proposed the grey system in 1982. This system can deal with the fuzzy and incomplete data. To update and complete the uncertain data, grey system uses related analysis methods, such as modeling, forecasting, and etc.

The grey forecasting model is the most common method in grey system theory. It can predict uncertain factors and tendency of case based on the history data. The grey forecasting model is often based on the differential equation, and $G(1,1)$ is the fundamental model of grey forecasting model.

4 Prediction Model

In this section, we first introduce the overview of our prediction model, including assumptions and prediction steps. Then we introduce these prediction algorithms and models in detail, which includes workload analysis algorithm, grey forecasting model and prediction algorithm.

4.1 Model Overview

The prediction model, PANP-GM, collects the historical workload, and then analyzes the characteristics of workload, to predict trends of upcoming workload. Meanwhile, two foundational assumptions are made by PANP-GM. The first one is that the workload is periodic fluctuation. The second one is that workload can't be too heavy so that cloud servers go down. In other words, the value of workload conforms to normal distribution law. In our research, we find that most of workload is in accordance with above two foundational assumptions, thus our prediction model is universal and efficient for most of workloads.

PANP-GM has two main step, workload analysis and workload prediction. For the first step, the proposed model analyzes the collected workload data, calculates growth rate of workload and estimates the period value of workload. The first step is based on the workload analysis algorithm. For the second step, the proposed model uses the growth rate of previous neighbor workload periodicity, which is proposed in first step, to predicate the upcoming workload. Meantime, to adapt to dynamic changes and abnormal increase and decrease, the grey forecasting model is applied for automatic error correction and improving prediction accuracy. To simplify the complexity of calculation, our prediction model use $G(1,1)$ as the grey forecasting model.

4.2 Prediction Algorithms

As described in above subsection, the prediction model includes three main algorithms and models, workload analysis algorithm, grey forecasting model and prediction algorithm.

(1) Workload analysis algorithm

The workload analysis algorithm is shown as Algorithm 1. Firstly, it calculates growth rate of workload data, V_o. In our research, the metabolic range of original workload data is high. However, the growth rate of workload data can reduce the impact of amplitude variation. So, this algorithm estimates the period value of workload based on analyzing V_o in the next step. In this algorithm, we use a high-efficiency period detection algorithm, ERPP, which is based on edit distance with real penalty and proposed in reference [15].

Algorithm 1. Workload analysis algorithm

Inputs:

X_o : original workload data

Outputs:

V_o : the growth rate of workload data

t : the period value of workload

---

1   **Intialize** $V_o = 0$, $t = 1$

2   **for** i=2 to n

3     $V_o(i) = \dfrac{X_o(i) - X_o(i-1)}{X_o(i-1)}$

4   **end for**

5   call algorithm ERPP to calculate the candidate value p of V_o

6   $t \leftarrow p$

7   **return** t

---

(2) Grey forecasting model

Grey forecasting model predicts the workload tendency based on the exiting workload data. $G(1,1)$ is the basic one of grey forecasting model, which includes three main steps described as follows.

(i) accumulation generating operation

For the original workload data $X^{(0)} = (x^{(0)}(1), x^{(0)}(2), \cdots x^{(0)}(n))$, the model uses one time accumulation generating operation to smooth the original data. The operation is shown as formula 1.

$$\begin{cases} X^{(1)} = (x^{(1)}(1), x^{(1)}(2), \cdots x^{(1)}(n)) \\ x^{(1)}(k) = \sum_{1}^{k} x^{(0)}(k), k = 1, 2, \cdots, n \end{cases} \tag{1}$$

Algorithm 2. Prediction algorithm

Inputs:

$X^{(0)}(k), k = 1, 2, \cdots m$: original workload sequence

α : the threshold of calling grey forecasting model

β : the original workload sequence length of $G(1,1)$

Outputs:

$\hat{X}^{(0)}(k), k = m+1,, \cdots n$: the predictive workload sequence

---

1   Intialize α, β

2   call Algorithm 1 to calculate the period value of workload and V_o

3   for i=m+1 to n

4   $\qquad \varphi_o(i-1) = \dfrac{\hat{x}^{(0)}(i-1) - x^{(0)}(i-1)}{x^{(0)}(i-1)}$

5   $\qquad V_o(i-1) = \dfrac{x^{(0)}(i-1) - x^{(0)}(i-2)}{x^{(0)}(i-2)}$

6   $\qquad$ if $\varphi_o(i-1) > \alpha$

7   $\qquad\qquad$ call $G(1,1)$ to predict $\hat{x}^{(0)}(i)$ based on $(x^{(0)}(i-1-\beta), \cdots, x^{(0)}(i-1))$

8   $\qquad$ else

9   $\qquad\qquad \hat{x}^{(0)}(i) = x^{(0)}(i) \cdot (1 + V_o(i-t))$

10 $\qquad$ end if

11 end for

12 return $\hat{X}^{(0)}(k)$

(ii) modeling

After getting data array $X^{(0)}$ and $X^{(1)}$, this model constructs a mean generating sequence $Z^{(1)}$, which is described as formula 2. Then, the $G(1,1)$ model can be described as formula 3, where a and b are adjusting factors.

$$\begin{cases} Z^{(1)} = (z^{(1)}(2), z^{(1)}(3), \cdots x^{(1)}(n)) \\ z^{(1)}(k) = 0.5 \left(x^{(1)}(k) + x^{(1)}(k-1) \right), k = 2, 3, \cdots, n \end{cases} \qquad (2)$$

$$x^{(0)}(k) + az^{(1)}(k) = b, k = 2, 3, \cdots, n \qquad (3)$$

(iii) solution

To get the predicting results, this model use least-square estimation method to solve the formula 3. The predictive result $\hat{x}^{(1)}(k)$ is presented in formula 4.

$$\hat{x}^{(1)}(k) = (x^{(1)}(1) - \frac{b}{a})e^{-at} + \frac{b}{a}, k = 1, 2, \cdots, n \tag{4}$$

So, the predictive value is described as formula 5.

$$\hat{x}^{(0)}(k+1) = (1 - e^a)(x^{(0)}(1) - \frac{b}{a})e^{-ak}, k = 1, 2, \cdots, n \tag{5}$$

Thus, the predictive sequence is $\hat{X}^{(0)} = (\hat{x}^{(0)}(1), \hat{x}^{(0)}(2), \cdots \hat{x}^{(0)}(n))$.

(3) **Prediction algorithm**

The prediction algorithm is the key factor of grey forecasting model. This algorithm uses the growth rate of previous neighbor periodicity as the present growth rate to predicate the upcoming workload. If the predicted data has a big difference with the real data, the prediction algorithm applies $G(1, 1)$ for automatic error correction and improving prediction accuracy. The difference percentage is described as $\varphi_o(k)$. The coefficient α is the threshold of calling grey forecasting model and β is the train sequence length of $G(1, 1)$. This algorithm is shown as Algorithm 2.

5 Performance Evaluation

This section presents results evaluating PANP-GM model. We first introduce the experiment setup and evaluation metrics. Then, we tune parameters of prediction model. At last, we present and analyze experiment results.

5.1 Experiment Setup

In our experiment, we use the traffic of data center as the workload, and we monitor and collect workload data for 456 h. The PANP-GM model is applied in workload prediction based on the collected data.

To evaluate the performance of our model, we compare our model with three baseline methods, including AR, MA and ARIMA. Meantime, we propose two different kinds of evaluation metrics, which includes prediction error and QoS evaluation metrics. These metrics are shown as follows.

(a) **Prediction error**

The mean of absolute percentage error (MAPE) is used to evaluate the prediction accuracy of PANP-GM model. The metric is defined as follows:

$$MAPE = \frac{1}{n}\sum_{i=1}^{n} \left| \frac{\hat{x}^{(0)}(i) - x^{(0)}(i)}{x^{(0)}(i)} \right| \tag{6}$$

Where, $x^{(0)}(i)$ is the original workload value and $\hat{x}^{(0)}(i)$ is the predicted workload value.

(b) **Qos evaluation metrics**

Time and resource are two important factors affecting the quality of service. To evaluate the improvement of QoS and reducing of SLO violations, we propose three QoS evaluation metrics, including lead time rate, under-provisioning and over-provisioning resource rate.

Leading time rate: leading time is the proportion of saved time obtained by the prediction model, which is defined as formula 8.

$$R_t = \frac{1}{n}\sum_{i=1}^{n}\frac{t_i - t_{pi}}{t_i} \tag{7}$$

t_i is the provisioning time without prediction, and t_{pi} is the provisioning time using the prediction framework.

Under-provisioning and over-provisioning resource rate: Under-provisioning can't meet demands of sudden surge workload, which causes SLO violations. Over-provisioning causes resource wasters. Thus, these metrics are considered for evaluate the prediction model. The under-provisioning resource (R_u) and over-provisioning resource (R_o) rates are defined as follow:

$$R_u = \frac{1}{n}\sum_{t=1}^{n}\frac{R_d - R_p}{R_d}, R_d \geq R_p \tag{8}$$

$$R_o = \frac{1}{n}\sum_{t=1}^{n}\frac{R_p - R_d}{R_d}, R_p > R_d \tag{9}$$

R_d is the demand resource of workload, and R_p is the prediction resource.

5.2   Parameters Turning

There are some parameters in our prediction algorithms should be adjusted to improve the prediction performance. So, we train and select optimal parameters based on experimental analysis.

(a) **Threshold and sequence length**

There are two parameters, α and β, in Algorithm 2. To improve the performance of prediction method, these parameters should be turned for getting the exact value. In this experiment, we change the values of parameters to select the optimal parameters.

α is the threshold of calling grey forecasting model, and β is the train sequence length of $G(1,1)$. To get optimal values of α and β, we analyze the relations between and among threshold, sequence length and prediction error. As shown in Fig. 2, the prediction error increases first, and then decreases with the increase of threshold value.

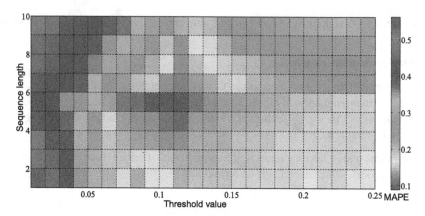

Fig. 2. Relations between and among threshold, sequence length and prediction error

Meantime, we can find that the prediction error is optimal when values of α and β are 0.11 and 5. Thus, we select these values to predict upcoming workload in the next experiments.

(b) **Period value**

To predict the trends of upcoming workload, we should analyze the periodicity of workload firstly. As shown in Fig. 3, the growth rate is more obvious than original workload in periodic changes. Therefor, we use the growth rate series to predict the trends of upcoming workload. Figure 3 shows that the period value is 24.

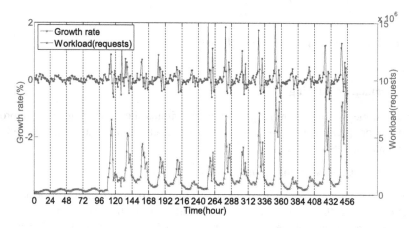

Fig. 3. Workload and growth rate analyzing

(c) **Prediction steps**

Algorithm 2 supports multi-step prediction. At the same time, prediction steps and leading time are equivalent in our algorithm, thus we should analyze the relations between and among leading time, prediction error, under-provisioning resource rate and over-provisioning resource rate. As shown in Fig. 4, with the leading time (prediction steps) increasing, the prediction error, under-provisioning resource rate and over-provisioning resource rate are increasing rapidly. So, synthesizing these results, we select one-step prediction in Algorithm 2.

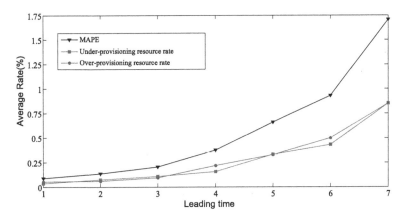

Fig. 4. Prediction performance varies along leading time

5.3 Experiment Results

Based on the above subsection analysis, we choose optimal parameters and conduct experiments using the prediction algorithm. Moreover, we also compare our model with three basic methods, including AR, MA and ARIMA. Experiment results are shown in Table 1 and Fig. 5.

As shown in Fig. 5 and Table 1, MAPE, under-provisioning resource rate and over-provisioning resource rate of our prediction method, PANP-GM, are significantly less than other three basic methods. The prediction error is less than 10%, and the under-provisioning resource rate and over-provisioning resource rate are above 5%. Further more, the leading time rate is more than 80%, which is more efficient than other methods.

Based on these experiment results, our method can achieve better prediction accuracy and significantly reduce SLO violations than other three basic methods. In other words, PANP-GM model can improve QoS of Cloud platform by workload prediction for resource provisioning.

Table 1. Evaluation results of different prediction methods

Evaluation metrics/methods	AR	MA	ARIMA	PANP-GM
MAPE	0.268	0.287	0.223	0.089
R_t	0.531	0.572	0.636	0.891
R_u	0.106	0.149	0.103	0.037
R_o	0.162	0.138	0.120	0.052

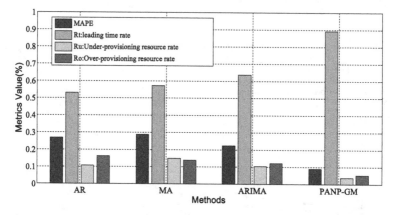

Fig. 5. Comparison of prediction performance of different methods

6   Conclusion and Future Work

This paper proposes a periodic adaptive neighbor workload prediction model based on grey forecasting (PANP-GM) for cloud resource provisioning. This model uses the growth rate of previous neighbor periodicity to predicate the trend of upcoming workload based on workload analysis. Furthermore, the grey forecasting model is applied for automatic error correction and adapting dynamic changes and emergencies. Experimental results demonstrate that PANP-GM can achieve better resource prediction accuracy than AR, MA and ARIMA model. Meanwhile, this model can effectively improve the QoS of cloud platform and reduce SLO violations.

In this paper, the model proposed achieves poor performance on irregular workload prediction and multi-step prediction. Therefore, efficiently dynamic and adaptive prediction methods for complex workload should be proposed. At the same time, the elastic scaling strategy based on the prediction results should be focused on in the future work.

Acknowledgments. This work is supported by the National High-Technology Research and Development Program of China (863 Program) (No. 2013AA01A215) and the National Natural Science Foundation of China (No. 61271252).

References

1. Jiang, Y., Perng, C., Li, T., et al.: Asap: a self-adaptive prediction system for instant cloud resource demand provisioning. In: 2011 IEEE 11th International Conference on Data Mining (ICDM), pp. 1104–1109. IEEE (2011)
2. Hoffmann, G., Trivedi, K.S., Malek, M.: A best practice guide to resource predicting for computing systems. IEEE Trans. Reliab. **56**(4), 615–628 (2007)
3. Almeida Morais, F.J., Vilar Brasileiro, F., Vigolvino Lopes, R., et al.: Autoflex: service agnostic auto-scaling framework for iaas deployment models. In: 2013 13th IEEE/ACM International Symposium on Cluster, Cloud and Grid Computing (CCGrid), pp. 42–49. IEEE (2013)
4. Khan, A., Yan, X., Tao, S., et al.: Workload characterization and prediction in the cloud: a multiple time series approach. In: 2012 IEEE Network Operations and Management Symposium (NOMS), pp. 1287–1294. IEEE (2012)
5. Roy, N., Dubey, A., Gokhale, A.: Efficient autoscaling in the cloud using predictive models for workload predicting. In: 2011 IEEE International Conference on Cloud Computing (CLOUD), pp. 500–507. IEEE (2011)
6. Reig, G., Guitart, J.: On the anticipation of resource demands to fulfill the QoS of saas web applications. In: Proceedings of the 2012 ACM/IEEE 13th International Conference on Grid Computing, pp. 147–154. IEEE Computer Society (2012)
7. Xu, W., Zhu, X., Singhal, S., et al.: Predictive control for dynamic resource allocation in enterprise data centers. In: 10th IEEE/IFIP Network Operations and Management Symposium, NOMS 2006, pp. 115–126. IEEE (2006)
8. Bankole, A.A., Ajila, S.A.: Cloud client prediction models for cloud resource provisioning in a multitier web application environment. In: 2013 IEEE 7th International Symposium on Service Oriented System Engineering (SOSE), pp. 156–161. IEEE (2013)
9. Imam, M.T., Miskhat, S.F., Rahman, R.M., et al.: Neural network and regression based processor load prediction for efficient scaling of Grid and Cloud resources. In: 2011 14th International Conference on Computer and Information Technology (ICCIT), pp. 333–338. IEEE (2011)
10. Islam, S., Keung, J., Lee, K., et al.: Empirical prediction models for adaptive resource provisioning in the cloud. Future Gener. Comput. Syst. **28**(1), 155–162 (2012)
11. Calheiros, R.N., Ranjan, R., Buyya, R.: Virtual machine provisioning based on analytical performance and QoS in cloud computing environments. In: 2011 International Conference on Parallel Processing (ICPP), pp. 295–304. IEEE (2011)
12. Jheng, J.J., Tseng, F.H., Chao, H.C., et al.: A novel VM workload prediction using Grey Predicting model in cloud data center. In: 2014 International Conference on Information Networking (ICOIN), pp. 40–45. IEEE (2014)
13. Saripalli, P., Kiran, G.V.R., Shankar, R.R., et al.: Load prediction and hot spot detection models for autonomic cloud computing. In: 2011 Fourth IEEE International Conference on Utility and Cloud Computing (UCC), pp. 397–402. IEEE (2011)
14. Julong, D.: Introduction to grey system theory. J. Grey Syst. **1**(1), 1–24 (1989)
15. Wang, Y., Gao, X., Wu, S., et al.: Periodicity detection method of periodic pattern mining in time series. Comput. Eng. **22**, 014 (2009)

Dynamic Load Balancing for Software-Defined Data Center Networks

Yun Chen, Weihong Chen, Yao Hu, Lianming Zhang$^{(\boxtimes)}$, and Yehua Wei

Key Laboratory of Internet of Things Technology and Application,
College of Physics and Information Science, Hunan Normal University, Changsha 410081, China
611cy@sina.com, 1018450155@qq.com, huyao9403@163.com,
zlm@hunnu.edu.cn, yehuahn@163.com

Abstract. In recent years, along with the increasing demand for cloud services, the network traffic is increased inside data center networks (DCNs). The inherent defects of TCP/IP network architecture have hindered the development of network technologies for a long time, and the software-defined network (SDN) has recently gained unprecedented attention from industry and research communities, and it has completely overturned the existing network architecture. In this paper, we have proposed a new network frame for software-defined data center network (SDDCN), and developed a dynamic schedule strategy of the network traffic by calculating available path coefficient of the SDDCN, then presented a schedule algorithm for the dynamic load balancing (SDLB) based on the path coefficient of network available bandwidth in real-time, and developed the components of the Ryu controller of the SDDCN, which is responsible for running the SDLB algorithm. Based on Mininet platform, the experimental results show that the SDLB algorithm has better performance of dynamic load balancing in the SDDCN, which has provided an effective solution for the load balancing of the existing DCNs.

Keywords: Software-defined data center network · Load balancing · Path coefficient

1 Introduction

With the rapid development of cloud computing, there are more and more data centers, which are pools of computational, storage and network resources using interconnection networks [1, 2], such as Internet. As the growing demand for the cloud services, the network traffic inside a data center network (DCN) has been increased, and it makes further demands on DCNs [3]. Today's data centers are constrained by the interconnection network [4]. For example, how to maximize the use of limited network resources has become an urgent problem needed to be solved in the field of the Internet, which uses TCP/IP architecture. One of the most commonly used methods is the load balancing technology. However, some inherent defects of the Internet architecture have hindered the development of network technology. At the same time, the problem of low bandwidth

© ICST Institute for Computer Sciences, Social Informatics and Telecommunications Engineering 2017
S. Wang and A. Zhou (Eds.): CollaborateCom 2016, LNICST 201, pp. 286–301, 2017.
DOI: 10.1007/978-3-319-59288-6_26

utilization also exists for a long time, which hinders the development of load balancing technology in the existing networks [5].

Against this background, the three-layer architecture of DCNs based on traditional interconnection networks is being challenged. Flat, virtualized, programmable and definable networks become the new trend in the DCNs architecture. Software-defined network (SDN) is an architecture which decouples network control and forwarding functions, and enabling to be directly programmable, dynamic, manageable, cost-effective and adaptable, and seeking to be suitable for the high-bandwidth, dynamic nature of today's applications, and providing a solution to the above problems [6–8]. For example, applying the software-defined idea can overturn the existing network architecture into DCNs, and can be better to solve the technical problem of load balancing in the distributed network architecture [9]. Paper [10] presents a load balancer for Open-Flow based the DCNs, and implements a dynamic routing algorithm in the load balancer. This paper extends these existing works.

The technical aim of the paper is to achieve dynamic load balancing for DCNs using software-defined method. In comparison with the existing literature on similar work, this paper has the following major contributions:

- To present a new software-defined frame for DCNs with fat-tree structure.
- To present a schedule algorithm for dynamic load balancing (SDLB) of software-defined data center networks (SDDCNs) based on the path coefficient of network available bandwidth in real-time.
- To develop the components of the Ryu controller for the SDLB algorithm, and to evaluate the performance of the SDLB algorithm under the simulation environment based on the DCNs with the fat-tree topology.

In the following sections, we first discuss existing research works on the load balancing technology for the DCNs and SDN in Sect. 2. Section 3 presents a SDLB algorithm based on the path coefficient of network available bandwidth in real-time. Section 4 presents the method for developing the Ryu controller component to running the SDLB algorithm. The experimental results and performance analysis of the SDLB algorithm are presented in Sect. 4. The paper is concluded in Sect. 5.

2 Related Works

With the popularization of the concept of SDN and the rapid development of OpenFlow technology, the researchers have gradually deepened the network innovation of traffic engineering, network security and load balancing in OpenFlow networks. The top–ranking network equipment manufacturers have introduced a number of SDN devices with markedly different characteristics, and the global deployment of SDN has gradually expanded from a small range.

OpenFlow-based SDN technology applied to data center deployment has become a hot topic of discussion on the SDN. A number of vendors, service providers and companies got into this field. For example, VMware is actively developing the software-defined data center approach [11]. Avaya, H3C, Big Switch Networks, Cisco, Dell and IBM are developing components and standards that enable the software-defined data center [12]. CloudGenix, VeloCloud and Viptela have already deployed a SDN in the data center and are now looking to expand those benefits to wide area networks [13], and so on.

Paper [14] has firstly proposed the introduction of OpenFlow technology and the NOX controller is used for achieving the mechanism of effective addressing and routing in the DCNs, such as PortLand [15] and VL2. ElasticTree [16] is mainly based on energy saving and emission reduction, and achieves energy saving according to the rules of dynamic adjustment of network equipment. Paper [17] has designed a load balancing solution for DCNs. The controller obtains the real-time traffic information of switches, and calculates the costs using simulated annealing algorithm, and makes the load balancing decision, however, the solution is mainly for the specific DCN, such as Port-Land [15].

The separation of forwarding element and control element based on OpenFlow has made the network innovation become a hot research direction, especially in traffic management, load balancing, and dynamic routing and so on. OpenTM gets the traffic information in the network node from the controller, and calculates the network load of each node, thus builds the traffic matrix for the whole network [18]. Paper [19] has applied the OpenFlow technology to the scalable streaming media application framework supporting the QoS, and the dynamic routing function of non-shortest path is used to schedule the video data stream. Paper [20] has proposed a server load balancing controller application to improve the QoS for video streaming over single operator OpenFlow network in case of server overload. Server load balance is achieved by continuously monitoring the load of each server, and dynamically redirecting activities or new service requests. In such a manner, the end user experiences the lowest delay and distortion when one or more servers are overloaded.

Paper [21] has described a dynamic load balancing method of server cluster based on OpenFlow to solve the problem of how to take load balancing into network virtualization data center. But there is no consideration of how the different services to make load balancing on the same path.

Paper [22] has presented a load balancing solution based on SDN for their campus network. Their aim is to cut costs and improve flexibility of the network. In this solution, their application shared elements with the distributed control plan of Kandoo [23], and there were a root controller and multiple local controllers. When an event comes, if it is not required to get overall information of the network, the local controller will handle it. Otherwise, it will be forwarded to the root controller, which keeps network-wide state and can process it best. However, the proposed scheme is mainly aimed at the load balancing in the campus network, and does not consider the scene of the data center.

Paper [10] has presented a dynamic load balancing algorithm based on the fat-tree topology for the DCN, and this algorithm calculates the shortest path for the network traffic by using of the network available bandwidth in real-time. Traffic from the source node to the top node is needed to visit in the fat-tree topology, and it determines the destination node of the downward transfer. For any traffic generated from the network, this algorithm firstly determines the source address, the destination address, and determines the highest layer node which the traffic needs to reach. It has realized dynamic path selection strategy based on the characteristic of the fat-tree topology, but only used the greedy algorithm for the real-time available bandwidth of the single hop path, then got the traffic adjusting decisions. This cannot consider the status of other link on the path, and may lead to the over load of part link on that path, causing the network congestion.

In this paper, we have proposed a new frame for the software-defined data center network (SDDCN), and discussed the link bottleneck problems caused by disequilibrium distribution of the available bandwidth of all the links on the path, and presented a schedule algorithm for the dynamic load balancing based on the path coefficient of network available bandwidth in real-time, and developed the components of the Ryu controller of the SDDCN which is responsible for running the SDLB algorithm. The presented algorithm has solved the local congestion problem which the DLB algorithm can easily lead to, and also provided a more efficient scheduling scheme for the load balancing of the fat-tree network.

3 Dynamic Load Balancing for the SDDCN

In this section, a new frame for the SDDCN is proposed based on the fat-tree topology in the existing DCNs and using software-defined method, and has designed a SDLB algorithm based on the path coefficient of network available bandwidth in real-time.

3.1 A Network Frame for the SDDCN

In order to realize the flexible control of network traffic, and to maximize the use of limited bandwidth and other resources in the DCNs, this paper presents a new frame for SDDCNs using the software-defined method. In comparison with the existing DCNs, the SDDCN has the following features:

- All routers and switches are only responsible for forwarding traffic, while control functions are completed by a special SDN controller.
- The network currently built and put into use is a tree topology generally composed of two or three layers of routers and switches.

Figure 1 presents a network frame for the SDDCN, and it is different from the structure of the DCN based the fat-tree topology in [24]. In this SDDCN, all switches, including core layer switches (s_{17}, s_{18}, s_{19} and s_{20}), convergence layer switches (s_9, s_{10}, s_{11}, s_{12}, s_{13}, s_{14}, s_{15} and s_{16}), and access layer (edge) switches (s_1, s_2, s_3, s_4, s_5, s_6, s_7 and s_8), are connected with a special SDN controller such as the Ryu. These switches are only responsible for forwarding traffic and are controlled by the SDN controller. For three-layer fat-tree topology with k variables, which contains $(k/2)^2$ core switches and k arrays; and each array is composed of k switches with k ports, among which the number of the convergence layer switches and the number of edge layer switches are the same; each edge switch directly is connected to the $k/2$ hosts.

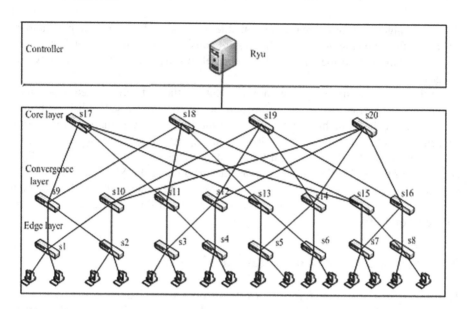

Fig. 1. A frame for the SDDCN

In general, we set the edge switches connecting to the host as the starting points of the paths. One of the important features of the fat-tree topology is that the traffic between all the hosts and the same edge switch in the same array only needs to visit the edge switches as the highest; the traffic between all the hosts and different edge switches within the same array only needs to visit the convergence layer switch as the highest; for the traffic between different arrays starting from the edge switches only needs to upward transfer to the highest core switches, and the downward path of the traffic is determined thereof. In this paper, the SDLB algorithm is designed based on the fat-tree topology of the SDDCN.

3.2 Detail Method

The SDLB algorithm designed in this paper needs to create and maintain three path tables: upward path table (UPT), downward path table (DPT), link load table (LLT) inside the SDN controller, thus to save all the up and down paths and the load information of each link, then the SDN controller accordingly calculates out the best path for the traffic transfer.

The structure of UPT is given in Table 1: Edge represents the start edge switch of the traffic, and each of the edge switches (s_1, s_2, ..., s_8) can be uploaded to one of the core layer switches through several paths; Core and Aggregation represent the high level switches that the data flow can reach, and A_1, A_2 respectively represents the first or second set of the convergence layer switches of each array; s_{17}, s_{18}, ..., s_{20} respectively represents the core layer switches; each cell represents the path of the traffic to the top switch. Through the load balancing decision of the UPT, the path information is provided, and the current minimum available bandwidth in each path for upward and downward is calculated.

Table 1. UPT

Edge / Path / Top	Aggregation		Core			
	A_1	A_2	s_{17}	s_{18}	s_{19}	s_{20}
s_1	{1,9}	{1,10}	{1,9,17}	{1,9,18}	{1,10,19}	{1,10,20}
s_2	{2,9}	{2,10}	{2,9,17}	{2,9,18}	{2,10,19}	{2,10,20}
s_3	{3,11}	{3,12}	{3,11,17}	{3,11,18}	{3,12,19}	{3,12,20}
s_4	{4,11}	{4,12}	{4,11,17}	{4,11,18}	{4,12,19}	{4,12,20}
s_5	{5,13}	{5,14}	{5,13,17}	{5,13,18}	{5,14,19}	{5,14,20}
s_6	{6,13}	{6,14}	{6,13,17}	{6,13,18}	{6,14,19}	{6,14,20}
s_7	{7,15}	{7,16}	{7,15,17}	{7,15,18}	{7,16,19}	{7,16,20}
s_8	{8,15}	{8,16}	{8,15,17}	{8,15,18}	{8,16,19}	{8,16,20}

The structure of DPT is shown in Table 2: contrast to UPT, in DPT, the Aggregation and Core represent the starting point of the downward traffic flow, which is the highest level node for upward flow to reach, and the node can be obtained by UPT; Edge represents the path needed to reach the destination; once the highest level nodes are determined, the downward flow transferring path is determined, and the load balancing algorithm determines the downward paths to reach the destination nodes based on the highest level nodes.

Table 2. DPT

Edge / Path / Top	Aggregation		Core			
	A_1	A_2	s_{17}	s_{18}	s_{19}	s_{20}
s_1	{9,1}	{10,1}	{17,9,1}	{18,9,1}	{19,10,1}	{20,10,1}
s_2	{9,2}	{10,2}	{17,9,2}	{18,9,2}	{19,10,2}	{20,10,2}
s_3	{11,3}	{12,3}	{17,11,3}	{18,11,3}	{19,12,3}	{20,12,3}
s_4	{11,4}	{12,4}	{17,11,4}	{18,11,4}	{19,12,4}	{20,12,4}
s_5	{13,5}	{14,5}	{17,13,5}	{18,13,5}	{19,14,5}	{20,14,5}
s_6	{13,6}	{14,6}	{17,13,6}	{18,13,6}	{19,14,6}	{20,14,6}
s_7	{15,7}	{16,7}	{17,15,7}	{18,15,7}	{19,16,7}	{20,16,7}
s_8	{15,8}	{16,8}	{17,15,8}	{18,15,8}	{19,16,8}	{20,16,8}

As shown in Table 3, each row of LLT represents a link between two adjacent nodes in the topology, which is represented by the starting and end points of the link, i.e., *<src, dst>*; each column represents an adjacent time interval. For definiteness and without loss of generality, we take the current available bandwidth of each link in a fixed cycle statistical topology, that is, B_i represents the current available bandwidth of link i. In the initialization phase, we set the available bandwidth as the maximum bandwidth of the link, and then calculate and update the LLT based on the port flow statistical information obtained at each cycle.

Table 3. LLT

Time B_i Link	T_0	T_-	T_+
$<s_1,s_9>$	1000	520	220
$<s_1,s_{10}>$	1000	395	395
$<s_3,s_{11}>$	1000	355	55
$<s_3,s_{12}>$	1000	545	545
$<s_9,s_{17}>$	1000	415	115
$<s_9,s_{18}>$	1000	600	600
$<s_{10},s_{19}>$	1000	300	300
$<s_{10},s_{20}>$	1000	350	350
$<s_{11},s_{17}>$	1000	450	150
$<s_{11},s_{18}>$	1000	175	175
$<s_{12},s_{19}>$	1000	485	485
$<s_{12},s_{20}>$	1000	220	220
...	...	...	...

3.3   Problem Descriptions

Definition 1:   Available bandwidth of the path. For all the possible paths that the traffic flow transfers to the highest layer or from the highest layer to the downward destination switches, the SDN controller will make a statistic on the available bandwidth of all the links inside each path, and through the principles of maximum and minimum to calculate the available bandwidth of that path [25]. We assume the available bandwidth of the kth upward and downward path are respectively Bu_k and Bd_k, and then we have

$$Bu_k = min\{b_0, b_1, \cdots, b_i\} \tag{1}$$

$$Bd_k = min\{B_0, B_1, \cdots, B_i\} \tag{2}$$

where B_i is the current available bandwidth for the ith link in the path, and $min\{\}$ is the minimum value in the sequence.

The size of the available bandwidth of the path can be used as the load state of the local network, which can be used as the basis of the load balancing algorithm. The greater the available bandwidth of the path is, the smaller the load on the path, the more difficult to cause local network congestion for choosing that path to transmit data packets.

Definition 2: Path variation coefficient. Based on the uploaded paths calculated from the source switch and the downward paths calculated according to the destination switch, the complete path is formed. But how to choose the best path for the traffic flow needs to calculate out the path variation coefficients (CV) respectively, that is

$$CV = \frac{\sigma_{AB_k}}{\overline{AB_k}} \times 100\% \tag{3}$$

where AB_k is the available bandwidth of the kth path, and $\overline{AB_k}$ is the average value of the available bandwidth of the upward path and the downward path in the kth path, the calculation formula is as follows:

$$\overline{AB_k} = \frac{Bu_k + Bd_k}{2} \tag{4}$$

Obviously, the smaller the $\overline{AB_k}$ value is, the greater the path variation coefficient is. The greater the available bandwidth variation of the path is, the worse the path transmission performance is, and the more prone to cause network congestion.

Among which, σ_{AB_k} is the standard deviation between the available bandwidths of upward path and the downward path inside the kth path, the calculation formula is as follows:

$$\sigma_{AB_k} = \sqrt{\frac{\left(Bd_k - \overline{AB_k}\right)^2 + \left(Bu_k - \overline{AB_k}\right)^2}{2}} \tag{5}$$

The smaller the σ_{AB_k} value is, the smaller the path variation coefficient is. The smaller the available bandwidth variation of the path is, the better the path transmission performance is, and the less prone to cause network congestion.

3.4   SDLB Algorithm

In order to dynamically select the best path and avoid local congestion in the network, the SDLB algorithm is designed, which is based on the real-time bandwidth of the link, and the pseudo code of the SDLB algorithm is as follows.

Algorithm 1. SDLB Algorithm

Input: `Flow(srcHost, dstHost),LLT,UPT,DPT`

Output: `bestPath`

```
1: SelectBestPath(){
2:     srcEdgeSw=getEdgeSwitch(srcHost);
3:     dstEdgeSw=getEdgeSwitch(dstHost);
4:     topLayer=getTopLayer(srcEdge, dstEdge);
5:     if srcEdgeSw==dstEdgeSw then
6:         return srcEdgeSw
7:     end if
8:     upwardPaths=getUpwardPaths(srcEdgeSw, topLayer)
9:     downwardPaths=getDownwardPath(topLayer, dstEdgeSw)
10:    paths=getPaths(upwardPaths, downwardPaths)
11:    bestPath=getBestPath(paths)
12:    return bestPath
13: }
```

According to the structural characteristics of the fat-tree network, the traffic flow only needs to determine the upward transmission path from the source node to the top layer node which is needed to reach, and then the downward transmission path is also determined. On the basis of the source address and destination address, the SDLB algorithm firstly calculates out the highest layer of switches that the traffic flow needs to reach in the shortest path, and provides basis for the calculation of the upward path. Once the highest layer needed to be visited by the traffic flow is determined, the SDLB algorithm can select out all the possible upward paths in the paths based on the source switch and the highest layer needed to reach of the traffic flow, then select the corresponding downward path according to the end of each upward path, and each upward path has only one downward path according to the characteristics of the fat-tree topology. Once all the possible upward path and downward path of the traffic flow has been determined, and formed a complete path, the SDLB algorithm will read the current available bandwidth B_i of all the links inside the link load table for each of the upward paths and its corresponding downward path, and calculate out the available bandwidth of that path based on the maximum and minimum principle, then calculate out the path coefficients of all the complete path through the calculation formula (3), and select the best transfer path for traffic flow accordingly. In the forwarding decision of traffic flow, the SDN controller can monitor the network state in real time and make statistics for the network information, then select the best path according to the SDLB algorithm, and update that path to all the switches of that path to realize scheduling of the traffic flow and achieve the load balancing effects.

For any n node of the fat-tree network, the time complexity of the SDLB algorithm is $O(n^3)$. Different from the case of single hop greedy of the DLB algorithm, the SDLB algorithm needs to maintain the link state information of the network to calculate the path coefficient, which leads to the computational overhead of the SDLB algorithm increasing larger continuously with the expansion of the network. However, the monitoring module of the SDLB algorithm in the initialization phase will complete all topology storage and update, so that the SDN controller can reach a balance between SDLB algorithm performance and the computational overhead.

4   Performance Evaluation and Discussion

In order to analyze the performance of the SDLB algorithm, we have established the experiment system. The SDN controller is to use Ryu, the switches are to use OpenFlow which will be integrated into the Ryu controller [26] to realize three relevant components, including *load_balance*, *load_sbalance* and *simple_monitor*. The component of the *load_balance* will realize the SDLB algorithm, and the component of the *load_sbalance* will realize the DLB algorithm, and the component of the *simple_monitor* will realize the all the basic statistical information needed for the load balancing algorithm. The three components exist under the Ryu controller's application files can communicate by using of the Ryu controller's API and other components in order to obtain the topology information and the load state of all the switches of the current network in time; then the component of the *load_balance* uses the component of the *simple_monitor* to obtain the data update link load table, upward path table and the downward table, and calculate the value of path variation coefficient *CV* to make path decision for the traffic flow and seal that path into *FlowMod* message and updated onto the flow tables of all the switches. Through the development of components, the SDLB algorithm can be realized in the Ryu controller which can be successfully started. The SDN controller can be connected to the network, and the traffic flow in the network can be dynamically scheduled. Then the performance of the SDLB algorithm is checked by comparing with the existing DLB algorithm.

4.1   Testing Environment

In this paper, we use the *Mininet* simulation platform [27] to test the performance of the SDLB algorithm. We generated a fat-tree network with $k = 8$ and connected to the Ryu controller. Two kinds of UDP traffic mode [28, 29] are set up for the fat-tree network to restore the traffic characteristics of the DCN.

(1) Random mode: the data flow randomly starts from one host, and is transferred to another host randomly.
(2) Centralized mode (i, j, k) (P_t, P_a, P_c): the host m sends data flow to the hosts: $m + i$, $m + j$ and $m + k$ at probabilities of P_t, P_a and P_c, and $P_t + P_a + P_c = 1$. Without loss of generality, the setting values are (1, 4, 64) (50%, 30%, 20%).

A host computer running Ryu 3.6 controller, and the other host running the fat-tree simulation environment generated by Mininet 2.1.0, and reintegrate the OVS into the virtualized OpenFlow switch of the OpenvSwitch 2.3.0 and connected to the Ryu controller. In order to evaluate the performance, we assume the maximum bandwidth of the host to the edge layer switch is 0.05 Mbps, and the data stream of different traffic loads is initiated in two modes, and each test time is 50 s.

4.2   Evaluation Parameters

In order to evaluate the performance of the SDLB algorithm, the following performance evaluation parameters are set up.

(1) Average bandwidth utilization ratio ρ. It is referring to in the average value of the ratio between the actual bandwidth and the specified bandwidth obtained by all data flows. The real bandwidth value that each flow can reach is often below the specified bandwidth when transferred, because the network status and performance is not ideal. By comparing the changes of these two, it can carry on the evaluation of the current network status and performance. The calculation formula of the average bandwidth utilization rate ρ is as follows:

$$\rho = \frac{\sum_{i=1}^{n} \frac{B_i}{B_0}}{n} \tag{6}$$

where B_i is the actual bandwidth of the ith flow, B_0 is the specified bandwidth of that flow, and n is the total amount of the flows.

(2) Average transmission delay τ. It is referring to the average value of time spend for all the data flow from the sending end to the receiving end, the flow transmission time is affected by the influence of network status and performance, through comparing the transmission delay of the flow can give effectively judgment on the network real-time performance status. The average transmission time delay calculation formula is as follows:

$$\tau = \frac{\sum_{i=1}^{n} t_{i-receive} - t_{i-send}}{n} \tag{7}$$

where $t_{i-receive}$ is the time of receiving the data flow at the receiving end, and t_{i-send} is the time of sending the data flow at the sending end.

4.3   Results Analysis

In order to verify the performance of the SDLB algorithm, we use the DLB algorithm to carry out the comparison tests, and performed several test on the two algorithms respectively in the centralized flow mode and the random flow mode. Figure 2 shows the relationship between the average bandwidth utilization and the traffic load. Under different traffic loads in random mode, the average bandwidth utilization of the SDLB algorithm is better than the DLB algorithm. When the traffic load is low, the bandwidth utilization rates of the DLB algorithm and the SDLB algorithm are all close to 1, and network performance is good. With the increase of traffic load, the performance of the two algorithms are all decreased, especially the traffic load is more than 0.5, a downward trend of the two algorithms is more obvious; but the utilization rate of the average bandwidth under the SDLB algorithm scheduling decreased slightly and gently, and was higher than that of the DLB algorithm. This is because the SDLB algorithm fully based on the available bandwidth of each link in the network to calculate the path coefficient of each complete path, and then select the best path for the flow scheduling, which is more comprehensive than the DLB algorithm, and can be better in avoiding the local network congestion and improving the network bandwidth utilization rate.

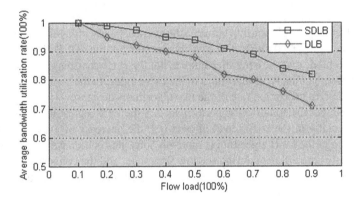

Fig. 2. Average bandwidth utilization in random mode

Figure 3 shows the relationship between the average transmission delay and the traffic load. Under different traffic loads in random mode, the average transmission delay of the SDLB algorithm is better than the DLB algorithm. When the traffic load is low, the available bandwidth of the network is enough, and the average transmission delay of the two algorithms is lower, and with the increase of the traffic load, the average transmission delay of the two algorithms is increasing, especially in the traffic load of more than 0.6, the average transmission delay is obviously high; when the network is close to full load, the network congestion is serious with higher average transmission delay. However, the SDLB algorithm can calculate the path coefficient to select path for the flow according to the actual available bandwidth, and can make a better load balancing decision than the DLB algorithm under the same flow load, and reduce the possibility of congestion in the network, and effectively decrease the average transmission delay in the network.

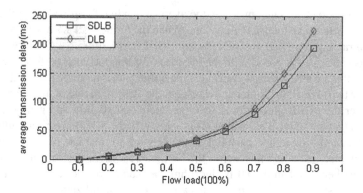

Fig. 3. Average transmission delay in random mode

Figure 4 shows the relationship between the average bandwidth utilization and traffic load under the centralized mode. The equilibrium effect of the SDLB algorithm is close in the random mode and the centralized mode, but the performances of the SDLB algorithm are better than the DLB algorithm in the two modes. In the centralized mode, the average bandwidth utilization rate of the two algorithms decreases with the increase of the traffic load, but the equalization performance of the DLB algorithm decreases more quickly, especially in the traffic load of over 0.3, the decrease of average bandwidth utilization rate of the DLB algorithm is more obvious, this is because the bandwidth of all the link paths are efficient during the low flow load, and the congestion rate is low. Based on simple greedy selection path, the DLB algorithm has increased the possibility of the local link congestion, which also confirms the effectiveness of the SDLB algorithm for solving this problem.

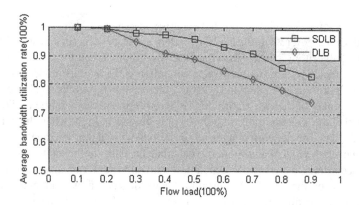

Fig. 4. Average bandwidth utilization in centralized mode

Figure 5 shows the relationship between the average transmission delay and the traffic load under the centralized mode. Quite similar to the situations in the random mode, the average transmission delay of the two algorithms increases with the increase of the traffic load, and the SDLB algorithm has a better performance than the DLB algorithm.

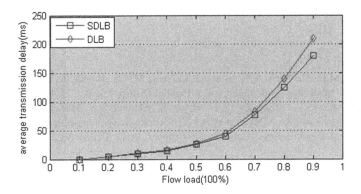

Fig. 5. Average transmission delay in centralized mode

In the meantime, we find that the tendency of the average bandwidth utilization along with flow load appears to be very similar though few difference (see Figs. 2 and 4), and so does the tendency of the average transmission delay along with flow load (see Figs. 3 and 5). This means that the performance of the SDLB algorithm is not affected by traffic mode, and this will show that the algorithm has well stability and applicability.

In summary, the SDLB algorithm has better average bandwidth utilization and average transmission delay in the above two test modes, which reflects the better performance of the network under that algorithm, and verifies the effectiveness of the proposed SDLB algorithm.

5   Conclusion and Future Work

The transfer-control-separation ideology of SDN architecture is one of the most promising technologies in the field of computer networks. In this paper, a new SDDCN architecture is proposed, based on this, a dynamic scheduling load balancing (DSLB) algorithm for the SDDCN based on fat-tree topology is designed. Based on the all possible available bandwidth of the upward paths and the downward paths, the SDLB algorithm has calculated the path coefficient of each complete path, and selected the best path for the traffic flow. The SDLB algorithm can make full use of the network bandwidth, ease the local congestion in the DCN, and provide a better solution for the traffic load balancing in the DCN.

Conflict of Interests
The authors declare that there is no conflict of interests regarding the publication of this paper.

Acknowledgment. This research is supported in part by the grant from the National Natural Science Foundation of China (61572191 and 61402170), the Hunan Provincial Science and Technology Program Project of China (No. 2013FJ4051), and the Hunan Provincial Education Department Scientific Research Fund of China (No. 13B065).

References

1. Assunção, M.D., Calheiros, R.N., Bianchi, S., Netto, M.A.S., Buyya, R.: Big data computing and clouds: trends and future directions. J. Parallel Distrib. Comput. **79–80**, 3–15 (2015)
2. Bilal, K., Khan, S.U., Zhang, L., Li, H., Hayat, K., Madani, S.A., Min-Allah, N., Wang, L., Chen, D., Iqbal, M., Xu, C.Z., Zomaya, A.Y.: Quantitative comparisons of the state-of-the-art data center architectures. Concurrency Comput. Pract. Experience **25**(12), 1771–1783 (2013)
3. Gang, D., Gong, Z., Hong, W.: Characteristics research on modern data center network. J. Comput. Res. Dev. **51**(2), 395–407 (2014)
4. Bilal, K., Khan, S.U., Zomaya, A.Y.: Green data center networks: challenges and opportunities. In: 11th International Conference on Frontiers of Information Technology (FIT 2013), Islamabad, Pakistan, pp. 229–234. IEEE (2013)
5. Pan, J., Paul, S., Jain, R.: A survey of the research on future internet architectures. IEEE Commun. Mag. **49**(7), 26–36 (2011)
6. Software-defined networking definition. https://www.opennetworking.org/sdn-resources/sdn-definition
7. Kim, H., Feamster, N.: Improving network management with software defined networking. IEEE Commun. Mag. **51**(2), 114–119 (2013)
8. Zuo, Q.Y., Chen, M., Zhao, G.S., Xing, C.Y., Zhang, G.M., Jiang, P.C.: Research on OpenFlow-based SDN technologies. J. Softw. **24**(5), 1078–1097 (2013)
9. Riforgiate, S., Sydney, A.: The evaluation of software defined networking for communication and control of cyber physical systems. Dissertations & Theses – Gradworks (2013)
10. Yu, L., Pan, D.: OpenFlow based load balancing for fat-tree networks with multipath support. In: 12th IEEE International Conference on Communications (ICC 2013), Budapest, Hungary (2013)
11. Davidson, E.A.: The software-defined-data-center: concept or reality? http://tinyurl.com/omhmbfv
12. Knorr, E.: OpenDaylight: a big step toward the software-defined data center. http://www.infoworld.com/article/2614152
13. Burt, J.: Startup CloudGenix aims to bring SDN to WAN. http://www.eweek.com/networking/startup-cloudgenix-aims-to-bring-sdn-to-wan.html
14. Tavakoli, A., Casado, M., Koponen, T., Shenker, S.: Applying nox to the datacenter. In: The Eighth ACM Workshop on Hot Topics in Networks (HotNets-VIII), New York City, NY, October 2009
15. Niranjan Mysore, R., Pamboris, A., Farrington, N., Huang, N., Miri, P., Radhakrishnan, S., Subramanya, V., Vahdat, A.: Portland: a scalable fault-tolerant layer 2 data center network fabric. ACM Sigcomm Comput. Commun. Rev. **39**(4), 39–50 (2009)
16. Heller, B., Seetharaman, S., Mahadevan, P., Yiakoumis, Y., Sharma, P., Banerjee, S., McKeown, N.: Elastictree: saving energy in data center networks. In: 7th USENIX Conference on Networked Systems Design and Implementation (NSDI 2010), San Jose, CA, USA, pp. 249–264. USENIX Association Berkeley (2010)

17. Al-Fares, M., Radhakrishnan, S., Raghavan, B., Huang, N., Vahdat, A.: Hedera: dynamic flow scheduling for data center networks. In: 7th USENIX Conference on Networked Systems Design and Implementation (NSDI 2010), San Jose, CA, USA, p. 19. USENIX Association Berkeley (2010)

18. Tootoonchian, A., Ghobadi, M., Ganjali, Y.: OpenTM: traffic matrix estimator for OpenFlow networks. In: Passive and Active Measurement, International Conference (PAM 2010), Zurich, Switzerland, pp. 201–210, 7–9 April 2010

19. Egilmez, H.E., Gorkemli, B., Tekalp, A.M., Civanlar, S.: Scalable video streaming over OpenFlow networks: an optimization framework for QoS routing. In: 18th IEEE International Conference on Image Processing (ICIP 2011), Brussels, Belgium, pp. 2241–2244. IEEE, September 2011

20. Yilmaz, S., Tekalp, A.M., Unluturk, B.D.: Video streaming over software defined networks with server load balancing. In: International Conference on Computing, Networking and Communications (ICNC 2015), Garden Grove, CA, USA, pp. 722–726. IEEE, February 2015

21. Chen, W., Shang, Z., Tian, X., Li, H.: Dynamic server cluster load balancing in virtualization environment with openflow. Int. J. Distrib. Sens. Netw., Article ID 531538 (2015)

22. Ghaffarinejad, A., Syrotiuk, V.R.: Load balancing in a campus network using software defined networking. In: Third GENI Research and Educational Experiment Workshop (GREE 2014), Atlanta, GA, pp. 75–76. IEEE, March 2014

23. Yeganeh, S.H., Ganjali, Y.: Kandoo: a framework for efficient and scalable offloading of control applications. In: First Workshop on Hot Topics in Software Defined Networks (HotSDN 2012), Helsinki, Finland, pp. 19–24, ACM, August 2012

24. Li, D., Chen, G., Ren, F., Jiang, C., Xu, M.: Data center network research progress and trends. J. Comput. 25(7), 87–89 (2014)

25. Amis, A.D., Prakash, R., Vuong, T.H.P., Huynh, D.T.: Max-min d-cluster formation in wireless ad hoc networks. In: IEEE International Conference on Computer Communications (INFOCOM 2000), Tel Aviv, pp. 32–41. IEEE, March 2000

26. Ryu. http://www.Ryu.org/

27. Mininet. http://mininet.org/

28. Benson, T., Anand, A., Akella, A., Zhang, M.: Understanding data center traffic characteristics. ACM SIGCOMM Comput. Commun. Rev. 40(1), 65–72 (2009)

29. Kandula, S., Sengupta, S., Greenberg, A., Patel, P., Chaiken, R.: The nature of data center traffic: measurements and analysis. In: 9th ACM SIGCOMM Conference on Internet Measurement Conference (IMC 2009), Chicago, IL, USA, pp. 202–208. ACM, November 2009

A Time-Aware Weighted-SVM Model for Web Service QoS Prediction

Dou Kai, Guo Bin, and Li Kuang[(✉)]

School of Software, Central South University Changsha, Changsha, 410075, China
{doukai,guobin,kuangli}@csu.edu.cn

Abstract. With the rapid development of Web services, how to identify services with high Quality of Service (QoS) becomes a hot research topic. Since time-series QoS records are highly nonlinear, complex and uncertain, it is difficult to make accurate predictions through conventional mathematic methods. In order to deal with the challenging issue, this paper proposes a novel personalized QoS prediction approach considering both the temporal dynamics of QoS attributes and the influence of different QoS records. First, slide-window based data grouping is firstly utilized to obtain training dataset for regression model. Then we take the different influence of history QoS records at different time into consideration and eventually propose a weighted-SVM model for QoS prediction. Compared to Auto-Regressive Moving Average Model (ARMA), standard SVM and Collaborative Filtering (CF), the proposed approach in the paper can improve significantly the accuracy in personalized QoS prediction.

Keywords: Web service · QoS prediction · Temporal dynamics · Support vector machine

1   Introduction

Web services have become a promising technology for the development of new Internet-based Software Systems. Web services have been boosting greatly due to the strong needs of industrial companies and end users. With the rapid development of Web services, it becomes puzzling how to identify the services with high Quality of Service (QoS) from a large number of services. Web service QoS prediction is an effective way to identify the Web service which possibly has the best performance.

Influenced by the unpredictable network condition and the server workload, the Quality of Service (QoS) is dynamically changing [1] from time to time. Inaccurate Web service QoS prediction will result in large deviations in service selection. Because of the large number of services and dynamic changes of Quality of Service, it is a critical problem to be addressed in the Web services recommendation [2] and selection [3] how to utilize the historical QoS data to predict the current or future QoS value.

In this paper, we propose a novel personalized QoS prediction approach based on weighted-SVM model. By analyzing the QoS records, we find that the QoS of Web Service is affected by that in the near prior time. And the closer the interval is, the greater the influence is. Therefore, in our prediction framework, first, a slide window is proposed

© ICST Institute for Computer Sciences, Social Informatics and Telecommunications Engineering 2017
S. Wang and A. Zhou (Eds.): CollaborateCom 2016, LNICST 201, pp. 302–311, 2017.
DOI: 10.1007/978-3-319-59288-6_27

for cutting the time series QoS data into multiple feature vectors as training dataset. And then, we take the different influence of history QoS records at different time into consideration through a weighted-SVM prediction model. The contributions of this paper include:

- We propose a slide to preprocess QoS historical records. Slide window is proposed for generating multiple feature vectors from one piece of time series QoS data.
- We propose a modified weighted Support Vector Machine by dynamically changing the SVM penalty factor. And we apply the weighted-SVM model to the Web services QoS prediction problem.
- By comparing with Auto-Regressive Moving Average Model (ARMA), standard SVM and Collaborative Filtering (CF), the proposed approach can improve the accuracy of personalized QoS prediction significantly.

The rest of the paper is organized as follows: Related works is discussed in Sect. 2. A Web service QoS Prediction Approach is illustrated in Sect. 3. And then the experiments and result analysis are given in Sect. 4. And finally the conclusion is drawn in Sect. 5.

2 Related Work

In the research literature, there are two mainstream technologies for QoS prediction: CF approaches and time series forecasting:

2.1 Collaborative Filtering

CF approaches are popular methods for personalized QoS prediction, which are mainly divided into two categories: model-based and neighborhood-based. Model-based approaches make predictions through learning a model. These kind of algorithms include the matrix factorization [4], the graph-based approaches [5], etc. Neighborhood-based approach utilizes historical QoS information from different users or services to measure their similarities on personalized QoS experiences. Then, QoS information from similar neighbors collected to make a personalized QoS prediction for a target user with a set of candidate Web Services. The neighborhood-based CF approaches include user-based [6], service-based [7] and hybrid [8, 9] methods. The user-based method utilizes the historical QoS experiences from similar users for personalized QoS prediction, while the service-based method uses those from similar services for prediction. The hybrid method is the combination of the previous two methods, so it can achieve higher prediction accuracy.

2.2 Time Series Forecasting

Time series forecasting approaches have been successfully applied to modeling and forecasting QoS data. They use different models to fit the past QoS values and then forecast their future changes. Godse et al. [10] proposed a method that combines monitoring technologies and extrapolation methods, which are based on ARIMA models, in order to predict future service performance. Amin et al. [11] presented an improved QoS forecasting approach which integrates ARIMA with GARCH models to address the constant variation of assumption limitation of ARIMA models. Zhang, Jinhong, Song, Jie, et al. [12] proposed a short-term prediction for QoS of web service, which are based on RBF neural networks. Zheng, Xiaoxia, et al. [13] proposed a dynamic prediction approach, which based on a time-series analysis for historical data.

Different from the above relevant work, our work is based on weighted-SVM. SVM is a machine learning method based on structural risk minimization principle [14]. Based on the analysis of QoS data, we find that different QoS records have different influence to other records. Therefore we propose a modified Support Vector Machine which has been modified by dynamically changing the SVM penalty factor, and based on the proposed weighted SVM model, we can predict the QoS based on historical records.

3   Problem Definition and Approach Overview

This section presents the problem definition and a detailed explanation of our proposed personalized QoS prediction approach.

3.1   Problem Definition

Suppose that a Web service mining system contains m users $U = \{ U_1, U_2, U_3 \cdots , U_m\}$ and n Web Services $S = \{ S_1, S_2, S_3 \cdots , S_n\}$. If user $U_i (U_i \in U)$ invoked service $S_j (S_j \in S)$ during the time interval $T_k (k = 1, 2, \cdots)$, the observed QoS value of this service invocation is recorded in the entry q_{U_i, S_j, T_k} of the matrix Q. The problem we have been discussing in this paper is how to efficiently and precisely predict the future perform based on the existing records. An illustrating example of QoS records is shown in Fig. 1.

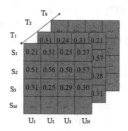

Fig. 1. Local QoS records

3.2   Theoretical Foundation

We use the dataset in WS-DREAM site [15]. The dataset consists of 142 users' invocation of 4532 Web services in 64 time slices.

We aim to find out the influence between each QoS data through statistical analysis of the dataset. Most of the QoS distributions are similar to Fig. 2. The current QoS value is close to the value at the previous and next time interval. In order to confirm whether the dataset fulfills the similar feature, we compare each QoS data with the data at next time slice by using First-order Difference function [16]. The result shows, there are 92.8% of data, the difference between the data and the next data is less than 0.1. We have a theoretical foundation that the QoS of different time periods are not independent and the QoS of Web service is affected by that of the near prior time.

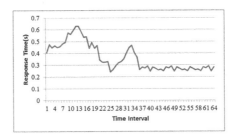

Fig. 2. Records of response-time

3.3 Approach Overview

As shown in Fig. 3, our approach mainly includes two phases: training phase and prediction phase. In the training phase, slide-window based data grouping is used to preprocess historical QoS data. Then a modified Weighted-SVM is proposed to derive the prediction model after parameter optimization. In the prediction phase, the QoS in the near future can be predicted from the derived model.

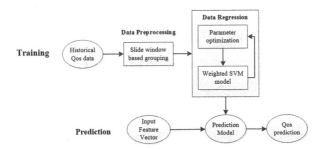

Fig. 3. Approach overview

Slide-Window based Data Grouping
In the stage of training phase, we divide each QoS sample x_i into multiple subsequences with a fixed-size slide window. A feature vector for each slide window can be generated. In order to derive a prediction model, we put the first m QoS records as training data and the size of slide window is l. We can get $m - l$ groups of mapping relationships. The

training   feature   vectors   are $(X_i, Y_i), i = (l + 1, l + 2, \cdots l + m)$,   where $X_i = (x_{i-l}, x_{i-l-1}, \cdots, x_{i-1})$ and $Y_i = x_i$.

Figure 4 illustrates an example of feature matrix. There is a QoS time sequence S_1. And the size of slide window is l here, because there are l QoS data in each slide window. Each slide window corresponds to a training data point. Figure 4 shows two training data points (X_1, Y_1) and (X_2, Y_2). X_1 is the vector $(q_1, q_2, \cdots q_{l-1})$ and X_2 is the vector $(q_2, \cdots, q_{l-1}, q_l)$. Y_1 and Y_2 represent the target value of QoS. It will cause information redundancy and introduce noise data when the size of slide window is too large. Otherwise, prediction model will get poor performance when the size of slide window is too small to contain the information we need for prediction.

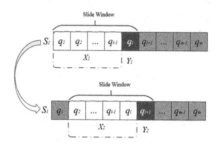

Fig. 4. Slide window

Personalized QoS Model Derivation

The basic idea of support vector regression is to map the input data X from the original input space into a high dimensional space with nonlinear map function $\varnothing(x)$. Then the problem becomes a linear regression in high dimensional space. Suppose that training samples are (x_i, y_i), $i = 1, 2, \cdots N$, where, $x_i \in R^m$ is the input vector, $y_i \in R$ is the corresponding output vector, $y = f(x)$ is the estimated output. Then we have:

$$y = f(x) = \omega^T \varnothing(x) + b \tag{1}$$

where ω^T is the weight vector, $b \in R$ is the bias term. The ε-insensitive loss function is defined by:

$$L_\varepsilon(x, y, f) = |y - f(x)|_\varepsilon = max(0, |y - f(x)| - \varepsilon) \tag{2}$$

In order to obtain weight vector ω^T and bias term b, we must minimize the sum of the ε-insensitive loss function:

$$\frac{1}{2}||\omega^2|| + C \sum_{i=1}^{N} L_\varepsilon(x_i, y_i, f) \tag{3}$$

where parameter C can measure the trade-off between complexity and losses. We can convert formula (3) into an equivalent formula (4) by introducing slack variables ξ_i and ξ_i^*.

$$\min[\frac{1}{2}||\omega||^2 + C\sum_{i=1}^{l}(\xi_i + \xi_i^*)]$$

$$s.t.\begin{cases} y_i - [\omega^T \emptyset(x) + b] \leq \varepsilon + \xi_i \\ [\omega^T \emptyset(x) + b] - y_i \leq \varepsilon + \xi_i^* \\ \xi_i, \xi_i^* \geq 0 \end{cases} \quad (4)$$

Because of the high dimensional feature space, it is not easy to find the answer of formula (4). We can convert it into a dual problem by introducing kernel function:

$$\max j(\alpha_j, \alpha_i^*) = \sum_{i=1}^{N}(\alpha_i^* - \alpha_i)y_i - \varepsilon\sum_{i=1}^{N}(\alpha_i^* + \alpha_i) - \frac{1}{2}\sum_{i,j=1}^{N}(\alpha_i^* - \alpha_i)(\alpha_j^* - \alpha_j)K(x_j, x) s.t. \begin{cases} \sum_{i=1}^{N}(\alpha_i - \alpha_i^*) = 0 \\ \alpha_i - \alpha_i^* \in [0, C] \end{cases} \quad (5)$$

where α_i, α_i^* are the corresponding Lagrange multipliers. And there are some kernel functions such as Linear kernel, Polynomial kernel, Sigmoid Kernel and RBF Kernel.

In the standard SVM, all the samples with deviation over ε have the same penalty factor C. Because of the different influence of various QoS samples, standard SVM have a poor performance on QoS prediction. To solve this problem, we give different penalty factor to the samples with deviation over ε. The closer the time is, the greater the penalty factor C is. The weighted function $W(i)$ can improve the accuracy of the prediction model. Therefore we modify formula (3) to (6).

$$\frac{1}{2}||\omega^2|| + C\sum_{i=1}^{N}W(i) * L_\varepsilon(x_i, y_i, f) \quad (6)$$

And we can modify formula (5) to formula (7):

$$\max J(\alpha_i, \alpha_i^*) = \sum_{i=1}^{N}(\alpha_i^* - \alpha_i)y_i - \varepsilon\sum_{i=1}^{N}(\alpha_i^* + \alpha_i) - \frac{1}{2}\sum_{i,j=1}^{N}(\alpha_i^* - \alpha_i)(\alpha_j^* - \alpha_j)K(x_i, x)$$

$$s.t.\begin{cases} \sum_{i=1}^{N}(\alpha_i - \alpha_i^*) = 0 \\ \alpha_i, \alpha_i^* \in [0, C * W(i)] \end{cases} \quad (7)$$

We choose exponential function as weighting function from linear function, quadratic parabolic function and exponential function based on extensive experiments:

$$W(i) = 1/(1 + \exp(-i))(i = 1, 2, \cdots l) \quad (8)$$

Where $i = 1$ represents the first QoS sample of training data, $i = l$ represents the last QoS sample of training data. $W(i)$ is a monotonically increasing function. Hsu [17] points out that RBF kernel has a good performance in most instances based on many years of research and analysis. So we select RBF kernel as kernel function.

$$K(x, y) = \exp\left(\frac{-||x - x_i||^2}{\sigma^2}\right) \quad (9)$$

By solving the above quadratic programming, we can obtain α_i and α_i^*. Through the expression (11), we can get our regression function.

$$\hat{Y} = \sum_{i=1}^{N} \left(\alpha_i - \alpha_i^* \right) exp\left(\frac{-||x - x_i||^2}{\sigma^2} \right) + b \qquad (10)$$

The weighted-SVM model is proposed here for Web services QoS prediction. SVM model can map the original nonlinear data in a low dimensional space into that with linear feature in a high dimensional space. And the kernel function is used to solve the optimization problem of the loss function. In the training phase, we aim to get the appropriate C, ε, σ^2 for our prediction model. Finally, QoS values can be predicted based on the trained weighted SVM model.

4   Implementation and Experiment

4.1   Dataset Collection

The experiment is implemented in a dataset from WS-DREAM site. In order to analyze the property of our data, we count the scale of the data. We find QoS data lies between 0 s and 20 s. The mean of these data is 2.328 s (Table 1).

Table 1. Information of data

Statistics	Response-time
Scale	0–20 s
Mean	2.328 s
Num. of users	142
Num. of service	4532
Num. of time slices	64

4.2   Evaluation Criterion

Mean Absolute Error (MAE) is used here for model evaluation. The definition of MAE is:

$$MAE = \frac{\sum_{ijk} |Y_{ijk}^\wedge - Y_{ijk}|}{N} \qquad (11)$$

In this formula, $Y_{ijk}^\wedge$ is the predicted value of the response time that user i invocate service j at time k. Y_{ijk} is the real value under the same condition. N is the number of QoS that we need to predict.

4.3   Analysis of Parameter

In our experiment, we aim to find appropriate C, ε, σ^2 and the size of slide window l. We divide the parameters adjustment experiment into four parts. First we adjust ε from 0.01 to 0.1. And then we adjust the parameter of σ^2 from 0.1 to 0.9 in the second part. Then we change C from 10 to 100. At last we change the size of the slide window from 1 to 8. Take the records of U_1 invoking services S_1 as an example, Fig. 6 shows that ε, σ^2, C, l are 0.03, 0.6, 30, 4 are the optimal values for the QoS prediction model of user U_1 invoking services S_1. The result is shown in Fig. 5

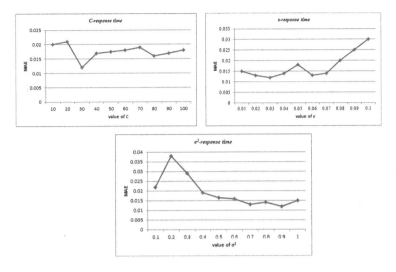

Fig. 5. Impact of C, ε, σ^2

In order to choose the size of slide window, we select 100 users and 50 different Web services as experimental data. We can see from Fig. 6 that the MAE of different QoS series is leveling off when the size of slide window is 5. So we choose $l = 5$.

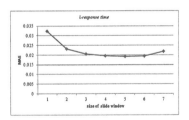

Fig. 6. Impact of l

4.4 Performance Comparisons

We choose the 100 users invoking the first 50 services records as the experimental data. And the size of slide window is 5. The former 54 feature vectors are selected as training data and the prediction is made on the latter 10 QoS values. We compare the prediction accuracy of the following methods:

- CF-This is a tensor factorization-based prediction method [12]. It applies tensor factorization on user-service-time tensor to extract user-specific, service-specific and time-specific characterizes.
- ARMA-ARMA is originally proposed by Box and Jenkins [18] and is a very popular model for time series forecasting.
- Standard SVM-SVM [14] is a novel machine learning method based on structural risk minimization principle.
- Weighted-SVM-This method is proposed in this paper. It is a modified SVM with dynamic penalty factor

The results can be seen from Fig. 7, the performance of CF is worse than other methods. Because prediction based on Collaborative Filtering only extracts the user-specific and service-specific features without considering the relationship between QoS changes in time intervals. Comparison between ARMA model and SVM prediction model, ARMA model shows a good performance when the QoS data are stable. But most of QoS record is highly nonlinear, complex and uncertain, it is difficult to make accurate predictions using ARIMA model. SVM have a better performance while solving nonlinear QoS regression problem. Comparison between standard SVM model and the proposed weighted-SVM model, standard SVM has a poor performance of QoS prediction because standard SVM cannot reflect the different influence between different QoS samples with a same penalty factor C.

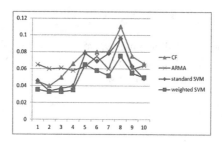

Fig. 7. Performance comparison

5   Conclusion

In this paper, we proposed a Web service QoS prediction framework based on weighted-SVM model. Firstly, we use a slide window for data modeling. Then a weighted-SVM model is employed to predict the QoS of Web services. In regard of practical application, our model has great space to be improved. Although it has achieved better accuracy compared to ARMA, CF and standard SVM, more improvement is needed in practical using. From the view of current stage, the combination of time and space is remarkable. But other ways of combination is worth to try to make a better model.

Acknowledgement. The research is supported by "Natural Science Foundation of Hunan Province" (No.2016JJ3154), "National Natural Science Foundation of China" (No.61202095), "Scientific Research Project for Professors in Central South University, China" (No. 904010001), and "Innovation Project for Graduate Students in Central South University" (No. 502210017).

References

1. Haner, M., Hinton, D., Klein, T.E.: Method of dynamically adjusting quality of service (QoS) targets: US, US 20060212594 A1[P] (2006)
2. Alrifai, M., Risse, T.: Combining global optimization with local selection for efficient QoS-aware service composition. In: Proceedings of the 18th International Conference on World Wide Web (2009)
3. Zheng, Z., Ma, H., Lyu, M.R., et al.: QoS-aware web service recommendation by collaborative filtering. IEEE Trans. Serv. Comput. **4**(2), 140–152 (2011)
4. Salakhutdinov, R., Mnih, A.: Probabilistic matrix factorization. Nips **1**(1), 1257–1264 (2012)
5. Fouss, F., Pirotte, A., Renders, J.M., et al.: Random-walk computation of similarities between nodes of a graph with application to collaborative recommendation. IEEE Trans. Knowl. Data Eng. **19**(3), 355–369 (2007)
6. Breese, J.S., Heckerman, D., Kadie, C.: Empirical analysis of predictive algorithms for collaborative filtering. In: Proceedings 14th Conference on Uncertainty Artificial Intelligence, pp. 43–52 (1998)
7. Deshpande, M., Karypis, G.: Item-based top-n recommendation algorithms. ACM Trans. Inf. Syst. **22**(1), 143–177 (2004)
8. Zheng, Z., Ma, H., Lyu, M.R., King, I.: WSRec: A collaborative filtering based Web service recommender system. In: ICWS, pp. 437–444 (2009)
9. Zheng, Z., Ma, H., Lyu, M.R., King, I.: QoS-aware Web service recommendation by collaborative filtering. IEEE Trans. Serv. Comput. **4**(2), 140–152 (2011)
10. Godse, M., Bellur, U., Sonar, R.: Automating QoS based service selection. In: ICWS, pp. 534–541 (2010)
11. Amin, A., Colman, A., Grunske, L.: An approach to forecasting QoS attributes of web services based on ARIMA and GARCH models. In: ICWS, pp. 74–81 (2012)
12. Zhang, J., Song, J.: A short-term prediction in web service QoS based on RBF neural network. J. Liaoning Eng. Technol. Univ. **29**(5), 918–921 (2010)
13. Zheng, X., Zhao, J., Cheng, Z., Xie, B.: A WebService response time dynamic prediction method. In: Mini-micro Systems, vol. 8 (2011)
14. Yang, J.F., Zhai, Y.J., Wang, D.F., et al.: Time series prediction based on support vector regression. Proc. CSEE **25**(17), 110–114 (2005)
15. Zhang, Y., Zheng, Z., Lyu, M.R.: WSPred: A time-aware personalized QoS prediction framework for web services. In: Proceedings of the 22th IEEE Symposium on Software Reliability Engineering (ISSRE 2011) (2011)
16. Kurogi, S., Koyama, R., Tanaka, S., et al.: Forecasting using first-order difference of time series and bagging of competitive associative nets. In: 2007 International Joint Conference on Neural Networks, IJCNN 2007, pp. 166–171. IEEE (2007)
17. Hsu, B.C., Chang, C.-C., Lin, C.-J.: A practical guide to support vector classification (2012)
18. Box, G.E., Jenkins, G.M.: Time Series Analysis: Forecasting and Control. Holden-Day, San Francisco (1976). revised ed.

An Approach of Extracting Feature Requests from App Reviews

Zhenlian Peng[1,2], Jian Wang[1(✉)], Keqing He[1], and Mingdong Tang[2]

[1] State Key Lab of Software Engineering, Computer School,
Wuhan University, Wuhan, China
{zlpeng,jianwang,hekeqing}@whu.edu.cn
[2] Computer School, Hunan University of Science and Technology, Xiangtan, China
mdtang@hnust.edu.cn

Abstract. With the rapid development of mobile technologies, developing high-quality mobile apps becomes increasingly important. App reviews, which are collaboratively collected from various users, are viewed as important sources for enhancing or evolving mobile apps, wherein how to accurately extract feature requests becomes an important issue. However, the scale of app reviews is so large that it is intractable to manually identify feature requests from these reviews. In this paper, we propose a semi-automated approach to extract feature requests based on machine learning approaches. In our approach, we firstly identify reviews on feature requests by defining suitable classification features and selecting appropriate classification approaches. Afterwards, these identified reviews are clustered using topic models, and phrases are extracted as feature requests, which serve as the basis of feature modeling. Experiments conducted on a real world data set show that the proposed approach can contribute to extracting feature requests from app reviews.

Keywords: Feature requests · App review · Classification · Word dependencies

1 Introduction

With the rapid development of mobile technologies, an increasing number of mobile apps have been developed and published. Similar to the traditional software development, the development of mobile apps also starts from requirements elicitation, where the quality of requirements plays a key role to assure the success of the software [1]. Since the approach of feature-oriented domain analysis (FODA) is proposed [2], the feature-oriented approach has been widely used in software development by software practitioners. According to IEEE standard glossary of software engineering terminology [3], a feature is defined as "a software characteristic specified or implied by requirements documentation". Due to the close relationship between requirements and features, extracting appropriate features will contribute to requirements elicitation, which will in turn promote the success of software development.

© ICST Institute for Computer Sciences, Social Informatics and Telecommunications Engineering 2017
S. Wang and A. Zhou (Eds.): CollaborateCom 2016, LNICST 201, pp. 312–323, 2017.
DOI: 10.1007/978-3-319-59288-6_28

Various sources can be used to extract feature requests. For example, online open forums have been used to elicit features by project managers [4,5]. Domain knowledge coming from domain experts can also be utilized to elicit features by recommending proper expert stakeholders [6,7]. In addition, descriptions of online software products can also be leveraged to elicit software features [8,9]. In particular, reviews can be viewed as a way for users to collaboratively propose feature requests for a certain mobile app. So many works have been conducted towards extracting feature requests from app reviews. For example, an unsupervised information extraction system named OPINES is proposed in [10], which builds a model of important product features by mining reviews. Various information retrieval techniques such as topic modeling are leveraged to extract topics and representative sentences of those topics from user comments, which will be used to revise requirements for next releases of software [11]. A prototype named mobile app review analyzer (MARA) for automatic retrieval of mobile app feature requests from app reviews is designed in [12]. As a whole, these approaches mainly leverage information retrieval techniques in identifying feature requests from user reviews and they do not classify app reviews in advance. An automated approach that helps developers filter, aggregate, and analyze user reviews is proposed in [13]. However, they mainly focus on sentiment analysis on reviews and feature requests mining is not the focus of their work. Several classification algorithms are compared in [14] to classify app reviews into four types: bug reports, feature requests, user experiences, and ratings. They comprehensively classify app reviews, but they do not consider the characteristics such as linguistic rules that are specific to feature requests.

An approach of extracting feature requests from app reviews is presented in this paper. We focus on how to select appropriate classification attributes and an optimal classification algorithm to identify feature requests from the app reviews. Specifically, various classification attributes such as bag of words, linguistic rules and metadata (e.g., rating, tenses and sentiment) are analyzed. Four classification algorithms including J48, Naive Bayes, Random Forest [15] and SVM (Support Vector Machine) [16] are compared to select an optimal classifier. Then LDA (latent Dirichlet allocation) [17] is used to cluster reviews on feature requests. Finally, phrases that represent feature requests are extracted by using the Stanford Parser [18], a tool that can generate word dependencies of sentences, based on the clustered topics and terms.

The main contributions of our work are as follows.

- An approach of extracting feature requests from app reviews is proposed. Various possible selected classification attributes from raw reviews and classification algorithms are discussed. In addition, we use LDA to cluster reviews on feature requests into various groups. Word dependencies are used to extract phrases that represent feature requests based on the clustered result.
- Experiments on a real world data set are conducted to identify reviews on feature requests and extract representative feature requests.

The remainder of the paper is organized as follows. Section 2 introduces feature requests extraction approach in detail. The evaluation of the proposed approach is discussed in Sect. 3. Section 4 discusses related work and we conclude the paper in Sect. 5.

2   Feature Requests Extraction

2.1   Overview of the Approach

An overview of the approach is described in Fig. 1, which mainly involves three steps:

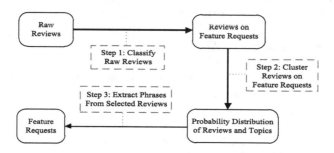

Fig. 1. Overview of feature requests extraction

Step 1: The objective of this step is to identify which reviews belong to feature requests using classification techniques. As depicted in Fig. 1, a classifier is trained by selecting appropriate classification attributes from these reviews. Then the classifier is utilized to predict whether unlabeled reviews belong to feature requests. To improve the prediction performance, it is important to select appropriate classification algorithms together with attributes.

Step 2: After raw reviews are classified, reviews on feature requests are clustered into semantically similar groups. Clustering algorithms have been widely used in mining features in the field of feature model extraction [8,9] and discovering Web service from text descriptions [19,20]. In this paper, LDA, a widely used topic model, is adopted to cluster these reviews based on identified latent topics.

Step 3: For each topic, the highly relevant reviews are selected, and then verb-noun phrases and noun phrases are extracted by analyzing from word dependencies of these selected reviews using the Stanford Parser. Finally, the phrases are filtered and selected as feature requests based on the relevance between its contained terms with the topic.

The extracted feature requests can be viewed as new requests of the mobile app, and therefore they can also serve as a basis of the mobile app evolution and the feature model change, which means that they will be developed or reused in the next release of the mobile app. Due to the space limitation, in this paper, we focus more on selecting appropriate classification algorithms and classification attributes.

2.2 Classification Attributes Selection

A review extracted from the Apple Store and the Google Play store [21] usually consists of the following attributes: app Id, review Id, review title, review comment, rating, reviewer, fee, date, and data source. However, not all the attributes are useful to train a classifier on identifying feature requests. Therefore it is necessary to select useful information from the review.

The title and comments are basic attributes of an app review, which can be treated as a document. In the document classification, bag of words (abbr. **BW**) are the basic classification attributes. The vectorization process of **BW** is usually described as follows: firstly a dictionary which includes all terms of reviews in the corpus is created; next, whether a term appears in the review and how often it appears is counted; and finally the *TF-IDF* of each term in a review is calculated. Some natural language processing techniques such as stop words removal and lemmatization are usually used during the process. In this paper, **BW** refers to bag of words together with stop words removal and lemmatization.

According to the analysis of the manually identified feature requests in the random sample described in [12], some keywords used for defining linguistic rules on feature requests have been identified in the title or comments. In order to reflect linguistic rules by using these keywords, they are classified into three categories: modal verbs (*abbr.* **MV**), general verbs or nouns (*abbr.* **VN**), and preposition phrase (*abbr.* **PP**), as shown in Table 1.

Table 1. Keywords in reviews on feature requests

Part of speech	Keywords
MV	could, maybe, must, need, should, will, wish, want, would, please
VN	add, allow, complaint, hope, improve, lack, look forward to, miss, prefer, request, suggest, wait for
PP	if only, instead of

TF-IDF of each category is calculated to quantify the textual attributes. *TF* of a category in a review is the ratio between the number of keywords of the category occurred in the review and the total number of words in the review. *IDF* of a category in a review is a logarithm between the number of all reviews and the number of reviews containing any keyword of this category. *TF-IDF* of a category is the product of the *TF* and *IDF* score of the category. They are calculated using Eqs. (1), (2) and (3), respectively.

$$TF(c,r) = \frac{\sum_{k \in c} \# \ of \ k \ occurs \ in \ r}{\# \ of \ words \ in \ r}, \tag{1}$$

$$IDF(c) = log \frac{\# \ of \ reviews}{\sum_{k \in c} \# \ of \ reviews \ containing \ k}, \tag{2}$$

$$TF\text{-}IDF(c,r) = TF(c,r) \times IDF(c), \tag{3}$$

where, k represents a keyword in a category c (**MV**, **VN**, or **PP**) and r represents a review. In addition, we use **LR** to represent the combination of **MV**, **VN**, and **PP**.

The metadata such as star **rating**, **tenses** of the verbs, and reviewer **sentiment** can be extracted from app reviews. The star **rating** is a numeric value between 1 and 5 given by the reviewer, which will be used as a classification attribute. The **tenses** of verbs which occur in the review is also selected as a classification attribute because the future tense reflects a larger possibility on an enhancement of the app or a new feature request. Different from [14] which used past, present, and future tenses by part of speech tagging provided in NLP libraries, we only distinguish the future tense and the non-future tense in this paper. The reviewer **sentiment** reflects the positive and negative emotions of the reviewer [13]. Thelwall et al. [22] propose a fine-grained sentiment extraction approach, where one negative sentiment score in a scale of -5 to -1 and one positive score in a scale of 1 to 5 are assigned for each review. Similar to [13,14], an absolute score combined by negative and positive scores is used as a classification attribute.

2.3 Feature Requests Clustering and Extraction

As one of the most widely used topic models, LDA can be used to extract unobserved factors that capture the underlying domain semantics within the given documents. Once the reviews on feature requests are identified, LDA is leveraged to cluster these reviews on feature requests and identify the latent topics among them. More specifically, according to the distribution of topics in these reviews and the distribution of terms in topics generated by LDA, we can cluster the reviews where the highly relevant reviews on each topic are grouped together and we can also identify the highly relevant terms of each topic.

In our opinion, the feature requests can be represented in the form of verb-noun phrases, e.g., "update screen", or noun phrases, e.g., "picture upload". Next, we pay our attention to extracting this kind of feature requests from the clustered reviews.

Inspired by our previous work on service goal extraction [23], in this paper we leverage the Stanford Parser [18] to extract the feature requests. The Stanford Parser can be used to perform linguistic analysis of sentences contained by reviews. The main linguistic analysis result we used is word dependencies, which describe the binary relations between words within a sentence. For example, amod(option-2, File-1) and compound(upload-6, picture-5) are two word dependencies in the review "File option such as picture upload will be loved". Based on these two word dependencies, we can get two potential feature requests: *file option* and *picture upload*. The Stanford Parser provides about 50 word dependencies, where we currently use a subset of them to extract feature requests, as shown in Table 2.

For each topic, we can extract feature requests from the reviews that are highly relevant to the topic using the above mentioned approach. Note that not all the phrases extracted from the word dependencies will be appropriate feature

Table 2. Used word dependencies

Dependency	Definition	Usage
dobj	A noun phrase which is the (accusative) object of the verb	Identify a "verb-noun" pair in an active clause
nsubjpass	A noun phrase which is the syntactic subject of a passive clause	Identify a "verb-noun" pair in a passive clause
nn(compound)	Any noun that serves to modify the head noun	Identify a "noun-noun" pair in a clause
amod	Any adjectival phrase that serves to modify the meaning of the noun phrase	Identify a "adj-noun" pair in a clause

requests relevant to the topic. A phrase can be viewed as a candidate feature request relevant to a topic if and only if it contains at least one highly relevant term of that topic. These candidate feature requests can be ranked according to their frequencies in the topic and the probabilities of its contained terms over the topic. In this way, we can get the feature requests from the reviews.

3 Evaluation

In this section, we evaluated the proposed extraction approach by a series of experiments. All the experiments are conducted on a PC with 3.19 GHz Intel Core i3 CPU and 4 GB RAM, running Windows 7 OS.

3.1 Experiment Data

In the experiments, we used the data set provided in [14], which was extracted from the Apple AppStore[1] and the Google Play[2]. In the data set, each review has the attributes of comment text, title, app name, category, store, submission date, and username. Furthermore, the metadata such as star rating, tenses of verbs and sentiment of the reviews were also extracted. Moreover, the types of reviews were manually analyzed and labeled, which were set as the grounding truth. In the data set, due to the great effort of manually labeling, 1924 reviews were labeled, where 295 reviews were feature requests, 600 reviews were non-feature requests, and 1029 reviews were labeled as other types such as bug reports, user experiences and ratings.

3.2 Evaluation Indicator

In order to evaluate the performance of various classification algorithms under different classification attributes, the standard metrics *precision*, *recall* and *F-measure* are used. In this paper, *Precision* is the fraction of reviews that are correctly classified to feature requests. *Recall* is the fraction of reviews on

---

[1] https://itunes.apple.com/us/genre/ios/id36.
[2] https://play.google.com/store?hl=en.

feature requests which are classified correctly. *F-measure* is a harmonic mean function of *precision* and *recall*. They are calculated by Eqs. (4), (5), and (6), respectively.

$$precision = TP/(TP + FP),\tag{4}$$

$$recall = TP/(TP + FN),\tag{5}$$

$$F\text{-}measure = \frac{2 \times precision \times recall}{precision + recall},\tag{6}$$

where, *TP* is the number of reviews that are classified as feature requests and actually are feature requests. *FP* is the number of reviews that are classified as feature requests but actually are not feature requests. *FN* is the number of reviews that are classified into non-feature requests but actually belong to feature requests.

3.3   Results and Analysis

Firstly, a group of experiments are conducted in order to evaluate the performance of various classification algorithms under different classification attributes. The values of *precision, recall, F-measure* and execution time are compared by using various classification algorithms such as Naive Bayes, SVM, J48, and Random Forest under different classification attributes. In order to reduce the sensitivity of the data, the mean values of *precision* (*abbr. pre*), *recall* (*abbr. rec*), *F-measure* (*abbr. F1*) and the execution time (*abbr.* time)under equal scale of training and testing data were calculated for five times. Every time 75% of all the reviews labeled as feature and non-feature requests were randomly selected as training data and the remaining 25% reviews were selected as testing data. The result of this group of experiments is shown in Table 3 (please note that rat, ten and sen denotes rating, tenses and sentiment respectively).

As can be seen from Table 3, if BW is solely used as the classification attribute, *precision, recall* and *F-measure* of each classification algorithm is on the scale of 63.5% to 70.9%, 52.7% to 68.9% and 60.5% to 69.4%, respectively. Wherein, SVM can get the best *precision*, but its *recall* is the smallest. Naive Bayes can achieve the best classification results on the whole and its executing time is the shortest. Random Forest is suboptimum on the whole but its executing time is the longest. If LR is solely used as the classification attribute, we find that *precision,recall* and *F* -measure of each classifier is about 57.7%, 60.8%, and 59.2%, respectively. It is obvious that the *F-measure* of using BW is generally superior to that of using LR, but the executing time is the opposite. The reason is that BW consists of much more classification information meanwhile it has far more dimensions to compute for training a classifier. If BW and LR are used as classification attributes together, *precision, recall* and *F-measure* of each classifier are on the scale of 66.7% to 76.8%, 58.1% to 75.7%, and 65.6% to 75.2%, respectively. Four classifiers have the similar comparison of classification results with only BW being used as the classification attribute. Each algorithm can get better results by using both of them to show that BW and LR can get mutual supplement for training a classifier.

Table 3. Comparison of various algorithms under different attributes

Attributes	Naive Bayes				SVM			
	pre	*rec*	*F1*	time/s	*pre*	*rec*	*F1*	time/s
BW	0.699	0.689	0.694	0.05	0.709	0.527	0.605	0.2
BW + rat	0.697	0.716	0.707	0.05	0.707	0.554	0.621	0.22
BW + rat + ten	0.74	0.76	0.75	0.05	0.758	0.642	0.695	0.23
BW + rat + ten + sen	0.76	0.77	0.765	0.05	0.778	0.662	0.715	0.26
LR	0.577	0.608	0.592	0.001	0.577	0.608	0.592	0.05
LR + rat	0.609	0.598	0.603	0.001	0.587	0.608	0.597	0.08
LR + rat + ten	0.632	0.618	0.625	0.001	0.736	0.519	0.609	0.09
LR + rat + ten + sen	0.639	0.622	0.63	0.001	0.75	0.527	0.619	0.18
BW + LR	0.747	0.757	0.752	0.05	0.768	0.581	0.662	0.26
BW + LR + rat	0.757	0.757	0.757	0.06	0.808	0.568	0.667	0.27
BW + LR + rat + ten	0.816	0.816	0.816	0.06	0.845	0.703	0.767	0.32
BW + LR + rat + ten + sen	**0.824**	**0.824**	**0.824**	**0.09**	0.852	0.703	0.77	0.4
Attributes	J48				Random Forest			
	pre	*rec*	*F1*	time/s	*pre*	*rec*	*F1*	time/s
BW	0.635	0.635	0.635	0.94	0.697	0.622	0.657	1.97
BW + rat	0.655	0.642	0.648	1	0.676	0.649	0.662	2.04
BW + rat + ten	0.737	0.651	0.691	1.06	0.73	0.622	0.672	2.88
BW + rat + ten + sen	0.742	0.662	0.7	1.1	0.771	0.73	0.75	3.01
LR	0.577	0.608	0.592	0.002	0.577	0.608	0.592	0.01
LR + rat	0.592	0.614	0.603	0.002	0.608	0.619	0.613	0.01
LR + rat + ten	0.706	0.681	0.693	0.003	0.687	0.622	0.652	0.02
LR + rat + ten + sen	0.718	0.689	0.703	0.01	0.71	0.662	0.685	0.03
BW + LR	0.749	0.584	0.656	0.89	0.667	0.649	0.658	1.78
BW + LR + rat	0.759	0.615	0.679	1.28	0.727	0.649	0.686	2.38
BW + LR + rat + ten	0.761	0.628	0.688	1.39	0.768	0.716	0.741	3.12
BW + LR + rat + ten + sen	0.772	0.643	0.702	2.18	0.809	0.743	0.775	5.74

Furthermore, adding the metadata such as rating, tenses and sentiment can effectively improve the performance of each classification algorithm. According to the results, using tenses can get better performance than using the other two because future tense and non-future tense are considered together. When LR and the metadata are used as classification attributes, J48 can get better *F-measure* than the other three since J48 is more suitable for the sample with the smaller size. SVM can often get the best *precision*, but its *recall* is almost the lowest, so its *F-measure* is not so good. The performance of Random Forest is rather moderate and its execution time is the longest. The performance of Naive Bayes is superior to other classifiers if BW is used as one of classification attributes. When BW, LR and metadata are used as classification attributes, Naive Bayes can get the best results and both of its *precision* and *recall* can reach 82.4%. Additionally, the executing time of Naive Bayes is the shortest.

Table 4. Some topics and representative terms

Topics / Terms	1	2	3	4	5
1	download$^{(0.031)}$	game$^{(0.053}$	give$^{(0.032)}$	love$^{(0.042)}$	update$^{(0.077)}$
2	note$^{(0.023)}$	fix$^{(0.050)}$	add$^{(0.032)}$	file$^{(0.032)}$	work$^{(0.043)}$
3	make$^{(0.020)}$	time$^{(0.030)}$	star$^{(0.027)}$	option$^{(0.027)}$	screen$^{(0.026)}$
4	version$^{(0.020)}$	play$^{(0.026)}$	feature$^{(0.021)}$	picture$^{(0.020)}$	open$^{(0.026)}$
5	way$^{(0.017)}$	phone$^{(0.026)}$	button$^{(0.019)}$	upload$^{(0.018)}$	video$^{(0.023)}$

Afterwards, LDA is conducted on the reviews on feature requests. Table 4 depicts some topics and top five representative terms in each topic. Wherein, each column represents a topic and each row shows terms and their probabilities in the corresponding topics.

Finally, for each topic, phrases are extracted from the clustered reviews by using the Stanford Parser. The top ranked feature requests in the data set are as follows: *update screen, fix game, game phone, add button, file download, open video, file option, picture upload, easy way,* and *proper version.* Clearly most of the identified feature requests are meaningful and can help requirements analysts in identifying new evolution requirements from app reviews. On the other hand, some resulting feature requests such as *easy way* and *proper version* are not satisfactory. How to further improve the identified feature requests using more word dependencies and more filtering rules will be our future work.

3.4 Threats to Validity

With respect to the internal validity, the main threat is that the proposed approach mainly considers various classification algorithms under different classification attributes for identifying whether a review belongs to feature requests. But it is also important to select proper clustering algorithms for grouping similar reviews into feature requests.

Threats to external validity concern the selection of keywords that occur in the reviews on feature requests. Since only some familiar keywords are selected for training a classifier, the value of recall is not high. Additionally, the scale of the experiments data needs to be extended. Due to the difficulty of getting the truth of the type of the app reviews by manually labeling, we only select 1924 reviews for the experiments. It inevitably limits the verification experiments on the performance of the classification algorithms.

4 Related Work

Many works have been presented to extract feature requests. Laurent et al. [5] explore the use of online forums to conduct the requirements engineering tasks of the open source projects which was led by the software vendor. Castro-Herrera et al. [6] present a hybrid recommender system to identify potential users who might be capable of responding to unanswered posts in open source forums. Castro-Herrera et al. [7] utilize the organizer and promoter of collaborative ideas (OPCI) recommendation system to recommend expert stakeholders of the field and the requirements are elicited by means of the domain knowledge from these expert stakeholders. These approaches focus on the problem of finding the proper stakeholders to participate in the process of requirements elicitation. Hariri et al. [8] and Dumitru et al. [9] leverage the data mining techniques to extract the common features from online products description and design a recommender system to elicit missing features.

App reviews have also been used to extract feature requests. Popescu et al. [10] introduce an unsupervised information extraction system named OPINE to build a model of important product features. Galvis Carreo et al. [11] adapt topic modeling from user comments to extract the topics mentioned and some sentences representative of those topics. These approaches do not consider sentiment of the user and they do not address the problem of the mis-classification or mix of topics. Iacob et al. [12] design a prototype named mobile app review analyzer (MARA) to automatic retrieve mobile app feature requests from app reviews, where they manually define linguistic rules and identify feature requests from reviews which match at least one linguistic rule. Because only part of the linguistic rules are listed in their paper, it is difficult to quantitatively compare their approach with ours. Their approach needs much manual labors and the output of their approach is the corresponding keywords relevant to the feature requests. In our approach, we use linguistic rules and bag of words as classification attributes to train a classifier for identifying reviews on feature requests. We also use the Stanford Parser to extract phrases to represent feature requests, which can be easily understood by users. Guzman et al. [13] propose an automated approach that helps developers filter, aggregate, and analyze user reviews. But they mainly focus on the emotion analysis on reviews and feature requests mining is not their research task. Maalej et al. [14] introduce several probabilistic techniques such as string matching, text classification, NLP (Natural Language Processing) and sentiment analysis, and compare the classification algorithms including Naive Bayes, Decision Tree and maximum entropy (MaxEnt) to classify app reviews into four types: bug reports, feature requests, user experiences, and ratings. They classify app reviews comprehensively, but they do not consider the characteristics such as linguistic rules only for feature requests. In contrast to their works, we add linguistic rules besides bag of words and metadata as classification attributes to identify the reviews on feature requests. Furthermore, we adopt the Stanford Parser to extract representative phrases as feature requests based on clustered topics and top relevant terms of each topic.

5   Conclusion and Future Work

An approach of extracting feature requests from app reviews is proposed in this paper. The approach can be applied in the early stage of software requirements engineering, which can be a supplement for mining features from the description of mobile apps. In order to accurately extract feature requests from reviews, it is important to identify whether a review belongs to feature requests. Therefore, different classification algorithms are compared under various classification attributes, which are validated by leveraging a real world data set of reviews from the AppleStore and the Google Play stores. In addition, phrases that represent feature requests are extracted by using word dependencies based on the clustered reviews.

In the future, we plan to extend our work from the following directions. Firstly, we will further investigate how to extract more meaningful phrases as feature requests from reviews. Secondly, we plan to evaluate the performance of various classification algorithms under different classification attributes when the experimental data set grows to a larger scale.

Acknowledgments. The work is supported by the National Basic Research Program of China under grant No. 2014CB340404, and the National Key Research and Development Program of China under grant No. 2016YFB0800400, and the National Natural Science Foundation of China under Nos. 61672387, 61373037, 61572186 and 61562073. The authors would like to thank anonymous reviewers for their valuable suggestions.

References

1. Tiwari, S., Rathore, S.S., Gupta, A.: Selecting requirement elicitation techniques for software projects. In: the CSI 6th IEEE International Conference on Software Engineering (CONSEG), pp. 1–10. IEEE Press, New York (2012)
2. Kang, K.C., Cohen, S.G., Hess, J.A., Novak, W.E., Peterson, A.S.: Feature-oriented domain analysis (FODA) feasibility study. Technical report, Carnegie Mellon University (1990)
3. Radatz, J., Geraci, A., Katki, F.: IEEE Standard Glossary of Software Engineering Terminology. IEEE Std **610121990**(121990): 3 (1990)
4. Cleland-Huang, J., Dumitru, H., Duan, C., Castro-Herrera, C.: Automated support for managing feature requests in open forums. Commun. ACM **52**(10), 68–74 (2009)
5. Laurent, P., Cleland-Huang, J.: Lessons learned from open source projects for facilitating online requirements processes. In: Glinz, M., Heymans, P. (eds.) REFSQ 2009. LNCS, vol. 5512, pp. 240–255. Springer, Heidelberg (2009). doi:10.1007/978-3-642-02050-6_21
6. Castro-Herrera, C.: A hybrid recommender system for finding relevant users in open source forums. In: 3rd IEEE International Workshop on Managing Requirements Knowledge, pp. 41–50. IEEE Press, New York (2010)
7. Castro-Herrera, C., Cleland-Huang, J., Mobasher, B.: Enhancing stakeholder profiles to improve recommendations in online requirements elicitation. In: Proceedings of the 17th IEEE International Conference on Requirements Engineering, pp. 37–46. IEEE Press, New York (2009)

8. Hariri, N., Castro-Herrera, H., Mirakhorli, M., Cleland-Huang, J.: Supporting domain analysis through mining and recommending features from online product listings. IEEE Trans. Softw. Eng. **39**(12), 1736–1752 (2013)

9. Dumitru, H., Gibiec, M., Hariri, N., Cleland-Huang, J., Mobasher, B., Castro-Herrera, C., Mirakhorli, M.: On-demand feature recommendations derived from mining public product descriptions. In: Proceedings of the 33rd IEEE International Conference on Software Engineering, pp. 181–190. IEEE Press, New York (2011)

10. Popescu, A.M., Etzioni, O.: Extracting product features and opinions from reviews. In: Anne, K., Stephen, R. (eds.) Natural Language Processing and Text Mining, pp. 9–28. Springer, London (2007)

11. Galvis Carreño, L.V., Winbladh, K.: Analysis of user comments: an approach for software requirements evolution. In: Proceedings of the 35th IEEE International Conference on Software Engineering, pp. 582–591. IEEE Press, New York (2013)

12. Iacob, C., Harrison, R.: Retrieving and analyzing mobile apps feature requests from online reviews. In: Proceedings of the 10th IEEE Working Conference on Mining Software Repositories (MSR 2013), pp. 41–44. IEEE Press, New York (2013)

13. Guzman, E., Maalej, W.: How do users like this feature? A fine grained sentiment analysis of App. reviews. In: Proceedings of the 22nd IEEE International Conference on Requirements Engineering, pp. 153–162. IEEE Press, New York (2014)

14. Maalej, W., Nabil, H.: Bug report, feature request, or simply praise? On automatically classifying app reviews. In: Proceedings of the 23rd IEEE International Conference on Requirements Engineering, pp. 116–125. IEEE Press, New York (2015)

15. Torgo, L.: Data Mining with R: Learning with Case Studies. Chapman & Hall/CRC, Boca Raton (2010)

16. Chang, C.C., Lin, C.J.: LIBSVM: a library for support vector machines. ACM Trans. Intell. Syst. Technol. (TIST) **2**(3), 271–2727 (2011)

17. Blei, D.M., Ng, A.Y., Jordan, M.I.: Latent Dirichlet allocation. J. Mach. Learn. Res. **3**, 993–1022 (2003)

18. Chen, D., Manning, C.D.: A fast and accurate dependency parser using neural networks. In: 2014 Conference on Empirical Methods in Natural Language Processing, pp. 740–750 (2014)

19. Wu, J., Chen, L., Zheng, Z., Lyu, M., Wu, Z.: Clustering web services to facilitate service discovery. Knowl. Inf. Syst. **38**(1), 207–229 (2014)

20. Chen, L., Wang, Y., Yu, Q., Zheng, Z., Wu, J.: WT-LDA: user tagging augmented LDA for web service clustering. In: Basu, S., Pautasso, C., Zhang, L., Fu, X. (eds.) ICSOC 2013. LNCS, vol. 8274, pp. 162–176. Springer, Heidelberg (2013). doi:10. 1007/978-3-642-45005-1_12

21. Pagano D., Maalej, W.: User feedback in the appstore: an empirical study. In: Proceedings of the 21st International Conference on Requirements Engineering, pp. 125–134. IEEE Press, New York (2013)

22. Thelwall, M., Buchley, K., Paltoglou, G.: Sentiment strength detection for the social web. J. Am. Soc. Inf. Sci. Technol. **63**(1), 163–173 (2012)

23. Wang, J., Zhang, N., Zeng, C., Li, Z., He, K.: Towards services discovery based on service goal extraction and recommendation. In: 2013 IEEE International Conference on Services Computing, pp. 65–72. IEEE Press, New York (2013)

QoS Prediction Based on Context-QoS Association Mining

Yang Hu[1,2(✉)], Qibo Sun[1], and Jinglin Li[1]

[1] State Key Laboratory of Networking and Switching Technology,
Beijing University of Posts and Telecommunications, Beijing, China
{hu.yang, qbsun, jlli}@bupt.edu.cn
[2] Science and Technology on Information Transmission and Dissemination
in Communication Networks Laboratory, Beijing, China

Abstract. Both the functional properties and the non-functional properties (known as quality of service, QoS) should be considered when recommending services. In mobile environment, the services are referred to under different contexts. Context-aware collaborative filtering is often employed to predict the QoS of candidate services when a user submits a service request. Existing collaborative filtering based methods seldom analyze the actual impact of each context property on the QoS properties in context-similarity mining. To address the problem, we propose a QoS prediction method based on the context-QoS association mining in this paper. The method is composed of two steps. We firstly propose an algorithm to mine the association between the context and the QoS properties. Then, a QoS prediction approach is proposed by taking the association and the context similarity into consideration. To study the effectiveness of our approach, we experiment on real world dataset. Experimental results show that our proposed method can improve the accuracy of QoS prediction.

Keywords: Web services · Mobile service · QoS · Context

1 Introduction

With the increase of the Web service providers, more and more Web services continue to be published. Therefore, many services could meet the functional requirements of the user. As a result, the user tends to prefer the Web service with the best Quality of Service performance [1]. QoS has become the key factor in service selection and service recommendation [2].

Collaborative filtering is widely used in QoS prediction by many Web services recommendation methods [3, 4]. Collaborative filtering is a very effectiveness mechanism in selecting the service with the optimal QoS values. In early collaborative filtering-based approaches, the contexts when the service is invoked are rarely taken care of.

In mobile environment, the services are referred to under different context. The QoS performance varies when the mobile Web service is invoked under different context. The context properties should be considered in QoS prediction for a specific user [5, 6]. Context-aware collaborative filtering-based methods are proposed to address the problem [7]. These web service QoS prediction methods work by collecting user observed QoS records and matching together users who invoke the web services under similar context. In others words, the users who refer to the service under similar context would have similar QoS experiences. Therefore, the QoS values are predicted based on the QoS data of the users with similar context.

However, current context-aware collaborative filtering-based methods assume that the QoS values are affected by many context properties [8]. Actually, some context properties may have strong correlation to the Web service QoS performance, while other context properties may have weak or no correlation to QoS performance. However, current methods are lack of accurate association analysis.

To address the problem, we propose a context-aware QoS prediction approach based on context-QoS association mining (QPAM). Our approach mainly consists of two steps. Firstly, we mine the association between the context properties and the QoS properties as a fundamental step for further work of QoS prediction. Secondly, we predict the QoS values of candidate service for current user based on the results of step 1. We filter out the irrelevant context properties so that the accuracy of prediction would not be affected. We experiment on real world dataset to study the effectiveness of our method. Experimental results show that our proposed method can improve the accuracy of QoS prediction.

The main contribution of this paper includes: (1) context-QoS mining to get the relevant context properties and filter out the irrelevant context properties. (2) a context-aware QoS prediction approach based on Context-QoS association mining to improve accuracy of QoS prediction.

The rest of paper is organized as follows. Section 2 introduces the related work. Section 3 defines some notations and describes the overview of our method. Section 4 describes the technical detail of our method. Section 5 shows the experimental results. Section 6 concludes the whole paper and presents future work finally.

2 Related Work

Considering that there are plenty of functionally equivalent candidates, the QoS performance plays a vital role in service selecting. A large number of QoS-aware methods has been employed in service recommendation [9]. Chen et al. [10] introduced a map containing visualized information regarding QoS among the recommended services, so that the service consumers can understand the service performance better.

The definitions of context and context-awareness are various. Dey [11] defined context as an information such as location, date, time, nearby things and nearby people and the situation of an entity is characterized by the information. The Web service QoS performance has strong correlation to some user contexts i.e. time interval, location. And they take the user contexts into account when predicting QoS values and selecting the optimal Web services. Chen et al. [12] proposed a LoRec (location-aware Web service recommender) system by employing the location information to improve the accuracy of the QoS prediction. Yu et al. [8] presented a time-aware Collaborative Filtering algorithm to predict the QoS values, by calculating the similarity between service users and candidates at different time intervals. Tang et al. [13] proposed a collaborative filtering algorithm base on location awareness to recommend Web services to the current user. Yu presented that the picture conversion service has low QoS performance at the intervals during which a discount is provided [8]. Tang presented that weather forecast services has relationship with the location so it is helpful to recommend the current user services through users with similar locations [13].

The service recommendation methods based on context-awareness are usually combined with the CF (collaborative filtering)–based methods.CF finds similar users or items and recommend items by employing information from them to the current user [14]. Zheng et al. [3] presented a collaborative filtering method based on the past experiences of collaborative service users by employing data from similar service users who have similar experience with the current service user. Jiang et al. [15] described an algorithm combining personalized user-based and item-based collaborative filtering called PHCF (Personalized Hybrid Collaborative Filtering) to recommend the current service user the optimal Web services accurately.

The above methods only assume that the QoS values are affected by many context properties. Actually, some context properties may have strong correlation to the Web service QoS performance, while other context properties may have weak or no correlation to QoS performance. There, current methods are lack of accurate association analysis. We will address the problem in this paper.

3   Overview

3.1   Problem Definition

Definition 1: Service.
Service set $S = \{s_1, s_2, \cdots, s_k\}$ is a set of functional equivalent mobile services that meets the need of the current user. The service set contains k services.

Definition 2: Users.
User $U = \{u_1, u_2, \cdots, u_l\}$ is a set of users that have invoked services at least once. The user set contains l users.

Definition 3: QoS properties.
QoS properties $Q = \{q_1, q_2, \cdots, q_m\}$ is a set of quality properties that is invoked by service users. Q contains m properties.

Definition 4: Context properties.
Context $C = \{c_1, c_2, \cdots, c_n\}$ is the set of context attributes of users that has invoked at least one services in S. The set contains n context properties. Context properties include location, time, season, temperature, network environment etc.

Definition 5: Record.
$R_{ij} = \left\{ < \left(q_1^{ij}, q_2^{ij}, \cdots, q_m^{ij}\right), \left(c_1^{ij}, c_2^{ij}, \cdots, c_n^{ij}\right) > \right\}$ is the set of historical service invocation records. R_{ij} is the service invocation record of s_i is invoked by u_j.

3.2 Framework of Our Method

Figure 1 shows the framework of our method. Our method mainly consists of two phases. The first phase is context-QoS association mining. This phase consists of two sub-phases: QoS-based service clustering and association mining. The second phase is QoS prediction based on mining results. This phase also consists of two sub-phases: properties filtering and QoS prediction.

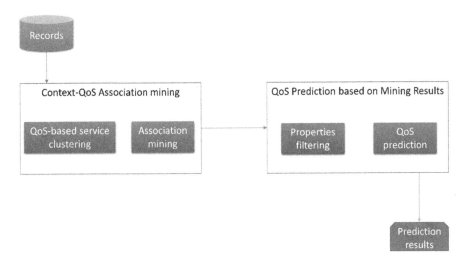

Fig. 1. Framework of our method

We will describe the technical detail of our proposed method in the next section.

4 Methodology

4.1 Context-QoS Association Mining

In this section, we analyze the association between each QoS property and each context property. Suppose R_i denotes all records that are related to service s_i. We now cluster the records based on QoS. To cluster the records, the distance between two records R_{i1} and R_{i2} on QoS property q_j can be calculated by the following:

$$Sim_{q_j}(R_{i1}, R_{i2}) = |R_{i1}.q_j - R_{i2}.q_j|. \tag{1}$$

Based on the calculation of distance between two records, we now mine the invocation records to obtain the context-QoS association. The algorithm is illustrated in Algorithm 1. Firstly, we cluster all records of a specific service s_i in the candidate services by using K-means clustering. Then, for each context property c_k, we calculate the overlapping degree between any two clusters g_1 and g_2. The values of the context property c_k are divided into a group of interval partitions $P = \{p_1, p_2, p_3 \ldots\}$. We now construct a vector $V_{gn} = \left\{ v_{gn}^1, v_{gn}^2, \ldots \right\}$ for each cluster g_n. The value of v_{gn}^1 is the number of records R_{gn} in g_n that the value of $R_{gn}.c_k$ belongs to p_1. We define the overlapping degree between any two clusters to measure the similarity between them. The overlapping degree is based on calculating vector similarity of two clusters. The overlapping degree between any two clusters g_1 and g_2 is calculated by the following:

$$degree(g_1, g_2) = \frac{V_{g1} * V_{g2}}{|V_{g1}| * |V_{g2}|} * e^{\varphi - 1}, \tag{2}$$

$$V_{g1} * V_{g2} = \sum_i v_{g1}^i * v_{g2}^i, \tag{3}$$

$$|V_{g1}| * |V_{g2}| = \sqrt{\sum_i v_{g1}^{i2}} * \sqrt{\sum_i v_{g2}^{i2}}, \tag{4}$$

$$\varphi = \frac{||V_{g1}| - |V_{g2}||}{||V_{g1}| + |V_{g2}||}, \tag{5}$$

$$|V_{g1}| \pm |V_{g2}| = \sqrt{\sum_i v_{g1}^{i2}} \pm \sqrt{\sum_i v_{g2}^{i2}}, \tag{6}$$

$$\bar{d} = \sum_{m,n} \varpi_{mn} * degree(g_m, g_n), \tag{7}$$

$$\varpi_{mn} = \frac{\sum_i v_{gm}^i * \sum_i v_{gn}^i}{\sum_{m,n} \sum_i v_{gm}^i * \sum_i v_{gn}^i}. \tag{8}$$

After we calculate the overlapping degree between any two clusters. Then, we calculate the average overlapping degree $\bar{d}$ of service S_i based on Eq. (7). The weight ϖ_{mn} of the overlapping degree between any two clusters is calculated in Eq. (8). If the average overlapping degree is smaller than σ, we consider the context property has impact on the QoS. Otherwise, the context property has no impact on the QoS.

Through context-QoS association mining, we can obtain $CI = \{ci_1, ci_2, ..., ci_{max}\}$. As we known, CI is a set of context properties that has impact on QoS property q_i.

4.2 QoS Prediction

After obtain the context-QoS association, the context properties that have impact on QoS are utilized for service recommendation. Euclidean distance is adopted by us to calculate The distance between two records r_1 and r_2 based on context properties. The distance between r_1 and r_2 in max context property dimensions is calculated by the following:

$$sim(r_1, r_2) = \sqrt{\sum_{ci \in CI} (r_1.c_i - r_2.c_i)^2} \tag{9}$$

Based on the calculation of distance between two services, we cluster all candidate services by using K-means clustering to predict the QoS values.

The algorithm consists of the following steps:

Step 1: Construct a virtual record Rv. The $CI\psi$ values of $Rv\psi$ are assigned according to the context environment of current user. Add $Rv\psi$ to *WSR*.

Step 2: Select $k\psi$ records from $WSR\psi$ as the centroids.

Step 3: Assign each record in the set $WSR\psi$ to the nearest centroid.

Step 4: $k\psi$ new centroids are calculated based on the clusters obtained from the previous step.

Step 5: Repeat steps 2 and 3 until all sub-clusters are stable. In other words, all centroids no longer move.

Step 6: Search for the sub-cluster C which $Rv\psi$ belongs to.

Step 7: The average values on q_i of the records in C is the prediction results.

Through the above seven steps, we can predict the QoS values.

Algorithm 1. Association mining algorithm

Input: all the record list R on a specific service, a QoS
     property q_j, a context property c_k

Output: the association between q_j and c_k

---

1 **For** R , select init k records as centrioles and assign the records to *tempCentrioList*;

2 **while** ! is stable **do**

3   *centrioList* = *tempCentrioList*;

4   **for each** r in R **do**

5   *bestCentri-> distance* $= \infty$;

6   **for each** *centri* in *centrioList* **do**

7   *distance* = *sim(r, centri)*;

8   **if** *bestCentri -> distance > distance* **then**

9   *bestCentri -> distance = distance*;

10   *bestCentri -> class = centri -> tag*;

11   **end**

12   **end**

13   *categoryList[bestCentri->class]*.Add(*r*);

14   **end**

15   relocate centriole based on categoryList, *centrioList* ;

16   assign the new centrioles to *tempCentrioList*;

17 **end**

18 Calculate the overlapping degree between any two clusters;

19 Calculate the average degree;

20 **If** the *average degree* $< \sigma$ **then**

21   return true;

22 **end**

23 **else**

24   return false;

25 **end**

5 Experiment

5.1 Experimental Setup

A set of experiments are conducted on the dataset WSDream published by Z. Zheng et al. Because we are the first to mine the context-QoS association, we compare our method with the RANDOM method. RADNOM refers to a set of methods that lack accurate association analysis when predicting the value of each QoS property based the context aware collaborative filtration, such as location-aware method [13] etc. Different from our method, RANDOM randomly decides whether a QoS property is affected by a context property. We use AE (the average error) to evaluate the QoS prediction accuracy. The definition of AE is demonstrated by the following:

$$AE = \frac{\sum_{i=0}^{N} \left| q_{prediction,i} - q_{real,i} \right|}{N}, \tag{10}$$

where $q_{prediction}$ denotes the predicted value of the QoS property q_j and q_{real} denotes the actual value of the QoS attribute q_j. σ is set to 0.4 in our experiments.

5.2 Performance Evaluation

We randomly select 12 services from WSDream for response-time prediction and select 12 services from WSDream for throughout prediction. For each service, the related records store the response-time, the throughout, the time, and the interval ID etc. The records are divided into two sets: the training set and the test set.

Figure 2 shows the AE of the response-time prediction. Figure 3 shows the AE of the throughout prediction. It is evident that our method can reduce the prediction error based on mining the association between each QoS property and each context property.

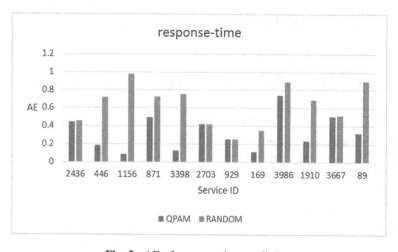

Fig. 2. AE of response-time prediction

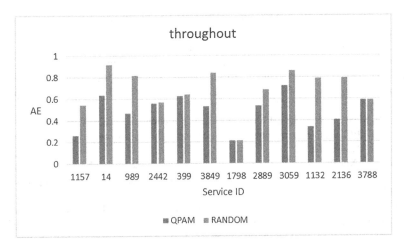

Fig. 3. AE of throughput prediction

RANDOM randomly decides whether a QoS property is affected by a context property. There is a higher chance that an important context property is ignored or an irrelevant context property is taken into consideration. Therefore, our method show a higher accuracy.

6 Conclusion and Future Work

We proposed a mobile service recommendation approach based on context-QoS association mining. The approach employs a context-QoS association mining algorithm and a recommendation algorithm to improve the accuracy of context-aware QoS prediction. The experiment results on WS-Dream dataset show the proposed method improves predictive accuracy and outperforms the compared methods.

Our future work will include (1) introduce other factors (trust, social information) to achieve better accuracy of recommendation; and (2) employ user preference to provide personalized services recommendation.

Acknowledgment. This work was supported by Science and Technology on Information Transmission and Dissemination in Communication Networks Laboratory. The research was supported by NSFC (61571066).

References

1. Ma, Y., Wang, S., Yang, F., Chang, R.N.: Predicting QoS values via multi-dimensional QoS data for web service recommendations. In: 2015 IEEE 22nd International Conference on Web Services, pp. 249–256 (2015)
2. Tao, C.H., Feng, Z.Y.: Novel QoS-aware web service recommendation model. Appl. Res. Comput. **27**, 3898–3902 (2010)

3. Zheng, Z., Ma, H., Lyu, M.R., King, I.: QoS-aware web service recommendation by collaborative filtering. IEEE Trans. Serv. Comput. **4**, 140–152 (2011)
4. Wu, X., Cheng, B., Chen, J.: Collaborative filtering service recommendation based on a novel similarity computation method. IEEE Trans. Serv. Comput. **5**, 1–11 (2015)
5. Xiao, H., Zou, Y., Ng, J., Nigul, L.: An approach for context-aware service discovery and recommendation. In: 2010 IEEE 17th International Conference on Web Services, pp. 163–170 (2010)
6. Liu, D., Meng, X.W., Chen, J.L.: A framework for context-aware service recommendation. In: 2008 IEEE 10th International Conference on Advanced Communication Technology, pp. 2131–2134 (2008)
7. Kuang, L., Xia, Y., Mao, Y.: Personalized services recommendation based on context-aware QoS prediction. In: 2012 IEEE 19th International Conference on Web Services, pp. 400–406 (2012)
8. Yu, C., Huang, L.: Time-aware collaborative filtering for QoS-based service recommendation. In: 2014 IEEE 21st International Conference on Web Services, pp. 265–272 (2014)
9. Moraru, A., Fortuna, C., Fortuna, B., Slavescu, R.R.: A hybrid approach to QoS-aware web service classification and recommendation. In: 2009 IEEE 5th International Conference on Intelligent Computer Communication and Processing, pp. 343–346 (2009)
10. Chen, X., Zheng, Z., Liu, X., Huang, Z., Sun, H.: Personalized QoS-aware web service recommendation and visualization. IEEE Trans. Serv. Comput. **6**, 35–47 (2013)
11. Dey, A.K.: Providing architectural support for building context-aware applications. Elementary Education, 25, pp. 106–111 (2000)
12. Chen, X., Zheng, Z., Yu, Q., Lyu, M.R.: Web service recommendation via exploiting location and QoS information. IEEE Trans. Parallel Distrib. Syst. **25**, 1913–1924 (2014)
13. Tang, M., Jiang, Y., Liu, J., Liu, X.: Location-aware collaborative filtering for QoS-based service recommendation. In: 2012 IEEE 19th International Conference on Web Services, pp. 202–209 (2012)
14. Herlocker, J.L., Konstan, J.A., Borchers, A., Riedl, J.: An algorithmic framework for performing collaborative filtering. In: International ACM SIGIR Conference on Research & Development in Information Retrieval, pp. 230–237 (1999)
15. Jiang, Y., Liu, J., Tang, M., Liu, X.: An effective web service recommendation method based on personalized collaborative filtering. In: 2013 IEEE 20th International Conference on Web Services, pp. 211–218 (2013)

Collaborate Algorithms for the Multi-channel Program Download Problem in VOD Applications

Wenli Zhang, Lin Yang, Kepi Zhang, and Chao Peng[(✉)]

School of Computer Science and Software Engineering,
East China Normal University, 3663 Zhongshan North Road, Shanghai 200062, China
{51141500065,51141500051,51141500059}@ecnu.cn, cpeng@sei.ecnu.edu.cn

Abstract. Video-on-demand (VOD) is a multimedia technology that allows users to watch video programs from a server flexibly at any time. In recent years, VOD applications are very popular in many networks, especially in internet of vehicles where video programs can often be collaboratively downloaded from multiple channels simultaneously. In this paper, we first study the Multi-Channel Program Download Problem (McPDP), which is to download a set of interested programs from different channels within limited time. We prove that McPDP is NP-complete by reduction from 3-SAT(3). For another version with neatly placed programs of equal length, the aligned multi-channel program download problem (AMcPDP), we present an algorithm by transforming it into a max-flow problem. Finally, we have also analyzed the performance of these proposed algorithms by simulation using MATLAB.

Keywords: Video-on-demand · Multi-channel Program Download Problem · NP-complete · Scheduling algorithms

1 Introduction

The last decades have witnessed the prevalence of multimedia technology, which has many different content forms, such as images, text, audio, animation and video. With the rapid development of science and technology, it has penetrated into all aspects of the national economy and improved the quality of our life. In recent years, more and more video services have become our research hotspots, especially, the video-on-demand (VOD) technology [1,2]. A VOD system allows users to watch video programs from a sever flexibly at any time, it is usually in a client-server architecture supported by certain transport networks such as cable TV systems (CATV) [3], LAN and community antenna television systems [4]. In a VOD system, a server will broadcast segments of a set of programs periodically in several channels. A group of clients can be served simultaneously, and will download their interested programs from channels if their local storage can accommodate [5–7]. Programs will be downloaded into the local storage of the client, and then the client can watch programs at any time without a break.

© ICST Institute for Computer Sciences, Social Informatics and Telecommunications Engineering 2017
S. Wang and A. Zhou (Eds.): CollaborateCom 2016, LNICST 201, pp. 333–342, 2017.
DOI: 10.1007/978-3-319-59288-6_30

The research objective of VOD, no matter the server side or the client side, is to find the fastest way collaboratively to download and watch interested programs as soon as possible. In recent years, much attention has been paid to broadcasting protocols on the server side. In [8], the authors develop an optimal bandwidth allocation algorithm for hybrid VoD streaming. This paper proposes a novel Demand Driven Max-Flow Formulation, which treats each peers bandwidth demand as the flow commodity. Authors in [5] present a permutation based pyramid scheme in which the storage requirements and disk transfer rates are greatly reduced, and yet the viewer latency is smaller as well. But they usually focus only on the tradeoff between bandwidth and delay, thus they are usually not efficient for the local storage. Authors in [4] proposed some new effective broadcasting protocols, which can intelligently adjust the solution according to available bandwidth and local storage to achieve an ideal waiting time. As for client side, authors in [9] presented a Program Download Problem (PDP) which is to download a set of desired programs from channels. But their assumption is that client can only download programs from one channel at one time. A client has to switch between different channels since his/her interested programs might be broadcasted in them.

However, this assumption may be inconsistent with the actual situation. For example, in vehicular networks [10], the Road Side Unit (RSU) plays the server role. It will keep broadcasting data, such as advertisements, local weather forecast, traffic situation etc. in multiple channels. Clients (video equipment in vehicles) within a range will be connected to the channel via wireless networks. To avoid the unnecessary waste of bandwidth, multiple channels downloading can be implemented by using MIMO technology [11]. But, many other factors such as limited buffer and conflicts in the client side should be considered, so it is necessary for us to find efficient algorithms to schedule the downloading process [12–15].

The remainder of this paper is organized as follows. Section 2 defines the Multi-Channel program download problem(McPDP) and proves McPDP is NP-Complete. In Sect. 3, the Aligned multi-channel program download problem(AMcPDP) is described, and we present an algorithm to solve it. In Sect. 4, we implement all the algorithms with Matlab, and analyze their performance. Finally, Sect. 5 concludes the paper.

2   Complexity of the Multi-channel Program Download Problem

Definition 1. *In an instance of the Multi-Channel program download problem (McPDP), there is a channel set C which contains n channels, said $\{c_1, c_2, \cdots, c_n\}$. The server (such as an RSU) broadcasts a set of programs U in these channels, and each program segment might appear multiple times. Each client (such as a video equipment in a vehicle) within range may have a target set of programs $P(P \subseteq U)$ to be downloaded as soon as possible. We assume that each program segment has a unit time interval length. A client can download* *any program from its starting time, and may switch between different channels at the end of the program. (Switching between different channels may take some time, it is very short and can be ignored here.) A client can download programs from up to $k(k < n)$ channels simultaneously. For any given target program set and a corresponding deadline d, the multi-channel program download problem (McPDP) asks whether we can download all programs in this set before d, it will be denoted as $McPDP(n, k, d)$. Notice that there is no limit on the appearance times of a program in each channel, next we will analyze the complexity of McPDP.*

Theorem 1. *Multi-Channel program download problem (McPDP) is NP-complete [16].*

Proof. We will reduce a simple version $McPDP(2, 1, d)$ into $McPDP$ $(n, k, d)(k < n)$ and then prove that $McPDP(2, 1, d)$ is NP-Complete. Both $McPDP(n, k, d)$ and $McPDP(2, 1, d)$ are obviously in NP, as we can check whether a download schedule is a yes certificate or not in polynomial time.

The first reduction process is rather simple. Given an instance of $McPDP$ $(2, 1, d)$, we will add $n - 2$ channels, $k - 1$ reading heads and some programs to keep these $k - 1$ heads busy. To do this, we simply put $(k - 1) \cdot d$ different programs into $k - 1$ channels and we join these programs into the original target set to make the final target set P. Then we put a peg program into the remain $n - k - 1$ channels.

The above transformation process can be finished in polynomial time, and it is not difficult to find out that any solution of the original version is corresponding to exact one solution of the $McPDP(n, k, d)$ version. That is because the later one has to use $k - 1$ heads to download those newly added programs at any time, and only one head can be used to download those old programs inherited from the original target set located in the first 2 channels.

Thus a solution to $McPDP(n, k, d)$ can be easily changed into one of $McPDP(2, 1, d)$ and vice versa.

Next, we will reduce 3-SAT(3), a known NP-complete problem to $McPDP(2, 1, d)$ to prove its NP-completeness. 3-SAT(3) is a special case of 3-SAT where each clause includes 3 items at most, and every literal will appear three times exactly (twice positively and once negatively or vice versa).

Given an instance of 3-SAT(3), we suppose the input formula F contains N variables x_i $(1 \le i \le N)$ and M clauses $C_1, C_2, \ldots, C_M$. Then we will build a corresponding new instance of $McPDP(2, 1, d)$.

For each clause C_i, we construct a unit-length program C_i and all these programs will form the target set P. Next we construct two channels c and $\bar{c}$, and evenly divide the two channels into segments with length of 4 time units.

Since each variable x_i will appear exactly three times in F, there will be three corresponding clause programs. W.o.l.g., we assume that the F contains two x_is and one $\overline{x}_i$, x_i appears in clause C^{i1} and clause C^{i2} while $\overline{x}_i$ appears in clause C^{i3}. These three clauses correspond to three unit-time programs C^{i1}, C^{i2} and C^{i3} in the new instance. We will put C^{i1} and C^{i2} in channel c, starting at time $4 \times (i-1) + 0.5$ and $4 \times (i-1) + 1.5$, followed by a unit-time peg program P_i starting at $4 \times (i-1) + 3$. On the other hand, C^{i3} will be put in channel $\bar{c}$ starting at $4 \times (i-1) + 1$, also followed by a peg program P_i. The case of one x_i and two $\bar{x}_i$s can be similarly handled.

Notice that a client can only download one program at one moment in the new instance of $McPDP(2, 1, d)$. Thus, a client cannot download C^{i1}, C^{i2} and C^{i3} in the meanwhile.

Now we will show that the formula F is satisfiable if and only if all the programs in P can be downloaded before deadline $d = 4n$.

($\rightarrow$) At first, we will show that formula F is satisfiable then all the programs in P can be downloaded by time $d = 4n$. Given a truth assignment of the formula F, for each clause C_i there will be at least one variable x_j in C_i that makes it true. So the client in $McPDP(2, 1, d)$ will correspondingly download clause program in the j th segment of channel c if x_j appears in C_i positively, or in the j th segment of channel $\bar{c}$ if x_j appears in C_i negatively. Since all clauses are true by this assignment, all the required programs will be downloaded before time $4n$.

($\leftarrow$) If all the required programs have been downloaded by time $4n$. Since we cannot download programs from channel c and channel $\bar{c}$ at the same time, we will assign $True$ to x_j if the client has downloaded clause programs C^i in the j-th segment of channel c. On the other hand, $False$ should be assigned to x_j if clause program C^i has been downloaded in the j-th segment of channel $\bar{c}$.

The above reduction takes polynomial time. Hence the theorem is proven. □

Here, we show a simple example of the instance. Given an instance of 3-SAT(3) where the input formula is as follows:

$$F = (x_1 \vee \bar{x}_2 \vee x_3) \wedge (x_1 \vee \bar{x}_3 \vee x_5) \wedge (\bar{x}_1 \vee \bar{x}_5 \vee x_4) \wedge (x_2 \vee x_3 \vee \bar{x}_4) \wedge (\bar{x}_2 \vee \bar{x}_4 \vee x_5) \quad (1)$$

The corresponding instance of $McPDP(2, 1, d)(P = \{C_1, C_2, C_3, C_4, C_5\})$ is in Fig. 1.

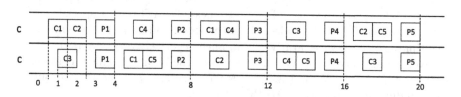

Fig. 1. The corresponding instance of formula F in Eq. 1

3   Aligned Multi-channel Program Download Problem

Definition 2. *The Aligned Multi-channel Program Download Problem (AMcPDP) is based on McPDP, it requires that all programs should be neatly aligned in the channels, thus if two programs overlap, they will start together and finish together.*

Instance. A program set U contains a series of programs which are neatly aligned in a set of channels C, where $|C| = n$. Similarly, each client within a range will have a target set of programs $P(P \subseteq U)$ to download, and we can download k programs at the same time. The Aligned multi-channel program download problem (AMcPDP) can be denoted as $AMcPDP(n, k, d)$, it aims to download all programs in the target set P with the least time by deadline d.

Theorem 2. *Aligned multi-channel program download problem (AMcPDP) is in P.*

Proof. To solve $AMcPDP(n, k, d)$, we can transform it into a maximum flow problem. Firstly, for each program in set P, we create a node $p_i(1 < i < |P|)$. We also need a set of nodes $r_t(1 \leq t \leq d)$ to represent time unit. A source node a and a sink node b are also necessary. We add a directed edge from a to all the p_i nodes. Then we connect node p_i to node r_t if program p_i can be downloaded at time unit t. Finally, we link all the nodes r_t to b. For the edge from r_t to b, we set a capacity of k, because programs can be downloaded from k channels at the same time. The remaining edges are all assigned one unit capacity.

Next we will prove that $AMcPDP(n, k, d)$ can be solved *iff* we can find a $|P|$-flow from a to b in the graph we have created.

($\rightarrow$) If we have downloaded all the programs in the target set P in the fastest way, then we can send $|P|$ units of flows from source node a to each node p_i, then it will flow to node r_t, and finally node b.

($\leftarrow$) Denote $G(r_t)$ as the subset of the graph whose path contains node $r_1, r_2, \cdots, r_t$, if we can find $|P|$ flow paths in total in $G(r_t)$, each of which is from source node a to node p_i, and r_t, finally to sink node b, correspondingly, we can make a schedule to download program p_i at the time unit of r_t. In this way, we can download all $|P|$ programs in the target set with the least time when we find the least t that contains $|P|$ flows in $G(r_t)$.   □

The following pseudo-code shows an algorithm to solve $AMcPDP(n, k, d)$. This algorithm is based on Ford-Fulkerson algorithm. To get the earliest time which contains $|P|$ flows, we shall find the possible earliest time $t_0(t_0 = max\{t, \lceil \frac{|P|}{K} \rceil\}$, where t is the earliest unit time when all the programs in P have appeared at least once and $\lceil \frac{|P|}{K} \rceil$ represents that at each time, the client can download K programs from n channels). If we cannot find $|P|$ flows within time t_0, then we increase the time unit t_0 time $t_0 + 1, t_0 + 2, \cdots, t_0 + i$ until d.

In Algorithm 1, we firstly construct a graph in which the number of nodes is $|V| = 2 + |P| + d$, and the edges are no more than $|E| = |P| + d \times n + d$. Since the graph can be done in $O(d \times n)$ time. The outer loop will execute at most $d - t_0 + 1$ rounds and the major part in each loop is the inner loop. To find an augmenting path in the graph will take $O(d \times n)$ time, therefore the inner loop will take at most $O(|P| \times d \times n)$ time, which is at most $O((d \times n)^2)$. Thus the total complexity of this algorithm is $O(d^3 \times n^2)$.

For example, we give a program broadcasting schedule in Fig. 2(a) as follows, the target set $P = \{S_1, S_2, S_3, S_4\}$ and $k = 2$, then construct the corresponding

---

Algorithm 1. $AMcPDP(n, k, d)$ algorithm

Input:
> A broadcasting schedule $I = \{(p_i, t)\}$ (program p_i broadcasts at time t) of a program set P

Output:
> The fastest download schedule W of programs;

1: Create node set $V = \{a\} \cup \{p_i\} \cup \{r_t\} \cup \{b\}, 1 \le i \le |P|, 1 \le t \le d$;
2: Create edge set $E = \{(a, p_i) \cup (r_t, b)\}$;
3: Add edge (p_i, r_t) to E iff program p_i can be downloaded at time t;
4: Set $f(e) \leftarrow 0$ for all the edge $e \in E$;
5: Set $t \leftarrow t_0 \leftarrow max\{t, \lceil \frac{|P|}{K} \rceil\}$ while r_t means time t;
6: **while** $t \le d$ **do**
7:    Set $G_f(r_t) \leftarrow G(r_t)$ while $G_f(r_t)$ is the residual graph;
8:    **while** $G_f(r_t)$ contains an a-b path **do**
9:       let m denote the a-b path;
10:      $f \leftarrow augment(f, m)$;
11:    **end while**
12:    **if** find a $|P|$ flow **then**
13:      break;
14:    **end if**
15:    $t \leftarrow t + 1$;
16: **end while**
17: Decompose f into $|P|$ unit-flow paths S;
18: build the schedule $W = \{(p_i, t)\}$ based on the path set S;
19: **return** W

---

graph as Fig. 2(b). At first, time $t_0 = max\{2, \lceil \frac{|4|}{2} \rceil\} = 2$. Next, we attempt to find the max flow in $G(r_2)$ but failed, then we try to continue searching for such a max flow. In this example, we can find it within time 3.

Based on Algorithm 1, we can try to apply binary search to find a relative optimal solution. Firstly, we find the possible earliest time t_0. Then, we can get the earliest time in the following way: we try to find a maximum flow within time t_0. If such a maximum flow exists, $AMcPDP(n, k, d)$ can be solved with the shortest time t_0. However, if there doesn't exist such a maximum flow, we should find another time t_i ($i = 1, 2, \cdots, d$) which is the earliest time with a $|P|$ flow and $t_i = 2^i \cdot t_0$. We use binary search to find a $|P|$ flow within the shortest time, and the searching range is from time $t_{i-1} + 1$ to t_i.

Next, we will show the pseudo-code of Algorithm 2, we call it $IAMcPDP$ (n,k,d) algorithm. In this algorithm, we use binary search to approach the earliest time. Denote $G(r_t)$ as the subset of the graph whose path contains node $r_1, \cdots, r_t$, and $G_f(r_t)$ as the residual graph of it, and this algorithm can solve $AMcPDP$ in polynomial time obviously.

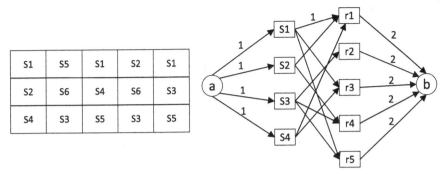

S1	S5	S1	S2	S1
S2	S6	S4	S6	S3
S4	S3	S5	S3	S5

(a) Broadcasting schedule of programs   (b) the corresponding maximum flow graph

Fig. 2. An AMcPDP example

Algorithm 2. $IAMcPDP(n, k, d)$ algorithm

Input:
  A broadcasting schedule $I = \{(p_i, t)\}$ (program p_i broadcasts at time t) of a program set P

Output:
  The fastest download schedule of programs;
  1: Create node set $V = \{a\} \cup \{p_i\} \cup \{r_t\} \cup \{b\}, 1 \leq i \leq |P|, 1 \leq t \leq d$;
  2: Create edge set $E = \{(a, p_i) \cup (r_t, b)\}$;
  3: Add edge (p_i, r_t) to E iff program p_i can be downloaded at time t;
  4: Set $f(e) \leftarrow 0$ for all the edge $e \in E$;
  5: Set $t \leftarrow t_0 \leftarrow max\{t, \lceil \frac{|P|}{K} \rceil\}$ while r_t means time t;
  6: **while** $t \leq d$ **do**
  7:     Set $G_f(r_t) \leftarrow G(r_t)$ while $G_f(r_t)$ is the residual graph;
  8:     **if** find $|P|$ flows in $G_f(r_t)$ **then**
  9:         **if** $t! = t_0$ **then**
 10:             use binary search to find the earliest time t which contains $|P|$ flows between the time $t_0 + 1$ and t
 11:         **end if**
 12:         Decompose f into $|P|$ unit-flow paths S;
 13:         build the schedule $W = \{(p_i, t)\}$ based on the path set S;
 14:         **return** W
 15:     **else**
 16:         $t = 2t$
 17:     **end if**
 18: **end while**

---

4   Performance Evaluation

In this section, we use Matlab to evaluate the performance of these proposed algorithms above.

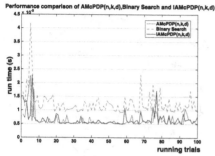
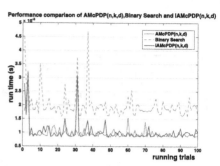

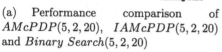

(a) Performance comparison of $AMcPDP(5, 2, 20)$, $IAMcPDP(5, 2, 20)$ and $Binary\ Search(5, 2, 20)$

(b) Performance comparison of $AMcPDP(5, 2, 40)$, $IAMcPDP(5, 2, 40)$ and $Binary\ Search(5, 2, 40)$

Fig. 3. Performance comparison of three algorithms where the program set U is $\{S_1, S_2, S_3, \cdots, S_{10}\}$ and the target set P is $\{S_1, S_2, S_3, \cdots, S_9\}$

4.1 AMcPDP(n,k,d), IAMcPDP(n,k,d) and Binary Search

In our experiment, for better comparison, besides $AMcPDP$ (n, k, d) and $IAMcPDP$ (n, k, d), we have also implemented the binary search algorithm, which finds maximum flow from the last time unit, and then use binary search to find the final target.

Firstly, we generate a $d \times n$ matrix to simulate our experiment environment: n channels and d time units. Each element in the matrix is a representation of a program. Then we run these three algorithms respectively, and compare the performance of them. In order to get a trustable conclusion, we have tried multiple parameters. The following figures show the run time of these three algorithms with different parameters over 100 trials.

In figures above, the green line represents the running time of Binary Search algorithm, while the blue line and the red line represent the running time of $IAMcPDP(n, k, d)$ and $AMcPDP(n, k, d)$ respectively. From these figures, we find that the binary search algorithm is inferior to the other two algorithms in all examples, and the running time of $AMcPDP(n, k, d)$ and $IAMcPDP(n, k, d)$ are nearly close to each other since our target programs are very easy to be found near time unit $t_0(t_0 = max\{t, \lceil \frac{|P|}{K} \rceil\})$, which is the reason why $IAMcPDP(n, k, d)$ doesn't have obvious advantages over $AMcPDP(n, k, d)$.

Obviously, there are some sharp fluctuations in the figures, which are caused by the complexity of the examples. The matrixes are generated randomly, so it inevitably will produce different examples. A hard example may lead to a peak value of a curve, while an easy example may cause a downward trend, and the fluctuating trend of two curves in the same figure almost keeps the same.

From Fig. 3(a) and (b), we see that curves in Fig. 3(b) is higher than that in Fig. 3(a). We conclude that the setting of deadline d will make a difference to the performance of the algorithms. The reasons are as follows: The first step of these algorithms is to check whether there exists a $|P|$ flow before deadline d, and a

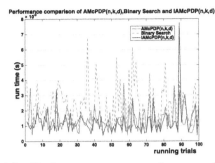
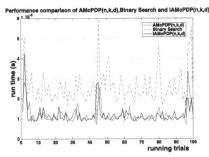

(a) Performance comparison of $AMcPDP(5,2,20)$, $IAMcPDP(5,2,20)$ and $Binary\ Search(5,2,20)$

(b) Performance comparison of $AMcPDP(5,2,40)$, $IAMcPDP(5,2,40)$ and $Binary\ Search(5,2,40)$

Fig. 4. Performance comparison of three algorithms where the program set U is $\{S_1, S_2, S_3, \cdots, S_{30}\}$ and the target set P is $\{S_1, S_2, S_3, \cdots, S_9\}$

later deadline will make the maximum flow algorithms more complex. Another possibility is that there doesn't exist such a $|P|$ flow before the early deadline, so the algorithms will stop executing under this situation. On the other hand, the latter deadline is later enough to find a $|P|$ flow, the following algorithms will continue running.

The only different parameters used in Fig. 3(a) and Fig. 4(a) is the program set U, we can see that the overall running time in Fig. 4(a) is slower than that in Fig. 3(a). This is an obvious difference as under the same conditions, the hitting ratio of selecting 9 specific programs from 10 ones is undoubtedly higher than that from 30 ones. Two maximum flow algorithms in Fig. 4(a) and (b) don't have a clear superiority over that in Fig. 3(a) and (b) as binary search algorithm will show its advantage when the hitting ratio of target programs isn't very high.

5 Conclusion

In this paper, we proved that the Multi-Channel program download problem (McPDP) is NP-complete by reducing 3-SAT(3) to it. We then find aligned multi-channel program download problem (AMcPDP) can be solved in polynomial time by reducing it to a max-flow problem, and we present two algorithms to solve it. Finally, we implement these algorithms in Matlab and the simulation results corroborate their efficiency.

References

1. Hanczewski, S., Stasiak, M.: Modeling of video on demand systems. In: Kwiecień, A., Gaj, P., Stera, P. (eds.) CN 2014. CCIS, vol. 431, pp. 233–242. Springer, Cham (2014). doi:10.1007/978-3-319-07941-7_24

2. Miesler, L., Gehring, B., Hannich, F., Wüthrich, A.: User experience of video-on-demand applications for smart TVs: a case study. In: Marcus, A. (ed.) DUXU 2014. LNCS, vol. 8520, pp. 412–422. Springer, Cham (2014). doi:10.1007/978-3-319-07638-6_40

3. Atzori, L., De Natale, F.G.B., Di Gregorio, M., Giusto, D.D.: Multimedia information broadcasting using digital TV channels. IEEE Trans. Broadcast. **43**(3), 242–251 (1997)

4. Peng, C., Tan, Y., Xiong, N., Yang, L.T., Park, J.H., Kim, S.-S.: Adaptive video-on-demand broadcasting in ubiquitous computing environment. Pers. Ubiquit. Comput. **13**(7), 479–488 (2009)

5. Aggarwal, C.C., Wolf, J.L., Yu, P.S.: A permutation-based pyramid broadcasting scheme for video-on-demand systems. In: Proceedings of the International Conference on Multimedia Computing and Systems, pp. 118–126 (1996)

6. Almeroth, K.C., Ammar, M.H.: The use of multicast delivery to provide a scalable and interactive video-on-demand service. IEEE J. Sel. Areas Commun. **14**(5), 1110–1122 (1996)

7. Juhn, L., Tseng, L.: Harmonic broadcasting for video-on-demand service. IEEE Trans. Broadcast. **43**(3), 268–271 (1997)

8. Tian, C., Sun, J., Wu, W., Luo, Y.: Optimal bandwidth allocation for hybrid video-on-demand streaming with a distributed max flow algorithm. Comput. Netw. **91**, 483–494 (2015)

9. Peng, C., Zhou, J., Zhu, B., Zhu, H.: Complexity analysis and algorithms for the program download problem. J. Comb. Optim. **29**(1), 216–227 (2015)

10. Xie, H., Boukerche, A., Loureiro, A.A.F.: MERVS: a novel multichannel error recovery video streaming protocol for vehicle ad hoc networks. IEEE Transaction on Vehicular Technology **65**(2), 923–935 (2016)

11. Yang, T., Liang, H., Cheng, N., Deng, R., Shen, X.: Efficient scheduling for video transmissions in maritime wireless communication networks. IEEE Transaction on Vehicular Technology **64**(9), 4215–4229 (2015)

12. Zaixin, L., Shi, Y., Weili, W., Bin, F.: Efficient data retrieval scheduling for multi-channel wireless data broadcast. In: Proceedings of the 31st IEEE International Conference on Computer Communications (INFOCOM), pp. 891–899 (2012)

13. Lu, Z., Wu, W., Fu, B.: Optimal data retrieval scheduling in the multi-channel data broadcast environments. IEEE Trans. Comput. **62**(12), 2427–2439 (2013)

14. Paris, J.-F., Carter, S., Long, D.D.E.: Efficient broadcasting protocols for video on demand. In: MASCOTS, pp. 127–132 (1998)

15. Aggarwal, V., Robert Calderbank, A., Gopalakrishnan, V., Jana, R., Ramakrishnan, K.K., Yu, F.: The effectiveness of intelligent scheduling for multicast video-on-demand. In: ACM Multimedia, pp. 421–430 (2009)

16. Darmann, A., Dcker, J.: Monotone 3-Sat-4 is NP-complete. CoRR abs/1603.07881 (2016)

Service Recommendation Based on Topics and Trend Prediction

Lei Yu[1,2(✉)], Zhang Junxing[1], and Philip S. Yu[3]

[1] Inner Mongolia University, Hohhot, China
yuleiimu@sohu.com
[2] State Key Laboratory of Networking and Switching Technology, BUPT, Beijing, China
[3] University of Illinois at Chicago, Chicago, USA

Abstract. Web service recommendation is a challenging task when the number of services and service consumers are growing rapidly on the Internet. Previous research used information retrieve methods, such as keyword search and semantic matching, to speculate the intent of service consumers. The intent is matched with contents or topics of existing data. These methods help service consumers to select appropriate services according to their needs. However, service evolution over time and topic correlation has not been given sufficient attention. Thus we propose a service recommendation approach that is able to extract service evolution patterns from history statistic data and correlated topics from semantic service descriptions. To this end, time series prediction is used to obtain evolution patterns; Latent Dirichlet Allocation (LDA) is used to model the extracted topics. Experiments results show that our approach has higher precision than existing methods.

Keywords: Service recommendation · Trend Prediction · Latent Dirichlet Allocation

1 Introduction

An important task is service discovery in an automated style, because service composition rely on the precision of automated service searching. Several web sites are collecting web services and mashups, such as ProgrammableWeb and myExperiment [1] in the recent years. myExperiment is used for sharing a variety of scientific workflows, such as Taverna and RapidMiner. Although this kind of web sites provide an easy way for web service consumers, searching desired and suitable services in large databases of services is still a time-consuming and tedious job for the service consumers. Service recommendation methods can facilitate consumers discover the suitable services.

Most of service recommendation methods search the information by keywords or semantic. Keyword-based search is inefficient, and semantic-based search needs much time to construct semantic information. A search method based on Latent Dirichlet Allocation (LDA) [2] was proposed for the challenge. In the method, a collections of

© ICST Institute for Computer Sciences, Social Informatics and Telecommunications Engineering 2017
S. Wang and A. Zhou (Eds.): CollaborateCom 2016, LNICST 201, pp. 343–352, 2017.
DOI: 10.1007/978-3-319-59288-6_31

words are extracted from WSDL, and assigned to several topics. Some other researchers [3] applied social network analysis for service recommendation.

In addition, temporal information has been ignored. The fact is that service topics change over time. Recommending services with popular topics may be reasonable for users, but how to decide which service is popular in the future is a problem. To deal with the problem, we collect the past usage of services at intervals, and predict the popularity in the future. Besides popularity, topics may be related each other. Using correlated topics can provide more related recommendation results in a recommendation-making system. It is especially useful when a search for one topic returns few recommendation results. In addition, we assume that services with similar functions aim to solve similar problems, thus these services are in the same topic.

We summarized contributions as follows: First, we extract a sequence of topic popularity from service usage history. Based on the sequence and Latent Dirichlet Allocation (LDA), we predict topic evolution and service popularity in the future. Second, based on the topic evolution model, we propose a method for service recommendation, called SRTT.

2   Related Work

Wang et al. [4] proposed an efficient QoS management approach for QoS-aware web service composition, and they classified web services according to similarity and then design a QoS tree to manage the QoS the classified web services. Chen et al. [5] proposed a collaborative filtering-based Web service recommender system to help users select services with optimal Quality-of-Service (QoS) performance. Their recommender system employed the location information and QoS values to cluster users and services, and made personalized service recommendation for users based on the clustering results. Lee et al. [6] developed a recommendation mechanism to predict user intention and activate the appropriate services. They chose to employ the event-condition-action model together with a rule induction algorithm to discover smartphone users' behavior patterns. Huang [7] proposed a three-phase network prediction approach (NPA) for evolution-aware recommendation. They introduced a network series model to formalize the evolution of the service ecosystem and developed a network analysis method to study the usage pattern with a special focus on its temporal evolution. In addition, a service network prediction method based on rank aggregation was proposed to predict the evolution of the network. Sun et al. [8] presented a new similarity measure for web service similarity computation and proposed a novel collaborative filtering approach, called normal recovery collaborative filtering, for personalized web service recommendation.

Cao et al. [9] designed a cube model to explicitly describe the relationship among providers, consumers and Web services. they presented a Standard Deviation based Hybrid Collaborative Filtering (SD-HCF) for Web Service Recommendation (WSRec) and an Inverse consumer Frequency based User Collaborative Filtering (IF-UCF) for Potential Consumers Recommendation (PCRec). Finally, the decision-making process of bidirectional recommendation was provided for both providers and consumers. Sets of experiments were conducted on real-world data provided by Planet-Lab.

Wu et al. [10] presented a neighborhood-based collaborative filtering approach to predict such unknown values for QoS-based selection. In addition, a two-phase neighbor selection strategy was proposed to improve its scalability. Zheng et al. [11] proposed a collaborative quality-of-service (QoS) prediction approach for web services by taking advantages of the past web service usage experiences of service users. They applied the concept of user-collaboration for the web service QoS information sharing. Based on the collected QoS data, a neighborhood-integrated approach was designed for personalized web service QoS value prediction.

Chen et al. [12] proposed a collaborative filtering algorithm designed for large-scale web service recommendation. The approach employed the characteristic of QoS and achieves considerable improvement on the recommendation accuracy. To avoid the time-consuming and expensive real-world service invocations, Zheng et al. [13] proposed a QoS ranking prediction framework for cloud services by taking advantage of the past service usage experiences of other consumers. The proposed framework requires no additional invocations of cloud services when making QoS ranking prediction. Two personalized QoS ranking prediction approaches were proposed to predict the QoS rankings directly. Zheng et al. [14] proposed two personalized reliability prediction approaches of Web services, that is, neighborhood-based approach and model-based approach. The neighborhood-based approach employed past failure data of similar neighbors (either service users or Web services) to predict the Web service reliability. On the other hand, the model-based approach fits a factor model based on the available Web service failure data and use this factor model to make further reliability prediction. Yu et al. [15] proposed a clustering method and a recommendation method for Web services. The clustering method combines TF-IDF (Term Frequency-Inverse Document Frequency) and ontology to compute the similarity of Web services, and it uses Ward's Distance to identify irregular shapes. The recommendation method uses matrix factorization to recommend proper services.

Related works mentioned above have some deficiencies. They do not consider the changing of service popularity, which may make high ranked services degradation. As a result, some usable services will not be recommended to the user. Third, the precision of recommendation results and speed of previous methods still have space to improve.

3   Service Recommendation Method

The recommendation will provide services according to a user query, in which the user query is matched with service description or mashup description.

After preprocessing on service descriptions, a collection of separated words w_1, w_2, ..., w_n can describe and represent the functions of a service. Likewise, a collection of separated words w_1, w_2, ..., w_n can describe and represent the functions of a mashup. A user search contains several words that indicate the intent of the user. These words can be represented by $Q = \{q_1, q_2, ..., q_n\}$, and will be matched with the first two collections. In the next step, a list of ranked services $R(m)$ will be generated. Higher $R(m)$ is more likely to be recommended to the user for creating a new mashup.

Considering service history information and content of services, we propose a service recommendation method. Thus, the components of our approach are TP (Trend Prediction) and CM (Content Matching) respectively.

(1) TP predict service activity according to service usage history. Regardless of functional requirements of a mashup, TP provides popularity scores of services in the near future. TP can offer a list of hot services invoked by a large amount of users. Hot services may be the result from low fee, high efficiency or lovely appearance viewing by majority of users, but may not be the required service by the current user. For complementation, CM and TC give higher score to the functional relevant services.
(2) By calculating semantic similarity between the requirements and the descriptions of services, CM selects services with similar functional requirements from existing mashups.

3.1   Trend Prediction

Popular services cater for users in many different ways, which is a common experience of users in every consumer market. That is the reason why new users like to consume prevalent services at current time. The prevalent services must have interesting topics. Analyzing the service usage history to recommend popular services is a reasonable idea to topic modeling. Topic modeling assumes that each service has several topics, or called latent topics which is needed to be calculated. LDA [16], a method for topic mining, can be used to describe the service generative process.

Suppose k_i^{t+1} is topic popularity for topic i at time $t + 1$. For every topic i, $(k_i^0, k_i^1, k_i^2, ..., k_i^{t+1})$ become a time series. The future popularity of topic i can be forecasted by Eq. 1. Several methods are able to solve the above problem, e.g. auto regression and linear weighted moving average [17]. We use the linear weighted moving average as follows.

$$k_i^{t+1} = \sum_{j=0}^{n} w_j \times k_i^{t-j} \tag{1}$$

w are weightings, which are positive real numbers, and satisfy the constraint $\sum w_i = 1$. Giving higher weightings to recent k will amplify the popularity.

According to LDA, a matrix can be represented by two matrices. For extension, we assume matrix C is represented by matrix Θ, matrix E(k) and matrix Φ. Matrix Θ and Φ are similar to that of LDA, but matrix E(k) is the extension. Θ is a word-topic matrix, as shown below. Its elements indicate the probability that a word belongs to a topic.

$$\Theta = \begin{pmatrix} a_{11} & \cdots & a_{1n} \\ \vdots & \ddots & \vdots \\ a_{m1} & \cdots & a_{mn} \end{pmatrix} \quad \Phi = \begin{pmatrix} b_{11} & \cdots & b_{1n} \\ \vdots & \ddots & \vdots \\ b_{m1} & \cdots & b_{mn} \end{pmatrix}$$

Φ is a topic-service matrix, as shown below. Its elements indicate the probability of a topic over a service. $E(k)$ is a coefficient matrix, as shown below. It is also a diagonal matrix that do not change the number of rows and columns of the matrix it is multiplied. Its elements, which are calculated from Eq. 1, indicate the popularity of each topic.

$$E(k_i^{t+1}) = \begin{pmatrix} k_1^{t+1} & & 0 \\ & \ddots & \\ 0 & & k_n^{t+1} \end{pmatrix}$$

C is a word-service matrix, indicating that each service is described by several words. Considering popularity of services, C should equal to the multiplication of matrix Θ, $E(k)$ and Φ.

$$C = \Theta \times E(k_i^{t+1}) \times \Phi$$

When a service consumer submits a query including several words (Q) for a new service (s), Eq. 2 shows the topic similarity between Q and service descriptions. Services with higher $P(Q|s)$ will be provided to the consumers.

$$P_{tp}(Q|s) = \prod_{q_n \in Q} \sum_{k=1}^{T} P(q_n|k_i^{t+1})E(k_i^{t+1})P(k_i^{t+1}|s) \tag{2}$$

3.2 Content Matching

Collaborative filtering is used broadly for recommendation [11] in many areas. It assumes that similar users possibly need similar items. Likewise, we calculate the mashups similarities by their descriptions, and then provide the component services from similar mashups for a new mashup based on historical information. For example, if the descriptions of a new mashup m_q is similar to an existing mashup m_e, and m_e is composed by services A and B, then m_q probably invokes A and B.

According to mashup descriptions, LDA is used to calculate the similarity among mashups. A collection of words, which describe functions of mashups, is the input of LDA. LDA uses Gibbs Sampling to obtain two posterior distributions, which are mashups-topics $p(k|m)$ and topics-words $p(w|k)$. When a user queries, by submitting with words $Q = \{q_1, q_2, \ldots, q_n\}$ for a new mashup m_q, the similarity between m_q and an existing mashup m_e can be computed as follows:

$$sim(m_q, m_e) = \prod_{q \in Q} \sum_{k=1}^{T} p(q|k)p(k|m_e) \tag{3}$$

After computing two mashups similarities, mashup m_q should use a component service s form similar mashups according to the following equation:

$$P_{cm}(Q|s) = \sum_{m_e \in U(k)} sim(m_q, m_e)d(m_e, s) \tag{4}$$

$U(k)$ contains the Top K mashups that are similar to m_q. $d(m_e, s)$ indicates that mashup m_e contains the service s. Comparing to Eq. 2, this method does not consider trend information.

4 Service Recommendation Framework

TP and CM have been introduced in the previous section. They will be integrated for service recommendation in this section. TP is used to obtain tendency. CM is used to obtain semantic similarity. The probability that a service s is invoked by a new mashup m_q is:

$$P(Q|s) = w_1 P_{tp}(Q|s) + w_2 P_{cm}(Q|s) \tag{5}$$

Where w_i are weightings. The ranked services for mashup m_q will provide to users in a descending order of $P_{tc}(Q|s)$. Alternatively, a technique from paper [18] can be used to aggregate each ranking produced by one component of our method in the last section to generate a final ranking.

We use approximate inference (e.g. Gibbs Sampling) to obtain the latent variables in LDA. Gibbs Sampling is formally a kind of Markov-Chain Monte Carlo.

Algorithm 1. Service Recommendation

Input:
    T: The number of topics in LDA
    SD: Service description texts
    α: the parameter of the Dirichlet prior distributions for topics
    β: the parameter of the Dirichlet prior distributions for words
    $Q = \{q_1, q_2, \ldots, q_n\}$: a user query containing n words

Output:
    Recommended services

Procedure:
1. Use Gibbs Sampling (α, β, SD) to obtain Matrix Θ and Φ
2. Compute tendency by Equ.1 and obtain E(k)
3. Obtain a user query
4. Calculate similarity by Equ.2 (TP) using parameters θ_1, ϕ_1
5. Calculate similarity by Equ.4 (CM) using parameters θ_1, ϕ_1
6. Calculate similarity between service descriptions and the user query by Equ.5
7. Recommend the high-ranked services

---

5   Experiments

Our experimental platform is: Operation system: Microsoft Windows 7. CPU: Intel Core i7, 2.5 GHz. RAM: 4 GB. Programming language: Java. Two data sources were used in our experiments. They are ProgrammableWeb.com and SAWSDL-TC [19]. The former data source is mainly used to evaluate the precision of each component of our method, and the latter data source is mainly used for comparing with other existing methods in the regard of advanced precision and response speed.

For more precise evaluation, we evaluate our algorithm by calculating the Precision@n (proportion of the top-n relevant services) and the Normalized Discounted Cumulative Gain (NDCG@n).

Precision@n computes the precision of the service discovery for the first n retrieved services. Precision@n indicates the relevance between the user query and retrieved n services. The Precision@n is given by:

$$Precision@n = \frac{r}{n}$$

n indicates the number of retrieved services. r indicates the number of relevant services from the set of retrieved services. DCG is defined as follows.

$$DCG_p = \sum_{i=1}^{p} \frac{2^{rel_i} - 1}{log_2(i + 1)}$$

Where p is a particular rank position, and rel_i is the graded relevance at position i. The normalized discounted cumulative gain is computed as:

$$NDCG_p = \frac{DCG_p}{IDCG_p}$$

We evaluated the effectiveness of our method based on CT by computing the Precision@n and NDCG@n. all of 42 queries are encoded by SAWSDL which contain semantic requirements. We compare our method with syntax-based methods, Apache Lucene [20] and SAWSDL-MX2 [21]. The queries are represented in a collection of words in our approach. The queries are submitted in the form of strings of text descriptions in the Apache Lucene. At last, the most relevant services will be selected for the user.

Comparing the averaged Precision@n and the NDCG@n, we evaluated different levels of concept lattices. The Precision@20 and NDCG@20 values are obtained in the three methods. The results are shown in Fig. 1.

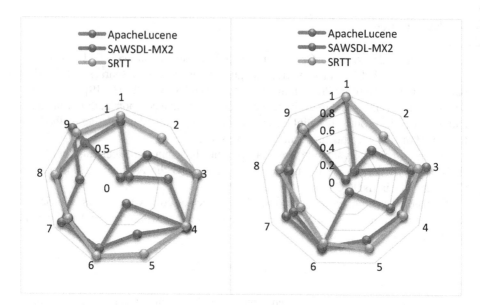

Fig. 1. Precision@20 and NDCG@20 for nine queries

In both cases, our SRTT method obtains higher Precision@20 and NDCG@20 for 9 queries. The Apache Lucene and SAWSDL-MX2 do not find the relevant services for three queries. Figures 2 and 3 show the average Precision@n and NDCG@n values of 42 queries. SRTT obtains the highest precision values than others.

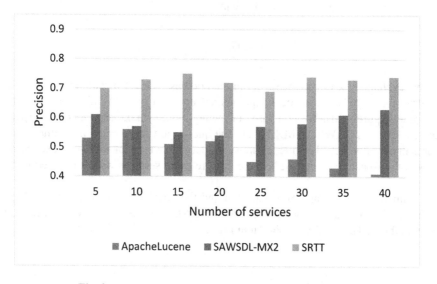

Fig. 2. Precision in each number of services for 42 queries

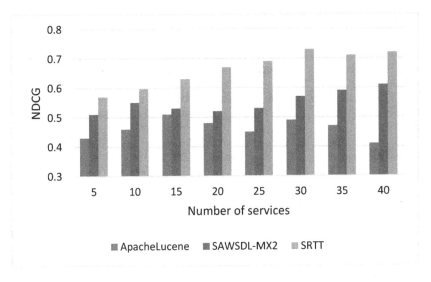

Fig. 3. NDCG in each number of services for 42 queries

In the future, we will improve SRTT method to adapt to big data environment [22]. We will propose a new service recommendation method that can be executed in parallel, with the help of Spark framework.

6 Conclusion

In this paper, we presented a method that combines service popularity and service content of services to recommend services to a mashup. We first extract topics from semantic service descriptions, and then analyze historic information to predict service popularity. In the experiment, the results of Precision@n and NDCG@n show that our method is better than the other two methods. We also conduct experiments on Programmable Web.com, a real-world data set. The results show that our method is better than content matching and collaborative filtering, with respect to mean average precision for service recommendation.

Acknowledgment. This work was supported by Scientific projects of higher school of Inner Mongolia [NJZY009], Open Foundation of State Key Laboratory of Networking and Switching Technology (SKLNST-2016-1-01), Programs of Higher-level talents of Inner Mongolia University [215005145143], Natural Science Foundation of Inner Mongolia Autonomous Region [2015BS0603].

References

1. De Roure, D., Goble, C., Stevens, R.: The design and realization of the myExperiment virtual research environment for social sharing of workflows. Future Gener. Comput. Syst. **25**, 561–567 (2009)
2. Li, C., Zhang, R., Huai, J., Guo, X., Sun, H.: A probabilistic approach for web service discovery. In: Proceedings of the IEEE International Conference on Services Computing, pp. 49–56 (2013)
3. Cao, J., Xu, W., Hu, L., Wang, J., Li, M.: A social-aware service recommendation approach for mashup creation. Int. J. Web Serv. Res. **10**, 53–72 (2013)
4. Wang, S.G., Zhu, X.L., Yang, F.C.: Efficient QoS management for QoS-aware web service composition. Int. J. Web Grid Serv. **10**(1), 1–23 (2014)
5. Chen, X., et al.: Web service recommendation via exploiting location and QoS information. IEEE Trans. Parallel Distrib. Syst. **25**(7), 1913–1924 (2014)
6. Lee, W., Lee, K.: Making smartphone service recommendations by predicting users' intentions: a context-aware approach. Inf. Sci. **277**, 21–35 (2014)
7. Huang, K., Fan, Y., Tan, W.: Recommendation in an evolving service ecosystem based on network prediction. IEEE Trans. Autom. Sci. Eng. **11**(3), 906–920 (2014)
8. Sun, H.F., et al.: Personalized web service recommendation via normal recovery collaborative filtering. IEEE Trans. Serv. Comput. **6**(4), 573–579 (2013)
9. Cao, J., et al.: Hybrid Collaborative Filtering algorithm for bidirectional Web service recommendation. Knowl. Inf. Syst. **36**(3), 607–627 (2013)
10. Wu, J., et al.: Predicting quality of service for selection by neighborhood-based collaborative filtering. IEEE Trans. Syst. Man Cybern. Syst. **43**(2), 428–439 (2013)
11. Zibin, Z., et al.: Collaborative web service QoS prediction via neighborhood integrated matrix factorization. IEEE Trans. Serv. Comput. **6**(3), 289–299 (2013)
12. Chen, X., et al.: Personalized QoS-aware web service recommendation and visualization. IEEE Trans. Serv. Comput. **6**(1), 35–47 (2013)
13. Zheng, Z., et al.: QoS ranking prediction for cloud services. IEEE Trans. Parallel Distrib. Syst. **24**(6), 1213–1222 (2013)
14. Zheng, Z., Lyu, M.R.: Personalized reliability prediction of web services. ACM Trans. Softw. Eng. Methodol. **22**(2), 1–25 (2013)
15. Yu, L., Wang, Z.-L., Meng, L.-M., et al.: Clustering and recommendation for semantic web service in time series. KSII Trans. Internet Inf. Syst. **8**(8), 2743–2762 (2014)
16. Blei, D.M., Ng, A.Y., Jordan, M.I.: Latent Dirichlet allocation. J. Mach. Learn. Res. **3**, 993–1022 (2003)
17. Matsubara, Y., Sakurai, Y., Faloutsos, C., Iwata, T., Yoshikawa, M.: Fast mining and forecasting of complex time-stamped events. In: Proceedings of the 18th ACM SIGKDD International Conference on Knowledge Discovery and Data Mining, pp. 271–279 (2012)
18. Sheng, X., et al.: SOR: an objective ranking system based on mobile phone sensing. In: IEEE 34th International Conference on Distributed Computing Systems, ICDCS 2014, June 30, Madrid (2014)
19. http://www.semwebcentral.org/projects/sawsdl-tc
20. http://lucene.apache.org/
21. http://projects.semwebcentral.org/projects/sawsdl-mx
22. Dobre, C., Xhafa, F.: Intelligent services for Big Data science. Future Gener. Comput. Syst. **37**, 267–281 (2014)

Real-Time Dynamic Decomposition Storage of Routing Tables

Wenlong Chen[1], Lijing Lan[1], Xiaolan Tang[1(✉)], Shuo Zhang[1],
and Guangwu Hu[2]

[1] College of Information Engineering, Capital Normal University,
Beijing 100048, China
tangxl@cnu.edu.cn
[2] Graduate School at Shenzhen, Tsinghua University, Shenzhen, China

Abstract. The decomposition storage of routing tables can effectively alleviate the storage problem caused by the Internet routing expansion. However, the existing researches based on certain routing tables cannot apply to unknown ones or support dynamic changes of routing tables. This paper presents a real-time dynamic decomposition storage model, named RDDS, which takes the IP prefix with 8 bits length mask as a pocket prefix and distributes the routing entries (REs) to different line cards (LCs) according to different pocket prefixes. In the light of the mapping relationship between the destination IP addresses of packets and the pocket prefixes, the forwarding engine determines the host LC of one IP packet and complete forwarding in the LC. RDDS needs a mapping table to locate the host LC in the process of packets forwarding, which only introduces very little logical processing. Therefore, RDDS hardly affect the overall performance of packets forwarding in routers. Experimental results show that RDDS achieves real-time part-storage and the load balancing of REs in LCs. Considering the frequent update of routing tables, RDDS is more significant than other storage models in real environments.

Keywords: Routing tables · Real-time · Dynamic · Decomposition storage · Pocket prefix · Mapping table

1 Introduction

With the rapid expansion of Internet, the kernel routing table of the Internet keeps fast growing and becomes a big challenge for backbone routers. At present, high performance routers use Ternary Content Addressable Memory (TCAM) to store routing tables. As opposed to Static Random Access Memory (SRAM), the storage space of TCAM is small, and the price is expensive. Hence, these undoubtedly increase the burden of storage. The current decomposition storage methods aim at routing tables with specific capacity. However, in the realistic environment, the routing table capacity in routers usually is unknown and it always change dynamically.

© ICST Institute for Computer Sciences, Social Informatics and Telecommunications Engineering 2017
S. Wang and A. Zhou (Eds.): CollaborateCom 2016, LNICST 201, pp. 353–362, 2017.
DOI: 10.1007/978-3-319-59288-6_32

This paper presents a real-time dynamic decomposition storage (RDDS) model to store routing tables in distributed routers. REs load-balanced means that total REs is allocated to each LC averagely, which prompts LCs to complete the routing and the packets forwarding together. In order to achieve the dynamic load balancing, we choose the first 8 bits of destination IP prefixes as distribution units. And according to the different 8 bits prefix, we decompose and store the routing table. Each LC stores only a partial routing table, and with the increase in the number of LCs, the number of dynamic REs in each LC will continue to decrease. At the same time, we use the first 8 bits prefix as an index value to form a mapping relationship between LCs and index values. For an IP packet to be forwarded, the forwarding engine locates the LC where the RE for the packet is stored, and finds the related information based on longest prefix matching (LPM). RDDS is more suitable for the dynamic changes of routing tables. In addition, the first 8 bits of destination IP prefix of each REs are unique, so the redundant storage phenomenon does not appear in each LC.

Compared to previous researches, RDDS has several obvious advantages. (1) The unknown routing tables can be dynamically decomposed and stored, hence, it has a strong random distribution capacity. (2) RDDS can locate the positions of LCs directly according to the index values. (3) As the value of the first 8 bits is unique, each LC does not store REs repeatedly.

2   Related Work

In recent years, an increasing number of researches strive to optimize the decomposition storage of routing tables and routing lookup engines.

The decomposition storage of routing tables can be expedited by various approaches. Lin et al. [4] introduce a logical caching mechanism where they expected to divide the routing tree into multiple sub-trees with identical sizes. Many other studies [5,6] develop more decomposition storage algorithms benefiting from a new feature of IP prefix bits. The key idea is to split the routing table into multiple sub-tables. For example, the Decomposed Storage of FIB (DSF) algorithm [5], Enhanced DSF (EDSF) [5], and the Speedy Packet Lookups (SPAL) algorithm [6].

There are also several efforts for performing other performance optimization in routers. Li et al. [7] use an alternative next hop Forwarding Information Base (FIB) aggregation algorithm to reduce the forwarding table sizes, which ensures packets can be forwarded to the destination IP address through any paths not the best path. Fast lookup and update of routing tables with a hash table is achieved according to the short prefix and the long prefix in [8]. The articles [10–12] are committed to improving routing tables lookup efficiency instead of the decomposition storage of routing tables.

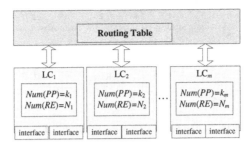

Fig. 1. Dynamic decomposition storage

3   Real-Time Dynamic Decomposition Storage Model

3.1   RDDS Overview

The full backup storage makes the load of routers increase as REs continue to increase [1–3,9]. And the existing decomposition storage methods do not apply to the dynamical update of routing tables. RDDS decomposes and stores REs to LCs on the basis of the non-full backup storage and ensures that the decomposition storage is dynamical and balanced. Our distribution principles are: (1) the REs attributed to the same PP are stored in the same LC. (2) each LC owns multiple PPs. (3) the RE capacity of each LC are as same as possible. As shown in Fig. 1, each LC just stores a portion of the routing table.

Definition 1. Equilibrium Degree (ED): ED is used to describe the relationship between the actual value of each LC's routing storage capacity and the average storage capacity of each LC. ED is calculated by (1):

$$ED = \frac{|RE\_LC_m - RE_{ave}|}{RE_{ave}} \qquad (1)$$

RE_LC_m is the actual routing capacity of LC_m in RDDS, RE_{ave} is the average capacity of each LC. This paper focuses on the real-time ED of RE's storage capacity, which ensures that ED is minimum as much as possible at any time. When the value of ED is 0, it indicates that all LCs are absolute load-balanced.

Definition 2. Reduction Ratio (RR): RR is the ratio that describes the relationship between RE's capacity of a LC in RDDS and the capacity in Full Backup Storage. We obtain the value of RR by (2):

$$RR = \frac{RE}{RE_{full}} \qquad (2)$$

Definition 3. Pocket Prefix (PP): Define the first n bits prefix of the routing address mask as a PP, the paper sets n as 8.

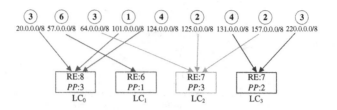

Fig. 2. Decomposition example in 4 LCs

In the dynamic decomposition storage of routing tables, there are 223 PPs (the multicast address is not taken into account) and each PP is independent. For example, the PP of 198.0.0.0/8 is 198.

We expect that in Fig. 1 RDDS ensures that N_1, N_2, ... , N_m are almost identical and the value of ED is the minimal. $Num_m[i]$ represents the RE number of i_{th} PP of m_{th} LC.

Equation (3) is the total number of REs stored in LC_m :

$$N_m = \sum_{i=1}^{k_m} Num_m[i] \tag{3}$$

3.2 Rules of Dynamic Decomposition Storage

RDDS dynamically decomposes and stores the routing table to achieve the load balancing of each LC. The decomposition storage ideas are as follows:

1. For each RE, we choose the first 8 bits of destination IP prefix as a PP and compare it with PPs of each LC. If there is the same PP_m, we store this RE to the LC that PP_m belongs to. Otherwise we use the first 8 bits of the mask prefix as a new PP, and assign the PP in the light of following steps.
2. For each allocation, according to the RE storage capacity of each LC, we preferentially assign the PP to the LC whose storage capacity is the smallest.
3. If there are multiple LCs with same minimum RE capacity, we preferentially assign the PP to the LC whose number of PP is the smallest.
4. If the minimum RE storage capacity and PPs of multiple LC are same, we assign the PP according to the serial number of LCs from small to large.
5. The new RE is stored in the LC owning the new PP.

As shown in Fig. 2, we choose 4 LCs as an example. The number in each circle is the number of REs that the corresponding PP contains.

In the process of assign PPs to LCs, We define the mapping relationship between PP and LC as $MR_{pre}(PRE_{sign}, LC_m)$. PRE_{sign} is the prefix sign of the RE, and LC_m represents the LC that the RE of PRE_{sign} belongs to. We use an array to save this relationship. So the relationship between PRE_{sign} and LC_m is expressed as: $MR_{pre}[PRE_{sign} - 1] = m$.

Real-Time Dynamic Decomposition Storage of Routing Tables

Table 1. Fourteen dynamic arrival REs

No.	RE	No.	RE
①	120.0.0.0/8	②	120.90.224.0/19
③	64.128.0.0/9	④	112.0.0.0/8
⑤	101.9.129.0/24	⑥	56.196.0.0/16
⑦	21.101.144.0/20	⑧	64.152.0.0/14
⑨	220.213.0.0/16	⑩	120.233.0.0/17
⑪	156.128.0.0/9	⑫	124.186.156.0/20
⑬	120.32.0.0/11	⑭	220.52.0.0/14

Table 2. The process of dynamic decomposition storage

Step	LC_0	LC_1	LC_2	LC_3	ED
(1)	A: ①				1.500
(2)	A: ① ②				1.500
(3)	A: ① ②	B:③			0.750
(4)	A: ① ②	B:③	C:④		0.500
(5)	A: ① ②	B:③	C:④	D:⑤	0.300
(6)	A: ① ②	B:③ E:⑥	C:④	D:⑤	0.335
(7)	A: ① ②	B:③ E:⑥	C:④ F:⑦	D:⑤	0.215
(8)	A: ① ②	B:③ ⑧ E:⑥	C:④ F:⑦	D:⑤	0.250
(9)	A: ① ②	B:③ ⑧ E:⑥	C:④ F:⑦	D:⑤ G:⑨	0.167
(10)	A: ① ② ⑩	B:③ ⑧ E:⑥	C:④ F:⑦	D:⑤ G:⑨	0.200
(11)	A: ① ② ⑩	B:③ ⑧ E:⑥ C:④ F:⑦ H:⑪		D:⑤ G:⑨	0.137
(12)	A: ① ② ⑩	B:③ ⑧ E:⑥ C:④ F:⑦ H:⑪	D:⑤ G:⑨ I:⑫		0
(13)	A: ① ② ⑩ ⑬	B:③ ⑧ E:⑥	C:④ F:⑦ H:⑪	D:⑤ G:⑨ I:⑬	0.116
(14)	A: ① ② ⑩ ⑬	B:③ ⑧ E:⑥	C:④ F:⑦ H:⑪ D:⑤	G:⑨ ⑭ I:⑬	0.143
	PP: 1 RE: 4	PP: 2 RE: 3	PP: 3 RE: 3	PP: 3 RE: 4	

We randomly select 14 dynamic REs and store them in 4 LCs. As shown in Table 1, the sequence number of REs is the order of REs arriving.

According to the definition of PP, we know that 14 REs belong to 9 different PPs respectively: A: 120, B: 64, C: 112, D: 101, E: 56, F: 21, G: 220, H: 156, I: 124. Initially, the storage capacity of the routing table and each LC are both 0. When ① arrives, we store it in LC_0. When ② arrives, we also store it in LC_0, because PP of ② is the same to ①. For ③ ④ ⑤, according to the different PP, we store them in LC_1, LC_2 and LC_3 by order. So far, the RE storage capacity of LC_0, LC_1, LC_2, LC_3 are 2, 1, 1, 1, respectively. For ⑥, we should choose the LC whose RE capacity is the smallest. There are three smallest RE capacities and they are all 1. Besides, the PP capacity in each LC is also all 1. According to the serial number of LCs, we preferentially store ⑥ in LC_1 and ⑦ in LC_2. Similarly, we distribute 14 REs to 4 LCs. Finally, the RE capacity of 4 LCs is: LC_0: ① ② ⑩ ⑬, LC_1: ③ ⑥ ⑧, LC_2: ④ ⑦ ⑪ and LC_3: ⑤ ⑨ ⑫ ⑭. After the dynamic decomposition storage of REs, we expect to achieve the same REs storage capacity for each LC and the minimum ED value. In this example, the PP capacities in each LC are different. But the storage capacities of REs in different LCs are almost same, namely: 4, 3, 3, 4. As shown in Table 2, we know that the result of routing storage is very balanced at any time.

In the implementation process, we first initialize the corresponding parameters. In this algorithm, RE_i indicates the dynamic RE; PP_j ($1 \leq j \leq 255$) represents a pocket prefix; LCm ($0 \leq m \leq n\text{-}1$) represents any LCs; $PP[m]$($0 \leq m \leq n\text{-}1$) represents an array that stores PPs of one LC; $RE[m]0 \leq m \leq n\text{-}1$ represents an array that stores REs of one LC; $MR_{pre}[PRE_{sign}\text{-}1]$ represents an array that stores the serial number of LC that PRE_{sign} belongs to, PRE_{sign} is the prefix sign of the RE. The implementation algorithm is shown in Algorithm 1.

Algorithm 1. Distribute Dynamic RE.

Input:
    RE_i;
Output:
    $PP[m]$;
    $RE[m]$;
1: Initialize $PP[m]$ and $RE[m]$ are 0;
2: Let LC_0 be the line card with the minimum amount of REs;
3: Set $min=0$;
4: Get the first 8 bits prefix of RE_i: j;
5: **if** $MR_{pre}[j\text{-}1]==\text{-}1$ **then**
6:    //The PP of RE_i does not exist.
7:    Send RE_i to the LC_{min};
8:    $MR_{pre}[j\text{-}1]=min$;
9:    $PP[min]++$;
10:    $RE[min]++$;
11:    Calculate the amount of REs of every LC;
12:    Get the serial number of LC with the minimum amount of REs: i;
13:    Set $min=i$;
14: **else**
15:    //The PP of RE_i already exists in one LC.
16:    $m=MR_{pre}[j\text{-}1]$;
17:    Send RE_i to the LC_m;
18:    $RE[m]++$;
19: **end if**
20: Return $RE[m]$, $PP[m]$;

3.3   Packet Forwarding Process

As for the packet forwarding, we define 3 different LC roles. The LC who has the RE that matches the destination IP address of the packet is called host LC (LC_{host}). At the same time, the LC that receives the packet is called its receiving LC (LC_{in}). The LC that sends out the packet is called its sending LC (LC_{out}). For each packet, we get the next hop through LPM in its LC_{host}. Therefore, a router receives an IP packet, it is necessary to find its LC_{host} according to the mapping table. Then, the packet is sent to the LC_{host} for LPM. When a LC receives a packet, the lookup process has two cases depending in the different LC_{in}. (1) LC_{in} is LC_{host}: When finding that LC_{in} of the packet is its LC_{host}, we get the forwarding information through LPM and forward this packet. (2) LC_{in} is not LC_{host}: We get its LC_{host}, where this packet will be sent to. Then we can get the out-interface and the next hop through LPM, and forward this packet. For both of the above cases, if the out-interface information is in LC_{host}, the packet is forwarded directly. Otherwise, it needs to be forwarded to the LC_{out} to complete the final transfer task.

During the packet forwarding of RDDS, some packets need once or twice inter-card communication. However, kernel routers commonly use TCAM to complete LPM, and the lookup speed of TCAM can reach nanosecond level. Therefore, it does not affect the network service quality. As for the internal switching bandwidth, due to the bottleneck of the processing speed of distributed routers is LCs rather than the inner switch network, we can solve this problem by improving the acceleration ratio of switch fabrics.

3.4   Routing Information Update

The RE adding is based on the allocating principles in Sect. 3.2. According to the mapping relationship between PRE_{sign} and LC, we know whether the PP of the new RE exists in LCs. If exists, the new RE will be stored in the LC that the PP belongs to; if not exists, the PP of this new RE will be served as a new PP. For the RE deletion: (1) If the PP that the deleted RE belongs to contains only this one RE, we delete both the RE and the PP. Furthermore, the mapping table will also be updated; (2) If the PP that the deleted RE belongs to contains multiple REs, we just delete this RE.

4   Performance Evaluation and Experimental Analysis

According to expression (1), we know that the value of ED is almost tiny at any time in RDDS. It indicates that RDDS achieves load balancing of LCs in dynamic changes. When n LCs store m REs in a complete balance, the desired capacity of REs required in each LC is m/n. In RDDS, the capacity of REs that each LC needs to store is shown in expression (3). Furthermore, the additional storage space that RDDS needs is also tiny. Each LC just needs additional 446 bytes to store a mapping table.

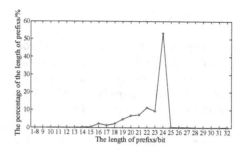

Fig. 3. The distribution of the length of prefixes

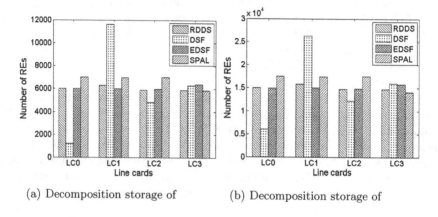

(a) Decomposition storage of   (b) Decomposition storage of

Fig. 4. REs decomposition storage in different models

In addition to the theoretical analysis, we have run a series of experiments to measure the RDDS's performance. This experimental data are selected from 9 different ASs [1,9]. In order to prove the credibility of RDDS, we make a statistical analysis of the prefix mask length of all REs in 9 different ASs, as shown in Fig. 3. According to the statistics on the percentage of each prefix mask length, we find that the prefix mask length of all REs less than 8 bits does not exist, so using the first 8 bits of the IP prefix of REs as a PP is feasible.

This experiment uses 5 PCs. PC_1 is the master card and $PC_2 \sim PC_5$ is $LC_0 \sim LC_3$, respectively. We inject all routing information about $data_1$ [9] and $data_2$ [9] to PC_1, and compare RDDS with other three models, namely DSF [5], EDSF [5], SPAL [6].

From Fig. 4(a) and (b), we know that EDSF achieves the load balancing of each LC, but it causes some consumption during decomposition and storage space. Although the RE capacity of each LC is almost identical in SPAL, it introduces uncontrolled redundancy. Compared with these three models, RDDS not only achieves a better load balancing of LC, but also does not introduce any redundant REs storage in each LC.

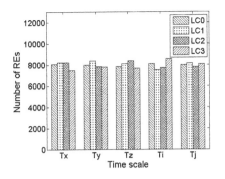

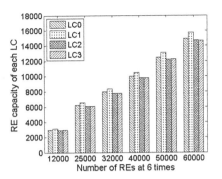

Fig. 5. REs capacity at random times   **Fig. 6.** REs capacity comparison

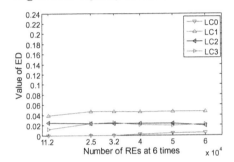

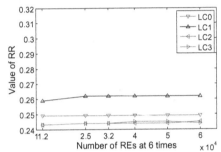

Fig. 7. 6 groups of ED values   **Fig. 8.** REs compression ratio in each LC

We have an experiment about the decomposition storage of routing tables in dynamic random changes, which is intended to prove that RDDS has a better randomness. As shown in Fig. 5, the number of REs in 4 LCs are most balanced at any time, and the maximum absolute difference of the REs capacity in each LC is no more than 900.

In order to better explain the characteristics of RDDS, we carry out 6 experiments with the different number of REs. Form Fig. 6, we find that the absolute difference between REs capacities in each LC and average REs capacities is no more than 600. Hence, it strongly proves that RDDS has a wonderful and stable performance.

As shown in Fig. 7, we know that RDDS effectively ensures that the storage capacity of REs in LCs at any moment are almost the same. When the value of ED is 0, RDDS achieves the absolute equilibrium storage of every LC. With the number of REs increasing, the ED of the REs capacity in each LC keeps the steady state. Figure 8 has a visual description of the compression ratio. Real experiments have indicated that the values of RR are uniformly distributed in the near of 0.25 (In the extremely balanced situation, the RR of routing tables in 4 LCs is 0.25.). Moreover, the minimum absolute difference between RR of RDDS and 0.25 is 0.

5   Conclusion

This paper proposes the RDDS that achieves real-time dynamic decomposition storage of REs in the distributed routers. It regards the first 8 bits of IP prefix as a pocket prefix. When REs arrive, they are stored on different LCs according to their pocket prefixes. And, RDDS ensures that the value of ED is always the minimum. Furthermore, compared with the full backup storage, the REs number of each LC is reduced sharply in RDDS. Experimental results show that RDDS not only ensures the non-full backup storage, but also is adaptable to the dynamic update of routing tables. Besides, RDDS does not produce redundant storage in LCs.

Acknowledgment. This work is supported by the National Natural Science Foundation of China under Grant No. 61373161, 61502320, 61300171. Science & Technology Project of Beijing Municipal Commission of Education under Grant No. KM201410028015, the Youth Backbone of Beijing Outstanding Talent Training Project under Grant No. 2014000020124G133, and Guangdong Natural Science Foundation No. 2015A030310492.

References

1. BGP Routing Table Analysis Reports. http://bgp.potaroo.net
2. Carpenter, B., Crowcroft, J.: IPv4 Address Behaviour Today. RFC 2101, February 1997
3. Gerich, E.: Guidelines for Management of Ip Address Space. RFC 1466, May (1993)
4. Lin, D., Zhang, Y., Hu, C., Liu, B., Zhang, X., Pao, D.: Route table partitioning and load balancing for parallel searching with TCAMs. In: IEEE International Parallel and Distributed Processing Symposium, Long Beach, CA, USA, pp. 1–10, March 2007
5. Chen, W., Xu, M., Yang, Y., Han, D.: Decomposed storage model of FIB for cluster router. Chin. J. Comput. **34**(9), 1611–1620 (2011)
6. Tzeng, N.-F.: Routing table partitioning for speedy packet lookups in high-performance distributed routers. IEEE Trans. Parallel Distrib. Syst. **17**(5), 481–494 (2006)
7. Li, Q., Wang, D., Xu, M., Yang, J.: On the scalability of router forwarding tables: Nexthop-selectable FIB aggregation. In: IEEE INFOCOM, Shanghai, China, vol. 42(4), pp. 321–325 (2011)
8. Zhang, X., Perrig, A., Zhang, H.: Centaur: A hybrid approach for reliable policy-based routing. In: IEEE 33rd International Conference on Distributed Computing Systems, Montreal, Quebec, Canada, pp. 76–84, June 2009
9. BGP Routing Table. http://www.cidr-report.org/as2.0/
10. Yang, T., Duan, R., Lu, J., Zhang, S., Dai, H., Liu, B.: CLUE: Achieving fast update over compressed table for parallel lookup with reduced dynamic redundancy. In: IEEE 32nd International Conference Distributed Computing Systems. Macau, China, pp. 678–687, June 2012
11. Li, Q., Xu, M., Chen, M.: NSFIB construction & aggregation with next hop of strict partial order. In: IEEE INFOCOM, Turin, Italy, pp. 550–554, April 2013
12. Chen, W., Liu, Y., Wang, H.: On storage partitioning of internet routing tables: A P2P-based enhancement for scalable routers. Peer-to-Peer Netw. Appl. **8**(6), 952–964 (2015)

Routing Model Based on Service Degree and Residual Energy in WSN

Zhenzhen Sun[1], Wenlong Chen[1(✉)], Xiaolan Tang[1], and Guangwu Hu[2]

[1] School of Information Engineering, Capital Normal University, Beijing, China
chenwenlong@cnu.edu.cn
[2] Graduate School at Shenzhen, Tsinghua University, Shenzhen, China

Abstract. Energy constraint of sensor nodes is a key problem in WSN. Energy-based routing mechanism can significantly prolong the lifetime of sensor networks, but the current researches do not consider the number of service objects of a senor node. In this paper, we propose a routing model based on service degree and residual energy, named SERM. We put forward the node service degree to represent the service scale of some node, and the path service efficiency to show the path's service capability. Then, a multi-path transmission system of wireless sensor networks is designed based on the 2-dimension: the service degree and the residual energy of nodes. Finally, the simulation experiments using OPNET prove that SERM can prolong the network lifetime and collect more sensor data.

Keywords: Service degree · Service efficiency · Residual energy · Lifetime

1 Introduction

In high density deployment environment, sensor nodes are rather small and usually carry limited energy. Normally, the energy of wireless sensor nodes are provided by the battery, and the nodes need work for a few months or even one year without adding energy [1]. Energy constraint of sensor nodes affects the stability of the network and the lifetime of the network [2]. Therefore, energy awareness and efficient using of energy have become a hot issue in the research of wireless sensor routing protocol [3–6].

For any wireless node, its forwarding service scale is different. Therefore, the number of service objects should be considered in the process of routing. But the existing routing protocols mainly consider the number of hops, residual energy and the path of consumption.

In Fig. 1, a circle indicates a node, the number in circles represents a node identifiers. Then, the two tuples outside the circles are the node's residual energy and the number of service objects whose traffic may be forwarded by the node. The direction of the arrow indicates the direction of data transmission. In Fig. 1, N_4 communicates with N_0. First of all, we assume that the costs of 2 paths are

© ICST Institute for Computer Sciences, Social Informatics and Telecommunications Engineering 2017
S. Wang and A. Zhou (Eds.): CollaborateCom 2016, LNICST 201, pp. 363–372, 2017.
DOI: 10.1007/978-3-319-59288-6_33

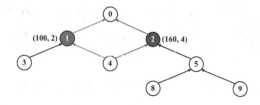

Fig. 1. Node service scale.

equal when data is forwarded from N_4 to N_1 or N_4 to N_2. If the path is selected only according to the residual energy, N_4 will select path: N_4-N_2-N_0. However, N_2 provides forwarding service for 4 nodes, and the average service capacity is 40. N_1 provides forwarding services for 2 nodes, and the average service capacity is 50. Obviously, it is reasonable that N_4 chooses N_1 as the next hop.

In this paper, we design a routing model based on service degree and residual energy (SERM). On account of the different service scale of some nodes, we put forward the node service degree, and path service efficiency which represents the path's service capability. Considering the residual energy and the service scale of the nodes, SERM chooses a optimal path to forward data.

SERM has the following characteristics: (1) SERM considers not only the node energy consumption but also the service capacity of nodes. (2) SERM chooses a different optimal path to forward data to sink node in different time. (3) SERM can prolong the network lifetime and the sink node can collect as many data as possible.

2   Related Work

As the main task of the WSN is to collect data from the sensor nodes to the observer, so the primary goal of the design of routing protocol is that sink node should collect the data information as much as possible in sensor network lifetime. Passive power supply environment has led to the energy of the sensor node is very limited [7], so another important goal of the routing protocol is to maximize the use of existing energy to improve the network's lifetime.

It is a focus of research that the shortest path routing design based on the minimum number of hops in recent years. Minimum hop routing protocol [8] is based on the flooding algorithm and directed diffusion algorithm, and adds the conception of hop count. But in the process of data transmission, nodes will send their packets to all the parent nodes, which results in the message redundancy and in the process of select the parent node only considers the nodes which close to sink one, but not considers the residual energy of nodes.

In some practical applications, the information transmission in sensor networks has a certain direction, so there is a directed diffusion routing protocol [9]. The routing protocol not only meets the feature of the direction of the information transmission in WSN, and still has potential advantage such as the shortest path, the minimal time delay, and the minimal energy consumption [10]. Through the simulated analysis of the directed routing network, the paper [11] gets the result that the gradient of the number of neighbor nodes and the nonuniformity of the distribution of data convergence flow can lead to the greater consumption of energy and delay.

Aiming at the problem of the excessive energy consumption of nodes caused by a single path, C. Shah Rahul proposed an energy multi-path routing mechanism [12]. The main principle of the routing mechanism design is to establish multiple paths between the source node and sink node, then according to the condition of residual energy and the path consumption, gives different paths a certain probability of selection. The model can balance the consumption of the whole network energy while forwarding data, and can prolong the lifetime of the network.

Multi-path routing strategy can not only balance the network traffic but also prolong the lifetime of the network. A routing mechanism for wireless sensor networks is proposed, which combines the residual energy of nodes and the maximum angle of nodes in [13]. Based on the residual energy and the node angle, the initial routing path of the network is established, and then the failure nodes in the network are replaced, and the path is selected again. In paper [14], the node degree, the residual energy and the transmission distance are regarded as the key factors in routing design. And the source node chooses the path to the sink node according to the forward cost which is calculated by the three factors.

Those related researches mentioned above have a good inspiration for this paper. But in this paper, the sensor nodes are distribution with a high density, so the path consume by the data transmission between nodes can be neglected. However, the scale of the service provided by the node is different, so the forward capability of the nodes is different. Therefore, the service scale of the nodes should be considered in the path selection.

3 Service Energy Efficiency Model

In general, there are multiple optional paths between the source nodes and sink node. In SERM, the source node chooses one path with the biggest service ability to forward data, based on the node residual energy and the service ability comprehensively. For instance, in Fig. 1, N_4 wants to send data to N_0. It has two optional paths, i.e. N_4-N_1-N_0 (the red path) and N_4-N_2-N_0 (the blue path). Since the former has a larger service capacity than the latter, the N_4-N_1-N_0 is selected to deliver data. Several important concepts in SERM are described below.

Note that the residual energy(RE) of a node changes with the network running. In this paper, we focus on the energy consumption of packets forwarding, so we compute the energy consumption by the unit of forwarding a packet. In Fig. 2, the residual energy of N_1 is 150, which indicates that N_1 has 150 units of energy. In other words, the residual energy of N_1 can still support the forwarding work for 150 packets.

Definition 1. Node Service Degree(SD): Node service degree represents the number of nodes that this node serve for. The service degree of the node N_k is m, which means there are m nodes which may deliver data to sink node through the node N_k. In the tree-like topology, it is apparent that node service degree is also the number of all descendants of this node.

In Fig. 2, only N_6 reaches N_0 via N_4, so the service degree of N_4 is 1.

Definition 2. Node Service Efficiency(NSE): Node service efficiency represents the node's service capability for its SD. It is computed as:

$$NSE(N_i) = RE(N_i)/SD(N_i) \qquad (1)$$

In Fig. 2, the $SD(N_8)$ is 2, and the $RE(N_8)$ is 60, so the $NSE(N_8)$ is 30.

Definition 3. Path Service Efficiency(PSE): Path service efficiency can reflex the optimal path from the node to sink node. That is:

$$PSE(N_i) = min\{max\{PSE(N_{f_1}), \cdots , PSE(N_{f_n})\}, NSE(N_i)\} \quad (2)$$

In Fig. 2, there are two paths from N_4 to N_0. Hence N_4 selects the maximum value of PSE_s of N_4's parent N_1 and parent N_2, which is 50. Then it selects the minimum value compared with $NSE(N_4)$. Eventually $PSE(N_4)$ is 50.

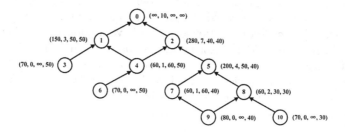

Fig. 2. The diagram of SERM.

A circle in Fig. 2 indicates a node, the numbers in circles are node identifiers, the four tuples outside the circles are: node residual energy, node service degree, node service efficiency, and path service efficiency. The arrows indicate the direction of data transfer.

4   SERM Implementation

SERM includes three parts: topology construction, routing, topology maintenance, etc.

4.1   Topology Construction

When sink node powers on, it means the beginning of the topology construction. The topology is a tree-like structure. In the topology construction process, each node has a "layer" attribute which is the hops from the node to sink node. Let sink node is layer 0, and the direct children nodes of sink node are layer 1.

Algorithm 1. the joining procedure of N_i

Input: The timer is T_1; the max number of child node is max_child;
Output: The parent of the node N_i;
1 **while** T_1 **do**
2 | N_i receives the service message from the nodes;
3 | if the number of it's child $<=$ max_child;
4 | then put the nodes into a set S_1;
5 | **if** T_1 *is expires and* S_1 *is NULL* **then**
6 | | reset the T_1;

7 select the nodes whose layer is minimum in S_1, put into a set S_2;
8 **return** the nodes in the set S_2;

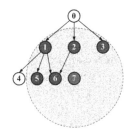

Fig. 3. Topology construction.

Let N_i is a node who has not connected the topology, then Algorithm 1 describes the joining procedure of N_i.

Suppose that the maximum of node connection number is 3. In Fig. 3, the dotted line circle represents the communication range of N_7. After N_7 starts to search parent nodes, it can receive the messages from N_1, N_2, N_3, N_5 and N_6. And then it will compare their connection numbers, so $S_1=\{N_2, N_3, N_5, N_6\}$. After that, N_7 selects the nodes whose layer are minimum, so $S_2=\{N_2, N_3\}$. It means N_7 joins the tree-like topology through N_2 and N_3.

4.2 Routing

After the topology construction, there may be multiple paths from a source node to sink node. In SERM, a node selects the transmission path based on the RE and SD. At any moment, the node always chooses the path whose PSE is maximum to forwarding packets.

In order to choose an optimal path, we need to get the RE and SD of nodes. We suppose nodes in WSN have self awareness of their energy, so we still need to get the SD of each node and PSE of each path.

We first define an array of the SD (referred to as SA), which contains the number of all nodes that reach the node. The SD is the size of the SA. Then Algorithm 2 describes the obtaining procedure of SD.

Algorithm 2. the obtaining procedure of $SD(N_i)$

Input: The number of the child node of N_i is Num_child
Output: The service degree of N_i as $SD(N_i)$
1 $SA_i = NULL$;
2 **for** $m = 1$; $m <= Num\_child$; $m{+}{+}$ **do**
3 | N_i receives the connect message from it's child N_m;
4 |__ $SA_i = SA_i + N_m$;
5 $SA_i = SA_i + N_i$;
6 the number of the SA_i is $SD(N_i)$;
7 **return** $SD(N_i)$;

In Fig. 2, N_9 and N_{10} send the connection messages in which the SA is empty to the parent N_8. After receiving the connection messages, N_8 counts its SA, $SA_8 = \{N_9, N_{10}\}$, the SD of N_8 is 2.

At present, the RE and SD of a node are already known, so the NSE of the node can be calculated according to expression (1). Then Algorithm 3 describes the obtaining procedure of PSE.

Algorithm 3. The obtaining procedure of $PSE(N_j)$

Input: The number of the parent node of N_j is Num_parent; the $RE(N_j)$; and
  the $SD(N_j)$;
Output: The path service efficiency of N_j as $PSE(N_j)$
1 $NSE(N_j) = RE(N_j)/SD(N_j)$;
2 $PSE(N_j) = NSE(N_j)$;
3 **for** $n = 1$; $n <= Num\_parent$; $n{+}{+}$ **do**
4 | N_j receives the price message from it's parent N_n;
5 |__ $PSE(N_j) = \min \{PSE(N_j), PSE(N_n)\}$;
6 **return** $PSE(N_j)$;

4.3 Topology Maintenance

During the operation of WSN, the RE of some nodes will decrease gradually, and there may be some failure nodes whose electricity drain out. These changes directly affect the selection of the transmission path.

Transmitting data, nodes select the path according to the PSE. When the RE of a node is changed, the PSEs of descendant nodes are updated according to the Algorithm 3. Once a node is failure, its child nodes first judge whether the node to the sink node still exist path, if there is no path, re-select the parent node according to Algorithm 1. Then the parent node first updates its own SD, and then the SDs of their ancestors are updated according to Algorithm 2, finally the PSEs of entire network are updated according to Algorithm 3.

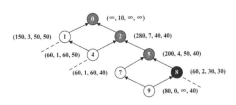

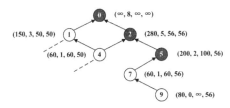

Fig. 4. Before the topology mainte- **Fig. 5.** After the topology maintenance.   nance.

Figures 4 and 5 show the topologies before and after N_8 failure respectively.
The two figures are both a partially views of Fig. 2. N_8 is a failure node, and
N_0, N_2 and N_5 are the nodes affected. N_8 fault, N_5 updates its SA, namely
$SA_5=\{N_7, N_9\}$, and the $SD(N_5)$ is 2. According to the Algorithm 2, N_5 sends
connection message to its ancestor node, and then the $SD(N_0)$ is 8. At last, the
topology and related parameters are updated according to Algorithm 3, which
are shown in Fig. 5.

5   Performance Analysis and Experimental Simulation

Compared with the shortest path model (Min Path) and the maximum energy
model (Max RE), SERM can prolong the network lifetime, but it needs some
cost for SD and PSE. In SERM, we do not care about the energy consumption
of sink node. Except sink node, every node needs to store the RE (2 bytes), SD
(1 bytes) and the PSE (1 bytes). Let M be the size of memory cost for SERM,
the formula is:

$$M = \begin{cases} 0, & if \ sink \ node \\ 4, & else \end{cases} \tag{3}$$

Except the leaf node, each node needs to send packets to convey energy
efficiency of paths downwards. Let BW_1 is the bandwidth cost of it. The packet
contains 8 bits of the PSE, and 224 bits of packet encapsulation. For any node
N_i, assuming the number of its direct son nodes is m, and a message be sent
every t time, then $BW_1=m*(224+8)$ /t. Take $m=2$, $t=100s$, then $BW_1 = 4.64$
bit/s. In addition to sink node, each node needs to send packets to convey service
information upwards. Let BW_2 is the bandwidth cost of it. The packet contains
all of the descendants of the node, and 224 bits of packet encapsulation. Suppose
the node N_i has the number of the parent node is n, the number of the descendant
node is k, then $BW_2=n*(224+k*8)/t$. Assuming the topology is the 5 layer of
the binary tree-like, we take the second layer node as an example, $n=2$, $k=9$,
$t=100s$, then $BW_2 = 5.92$ bit/s. So the cost of memory and bandwidth are both
small in SERM.

To verify the performance of SERM, we use the OPNET to simulation experiments. The parameters used in the simulation are shown in Table 1. In order

Table 1. Table of simulation parameters

Parameters	Value
The regional scale (m)	1000*1000
The communication radius (m)	100
The number of nodes	60, 100
The packet delivery (pkts/min)	0.5, 1, 1.5, 2

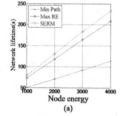
(a)

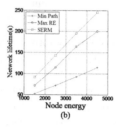
(b)

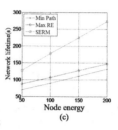
(c)

Fig. 6. The lifetime of 60 nodes.

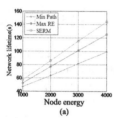
(a)

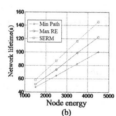
(b)

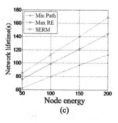
(c)

Fig. 7. The lifetime of 100 nodes.

to reflect the reliability of the experimental data, we compare SERM with Min Path and Max RE in same topology.

In this paper, the lifetime of network is defined as the time from beginning of the network to energy exhaustion of any node [15]. Figure 6 shows the lifetime of 60 nodes in different energy distribution. The abscissa represents the energy value of the node, the ordinate indicates the time when the first node failure. In Fig. 6.a, all of the node energy are same. In Fig. 6.b, the energy is a random value in range. In Fig. 6.c, the energy of leaf nodes is 1000, each reducing one layer, the energy is increased by 50, 100, 150 and 200.

No matter what kind of energy distribution, the lifetime of SERM is always longer than Min Path and Max RE. And the slope of SERM is the largest, which reflects the greater the energy, the advantage of SERM is more obvious. Figure 7 shows the lifetime of 100 nodes in different energy distribution.

We define the network throughput as the number of packets that sink node is collected in the lifetime of the network. Figure 8 shows the throughput of 60 nodes in different energy distribution, and the frequency of the packet delivery is

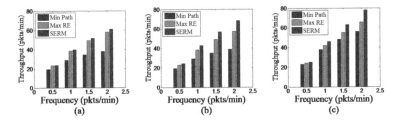

Fig. 8. The throughput of 60 nodes.

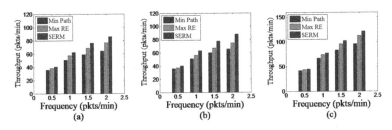

Fig. 9. The throughput of 100 nodes.

0.5, 1, 1.5 and 2 per minute respectively. In Fig. 8.a, all the node energy is same, which is 1000. In Fig. 8.b, the energy of nodes is different, which is a random value in [1000,2000]. In Fig. 8.c, the energy of nodes is increased layer by layer. The energy of leaf nodes is 1000, and each reducing one layer, the energy is increased by 50. The simulation results show that SERM in different contract frequency, different node energy distributions, the throughput of the network are better than Min Path and Max RE. So during the lifetime, sink node can collect more packets with SERM. Figure 9 shows the throughput of 100 nodes in different energy distribution.

6   Conclusion

In wireless sensor networks, nodes resources are limited. Thus for a routing model, one of the most significant tasks is to maximize the energy utilization of nodes. In dense networks, there usually exist multiple paths for a node to send data to sink node. Therefore, in SERM, the path selection considers not only the remaining energy of nodes, but also their service degree. Simulation experiments prove that SERM has certain advantages in terms of network throughput and network lifetime, in spite of some additional cost for the storage and transmission of SD and PSE.

Acknowledgment. This research is supported by the National Natural Science Foundation of China (Nos.61373161, 61502320, 61300171), Youth Backbone of Beijing Outstanding Talent Training Project (No. 2014000020124G133), and the Fundamental Research Project of Shenzhen Municipality (No.JCYJ20160228172531429).

References

1. Liu, M., Cao, J.N., Zheng, Y., Chen, L.J., Xie, L.: Analysis for multi-coverage problem in wireless sensor networks. J. Softw. **18**(1), 127–136 (2007)
2. Kaur, R., et al.: Optimized cluster based deployment of sensor nodes to enhance the network lifetime in wireless sensor network. In: Fifth International Conference on Advanced Computing & Communication Technologies (ACCT), pp. 658–665. IEEE Computer Society (2015)
3. Yao, Y., Cao, Q., Vasilakos, A.V.: EDAL: An energy-efficient, delay-aware, and lifetime-balancing data collection protocol for heterogeneous wireless sensor networks. IEEE/ACM Trans. Netw. **23**(6), 810–823 (2015)
4. Lee, A., Ra, I.: Adaptive-gossiping for an energy-aware routing protocol in wireless sensor networks. In: International Conference on Wireless Communications & Mobile Computing, pp. 1131–1135. ACM (2010)
5. Rachamalla, S., Kancharla, A.S.: Power-control delay-aware routing and MAC protocol for wireless sensor networks. In: IEEE International Conference on Networking, Sensing & Control, pp. 527–532 (2015)
6. Zaman, N., Low, T.J., Alghamdi, T.: Enhancing routing energy efficiency of wireless sensor networks. In: International Conference on Advanced Communication Technology (ICACT), pp. 587–595. IEEE (2015)
7. Chang, J.H., Tassiulas, L.: Maximum lifetime routing in wireless sensor networks. IEEE/ACM Trans. Netw. **12**(4), 609–619 (2004)
8. Han, K.H., Ko, Y.B., Kim, J.H.: A novel gradient approach for efficient data dissemination in wireless sensor networks. In: IEEE Vehicular Technology Conference, pp. 2979–2983 (2004)
9. Chiang, S.S., Huang, C.H., Chang, K.C.: A minimum hop routing protocol for home security systems using wireless sensor networks. IEEE Trans. Consum. Electron. **53**(4), 1483–1489 (2007)
10. Akyildiz, I.F., Su, W., Sankarasubramaniam, Y., et al.: Wireless sensor networks: A survey. Comput. Netw. **38**(4), 393–422 (2002)
11. Wang, W., Li, Y., Li, H.S., et al.: The analysis of link availability for directional routing in mobile ad hoc network. In: International Conference on Computer Application and System Modeling (ICCASM), pp. 353–356. IEEE (2010)
12. Shah, R.C., Rabaey, J.M.: Energy aware routing for low energy ad hoc sensor networks.In: Wireless Communications and Networking Conference, pp. 350–355. IEEE (2002)
13. Wei, M., Huang, X., Wu, C., et al.: Network coding based energy-efficient multipath routing for wireless sensor network. In: International Conference on Advances in Mobile Computing & Multimedia, pp. 240–244. ACM (2012)
14. Qi, X.G., Wang, H.F., Zheng, G.Z., Xie, M.D., Duan, L.: Analysis on resilience of wireless sensor networks growth model. J. Softw. **25**(1), 131–138 (2014). (in Chinese)
15. Mak, N.H., Seah, W.K.G.: How long is the lifetime of a wireless sensor network? In: International Conference on Advanced Information Networking & Applications, pp. 763–770. IEEE (2009)

Abnormal Group User Detection in Recommender Systems Using Multi-dimension Time Series

Wei Zhou$^{(\boxtimes)}$, Junhao Wen, Qingyu Xiong, Jun Zeng, Ling Liu, Haini Cai, and Tian Chen

College of Software Engineering, Chongqing University,
174 Shazheng Street, Chongqing, China
{zhouwei,wjhcqu,xiong03,zengjun,liuling,hainic,chengtian}@cqu.edu.cn

Abstract. Collaborative filtering based recommender systems are capable of generating personalized recommendations, which are tools to alleviate information overload problem. However, due to the open nature of recommender systems, they are vulnerable to shilling attacks which insert forged user profiles to alter the recommendation list of targeted items. Previous research related to robustness of recommender systems has focused on detecting malicious profiles. Most approaches focus on profile classification but ignore the group attributes among shilling attack profiles. A method for detecting suspicious ratings by constructing multi-dimension time series *TS-TIA* is proposed. We reorganize all ratings on each item sorted by time series, each time series is examined and suspicious rating segments are checked. Then statistical metrics and target item analysis techniques are used to detect shilling attacks in these anomaly rating segments. Experiments show that our proposed method can be effective and less time consuming at detecting items under attacks in greater datasets.

Keywords: Abnormal group users · Shilling attack detection · Time series · Recommender system

1 Introduction

Information overload [1] is a problem people have to face in modern society. Collaborative Filtering based recommender systems play an increasing role in information filtering, which is an important tool to alleviate this contradiction [2]. In recent years, recommender systems have become extremely popular and are applied in a variety of areas. Recommender systems have been developed to recommend movies, music, news, books, research articles, social tags, and other products.

However, recent research has shown that traditional collaborative filtering based techniques are vulnerable to attacks [3–5]. Recent work has shown that

© ICST Institute for Computer Sciences, Social Informatics and Telecommunications Engineering 2017
S. Wang and A. Zhou (Eds.): CollaborateCom 2016, LNICST 201, pp. 373–383, 2017.
DOI: 10.1007/978-3-319-59288-6_34

even modest attacks are sufficient to manipulate the behavior of the most commonly used recommendation algorithm [6]. Attackers change the recommendation list by introducing biased profiles into the rating matrix, which is called shilling attack. Attacks against recommender systems can affect the quality of predictions, resulting in crisis of confidence.

In order to preserve order and fairness of recommender systems, attack profiles should be detected and removed. In this paper, we propose a novel technique based on statistical metrics and rating time stamps. The main contribution of this technique is that we divide the rating matrix into rating segments (windows) and find suspicious rating segments. We examine the suspected rating segments instead of the whole rating matrix, which reduces the algorithm complexity and time consuming. The paper is organized as follows. In next section we look at previous work in the area. In Sect. 3 we discuss preliminary knowledge that used in this paper, including detecting metrics and how to construct time series. Section 4 describes the detailed metrics used in detecting attacks and algorithms and experimental methodology for our detection model. In Sect. 5 we present our experimental results and a conclusion in Sect. 6.

2   Related Work

Attack profiles that are introduced into recommender systems in order to alter recommendation lists of a set of target items. There are two types of main attacks according to the intent of attackers. A push attack is an attack that aims to promote an item and boost its ranking, whereas a nuke attack is an attack designed to demote an item and lower its rankings.

The word "shilling" was first termed in [7]. There have been some recent research efforts aiming at detecting and reducing the effects of profile injection attacks [8,9]. These attacks consist of a set of attack profiles, each containing biased rating data associated with a fictitious user identity. Since "shilling" profiles look similar to authentic profiles, which is difficult to identify. Many attack profiles are based on random and average attack models which were introduced originally in Lam and Reidl [10]. There are three categories of attack detection algorithms: supervised, unsupervised, and semi-supervised.

In the first category, attack detection techniques are modelled as a classification problem. Most early detection algorithms [11] exploited signatures of attack profiles. These techniques were considered less accurate, since they looked at individual users and ignored the combined effect of such malicious users. Moreover, these algorithms do not perform well when the attack profiles are obscured. Some of these techniques use nearest neighbours classifiers, decision tree methods, rule based classifiers, Bayes classifiers, Neural Networks classifiers, or SVM based classifiers [12,13].

In the second category, unsupervised detection approaches address these issues by training on an unlabeled dataset. The benefit of this is that these techniques facilitate online learning and improve detection accuracy. Some of the techniques use clustering, association rules methods [14] and other statistical approaches [15,16]. Zhang et al. [17] used a Singular Value Decomposition (SVD) method to learn a low-dimensional linear model. Wei et al. [18,19] proposed a novel technique for identifying group attack profiles which uses an improved metric based on Degree of Similarity with Top Neighbors ($DegSim$) and Rating Deviation from Mean Agreement ($RDMA$) using statistical strategy. They also extend a detailed analysis of target item rating patterns. The proposed methods improve the detection accuracy of detection using target item analysis method.

In the third category, semi-supervised detection approaches make use of both unlabelled and labelled user profiles for multi-class modelling. Wu et al. [20] proposed a system called $HySAD$ for hybrid attack detection. In general, $HySAD$ is a semi-supervised learning system that makes use of both unlabeled and labeled user profiles for multi-class modeling.

Time series have been used to detect shilling attacks in recommender systems. The intuition of the idea is that all attack models cause changes in the rating distributions of target items. [17] postulates that the distribution of item ratings in time can reveal the presence of a wide range of shilling attacks given reasonable assumptions about their duration. In this paper, we borrow this idea, all ratings on each item are sorted by time series, each time series is examined and suspected rating segments are checked. Then techniques of our previous study are used to detect shilling attacks in these anomaly rating segments using statistical metrics and target item analysis.

3   Preliminary Knowledge

In this section, some preliminary knowledge are introduced. Section 3.1 introduces the detecting structure of the proposed method. Section 3.2 introduces how a multi-time series data stream are constructed. Section 3.3 reviews two different detecting metrics in collaborative filtering algorithms.

3.1   Structure of Detecting

There are millions of profiles and items in real time recommender systems; it is time consuming to carry out detecting on the whole system. Group attributes and time clustering characteristics are found exist in shilling attacks. Most of profiles and ratings are low suspected of being attackers. We intend to divide the whole dataset into a group of subsections, and then suspected subsections are checked. In the end, techniques we proposed in our previous studies are used focusing on rating matrix that composed of suspected subsections. The scope of the target dataset will be reduced greatly, which would be time saving and efficiency.

There are two phases in the detecting structure. In the first phase, we find the suspected ratings on an item and then find suspicious rating segments that rated on the item during the specific time. Suspected rating segments are determine by

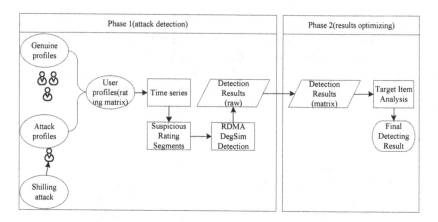

Fig. 1. Detecting structure of the proposed method *TS-TIA*

constructing a time series. The number of profiles are reduced by a wide margin in this phase. Then we detect shilling attacks in these anomaly rating segments using statistical metrics and target item analysis method. In the second phase, a fine-tuning phase whereby the target items in the potential attack profiles set are analyzed. Figure 1 shows the detecting process of the proposed method *TS-TIA*.

3.2   Constructing Time Series

To construct the time series of the above measure for an item, we first sort all the ratings for the item by their time stamps into a data stream, and then group every disjoint w consecutive ratings into a window. w is referred as the window size. In this paper, window size is set to 20. According to the attribute of characteristic of abnormal groups, multi-dimension time series are chose, including number of rating in unit time, average rating and review frequency. For example, in a online store, sort rating on an item according to the time stamps in ascending order. We can get:

$$R(s) = \{r_1, r_2, r_3, \cdots, r_i, \cdots, r_j, \cdots, r_{n_s}\} \tag{1}$$

$$TS(s) = \{t_{s_1}, t_{s_2}, t_{s_3}, \cdots, t_{s_i}, \cdots, t_{s_j}, \cdots, t_{s_n}\} \tag{2}$$

While $R(s)$ is the rating series of an item by all users that rate on the item, and $TS(s)$ is the time series of ratings on the item. For all ratings, $1 \leq i \leq j \leq n$, $t_{s_i} \leq t_{s_j}$. For example, t_{s_i} is the time stamp of rating r_i.

A time window Δt is used to divide the rating time interval $I = [t_0, t_0 + T]$ into $n = T/\Delta t$ time windows, while the length of every time window is Δt, t_0 is the starting time stamp. For the ith time window I_i, $I_i = [t_0 + (i-1)\Delta t, t_0 + it_0]$, while $I = \bigcup\limits_{i=1}^{n} I_i$. For every time window in the time series I_i, the value of characteristic is calculated. So, in a rating dataset, given the time interval $[t_0, t_0 + T]$ and the time window Δt, a time series can be achieved:

$$F_s (I, \Delta t) = \begin{bmatrix} I_1 (1), I_1 (2), \cdots, I_1 (i), \cdots, I_1 (j), \cdots I_1 (n) \\ I_2 (1), I_2 (2), \cdots, I_1 (i), \cdots, I_1 (j), \cdots I_2 (n) \\ I_3 (1), I_3 (2), \cdots, I_1 (i), \cdots, I_1 (j), \cdots I_3 (n) \end{bmatrix} \tag{3}$$

Abnormal group user discovery based on multi-dimension time series can disclose the group attribute of abnormal users. If multi-dimension characteristics are abnormal in the time series, then all the ratings in the time interval is recognized as abnormal. For example, time interval $[t_0, t_0 + T]$ is abnormal in Fig. 2. A set of suspicious ratings can be get in this step. It is necessary to filter normal ratings from the suspicious ratings set. Figure 2 is the schematic diagram that shows how suspicious rating segments (windows) are located.

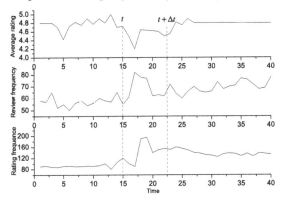

Fig. 2. Abnormal group users discovery based on multi-time series

3.3 Detecting Metrics

Attack profiles differ from that of genuine profiles in a statistical way. There are two main differences: the rating given to the target item (items); the rating distribution among the filler items. Due to this there are different metrics that have been proposed to measure the difference between rating profiles. In this section we will look at two metrics, *RDMA* and *DegSim* [6]. RDMA value of attack profiles is higher than that of genuine profiles; while DegSim value of attack profiles is lower than that of genuine profiles.

Rating Deviation from Mean Agreement. *RDMA* measures the deviation of agreement from other users on a set of target items, combined with the inverse rating frequency for these items. *RDMA* can be calculated in the following way:

$$RDMA_u = \frac{\sum_{i=0}^{N_u} \frac{|r_{u,i} - \overline{r_i}|}{NR_i}}{N_u} \tag{4}$$

where N_u is the number of items user u rated, $r_{u,i}$ is the rating given by user u to item i, NR_i is the overall number of ratings in the system given to item i.

Degree of Similarity with Top Neighbours. The *DegSim* attribute is based on the average Pearson correlation of the profile's k nearest neighbours and is calculated as follows:

$$DegSim = \frac{\sum_{u=1}^{k} W_{uv}}{k} \tag{5}$$

where W_{uv} is the Pearson correlation between user u and user v, and k is the number of neighbours.

In paper [18], we proposed a novel technique for identifying group attack profiles which uses an improved metric based on Degree of Similarity with Top Neighbors (*DegSim*) and Rating Deviation from Mean Agreement (*RDMA*). We also extended our work with a detailed analysis of target item rating patterns. Experiments show that the combined methods can improve detection rates when the dataset is in a small scale. However, the efficiency becomes lower when the datasets increase. In the next section, time series will be constructed and suspected rating segments are checked.

4   Detecting Profile Injection Attacks

In the first phase, a suspicious rating segment is get by constructing a time series. The scope of attack profiles are greatly narrowed, which saves time and reduces the computing complexity. However, genuine profiles and attack profiles are mixed together. We use statistical metrics and target item analysis techniques in our previous research to filter out genuine profiles.

Overall attackers should have a high influence in the system in order to promote the target items effectively. However, there are three different features in attack profiles, which enable us to differentiate between genuine and attack profiles. Firstly, filler items are randomly chosen thus the similarity based on these filler items between attack and genuine profiles should be lower. Secondly, since shilling attacks usually try to push items with low ratings or vice versa in nuke attacks, the users mounting such an attack will assign a rating that deviates from the average rating value assigned by the genuine profiles. Last but not least, all target items are assigned a highest or lowest value, the count number of this value should be greater than other values among items. Based of these three reasons, we choose the *RDMA* and *DegSim* metrics, which reveal these distinctive features in the rating patterns. Attackers should therefore have relatively high values for *RDMA*, as well as very low values in *Degsim*. The pseudocode of the method is shown in Algorithm 1.

In this phase, an *RDMA* value for each profile is calculated. If the *RDMA* value for a profile is above a maximum ϵ_{RDMA} threshold then we consider this profile as a suspicious profile.

$$RDMA_u = \frac{\sum_{i=0}^{N_u} \frac{|r_{u,i} - \overline{r_i}|}{NR_i}}{N_u} \geq \epsilon_{RDMA}$$

From this process, we get a pool of suspicious profiles, SP_{RDMA}, that had *RDMA* values above the assigned threshold. We also calculate the *DegSim* value for each

Algorithm 1. Applying target item analysis method on abnormal rating segments.

Input: The set of suspected profiles $SUSSEG$;item set I;
Output: Final detect result set $DetectedResult$;

1: $SUSSEG = SUSSEG - RDMA_u \geq \epsilon_{RDMA} \cap DegSim_u \leq \epsilon_{DegSim}$
2: $DetectedResult = \emptyset$;
3: $\forall i \in I, count_i \leftarrow$ number of ratings in $item_i$ equal to r;
4: **while** $\max(count) > \theta$ **do**
5: $\quad item_t \leftarrow \{item_i | count_i = \max(count)\}$;
6: $\quad \forall p \in SUS_{RD}, P \leftarrow p$ rate $item_t$ with r;
7: $\quad DetectedResult \leftarrow P \cup DetectedResult$;
8: $\quad SUS_{RD} \leftarrow SUS_{RD} - P$;
9: **end while**
10: **return** $DetectedResult$.

of the profiles. If the $DegSim$ value for a profile u is below a minimum ϵ_{DegSim} threshold then we consider this profile as a suspicious profile.

$$DegSim = \frac{\sum_{u=1}^{k} W_{uv}}{k} \leq \epsilon_{DegSim}$$

From this process, we get a pool of suspicious profiles, SP_{DegSim}, that had $DegSim$ values below the assigned threshold. Lastly we consider the intersection between the pool of SP_{RDMA} and SP_{DegSim}, as our $SuspectedAttackers$.

$$SuspectedAttackers = SP_{DegSim} \cap SP_{RDMA}$$

We set generous thresholds ϵ_{RDMA} and ϵ_{DegSim}, allowing more profiles to be considered as suspicious. We then filter out the misclassified profiles in the second phase.

For example, Table 1 is an example of a rating matrix and attack profiles. The matrix is an $m \times n$ matrix. Each row in the matrix is the rating for the m items by a user. Table 1 shows genuine user profiles from $User_1$ to $User_m$ and attackers profiles from $Attacker_1$ to $Attacker_p$. The last row is the count number of rating 5, in this example, $Item_5$ is the target item.

5   Experiments and Results

5.1   Experiment Setup

The datasets used in the experiments are the widely used *MovieLens* Datasets, Including MovileLens 100k Dataset, 1 Million and 10 Million Dataset by the GroupLens Research Project at the University of Minnesota and a subset of Netflix dataset. The platform we implement all the experiments as flows: Hardware: CPU is Intel Core i7 processors, Windows 7, with 16 G RAM. Software: All of our tests is on Matlab 2012b.

Table 1. An example of rating matrix and attack profiles.

	Item$_1$	Item$_2$	Item$_3$	Item$_4$	Item$_5$	....	Item$_n$
User$_1$	5	2	3	0	0	....	5
User$_2$	2	0	4	1	2	....	3
User$_3$	4	2	3	0	5	....	0
User$_4$	0	3	0	3	4	....	3
....	....	....	....	....	....	....	....
User$_m$	2	0	4	1	2	....	3
Attacker$_1$	2	1	0	0	5	....	4
Attacker$_2$	2	2	0	0	5	....	3
Attacker$_3$	1	2	0	0	5	....	2
....	....	....	....	....	....	....	....
Attacker$_p$	2	0	0	0	5	....	4
Count(5)	2	2	2	2	9	....	3

5.2 Experiment Results

In order to simulate real attacks in recommender systems, we injected attack profiles generated by certain attack models. In the experiments we varied two different variables: the attack size and the filler size. Because the median filler size of all profiles is 3%, we did not consider situations where the filler size is greater than 10%. In order to get certain prediction shift, the minimum number of attack profiles are set to 20. The attack size are varied from 20 to 200 and the filler size are varied from 3% to 9% (Table 3).

Experiments Result and Comparisons. Table 2 shows the attack detection results when attack size and filler size varies. The detection rate increase while the false positive rate decrease with the increase of attack size and filler size.

Table 2. Detection results of *TS-TIA* when the filler size and attack size varies

Attack size	Filler size	20	40	60	80	100	120	140	160	180	200
Detection rate	3%	65%	74%	78%	85%	86%	88%	91%	93%	95%	98%
	5%	68%	76%	80%	86%	87%	92%	93%	94%	95%	98%
	7%	78%	80%	86%	89%	91%	93%	93%	95%	95%	98%
	9%	82%	84%	87%	90%	92%	93%	94%	96%	97%	99%
False positive rate	3%	5%	5%	4%	4%	3%	3%	2%	2%	3%	2%
	5%	4%	4%	4%	4%	3%	3%	3%	2%	2%	2%
	7%	4%	4%	3%	4%	3%	5%	2%	1%	2%	2%
	9%	4%	4%	3%	4%	2%	2%	2%	1%	2%	1%

Table 3. Comparison of detection results of different methods when filler size is 7% and attack size varies

Attack size	Method	20	40	60	80	100	120	140	160	180	200
Detection rate	DeR-TIA	78%	80%	90%	98%	100%	100%	100%	100%	100%	100%
	RD-TIA	92%	95%	100%	100%	100%	100%	100%	100%	100%	100%
	TS-TIA	60%	82%	86%	89%	91%	93%	93%	95%	95%	98%
	bp-based	70%	60%	78%	85%	90%	96%	100%	100%	100%	100%
False positive rate	DeR-TIA	3%	3%	2%	0%	0%	0%	0%	0%	0%	0%
	RD-TIA	2%	2%	2%	0%	0%	0%	0%	0%	0%	0%
	TS-TIA	4%	4%	3%	4%	3%	5%	2%	1%	2%	2%
	bp-based	12%	11%	11%	12%	11%	12%	12%	12%	12%	12%

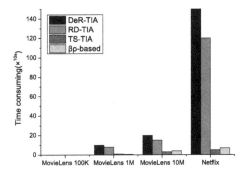

Fig. 3. Time consuming of different detecting methods when the datasets are different

The detection rate reaches 90% or more when the attack size greater than 140. The false positive rate is less than 10%, and became stable around 3% when the attack size is greater than 100. The false positive rate of algorithms using target item analysis method is lower than that of $\beta\rho$-based method.

Table 2 shows comparison of detection rate of different methods. The detection rate increase while the false positive rate decrease with the increase of attack size. The detection rate of the proposed algorithm is lower than that of other detecting algorithms. The false positive rate of the proposed algorithm is higher than that of DeR-TIA and RD-TIA, which all of them using target item analysis method, but lower than that of $\beta\rho$-based algorithm. The false positive rate is less than 5%, and became stable around 2% when the attack size is greater than 100.

Figure 3 shows time consuming of different algorithms when attack size varies. All Algorithms consume more time when detecting greater datasets. DeR-TIA consumes the most time in all detections and RD-TIA gets the second most time consuming, which is intolerable in greater datasets. TS-TIA consumes the least time. $\beta\rho$-based method consumes more time than TS-TIA but less than other two target item analysis based methods. Generally speaking, even the detection rate of *TS-TIA* is not better than that of $\beta\rho$-based method, but consumes less time and the false positive rete is lower.

6 Conclusion

Collaborative filtering based recommender systems suffer from shilling attacks. In most cases, attackers inject masses of forged profiles in order to get a substantial prediction shift. When a large number of forged profiles are injected into the rating matrix in a short period of time, the group feature would stand out. In this paper, a data stream by sorting ratings of an item is constructed, time series are built and suspicious profiles are filtered, then two statistical metrics are used to detect forged profiles; last but not least, target item analysis method reduce the false positive rate of the final detecting result. Experiments showed that the proposed method gets lower precision in great datasets, but occupies less computing capacity.

Acknowledgement. This research is supported by NSFC under grant No. 61602070, 61502062, 61379158 and China Postdoctoral Science Foundation under Grant No. 2014M560704.

References

1. Ma, Y., Wang, S., Yang, F., Chang, R.N.: Predicting QoS values via multi-dimensional QoS data for web service recommendations. In: 2015 IEEE International Conference on Web Services (ICWS), pp. 249–256. IEEE (2015)
2. Herlocker, J.L., Konstan, J.A., Terveen, L.G., Riedl, J.T.: Evaluating collaborative filtering recommender systems. ACM Trans. Inf. Syst. (TOIS) **22**(1), 5–53 (2004)
3. Sarwar, B., Karypis, G., Konstan, J., Riedl, J.: Item-based collaborative filtering recommendation algorithms. In: Proceedings of the 10th International Conference on World Wide Web, pp. 285–295. ACM (2001)
4. Xia, H., Fang, B., Gao, M., Ma, H., Tang, Y., Wen, J.: A novel item anomaly detection approach against shilling attacks in collaborative recommendation systems using the dynamic time interval segmentation technique. Inf. Sci. **306**, 150–165 (2015)
5. Cao, J., Wu, Z., Mao, B., Zhang, Y.: Shilling attack detection utilizing semi-supervised learning method for collaborative recommender system. World Wide Web **16**(5–6), 729–748 (2013)
6. Chirita, P.-A., Nejdl, W., Zamfir, C.: Preventing shilling attacks in online recommender systems. In: Proceedings of the 7th Annual ACM International Workshop on Web Information and Data Management, pp. 67–74. ACM (2005)
7. Lam, S.K., Riedl, J.: Shilling recommender systems for fun and profit. In: Proceedings of the 13th International Conference on World Wide Web, pp. 393–402. ACM (2004)
8. Zhang, S., Ouyang, Y., Ford, J., Makedon, F.: Analysis of a low-dimensional linear model under recommendation attacks. In: Proceedings of the 29th Annual International ACM SIGIR Conference on Research and Development in Information Retrieval, pp. 517–524. ACM (2006)

9. O'Mahony, M.P., Hurley, N.J., Silvestre, G.: Detecting noise in recommender system databases. In: Proceedings of the 11th International Conference on Intelligent User Interfaces, pp. 109–115. ACM (2006)

10. Fu, L., Goh, D.H.-L., Foo, S.S.-B., Na, J.-C.: Collaborative querying through a hybrid query clustering approach. In: Sembok, T.M.T., Zaman, H.B., Chen, H., Urs, S.R., Myaeng, S.-H. (eds.) ICADL 2003. LNCS, vol. 2911, pp. 111–122. Springer, Heidelberg (2003). doi:10.1007/978-3-540-24594-0_10

11. O'Mahony, M.P., Hurley, N.J., Silvestre, G.C.M.: Promoting recommendations: An attack on collaborative filtering. In: Hameurlain, A., Cicchetti, R., Traunmüller, R. (eds.) DEXA 2002. LNCS, vol. 2453, pp. 494–503. Springer, Heidelberg (2002). doi:10.1007/3-540-46146-9_49

12. Grčar, M., Fortuna, B., Mladenič, D., Grobelnik, M.: KNN versus SVM in the collaborative filtering framework. In: Batagelj, V., Bock, H.H., Ferligoj, A., Žiberna, A. (eds.) Data Science and Classification. Studies in Classification, Data Analysis, and Knowledge Organization, pp. 251–260. Springer, Heidelberg (2006)

13. Su, X., Khoshgoftaar, T.M.: A survey of collaborative filtering techniques. Adv. Artif. Intell. 2009, 4 (2009)

14. Lee, C.-H., Kim, Y.-H., Rhee, P.-K.: Web personalization expert with combining collaborative filtering and association rule mining technique. Expert Syst. Appl. 21(3), 131–137 (2001)

15. Hurley, N., Cheng, Z., Zhang, M.: Statistical attack detection. In: Proceedings of the Third ACM Conference on Recommender Systems, pp. 149–156. ACM (2009)

16. Wang, S., Ma, Y., Cheng, B., Chang, R., et al.: Multi-dimensional QoS prediction for service recommendations (2017)

17. Zhang, S., Chakrabarti, A., Ford, J., Makedon, J.: Attack detection in time series for recommender systems. In: Proceedings of the 12th ACM SIGKDD International Conference on Knowledge Discovery and Data Mining, pp. 809–814. ACM (2006)

18. Zhou, W., Wen, J., Koh, Y.S., Alam, S., Dobbie, G.: Attack detection in recommender systems based on target item analysis. In: 2014 International Joint Conference on Neural Networks (IJCNN), pp. 332–339. IEEE (2014)

19. Zhou, W., Koh, Y.S., Wen, J., Alam, S., Dobbie, G.: Detection of abnormal profiles on group attacks in recommender systems. In: Proceedings of the 37th International ACM SIGIR Conference on Research & Development in Information Retrieval, pp. 955–958. ACM (2014)

20. Wu, Z., Wu, J., Cao, J., Tao, D.: HySAD: A semi-supervised hybrid shilling attack detector for trustworthy product recommendation. In: Proceedings of the 18th ACM SIGKDD International Conference on Knowledge Discovery and Data Mining, pp. 985–993. ACM (2012)

Dynamic Scheduling Method of Virtual Resources Based on the Prediction Model

Dongju Yang[✉], Chongbin Deng, and Zhuofeng Zhao

Beijing Key Laboratory on Integration and Analysis of Large-Scale Stream Data, Research Center for Cloud Computing, North China University of Technology, Beijing 100144, China
{yangdongju,edzhao}@ncut.edu.cn, xgybdcb@163.com

Abstract. Deploying applications to the cloud has become an increasingly popular way in the industry due to elasticity and flexibility. It uses virtualization technology to provide storing and computing resources to the applications. So how to efficiently schedule virtual resources to ensure the quality of services during the peak, and avoid the waste of resources during the idle is an important research topic in the cloud computing, which aims to minimize the execution cost and to increase the resource utilization. The way based on the monitoring data to scale up or scale down the virtual resources may let virtual resources suffer from over seriously. In this paper, we present a dynamic scheduling method for the virtual resources based on the prediction model. Firstly, we use prediction model to predict the request quantity. And then we combined the prediction result with the load capacity of current resources to compute whether to increase or decrease the virtual resources. Finally, we choose the suitable physical machine to create or recycle the virtual machine. The experimental results show that the prediction model can fit our scene well, and the resource scheduling algorithm can be used to ensure the quality of service in a timely and effective manner.

Keywords: Cloud application · Surge in traffic · Quality of service · Prediction model · Dynamic resource scheduling

1   Introduction

Cloud computing provides an on-demand and scalable delivery model for the users [1]. It has been used to solve the complicated computation and storage problems by more and more governments, research institutions and industries [2] due to provide resources as a service to the users. Effective virtual resource scheduling can improve the utilization of resources and meet the needs of users. The virtual resource scheduling problem is considered to be a combinatorial optimization problem, but also a NP complete problem [3].

The workload of each virtual machine (VM) is always changing, and some may exhibit cyclical changes. We usually tend to over allocate virtual resources in order to ensure the application to have a better performance during the peak [4], which will inevitably lead to low utilization of resources. To operate and manage resources more conveniently, effective monitor is often used [5]. But there will be a traffic surge for

© ICST Institute for Computer Sciences, Social Informatics and Telecommunications Engineering 2017
S. Wang and A. Zhou (Eds.): CollaborateCom 2016, LNICST 201, pp. 384–396, 2017.
DOI: 10.1007/978-3-319-59288-6_35

quite a time after application is deployed and then decline gradually based on the monitoring. For example, in the school's teaching information system, a few students will visit this website in ordinary time, but a huge amount of traffic will be generated when students need to select the course. Then the application system needs to extend resources to deal with the requests traffic. We usually monitor the system and warn system managers to deal with the lack of resources. But there is often a delay to schedule resources by monitor and warning.

To deal with the above challenges and to improve the utilization of virtual resources and flexibility of scheduling, we propose a method to dynamically schedule the virtual resources based on the Autoregressive Integrated Moving Average Model (ARIMA) prediction model. Resources will be allocated in advance on the basis of the prediction data. Our paper addresses the following problems:

Find a prediction model to accurately predict the possible application workload of the next time interval.

Dynamic scheduling of virtual machine resources according to the change of workload and prediction data to ensure more efficient use of resources.

The rest of our paper is organized as follows. Section 2 is an overview of the current state of the academic research on the virtual resource scheduling. Section 3 describes the system architecture. Section 4 focuses on the prediction model we will use. Section 5 describes the virtual machine scheduling strategy and the corresponding experiment details are illustrated in Sect. 6. Section 7 presents conclusions and future work.

2 Related Works

Since cloud computing uses virtualized resources, scheduling and resource allocation are the important research topics [6]. It is a hot research topic that how to use effective scheduling strategies to reduce the cost of execution and improve the utilization of resources.

Silpa et al. [6] discuss the current scheduling algorithm that has been published in cloud computing, in this paper, 15 different algorithms are studied and compared, such as fuzzy genetic algorithm based on task scheduling.

Some resource scheduling frameworks are put forward. Singh et al. [7] present an efficient cloud workload management framework under the premise of certain workload and quality of service. Shuja et al. [8] introduce a resource scheduling framework for efficient utilization.

Hassan et al. [9] present Nash bargaining to save resources and optimize the number of servers. Singh et al. [10] propose service quality indicators to optimize the execution time and avoid waste of resources. And some studies about resource optimization algorithms, such as the article [11, 12].

Zheng et al. [13] point out that virtual machine placement is also a way to optimize the resources, two kinds of virtual machine placement method, incremental placement and consolidated placement, are discussed and a new virtual machine placement strategy is proposed. Wang et al. [14] explore an energy and QoS-aware VM placement optimization approach based on particle swarm optimization.

Liu et al. [15] present an approach to process the dynamic user service requests more cost-effectively. Zhou et al. [16] introduce a dynamically adjust the virtual resource rental strategy to help cloud service providers maximizing profits.

There are also some researches on prediction methods. Salah et al. [17] use Markov chains to estimate the number of virtual machine instances that are required to be allocated under a given Service Level Object (SLO) standard. Shyama et al. [18] study a Bayesian model to predict resource needs of CPU and memory intensive applications in the short term and long term. However, the article [17] focus on load balance, and in [18] mainly focus on CPU cores and RAM, but they are not very suitable for our scenarios.

3   System Architecture

3.1   Architecture Description

The system architecture used in this paper showed in Fig. 1 includes the following layers User Layer, Application Layer, Control Layer, Virtual Layer, Physical Layer.

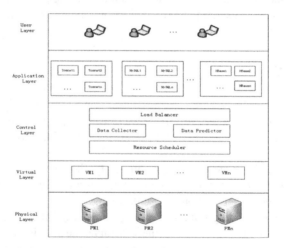

Fig. 1. System architecture diagram

User Layer: Users who use the application in cloud plateform.

Application Layer: It provides basic application environment, such as tomcat server, MySQL database, Hbase, etc.

Control Layer: It includes Load Balance Module, Data Collector Module, Data Predictor Module, Resource Scheduler Module.

Load Balancer Module: All requests submitted by the users will be forwarded through the Load Balancer to our web server. We use Nginx as a load balancing server in the system architecture.

Data Collector Module: This module is mainly to get the data through real-time monitoring. Some data will be collected by this module, such as CPU, memory, request quantity, etc., and then data will be pre processed. We store the requests per second to database in order to analyze historical data in the future. The module will calculate the response time for each request, which is ready for us to assess the application response time.

Data Predictor Module: The module uses the data collected in the Data Collector Module to calculate the number of requests to be reached at the next time interval of the application. The next time interval is the amount of user requests that the application will achieve after 5 min. On one hand, we mainly study the prediction of the application workload in the short term; On the other hand, the high frequency statistics and calculation will cause some pressure on our server. Generally each virtual machine can be completed in 30–96 s from creation to deployment [17], so the time is enough for us to deal with the coming pressure on the system. Of course, you can adjust the time interval.

Resource Scheduler Module: Using the Data Predictor Module to get the predicted requests of the application to decide to increase or reduce the virtual resource.

Virtual Layer: It supply virtual resource and composes a virtual resource pool.

Physical Layer: It is infrastructure and mainly includes the physical servers and the virtual machines deployed on the physical servers, which provides the underlying resources for the application.

4   Workload Prediction Methods

In this section we will discuss several methods for predicting the workload. We simplify the workload to the number of user requests in our scenario. But the requested quality of service has been taken into account, we assume that the response time of the request is satisfied in the range of 0 to 2 s, the maximum workload of the server is considered under such a condition. We mainly discuss three prediction methods: Moving Average method, Polynomial Fitting method, ARIMA Model method. We have also introduced the error to analyze the three methods which is more suitable for our scenario.

① Moving Average: Moving Average is one of widely known technical indicator used to predict the future data in time series analysis [19]. In statistics, a moving average is a calculation to analyze data points by creating series of averages of different subsets of the full data set. It includes simple moving average, the cumulative moving average and weighted moving average [20]. We use simple moving average in this paper.

We assume that the requests for a certain time of application is r_i, then the sequence of requests can be expressed as $R = \{r_1, r_2 \ldots r_i \ldots r_n \mid n < T\}$, where T is our measurement time. According to the definition of the moving average, we can predict the amount requested at time n + 1 is:

$$Pre\_R = (r_1 + r_2 + \ldots + r_n)/n. \tag{1}$$

Pre_R is the predicted value at time n + 1 in Eq. (1), n denotes the average movement cycle, r_1 to r_n are the first n values.

② Polynomial Fitting method: Polynomial regression is a form of linear regression in which the relationship between the independent variable x and the dependent variable y is modelled as an nth degree polynomial [21]. Linear relationship is not a good description of the relationship between the amounts of application requests at different times, so the polynomial method is one aspect to consider.

We assume that the ti time corresponds to a request amount of r_i, and (t_i, r_i) is a point on a two curve, namely:

$$r_i = at_i^2 + bt_i = c. \tag{2}$$

Since it is the conic section, we only need to use three sets of values to be able to seek out a, b and c solution. If we predict r_{i+1}, just need three points, that is, $(t_{i-2}, r_{i-2}), (t_{i-1}, r_{i-1}), (t_i, r_i)$.

③ ARIMA Model: The ARIMA model is built based on Markov random process, which not only absorbs the dynamic advantages of the regression analysis, but also the advantages of moving average [22]. Non-seasonal ARIMA model use ARIMA (p, d, q) to express, wherein p, d, q are non-negative integers, p is the order of autoregressive model; d indicates the degree of differencing, q represents the moving average model order. Seasonal ARIMA model using ARIMA (p, d, q) (P, D, Q) m, m refers to the number of cycles per season, P, D, Q, respectively, refers to the autoregressive, moving average and differential [23].

5   Scheduling Algorithm and Implementation

5.1   VM Provisioning Algorithm and Implementation

We assume that a certain time point T, the requests for our application is R. We simplify the application workload to the user's request. Our machine (Web Server) number is N in the current state. We adopt a polling workload allocation strategy. The number of requests for each web server shared by the load balancer is R/N.

We use Data Collector Module to collect raw data and pre-processing data. We use $T_{response}$ to denote the response time for each request, and pass the request of the pre processed data to the ARIMA module. Each time the user requests for the application will be recorded in the database, we can calculate the amount of user requests of each interval, abbreviated R_i. We predict requests of the next time interval, assumed to be $S_{predict}$ based on R_i. $S_{predict}$ and $S_{current\_max}$, the maximum workload that the virtual machines can bear under the current scale, will be passed to the Dynamic Scheduling Module. If $S_{predict}$ is greater than $S_{current\_max}$, then the DSM will find the right virtual machine template in physical servers to configure virtual resources. The way we are using is to randomly select a virtual machine that is providing services for the application and obtain its information (the using operation system, CPU kernel number, memory, etc.). Finding the information from the template in physical servers and here we assume that each virtual machine that has been used is created by a template in the physical machine server. In order to reduce the false positive rate, we can set the number of times to meet the judgment. We begin to configure virtual resources, when the times are more than a specified number of times. Assuming that each virtual machine created by virtual machine template can withstand the maximum workload of MHVMW. The difference between the predicted workload and the maximum workload that the current size of the virtual machines can withstand is the workload that we need to create virtual machines to support. We can roughly calculate the number of virtual machines that need to be created at a time combined with MHVMW, using N_{need} to denote the calculated number. To determine the location of the virtual machine created, first of all, physical machines workload will be sorted from least to most, and we use the word "size" to denote the number of physical machines that meet the conditions for creating virtual machines, then taking the remainder of "size" from 0 to N_{need}. The purpose of this is to create a virtual machine in a low workload physical machine. Finally, the strategy returns the positions of the virtual machine to be created.

Symbol definition:

$LVMW_i$: Lowest Virtual Machine Workload, the minimum workload value allowed by each virtual machine, if the current workload is lower than the value, we will consider it to be an idle virtual machine.

$HVMW_i$: Highest Virtual Machine Workload, the maximum workload value allowed by each virtual machine, if the current workload is higher than the value, we will believe that the quality of service provided can not meet the needs of users.

$S_{predict}$: The predicted workload value obtained from the prediction model.

$N_{current}$: Number of current virtual machines.

$S_{current\_max}$: The maximum workload that the virtual machines can bear under the current scale.

$$S_{current\_max} = \sum_{i=1}^{Ncurrent} HVMW_i \tag{3}$$

S_{curent_min}: The minimum workload required for the virtual machines at the current scale.

$$S_{curent\_min} = \sum_{i=1}^{Ncurrent} LVMW_i. \tag{4}$$

MHVMW: Model Highest Virtual Machine Workload, the virtual machine can be made into a template, this variable represents the maximum workload that it can take after the template is turned into a virtual machine.

PM: Physical Machine, $PM = \{PM_1, PM_2 \ldots PM_i \mid i < PMCount\}$.

VM: Virtual Machine, $VM = \{VM_1, VM_2 \ldots VM_j \mid j < VMCount\}$.

Algorithm 1. VM Provisioning

```
Input: S_predict, N_current, S_current_max, MHVMW, PM, VM
Output: postions that VM will place.

1: while true do
2:    if  S_predict >= S_current_max  then
3:                MHVMW = findTemplate(PM, VM)
4:                N_need = (S_predict  - S_current_max) / MHVMW
5:        return addVMPos(PM, Nneed)
6:    else
7:                break;
8: end while
9:    function findTemplate(PM, VM)
10:           randomly select VM[j] from VM
11:           for(template in PM)
12:            if(VM[j]== template)
13:               MHVMW = VM[j]
14:               break;
15:            else
16:               continue
17:           end for
18:           return MHVMW
19: function addVMPos(PM, Nneed)
20:           list = {}
```

```
21:        for pm in PM do

22:           if (pm.currentWorkload <
pm.higestworkload())&& pm.hasResource() then

23:              list.add(pm)

24:        end for

25:        sortByAsc(list)

26:        size = list.size()

27:        for i=0;i< N_need ;i++ do

28:           positions.add(list.get(i % size))

29:        end for

30:        return positions
```

Algorithm 2: VM Recycling

Input: $S_{predict}$, S_{curent_min} , VM

Output: Recycling virtual machine success (true) or
failure (false)

```
1:        while true do

2:           if S_predict <= S_curent_min then

3:              rmPos = delVMPos(VM)

4:             return destoryVM(rmPos)

5:           else

6:             break;

7:           end while

8:        function delVMPos(VM)

9:           sortByAsc(VM)

10:           return VM.get(0)
```

5.2 VM Recycling Algorithm and Implementation

It is obviously a waste of resources that virtual resources remain the largest scale after the peak of the traffic is over. VM recycling Algorithm will be enabled when the current workload is less than the specified minimum workload. We will carry out an ascending sort to workload of all virtual machines when the recycling algorithm is enabled. In order to reduce the false positive rate, we can also use the method that predicted times reach the number of count times specified to enable VM Recycling Algorithm. We will poll the VM workload and recycle the VM that is the minimum workload until the remaining one virtual machine to provide services.

6   Experimental Design and Results

6.1 Experimental Environment

In order to verify whether the prediction model and the resource scheduling algorithms are effective, we do some experiments in this part. The experimental environment used is: 2 LoadRunner servers, 1 load balance server, 4 application servers, 1 MySQL servers and 3 physical machines (Table 1).

Table 1. Configuration information

Name	CPU	Memory	Hard disk
LoadRunner1	2 cores 2.0 GHz	4 GB	130 GB
LoadRunner2	2 cores 2000 MHz	4 GB	100 GB
LoadBalance	1 core 2000 MHz	2 GB	100 GB
VM1 (Application Server)	1 core 2000 MHz	2 GB	100 GB
VM2 (Application Server)	1 core 2000 MHz	2 GB	100 GB
VM3 (Application Server)	2 core 2600 MHz	2 GB	100 GB
VM4 (Application Server)	1 core 2000 MHz	2 GB	100 GB
MySQL	2 core 2.67 GHz	4 GB	100 GB
PM1	48 core 2.6 GHz	64 GB	830 GB
PM2	48 core 2.6 GHz	32 GB	550 GB
PM3	48 core 2.6 GHz	32 GB	550 GB

6.2 Experiment and Result Analysis of the Predict Methods

We deploy our application in two groups of two virtual machines, one group using the default policy, another group using the proposed strategy in this paper. Using 2 LoadRunner servers to simulate the request, and then using our prediction model to predict. We will show the number of requests for the site below and the curve drawing of the real value and the predictive value obtained by using the methods in the Sect. 4.

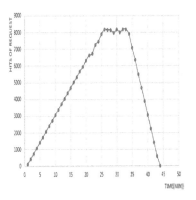

Fig. 2. Site request volume graph

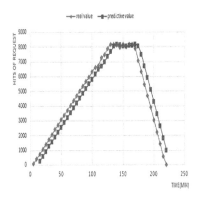

Fig. 3. The real value and predictive value of MA

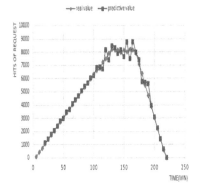

Fig. 4. The real value and predictive value of polynomial fitting

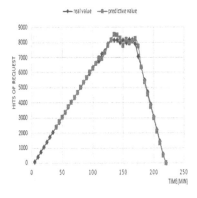

Fig. 5. The real value and predictive value of ARIMA

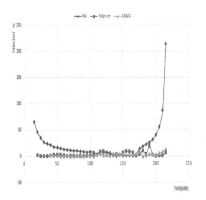

Fig. 6. Relative error curve of MA, Polynomial and ARIMA

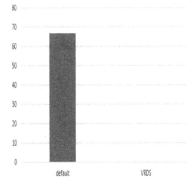

Fig. 7. Default policy and VRDS comparison graph with failed requests

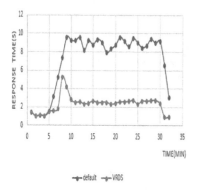
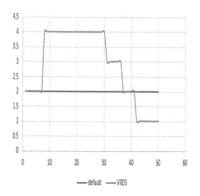

Fig. 8. Default policy and VRDS response time comparison graph

Fig. 9. Changes in the number of VMs under the default policy and VRDS

Figure 2 is the general trend of accepting requests from our website. The number of requests for the site is a gradual increase from less to more, after a certain period of time, the requests will gradually decline. This is the scenario we need to deal with in the project. Figure 3 uses moving average method to fit our scenarios, and the overall trend is well fitted, but we can find out from the graph, the fitting curve of this method is relatively backward, which cannot be very good to help us to predict the future trend of requests. Figure 4 method is very good at the request of the amount of the increase and decrease of the scene, but the volatility of prediction results is larger in the peak period of requests. In our scenario, the Fig. 5 method can be well fitted with both increasing and decreasing values. In order to observe the real value and the predicted value of the scene, we introduce the error analysis. Figure 6 shows the relative error of the three methods.

From Fig. 6, we can see that the relative error of ARIMA is relatively stable, and the error is the smallest of the three methods, we will use the model to predict in our scene.

6.3 Resource Scheduling Experiment Results and Analysis

We use our prediction model in the virtual machine scheduling algorithm. By prediction, it will inform our Virtual Resource Dynamic Scheduling (VRDS) algorithm when the user's traffic continues to increase. And then our VRDS algorithm calculates the size of the required resources, select a reasonable resource scheduling and decide to create or recycle the virtual machine. In the default policy we give a fixed number of virtual machines, and in the VRDS strategy will base on the load situation to do resource scheduling. In Fig. 7, it shows the comparison of the number of requests for the users to access the web site under the two different strategies. VRDS strategy can effectively reduce the number of failed requests. It is assumed that the maximum response time for each user to request is 2 s. The response time of the user request is illustrated in the case of Fig. 8 with two strategies, which are continuously increasing with the number of requests on the website. VRDS strategy can be more close to the response time we set.

Figure 9 shows the change in the number of VMs, VRDS can create and recycle VMs in different stages.

In summary, in our scenario, the prediction model used in this article can be more fitting site requests constantly increasing amount of requests to the maximum amount and gradually decreasing after the scene. VRDS algorithm combined with the prediction model in this paper can effectively and timely response to the site of the high workload situation.

7   Conclusion and Future Work

With the advent of big data era, the data is growing geometrically. Our web site or application is likely to generate a huge surge in traffic because of sudden or hot events. Relying solely on the traditional way apparently is unable to cope with such pressure, and cloud computing brings us a new revolution. Deploying our applications in the cloud will help us to avoid the collapse of the application because of heavy workload. However, there are still many deficiencies in the dynamic scheduling of cloud resources.

In this paper, we proposed a method for dynamic scheduling of virtual resources based on prediction. The prediction will help us to make the decision to deal with the load too much earlier, and change the passive into the initiative. By actively calculating the size of the virtual resources that are needed to cope with the current workload and the decision to create a reasonable location for the virtual machine, we will be more rapid in response to the heavy workload of cloud applications and ensure that the application can easily cope with the massive use of access.

Of course, that we simplify the server workload to the user's request for the application is not enough to completely express the actual situation of the workload, and the workload prediction method is still not fine enough, the scene is relatively simple. In future work we will consider more factors that are more close to the actual situation and simulate our experiments, and apply our algorithm to more practical scenarios.

Acknowledgments.   This work is supported by Key Program of Beijing Municipal Natural Science Foundation "Theory and Key Technologies of Data Space Towards Large Scale Stream Data Processing" (No. 4131001).

References

1. Somasundaram, T.S., Govindarajan, K.: CLOUDRB: a framework for scheduling and managing High-Performance Computing (HPC) applications in science cloud. Future Gener. Comput. Syst. **34**, 47–65 (2014)
2. Zhao, Y., Li, Y., Raicu, I., Lu, S., Tian, W., Liu, H.: Enabling scalable scientific workflow management in the Cloud. Future Gener. Comput. Syst. **46**, 3–16 (2015)
3. Yuan, H., Li, C., Du, M.: Optimal virtual machine resources scheduling based on improved particle swarm optimization in cloud computing. J. Softw. **9**(3), 705–708 (2014)
4. Huang, Q., Shuang, K., Xu, P., Li, J., Liu, X., Su, S.: Prediction-based dynamic resource scheduling for virtualized cloud systems. J. Netw. **9**(2), 375–383 (2014)

5. Aceto, G., Botta, A., de Donato, W., Pescape, A.: Cloud monitoring: a survey. J. Comput. Netw. **57**(9), 2093–2115 (2013)
6. Silpa, C.S., Basha, M.S.S.: A comparative analysis of scheduling policies in cloud computing environment. Int. J. Comput. Appl. (0975–8887) **67**(20), 16–24 (2013)
7. Singh, S., Chana, I.: QRSF: QoS-aware resource scheduling framework in cloud computing. J. Supercomput. **71**, 241–292 (2015)
8. Shuja, J., Bilal, K., Madani, S.A., Khan, S.U.: Data center energy efficient resource scheduling. Cluster Comput. **17**, 1265–1277 (2014)
9. Hassan, M.M., Alamri, A.: Virtual machine resource allocation for multimedia cloud: a Nash bargaining approach. Procedia Comput. Sci. **34**, 571–576 (2014)
10. Singh, S., Chana, I.: Q-aware: quality of service based cloud resource provisioning. Comput. Electr. Eng. **47**, 138–160 (2015)
11. Liu, Z., Zhou, H., Fu, S., Liu, C.: Algorithm optimization of resources scheduling based on cloud computing. J. Multimedia **9**(7), 977–984 (2014)
12. Shao, Y.: Virtual resource allocation based on improved particle swarm optimization in cloud computing environment. Int. J. Grid Distrib. Comput. **8**(3), 111–118 (2015)
13. Zheng, Q., Li, R., Li, X., Shah, N., Zhang, J., Tian, F., Chao, K.-M., Li, J.: Virtual machine consolidated placement based on multi-objective biogeography-based optimization. Future Gener. Comput. Syst. **54**, 95–122 (2016)
14. Wang, S., Zhou, A., Hsu, C.H., et al.: Provision of data-intensive services through energy- and QoS-aware virtual machine placement in national cloud data centers. IEEE Trans. Emerg. Top. Comput. **4**(2), 290–300 (2016)
15. Liu, Z., Wang, S., Sun, Q., et al.: Cost-aware cloud service request scheduling for SaaS providers. Comput. J. **57**(2), 291–301 (2014)
16. Zhou, A., Wang, S., Sun, Q., et al.: Dynamic virtual resource renting method for maximizing the profits of a cloud service provider in a dynamic pricing model. In: International Conference on Parallel and Distributed Systems, pp. 944–945. IEEE Computer Society (2013)
17. Salah, K., Elbadawi, K., Boutaba, R.: An analytical model for estimating cloud resources of elastic services. J. Netw. Syst. Manage. **24**, 285–308 (2016)
18. Shyama, G.K., Manvi, S.S.: Virtual resource prediction in cloud environment: a Bayesian approach. J. Netw. Comput. Appl. **65**, 144–154 (2016)
19. Hansun, S.: A new approach of moving average method in time series analysis. In: 2013 Conference on New Media Studies (CoNMedia), pp. 1–4 (2013)
20. Wikipedia. https://en.wikipedia.org/wiki/Moving_average
21. Wikipedia. https://en.wikipedia.org/wiki/Polynomial_regression
22. Li, J., Shen, L., Tong, Y.: Prediction of network flow based on wavelet analysis and ARIMA model. In: International Conference on Wireless Networks and Information Systems, 2009, WNIS 2009, pp. 217–220 (2009)
23. Wikipedia. https://en.wikipedia.org/wiki/Autoregressive_integrated_moving_average

A Reliable Replica Mechanism for Stream Processing

Weilong Ding[1(✉)], Zhuofeng Zhao[1], and Yanbo Han[2]

[1] Data Engineering Institute, North China University of Technology, Beijing, China
dingweilong@ncut.edu.cn
[2] Beijing Key Laboratory on Integration and Analysis of Large-Scale Stream Data, Beijing, China

Abstract. In Internet of Things, data would be fast generated from massive sensors as real-time data stream, and the replica mechanism is essential to guarantee availability during stream processing. Traditional mechanisms always assume the redundant replicas were exactly correct, but in the practical conditions even slight errors of replica would lead to the calamity for recovery. In this paper, a reliable mechanism is proposed in which space-bounded signature of checkpoint is used for validation during the replica placement. The mechanism has been analyzed theoretically, and also demonstrated by extensive experiments in various conditions.

Keywords: Stream processing · Replica · Availability · Space-bounded · Signature

1 Introduction

In Internet of Things, data is fast generated from massive sensors of many business scenarios, and these real-time, continuous and no-boundary data is termed as data stream. For stream processing, low latency and high throughput is elementary requirements, the failure of any processing element (**PE** for short) not only cuts off the data flow to the downstream, but may also overflow the memory of upstream in chain reaction [1]. Therefore, high availability (**HA** for short) guarantee for stream processing is necessary due to the velocity nature of data stream [2, 3]. As the most favorite HA, the replica of PEs can keep partial data, and would rebuild status of failed PE. Traditional replica mechanisms assume the redundant replicas were exactly correct, but even the slight errors of replica would lead to the calamity for recovery. In this paper, we propose a reliable replica mechanism through space-bounded signature, which is used to validate checkpoint when the replica is placed. We also balance extra overheads during the backup phase, such as bandwidth, memory and CPU. Our contributions conclude as follows. (1) The replicas can be fast validated through space-bounded signature. The validation is efficient in high probability. (2) The optimal tradeoff between overheads is well studied according to physical capacities. The performance holds steady when data scales up.

© ICST Institute for Computer Sciences, Social Informatics and Telecommunications Engineering 2017
S. Wang and A. Zhou (Eds.): CollaborateCom 2016, LNICST 201, pp. 397–407, 2017.
DOI: 10.1007/978-3-319-59288-6_36

This paper is organized as follows. Section 2 shows the background including motivation and related works. Section 3 elaborates our replica mechanism with checkpoint algorithm. Section 4 quantitatively evaluates performance and availability guarantee through extensive experiments in various conditions. Section 5 summarizes the conclusion.

2 Background

2.1 Motivation

Our work comes from the practical project *Grid Transportation* in Chinese city Shenzhen. In this metropolitan city, thousands of cameras are deployed on trunk roads to recognize the passing vehicles for traffic analysis. A basic data unit *tuple* would be packaged by a camera in one second, which includes a recognized vehicle-plate, vehicle type, capture time, lane number, camera number, two photos (front and back view) and other 22 attributes. We have developed a backend system in Cloud to do more than 10 business jobs, such as fake-plate detection, copy-plate detection, black-list detection and accompanied-vehicle analysis, etc. It is typical requirement of stream processing that any tuple should respond within no longer than three seconds since its arrival. In our system, more than 40 distributed machines in Cloud are involved, and each processing unit on one machine is termed as *PE* [1, 4]. The periodical checkpoint as replica is required for specific PE, because that PE is apt to overload and then fail when the data stream is in high velocity. We found it difficult to guarantee replica's validity especially in unstable network condition. For example, in our system a PE executes quantile aggregation on the tuples in recent 30 s to detect traffic jam. When fails in rush hour, its recovery may not complete from replica due to the network congestion or some errors in replica. However, current replica mechanisms assume the replica is always correct and neglect the slight errors from network in practice. A reliable mechanism for stream processing is required to validate the replica efficiently. That is just our original motivation.

2.2 Related Work

For stream processing, the replica mechanisms can be classified by two perspectives [5], which imply different tradeoffs between performance and overheads. (1) In backup phase at run-time, replica mechanism has three types: active standby, passive standby and upstream backup. The replicas in those three types have the decreasing independence, while the more independent the replica is, the higher overheads and lower latency would cost. (2) In recovery phase at fail-time, replica mechanism could have three types either: gap recovery, rollback recovery and precise recovery. Those three types have increasing precision after recovery, while the more precise the recovery guarantees, the higher overheads and longer latency would suffer. Each type has its own advantages and limitations, and both perspectives have to be considered in current systems. For example, Borealis [6] adopts active standby with precise recovery; SAND [7] uses upstream backup and passive-standby to guarantee precise recovery; MillWheel [8] provides passive standby with gap recovery; Flume [9] and Storm [10] uses upstream backup to implement rollback or precise recovery. Our work employs the passive standby at run-time to guarantee gap recovery at fail-time.

Due to the flexible tradeoff, the PE's checkpoint as replica is the most commonly used mechanism in current systems [2], and current works focus on the optimization in certain conditions. However, the assumptions that the replica would be correctly transferred through network may not always hold in practice, because real network condition is unpredictable. There is no validation for the replicas' correctness. The replica mechanism in SAND [7] can solve the uncertainty from the disordered tuples by new type PE *coordinator*; but its strong consistency guarantee restricts the throughput of stream processing. In our work, limited extra bits as signature are included in the replica, by which the checkpoint can be validated fast and correctly enough. Moreover, this configurable signature can balance between the correctness and the bandwidth overhead during the backup phase.

3 Replica with Space-Bounded Signature

3.1 PACK Protocol for Passive Standby

We propose the PACK (Passive replica with check) protocol to provide reliable replica, with the help of a monitor module to manage status and the configurations. For passive standby, traditional replica is a synonym for checkpoint, but the replica through PACK includes checkpoint and its signature. The sequence diagram of PACK is showed in Fig. 1. (1) In Step 1, a checkpoint algorithm is employed to build replica with signature, which would be discussed in the next section. (2) In Steps 2–6, replica is placed among machines; in Steps 4–6, the checkpoint would be validated by monitor module. Therefore at fail-time, after detecting a PE's failure, the monitor selects one of its replicas on another machine, downloads the program package of the failed PE and transfers it to that machine. The PE would be initiated from the program package and then rebuilt from the replica.

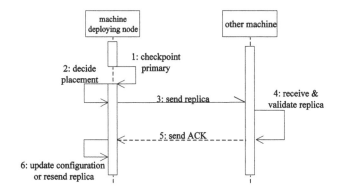

Fig. 1. The PACK protocol at run-time

PACK extends the Sweeping Checkpointing protocol (**SC** for short) [11] in IBM CLASP whose validity has been proved formally. Compared with SC, PACK has the advantages below. First, the checkpoint is programmable, and a signature of checkpoint is attached in the replica. The content of replica can be tuned via the signature. Second, the checkpoint can be validated from its signature after the replica is placed. If unsuccessful, the replica is abandoned and the monitor would resend a replica again after the notification. Third, the replicas are built asynchronously with their own timer and configurable intervals. It is more suitable for stream processing especially in high velocity.

There are two assumptions in our work. (a) All PEs are in clock-synchronization. It can be easily ensured through NTP (Network Time Protocol) servers. (b) The PEs' failure comes from machines' fail-stop. It is sensible because we focus on the replicas among distributed machines. One PE cannot be recovered only if all its replicas are inaccessible in the system.

3.2   Checkpoint Algorithm

To validate the checkpoint, some extra bits as the signature are required. But how many bits are adequate is the very problem, which implies how much the additional bandwidth overhead would cost. In the following, we assume that the checkpoint own m binary bits and its size is M. That is, $M = 2^m$ and $m = \ln M$ where $\ln x$ expresses the logarithmic value based on 2. A lemma is proved below to show that problem is hard.

Lemma 1. To correctly validate a checkpoint containing m bits, at least m bits have to be checked through a deterministic algorithm.

Proof. The least erroneous case is that only the rth bit in the checkpoint is reversed during the transfer. $1 <= r <= m$. In this case, r uniformly and randomly lies in $[1..m]$ and could not be determined in advance. Therefore, to definitely and correctly locate r in a deterministic algorithm, at least m bits have to be checked in this replica. ∎

In deterministic algorithm, the extra bits for validation have the same magnitude as the checkpoint itself. It is impossible and impractical due to the doubled the bandwidth. Therefore, we propose a checkpoint algorithm to build replica using space-bounded bits as signature to balance the validation correctness and bandwidth overhead. We name this algorithm as SCC (Sweeping Checkpoint with Check).

```
Input: a natural number i bigger than 2
Output: a replica including checkpoint with signature

SCC algorithm
1 begin
2   if (checkpoint needs inputQueue)
3     checkpoint += inputQueue;
4   end if
5   while (state && (checkpoint needs state))
6     stateMap.add(state);
7   end while
8   checkpoint += stateMap;
9   checkpoint += outputQueue;
10  p = randomPrime(i);
11  rem = checkpoint mod p;
12  replica = [checkpoint, p, rem];
13  return replica;
14 end
```

The parameter i of a natural number bigger than 2 is termed as **check index**. The **signature** of given checkpoint is composed by p and rem, and the replica include checkpoint with its signature. As the line 9, the output queue is always included in the checkpoint, while the input queue or internal states are optional on demand. The signature of checkpoint is generated at lines 10–11: p is random prime and rem is the remainder of *checkpoint* as binary values divided p. The function $randomPrime(i)$ generates $p <= 2^{i*\ln m}$, where m is the bits of the checkpoint and i restricts the range of p. To get this random prime, it is the straightforward method to generate a random number and test whether it is a prime or not; if not repeat until the test is true. However, the classical prime test algorithms like Miller-Rabin [12, 13] or AKS [14] have high time complexity. For that reason, a trick is adopted here to fast find a random prime: we maintain enough primes [15] beforehand as a table in memory, and select a required prime (less than $2^{i*\ln m}$) randomly in that table.

Accordingly, the replica validation can be deduced as these steps. First, the replica is unpacked as three pieces *checkpoint*, p and rem. Second, if the remainder of *checkpoint* dividing p equals rem, the validation is claimed to be true; otherwise is false. Due to the random prime p, there is the opportunity to get a false claim for the validation, when the remainder equals rem but the checkpoint is not identical than the original one. We then prove that error probability is bounded and small enough.

Theorem 1. Through the replica built by SCC algorithm, the error probability of validation is less than i/m^{i-2}. Here, i is check index, m is the bits of the checkpoint, and the random prime $p <= 2^{i*\ln m}$.

Proof. Assume an original checkpoint C becomes the C' after the transfer through network, $\#$ is the set size, *Prime* is the set of primes, and $length(p)$ returns the bit-length of random prime p. The error probability $\Pr_{err}$ of validation can be deduced as:

$$\Pr err = \Pr((C - C') \bmod p = 0 | C \neq C')$$

$$= \frac{\#\{p | p \in Prime, \text{length}(p) <= i * \ln m, (C - C') \bmod p = 0\}}{\#\{p | p \in Prime, \text{length}(p) <= i * \ln m\}}$$

$$< \frac{m}{\Pi(m^i)} < \frac{i * m}{m^{i-1}} = \frac{i}{m^{i-2}}$$

Here, the first inequality holds due to these facts. $C, C' \in \{1, 2, 2^2, ..., 2^m\}$, so $(C - C') \in \{1, 2, 2^2, ..., 2^m\}$. $(C - C') \bmod p = 0$ implies $(C - C')$ is a composite number and could be expressed as the multiplication of a series of primes. That is, $(C - C') = 2 * 3 * 5... * p' < 2^m$. Here, p' is at most the mth prime, which makes the numerator less than m. Meanwhile, the denominator is the number of all the primes whose bits are less than $i*\ln m$, and can be expressed as $\Pi(2^{i * \ln m}) = \Pi(m^i)$, where $\Pi(x)$ is the number of the prime which is less than x.

The second inequality is holds due to these facts. According to prime number theorem [16], $\Pi(x) \approx x/\ln x$. Therefore, $\Pi(m^i) \approx m^i/(i*\ln m) > m^i/(i*m) = m^{i-1}/i$. Then, considering the numerator, we conclude $\Pr_{err} < m/\Pi(m^i) < i/m^{i-2}$. ∎

Therefore the upper bound i/m^{i-2} of error probability correlates with the check index i and m like Fig. 2. The larger i or larger checkpoint size (larger m) would make this bound tighter exponentially, which implies lower error probability of validation.

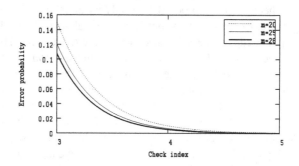

Fig. 2. Theoretical upper bound of error probability for validation.

Moreover, we prove that the extra required bandwidth overhead from the signature is also bounded as the theorem below.

Theorem 2. The extra bandwidth from the signature generated by algorithm SCC in the replica is less than $2^{1+i*\ln m}$. Here, m is the bits of checkpoint and i is check index.

Proof. The bandwidth increase comes from the signature in replica which includes two pieces p and rem. As the remainder on the divisor p, rem must be smaller than p. Therefore, the extra bandwidth is $p + rem < 2*p <= 2*2^{i*\ln m} = 2^{1+i*\ln m}$. ∎

This upper bound of bandwidth overhead correlates with the check index i and the checkpoint size either. The larger i or larger checkpoint size (as larger m) would make this bound looser, which implies larger bandwidth consumption. In fact, we can tune the tradeoff through the check index: larger i is required when checkpoint correctness is the emphasis; otherwise smaller i should be set due to the economical bandwidth.

4 Experiment and Evaluation

For the quantitative and qualitative evaluation, a distributed data stream processing system VINCA-CCS [1, 4, 17] is used for experiments. Any machine in this system owns 4 core CPU, 8 GB RAM, 100 GB storage and CentOS 5.5 × 86 64 bit, which is the virtualized one via VMware vSphere™ 5.1 in our private Cloud on eight Dell PowerEdge™ rack servers in local area network. A data generator [1, 4, 17] is employed to simulate streams from the offline data in our practical project. By default, the generator simulates 1000 connections, and sends data as the speed 1 tuple/s per connection. The tuple as data unit includes 22 attributes including vehicle-plate and photos. Both the PACK protocol and original SC protocol are implemented in VINCA-CCS for comparison, and we would evaluate the tradeoff between the correctness and extra bandwidth from SCC algorithm.

In the topology as Fig. 3, the PE *communicator* and its downstream PE *mq* are deployed in different machines, where *communicator* receives the raw data and packs them as structural tuples; *mq* receives tuples and keeps the payload in given JMS (Java Message Service) topics. Moreover, an endpoint-to-endpoint connector HAC-node [17] is used as the monitor module, which run as PACK or original SC respectively to build replica *cp* for *communicator* periodically. Here, the check index of SCC algorithm of PACK is set 3 by default.

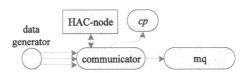

Fig. 3. Topology sample for experiments

Experiment 1. In data generator, the concurrency is set as 1000 TCP connections and the data speed is kept as 1 tuple/s/connection. The checkpoint interval for *communicator* is set 500 ms. Through both protocols, the memory of *communicator* is monitored at run-time.

Experiment 2. In data generator, the concurrency is set 30 and the data speed is kept as 1 tuple/s/connection in data generator. Record the memory used by *communicator* through two protocols respectively.

Experiment 3. In data generator, the concurrency is set 10000 and the data speed is kept as 1 tuple/s/connection. Record the memory used by *communicator* through two protocols respectively.

The replica size is the same magnitude of the memory consumed, which is also the bandwidth overhead. In experiment 1, we find the memory used is about 4 MB and deduce the bits of checkpoint $m = \lceil \ln4\ MB \rceil = 25$. Accordingly in the experiments 2 and 3, we find the used memory is about 100 KB and 30 MB and deduce the m is 20 and 28 respectively. For those experiments, the Fig. 4 presents the theoretical worst of bandwidth overhead.

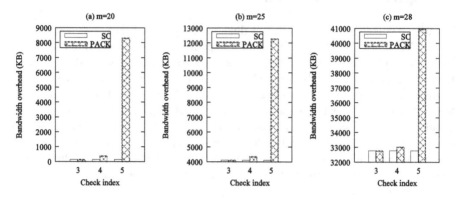

Fig. 4. Upper bound of bandwidth overhead

We can discuss the tradeoff theoretically. (1) As the Theorem 1, the upper bound decreases exponentially when i increase, and the larger checkpoint has tighter upper bound for the same check index. Take the given checkpoint in experiment 1 ($m = 25$) as an example. When i is set 3, the size of *rem* is $\lceil 3 * \ln m \rceil = 3 * 5 = 15$ bits. According to the Theorem 2, the extra bandwidth is less than $2 * 2^{15} = 8$ KB. Meanwhile, according to the Theorem 1, the upper bound of error probability for validation is less than $3/25 \approx 12\%$. While if i is set 4, the size of *rem* is $\lceil 4 * \ln m \rceil = 4 * 5 = 20$ bits. The extra bandwidth is less than $2 * 2^{20} = 256$ KB and the upper bound of error probability for validation is less than $4/25^2 \approx 0.64\%$. Then, compare the checkpoints in experiment 1 ($m = 25$) and 3 ($m = 28$). When i is set 4 in both experiment, the checkpoint in experiment 3 would be validated correctly in higher possibility, because it is larger (30 MB > 4 MB) with the tighter error bound. (2) Larger check index implies less error but more bandwidth overhead, which is tunable in practice. Note that check index cannot be set too large either. In those experiments, when i is set 3, 4 or 5, theoretical worst extra bandwidth through PACK are 8 KB, 256 KB and 8 MB respectively. However, when $i = 4$, 256 KB signature is larger than the 100 KB checkpoint ($m = 20$) itself; when $i = 5$, 8 MB signature is much larger than 100 KB checkpoint ($m = 20$) or 4 MB checkpoint ($m = 25$). It seems that huge checkpoint has more options on check index and more flexible tradeoff.

In brief, by the check index, it is the tunable tradeoff between the bandwidth and the replica correctness. Next we evaluate the performance through both protocols.

Experiment 4. In data generator, the data rate is set from 1 to 10 tuples/s/connection and the data speed is kept as 1 tuple/s/connection. In HAC-node through PACK, the check index is set 4. Repeat tests to get the average of the system response time under each data rate.

The result is showed in Fig. 5(a).

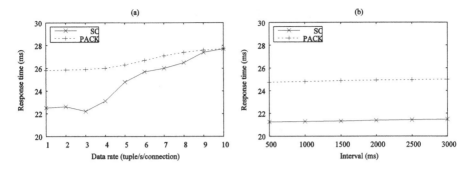

Fig. 5. Performance through both protocols

Experiment 5. In data generator, the concurrency is set as 1000 and the data speed is kept as 1 tuple/s/connection. In HAC-node, the checkpoint interval is set from 500 ms to 3 s and the check index through PACK is set 4. Repeat tests to get the average of the system response time under each interval.

The result is showed in Fig. 5(b).

We found the response time grows as data rate increases through both protocols, but the relative increment shrinks through PACK than SC under the same data rate. The growth of data rate makes larger checkpoint at given backup interval, but the relative increment through PACK becomes smaller because the proportion of signature in replica relatively decreases for larger checkpoint. Moreover, we found the response time is steady when backup interval increases through both protocols; the difference between PACK and SC is no more than 3 ms under the same interval. It is the reason that the CPU consumption for checkpoint through PACK is small enough due to the space-bounded signature. It also demonstrates the Theorem 2 in Sect. 3.2.

In brief, through PACK, the performance holds in multiple conditions. Next we simulate the errors of replica to evaluate the availability guarantee.

Experiment 6. In data generator, the concurrency is set as 1000 and the data speed is kept as 1 tuple/s/connection. In HAC-node, the checkpoint interval is set as 500 ms and the check index through PACK is set 3. In HAC-node, we simulate errors by flipping random bits of checkpoint before the replica is sent to another machine. The size of flipped bits is set 2, 5 and 10 respectively. After replica placement, we can compare the replica with the original one to find whether error appears. Repeat tests hundreds of times to get the average ratio of errorless replica under each size of flipped bits.

The result is showed in Fig. 6. The ratio here reflects the reliability in the unstable network condition. When flipped bit grows, we found the errorless ratio through PACK remains above 95%, but that of SC drops dramatically. The difference between them comes from the replica validation through PACK. In PACK, there are three possibilities for the flipped bits: first, the flipped bits entirely lie in the checkpoint; second, flipped ones entirely lie in the signature; third, those ones span the checkpoint and the signature. By our SCC algorithm, the signature is far small than the other, so that the first case remains relatively high possibility. In the first case the validation must be unsuccessful, and the replica has to be resent until the validation is successful. PACK makes the correct replica in high possibility; contrarily, SC has to appear errors as long as at least one bit is flipped.

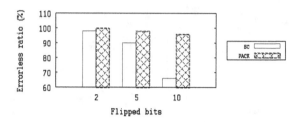

Fig. 6. Errorless ratio through both protocols

In brief, through PACK high availability is guaranteed.

5   Conclusion

We propose a reliable replica mechanism for stream processing to guarantee the correctness of the checkpoint. The replicas can be validated using space-bounded signature fast and correctly with high probability. In various conditions, the performance can hold by the tunable tradeoff and high availability is guaranteed.

Acknowledgment. This work was supported by the R&D General Program of Beijing Education Commission (No. KM2015_10009007), the Key Young Scholars Foundation for the Excellent Talents of Beijing (No. 2014000020124G011) and Foundation for the Excellent Youth Scholars of North China University of Technology (XN072-006).

References

1. Ding, W., Han, Y., Wang, J., Zhao, Z.: Feature-based high-availability mechanism for quantile tasks in real-time data stream processing. Softw. Pract. Experience **44**, 855–871 (2014)
2. Bockermann, C.: A Survey of the Stream Processing Landscape. Lehrstuhl furk unstliche Intelligenz Technische Universität Dortmund (2014)
3. Barlow, M.: Real-Time Big Data Analytics: Emerging Architecture. O'Reilly Media Inc., Sebastopol (2013)
4. Ding, W., Han, Y., Wang, J., Zhao, Z.: Feature-based high availability mechanism for extreme aggregation tasks in real-time data stream processing. J. Internet Technol. **14**, 327–340 (2013)
5. Hwang, J.H., Balazinska, M., Rasin, A., Cetintemel, U., Michael, S., Stan, Z.: High-availability algorithms for distributed stream processing. In: The 21st International Conference on Data Engineering, pp. 779–790 (2005)
6. Balazinska, M., Balakrishnan, H., Madden, S.R., Stonebraker, M.: Fault-tolerance in the borealis distributed stream processing system. In: Proceedings of the 2005 ACM SIGMOD International Conference on Management of Data, pp. 13–24. ACM (2005)
7. Liu, Q., Lui, J.C., He, C., Pan, L., Fan, W., Shi, Y.: SAND: a fault-tolerant streaming architecture for network traffic analytics. In: The 44th Annual IEEE/IFIP International

Conference on Dependable Systems and Networks (DSN 2014), Atlanta, Georgia, USA, pp. 80–87 (2014)

8. Akidau, T., Balikov, A., Bekiroglu, K., Chernyak, S., Haberman, J., Lax, R., McVeety, S., Mills, D., Nordstrom, P., Whittle, S.: MillWheel: fault-tolerant stream processing at internet scale. Proc. VLDB Endow. **6**, 1033–1044 (2013)

9. http://archive.cloudera.com/cdh/3/flume/

10. Toshniwal, A., Taneja, S., Shukla, A., Ramasamy, K., Patel, J.M., Kulkarni, S., Jackson, J., Gade, K., Fu, M., Donham, J., Bhagat, N., Mittal, S., Ryaboy, D.: Storm@twitter. In: Proceedings of the 2014 ACM SIGMOD International Conference on Management of Data, pp. 147–156. ACM, Snowbird (2014)

11. Gu, Y., Zhang, Z., Ye, F., Yang, H., Kim, M., Lei, H., Liu, Z.: An empirical study of high availability in stream processing systems. In: Proceedings of the 10th ACM/IFIP/USENIX International Conference on Middleware, pp. 1–9. Springer, New York (2009)

12. Miller, G.L.: Riemann's hypothesis and tests for primality. J. Comput. Syst. Sci. **13**, 300–317 (1976)

13. Rabin, M.O.: Probabilistic algorithm for testing primality. J. Number Theory **12**, 128–138 (1980)

14. Agrawal, M., Kayal, N., Saxena, N.: PRIMES is in P. Ann. Math. **160**, 781–793 (2004)

15. http://primes.utm.edu/lists/small/millions/

16. http://en.wikipedia.org/wiki/Prime_number_theorem

17. Ding, W., Zhao, Z., Han, Y.: A framework to improve the availability of stream computing. In: 23rd IEEE International Conference on Web Services (ICWS 2016), pp. 594–601. IEEE (2016)

Exploring External Knowledge Base for Personalized Search in Collaborative Tagging Systems

Dong Zhou[1(✉)], Xuan Wu[1], Wenyu Zhao[1], Séamus Lawless[2], and Jianxun Liu[1]

[1] School of Computer Science and Engineering, Hunan University of Science and Technology,
Xiangtan 411201, Hunan, China
dongzhou1979@hotmail.com
[2] ADAPT Centre, Knowledge and Date Engineering Group, School of Computer Science
and Statistics, Trinity College Dublin, Dublin 2, Ireland

Abstract. Alongside the enormous volume of user-generated content posted to World Wide Web, there exists a thriving demand for search personalization services, especially those utilizing collaborative tagging data. To provide personalized services, a user model is usually required. We address the setting adopted by the majority of previous work, where a user model consists solely of the user's past information. We construct an augmented user model from a number of tags and documents. These resources are further processed according to the user's past information by exploring external knowledge base. A novel generative model is proposed for user model generation. This model leverages recent advances in neural language models such as Word Embeddings with latent semantic models such as Latent Dirichlet Allocation. We further present a new query expansion method to facilitate the desired personalized retrieval. Experiments conducted by utilizing real-world collaborative tagging data show that the methods proposed in the current paper outperform several non-personalized methods as well as existing personalized search methods by utilizing user models solely constructed from usage histories.

Keywords: Personalized search · Collaborative tagging systems · Latent semantic models · Word embeddings · Query expansion

1 Introduction

The amount of digital content online has increased exponentially recently. The use of personalized Web search systems has become crucial in retrieving relevant information. Such system fetches relevant information that are most correlated to an individual user rather than only to the issued query [1, 2]. Recording of the individual's interests and past behaviors in user models has been widely adopted. Subsequently the information inside the user model can be used for query and/or results personalization.

With this increasing volume of digital content comes an increasing number of social tagging Websites for Web pages and documents. Collaborative tagging systems like

© ICST Institute for Computer Sciences, Social Informatics and Telecommunications Engineering 2017
S. Wang and A. Zhou (Eds.): CollaborateCom 2016, LNICST 201, pp. 408–417, 2017.
DOI: 10.1007/978-3-319-59288-6_37

del.icio.us[1] and *BibSonomy*[2],etc., have become more and more popular. The tags and documents added by different users to the platforms are closely linked to that individual and their interests, providing abundant information for constructing more rigid and characteristic user models. Therefore, constructing user models from collaborative tagging systems has the potential to be instrumental for personalized search. In the collaborative tagging platform, users are freely to choose whatever words/terms to be used in tagging. This behavior makes the information search process even more difficult than normal web search systems. To deal with this problem, personalized search results re-ranking [3–6] and personalized query expansion [7–9] have been widely adopted.

However, there are several drawbacks in the process of searching in such type of systems, including the following. (i) In the approaches that a user model contains potential expansion terms, past researchers used relationships between tags and lexical matching methods between terms and queries. For the most of the cases, tags can not be viewed as accurate summarization of documents, henceforth the search experiences are somewhat depressed [10]. Moreover, lexical matching may miss some latent semantic information exhibited in the user model. (ii) All the previously proposed personalized search methods require a user's past click/browse information stored in a user model. However, we argue that using this information alone is not sufficient. In some cases, a user may have clicked and/or browsed only a few documents. It is relatively hard to personalized search with this little usage information to hand.

To handle these limitations, we construct an augmented user model from a number of tags and documents. These resources are further processed according to the user's past information by exploring external knowledge base. A novel generative model is proposed for user model generation. This model leverages recent advances in neural language models such as Word Embeddings (WE) [11] with the traditional Latent Dirichlet Allocation (LDA) model [12]. We learn latent topics that generate word embeddings and words simultaneously. Based on the topics learnt, we further propose a novel topical query expansion model to be used in collaborative tagging systems. In this model, queries are expanded not only by their lexical similarity with the potential terms, but are also based on their topical relevancy. Observing the obtained evaluation results from a collaborative dataset sourced from a real-world platform, we can find that the personalized search methods provide very good performance improvements over various baseline methods.

Our contribution in the current paper are: (i) We introduce augmented user profiles by exploiting an external knowledge base to perform personalized search in a novel way. (ii) We suggest and evaluate a novel generative model that leverages recent advances in neural language models with latent semantic models.

---

[1] http://www.delicious.com/.
[2] http://www.bibsonomy.org.

2   Related Work

There exist sufficient researches in personalized search [1, 2]. These can be roughly allocated into two categories. The first one is known as results processing. This is usually done with results re-ranking by re-ordering retrieved results using the information from a user model [13]. Another is query expansion [14]. In this category, new terms selecting from a user model can be utilized to expand the original query, or terms inside the initial query can be re-weighted according to the user model [15].

The problem studied in the current paper falls in one of the above two strategies. Tags and documents crawled from a collaborative tagging system can be used to construct a test collection. This collection can be further utilized to advance the research in search personalization. For example, tags and documents can be employed to automatically learn an individual's preferences. The retrieval results can be personalized based on the topical relevance between documents and information from the user model [3]. Signals from multiple rather than single collaborative systems can be used for search personalization [16]. Bouadjenek et al. [4] presented an enhanced document representation based on user relationships to re-rank documents on a social platform. Cai et al. [17] treated the relevance as fuzzy satisfaction between users and queries. However, if the relevant documents cannot be returned in the retrieval list, the strategy has no way to fetch more relevant results.

Another strategy expands a user's issued query with potential terms from user models. Relationships between tags have been used for personalized query expansion. If a tag appears in a query, the most related tags will be selected from the user model to expand the query [10]. Researchers also considered using lexical matching methods such as co-occurrence-based method to expand the query based on a user's past information [15]. Recently, a query expansion method for personalization has been proposed [8], which is state-of-the-art. This method captures term relationships through a Tag-Topic model. Mutual information between the terms is then utilized to choose the potential expansion terms.

All of the above systems consider building user models from his/her past information only. In contrast, in this paper we explore an external knowledge base to build augmented user models. We also propose a novel topical query expansion model for personalization.

3   User Model Generation

We now define the research problem studied in the current paper. Subsequently we describe the user model generation process. Formally, data in collaborative tagging systems can be represented by $\mathcal{P}$: $=(\mathcal{U}, \mathcal{D}, \mathcal{T}, \mathcal{A})$. The elements in the ternary relation $\mathcal{A} \subseteq \mathcal{U} \times \mathcal{D} \times \mathcal{T}$ are called annotations, or bookmarking activities performed by different users. $\mathcal{A}^u := \{(t, d) | u \in \mathcal{U},\ d \in \mathcal{D}, t \in \mathcal{T}\}$ represents a user's annotations. $\mathcal{D}^u := \{d | (t, d) \in \mathcal{A}^u\}$ represents all documents annotated by a user u. $\mathcal{T}^u := \{t | (t, d) \in \mathcal{A}^u\}$ represents the total tags used by a user. $term^{\mathcal{D}^u} := \{w | w \in \mathcal{D}^u\}$ represents all terms from $\mathcal{D}^u$, w is a word/term extracted from $\mathcal{D}^u$. Similarly,

$term^{\mathcal{D}^u_{exter}} := \{w | w \in \mathcal{D}^u_{exter}\}$ represents all terms extracted from $\mathcal{D}^u_{exter}$. $\mathcal{D}^u_{exter}$ represents all external documents extracted from an corpus $\mathcal{D}_{exter}$ different from $\mathcal{D}$.

Algorithm 1. Generative process for Enhanced User Model Generation

---

Require: the total tags used by a user $\mathcal{T}^u$
Require: all documents annotated by a user $\mathcal{D}^u$
Require: a user's set of external documents $\mathcal{D}^u_{exter}$
Require: word embeddings calculated by Skip-Gram for all words in $\mathcal{T}^u \cup \mathcal{D}^u \cup \mathcal{D}^u_{exter}$ $(\mathcal{D}')$
1. **for** $k \in [1, K]$
2.   draw mixture components $\varphi_k \sim Dirichlet(\beta)$
3. **for** d_j in $\mathcal{D}'$
4.   draw mixture proportion $\theta_j \sim Dirichlet(\alpha)$
5.   **for** $w_i \in [1, N_{d_j}]$
6.   draw topic index $z_{j,i} \sim Multinomial(\theta_{d_j})$
7.   draw term for word $w_{j,i} \sim Multinomial(\varphi_{z_{j,i}})$
8.   for each dimension of the embedding of $w_{j,i}$, draw $f^e_{j,i} \sim \mathcal{N}(\mu^e_{z_{j,i}}, \sigma^e_{z_{j,i}})$

In the problem studied here, we construct a user model contains a number of words/terms $\{w_1, w_2 \ldots w_n\} \in term^{\mathcal{D}^u} \cup term^{\mathcal{D}^u_{exter}} \cup \mathcal{T}^u$. If a user submits a query, potential expansion terms will be selected from a sorted list of terms.

The user model generation has two steps: external documents fetch and user model construction. We augment a user's past information in step 1. All tags t in $\mathcal{T}^u$ are joined to form a query $q^{\mathcal{T}^u}$. We iterate through d in $\mathcal{D}^u$ to extract high weighted terms to form a number of queries $Q^{\mathcal{D}^u}$ (inverted document frequency used here and we extract top λ terms). Then we issue queries in $q^{\mathcal{T}^u} \cup Q^{\mathcal{D}^u}$ to an external corpus $\mathcal{D}_{exter}$ to fetch γ number of documents to form $\mathcal{D}^u_{exter}$.

In step 2, we integrate $\mathcal{T}^u$, $\mathcal{D}^u$ and $\mathcal{D}^u_{exter}$ into a novel generative model. In this model, multinomial distribution of topics of each single document can be easily acquired. The procedure is described in the remaining of this section.

It is well known that the LDA model can mine the thematic structure of documents. Recently, WE has played an increasingly vital role in building continuous word vectors based on their context in a corpus. There are also some attempts to integrate LDA with WE for different purposes [18, 19]. Inspired by those works, a novel generative model for user model generation is presented in this paper. We named this model enhanced user model generation (EUMG).

To jointly model words and word embeddings produced by WE, EUMG learns a shared latent topic space to generate words in documents and corresponding word embeddings. The WE are all pre-trained, together with documents as input to the model. Skip-Gram model [11] is utilized here before running our model to learn WE. A normal distribution is used for WE to learn latent topics from the documents as well as the words. With the WE and documents trained by the Skip-Gram model, the generation process of the EUMG model can be summarized as in Algorithm 1.

In Algorithm 1, the mean and deviation of the normal distribution are defined as μ and σ respectively. The parameters of a topic Dirichlet prior and word Dirichlet prior are defined as α and β. θ_j is the multinomial topic distribution of document d_j. $f^e_{j,i}$ are word embeddings. The number of latent topics and dimensions for WE are both fixed. Both the words and WE determine posterior distribution of topics.

In the proposed model, Gibbs Sampling is used to solve the intractable inference problem. A conjugate prior is used here. We also integrate out θ and φ. The conditional distribution $p(z_{j,i} = k)$ has to be calculated in sampling. Specifically, the topic is chosen from the following equation for each word:

$$p(z_{j,i} = k) \propto \frac{n_{j,k,\neg i} + \alpha}{n_{j,\cdot,\neg i} + K \cdot \alpha} \times \frac{v_{k,w_{j,i},\neg} + \beta}{v_{k,\cdot,\neg} + V \cdot \beta} \times \prod_{e=1}^{E} \frac{1}{\sqrt{2\pi}\sigma_{z_{j,i}}} \exp\left(-\frac{\left(f_{j,i}^{e} - \mu_{z_{j,i}}\right)^2}{2\sigma_{z_{j,i}}^2}\right) \quad (1)$$

The amount of times that topic k is added up in $n_{j,k,\neg i}$ (from multinomial distribution of the document j). Note that the present $z_{j,i}$ is not included. The amount of times $w_{j,i}$ is generated by topic k is added up in $v_{k,w_{j,i},\neg}$. The present $w_{j,i}$ is not included. The summation over all values of the variable is denoted by a dot. E is the dimensions of word embeddings. The posterior estimate of θ and φ can then be easily obtained.

4   Topical Query Expansion

Next, The output from step 2 of the last section can be utilized to build a query expansion model that ranks terms from the user model to be added to the query. We only layout the key steps in this section because of space constrains.

We assume there exists a query $q = \{w_a\}_{a=1}^{n}$, where $\{w_a\}_{a=1}^{n}$ denotes n independent query words. We approximate the probability of q generating w from a hidden model H is by: (see also [20, 21]):

$$P(w|H) \approx P(w|q) \quad (2)$$

We further define a number of relevant documents $\{d_b\}_{b=1}^{M}$. These documents have relationships with both the query and the words in a user model. M represents total number of documents. Associate $\{d_b\}$ into Eq. (2) leads to:

$$P(w|q) = \sum_{b=1}^{M} P(w|d_b)P(d_b|q) \quad (3)$$

The uniform prior of documents is also put outside of the summation. $P(q)$ has been eliminated here as a uniform prior.

The output form step 2 of the last section (i.e. the documents in the user model) can be treated as $\{d_b\}_{b=1}^{M}$ in the above equation. In Eq. (3), w has a direct dependency on d_b and w_a also has a direct dependency on d_b, the assumption is too simplistic. Through the EUMG model, we obtain latent topics. These topics can be used to re-calculate the probability of q generating w:

$$P(w|q) \propto \frac{1}{M} \sum_{b=1}^{M} (\sum_{k=1}^{K} P(w|topic_k)P(topic_k|d_b))(\prod_{a=1}^{n} \sum_{k=1}^{K} P(w_a|topic_k)P(topic_k|d_b)) \quad (4)$$

$topic_k$ represents a particular topic learnt. After we obtain the probability scores, we sort all the terms and select the top δ terms as the final expansion query terms.

5 Experiments

5.1 Evaluation Setup

To examine the performance of the user model generation and query expansion methods, we perform the experiments in a dataset which merges two real-world sub-datasets from a collaborative tagging system *del.icio.us*: *socialbm0311* and *deliciousT140*. Please refer to [22, 23] for details about the two datasets. There are 5,153,720 annotation activities, 259,511 users, 137,870 tags and 131,283 documents in our merged dataset. An external knowledge base is constructed from Wikipedia[3]. This knowledge base contains 4,634,369 documents. It was crawled on 14/08/2014. To evaluate the effects of augmented user models, foursets of users with different size are chosen as test users. This includes: users with no more than 50 annotation activities (**User50**), users with 50–100 annotation activities (**User100**), users with 100–500 annotation activities (**User500**) and users with more than 500 annotation activities (**UserG500**). These sets represent users with small, moderate and rich amounts of past usage information respectively. We randomly choose 200 users from each set. We select 25% of each user's annotations for evaluation, and the remaining 75% are utilized to build the user model.

We follow the evaluation procedure of previous research [3, 8, 16]. If a user u issues a query t, this query is viewed as a personalized query. In this case, relevant documents are the documents annotated by u with t.

We use the evaluation metrics that are typically utilized in Web search evaluation: mean average precision (MAP), which is usually employed to report search accuracy; normalized discounted cumulative gain (NDCG), a natural choice for search engine evaluation; as well as another commonly adopted evaluation metric mean reciprocal rank (MRR). Paired t-test is used for significance evaluation. We set the confidence level at 95%. The average performance is computed for all users in the same set.

The methods proposed in this paper are compared with several query expansion methods. This includes non-personalized methods and personalized baselines. We now describe them in detail.

LM A language model based retrieval method. This model is quite popular and produces good results before. We use the model described in [24].

LM + RM-wiki This is a relevance model which uses Wikipedia to obtain the relevance documents, as in [25]. It is a strong non-personalized baseline for comparison because that we also used external corpus in our approach.

---

[3] http://www.wikipedia.org.

Cooccur + QE This is a personalized baseline method, utilized by many previous researchers [6, 11]. The method calculates co-occurrence scores between terms from a user model and terms from a query [15].

Tag-topic + QE This method captures term relationships through a Tag-Topic model. Mutual information between the terms is then utilized to choose the potential expansion terms [8]. The highest performing method from [8] is selected here as a strong personalized baseline.

EUMG + TQE finally, our approach uses the EUMG model and the query expansion method proposed in Sect. 4 for personalized search in collaborative tagging systems.

5.2 Experimental Results

Results are now fully examined in this section. The overall performance is demonstrated in Table 1, including our new approach presented in the paper together with baseline methods on the test users in four sets. Statistically significant differences between a method with the best performing non-personalized baseline (***LM + RM-wiki***) and the best performing personalized baseline (***Tag-topic + QE***) are indicated by *, # respectively. From the results, we learn that ***LM*** model performs the worst in all different sets of users by using all evaluation metrics. ***LM + RM-wiki*** method performed steadily better than ***LM***. This illustrates the effectiveness of utilizing an external corpus. The results are consistent with previous research [25]. These two methods are surpassed by the three personalized methods with statistically significance. This includes the method ***EUMG + TQE*** proposed in this paper. This shows that terms in the user models can improve the effectiveness of search significantly. Non-personalized query expansion methods only select terms from top documents. There are only limited improvements observed.

The personalized baselines ***Cooccur + QE*** and ***Tag-topic + QE*** expand the queries by using the user's historical information only while our approach explores an external knowledge base. We now analyze the results for these three methods. As seen from Table 1, several conclusions can be drawn. First, ***EUMG + TQE*** out performs the two personalization methods ***Cooccur + QE*** and ***Tag-topic + QE***, in all foursets of users by using different metrics. The differences are consistently significant. The possible reason is that we use an external knowledge base in addition to the user's past information to build an augmented user model for personalized search. Secondly, ***EUMG + TQE*** achieves consistent improvements over baseline approaches across four sets of users. The improvements in **User50** are more remarkable than in other sets of test users. In reality, we often face the situation where a user has little interactions with the search platform. Under such circumstances, personalized search experience is usually unsatisfactory. However, with enhanced content, our method can obtain reasonably better results for this set of users. This result also confirms that our approach performs well for users with small or moderate volumes of past information and those with a rich set of historical data. Third, using Wikipedia seems a good choice of the external corpus. The possible reason, as pointed out in [25], is that if an external knowledge base has good coverage of topics, it is more likely that good expansion terms can be selected from it.

Finally, we examine the optimum number of latent topics and dimensions for WE. The number of topics is chosen from [5, 50]. The dimension numbers is chosen from [10, 100]. Because of the space constraints, we only report the results here. When there are 15 latent topics and 50 dimensions for WE, we obtain the highest performance. When both numbers grow beyond 15 and 50, we have a lower performance. However, comparing to baseline models, *EUMG + TQE* always performs better than them, even the lowest performed runs.

Table 1. Overall performance

	User50				User500		
	MAP	NDCG	MRR		MAP	NDCG	MRR
LM	0.0163	0.0309	0.0184	*LM*	0.0167	0.0283	0.0203
LM + RM-wiki	0.0211	0.0501	0.0232	*LM + RM-wiki*	0.0242	0.0468	0.0263
Cooccur + QE	0.0674^*	0.0975^*	0.0779^*	*Cooccur + QE*	0.0886^*	0.1195^*	0.0993^*
Tag-topic + QE	0.1525^*	0.1924^*	0.2009^*	*Tag-topic + QE*	0.1655^*	0.2036^*	0.203^*
EUMG + QE	$0.2440^{*,\#}$	$0.2868^{*,\#}$	$0.2980^{*,\#}$	*EUMG + QE*	$0.2154^{*,\#}$	$0.2592^{*,\#}$	$0.2424^{*,\#}$
	User100				UserG500		
	MAP	NDCG	MRR		MAP	NDCG	MRR
LM	0.0125	0.0314	0.0136	*LM*	0.019	0.0349	0.0193
LM + RM-wiki	0.0225	0.0384	0.0238	*LM + RM-wiki*	0.0319	0.0674	0.0333
Cooccur + QE	0.0843^*	0.1216^*	0.0897^*	*Cooccur + QE*	0.0916^*	0.1246^*	0.1015^*
Tag-topic + QE	0.1586^*	0.1647^*	0.1721^*	*Tag-topic + QE*	0.2004^*	0.2405^*	0.2528^*
EUMG + QE	$0.2117^{*,\#}$	$0.2476^{*,\#}$	$0.2377^{*,\#}$	*EUMG + QE*	$0.2385^{*,\#}$	$0.2897^{*,\#}$	$0.2802^{*,\#}$

6   Conclusions

We study the problem of personalized search utilizing collaborative tagging data in the current paper. In particular, we investigated augmented user models and query expansion methods. We construct an augmented user model from a set of tags and documents, together with an external knowledge base. A novel generative model is proposed, which leverages word embeddings with Latent Dirichlet Allocation for user model generation. Based on the user models constructed, we further present a query expansion model to facilitate the desired personalized retrieval based on topics learnt. The proposed method performed well on a real-world collaborative tagging dataset. It demonstrates statistically significant improvements over several baseline systems including non-personalized and personalized methods. In future research, automatically determination of the number of topics and dimensions will be studied. The effectiveness of different external knowledge bases will also be examined in our subsequent experiments.

Acknowledgments. This research was supported by the National Natural Science Foundation of China (61300129, 61572187 and 61272063), Scientific Research Fund of Hunan Provincial Education Department of China (16K030), Hunan Provincial Innovation Foundation For Postgraduate (CX2016B575). This research was also supported by the ADAPT Centre for Digital

Content Technology, which is funded under the Science Foundation Ireland Research Centres Programme (13/RC/2106) and is co-funded under the European Regional Development Fund.

References

1. Ghorab, M.R., Zhou, D., O'Connor, A., Wade, V.: Personalised information retrieval: survey and classification. User Model. User-Adap. Inter. **23**, 381–443 (2013)
2. Zhou, D., Lawless, S., Wu, X., Zhao, W., Liu, J.: A study of user profile representation for personalized cross-language information retrieval. Aslib J. Inf. Manage. **68**, 448–477 (2016)
3. Xu, S., Bao, S., Fei, B., Su, Z., Yu, Y.: Exploring folksonomy for personalized search. In: Proceedings of the 31st Annual International ACM SIGIR Conference on Research and Development in Information Retrieval, pp. 155–162. ACM (2008)
4. Bouadjenek, M.R., Hacid, H., Bouzeghoub, M.: Sopra: a new social personalized ranking function for improving web search. In: Proceedings of the 36th International ACM SIGIR Conference on Research and Development in Information Retrieval, pp. 861–864. ACM, Dublin (2013)
5. Xie, H., Li, X., Wang, T., Chen, L., Li, K., Wang, F.L., Cai, Y., Li, Q., Min, H.: Personalized search for social media via dominating verbal context. Neurocomputing **172**, 27–37 (2016)
6. Xie, H., Li, X., Wang, T., Lau, R.Y.K., Wong, T.-L., Chen, L., Wang, F.L., Li, Q.: Incorporating sentiment into tag-based user profiles and resource profiles for personalized search in folksonomy. Inf. Process. Manage. **52**, 61–72 (2016)
7. Bouadjenek, M.R., Hacid, H., Bouzeghoub, M., Daigremont, J.: Personalized social query expansion using social bookmarking systems. In: Proceedings of the 34th International ACM SIGIR Conference on Research and Development in Information Retrieval, pp. 1113–1114. ACM, Beijing (2011)
8. Zhou, D., Lawless, S., Wade, V.: Improving search via personalized query expansion using social media. Inf. Retr. **15**, 218–242 (2012)
9. Zhou, D., Lawless, S., Wade, V.: Web search personalization using social data. In: Zaphiris, P., Buchanan, G., Rasmussen, E., Loizides, F. (eds.) TPDL 2012. LNCS, vol. 7489, pp. 298–310. Springer, Heidelberg (2012). doi:10.1007/978-3-642-33290-6_32
10. Bender, M., Crecelius, T., Kacimi, M., Michel, S., Neumann, T., Parreira, J.X., Schenkel, R., Weikum, G.: Exploiting social relations for query expansion and result ranking. In: Proceedings of the IEEE 24th International Conference on Data Engineering Workshop, ICDEW 2008, pp. 501–506. IEEE (2008)
11. Mikolov, T., Sutskever, I., Chen, K., Corrado, G.S., Dean, J.: Distributed representations of words and phrases and their compositionality. In: Advances in Neural Information Processing Systems, NIPS 2013, pp. 3111–3119 (2013)
12. Blei, D.M., Ng, A.Y., Jordan, M.I.: Latent dirichlet allocation. J. Mach. Learn. Res. **3**, 993–1022 (2003)
13. Dou, Z., Song, R., Wen, J.-R.: A large-scale evaluation and analysis of personalized search strategies. In: Proceedings of the 16th International Conference on World Wide Web, pp. 581–590. ACM, Banff (2007)
14. Zhou, D., Lawless, S., Liu, J., Zhang, S., Xu, Y.: Query expansion for personalized cross-language information retrieval. In: Proceedings of the 10th International Workshop on Semantic and Social Media Adaptation and Personalization, SMAP 2015, pp. 1–5. IEEE, Trento (2015)

15. Chirita, P.-A., Firan, C.S., Nejdl, W.: Personalized query expansion for the web. In: Proceedings of the 30th Annual International ACM SIGIR Conference on Research and Development in Information Retrieval, pp. 7–14. ACM, Amsterdam (2007)

16. Wang, Q., Jin, H.: Exploring online social activities for adaptive search personalization. In: Proceedings of the 19th ACM International Conference on Information and Knowledge Management, pp. 999–1008. ACM, Toronto (2010)

17. Cai, Y., Li, Q.: Personalized search by tag-based user profile and resource profile in collaborative tagging systems. In: Proceedings of the 19th ACM International Conference on Information and Knowledge Management, pp. 969–978. ACM, Toronto (2010)

18. Das, R., Zaheer, M., Dyer, C.: Gaussian LDA for topic models with word embeddings. In: Proceedings of the 53rd Annual Meeting of the Association for Computational Linguistics and the 7th International Joint Conference on Natural Language Processing of the Asian Federation of Natural Language Processing, ACL 2015, pp. 795–804. ACL, Beijing (2015)

19. Liu, Y., Liu, Z., Chua, T.-S., Sun, M.: Topical word embeddings. In: Proceedings of the Twenty-Ninth AAAI Conference on Artificial Intelligence, AAAI 2015, pp. 2418–2424. AAAI Press, Austin (2015)

20. Lavrenko, V., Croft, W.B.: Relevance based language models. In: Proceedings of the 24th Annual International ACM SIGIR Conference on Research and Development in Information Retrieval, pp. 120–127. ACM, New Orleans (2001)

21. Ganguly, D., Leveling, J., Jones, G.J.F.: Topical relevance model. In: Hou, Y., Nie, J.-Y., Sun, L., Wang, B., Zhang, P. (eds.) AIRS 2012. LNCS, vol. 7675, pp. 326–335. Springer, Heidelberg (2012). doi:10.1007/978-3-642-35341-3_28

22. Zubiaga, A., Garcia-Plaza, A.P., Fresno, V., Martinez, R.: Content-based clustering for tag cloud visualization. In: Proceedings of the International Conference on Advances in Social Network Analysis and Mining, ASONAM 2009, pp. 316–319. IEEE (2009)

23. Zubiaga, A., Fresno, V., Martinez, R., Garcia-Plaza, A.P.: Harnessing folksonomies to produce a social classification of resources. IEEE Trans. Knowl. Data Eng. **25**, 1801–1813 (2013)

24. Zhai, C., Lafferty, J.: Model-based feedback in the language modeling approach to information retrieval. In: Proceedings of the Tenth International Conference on Information and Knowledge Management, pp. 403–410. ACM (2001)

25. Diaz, F., Metzler, D.: Improving the estimation of relevance models using large external corpora. In: Proceedings of the 29th Annual International ACM SIGIR Conference on Research and Development in Information Retrieval, pp. 154–161. ACM, Seattle (2006)

Energy-and-Time-Saving Task Scheduling Based on Improved Genetic Algorithm in Mobile Cloud Computing

Jirui Li[✉], Xiaoyong Li, and Rui Zhang

Key Laboratory of Trustworthy Distributed Computing and Service, Ministry of Education, Beijing University of Posts and Telecommunications, Beijing 100876, China
ljrokyes@163.com

Abstract. With the collaboration of 5G network and mobile cloud computing(MCC), mobile devices can be offered important opportunities and new challenges in terms of energy saving and performance enhancement, sophisticated applications running on smart phones, which are called tasks in MCC environment, may be same or different. The paper studies the problem of task scheduling in MCC. Firstly, a task-virtual machine (VM) assignment strategy is presented; Secondly, on the basis of the strategy, we improve genetic algorithm (GA) which uses grouping multi-level encoding and dual fitness function (GMLE-DFF), GMLE means that the individual adopts hierarchical coding according to VMs grouping and tasks queuing. DFF refers to the reasonable combination of the optimal time span and the maximum resources utilization and minimum opened number of VMs. By simulating and realizing traditional GA, Sufferage algorithm and our improved GA, the results show the improved GA is superior to other two algorithms for reducing energy consumption while the task completion time is satisfied.

Keywords: Mobile cloud computing · 5G · Task scheduling · Genetic algorithm · Energy consumption

1 Introduction

Nowadays, the combination of 5G network and cloud computing will give rise to newer and hotter attention, and can give more additional advantages, in particular, longer lasting battery lifetime and more powerful computing ability for mobile devices. These merits have brought much changes of services and applications, significantly faster growth number and richer forms, both of which require offloading heavy computing from mobile terminals to cloud in order to realize longer lasting services [1]. But, if a cloud is used to provide services, in cloud server, a heavy energy consumption problem must be paid special attention. With the rapid growth of richer applications running on mobile devices, the energy consumption problem is worse and worse. The solutions of software and hardware are urgently needed to determine which methods will be greener or more energy efficient.

© ICST Institute for Computer Sciences, Social Informatics and Telecommunications Engineering 2017
S. Wang and A. Zhou (Eds.): CollaborateCom 2016, LNICST 201, pp. 418–428, 2017.
DOI: 10.1007/978-3-319-59288-6_38

In MCC, the study of task scheduling is very important for reducing energy consumption and improving the system performance, and scheduling efficiency can largely affect the execution of applications running on mobile devices, especially in 5G network. The methods of task scheduling have been proposed in many studies. Two non-cooperative game methods (symmetric non-zero-sum game and asymmetry stein's game) were proposed by Kolodziej and Xhafa [2] by modeling the user requirements as the grid user's behavior, and designed and realized hybrid tuning scheduler based GA to balance the two game. Li Zhi-Yong et al. [3] implemented a multi-objective memetic algorithm for the problem of multi-objective scheduling optimization on the heterogeneous cloud, which used memetic local search technique based on the related information of solution structure to improve the local optimization ability, the technique could reduce the computational overhead of algorithm. Li et al. [4] presented a resource optimization mechanism, which included two online dynamic task scheduling algorithms: dynamic cloud list scheduling and dynamic cloud min-min scheduling. Heuristic algorithm [5] has two main goals, minimizing the task execution time and minimizing the task execution cost. Li et al. [6] designed a kind of Normal Best-Oriented Ant Colony Optimization by applying improved heuristic algorithm. Taheri et al. [7] proposed a job data scheduling algorithm based on colony. Xue Lin et al. [8] presented a task scheduling algorithm with dynamic voltage and frequency scaling (DVFC), which mainly solves the energy minimization problem in MCC environment. Neeraj Kumar et al. [9] proposed a Bayesian coalition Game-based VM migration method in vehicular mobile cloud to avoid wasting energy. In the aforementioned methods, energy consumption was the product of the finished time of tasks times the power consumption per unit, the computation method is partial and cannot objectively reflect the whole energy consumption of cloud server center, which is usually to maximize the resources utilization and minimize opened number of VMs, meanwhile, minimize the execution time of task sets [10].

Because of the mobility of terminals, tasks must be finished in the limited time, or else, the execution result may not return the terminals if the link between mobile device and cloud server is lost, and it must product large and additional energy consumption in cloud computing. In this paper, basing on the "intensive" characteristic of 5G, a task-VM allocation strategy is presented and applied to GMLE-DFF-based GA for improving the applications performance and the resource utilization of cloud server.

2   Task Scheduling Based on Improved GA

In 1975, J.H. Holland professor put forward the basic theory and method of GA [11], which is based on nature selection and genetic theory and adopts the principle of "survival of the fittest" in nature. GA contains chromosome encoding, initial population, the design of fitness function, genetic operation (selection, crossover and mutation) and parameters settings. At present, GA has been widely used in artificial intelligence, information technology, computer science and engineering practice. With the in-depth theory study and practice proving, although GA develops rapidly, its shortcomings are gradually revealed. GA slows for the selection of the optimal solution and is easy to form a pseudo solution. To improve GA, the key is to avoid a false solution and shorten the time for finding the optimal solution. In this paper, combining with resource characteristic in MCC system, an improved GA based on GMLE-DFF is proposed, which applies task-VM allocation strategy orienting multidimensional resources, and its flow figure is shown in Fig. 1.

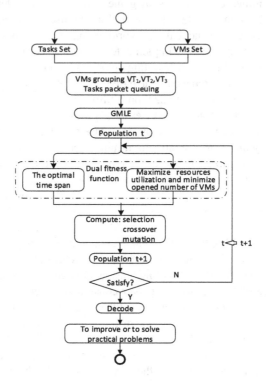

Fig. 1. The flow figure of improved GA based on GMLE-DFF.

2.1 Task-VM Assignment Strategy

Improved GA uses packet queuing method for tasks and VMs before encoding. In MCC environment, any one of mobile users may trigger tasks, and the distribution of tasks may be asymmetry. If considering only performance indicators of tasks, the uneven distribution of the tasks will happen, how to get good compromise between the task performance indexes and system load balancing is always a key point for task scheduling strategy. In order to solve this problem, we model task allocation process and present a two-stage task scheduling method, that is to say, task scheduling can be divided into VMs grouping and tasks allocation. The first stage, according to the computing power each VM provides, we divide VM collection into three groups, which are fixed sequence respectively: interaction intensive type (vt_1), computation intensive type (vt_2), and other type (vt_3). The second phase, for tasks waiting to be allocated, according to the demand for resources, each task selects the group and stands in line. Task-VM allocation strategy is shown in Fig. 2.

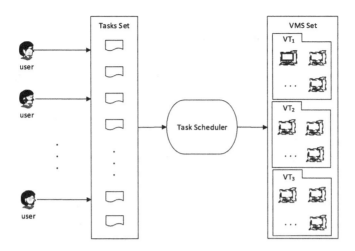

Fig. 2. Task-VM allocation strategy.

At Fig. 2, after tasks arrive at the request queue (Tasks set), in accordance with the principle of "First Come, First Service (FCFS)" [12], tasks are sent to the task scheduler, then, according to the running status of each VM, the scheduler calculates the corresponding VM set, if the current task is not to violate the Service Level Agreement (SLA) of VM, and deploys task on the VM, if the collection which does not violate the SLA is empty, then creates a new VM for the task.

2.2 Grouping Multi-level Encoding (GMLE) Mode

In MCC, mobile devices differ in thousands ways, different mobile devices may complete different tasks, so, it will trigger a greater difference of resources utilization between different VMs, even lead to load imbalance of cloud computing system. In order to solve the problem and promote the resources utilization, based on 2.1, we build a multi-level chromosome encoding rules, which use genetic box to signify VM and use gene to expresses task, one genetic box may include many genes, genes in box are no order, but the box capacity is limited, lots of genetic boxes make up a type of VM sets. These genetic boxes arrange in fixed order according to the category to form a chromosome. There are three genetic box sets, which are respectively vt_1, vt_2 and vt_3, tasks coming from mobile devices will be also classified following the same criterion. Table 1 illustrates the encoding rules.

At Table 1, it refers to the scheduling of m tasks allocated to n VMs. Firstly, n VMs are divided into three queues according to the special criterion; there is p, q, and $n - p - q$ VMs respectively in vt_1, vt_2, vt_3; then, on the basis of the same rules, the tasks are classified and fall in. The corresponding encoding is shown in formula (1).

$$
\begin{aligned}
D_i &= \left\{ vt_1, vt_2, vt_3 \right\} = \left\{ \{ v_1 \dots v_p \}, \{ v_{p+1} \dots v_{p+q} \}, \{ v_{p+q+1} \dots v_n \} \right\} \\
&= \left\{ \{ v_1 : \{2, 5, 7, 38, 79\}, \dots, v_p : \{9, \dots, m\} \}, \{ v_{p+1} : \{3, 52, m - 2\}, \dots, v_{p+q} : \{4, \dots, 32\} \}, \right. \\
&\quad \left. \{ v_{p+q+1} : \{m - 3, m - 1\}, \dots, v_n : \{14, \dots, m - 10\} \} \right\},
\end{aligned}
\tag{1}
$$

Table 1. The Chromosome Coding.

Interaction	VM ID	v_1	v_2	...	v_p
intensive type vt_1	Task ID	{2,5,7,38,79}	{1,20,21,22}	...	{9,15,28,44,101,116, m}
Computation	VM ID	v_{p+1}	v_{p+2}	...	v_{p+q}
intensive type vt_2	Task ID	{3,52, m-2}	{18,27,49,63,70,92}	...	{4,8,66,87,32}
Other type vt_3	VM ID	v_{p+q+1}	v_{p+q+2}	...	v_n
	Task ID	{m-3,m-1}	{25,56,43,120,10}	...	{14,77,96,131,158,m-10}

After the chromosome encoding is determined, the population will be initialized. Because of the diversity and uncertainty of the initial population, the paper uses the random method product the initial population, which size is S.

2.3   Energy-and-Time-Aware Double Fitness Function

Improved GA makes use of DFF to reality the compromise between promoting the performance and reducing energy consumption. DFF refers to the optimal time span and the maximum resources utilization and minimum opened number of all VMs.

2.3.1   The Optimal Time Span
For a task-VM allocation scheme, its optimal time span means the completion time of a task which is the longest in all the tasks of VM. $cost_j^i$ expresses the completing time of the task t_i running on VM v_j. If the number of tasks allocated to v_j is ats, the finishing time of total task is shown in formula (2).

$$T_{j,total} = \sum_{i=1}^{ats} cost_j^i, \tag{2}$$

Therefore, the fitness function based on the optimal time span is formula (3).

$$f(j) = max_{1 \leq k \leq n} T_{k,total}, 1 \leq j \leq S, \tag{3}$$

In the initial evolution stage of the population, the part individuals which have superior fitness value may mislead the development direction of population; near the convergence phase, the individuals which fitness values are close are difficult to continue to evolve, thus, it is difficult to find the optimal solution. In the above two cases, the fitness function must be adjusted, after adjusting, $f_{ad}(j)$ is formula (4).

$$f_{ad}(j) = \frac{f(j) + |f_{min}|}{f_{max} + f_{min} + \delta}, 1 \leq j \leq S, \tag{4}$$

Of which, $f(j)$ is the original fitness value; f_{max} is an upper bound of $f(j)$; f_{min} is a lower bound of $f(j)$; δ is a real number, $\delta \in (0, 1)$, which aim is to prevent the denominator as zero and increase the randomness of GA. If f_{max} or f_{min} is unknown, their value is replaced by the maximum or minimum value of the current generation so far, respectively; $|f_{min}|$ is to ensure that the fitness values are not negative after the calibration; if there is larger difference between f_{max} and f_{min}, the discrepancy is smaller after adjusting, this can prevent the exceptional individuals from ruling the whole population; if f_{max} and f_{min} are more close, the discrepancy is bigger after adjusting, thus this can increase the differences between individuals in the group and expand the search space to find the optimal solution.

2.3.2 Maximizing Resources Utilization and Minimizing Opened Number of VMs

Firstly, defining the fitness of the genetic box(VM). Consider the average utilization of all resources on VM as the comprehensive utilization(ϑ_c), as shown in formula (5).

$$\overline{\vartheta}_c = \frac{\sum \vartheta_k^c}{4}, \quad k \in \{mem, cpu, stor, net\}, \tag{5}$$

Among, ϑ_k^c denotes the utilization of the k-dimensional resource on VM v_c.

However, $\overline{\vartheta}_c$ cannot completely measure VM utilization, for example, v_c has two dimensions, the utilization of one is 85%, the other is 15%, then $\overline{\vartheta}_c = 50\%$; if the utilization of two dimensions on v_i is 45% and 55% respectively, then $\overline{\vartheta}_i = 50\%$. It is obvious that the resources usage of v_i is superior to v_c. Considering the balance between each resource dimension on VM, based on $\overline{\vartheta}_c$, designing a new genetic box evaluation parameter θ_c, which is expressed in formula (6).

$$\theta_c = \frac{\overline{\vartheta}_c}{\sqrt{\sum \left(\vartheta_k^c - \overline{\vartheta}_c\right)^2}}, \quad k \in \{mem, cpu, stor, net\}, \tag{6}$$

θ_c reflects the utilization of a genetic box and the equilibrium degree between the resources. θ_c is higher, corresponding VM has a higher efficiency, at the same time, the difference of the utilization between multiple resource dimensions on VM is small.

If using $usage_j$ to depict the overall utilization and resource equilibrium degree of the chromosome j (VM sets), as shown in formula (7).

$$usage_j = \frac{\sum \theta_c}{open\_num_z}, \tag{7}$$

Therein to, $open\_num_z$ signifies the number of opening VMs in the allocation scheme. $usage_j$ reflects an average utilization of all VMs which are deployed the tasks in the task migration plan corresponding with chromosome j.

Secondly, the fitness of chromosome j is made up of two parts: (1) overall utilization and resource equilibrium degree $usage_j$; (2) the number of opening VMs $open\_num_z$. Then, the fitness function of chromosome j is formula (8).

$$f(chr_j) = \varepsilon_1 * usage_j - \varepsilon_2 * \frac{open\_num_z}{n},\tag{8}$$

n is the number of VMs in the whole system; ε_1 and ε_2 are the weight coefficient.

Finally, in order to facilitate screening of individuals in the phase of selection stage, before selection, using the normalization and information entropy methods [13] to handle DFF, the purpose is to control the production of population objectively.

2.4 Genetic Operation and the Stopping Criterion

In GA, the goal of selection operator is to simulate the evolution model in the nature, excellent individuals have greater provability to survive to the next generation and poor individuals are likely to be eliminated. this paper uses the selection method of roulette wheel to select individuals, the computation of the individual fitness is formula (9).

$$p_k = \frac{\varphi_{a_k}(i)}{\sum_{k=1}^{S} \varphi_{a_k}(i)}, \quad k = 1, 2, \ldots, S,\tag{9}$$

i shows the i generation chromosomes set, $\varphi_{a_k}(i)$ is the fitness value of individual which will variant.

The crossover operator is the main method to generate new individual, it determines the global search ability of GA and looks for the crossover pair from the whole population. The selection of the crossover position uses formula (10) to calculate.

$$p_c = \begin{cases} p_{c_1} * e^{\frac{\varphi'_{a_k}(i) - \varphi_{a_k}^{avg}(i)}{\varphi_{a_k}^{max}(i) - \varphi_{a_k}^{avg}(i)}}, & \varphi'_{a_k}(i) \geq \varphi_{a_k}^{avg}(i) \\ p_{c_1}, & \varphi'_{a_k}(i) < \varphi_{a_k}^{avg}(i) \end{cases}\tag{10}$$

$\varphi_{a_k}^{max}(i)$ is the maximum value of the population fitness, $\varphi_{a_k}^{avg}(i)$ is the average value of the population fitness, $\varphi'_{a_k}(i)$ is the one of two crossover individuals which fitness value is bigger, p_{c_1} is set as the maximum crossover probability.

The mutation operator is the aiding method to produce new individuals. The mutation operator is as follow.

$$p_m = \begin{cases} p_{m_1} * e^{\frac{\varphi_{a_k}(i) - \varphi_{a_k}^{avg}(i)}{\varphi_{a_k}^{max}(i) - \varphi_{a_k}^{avg}(i)}}, & \varphi_{a_k}(i) \geq \varphi_{a_k}^{avg}(i) \\ p_{m_1}, & \varphi_{a_k}(i) < \varphi_{a_k}^{avg}(i) \end{cases}\tag{11}$$

Among, p_{m_1} is set as the maximum mutation probability in the algorithm.

In this paper, using the standard deviation of the fitness function value of the optimal time span as the terminal convergence conditions.

$$tc = \sqrt{\frac{\sum_{k=1}^{S}(\varphi_{a_k}(i) - \varphi_{a_k}^{avg}(i))^2}{S}} < \sigma, \tag{12}$$

σ is the convergence threshold, $\sigma \in (0, 1)$, if the standard deviation tc is smaller than σ, the iteration terminates, or to continue their genetic evolution.

3   Performance Evaluation

In the simulation experiment, the host is configured as follow, CPU is Intel 3.2 GHz, Memory is 12.0 GB, and the capacity of hardware is 500 GB. The parameters and their value are shown at Tables 2 and 3.

Table 2.   The number settings of tasks and VMs.

Configuration groups	conf1	conf2	conf3	conf4	conf5	conf6
Number of VMs	20	60	100	200	300	500
Number of tasks	60	180	300	600	900	1500

Table 3.   The parameters settings of simulation environment.

Parameters	Settings	Illustration
Population	44	Population size
ε_1	0.75	Weight coefficient of resources utilization
ε_2	0.25	Weight coefficient of the number of opening VMs
p_{c_1}	0.69	Maximum crossover probability
p_{m_1}	0.008	Maximum mutation probability
σ	0.1	Convergence threshold

At Table 2, the number of VMs in vt_1, vt_2, vt_3 is respectively gotten by summarizing the numbers of VMs after which are partitioned according to the VM parameters generated randomly; the number of tasks in each VM type vt_1, vt_2, vt_3 is also gained by using the same summarizing method.

3.1   Evaluate Experimental Results

3.1.1   Comparing Tasks Completion Time

Under the different number configurations of tasks and VMs, the completion time of tasks in the three algorithms are recorded at Table 4.

Table 4. Task completion time.

Algorithms	The completion time under the difference configurations(t)					
	conf1	conf2	conf3	conf4	conf5	conf6
GMLE-DFF	198	630	6465	40720	125608	300225
Sufferage	150	558	6278	40610	125608	300255
GA	180	594	6398	40640	125698	301650

Known from Table 4, task completion time of the three algorithms is nearly the same from conf1 to conf6 respectively, Improved GA is no obvious advantage. Based on Table 2, maintaining the number of tasks is constant at 4500, respectively recording task completion time, the result is in Fig. 3.

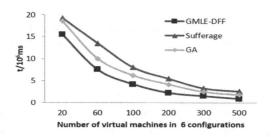

Fig. 3. Task completion time with the number of VMs changing.

Known from Fig. 3, when the number of VMs is less, the completion time of GMLE-DFF is far less than Sufferage and GA. But, as the number of VMs increasing, task completion time of all the three algorithms are declining and roughly equal finally. The cause is when the number of VMs increases, handling ability of VMs can well meet tasks demand, the conditions of task preemption resources and FCFS do not exist.

3.1.2   Comparing Resources Utilization

Under 6 configurations of Table 2, comparing resources utilization of improved GA and Sufferage algorithm, the average resources utilization is recorded in Fig. 4.

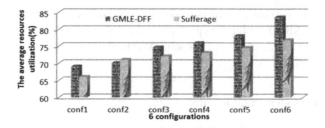

Fig. 4. Average resources utilization.

Seen from Fig. 4, when the number of tasks and VMs is both small, the difference of improved GA and Sufferage is not large in terms of average resources utilization, even in the conf2, Sufferage is better than improved GA. However, as the number of tasks and VMs increases gradually, the advantage of improved GA emerges little by little, for example, to conf6, the average resources utilization of improved GA is 83.5%, and Sufferage is 76.8%, the former is 6.7% higher than the latter. This is ascribed to redundant free VMs closed in improved GA based on GMLE-DFF.

3.1.3   Algorithm Convergence Situation

Supposing the number of tasks is 4500 in conf2, algorithm convergence result of improved GA based on GMLE-DFF and GA is shown in Fig. 5.

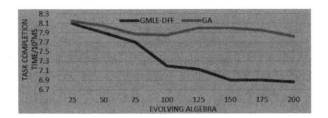

Fig. 5. Algorithm convergence result.

Seen from Fig. 5, at the early stage of algorithm iteration, the performance of two algorithms is more or less, but the convergence speed of improved GA based on GMLE-DFF is faster. After 150 generations, improved GA has started to restrain oneself, while GA presents the tendency of convergence when it is close to 200 generations. In addition, in the initial phase of evolution, it is about 65 generations, in GA, parts of exceptional individuals mislead the population evolution direction and make GA evolve to the direction of the extraordinary value from 65 to 100 generations, but the superior value is not the ideal optimal solution; Improved GA does not emerge the situation, meanwhile, improved GA adopts adaptive crossover probability and mutation probability, and adjusts the fitness function in the close to the algorithm convergence, therefore, finally the optimal solution gained by improved GA based on GMLE-DFF is more ideal than GA.

4   Conclusion

Reducing energy consumption is an important method to implement green computing. With the development of MCC and the coming of 5G, the related energy consumption problems give rise to new and hot attention for green MCC. Based on the intensive characteristic of 5G, the paper studies the problem of task scheduling in MCC. While guarantying system performance, in order to solute load imbalance and promote the resources utilization of the cloud computing system, a task-VM assignment strategy is put forward and applied to GA, which is improved based on GMLE-DFF. Experiments show that convergence speed of improved GA based on GMLE-DFF is faster than GA, and its performance is more outstanding, not only the task execution time is the shortest, but also it could meet resources utilization maximizing and load balancing of VMs. Therefore, it can be well applied to task scheduling for reducing energy consumption and shortening the execution time in MCC.

Funding Acknowledgments. The work is supported by the National Nature Science Foundation of China (No. 61370069, 61672111), Fok Ying Tung Education Foundation (No. 132032), Beijing Natural Science Foundation (No. 4162043), and the Cosponsored Project of Beijing Committee of Education.

References

1. Liu, F., Shu, P., et al.: Gearing resource-poor mobile devices with powerful clouds: architectures, challenges, and applications. Wirel. Commun. IEEE **20**(3), 14–22 (2013)
2. KołOdziej, J., Xhafa, F.: Modern approaches to modeling user requirements on resource and task allocation in hierarchical computational grids. Int. J. Appl. Math. Comput. Sci. **21**(2), 243–257 (2011)
3. Li, Z.-Y., Chen, S.-M., Yang, B., et al.: Multi-objective memetic algorithm for task scheduling on heterogeneous cloud. Chin. J. Comput. **2016**(2)
4. Li, J., Qiu, M., Ming, Z., et al.: Online optimization for scheduling preemptable tasks on IaaS cloud systems. J. Parallel Distrib. Comput. **72**(5), 666–677 (2012)
5. Guo, L., Zhao, S., Shen, S., et al.: Task scheduling optimization in cloud computing based on heuristic algorithm. J. Netw. **7**(3), 547–553 (2012)
6. Li, J., Qiu, M., Niu, J., et al.: Feedback dynamic algorithms for preemptable job scheduling in cloud systems. In: 2010 IEEE/WIC/ACM International Conference on Web Intelligence and Intelligent Agent Technology (WI-IAT), vol. 1, pp. 561–564. IEEE (2010)
7. Taheri, J., Lee, Y.C., Zomaya, A.Y., et al.: A Bee Colony based optimization approach for simultaneous job scheduling and data replication in grid environments. Comput. Oper. Res. **40**(6), 1564–1578 (2013)
8. Lin, X., Wang, Y., Xie, Q., et al.: Task scheduling with dynamic voltage and frequency scaling for energy minimization in the mobile cloud computing environment. IEEE Trans. Serv. Comput. **8**(2), 175–186 (2015)
9. Kumar, N., et al.: Performance analysis of Bayesian coalition game-based energy-aware virtual machine migration in vehicular mobile cloud. Netw. IEEE **29**(2), 62–69 (2015)
10. Zomaya, A.Y., Teh, Y.H.: Observations on using genetic algorithms for dynamic load-balancing. IEEE Trans. Parallel Distrib. Syst. **12**(9), 899–911 (2001)
11. Thede, S.M.: An introduction to genetic algorithms. J. Comput. Sci. Coll. **20**(1), 115–123 (2004)
12. Prasad Acharya, G., Asha Rani, M.: Fault-tolerant multi-core system design using pb model and genetic algorithm based task scheduling. In: Satapathy, S.C., Rao, N.B., Kumar, S.S., Raj, C.D., Rao, V.M., Sarma, G.V.K. (eds.) Microelectronics, Electromagnetics and Telecommunications. LNEE, vol. 372, pp. 449–458. Springer, New Delhi (2016). doi: 10.1007/978-81-322-2728-1_41
13. Li, X., et al.: Service operator-aware trust scheme for resource matchmaking across multiple clouds. IEEE Trans. Parallel Distrib. Syst. **26**(5), 1419–1429 (2015)

A Novel Service Recommendation Approach Considering the User's Trust Network

Guoqiang Li[1], Zibin Zheng[2], Haifeng Wang[1(✉)], Zifen Yang[1],
Zuoping Xu[1], and Li Liu[1]

[1] School of Informatics, Linyi University, Linyi 276000, Shandong, China
lgq_2005@126.com,
{wanghaifeng,yangzifen,xuzuoping,liuli}@lyu.edu.cn
[2] Mobile Internet and Financial Big Data Lab, Sun Yat-Sen University,
Guangzhou 510006, China
zibin.gil@gmail.com

Abstract. Web services are ever increasingly published on the network as core components of Service-oriented architecture (SOA). An attendant problem is how to help users select their satisfied services that meet their functional and non-functional requirements from the mass services. Service recommendation technology is adopted and studied as an effective approach currently. This paper focuses on the user's trust network, where the users share their experience and rating for the invoked services. To attack the data sparsity and cold-start problems in the user-service rating matrix, an improved random walk algorithm is proposed. Firstly, we employ the non-negative matrix factorization method to compute the similarities between users and services separately. Then our method introduces the trust relationship in iterations of the random walk to select the trust users accurately. At last, the real dataset is used to validate our approach. Experimental results show the effectiveness of our approach compared with the state-of-art algorithms.

Keywords: Web service · Service recommendation · Social network · Random walk

1 Introduction

There are growing number of web services occurring on the internet, e.g. WebserviceX^1 and ProgrammableWeb^2. More and more users invoke these services, e.g. there 6,000,000+ web services transactions for WebServiceX services every day. So, how to help users select appropriate web services among a large number of candidates to fulfill their needs is an important task and full of challenge. Quality of Services (QoS) is usually adopted to differentiate between web services that share similar functionalities [1]. It is difficult to acquire the QoS information by invoking the services in advance. The reason

---

[1] WebserviceX.Net: http://www.webservicex.net/ws/default.aspx.
[2] http://www.programmableweb.com/.

© ICST Institute for Computer Sciences, Social Informatics and Telecommunications Engineering 2017
S. Wang and A. Zhou (Eds.): CollaborateCom 2016, LNICST 201, pp. 429–438, 2017.
DOI: 10.1007/978-3-319-59288-6_39

is that it is time-consuming and pay-per-use to invoke the services. So, QoS prediction becomes a reasonable way to select service via collaborative filtering (CF). e.g. [2]. But it seems inadequate to cope with the cold-start users and sparse data questions [3]. Recently, users are connected by online social networks, e.g. Facebook. In view of the idea that we will refer to the advice from our friends, social network is explored to improve recommendations.

This paper takes the trust information into account in the random walk model. The main contributions of this paper include: (1) For the cold-start users, we employ the random walk model to enhance the recommendation accuracy. In any iteration of walk, the trust relation and similarity of users are both considered at the same time. (2) We also provide many metrics to compare and assert the efficiency of our algorithms with the state-of-the-art algorithms.

The rest of this paper is organized as follows. Section 2 introduces the related work about services recommendation. A recommendation model based on random walk is described in detail in Sect. 3. We conduct the extensive experiments in Sect. 4. Finally, Sect. 5 concludes this paper and presents the future work.

2   Related Work

Predicting the Quality of Services is one way to choose or recommend services to users. E.g. [2, 4–6]. To attack the data sparse, Matrix Factorization technique is also adopted in many works, e.g. [7–10]. Using the user-service rating matrix, A. Abdullah proposes an integrated-model QoS based on graph (IMQG), then a random walk algorithm is conducted on IMQG [11]. For these approaches, the social network of users is not considered completely.

A trust-aware recommender system (RS) architecture is proposed to confirm that trust-awareness can solve some problems of the traditional problems of RSs [3], e.g. data sparsity. For TidalTrust [12], the shortest path between two users are hired to compute the ratings and the trust values of them are taken to be weights. On the base of item-level trust model, the target neighbors are selected by double neighbor choosing strategy considering the user's similarity and trust degree [13]. Even though trust is employed in [14], direct neighbors of the target user are only used.

Three weightage schemes for rating predictions are proposed and compared in [15]. A linear combination model is proposed using an enhanced PCC similarity and hiring the product of trust degree one a trust path to compute the non-adjacent users' trust value [16]. A random walk method is used to combine trust-based and item-based recommendations, meanwhile the confidence in the predictions are introduced [17]. The most similar work with our method is [18], which proposes trust relevancy to reconstruct the social network where the weight between users is computed by multiplying the trust value and the user similarity. Different from existing random walk model, we distinguish direct neighbors from indirect neighbors. That is to say, the trust relationship between the source user and selected user will be taken into account, instead of only using the similarity between the current user and the to-be-selected user [17–19].

3   Recommendation Model Based on Random Walk

In recommendation systems, there are two basic sets: users and items (services used as synonyms). A rating matrix R expresses the ratings on items by users, and usually the rating value is in the rang [1, 5]. After introducing the trust network of users, a trust rating matrix is formed by each user u giving the ratings to his direct neighbors.

3.1   Similarities Computation with Rating Matrix

In this paper, we make use of the Non-negative Matrix Factorization (NMF) [20] Model to compute the similarities of users and items. Its key idea is to decompose a rating matrix R into two latent feature matrices of users and services with a lower dimensionality d. $R \approx PQ^T$, where $P(m \times d)$ and $Q(n \times d)$ represent the latent feature matrices of users and services separately. Then each line of rows in the respective matrix denotes the latent feature vector of a user or service. Then, we employ the cosine similarity measure to calculate the similarities as follows:

$$simS(u_a, u_b) = \cos(\overline{u_a}, \overline{u_b}) = \frac{\overline{u_a} \cdot \overline{u_b}}{|\overline{u_a}| \cdot |\overline{u_b}|} \tag{1}$$

where $\overline{u_a}$ and $\overline{u_b}$ denotes the latent feature vectors of users u_a and u_b. Similarly,

$$simS(s_i, s_j) = \cos(\overline{s_i}, \overline{s_j}) = \frac{\overline{s_i} \cdot \overline{s_j}}{|\overline{s_i}| \cdot |\overline{s_j}|} \tag{2}$$

where $\overline{s_i}$ and $\overline{s_j}$ denotes the latent feature vectors of services s_i and s_j.

3.2   Random Walk with Trust Network

This section presents our algorithm TSWSWalker (Web Services Walker based on Trust Similarity) by improving the random walk algorithm [17, 18]. All notations used in our algorithm are listed in Table 1.

1.   A Single Random Walk

For the to-be-recommended service s_0, the random walk starts from the source user u_0. At each step k, a certain user u is reached. If u already rated s_0, then the random walk stops and return $r_{u,0}$ as the result. If not, there are two options as follows:

(1)   The random walk will stop at u_c with a certain probability $\varphi_{u,k}$. Then, the service s_i is selected from RS_u based on the selection probability $SP_u(s_i)$. The rating of s_i given by u is returned as a result.

The probability $\varphi_{u,k}$ is affected by the similarity of the service of RS_u. A bigger similarity between the selected service s_i and s_0 incurs the greater probability to stop.

Table 1. All notations in our algorithm

Symbols	Description
$r_{u,s}$	The rating of service s given by user u
$r'_{u,s}$	The predicted rating of service s given by user u
u_c	The current user u
$\varphi_{u,k}$	The probability that the random walk stops at user u in the kth step
RS_u	The set of services which user u rated
$SP_u(s_i)$	The probability that s_i is selected from RS_u to gain the u's rating for s_i
TS_u	The set of users which user u give trust value directly in the dataset
$UP_u(u_a)$	The probability that u_a is selected from TS_u to gain $r_{u,s}$
$simS(s_i, s_j)$	The similarity of services s_i and s_j
$simS(u_a, u_b)$	The similarity of users u_a and u_b

To get more trust users, the probability of keeping random walk $\varphi_{u,k}$ should increase by considering the walk distance k. The following equation is adopted as [18, 19].

$$\varphi_{u,k} = \max_{s_i \in RS_u} Sim(s_i, s_0) \times \frac{1}{1 + e^{-\frac{k}{2}}} \qquad (3)$$

When this walk stops at the user u, the method needs to select a service from RS_u. The probability $SP_u(s_i)$ is computed according to the following equation:

$$SP_u(s_i) = \frac{simS(s_i, s_0)}{\sum_{s_j \in RS_u} simS(s_j, s_0)} \qquad (4)$$

Once one service s_i is selected, the rating of s_i given by u is returned as the result.

(2) Another possibility is that the walk continues with a probability $1 - \varphi_{u,k}$. A user is selected from the set of direct trust neighbors for the next walk. Meanwhile this user is the most trusted by the source user u_0.

In the trust network, It is proved that choosing a user randomly will decrease the predication accuracy in [18], different from which we consider the trust similarity and rating similarity between the source user S_0 and to-be-selected user comprehensively instead of the single similarity of the current u_c and to-be-selected user.

① We propose that the trust similarity which is employed in the users' selection phase is computed by Jaccard similarity. The equation is as follows:

$$J_{a,b} = \frac{|T_a \cap T_b|}{|T_a \cup T_b|} \qquad (5)$$

where T_a and T_b denote the set of trusted users of user a and user b.

② For the condition that there are two users, who have the same number of trust users between source user. To differentiate from them, we design an improved Jaccard similarity equation as follows:

$$J_{a,b}^{+} = \frac{\sum\limits_{u \in T_a \cap T_b} 1 * \dfrac{1}{d_{u_0,u}}}{|T_a \cup T_b|} \tag{6}$$

where $d_{u_{0,u}}$ denotes the minimum distance between the source user u_0 and the user u who is in the intersection of users a and b. It is obviously, Eq. (6) is a general formation of Eq. (5) when the common users come from the direct trust users intersection of two users a and b.

③ Another condition is that there are no users who are commonly trusted by two users. The user is selected by the bigger similarity between $simS(u_a, u_g)$ and $simS(u_a, u_h)$.

All in all, the user selection similarity is decided as follows:

$$UP_u(U_a) = \begin{cases} \sum\limits_{a \in TS_u} \max\left(J_{u_0,a}^{+}\right) & T_{u_0} \cap T_a \neq \emptyset \\ \sum\limits_{a \in TS_u} \max\left(simS(u_a, u_{u_0})\right) & T_{u_0} \cap T_a = \emptyset \end{cases} \tag{7}$$

The random walk is likely to run and never stop. Here three cases to stop it are listed as follows:

(1) Stopping at a user who has rated the service s_0.
(2) A user node is stayed and a service is selected to return its rating.
(3) To avoid walking forever, the maximum depth is set to 6 to terminate the walk according to the "six-degrees of separation" in the social networks.

   2. Ratings predication

The final predicated ratings can be gained via the results returned from multiple walks. The equation is:

$$r'_{u_0,s} = \frac{1}{n} \sum_{i=1}^{n} r_i \tag{8}$$

where r_i is the returned result of each walk, n is the number of total walks. To decide the number of random walks, the variance of the predicted values is employed. Let r_j denotes the returned value of the jth random walk and $\bar{r}$ denotes the average value returned by n random walks. The calculation equation of variance σ^2 of i iterations is as follows:

$$\sigma_i^2 = \frac{1}{i} \sum_{j=1}^{i} (r_j - \bar{r})^2 \tag{9}$$

We also set a tunable parameter ε to guide the termination of walk satisfying the condition $\left| \sigma_{i+1}^2 - \sigma_i^2 \right| \leq \varepsilon$. In our experiments, this parameter is set to be 0.0001.

4 Experiments and Evaluation

4.1 Experiment Setup

We extract a subset from the extended Epinions dataset used in many works, e.g. [21]. There are 237 users and 31319 articles in our dataset where 48 users do not rate any article(an article is taken as a service). The total number of ratings is 371140. The density of the user rating matrix is 0.06. For the social trust network, there are 23515 trust statements (distrusts are excluded). The density of the trust statements matrix is 0.42. There are about 51% users whose rated articles less than 5, so these users can be identified as cold-start users. Our experiments are conducted using python 2.7.

We compare with the following state-of-the-art algorithms:

(1) User-based CF: It is the classic user-based collaborative filtering method.
(2) TidalTrust [12]: It treat the trust as the weight to compute the ratings.
(3) MoleTrust [22]: It predicts the trust score using the trust propagation method.
(4) TrustWalker [17]: It is based on the random walk considering trust and item similarity.
(5) RelevantTrustWalker [18]: This algorithm introduces trust relevancy concept.

We will not compare our method with the WSWalker [19], because the trust network of users is constructed according to the user's location and the user's similarity.

4.2 Evaluation Metrics

We work with the leave-one-out method, which consists of hiding a rating and trying to predict its value. The following metrics will be considered in the experiments. These equations of above metrics are same as the equations in [18].

(1) Root Mean Squared Error (*RMSE*): $R_{u,s}$ is the actual rating given to service s by user u. $R_{u,s}'$ is the predicted rating given to service s by u employing the recommendation algorithms. N denotes the total number of tested ratings. Smaller *RMSE* value indicates that the recommendation algorithm performs more precisely.

$$RMSE = \sqrt{\frac{\sum_{u,s} \left(R_{u,s} - R_{u,s}' \right)^2}{N}} \tag{10}$$

(2) Coverage: Due to sparsity of the dataset, coverage metric can be used to verify that trust information can not only enhance this metric but also not sacrificing the precision. Its equation defined as:

$$Coverage = \frac{Np}{M} \tag{11}$$

Where N_p is the number of pairs <user,service> successfully predicted by using the recommendation algorithms and M is the number of tested pairs <user, service>.

(3) F-measure: it will be hired to examine the tradeoffs between accuracy and coverage. Firstly, we convert *RMSE* into a precision metric whose values are in the range [0,1]. The equation is as follows:

$$Precision = 1 - \frac{RMSE}{Maxrating - Minrating} \tag{12}$$

where the *Maxrating* is 5 and *Minrating* is 1 in the dataset used in this paper. Then, we use the equation to compute the *F-measure*:

$$F - measure = \frac{2 \times Precision \times Coverage}{Precision + Coverage} \tag{13}$$

4.3   Experimental Results and Analysis

We measure their performance on the cold-start users and all results are shown as Fig. 1. Obviously, the User-based CF fails to recommend with 15.73% coverage. The reason is that the cold-start users rate few services, so it is difficult to compute the similarities. After introducing the trust relationships, the *Coverage* of TidalTrust and MoleTrust is bigger than User-based CF. At the same time, the *RMSE* decrease. But the precision does not improve obviously. The trust-related algorithms based on random walk model gain the significant improve on the coverage and precision according to the users' selection strategy. And the *RMSE* of TSWSWalker is the smallest because the selected users of one walk are the most trustful and similar with the source user. After analyzing the data, there are about 26% users from the selected users in our algorithm are not considered in the RelevantTrustWalker algorithm. Finally, the *F-measure* of the TSWSWalker is better than the other algorithms.

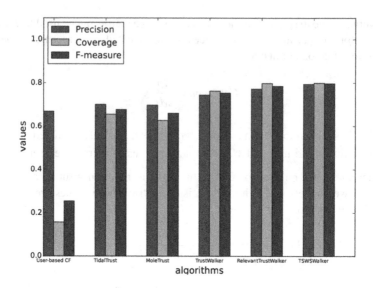

Fig. 1. Comparison results for cold start users

From the Fig. 2, we can see that all the trust-related algorithms outperform the User-based CF for all considered metrics. For the algorithms based on the random walk, it is better to design the user-selection strategy in the walk process, i.e., the *RMSE* of TSWSWalker and RelevantTrustWalker are less than TrustWalker's. Even though the

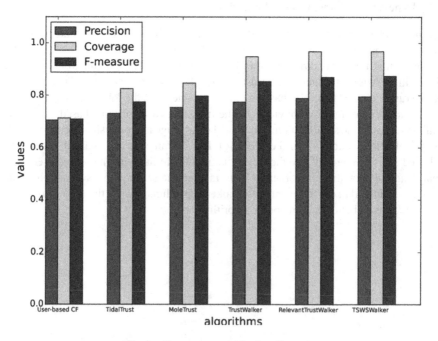

Fig. 2. Comparison results for all users.

coverage of TSWSWalker and RelevantTrustWalker are very close, TSWSWalker's *RMSE* is smaller than RelevantTrustWalker. The reason is that there are about 89% users who have common trusted users with others after analyzing the dataset. In the same way, the recommendation performance of the TSWSWalker outperforms the other algorithms for all users.

5   Conclusion

In this paper, an improved random walk algorithm is proposed to recommend the services. The non-negative matrix factorization technique is hired to compute the similarities of users and services. In each walk, we not only consider the rating similarity between users but their trust value. At last, the extensive experiments are conducted and the results validate that our proposed approach outperforms the other recommendation algorithms.

In the used dataset, there exist distrust relationships. These distrust users' influence on the recommendation accuracy will be deeply studied as a future work. And we will compare more algorithms with our algorithm.

Acknowledgments. This work was funded by the Natural Science Foundation of Shandong Province (NSFS Grant No. ZR2014FL013) and the Independent Innovation and Achievements Transformation Special Project of Shandong Province (No. 2014ZZCX02702). The authors acknowledge the support of the Opening Fund of Shandong Provincial Key Laboratory for Network Based Intelligent Computing.

References

1. Al-Masri, E., Mahmoud, Q.H.: QoS-based discovery and ranking of web services. In: The 16th International Conference on Computer Communications and Networks, pp. 529–534. IEEE Press, Honolulu, Hawaii (2007)
2. Zheng, Z., Ma, H., Lyu, M.R., King, I.: WSRec: a collaborative filtering based web service recommender system. In: The 16th International Conference on Web Services, pp. 437–444. IEEE Computer Society, Los Angeles (2009)
3. Massa, P., Avesani, P.: Trust-aware collaborative filtering for recommender systems. In: Meersman, R., Tari, Z. (eds.) OTM 2004. LNCS, vol. 3290, pp. 492–508. Springer, Heidelberg (2004). doi:10.1007/978-3-540-30468-5_31
4. Wang, S., Hsu, C.-H., Liang, Z., Sun, Q.: Multi-user web service selection based on multi-QoS prediction. Inf. Syst. Front. **16**(1), 143–152 (2014)
5. Chen, X., Zheng, Z., Yu, Q., Lyu, M.R.: Web service recommendation via exploiting location and QoS information. IEEE Trans. Parallel Distrib. Syst. **25**(7), 1913–1924 (2014)
6. He, P., Zhu, J., Zheng, Z., Xu, J., Lyu, M.R.: Location-based hierarchical matrix factorization for web service recommendation. In: The 21st International Conference on Web Services, pp. 297–304. IEEE Computer Society, Alaska (2014)
7. Zheng, Z., Ma, H., Lyu, M.R., King, I.: Collaborative web service QoS prediction via neighborhood integrated matrix factorization. IEEE Trans. Serv. Comput. **6**(3), 289–299 (2013)

8. Yu, Q., Zheng, Z., Wang, H.: Trace norm regularized matrix factorization for service recommendation. In: 20th IEEE International Conference on Web Services, pp. 34–41. IEEE Computer Society, Santa Clara (2013)

9. Li, Z., Cao, J., Gu, Q.: Temporal-aware QoS-based service recommendation using tensor decomposition. J. Web Serv. Res. **12**(1), 62–74 (2015)

10. Zhang, R., Li, C., Sun, H., Wang, Y., Huai, J.: Quality of web service prediction by collective matrix factorization. In: 11th International Conference on Service Computing, pp. 432–439. IEEE Xplore Press, Bangalore (2014)

11. Abdullah, A.: An integrated-model QoS-based graph for web service recommendation. In: 22nd International Conference on Web Services, pp. 416–423. IEEE Computer Society, New York (2015)

12. Golbeck, J.A.: Computing and applying trust in web-based socail networks, University of Maryland (2005)

13. Dongyan, J., Fuzhi, Z.: A collaborative filtering recommendation algorithm based on double neighbor choosing strategy. J. Comput. Res. Dev. **50**(5), 1076–1084 (2013)

14. He, J., Chu, W.W.: Social networ-based recommender system (SNRS). In: Memon, N., Xu, J.J., Hicks, D.L., Chen, H. (eds.) Data Mining for Social Network Data. Annals of Information Systems, vol. 12, pp. 47–74. Springer, Heidelberg (2010)

15. Ray, S., Mahanti, A.: Improving prediction accuracy in trust-aware recommender systems. In: 43rd International Conference on System Sciences, pp. 1–9. IEEE Computer Society, New York (2010)

16. Tang, M., Xu, Y., Liu, J., Zheng, Z., Liu, X.F.: Trust-aware service recommendation via exploiting social networks. In: 10th IEEE International Conference on Services Computing, pp. 376–383. IEEE Computer Society, Santa Clara (2013)

17. Jamali, M., Ester, M.: TrustWalker: a random walk model for combining trust-based and item-based recommendation. In: 15th International Conference on Knowledge Discovery and Data Mining, pp. 397–406. ACM, Paris, France (2009)

18. Deng, S., Huang, L., Xu, G.: Social network-based service recommendation with trust enhancement. Expert Syst. Appl. **41**(18), 8075–8084 (2014)

19. Tang, M., Dai, X., Cao, B., Liu, J.: WSWalker: a random walk method for Qos-aware web service recommendation. In: 22th International Conference on Web Services, pp. 591–598. IEEE Computer Society, New York (2015)

20. Hoyer, P.O.: Non-negative matrix factorization with sparseness constraints. J. Mach. Learn. Res. **5**, 1457–1469 (2004)

21. Victor, P., Cornelis, C., De Cock, M., Teredesai, A.: Trust-and distrust-based recommendations for controversial reviews. IEEE Intell. Syst. **26**(1), 48–55 (2011)

22. Massa, P., Avesani, P.: Trust-aware recommender systems. In: 1st Conference on Recommender Systems, pp. 17–24. ACM (2007)

3-D Design Review System in Collaborative Design of Process Plant

Jian Zhou[1](✉), Linfeng Liu[1], Yunyun Wang[1], Fu Xiao[1], and Weiqing Tang[2]

[1] College of Computer, Nanjing University of Posts and Telecommunications,
Nanjing 210003, China
zhoujian@njupt.edu.cn
[2] Institute of Computing Technology, Chinese Academy of Sciences, Beijing 100190, China

Abstract. Design review is important in collaborative design of process plants. To satisfy the actual work demands of design review, a 3-d design review system is developed and the key technologies such as information organization model and multi-resolution rendering approach are proposed. The information organization model combining scene tree and attribute tree can organize the information from different CAD systems with a unified structure, and optimize the information query speed. The multi-resolution rendering approach based on programmable graphics pipeline can improve rendering efficiency within less preprocessing time, without using extra hard-disk space. Examples show that the 3-d design review system can work on a general PC to review a large quantity of design information from different subjects, and ensure real-time interaction at the same time.

Keywords: Design review · Information organization model · Multi-resolution rendering · Collaborative design

1 Introduction

Process plants, such as refineries and petrochemical plants, are complex facilities mainly consisting of pipelines and equipment [1]. As shown in Fig. 1, process plants are used in industries such as petrochemical, power, metallurgical industries. With increasing product complexity and intensive global competition in the process plant industry, companies are increasingly relying on collaborative design techniques to shorten the design cycle and to sustain the optimum productivity [2].

In collaborative design of process plants, there are constraints among stages or subjects. The relevant design must meet the constraints, otherwise there will be confliction. So design review is important in collaborative design of process plants. A reviewer has to check the results of different stages or subjects to find the design errors and conflicts, and then inform relevant designers the review results. When the review efficiency is improved, the rework in construction and the corresponding cost waste can be reduced, which helps to avoid the extension of period. So far, many review systems have

© ICST Institute for Computer Sciences, Social Informatics and Telecommunications Engineering 2017
S. Wang and A. Zhou (Eds.): CollaborateCom 2016, LNICST 201, pp. 439–450, 2017.
DOI: 10.1007/978-3-319-59288-6_40

been developed by major CAD companies for their own CAD products, e.g. Navis-Works, SmartPlant Review and PDMS Review. But none of them works well in large CAD datasets especially on current desktop PCs.

A
Urumqi Petrochemical Company Refinery 110 million tons / year delayed coking unit expansion project

B
Wastewater treatment project in Shanghai Baoshan Iron and Steel Dedigned by South Metallurgical Engineering design Company

Fig. 1. Instances of process plants

First, the design institutes adopt different CAD systems, leading to the heterogeneity of design information. Second, limited by economic conditions, the design institutes usually work with general PC. Finally, as the collaborative design technology is getting more widely used in design of large-scale process plants, the quantity and complexity of information in design review have been raised rapidly [1]. To solve the problems mentioned above, a new 3-d design review system needs to be developed, which can process large quantity of design information from different CAD systems while working on a general PC.

The remainder of this paper is structured as follows. We introduce the problems and some related works in Sect. 2. The architecture of our review system is described in Sect. 3. In Sect. 4, the key technologies such as information organization model and multi-resolution rendering approach are proposed. Section 5 presents and discusses the function and the performance of our review system. Finally, conclusions are drawn in Sect. 6.

2   Problems and Related Work

During design review, the reviewer could find the design errors and conflicts among subjects or stages by real-time 3-d navigation, either by referring to the attributes and design conditions, or through automatic collision check and design condition check by the computer. To achieve the above functions, some technologies must be improved and adopted in review system, e.g., fast rendering, human-computer interaction, information organization and collision detection. In this paper, we focus on two problems, how to organize the design information from different CAD systems, and how to fast render a large-scale process plant model.

2.1   Information Organization Model

The information of graphics, topology, attributes and design conditions should be included in design review. The model of triangular surface piece, which is usually used in virtual environment, is not suitable for design review because it has lost topological information and attribute information [3]. Various information organization models have been proposed to solve this problem [4–7], and most of them were oriented to satisfy the requirements for application of virtual assembly. Compared to virtual assembly, the structure of graphics information is much simpler, and no behavior information is required. But there are a large number of graphics in design review, with more complex topological relations and a large quantity of engineering attributes. Therefore, neither the triangular surface piece model nor the information organization model for virtual assembly can satisfy the demands of design review, so it is important to study the information organization model that can simultaneously organize the information from different CAD systems with a unified structure and optimize the information query speed.

2.2   Multi-resolution Rendering Approach

During design review, a large-scale process plant model usually involves hundreds of millions, even thousands of millions of triangular faces. In order to improve the real-time performance of human-computer interaction, the number of polygons rendered in each frame should be reduced while the realisticness of the scene has been satisfied. Level-of-Detail (LOD) proposed by Clark [8] in 1976 is an effective method. There are two types of LOD: static LOD and dynamic LOD. Although the latter provides high quality images, it increases the computing cost in the rendering process. On the contrary, the static LOD could reduce the computing cost by constructing a multi-resolution model in advance. Therefore the static LOD is usually preferred in an actual real-time rendering system for a large-scale complex scene. On one hand, it takes a long time to preprocess a multi-resolution model with the traditional static LOD. To solve this problem, multi-resolution model in parallel with PC cluster [9, 10] or with GPU [11, 12] were constructed. However, it still takes minutes or even hours. In order to improve the design review efficiency, the preprocessing time on general PC should be reduced effectively. On the other hand, main memory could not contain large quantity of multi-resolution model of large-scale complex scene with the traditional static LOD. To solve this problem by out-of-core techniques, experts [13–15] start to develop multi-resolution rendering approaches based on external memory. But these approaches require large extra hard-disk space. Therefore, a new multi-resolution rendering approach which requires less preprocessing time and less hard-disk space for design review of process plants should be studied.

3   Architecture of 3-D Design Review System

A new 3-d design review system which adopts novel information organization model and multi-resolution rendering approach is developed in this paper, and its bottom-up structure includes layers of "resource supply", "review data", "review core service", and "review functional application". "Resource supply" derives the design information from different CAD systems and transports to "review data". "Review data" stores and manages the design information using database. "Review core service" acquires the information and organizes it by access to "review data", and provides "review functional application" services for querying. Reviewers use the functions provided by "review functional application", and return the results to the data layer.

The design information includes graphics, topology, attributes and design conditions. These types of information would be queried real time but not be modified in design review of process plants.

Graphic information describes the geometric figure of an object. In this paper, "Object" is the minimum unit in engineering description, e.g. a pipe and a valve. In design review, what the reviewer concerns about is only the graphic's surface information of an object, rather than the internal conditions. An object is mainly composed of basic voxels, such as box, cylinder, prism, and sphere. Figure 2 shows the basic voxels used in our process plant model.

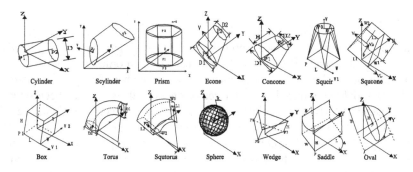

Fig. 2. Basic voxels used in process plant model

Topological information describes the connection relation between objects. As shown in Fig. 3, pipe A1 is connected with valve B, and valve B is also connected with pipe A2. In hard collision check, it is supposed that no collision occurs between the connected objects.

Fig. 3. Topological information in one particular pipe

Attribute information includes category attribute and engineering property. Category attribute is the category which the objects belong to and hierarchical relations between the categories. Engineering property is the object's attributes and corresponding value in the engineering application, e.g. pipeline rank, size, end-category, thickness, material, and flow direction.

Design condition information describes a related design condition for other design subjects requested. For example, equipment subject requests structure subject in ground bearing ability, due to the need of using large equipment.

4 Key Technology

4.1 Information Organization for Design Review

On one hand, design information is from different CAD systems and in this way it has problem of information heterogeneity. On the other hand, the efficiency of design review depends on the efficiency of information queries. Therefore, an information organization model combining scene tree and attribute tree is proposed in this paper. We use this model to organize the design information with a unified structure, and optimize the information query speed.

4.1.1 Information Organization Mode Combining Scene Tree and Attribute Tree

The information organization mode combining scene tree and attribute tree is shown in Fig. 4, with objects as the minimum organizational unit. Under the subject node, the scene tree is on the left and the attribute tree on the right. The subject node is used to describe the corresponding information and address of review database of the subject. The scene tree describes the subject's graphic information and topological information, using the octree structure to organize the objects. The octree structure helps in view frustum culling and occlusion culling, which can finally improve the rendering speed. The attribute tree describes the category attribute and engineering property, using category to organize objects. Due to the large quantity of engineering property information and low using frequency, on-demand mode is applied to read in the engineering property, thereby saving the cost on main memory.

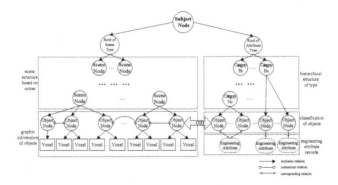

Fig. 4. Information organization model combining scene tree and attribute tree

4.1.2   Storage and Acquisition of Design Information

Database has some advantages, such as accurate data retrieval, convenient remote access, reasonable resource utilization and easy data recovery. In this paper, the design information extracted from CAD systems and the results returned from review are stored in database in the form of tables. An independent database is established for each subject, and the structure of the tables is shown in Table 1. The information organization mode combining scene tree and attribute tree is constructed according to information in the tables.

Table 1. Information in the tables of database

Table name	Table description
Meta	Subject information, including name, CAD system, version, and units
Category	Category information, including category id (cid), category name, father category id and engineering property table id (pdid)
Property_*	Engineering property information, including engineering property id (pid) and fields of engineering attribute. * means pdid
Object	Relationship between object and category, and engineering property, including object id (oid), the corresponding cid and pid
Graph	Graphic and topological information of an object, including oid, RGB valuet, axis-aligned bounding box, and the voxels included in the object
Condition	Design condition information proposed for other subjects, including design condition id, other subjects' names, oid of the subject corresponded and text description of the design conditions
Result	Review results, including review result id, type, location, and set of objects related to the problem

The review system is not required to build model. The design information is acquired from CAD system and reconstructed in review system. A CAD system usually provides a development interface, such as ObjectArx provided by AutoCAD and Pro/ToolKit provided by Pro/Engineer. In this paper, information is exported through the development interface, based on the category definition files (XML format) provided by each design subject.

4.1.3   Query of Information

In 3-d design review, we query engineering property by obtaining the objects according to human-computer interaction. The specific steps are as follows:

Step 1.   Intersection of ray with scene node's axis-aligned bounding box of scene tree in the information organization mode. If there's no intersection, traverse process ends. If the intersection obtained, then traverse the child nodes of this node. If the child node is a scene node, repeat Step 1. If the child node is an object node, execute Step 2.

Step 2.   Intersection of ray with object node's axis-aligned bounding box. If intersection obtained, then traverse the child nodes of this node. Otherwise the traverse process ends.

Step 3. Intersection of ray with voxel node's oriented bounding box. If intersection obtained, then traverse the corresponding triangular faces of this voxel node. Otherwise the traverse process ends.

Step 4. Intersection of ray with triangular faces. If intersection obtained, then record the oid of the object which the voxel belongs to. Otherwise the traverse process ends.

Step 5. Acquire the corresponding pid and pdid of the object by oid, according to the structure of attribute tree in the information organization mode.

Step 6. Acquire the engineering property by querying the "Property_pdid" table in the object database based on pid.

4.2   Multi-resolution Rendering Approach for Design Review

In recent years, fixed graphics pipeline has been replaced by programmable graphics pipeline in GPU, which provides a flexible control interface to vertex buffer and index buffer in display memory [16]. It provides good opportunity for solving the problems in fast rendering of large-scale complex scene. A multi-resolution rendering approach of large-scale process plant model based on programmable graphics pipeline is proposed in this paper.

4.2.1   Construction of Multi-resolution Model

As mentioned above, an object is mainly composed of basic voxels. A multi-resolution model of objects is constructed according to the multi-resolution model of the basic voxels. In the generation of multi-resolution model, the proposed approach ensures that the vertex set of a low resolution model is the subset of that of a high resolution model. So only the vertex information of its highest resolution mode and some of the vertex indexes are needed to be saved for each object.

In advance, a multi-resolution model of the basic voxels is constructed on basis of the number of subdivisions in the following steps:

Step 1. The voxel is subdivided uniformly. In a cylinder, for example, both its bottom and top circles are divided into N sections, then its flank is turned into $2 \times N$ rectangular meshes, and the two circles are turned into regular N-polygon with totally $4 \times N$ vertexes. The multi-resolution model of the basic voxels is constructed by the number of subdivisions (N).

Step 2. The maximum and minimum of N (N_{max} and N_{min} respectively) are obtained based on the voxel size. In order to subdivide a voxel uniformly, we define $N_{max} = 2^{n_{max}}, N_{min} = 2^{n_{min}}$, where $n_{max} \geq n_{min} \geq 2$ are integers.

Step 3. Define N of the i-th resolution model of voxels as $N_i = 2^{n_i}$, where $n_i = n_{min} + \lfloor i \cdot (n_{max} - n_{min})/(L - 1) \rfloor$ is an integer, and L is the number of multi-resolution model. The first subdivision points of different resolution models are the same.

If the voxel subdivision number is larger, the voxel has more triangular faces, and the resolution of the model is higher. The voxel is symmetric, and subdivision number of a high resolution model of voxels is 2^x times that of a low resolution model. So the vertex set of the low resolution model is the sub-set of that of the high resolution model.

In a cylinder, for example, its size is determined by diameter D. If $D \in [0, 1]$ (meter), then $N_{max} = 2^5 = 32, N_{min} = 2^2 = 4$. The subdivision of the circles and cylinder graphics of a multi-resolution model when $L = 4$ are shown in Fig. 5.

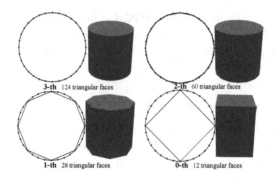

Fig. 5. Subdivision of the circles and cylinder graphics of multi-resolution model

4.2.2   Transformation of Multi-resolution Model

Based on the construction of a multi-resolution model, with effective management of vertex buffer and index buffer, a multi-resolution model can be transformed according to the vertex index transform in the rendering process. The relationship between main memory, display memory and graphics pipeline is shown in Fig. 6.

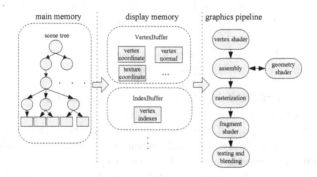

Fig. 6. Relationship between main memory, display memory and graphics pipeline

Concrete steps are as follows:

Step 1. Generate vertex information (vertex coordinate, vertex normal and texture coordinate) of the objects and vertex indexes of the resolutions, which are stored in the object nodes. Suppose the total size of the vertex information is M.

Step 2. Suppose $S_{VertexBuffer}$ is the size of the vertex buffer in display memory. If $M < S_\partial < S_{VertexBuffer}$ (S_∂ is a threshold), the vertex information of all objects is sent to the vertex buffer by main memory before rendering and is kept there the whole duration. Otherwise, combine the visibility culling and prefetching policy, transport the vertex indexes of objects which are visible or might visible into the vertex buffer from main memory.

Step 3. In the rendering process, determine the resolution model which should be used by the object, referring to the ratio of distance of viewpoint to its bounding box to the volume of its bounding box. Suppose the l-th resolution model should be used currently. If the current resolution is not l, go to Step 4.

Step 4. Delete the vertex indexes and triangular faces information of the object in the display memory, and send $Index_l$ stored in the object node to the index buffer in the display memory directly. Organize the triangular faces of the current resolution in the assemble stage of graphics pipeline, according to the vertex information in the vertex buffer and the new vertex indexes in the index buffer.

Since LOD does not need to be stored on hard drive, data exchange with external storage can be avoided. Since the multi-resolution model of the basic voxels is created by rule, the preprocessing time can be reduced. With this approach, data exchange between the main memory and display memory during the rendering process can be reduced effectively. During the whole rendering process, the vertex coordinate, vertex normal and texture coordinate of the objects do not need to be recalculated, although the resolution might change dynamically. Therefore, this approach can improve the rendering efficiency.

5   System and Applications

The 3-d design review system is developed by C++ and Open GL on Windows. And the derived plug-in of design information on AutoCAD is developed based on Objectarx, using MySQL as database.

5.1   Function

In the design review of multi-subjects of one chemical plant for example, it refers to subjects of pipe, equipment and structure. The three subjects are all designed on AutoCAD. Review database, CAD systems and review system are all deployed in LAN. First, designers of each subject derive the design information of its own subject from CAD system by the derived plug-in. Then the reviewer acquires the information from the database through the review system and reviews the design of multi-subjects, with the help of functions, such as real-time 3-d navigation, attribute query, and collision check. As shown in Fig. 7 A, the reviewer queries the design conflict manually in long distance by 3-d navigation with the review system. As shown in Fig. 7 B, the reviewer queries the engineering property of one particular valve in short distance with the review system.

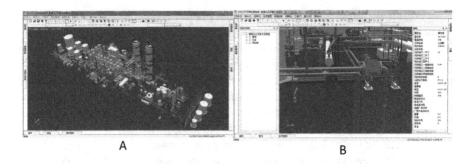

A   B

Fig. 7. Reviewer views the model with the review system

5.2 Performance

In review of subjects such as pipe, equipment and structure, the number of triangular faces will be larger than 21 million, and the data of engineering property will be larger than 300 M bytes. Meanwhile, the 3-d design review system developed in this paper is applied, with the computer configuration: CPU, IntelCore2 2.2 GHz; graphics card, GeForce9400 (512 M); and 2G RAM. Each object has 4 LODs with average distances of [0 m, 50 m), [50 m, 75 m), [75 m, 100 m), [100 m, +∞). Our approach preprocesses this model within 10 s and achieves an average smooth frame rate of 31 fps, without using extra hard-disk space. The query time for engineering property of a single object could be reduced to less than 0.1 s, and the requirement of real-time interactive could be satisfied. Table 2 illustrates the performance of our approach by rendering this model over the same path on the same PC, compared with other approaches.

Table 2. Results of comparison

	Average frame rate/f/s	Preprocessing time/s	Extra hard-disk space/M
LOD is not used	9.3	5	0
Approach in paper [17]	40.3	336	932
Our approach	31.7	7	0

Table 2 shows that the rendering performance of our approach is not as high as that in paper [17]. However, the real-time interaction can be satisfied with our approach. It is significant that the preprocessing time is controlled within 10 s and no extra hard-disk space is required with our approach, while the preprocessing time is more than 5 min and more than 900 M hard-disk is required with the approach in paper [17].

In a piece of pipe including multi-objects and multi-voxels, for example, the models of the highest resolution and the lowest resolution are compared as shown in Fig. 8a and b. Obviously, model simplification leads to deformed appearance, but the graphics characteristics and topological relation are still clear. The low resolution models are used in long distance (Fig. 8c), and in that condition, this type of model will not be the subject concern of the reviewer. Therefore, vision errors caused by simplification are acceptable.

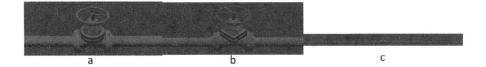

a   b   c

Fig. 8. Multi-resolution model of one particular pipeline

6   Conclusions

Process plants are used in many industries which have a significant effect on the national economy sectors. Design review is important in the collaborative design of process plant. A 3-d design review system is developed to improve review efficiency in this paper. The key technologies of this system are proposed, such as information organization model and multi-resolution rendering approach. This information organization model organizes the information from different CAD systems with a unified structure, and optimizes the design information query speed through the good organization structure. This multi-resolution rendering approach based on programmable graphics pipeline ensures that the vertex set of a low resolution model is the subset of that of a high resolution model, so only the vertex information of its highest resolution mode and some of the vertex indexes need to be saved for each object. On this basis, with effective management of the vertex buffer and the index buffer, multi-resolution model transform can be implemented according to the vertex index transform in the rendering process. Examples prove that our review system could satisfy actual work demands of design review. It could work on a general PC to review a large quantity of design information from different subjects, and ensure real-time interaction at the same time. Our review system is used currently in many design institutes in China.

Acknowledgements. This work is sponsored by the National Natural Science Foundation of China (No. 71301081, 61373139, 61300165, 61572261), Natural Science Foundation of Jiangsu Province (No. BK20130877, BK20140895), Postdoctoral Science Foundation of China (No. 2014M551637), Postdoctoral Science Foundation of Jiangsu Province (No. 1401046C).

References

1. Su, Z.Y., Li, W.Q., Kong, J.S., Dai, Y.W., Tang, W.Q.: Watermarking 3D CAPD Models for Topology Verification. Comput. Aided Des. **45**, 1042–1052 (2013)
2. Su, Z.Y., Zhou, L., Liu, G.J., Kong, J.S., Dai, Y.W.: Authenticating topological integrity of process plant models through digital watermarking. Multimedia Tools Appl. **73**, 1687–1707 (2014)
3. Ma, W.Y., Zhong, Y.M., Tso, S.K., Zhou, T.X.: A hierarchically structured and constraint-based data model for intuitive and precise solid modeling in a virtual reality environment. Comput. Aided Des. **36**, 903–928 (2004)

4. Gonzalez-Badillo, G., Medellin-Castillo, H., Lim, T., Ritchie, J., Garbaya, S.: The development of a physics and constraint-based haptic virtual assembly system. Assem. Autom. **34**, 41–55 (2014)
5. Wang, P., Li, Y., Yu, L., Zhang, J., Xu, Z.J.: A novel assembly simulation method based on semantics and geometric constraint. Assem. Autom. **36**, 34–50 (2016)
6. Wang, X., Ong, S.K., Nee, A.Y.C.: Real-virtual components interaction for assembly simulation and planning. Robot. Comput. Integr. Manufact. **41**, 102–114 (2016)
7. Johnston, B., Bulbul, T., Beliveau, Y., Wakefield, R.: An assessment of pictographic instructions derived from a virtual prototype to support construction assembly procedures. Autom. Constr. **64**, 36–53 (2016)
8. Clark, J.H.: Hierarchical geometric models for visible surface algorithms. Commun. ACM **19**, 547–554 (1976)
9. Goswami, P., Erol, F., Mukhi, R., Pajarola, R., Gobbetti, E.: An efficient multi-resolution framework for high quality interactive rendering of massive point clouds using multi-way Kd-trees. Vis. Comput. **29**, 69–83 (2013)
10. Han, L.H., Hu, X.Y., Adams, N.A.: Adaptive multi-resolution method for compressible multi-phase flows with sharp interface model and pyramid data structure. J. Comput. Phys. **262**, 131–152 (2014)
11. Ripolles, O., Chover, M., Ramos, F.: Visualization of level-of-detail meshes on the GPU. Vis. Comput. **27**, 793–809 (2011)
12. Kang, H., Jang, H., Cho, C.S., Han, J.: Multi-resolution terrain rendering with GPU tessellation. Vis. Comput. **31**, 455–469 (2015)
13. Aguilera, A., Melero, F.J., Feito, F.R.: Out-of-core real-time haptic interaction on very large models. Comput. Aided Des. **77**, 98–106 (2016)
14. Park, J., Lee, H.: A hierarchical framework for large 3D mesh streaming on mobile systems. Multimedia Tools Appl. **75**, 1983–2004 (2016)
15. Afra, A.T.: Interactive ray tracing of large models using voxel hierarchies. Comput. Graph. Forum **31**, 75–88 (2012)
16. Graham, S., Richard, S.W.J., Nicholas, H.: OpenGL Superbible: Comprehensive Tutorial and Reference, 7th edn. Addison-Wesley Professional, Boston (2015)
17. Su, Z.Y., Xia, M., Li, W.Q., He, T., Tang, W.Q.: Feature-based simplification of process plant models over network. Int. J. Virtual Reality **8**, 51–58 (2009)

Industry Track Papers

Review of Heterogeneous Wireless Fusion in Mobile 5G Networks: Benefits and Challenges

Yuan Gao[1,2,3(✉)], Ao Hong[2], Quan Zhou[2], Zhaoyang Li[2], Weigui Zhou[2], Shaochi Cheng[1], Xiangyang Li[1], and Yi Li[3,4(✉)]

[1] China Defense Science and Technology Information Center, Beijing, China
[2] Xi Chang Satellite Launch Center, Xichang, China
[3] State Key Laboratory on Microwave and Digital Communications, National Laboratory for Information Science and Technology, Tsinghua University, Beijing, China
yuangao08@tsinghua.edu.cn
[4] The High School Affiliated to Renmin University of China, Beijing, China
liyi@rdfz.cn

Abstract. The 5th generation wireless network has become popular in recent days, the system could provide higher transmission speed, lower latency, enhanced spectrum efficiency and energy efficiency. However, the improvements are mainly focused on mobile base stations such as large scale MIMO, full duplex, etc. The resources of integrated multi-functional mobile terminals are wasted. In this work, we discuss the fusion technology in 5G wireless networks, to make full utilization of multi-functional terminals, the fusion of 5G, Wi-Fi, ZigBee, Bluetooth will greatly increase the transmission speed and reduce the latency, both benefits and challenges are summarized. In heterogeneous architecture, simulation results indicate that the fusion of mobile terminals could increase system capacity and reduce transmission latency significantly.

Keywords: Wireless fusion · Mobile terminal · Heterogeneous networks · 5G

1 Introduction

In the past five years, the rapid development of mobile communication technology has brought changes in the communications industry, especially the number of mobile terminals and processing ability has been greatly improved. The 2016 National Science and Technology R & D program focused on "broadband communications and networking" has mentioned that, to speed up the establishment process of the fifth generation mobile communication (5G) systems and further improve the transmission speed and efficiency of the wireless network is the major mission of the upcoming 5 years. In order to meet growing demand of customers for QoS, 3GPP LTE Advanced Pro (LTE Rel.14) [1, 2] and the 5G IMT-2020 white paper are network architecture and key technologies for future mobile communication systems were discussed, especially the ultra-high dense networks with Device to Device communication (D2D), which could improve the transmission rate and reduce transmission delay of technical breakthroughs [3].

© ICST Institute for Computer Sciences, Social Informatics and Telecommunications Engineering 2017
S. Wang and A. Zhou (Eds.): CollaborateCom 2016, LNICST 201, pp. 453–461, 2017.
DOI: 10.1007/978-3-319-59288-6_41

As an important method to enhance the transmission rate, many researchers tried to optimize the transmission schemes in base station side, such as using distributed antenna systems (DAS), base stations cooperation (CoMP), large-scale MIMO, etc., which could significantly enhance the user's transmission speed. However, these improvements are mainly in the base station side, the multi-functional mobile terminals are omitted and the resources are wasted. Considering the amount of mobile terminals are large with satisfied performance, so how to make full use of such integrated wireless transmission methods becomes a new chance [5].

Current researches on D2D collaborative technology has been discussed for a long time [6]. Researches on Cooperative D2D communication contains two major aspects:

D2D relay system: In order to shorten the distance between the base station and the target user, users located between base stations and target users will be considered as relay node, data is transmitted to destination via point to point transmission, and such operation could help reduce the loss of long-distance transmission. The main contribution of such problems are summarized in reference [7–10], where the joint optimization of relay selection and resource allocation in single-hop and multi-hop scenario. Traditional solution is to form a continuous convex optimization problem and find out optimal relay nodes and optimal resource allocation policy. There are still problems remaining in this scenario, such as the assumption of ideal channel estimation and mobility.

D2D cooperative multi-functional terminal design: This is the most complex research in D2D, including the cooperative node selection [11], selection of cooperative scheme [12, 13], the optimization of cooperative transmission design (including power allocation [14], bandwidth allocation [15–18] and optimization of spectral efficiency [19, 20]) as well as constraint cooperating scenarios optimization design [21] and other studies. The above references are mainly about the selection of cooperative terminals using information of UE position, transmission power, etc. in multi-UE scenario, and then perform cooperative resource allocation and transmission optimization. The above-mentioned problems can be solved by modeling and solving the typical convex optimization problem, and then get the optimal solution. The literature [22, 23] considered the fusion between UE terminals, that is, different types of traffic need different bandwidth and power resources, and how to make full use of system resources and improve system capacity becomes the major target.

The rest of this paper is organized as follows: in part 2, we introduce the wireless fusion technology in 5G related networks, both architecture and principle are discussed; in part 3, we discuss the advantage and challenge in wireless fusion, the advantages include spectrum efficiency and energy efficiency, the challenges are mainly about the interface and heterogeneous networks architecture, practical simulation results are also discussed in this part; in part 4, conclusions are presented and further discussion are planned.

2   Wireless Fusion in 5G Mobile Networks

The construction of 5G wireless network will mainly increase transmission speed and reduce latency to satisfy the need of users. Current 3GPP specifications do not restrict the utilization of multi-functional terminals, so there are some chances to improve system performance by using the multi-functional mobile terminals.

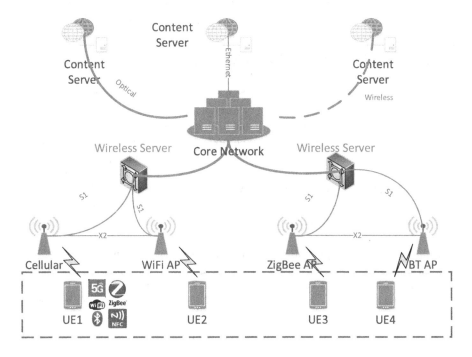

Fig. 1. Network architecture of heterogeneous network with multi-functional mobile terminals, varieties of transmission technology are integrated together in one terminal and chances are introduced in such scenarios.

As shown in Fig. 1, the heterogeneous network architecture may support many types of base stations and service mode, which serve the minorities of users. To tackle the different types of services, many mobile terminals support multi-functional services by installing multi-functional antennas and software defined radio and signal processing core, such as 5G cellular networks, the 802.11 family Wi-Fi (2.4 GHz and 5 GHz), Bluetooth 4.2, ZigBee, NFC and so on. Because such service providers are all connected to Internet cloud service, so the effects of different service base stations are the same, the only differences are the QoS and cost. Typically, users use only one of the transmission methods at the same time, e.g. using the cellular network when making a phone call or SMS, free Wi-Fi for high speed download or online video, Bluetooth or ZigBee for some specific point to point transmission scenarios. However, the decision that which method (s) is selected to perform transmission not only depend on the network providers, but also the prices and QoS (such as 802.11n Wi-Fi could afford 300Mbps in general,

5G cellular network could provide the maximum speed of 1 Gbps when paying some fees, Bluetooth version 4.2 is 60 Mbps, etc.).

In fact, the UE terminal that supports multiple transmission mode is common in recent wireless systems, and the current operator-centric network operation mode causes a waste of system resources in UE terminals. The UE terminal cannot perform better scheduling according to the actual needs of the traffic under the constraint of quality of service requirements (QoS) or money. So wireless fusion technology is proposed to make full use of the terminal resources and reduce the load of traditional base stations.

3   Benefits of Wireless Fusion in SE and EE

The fusion of multi-functional terminals brings the chance to utilize all the types of wireless transmission at a proper way. For example, when target user is located at the coverage of 5G wireless network, he will find out the balance between charge and transmission speed while only one transmission mode could be selected. However, when wireless fusion is enabled, users could receive signal from multiple types of base stations, that means, when users are requiring a large video clip, traditional method using 5G will cost much money when there is no Wi-Fi coverage, when fusion is enabled, this video clip would be divided into multiple slices and provided by different types of providers at the same time, so the target user will receive satisfied QoS in a very low cost.

Such fusion technology will enable the transmission from multiple functional antennas at the same time, so from the terminal side of view, it is a proper and workable method. But there is much work to do at the network operator side.

To describe the benefits of the fusion technology, we make some simple but promising simulations to quantize the benefits of the wireless fusion under the widely used system level simulation platform. Simulation parameters and assumptions are listed in Table 1.

Considering the ultra-dense network in 5G scenario, we take SCME urban micro as channel model. The carrier frequency is set to 2.2 GHz according to LTE-R14, the antenna configuration is set to 8 by 8 at the most, and 2 by 2 MIMO is configured in regular, the configuration is dynamically changed according to channel environment. The number of typical 5G base stations is set to 7 with 3 sectors per cell, the affiliated service nodes such as Wi-Fi and Bluetooth are deployed in conjunction with the primary 5G base stations. The bandwidth for 5G transmission is 100 MHz and the inter site distance is 50 meters.

For system level simulation platform, the mapping from link level to system level is set to EESM and the speed of users is set to 1 m/s in average and the density is set to 3 UE/cell. Note that the channel state information is assumed global to reduce the complexity of the evaluation, and higher order modulation is not adopted because complex signal processing method such as ML detector is not considered.

Table 1. Simulation parameters and assumptions according to our SL simulation platform.

Name	Value
Channel model	SCME, urban micro
Carrier frequency	2.2 GHz
Tx antenna	8 (maximum)
Rx antenna	8 (maximum)
Transmit power	38 dBm
BS number	7
Sectors per BS	3
Users in simulation	3 per cell
Bandwidth	100 MHz
SL to LL mapping	EESM
Inter-site distance	50 m
Pathloss model	$L = 128.1 + 37.6\log10(R)$
Shadowing Std	4 dB
HARQ scheme	CC
AMC table	QPSK(R = {1/8, 1/7, 1/6, 1/5, 1/4, 1/3, 2/5, 1/2, 3/5, 2/3, 3/4, 4/5}) 16QAM(R = {1/2, 3/5, 2/3, 3/4, 4/5})
UE Sig processing	MMSE
Max Re-trans times	4
UE speed	1 m/s
Channel estimation	Ideal
Simulation TTIs	2000

3.1   Benefits in Spectrum Efficiency

Spectrum efficiency is the key technique to evaluate the system performance. In 5G related works, the spectrum efficiency is the leaf of the 5G flower. In 5G communication systems, the bandwidth resource becomes prosperous when carrier aggregation, high frequency transmission and full duplex transmission technology are adopted.

The spectrum efficiency is defined the fraction of transmission capacity and the bandwidth. In previous version of LTE related systems, due to the limitation of transmission capacity, the spectrum efficiency is limited. When wireless fusion is adopted, the maximum capacity will increase due to the allocation of multi-functional antennas, user could acquire information from different types of service nodes. In Fig. 2, we make a comparison of spectrum efficiency between HSDPA, LTE, LTE-A, 5G (LTE-Rel 14) and 5G with fusion. The x-axis is the index of different technologies and the y-axis is the spectrum efficiency in bit/s/Hz. The spectrum efficiency is gradually increased along with the advance of wireless transmission technology, in 5G fusion method, the additional frequency is not taken into account, so the benefits in spectrum efficiency is a little bit higher than 5G. In real transmission systems, the fusion with 2.4Ghz public spectrum will not introduce additional spectrum waste to 5G systems.

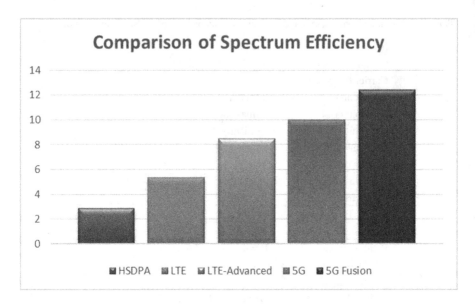

Fig. 2. Comparison of Spectrum Efficiency.

So in this way, the wireless fusion could increase system spectrum efficiency by introducing additional spectrum resources to this system and make full use of the limited resources to achieve higher transmission rates.

3.2 Benefits in Energy Efficiency

The energy efficiency is defined in bit/Joule, where this parameter reflect the fact that how much energy will be consumed to transmit a single bit information. The energy efficiency becomes key technique in 5G communication system because the increasing amount of base stations and the terrible electricity consumption in current wireless networks.

To increase the energy efficiency, the most effective way is to reduce the energy consumption of base stations. Traditional researches on EE are mainly focused on how to turn down idle base stations, which is proved effective in current 5G architectures. However, the on-off control of base stations meet the bottleneck of EE, because the energy consumption could not be reduced any more. So we are trying to increase the ability of per usage of electric power to transmit information as much as possible.

In wireless fusion technology, a large video clip will be divided into many parts, and these parts could be transmitted through different method. For example, within 1 min, the 5G network could transmit 60 Gbit at the most, but with the help of Wi-Fi and Bluetooth, this value could be increased to 100 Gbit.

In Fig. 3, we make a comparison of different types of transmission and power. The x-axis is the index and the y-axis is the energy efficiency. It is clear that the EE will increase when transmit power is low at the same scenario. That means, the cell-edge user will not affect the EE in a significant way. With the advance of transmission technology, the energy efficiency increases at a low speed, but the 5G system has brought significant changes in EE for the on-off control of base stations are introduced. The wireless fusion help increase the EE in advance, because the time consumption to serve a practical traffic is reduced, so the leisure time of the 5G base station is increased, by utilizing the on-off control of base stations, the EE will be increased.

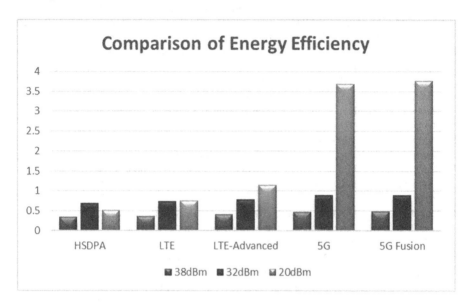

Fig. 3. Comparison of Energy Efficiency.

4 Conclusion

In this paper, we discuss the wireless fusion in 5G related networks as a review. First of all, we point out the fact that the ability of integrated multi-functional terminal are wasted for only one transmission method could be selected at one time, then we propose the possible wireless fusion technology in heterogeneous architecture to enhance the system capacity. Evaluation under the system level simulation has been given both in SE and EE.

Acknowledgments. This work is funded by China's 973 project under grant of 2012CB316002 and China's 863 project under grant of 2013AA013603, 2012AA011402, National Natural Science Foundation of China (61201192), The Open Research Fund of National Mobile Communications Research Laboratory, Southeast University (2012D02); International Science and Technology Cooperation Program (2012DFG12010); National S & T Major Project (2013ZX03001024-004), Operation Agreement Between Tsinghua University and Ericsson, Qualcomm Innovation Fellowship, whose funding support is gratefully acknowledgment. The author would also like to thank all the reviewers, their suggestions help improve my work a lot.

References

1. RP-150041, ITU-R WP5D liaison statement to external organizations on the detailed WORK PLAN, TIMELINE, PROCESS AND DELIVERABLES for the future development of IMT (2016)
2. 3GPP Release 14 Overview, March 2016. http://www.3gpp.org/release-14
3. Silva, B.M.C., Rodrigues, J.J.P.C., Kumar, N., Han, G.: Cooperative strategies for challenged networks and applications: a survey. IEEE Syst. J. **PP**(99), 1–12 (2015)
4. Mustafa, H.A.U., Imran, M.A., Shakir, M.Z., Imran, A., Tafazolli, R.: Separation framework: an enabler for cooperative and D2D communication for future 5G networks. IEEE Commun. Surv. Tutor. **18**(1), 419–445 (2016). Firstquarter
5. Seferoglu, H., Xing, Y.: Device-centric cooperation in mobile networks. In: 2014 IEEE 3rd International Conference on Cloud Networking (CloudNet), Luxembourg, pp. 217–222 (2014)
6. Hwang, D., Kim, D.I., Choi, S.K., Lee, T.J.: UE relaying cooperation over D2D uplink in heterogeneous cellular networks. IEEE Trans. Commun. **63**(12), 4784–4796 (2015)
7. Zhang, G., Yang, K., Liu, P., Wei, J.: Power allocation for full-duplex relaying-based D2D communication underlaying cellular networks. IEEE Trans. Veh. Technol. **64**(10), 4911–4916 (2015)
8. Deng, J., Dowhuszko, A.A., Freij, R., Tirkkonen, O.: Relay selection and resource allocation for D2D-relaying under uplink cellular power control. In: 2015 IEEE Globecom Workshops (GC Wkshps), San Diego, CA, USA, pp. 1–6 (2015)
9. Douik, A., Sorour, S., Al-Naffouri, T.Y., Yang, H.C., Alouini, M.S.: Delay reduction in multi-hop device-to-device communication using network coding. In: 2015 International Symposium on Network Coding (NetCod), Sydney, NSW, pp. 6–10 (2015)
10. Castagno, P., Gaeta, R., Grangetto, M., Sereno, M.: Device-to-device content distribution in cellular networks: a user-centric collaborative strategy. In: 2015 IEEE Global Communications Conference (GLOBECOM), San Diego, CA, USA, pp. 1–6 (2015)
11. Wang, Z., Wong, V.W.S.: A novel D2D data offloading scheme for LTE networks. In: 2015 IEEE International Conference on Communications (ICC), London, pp. 3107–3112 (2015)
12. Mustafa, H.A., Shakir, M.Z., Imran, M.A., Tafazolli, R.: Distance based cooperation region for D2D pair. In: 2015 81st IEEE Vehicular Technology Conference (VTC Spring), Glasgow, pp. 1–6 (2015)
13. Lee, N., Lin, X., Andrews, J.G., Heath, R.W.: Power control for D2D underlaid cellular networks: modeling, algorithms, and analysis. IEEE J. Sel. Areas Commun. **33**(1), 1–13 (2015)
14. Melki, L., Najeh, S., Besbes, H.: Radio resource allocation scheme for intra-inter-cell D2D communications in LTE-A. In: 2015 IEEE 26th Annual International Symposium on Personal, Indoor, and Mobile Radio Communications (PIMRC), Hong Kong, pp. 1515–1519 (2015)
15. Botsov, M., Klugel, M., Kellerer, W., Fertl, P.: Location-based resource allocation for mobile D2D communications in multicell deployments. In: 2015 IEEE International Conference on Communication Workshop (ICCW), London, pp. 2444–2450 (2015)
16. Ye, Q., Al-Shalash, M., Caramanis, C., Andrews, J.G.: Distributed resource allocation in device-to-device enhanced cellular networks. IEEE Trans. Commun. **63**(2), 441–454 (2015)
17. Kai, Y., Zhu, H.: Resource allocation for multiple-pair D2D communications in cellular networks. In: 2015 IEEE International Conference on Communications (ICC), London, pp. 2955–2960 (2015)

18. Lin, X., Heath, R.W., Andrews, J.G.: Spectral efficiency of massive MIMO systems with D2D underlay. In: 2015 IEEE International Conference on Communications (ICC), London, pp. 4345–4350 (2015)
19. Al Haija, A.A., Vu, M.: Spectral efficiency and outage performance for hybrid D2D-infrastructure uplink cooperation. IEEE Trans. Wirel. Commun. **14**(3), 1183–1198 (2015)
20. Lee, S., Shin, D., Jeong, H., Kim, Y.: Distributed bargaining strategy for downlink virtual MIMO with device-to-device communication. IEEE Trans. Commun. **PP**(99): 1
21. Cao, Y., Maaref, A.: Soft forwarding device cooperation strategies for 5G radio access networks. In: 2014 IEEE 25th Annual International Symposium on Personal, Indoor, and Mobile Radio Communication (PIMRC), Washington DC, pp. 359–364 (2014)
22. Pierleoni, P., Belli, A., Palma, L., Pernini, L., Valenti, S.: An accurate device for real-time altitude estimation using data fusion algorithms. In: 2014 IEEE/ASME 10th International Conference on Mechatronic and Embedded Systems and Applications (MESA), Senigallia, pp. 1–5 (2014)
23. Yen, H.C., Wang, C.C.: Cross-device Wi-Fi map fusion with gaussian processes. IEEE Trans. Mob. Comput. **PP**(99): 1. doi:10.1109/TMC.2016.2539966

Optimal Control for Correlated Wireless Multiview Video Systems

Yi Chen[1]([✉]) and Ge Gao[2]

[1] School of Computer Science, Huazhong Normal University, Wuhan, Hubei, China
chenyi30@mail.ccnu.edu.cn
[2] School of Computer Science, Wuhan University, Wuhan, Hubei, China
gaoge@whu.edu.cn

Abstract. Emerging multimedia Multiview video systems consist of a dense deployment of multiple partial-overlapped wireless cameras, as well as some access points (Aps) and many wireless distributed relay nodes. Correlated views are captured by cameras followed being transmitted to destination by different Aps and networks links. Packet expiration of one camera flow may harm the whole task. To effectively integrate multiple viewpoints into a whole image, the correlated data rate and deadline of flows from multiple cameras are meaningful. There is a trade-off between data redundancy and time deadline among correlated multi-views subjecting to the constraints of limited buffer length. However, most researches in this field have not considered packet expiration suffering from varieties of delays after multipath. In this paper, we conduct this problem to optimally adjust multiple flows of viewpoints by exploiting spatial and temporal correlations among cameras to reduce delay variances. A global optimization algorithm based on joint rate-distortion and delay-distortion model is proposed. Simulation results show that quality of service for Multiview streaming can be improved by allocating suitable transmission rates among correlated cameras as well as appropriate playout deadline. The PSNR quality shows that better performance can be achieved compared with baseline policies.

Keywords: Correlation · Multiview streaming · Packet scheduling · Delay

1 Introduction

In recent years, the progress in multimedia technology has given rise to the demand for Multiview wide-area video applications over wireless networks. We consider a system that generates a wide area scene by acquiring images and depth information from many different viewpoints. However, network is unable to transmit all video packets from each camera. To sure a satisfactory viewing experience for end users, it is important to consider temporal and spatial masking effects to help compressed code work optimally that result in efficient usage of network resource for video service with cost-based quality. Our goal is to improve multi-camera wide area system's performance with respect to network constraints.

© ICST Institute for Computer Sciences, Social Informatics and Telecommunications Engineering 2017
S. Wang and A. Zhou (Eds.): CollaborateCom 2016, LNICST 201, pp. 462–467, 2017.
DOI: 10.1007/978-3-319-59288-6_42

For instance, Fig. 1 shows a wide area field image generated by combining sources from more than three cameras through wireless networks.

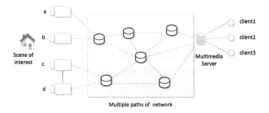

Fig. 1. An example of multimedia wide area view field system with multi-cameras

Resource allocation for video application has been an important research topic [1, 2], and there exists several works addressing the problem of scheduling of correlated video sources [3–5]. Some studies addressed the problem of Multiview transmission and view-switching delay [6–8]. The work in [9] coded multiple views at the minimum level of redundancy in order to speed up the view switching. The work in [10, 11] mainly focused on the transmission of Multiview video coded streams based on multicast whose aim was to maximize the coding optimization to facilitate accessing to different views. However, they have a common shortcoming that the dynamics of networks are not efficiently exploited to improve protocol performance of Multiview video [12].

Although packet loss and transmission delay is considered in [13], it does not solve the problem of correlated multiple flows in Multiview video.

A video transmission control is presented in [14] to jointly control channel rate and relay node. In [15], Yanzhi Dou et al. utilized correlation of application users to monitor control flows and data flows for cognitive radio.

In this paper, a packet scheduling optimization algorithm for correlated multiple flows is proposed, enabling maximizing Multiview video quality performance by exploiting spatial and temporal correlation of multiple flows to reduce the costs of delay variance among flows as well as transmission redundancy among them.

2   Problem Formulation

By using distributed source code, an image $f(t)$ can be recovered from either temporal or spatial correlated frames, under the condition that those reference frames should be in encoder's buffer already. So we have

$$f(t) = \begin{cases} [1 - \rho(f(t))|\theta^S(t)] \cup [1 - \rho(f(t)|\theta^T(t-\tau))], & if \ f(t) \in K \\ f(t), & if \ f(t) \notin K \end{cases} \tag{1}$$

where K means pure key frames set. At the decoder side, key frame is decoded independently without the help of other frames, and dependent frame can be recovered from temporal or spatial correlated frames.

We use D_τ to denote this kind of video distortion of wide screen video streaming. Assume the packet length is S, the transmission delay of a camera m is represented by

$$\tau_m = \frac{S \times n(L_m)}{R_m} \tag{2}$$

where $n(L_m)$ is the number of hops from the camera m to decoder.

We use I_m to denote the encoding importance of camera m compared to other cameras, with $\sum_m I_m = 1$. The delay distortion of multi-camera is described as:

$$D_\tau(F(t)) = \sum_m I_m d_\tau(f_m(t)) = \sum_m I_m e^{-\frac{t_{dex}}{t_0 + \tau_m}} \tag{3}$$

We use $\rho(f_m(t))f_k(t_k)$ to describe the recovery degree of an image $f_m(t)$ from its neighbor $f_k(t)$. Then the data amount of $f_m(t)$ is

$$f_m(t) = (1 - \rho_{m,k})f_k(t) \quad t \geq \tau_m, t \geq \tau_k\, m \neq k. \tag{4}$$

If the image is recovered from time correlated relationship, then the data rate of $f_m(t)$ is

$$f_m(t) = (1 - \rho_{m,m})f_m(t - \tau_{m,m})\, t \geq \tau_m + \tau_{m,m} \tag{5}$$

where $\tau_{m,m}$ represent the gap of time between two successive images from the same camera m.

So the effective frames in the decoder's buffer can be described as:

$$F(t_{dec}) = \sum_{m=1}^{M} \sum_{t=\tau_m}^{t_{dec}} \{\alpha_1(1 - \rho_{m,k})R_k(t) + \alpha_2(1 - \rho_{m,m})R_m(t - \tau_{m,m})\} \tag{6}$$

where

$$\sum_{i=1}^{2} \alpha_2 \leq 1, \quad \alpha_i \geq 0 \tag{7}$$

and

$$R_m, R_k \in [R_L, R_M] \tag{8}$$

In Eq. (7), α_i denotes the weight of decoding dependence.
We express the frame rate distortion as:

$$D_R(F(t)) = D_0 + \frac{\theta_0}{F(t) - R_0} \tag{9}$$

The wide area video is measured in terms of PSNR, which is a monotonically decreasing function of the mean-square error (MSE) [13].

$$PSNR(F) = 10 \log_{10}(\frac{\dot{D}_{max}}{D(F)})$$ (10)

The events of packet loss occur only when deadline cannot be met. So the distortion of wide screen video streaming might be represented as

$$D(F(t)) = D_R(F(t)) + D_\tau(F(t))$$ (11)

We can now formulate the problem of maximizing the sum-PSNR of multiple cameras by jointly controlling the video encoding rate, delay distortion of a wide screen as followings.

P: Maximize

$$PSNR_d(F)$$ (12)

Subject to: (1)–(11)

$$\sum_{m \in M} \sum_{t=\tau_m}^{t_{dec}} R_m(t) \le C_{dec}$$ (13)

$$\tau_m \le t_{dec} \quad (m \in M)$$ (14)

3   Simulation Results

We consider a 3-camera system where video packets experience different delays to reach decoder. Using same packet length and same transmission rate, the delays are proportional to hop number. For simplicity, the arriving intervals of packets from two cameras are calculated in terms of constant time slot ΔT. we use $F(t)$ to denote reconstructed wide area frame rate by conventional camera transmission scheduling [7], which does not consider joint packet scheduling and delay minimization, and use $FF(t)$ to denote our algorithms.

In Fig. 2(a), we observe that when the playout deadline is 400 ms the effective frame rate is maximized. In Fig. 2(b), the playout deadline is 500 ms at the maximal video frame rate. This means that relaxing delay constraint can improve effective frame rate with its maximum determined by decoder capability. We can observe that $FF(t)$ is about 400 bits more than $F(t)$ when time constraints are 400 ms and $C_{dec} = 1800$ bits. A similar phenomenon happens when $C_{dec} = 1400$ bits.

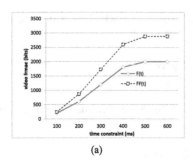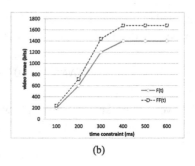

(a)	(b)

Fig. 2. Video frame of wide area display for different playout deadline ($\rho_{s,m} = 0.8$, $\rho_{\tau,m} = 0.8$, $R_m = 200\,\text{bit}/\,\text{ms}$). (a) $C_{dec} = 2000\,\text{bits}$. (b) $C_{dec} = 1400\,\text{bits}$.

In Fig. 3, we use *PSNR* to denote conventional camera transmission scheduling [7], and *PSNR − A* to denote our algorithms. With changing values of playout deadline, *PSNR* and *PSNR − A* become larger. But *PSNR − A* is still more than *PSNR* about 0.7 db. That is, our algorithm can allow cameras to exploit correlation information to schedule packets for higher PSNR.

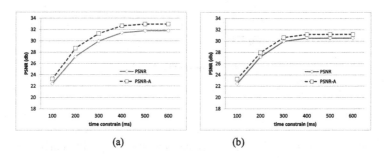

(a)	(b)

Fig. 3. PSNRs of wide area display for different playout deadline ($\rho_{s,m} = 0.8$, $\rho_{\tau,m} = 0.8$, $R_m = 200\,\text{bit}/\,\text{ms}$). (a) $C_{dec} = 2000\,\text{bits}$. (b) $C_{dec} = 1400\,\text{bits}$.

4 Conclusion

We studied correlated time constraints on Multiview multimedia system under certain network limitations. We have proposed a novel rate-distortion and delay-distortion model to take the advantages of the correlation level among cameras themselves and their neighborhood. Based on joint rate-distortion and delay distortion function, a distributed packet scheduling and delay control algorithm is proposed, which can optimally control resource allocation based on network capability and camera correlation. The proposed algorithm adjusts the amounts of video among sources to minimize the transmission delay variances, by which to maximize the effective video frame rate and minimize the packet loss due to exceeding playout deadline. In the simulation, we have analyzed the spatial and time constraints impacts on multimedia system. The results demonstrate the gain of our algorithm compared with classical method. We also have pointed out that the video reconstruction quality can be achieved by manipulating the correlation relationship among cameras.

Acknowledgments. This work was supported by the National Science Foundation of China under Grant (No. 61202470, No. 61471271), Wuhan Science and Technology Project (No. 2013010501010148, No. 2014010202010108), Chin Postdoctoral Science Foundation (No. 2013M531711), Financially supported by self-determined research funds of CCNU from the colleges' basic research and operation of MOE (No.CCNU14A05016, No. CCNU15A02017).

References

1. Chou, P., Miao, Z.: Rate-distortion optimized streaming of packetized media. IEEE Trans. Multimed. **8**(2), 390–404 (2006)
2. Fu, F., van der Schaar, M.: Structural solution for dynamic scheduling in wireless multimedia transmission. IEEE Trans. Circ. Syst. Video Technol. **22**(5), 727–739 (2012)
3. Wang, P., Dai, R., Akyildiz, I.F.: Visual correlation-based image gathering for wireless multimedia sensor networks. In: IEEE Proceedings INFOCOM, pp. 746–749. IEEE Press (2011)
4. Chakareski, J.: Transmission policy selection for multi-view content delivery over bandwidth constrained channels. IEEE Trans. Image Process. **23**(2), 931–942 (2014)
5. Toni, L., Maugey, T., Frossard, P.: Correlation-aware packet scheduling in multi-camera networks. IEEE Trans. Multimed. **16**(2), 496–509 (2014)
6. Kurutepe, E., Civanlar, M.R., Tekalp, A.M.: Client-driven selective streaming of multiview video for interactive 3DTV. IEEE Trans. Circ. Syst. Video Technol. **17**(11), 1558–1565 (2007)
7. De Abreu, A., Frossard, P., Pereira, F.: Optimizing multiview video plus depth prediction structures for interactive multiview video streaming. IEEE J. Sel. Topics Signal Process. **9**(3), 487–500 (2015)
8. Chakareski, J: Scheduling space-time dependent packets in multi-view video streaming. In: IEEE 15th International Workshop on Multimedia Signal Processing (MMSP), pp. 070–075 (2013)
9. Cheung, G., Ortega, V., Cheung, N.-M.: Interactive streaming of stored multiview video using redundant frame structures. IEEE Trans. Image Process. **20**(3), 744–761 (2011)
10. Lou, J.-G., Cai, H., Li, J.: Interactive multiview video delivery based on IP multicast. J. Adv. Multimed. **2007**(1), 13 (2007)
11. Li, Z., Begen, A.C., Gahm, J., Shan, Y., Osler, B., Oran, D.: Streaming video over HTTP with consistent quality. In: Proceedings of ACM Multimedia System Conference, pp. 248–258 (2014)
12. Cheung, G., Ortega, A., Cheung, N.: Interactive streaming of stored multiview video using redundant frame structures. IEEE Trans. Image Process. **3**(3), 744–761 (2011)
13. Stuhlmuler, K., Faber, N., Link, M., Girod, B.: Analysis of video transmission over lossy channels. IEEE J. Sel. Areas Commu. **18**(6), 1012–1032 (2000)
14. Guan, Z., Melodia, T., Yuan, D.: Joint optimal rate control and relay selection for cooperative wireless video streaming. IEEE/ACM Trans. Netw. **21**(4), 1173–1186 (2013)
15. Dou, Y., Zeng, K.C., Yang, Y., Yao, D.D.: MadeCR: correlation-based malware detection for cognitive radio. In: IEEE Conference on Computer Communications INFOCOM (2015)

A Grouping Genetic Algorithm for Virtual Machine Placement in Cloud Computing

Hong Chen[✉]

State Grid Info-Telecom Great Power Science and Technology Co., Ltd., Beijing, China
hongchengrid@sina.com

Abstract. Virtual machine placement is a process of mapping virtual machines to physical machines. The optimal placement is important for improving power efficiency in a cloud computing environment. In this paper, we exploit a grouping genetic algorithm to solve the virtual machine placement problem. The goal is to efficiently obtain a set of non-dominated solutions that minimize power consumption. The proposed algorithm is tested with some instances from the related literatures. The experimental results show that the proposed algorithm is more efficient and effective than the other related algorithms.

Keywords: Virtual machine placement · Grouping genetic algorithm · Power consumption

1 Introduction

In recent year, cloud computing has become a popular computing paradigm for hosting and delivering services over the Internet [1]. To the consumer, the cloud appears to be infinite, and the consumer can purchase as much or as little computing power as they need. From a provider's perspective, the key issue is to maximize profits by minimizing the operational costs. In this regard, power management in cloud data centers is becoming a crucial issue since it dominates the operational costs. Moreover, power consumption in large-scale computer systems like clouds also raises many other serious issues including carbon dioxide and system reliability.

The emergence of cloud computing has made a tremendous impact on the information technology (IT) industry over the past few years, where large companies such as Amazon, Google, Salesforce, IBM, Microsoft, and Oracle have begun to establish new data centers for hosting cloud computing applications in various locations around the world to provide redundancy and ensure reliability in case of site failures. There are a number of key technologies that make cloud computing possible. One of the most importance is virtualization. Virtualization provides a promising approach through which hardware resources on one or more machines can be divided through partial or complete machine simulation, time-sharing, hardware and software partitioning into multiple execution environments, each of which can act as a complete system. Virtualization enables dynamic sharing of physical resources in cloud computing environments, allowing multiple applications to run in different performance-isolated platforms called

© ICST Institute for Computer Sciences, Social Informatics and Telecommunications Engineering 2017
S. Wang and A. Zhou (Eds.): CollaborateCom 2016, LNICST 201, pp. 468–473, 2017.
DOI: 10.1007/978-3-319-59288-6_43

virtual machines (VMs) in a single physical machine (PM). This technology also enables on-demand or utility computing-a just-in time resource provisioning model in which computing resources such as CPU, memory, and disk space are made available to applications only as needed and not allocated statically based on the peak workload demand [2]. Through virtualization, a cloud provider can ensure the quality of service (QoS) delivered to the users while achieving a high server utilization and energy efficiency.

VM placement is a process of mapping VMs to PMs. As virtualization is a core technology of cloud computing, the problem of VM placement has become a hot topic recently. This VM placement is an important approach for improving power efficiency and resource utilization in cloud infrastructures. Several research works [3, 4] addressed the importance of placing VMs appropriately. Vogels [5] quoted the benefit of packing VMs efficiently in server consolidation. The proxy placement [6] and object placement/replacement [7] for transparent data replication bear some resemblance to the issues we face since they all attempt to exploit the flexibility available in determining proper placement. The following are some of the approaches that have been used to solve the VM placement problem. Chaisiri et al. [8] presented a nice algorithm for optimal placement of VMs on PMs. The goal is that the number of used nodes is minimum. They provided approaches based on linear and quadratic programming. Mi et al. [9] proposed a GA based approach, namely GABA, to adaptively self-reconfigure the VMs in cloud data centers consisting of heterogeneous nodes. GABA can efficiently decide the optimal physical locations of VMs according to time-varying requirements and the dynamic environmental conditions. Hermenier et al. [10] proposed the Entropy resource manager for homogeneous clusters, which performs dynamic consolidation based on constraint programming and takes into account both the problem of allocating the VMs to the available nodes and the problem of how to migrate the VMs to these nodes.

The scenario considered is a virtualized cloud data center that provides a shared hosting infrastructure to customers, who need resources as cloud services on a virtualized platform. Each cloud service runs inside of its own VM which can be provisioned and managed on-demand. The data center manager must respond to various on-demand resource requests by determining where VMs are placed and how the resources are allocated to them. This is a time-consuming complex task that cannot be performed by human operators in a timely fashion in increasingly larger data centers. In this paper, we exploit a grouping genetic algorithm (GGA) to solve the VM placement problem. The goal is to efficiently obtain a set of non-dominated solutions that minimize power consumption. The proposed algorithm is tested with some instances from the related literatures. The experimental results show that the proposed algorithm is more efficient and effective than the other related algorithms.

The remainder of this paper is organized as follows. In Sect. 2, we introduce a VMP optimization problem, and present a simple procedure to perform VM placement in a virtualized cloud environment. The computational results on benchmark problems are given in Sect. 3. We conclude this paper in Sect. 4.

2 VMP Optimization

In this section, we will exploit GGA to solve the VMP discrete optimization problem.

2.1 Power Consumption Model

The power consumption of PMs in cloud data centers depends on the comprehensive utilization of the CPU, memory, disk storage and network interfaces. Some studies [11] have shown that on average an idle PM consumes approximately 70% of the power consumed when it is fully utilized [12] and a linearly relationship between the power consumption and CPU utilization. Therefore, we defined the power consumption model of the j-th PM as follows.

$$P(u_j^{CPU}) = k * P_{max} + (1 - k) * P_{max} * u_j^{CPU} \tag{1}$$

where P_{max} is the maximum power consumed when the j-th PM is fully utilized; k is the fraction of power consumed by an idle PM; and u_j^{CPU} is the CPU utilization, which is a function of the time: $u_j^{CPU}(t)$ $(u_j^{CPU}(t) \in [0, 1])$. Therefore, the total power consumption by the j-th PM (E_j) can be modeled as as follows.

$$E_j = \int_{t_0}^{t_1} P(u_j^{CPU}(t))dt \tag{2}$$

where $P(u_j^{CPU}(t))$ is the power consumption of this PM at time t [13].

Next, an optimization formulation is proposed to minimize the power consumption.

2.2 Optimization Formulation

In this section, the optimization objective of the VM placement optimization problem to minimize the overall power consumption. The multi-objective optimization problem can therefore be formulated as:

$$\text{Minimize:} \qquad \sum_{j=1}^{N} \sum_{i=1}^{M} E_j x_{ij} \tag{3}$$

Such that

$$\sum_{j=1}^{N} x_{ij} = 1, \; x_{ij} = 0 \; or \; 1 \tag{4}$$

$$\sum_{i=1}^{M} R_i^{mem} x_{ij} < T_j^{mem} \cap \sum_{i=1}^{M} R_i^{cpu} x_{ij} < T_j^{cpu} \cap \sum_{i=1}^{M} R_i^{bw} x_{ij} < T_j^{bw} \tag{5}$$

$$y_j, x_{ij} \in \{0, 1\} \quad i = [1, 2, \dots, M], j = [1, 2, \dots N] \tag{6}$$

where N is the number of PMs in the cloud data center; M is the number of VMs in the cloud data center; Eqs. (4) and (6) define the range of the variables y_j and x_{ij} and show that a VM can only be placed on one PM, such that $x_{ij} = 1$ if i-th VM is run on the j-th PM, and $x_{ij} = 0$ otherwise; Eq. (5) shows that the sum of the resource requirements for VMs must be less than the PM's idle resource capacity.

Next, we will exploit an adaptive heuristic algorithm based on the improved GGA to solve the optimization problems.

2.3 Grouping Genetic Algorithm

Since a classic GA performs poorly on grouping problems (e.g., bin-packing) which is to group a set of items into a collection of mutually disjoint subsets, the GA is heavily modified into the GGA and to suit the structure of grouping problems [15]. In the GGA, a special encoding scheme is exploited to make the relevant structure of grouping correspond to genes in chromosomes. Meanwhile, crossover and mutation operators are redefined to suit the structure of chromosomes.

Encoding: Since the objective function is defined over groups rather than isolated objects, the encoding in GGA is group oriented.

Crossover: In order to produce the offspring out of two parents, this operator inherit as much as possible of useful information from both parents. Specially, it randomly selects a portion of the first parent (i.e., some of the VM groups) and injects it into the second parent. In this way, some VMs could be contained by the groups eliminated in the second parent, this is because that they could appear twice in the solution. Therefore, GGA exploits a local heuristic (e.g., first-fit) to reinsert these missing VMs.

Mutation: Since the operator is also group oriented, it randomly select and eliminate a few VM groups. Finally, it inserts the VMs in those groups back in a random order using first-fit heuristic algorithm.

3 Experiment

In this section, we compare it with four other approaches in terms of the overall power consumption. We use CloudSim to simulate our experimental environment. In our experiment [3], we simulate a cloud data center comprising 1024 heterogeneous PMs and 2000 heterogeneous VMs. To assess the performance of our proposed algorithm (VMPGGA), we compare our algorithm with four other heuristic algorithms: Random First-fit (RFF), First-fit (FF), Best-fit algorithm (BF), and MBFD [13].

As depicted in the Fig. 1, the experiment aims at estimating the overall power consumption incurred due to the PMs used and the VMs hosted by these PMs. The experimental results indicate that our proposed algorithm (VMPGGA) has the least amount of the overall power consumption compared to other four related algorithms. This is because that our algorithm exploits the improved GGA-based approximation algorithm to search the near-optimal PMs for these VMs allocated. Therefore, when these VMs are allocated to some near-optimal PMs, the overall power consumption is minimum. Other related algorithms do not adopt heuristic algorithm. RFF, FF, and BF have similar higher overall power consumption, since these algorithms do not consider the power consumption during the allocation of these VMs.

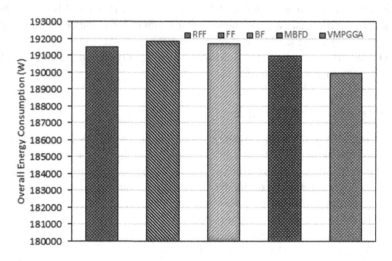

Fig. 1. Comparison of overall power consumption

4   Conclusions

In this paper, the problem of VM placement is formulated as an optimization problem aiming to optimize possibly the objective. A modified GA is exploited to effectively deal with the potential large solution space for large-scale data centers. The simulation-based experimental results showed the superior performance of the proposed approach compared with well-known bin-packing algorithms. Future work focus on implement our approach for green cloud data center [12–14].

References

1. Wang, S., Zhou, A., Hsu, C., Xiao, X., Yang, F.: Provision of data-intensive services through Energy- and QoS-aware virtual machine placement in national cloud data centers. IEEE Trans. Emerg. Top. Comput. **4**(2), 290–300 (2016)
2. Wang, S., Sun, Q., Zou, H., Yang, F.: Towards an accurate evaluation of quality of cloud service in service-oriented cloud computing. J. Intell. Manuf. **25**(2), 283–291 (2014)
3. Liu, J., Wang, S., Zhou, A., Kumar, S.A.P., Yang, F., Buyya, R.: Using proactive fault-tolerance approach to enhance cloud service reliability. IEEE Trans. Cloud Comput. PP(99), 1–1 (2016). doi:10.1109/TCC.2016.2567392
4. Grit, L., Irwin, D., Yumerefendi, A., Chase, J.: Virtual machine hosting for networked clusters: Building the foundations for autonomic orchestration. In: Proceedings of the 2nd International Workshop on Virtualization Technology in Distributed Computing, p. 7 (2006)
5. Vogels, W.: Beyond server consolidation. Queue **6**(1), 20–26 (2008)
6. Keqiu, L., Hong, S.: Optimal proxy placement for coordinated en-route transcoding proxy caching. IEICE Trans. Inf. Syst. **87**(12), 2689–2696 (2004)

7. Li, K., Shen, H., Chin, F.Y., Zheng, S.Q.: Optimal methods for coordinated enroute web caching for tree networks. ACM Trans. Internet Technol. **5**(3), 480–507 (2005)
8. Chaisiri, S., Lee, B.-S., Niyato, D.: Optimal virtual machine placement across multiple cloud providers. In: IEEE Asia-Pacific Services Computing Conference, pp. 103–110 (2009)
9. Mi, H., Wang, H., Yin, G., Zhou, Y., Shi, D., Yuan, L.: Online self-reconfiguration with performance guarantee for energy-efficient large-scale cloud computing data centers. In: IEEE International Conference on Services Computing, pp. 514–521 (2010)
10. Hermenier, F., Lorca, X., Menaud, J.-M., Muller, G., Lawall, J.: Entropy: A consolidation manager for clusters. In: Proceedings of the 2009 ACM SIGPLAN/SIGOPS International Conference on Virtual Execution Environments, pp. 41–50 (2009)
11. Fan, X., Weber, W.-D., Barroso, L.A.: Power provisioning for a warehouse-sized computer. ACM SIGARCH Comput. Archit. News **35**(2), 13–23 (2007)
12. Beloglazov, A., Buyya, R.: Adaptive threshold-based approach for energy-efficient consolidation of virtual machines in cloud data centers. In: Proceedings of the 8th International Workshop on Middleware for Grids, Clouds and e-Science (2010)
13. Wang, S., Zhou, A., Hsu, C., Xiao, X., Yang, F.: Provision of data-intensive services through energy- and QoS-aware virtual machine placement in national cloud data centers. IEEE Trans. Emerg. Top. Comput. **4**(2), 290–300 (2016)
14. Wang, S., Zhou, A., Yang, F., Chang, R.: Towards network-aware service composition in the cloud. IEEE Trans. Cloud Comput. doi:10.1109/TCC.2016.2603504
15. Xu, J., Fortes, J.A.: Multi-objective virtual machine placement in virtualized data center environments. In: Proceedings IEEE/ACM International Conference on Green Computing and Communications (GreenCom 2010), pp. 179–188 (2010)

Towards Scheduling Data-Intensive and Privacy-Aware Workflows in Clouds

Yiping Wen[1,2(✉)], Wanchun Dou[1], Buqing Cao[2], and Congyang Chen[2]

[1] State Key Laboratory for Novel Software Technology, Nanjing University, Nanjing, China
ypwen81@gmail.com, douwc@nju.edu.cn
[2] Key Laboratory of Knowledge Processing and Networked Manufacture,
Hunan University of Science and Technology, Xiangtan, China

Abstract. Nowadays, business or scientific workflows with a massive of data are springing up in clouds. To avoid security and privacy leakage issues, users' privacy or sensitive data may be restricted to being processed in some specified and trusted cloud datacenters. Meanwhile, users may also pay attention to the cost incurred by renting cloud resources. Therefore, new workflow scheduling algorithms should be developed to achieve a balance between economically utilizing the cloud resources and protection of users' data privacy and security. In this paper, we propose a cost-aware scheduling algorithm for executing multiple data-intensive and privacy-aware workflow instances in clouds. Our proposed algorithm is based on the strategy of batch processing, the ideas of simulated annealing algorithm and the particle swarm optimization, the coding strategy of which is devised to minimize the total execution cost while meeting specified privacy protection constraints. The experimental results demonstrate the effectiveness of our algorithm.

Keywords: Privacy protection · Cloud · Workflow scheduling · Cost · Batch processing · Particle swarm optimization

1 Introduction

Workflow scheduling in clouds is an important research topic [1], which tries to map the workflow tasks to the dynamically provisioned resources based on different functional and non-functional requirements. However, existing cloud workflow scheduling algorithms normally do not consider the security requirement of meeting privacy protection constraints when making resource allocation decisions, yet protection of privacy or sensitive data involved in tasks is important in the cloud workflows for business or scientific purpose, which may contain one or several data intensive tasks (with huge data) in the big data era. These data intensive cloud workflows usually are abstract of cross-organizational business processes which include trade secrets or personal privacy data. For security reason, they may not be allowed to be scheduled to some cloud datacenters though these cloud datacenters can speed up more efficiently or much cheaper. For example, financial data and customers consuming data may be secret information for some enterprises and they usually may be restricted to being processed in specified

© ICST Institute for Computer Sciences, Social Informatics and Telecommunications Engineering 2017
S. Wang and A. Zhou (Eds.): CollaborateCom 2016, LNICST 201, pp. 474–479, 2017.
DOI: 10.1007/978-3-319-59288-6_44

and trusted datacenters to provide privacy protection. Hence, scheduling algorithms for such privacy-aware workflow in clouds should be developed to solve such new issue.

Based on our previous works in [2], this paper proposes a cost-aware scheduling algorithm for executing multiple data-intensive and privacy-aware workflow instances in clouds, which is called BCP-PSO and aims at optimizing the total workflow execution cost while meeting specified privacy protection constraints.

To the best of our knowledge, our work is the first approach considering both privacy protection constraints and batch processing strategy in workflow scheduling. It can be viewed as an improvement to our previous work in [2], which only focuses on optimizing the execution cost of one workflow instance with privacy protection constraints while we focus on that of a set of concurrent workflow instances in this paper. In addition, we further employ the particle swarm optimization (PSO) [3], the ideas of simulated annealing (SA) algorithm [4] and batch processing strategy to reduce the execution cost. The resource utilization is also improved by further utilize the idle time fragments in the rented virtual machine instances according to the time unit-based pricing model.

2   Design of Scheduling Algorithm

In our work, we introduce the ideas of the SA into PSO and construct a variant inertia weight function featured in annealing mechanism. Meanwhile, we adopt the batch processing strategy to optimize scheduling a group of instances of the same task simultaneously. The pseudo code for our proposed algorithm is described as Fig. 1, and the following sections provide their related steps in detail.

2.1   Group Unscheduled Ready Task Instances

The step of grouping unscheduled ready task instances (Line 3) adopts the strategy of batch processing to handle task instances from multiple concurrent instances with the same workflow model. A ready task instance is either the instance of the entry task in the workflow or the other task's instance whose predecessors have all been allocated. Each ready task instance will belong to only one group and all task instances in the same group have the same task type. By grouping task instances, cloud resources can be reused to reduce execution cost, which will be explained in Sect. 2.3.

2.2   Coding and Privacy Protection Constraints Handling Strategy

In PSO, each alternative solution is called as a particle. Therefore, we need to establish the meaning of a particle and deal with the privacy protection constraints to get alternative feasible solutions for our problem.

To promote efficiency, we firstly create a feasible resource list according to privacy protection constraints and the corresponding task type of instances in current task instance group. For example, if all task instances in a group are instances of the task t_k with privacy or sensitive data, which are restricted to being processed only in the datacenter dc_i, only the cloud resources in dc_i are included in the feasible resource list and

Algorithm 1. Pseudo code of BCP-PSO algorithm

Input: Set of resources, set of workflow instances, N: number of particles
Output: FS: a workflow scheduling solution
1:   $FS \leftarrow \varnothing$, set initial parameters for PSO and SA;
2:   **While** there are unscheduled "ready" task instances
3:       Generate unscheduled "ready" task instance group set $RTIG$ so that instances of the same task are in the same group;
4:       **For** each group in $RTIG$ **do**
5:           Generate a new feasible resource list RL according to privacy protection constraints and the task type of current group;
6:           Set particle dimension equal to the size of current group;
7:           Initialize particles position randomly from $\{1, ..., |RL|\}$ and velocity randomly;   // $|RL|$ is the number of resources in RL
8:           **Repeat**
9:               **For** each particle $i = 1$ to N **do**
10:                  Calculate its fitness value;
11:                  If current fitness value is better than the fitness value of its $pbest_i$, set current location as the new $pbest_i$;
12:                  Modify the inertia weight and update the velocity and position of each particle;
13:              **End for**
14:              Modify $gbest$ by the particle with the best fitness value of all the particles, and annealing temperature $T = \alpha \cdot T$;
15:          **Until** maximum iteration is satisfied
16:          Add the schedule of task instances in current group to FS;
17:      **End for**
18: **End while**
19: **return** FS

Fig. 1. Pseudo code of BCP-PSO algorithm

each cloud resource is assigned a unique positive integer index for allocating them to task instances in such group.

Our coding strategy is devised based on the generated feasible resource list and task instance group. We set the dimension of each particle equal to the size of task instance group and each position in each particle represents a task instance, the value of which represents the index of a cloud resource in feasible resource list.

2.3   Generate a Schedule of a Task Instance Group

According to the coding strategy described above, we can convert a particle's position into a schedule of a task instance group and calculate the total execution cost so far. Because commercial cloud providers typically charge users by an hourly-based pricing model, it may leave much idle time. For example, suppose t_{ik} and t_{jk} are two instances of the task t_k; if the processing time of is 20 min, we still lease the cloud resource (e.g., VM) for one hour. Thus, the VM will be in idle for 40 min which can be reused by t_{jk}. In this case, if t_{ik} and t_{jk} have been mapped to the same VM, this VM can be reused to reduce execution cost. By using PSO and the strategy of batch processing, VM reuse can be accomplished more effectively for scheduling multiple workflow instances in clouds.

2.4 Update Velocity and Position of Particles

In the iterative phase (Line 8–15) of our algorithm, to ensure that the search is done inside the positive integer space, the velocity and position of a particle are updated based on the Eqs. 1 and 2 respectively:

$$v_i^{k+1} = \left\lceil \omega_i^k \cdot v_i^k + c_1 \cdot r_1 \cdot \left(pbest_i^k - x_i^k \right) + c_2 \cdot r_2 \cdot \left(gbest^k - x_i^k \right) \right\rceil \tag{1}$$

$$x_i^{k+1} = x_i^k + v_i^{k+1} \tag{2}$$

where v_i^{k+1} is the velocity of particle i in iterative $k + 1$, ω_i^k is the inertia weight of particle i in iterative k, c_1 and c_2 are two positive numbers termed learning factors, r_1 and r_2 are two random numbers with uniform distributed in the range $[0, 1]$, x_i^k is the position of particle i in iterative k, $pbest_i^k$ is the individual best position for particle i after k iterations, $gbest^k$ is the best position for all the particles after k iterations.

The inertia weight ω_i^k in Eq. 1 keeps particle i with the movement inertia. When ω_i^k is larger, particle i has better ability to search for a global optimum solution, otherwise the local search capability of particle i is better. Therefore, we dynamically adjust ω_i^k on the basis of the ideas of the SA to improve the probability and particle's ability of finding the global or near optimum solution. ω_i^k is updated based on Eqs. 3 and 4:

$$\omega_i^k = \begin{cases} 1 + \dfrac{ran}{2} & \rho_i^k \geq ran \\[2mm] \dfrac{ran}{2} & \rho_i^k < ran \end{cases} \tag{3}$$

$$\rho_i^k = \begin{cases} 1 & fitness\left(x_i^{k-1}\right) > fitness\left(x_i^k\right) \\[2mm] e^{\dfrac{fitness\left(x_i^{k-1}\right) - fitness\left(x_i^k\right)}{T}} & fitness\left(x_i^{k-1}\right) \leq fitness\left(x_i^k\right) \end{cases} \tag{4}$$

where ran is a random number with uniform distributed in the range $[0, 1]$, T represents current annealing temperature. If $fitness\left(x_i^{k-1}\right) > fitness\left(x_i^k\right)$, meaning that, the position of particle i in iterative k is better than the previous iterative $k-1$ for the fitness function.

Besides, the updates of velocity and position are liable to cause particles to exceed the search boundaries. Our algorithm adopts the handling method in [5] to keep particles within the search space.

3 Experiments and Evaluation

In order to test the algorithm performance, we use the CloudSim framework to simulate a cloud environment and make up three datacenters and ten virtual machines with four types. The CP-GA algorithm [2] and SPSO algorithm are tested against the proposed BCP-PSO algorithm, where the SPSO algorithm is based on PSO [3] while using the coding and privacy protection constraints handling strategy of the BCP-PSO algorithm to schedule multiple data-intensive and privacy-aware workflow instances in clouds. In our experiments, the numbers of particles are equal to 20, and the values of learning factors are equal to 1.49445.

Figure 2 demonstrates the evaluation results of three algorithms with specified privacy protection constraints on task t_3 and task t_5. Figure 2a shows that the BCP-PSO algorithm outperforms the CP-GA and SPSO algorithms in terms of the cloud resources cost of workflow instances. With the growth of the size of workflow instances, the optimization on cost of BCP-PSO is better. The main reason is that the BCP-PSO algorithm adopts the batch processing strategy to reuse the VM and reduce execution cost. However, this will increase the completion time of workflow instances compared to the CP-GA algorithm, which is shown as Fig. 2b.

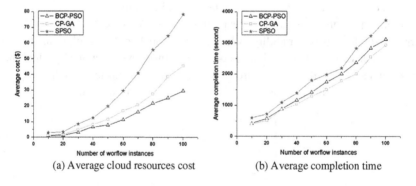

(a) Average cloud resources cost   (b) Average completion time

Fig. 2. Evaluation results of three algorithms with specified privacy protection constraints

Figure 3 demonstrates the evaluation results of these three algorithms without specified privacy protection constraints on task t_3 and task t_5. In terms of the cloud resources cost of workflow instances, the BCP-PSO algorithm also outperforms the other two algorithms.

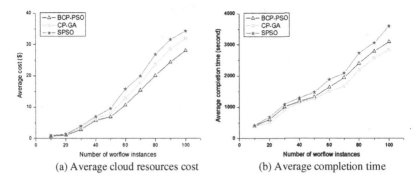

(a) Average cloud resources cost   (b) Average completion time

Fig. 3. Evaluation results of three algorithms without specified privacy protection constraints

4 Conclusion

In this paper, we analyze the cost optimization problem of scheduling workflow with privacy protection constraints and propose a cost-aware scheduling algorithm for executing multiple data-intensive and privacy-aware workflow instances in clouds. In our algorithm, we use the strategy of batch processing to group task instances according to their task type, and incorporate the privacy protection constraints to devise the coding strategy of particles. We also introduce the ideas of the SA into PSO and construct a variant inertia weight function to overcome premature convergence. The comparative experiments show the effectiveness of our algorithm.

Acknowledgments. This paper was supported by National Natural Science Fund of China, under grant number 61402167, 61572187, 61402168, and National Science and Technology Support Project of China, under grant number 2015BAF32B01.

References

1. Smanchat, S., Viriyapant, K.: Taxonomies of workflow scheduling problem and techniques in the cloud. Future Gener. Comput. Syst. **52**, 1–12 (2015)
2. Chen, C., Liu, J., Wen, Y., Chen, J., Zhou, D.: A hybrid genetic algorithm for privacy and cost aware scheduling of data intensive workflow in cloud. In: Wang, G., Zomaya, A., Perez, G.M., Li, K. (eds.) ICA3PP 2015. LNCS, vol. 9528, pp. 578–591. Springer, Cham (2015). doi: 10.1007/978-3-319-27119-4_40
3. Kennedy, J., Eberhart, R.: Particle swarm optimization. In: Proceedings of IEEE International Conference on Neutral Networks. pp. 1942–1948. IEEE Service Center, Piscataway (1995)
4. Kirkpatrick, S., Gelatt, C., Vecchi, M.: Optimization by simulated annealing. Science **220**, 671–680 (1983)
5. Li, Z.J., Ge, J.D., Yang, H.J., Huang, L.G., Hu, H.Y., Hu, H., Luo, B.: A security and cost aware scheduling algorithm for heterogeneous tasks of scientific workflow in clouds. Future Gener. Comput. Syst. **65**, 140–152 (2016)

Spontaneous Proximity Clouds: Making Mobile Devices to Collaborate for Resource and Data Sharing

Roya Golchay, Frédéric Le Mouël$^{(\boxtimes)}$, Julien Ponge, and Nicolas Stouls

University of Lyon, INSA-Lyon, INRIA CITI Lab, 69621 Villeurbanne, France
{roya.golchay,frederic.le-mouel,julien.ponge,nicolas.stouls}@insa-lyon.fr

Abstract. The base motivation of Mobile Cloud Computing was empowering mobile devices by application offloading onto powerful cloud resources. However, this goal can't entirely be reached because of the high offloading cost imposed by the long physical distance between the mobile device and the cloud. To address this issue, we propose an application offloading onto a nearby mobile cloud composed of the mobile devices in the vicinity - a Spontaneous Proximity Cloud. We introduce our proposed dynamic, ant-inspired, bi-objective offloading middleware - ACOMMA, and explain its extension to perform a close mobile application offloading. With the learning-based offloading decision-making process of ACOMMA, combined to the collaborative resource sharing, the mobile devices can cooperate for decision cache sharing. We evaluate the performance of ACOMMA in collaborative mode with real benchmarks - Face Recognition and Monte-Carlo algorithms - and achieve 50% execution time gain.

Keywords: Mobile Cloud Computing · Spontaneous Proximity Cloud · Collaborative application offloading · Resource sharing · Decision cache · Offloading middleware · Learned-based decision-making

1 Introduction

Mobile Cloud Computing is the emerging paradigm of recent decades that focuses on overcoming the inherent shortages of mobile devices regarding processing power, memory and battery via application offloading, by total or partial execution of mobile applications on a distant cloud. Hence, the application offloading might not always be helpful because of the long physical distance between the mobile device and the cloud. The concept of the cloudlet [14] has been raised to response to this issue of distance. The cloudlet is a predefined cloud in proximity that consists of some static stations and is generally installed in public domains, but with no guaranty of availability near a mobile device.

As a solution to this cloud distance problem, we propose to offload application onto a Spontaneous Proximity Cloud (SPC) - a cloud in the proximity of the mobile device, composed of a set of mobile devices in the vicinity.

© ICST Institute for Computer Sciences, Social Informatics and Telecommunications Engineering 2017
S. Wang and A. Zhou (Eds.): CollaborateCom 2016, LNICST 201, pp. 480–489, 2017.
DOI: 10.1007/978-3-319-59288-6_45

This SPC is a collaborative group of moving devices in proximity with members that occasionally join and leave. The short distance between the mobile device and the SPC overcomes the issue of latency in data transfer to distant clouds, especially in high network traffic conditions. Offloading onto SPC could also prevent imposing bandwidth allocation overhead onto a communication network that experiences a shortage of capacities, due to the continuous traffic growth. Besides, the energy consumption of a 3G cellular data interface, associated with the cloud, is 3 to 5 times much higher than WiFi transmissions, used between mobile devices [4,10]. Another motivating factor to use SPC is the popularity of mobile devices. Inadequate network coverage, natural or man-made disasters may damage the data centres and significant technical failures - such as experimented by Amazon cloud [1] - can make remote clouds temporarily unavailable. While, because of the increasing number of mobile devices and the wide frequency of use - per user or household [2] - a mobile device presents a great chance to be surrounded by a group of mobile devices. Finally, the use of SPC is a perfect incentive for green computing, with individual devices powered under the user responsibility that can use human body kinetic energy harvesting or solar panels [1].

We found all these factors motivating enough to design and implement ACOMMA, an Ant-inspired Collaborative Offloading Middleware for Mobile Applications, that performs offloading on either distant cloud or SPC. ACOMMA is an automated offloading middleware that takes offloading decisions dynamically by applying an ant-inspired bi-objective decision-making algorithm. The details of offloading onto distant cloud are already explained and evaluated in our previous article [8]. In this paper, we demonstrate that taking a decision in a mobile device can benefit to all the other mobile devices in the vicinity and so better the application execution performances. We create a decision cache composed of the execution trails of mobile applications and, by using learning-based decision-making algorithm, ACOMMA could reuse previous offloading decisions instead of running its Ant Colony Optimization (ACO) decision-making algorithm.

In this paper, we focus on the extension of ACOMMA in a way that it can be able to perform offloading in a collaborative manner. In collaborative offloading, instead of communicating with a distant cloud, the mobile device cooperates with SPC's members, for either resource or data sharing. Our main contributions consist of:

- Developing a decision-making process performing multi-destination offloading. To this end, we need to modify the ACO algorithm to take potential offloading decisions to remote clouds as well as mobile devices in the SPC, without any lock-in considerations to the number of devices. In this case, the mobile devices collaborate for resource sharing.
- Developing a learned-based decision-making process to use the collaborative decision cache instead of the local cache. In this case, the mobile devices collaborate for data sharing. They share their local caches to create a richer collaborative cache that permits more efficient and relevant offloading decisions.

The remainder of the paper is structured as follows: Sect. 2 discusses the existing offloading approaches. Section 3 explains the architecture of our proposed offloading middleware - ACOMMA. Sections 4 and 5 show how ACOMMA is enhanced to make mobile devices collaborate for resource and cache sharing. Section 6 evaluates our offloading middleware under a range of scenarios and using different benchmarks. Finally, Sect. 7 provides a summary, conclusion and outline of future work.

2   Related Work

Recently, delegating total or partial application execution to more powerful machines instead of local devices - known as application offloading - has attracted attention to overcome resource limitations and to save the battery of mobile devices. A significant amount of researches has been performed in this domain to propose solutions to bring the cloud to the vicinity of the mobile device [6,7].

MAUI [4] and ThinkAir [9] are the most prominent works in this domain. They are focusing on optimising energy consumption or execution time using linear programming. They use the virtual machine migration techniques to execute application methods onto the cloud. However, these virtualized environments are heavy for limited mobile devices. CloneCloud [3] is a lighter approach since it cuts the application into two thread level partitions using linear programming, with only one of them offloaded onto the cloud. Some approaches perform offloading onto a closer surrogate, a cloudlet [14], that is composed of static stations. However, a cloudlet does not necessarily exist near a mobile device.

Few studies focused on the use of adjacent mobile devices as offloading surrogates. Transient cloud [13] uses the collective capabilities of nearby devices in an ad-hoc network to meet the needs of the mobile device. A modified Hungarian method is applied as an assignment algorithm to assign tasks to devices that are to be run according to their abilities. The execution of each task by any device imposes some cost, and the assignment algorithm aims to find the minimum total cost assignment. To that end, [13] has proposed a dynamic cost adjustment to balance the tasks based on costs between devices. Miluzzo et al. [10] proposed an architecture named mCloud that runs resource-intensive applications on collections of cooperating mobile devices and discuss its advantages. Kassahun et al. [1] have gone one step further and formulated a decision algorithm for global adaptive offloading. They implemented the program components on mobile devices set to optimise Time to Failure (TTF) while taking into account the limitations of the effectiveness of the program. Having highlighted the benefits of collaboration for mobile task offloading, Mtibaa et al. also implemented computational offloading schemes to maximise the longevity of mobile devices [11,12].

3   The General Architecture of ACOMMA

The proposed architecture of ACOMMA makes application offloading possible onto remote clouds and SPC as a single or multiple destination offloading process. The building blocks of ACOMMA are illustrated in Fig. 1.

ACOMMA considers a mobile application as a dependency graph, where the nodes represent the function/method calls of the application and the edges are their dependency in terms of function/method invocations. The offloading decision-making process partitions this call graph to define which function/method should be executed locally - on the mobile device, near-remotely - on a device of the SPC, or far-remotely - on the distant cloud.

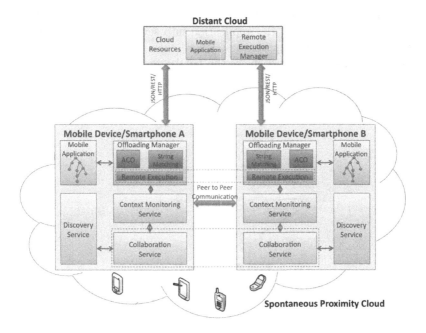

Fig. 1. The general architecture and building blocks of ACOMMA

The offloading middleware is composed of a group of services to offload this application. The *Offloading Manager* is in charge of taking offloading decisions using (1) an Ant Colony Optimization algorithm for the initial decision-making or (2) String matching algorithm for learning-based decision-making. In the learning-based mode, the decision-making relies on previous application execution traces, saved in a local or collaborative decision cache. Coming to the collaborative mode, the *Collaboration Service* takes the responsibility of offloading onto SPC with the help of *Offloading Manager*. The *Collaboration Service* makes nearby devices collaborate using the neighbours' information prepared by the *Discovery Service*. This service finds the nearby devices and saves their address and information. To perform a dynamic offloading considering the current state of mobile devices, ACOMMA needs to be aware of current conditions and requirements. The mobile devices' information, such as the available battery and memory, and their environment such as the available networks, the available bandwidth, as well as cloud kind and theirs costs, are collected by

Context Monitoring Service. This contextual information helps ACOMMA to choose in-between the SPC or the remote clouds.

4   Collaborative Resource Sharing in Application Offloading

As mentioned before, the decision-making process of ACOMMA is based on the application call graph partitioning. To perform offloading onto SPC, the decision engine breaks apart the application into several parts - instead of two in traditional partitioning approaches, where each part represents an executing device. For example, Fig. 2 shows the partitioning for offloading onto three nearby devices, where nodes a, c, f execute locally, node b executes on device A, node e and g execute on device B and finally mobile device C executes node d.

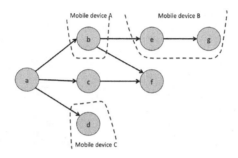

Fig. 2. Application partitioning for multi destination offloading

To perform such a graph partitioning for multi-destination offloading, the ACOMMA collaboration service modifies the application call graph in a way that for each method, several nodes are added to the graph, depending on the number of potential executing devices, one for each device. The modification process of the call graph is shown in the Fig. 3.

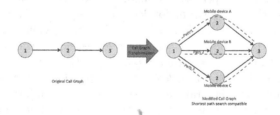

Fig. 3. Call graph modification for multi destination offloading

The original graph is composed of three nodes, where the start and end nodes (node 1 and 3) have to execute locally. Assuming that there are two devices in

SPC in addition to the current mobile device, the node 2 is then duplicated two times - as often as the number of possible execution targets. The ACOMMA decision engine partitions the graph using an ACO algorithm that finds the shortest path between the start and end points of the graph. The choice of the first path shows the local execution of method 2 on device A, where the choice of the second and the third path represents the execution of method 2 on device B and device C respectively.

Finding shortest path is done according to weights assigned to the edges of the graph. Since the different devices can have different optimisation goals, to reach a consensus in the objective function, we apply a multi-objective decision-making process - illustrated by a bi-objective decision-making with the execution cost of the related method regarding CPU usage and execution time. To take dynamic offloading decisions based on the current state, the shortest path is calculated for each function/method call in the total graph.

5 Collaborative Decision Cache Sharing

Learning is one of the primary functions of dynamic systems - such as in sensor networks and mobile networks. It is mainly used for the establishment of a relevant situation and the adaptations to the environment. In existing SPC, the learning process stays local. We argue that, when a mobile device takes a decision, this decision could benefit to the other devices nearby.

To distribute the local decisions, we rely on a sharing decision cache. The sharing decision cache between nearby devices makes collaborative decisions possible. In this learning-based decision-making process, the mobile devices in the same state and environmental conditions could perform offloading in the same way as their neighbours. Moreover, even if the execution conditions are not exactly the same, in case of common applications, the decision is relevant enough.

To take collaborative decisions, the collaborative cache is created by merging local cache of nearby devices. They could receive and send respecting different dissemination, merging and invalidating policies. For receiving neighbour's local decisions, we propose on-demand, periodical and on-change policies. Using an on-demand method, a mobile device broadcasts a cache request to the nearby devices whenever needed. In the periodic method, each mobile device periodically sends their decision caches to their neighbours without any concerns about their requirement. Also, in the on-change method, the source device sends its decision cache whenever it is modified either by adding a new execution trail or deleting old ones. The merge could be done simply by adding the new executing trail at the end of the local cache. Alternatively, another way is to implement a collaborative cache with unique rows by deleting the duplicate traces. Creating a weighted cache is also an implementation available. The weight of each executing trace corresponds to the number of decisions already taken - implying that an already optimisation decision have more chance to be reselected. As cache invalidation policies, we propose periodic and on-change methods. While the offloading decisions highly depend on the current status of the mobile device itself and its environment, the cache could reset when these conditions change.

Applying different combinations of these policies for cache management may greatly impact the performance of ACOMMA for offloading using collaborative decision-making.

6 Implementation and Evaluations

6.1 Benchmark Applications and Experimental Platform

To evaluate the performance of ACOMMA, we first test micro-benchmarks mathematical functions: Matrix determinant and Integral - consuming enough resources to make offloading valuable. Their small number of methods helps us to trace function call executions accurately. To be closer to real applications, we also implement macro-benchmarks with popular offloading applications of Chess and Face Recognition including Monte Carlo and Eigenfaces algorithms [5].

As mobile devices, we use Samsung Galaxy SII with 1,2 GHz dual-core processor and 2 GB of memory running Android version 4.1.2 (Jelly Bean) and Asus Google Nexus 7 pad with quad-core 1.2 GHz processor and 1 GB of memory running Android version 5.1.1 (Lollipop). To successfully validate collaborative offloading of ACOMMA using SPC, we need to show that ACOMMA can detect the SPC and correctly dispatch the methods of running application between detected nearby devices according to their processing power.

6.2 Results

To evaluate the efficiency of offloading onto the SPC, we apply a scenario where a Galaxy SII makes offloading onto an SPC that consists in 2 Galaxy SII and 3 Google Nexus 7 pads. We compare the performance of offloading onto this SPC with offloading onto a MacBook Pro with 8 GB of memory, a 250 GB hard disk and a 2,53 GHz Intel processor dual-core as a remote server. This server has OS X 10.9.5 Mavericks as operating system. The result shows that the local execution is rather slow - 1200 ms for the Monte Carlo application, and offloading onto the MacBook presents a significant gain in terms of execution time - 60–70 ms [8]. Offloading to the SPC - less powerful than a remote cloud, but with a better latency - results in a less efficient execution time - 100 ms, but interesting enough to test the benefit of a collaborative cache.

Coming to the evaluation of dispatching onto SPC, we ran Determinant and Integral 10 times with a SPC composed of four devices in addition to the source device. In this scenario, D1, D2, D3 - Google Nexus pads - and D4 - Samsung Galaxy SII - are offloading destination devices.

Figures 4(a) and (b) show the percentage of successful offloading for each application method. Considering the four methods of Integral benchmark, the method D is never offloaded. Considering the five methods of Determinant, method B and method C were always executed locally. These are the methods that consume a negligible amount of resources, when offloading them impose more cost to the system compared to their local execution.

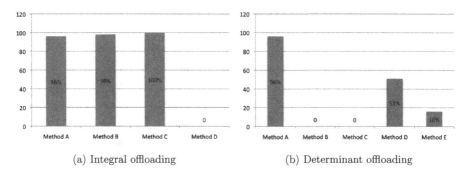

(a) Integral offloading   (b) Determinant offloading

Fig. 4. Successful method offloading rate (%)

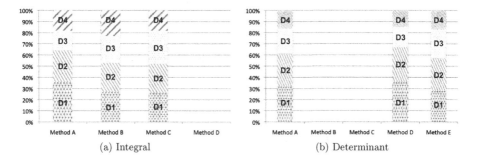

(a) Integral   (b) Determinant

Fig. 5. Contribution of devices to execute offloaded methods (%)

Figures 5(a) and (b) shows the offloading proportion and the contribution of each device to the offloading process. As expected, in most of the cases the device D4 has the lighter portion of execution as it is the less powerful device. The devices D1, D2 and D3 that have the same hardware characteristics, have almost the same execution contribution, even if their loads are not exactly equal. These results show that ACOMMA is really context- and application-aware to make multi-destination offloading and to dispatch the application methods between SPC's members correctly.

To evaluate the sharing benefits, we compare the execution time of the different benchmarks between ACO and string matching based on a local cache [8] and the collaborative cache. We evaluate the decision-making based on the collaborative cache with an on-changed dissemination policy, and a unique weighted cache merge policy (the invalidating policy has been shown to have a neglectable impact on results [8]). We run Determinant, Integral, Face detection and Monte-Carlo 10 times for two series of inputs on Galaxy SII. First, the ACO algorithm offloads and populates the local cache with maximum 10 rows. Secondly, when the source device has finished its executions, we run the same application on destination devices while making the offloading decision using collaborative cache and a string matching algorithm.

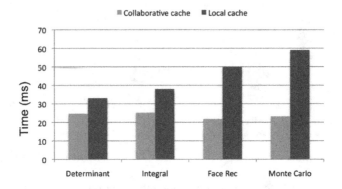

Fig. 6. Learned based offloading using local and collaborative cache

The results in Fig. 6 show that learning-based decision-making using a collaborative cache is more efficient than using a local cache. The gain in terms of execution time depends on the graph size. Small applications - Determinant and Integral - presents 30–40% gain (10 ms) and more complex ones - Face Recognition and Monte Carlo - up to 60% (35 ms).

7   Conclusion and Future Work

In this work, we propose the Spontaneous Proximity Cloud concept to offload applications onto mobile devices in the vicinity. We enriched our ant-inspired bi-objective offloading middleware, ACOMMA, with a learning-based decision-making using a collaborative resource and data cache sharing. We evaluate the performance of ACOMMA in collaborative mode with real benchmarks - Face Recognition and Monte-Carlo algorithms - and achieve 50% execution time gain. Several issues need further work. Testing the robustness and the scalability of the offloading to the mobility and connection interferences is a major one. A balance between the caching cost - storage and network - and the better decision to take has to be carefully studied.

References

1. Adem, K., Ryan, C., Abebe, E.: Crowdsourcing the cloud: energy-aware computational offloading for pervasive community-based cloud computing. In: Proceedings of PDPTA 2015, p. 415 (2015)
2. Ahonen, T.: Household penetration rates for technology across the digital divide. In: VR World (2011)
3. Chun, B.G., Ihm, S., Maniatis, P., Naik, M., Patti, A.: CloneCloud: elastic execution between mobile device and cloud. In: Proceeding of EuroSys 2011, pp. 301–314. ACM, New York (2011)
4. Cuervo, E., Balasubramanian, A., Cho, D.K., Wolman, A., Saroiu, S., Chandra, R., Bahl, P.: MAUI: making smartphones last longer with code offload. In: Proceeding of MobiSys 2010, pp. 49–62. ACM, New York (2010)

5. Face recognition algorithm. https://code.google.com/p/javafaces/
6. Gao, B., He, L., Liu, L., Li, K., Jarvis, S.: From mobiles to clouds: developing energy-aware offloading strategies for workflows. In: Proceeding of 13th International Conference on Grid Computing (GRID), pp. 139–146. ACM/IEEE (2012)
7. Giurgiu, I., Riva, O., Juric, D., Krivulev, I., Alonso, G.: Calling the cloud: enabling mobile phones as interfaces to cloud applications. In: Bacon, J.M., Cooper, B.F. (eds.) Middleware 2009. LNCS, vol. 5896, pp. 83–102. Springer, Heidelberg (2009). doi:10.1007/978-3-642-10445-9_5
8. Golchay, R., Le Mouël, F., Ponge, J., Stouls, N.: Automated application offloading through ant-inspired decision-making. In: Proceedings of the 13th International Conference on New Technologies in Distributed Systems (NOTERE'2016). IEEE (2016)
9. Kosta, S., Aucinas, A., Hui, P., Mortier, R., Zhang, X.: Thinkair: dynamic resource allocation and parallel execution in the cloud for mobile code offloading. In: Proceedings of INFOCOM, pp. 945–953. IEEE (2012)
10. Miluzzo, E., Cáceres, R., Chen, Y.F.: Vision: mClouds - computing on clouds of mobile devices. In: Proceedings of the Third ACM Workshop on Mobile Cloud Computing and Services, MCS 2012, pp. 9–14. ACM, New York (2012)
11. Mtibaa, A., Abu Snober, M., Carelli, A., Beraldi, R., Alnuweiri, H.: Collaborative mobile-to-mobile computation offloading. In: Proceedings of the International Conference on Collaborative Computing: Networking, Applications and Worksharing (CollaborateCom), pp. 460–465 (2014)
12. Mtibaa, A., Fahim, A., Harras, K.A., Ammar, M.H.: Towards resource sharing in mobile device clouds: power balancing across mobile devices. In: Proceedings of the Second ACM SIGCOMM Workshop on Mobile Cloud Computing, vol. 43(4), pp. 51–56 (2013)
13. Penner, T., Johnson, A., Van Slyke, B., Guirguis, M., Gu, Q.: Transient clouds: assignment and collaborative execution of tasks on mobile devices. In: Proceedings of GLOBECOM 2014, pp. 2801–2806. IEEE (2014)
14. Satyanarayanan, M., Bahl, P., Caceres, R., Davies, N.: The case for vm-based cloudlets in mobile computing. In: Pervasive Computing, vol. 8(4), pp. 14–23. IEEE (2009)

E-commerce Blockchain Consensus Mechanism for Supporting High-Throughput and Real-Time Transaction

Yuqin Xu[1], Qingzhong Li[1,3(✉)], Xingpin Min[1], Lizhen Cui[1], Zongshui Xiao[2,3], and Lanju Kong[1]

[1] School of Computer Science and Technology, Shandong University, Jinan, China
xuyuqin_sdu@163.com, {Lqz,clz,klj}@sdu.edu.cn,
minxingpin0105@163.com
[2] Electronic Commerce Research Center of Shandong University, Jinan, China
xzs@sdu.edu.cn
[3] Dareway Software Co., Ltd, Jinan, China

Abstract. Transactions may be altered, which leads to low credibility of transactions that restricts the rapid development and popularization of E-commerce. Although blockchain can ensure high stability and credibility of data, existing solutions still have some significant scalability barriers, such as low-throughput and high-latency. To improve credibility, this paper presents an e-commerce blockchain consensus mechanism (EBCM). EBCM does not rely on computing power and token but with the same level of security and credibility as Nakamoto consensus. Meanwhile, EBCM achieves real-time transaction and high-throughput. By introducing validation blockchain, we can ensure transactions cannot be altered. In order to realize high-throughput and real-time transaction, this paper constructs a two-layer blockchain. EBCM has been compared with Bitcoin in performance, and demonstrates better on throughput, latency.

Keywords: Credibility · Consensus mechanism · Blockchain scalability

1 Introduction

Shopping online which brings convenience to people's life is becoming more and more popular. So it is very important to build a secure and credibility e-commerce transaction network. Nowadays the lack of transactions' credibility is an urgent problem to be solved [1], because low credibility will seriously restrict the development of e-commerce. One possible method is to apply blockchain [2] to e-commerce, which can ensure high stability and credibility of data.

Consensus mechanism of Blockchain can solve the problem of trust and safety in distributed network. It is the key to building a safe and credible e-commerce transaction network, But existing blockchain mechanisms cannot support real-time transaction and high-throughput that e-commerce requires. In bitcoin [2], a transaction's confirmation time is an hour or so, that is fatal for e-commerce. Moreover, bitcoin's block size is not more than 1 MB, it only achieves a very small throughput [3]. So we propose an EBCM

© ICST Institute for Computer Sciences, Social Informatics and Telecommunications Engineering 2017
S. Wang and A. Zhou (Eds.): CollaborateCom 2016, LNICST 201, pp. 490–496, 2017.
DOI: 10.1007/978-3-319-59288-6_46

which is suitable for e-commerce can help to build a safe, credible, public, autonomous e-commerce transaction network.

EBCM supports the similar blockchain data structure format as Bitcoin, we propose a modification that permits better efficiency. It guarantees credibility by introducing validation blockchain, and constructs a two-layer blockchain called peer blockchain to ensure high-throughput and real-time transaction. The contributions of our research are two-folds:

- We put forward EBCM which does not relay on computing power and token, but with the same level of security and credibility as Nakamoto consensus.
- EBCM can realize High-throughput, real-time transaction and no forks in blockchain.

The remainder of the paper is organized as follow: Sect. 2 introduces related work which had done lots of work for improving the performance of blockchain. In Sect. 3, we introduce an e-commerce transaction network. Section 4 describe consensus mechanism of creating blocks in detail. Section 5 introduces the experiment about EBCM.

2   Related Work

After POW [2], lots of researchers put forward some other mechanisms which can solve bad performance of blockchain. Sunny King proposed proof-of-stake (POS) [4], he thinks that blockchain should be created by those who have stakes. Although POS reduces transaction latency, it is far away from e-commerce requirement. Dan Larimer put forward Delegated Proof-of-Stake (DPOS) [5] which is similar to the voting mechanism of board, but it relies on tokens. Ittay Eyal presented Bitcoin-NG [3] which decouples Bitcoin's blockchain operation into two planes and divides time into epochs. Bitcoin-NG has better performance than bitcoin, and also relies on peer's computing power which does not apply to e-commerce. GHOST [6] introduced by Sompolinsky Y et al. modified the rule to accept the main valid blockchain in order to push more transactions to the network. But it requires higher bandwidths [7]. Loi Luu [8] designed SCP which can allow to reach consensus on blocks without broadcasting actual block data, while still enabling efficient block verification. But the performance of SCP are not enough for e-commerce.

3   E-commerce Transaction Network

In this section, we will introduce an e-commerce transaction network (BCTN) using EBCM based on p2p, which is showed in Fig. 1. BCTN integrates e-commerce trading center, which is convenient to the supervision department to audit. It composes of multiple peers and a Verification Network (VENT).

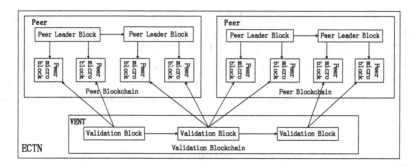

Fig. 1. E-commerce transaction network

Definition 1: Peer. A peer represents an e-commerce trading center or a logistics platform, such as Tmall. Each peer has an identity authentication, which can get public key for encrypting messages and private key for signing blocks. It can ensure the security of message and blocks cannot be forged.

Definition 2: Verification Network (VENT). Verification Network is composed of peers which has verification right, its function is to ensure that all peer micro blocks cannot be altered. Verification right means that the peer called verification peer (VP) has the right to construct validation blocks.

Peer blockchain designed as a two-layer blockchain ensures high-throughput and real-time transaction, it contains peer leader blocks and peer micro blocks. The structure of blocks are shown in Fig. 2. Peer micro block header contains: signature is used to identify the creator of the block, the GMT time is the creation time; the hash value of data is calculated transactions' hash by Sha256 algorithm which can ensure uniqueness and irreversibility. Peer leader block header includes all mentioned above, but with the hash value of previous block which can link peer leader block as blockchain.

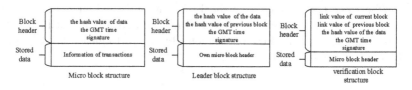

Fig. 2. Block structure

Validation blockchain shown in Fig. 2 stores all peer micro block headers to ensure that each peer micro block cannot be altered. The link value of current block and previous block can link all verification blocks into blockchain. How to calculate the link value will describe completely in Sect. 4.

The size of the micro block is fixed and the creation time is not greater than a predetermined value T_M, which can ensure real-time transaction. The number of block headers stored in peer leader block and verification block is also fixed value.

4   Consensus Mechanism of BCTN

In this section, we will describe EBCM in detail. In order to ensure EBCM has a same level of safe and credible, the process of creating blocks must promise that all blocks cannot be forged and altered.

4.1   The Creation Strategy of Peer Blockchain

We construct peer blockchain as two-layer blockchain to ensure high-throughput and real-time transactions. All transactions that saved in blocks are in chronological order. Peers cannot change transactions, cannot eliminate transactions, and cannot sort transactions artificially.

Each peer processes transactions which occur in it and verifies the legitimacy of transactions. After verification, transactions are temporarily stored in the memory pool. Transactions will be packaged into peer micro block until its size can satisfy or the time is more than T_M. After creating a complete peer micro block, the peer will send its header to all VPs in VENT and transactions store in the peer micro block can take effect. Multiple peer micro blocks can be created at the same time, which can realize high-throughput. Peers also need to create peer leader block as index which stored its own peer micro block headers. After calculating hash value of data and signing, the peer creates a complete peer leader block and then linked it to the leader blockchain. Peer leader block can be created only one at the same time.

4.2   Dynamic Verification Network

The process of creating verification block must be credibility to ensure peer micro blocks cannot be altered. We take two measures. Firstly, VPs in VENT is dynamically changed. Secondly, we propose a negotiated consensus algorithm which can promise that verification block cannot be forged as long as an honest peer existed in VENT.

This paper uses the credibility of peer (CRE), busy degree (B), computing power, and the number of times who had been as VP (T) to calculate peer's comprehensive value (C_V). Formula is as follows:

$$C\_V = \frac{CRE * (P/B)}{\sqrt{T}} \tag{1}$$

CRE is used to indicate the degree of peer's credibility, each peer's initial value is the same. And peer's CRE will reduce directly because of its malicious behavior. We use the number of peer micro blocks per hour to represent busy degree, its initial value is peer's average number of transactions per hour. To ensure VENT is dynamically changed, T is used as a limiting factor.

By using C_V, VENT sorts peers from big to small, the sequence is referred to as R_{C_V}. Assuming that the number of VPs in the verification network is N_V, and the VP set is constructed with peers which are in the top N_V of R_{C_V}.

4.3 Negotiated Consensus Algorithm

We propose a negotiated algorithm that does not rely on computing power, which can make sure the process of creating verification block is safe and credible.

First of all, all VPs reach a consensus on link value of validation block. Each VP in VENT creates a random number and signs, then sends it to other VPs. When a VP receives all VPs' random number, it can combine all VPs' random number as the link value. Considering information that may be lost or peer failure, we set two time thresholds T_{V1} and T_{V2} to prevent such situations. If the time that peer A waits for peer B's random number is more than T_{V1}, peer A requests peer B's random number to VENT. And If the time is more than T_{V2}, we will remove peer B from VENT. The remaining peers reach a consensus on the link value.

Secondly, VENT selects a VP to create a complete validation block by random numbers. A VP whose random number is the closest to the average of all random numbers and produces random number earlier, it will be selected. If other VPs do not receive validation block and the waiting time is more than T_D, the VP will lose the chance and the next VP gets the chance. After creating a complete validation block, the VP should send the feedback information to the peer whose micro block header has already been saved in it. The complete algorithm description of negotiated consensus is given in Algorithm 1.

Algorithm 1 **Negotiated Consensus Algorithm**	
Input: the VP set	14: Jump to step 3
Output: validation block	15: **End if**
1: Each peer creates a random number	16: Average value = block's link value / the number
2: Send random number with signature to other peers	of VP
3: **If** (the number of random numbers had been received	17: Each peer's DIFF = Each peer's random number -
= the number of VP -1)	Average value
4: block's link value = the sum of all the random	18: Sort peer according to DIFF from small to large
number	16: **For**(i=1,i<= the number of VP, i++)
5: **Jump to** step 16	19: **If** (the rank of peer=i)
6: **End if**	20: The peer is selected for creating block
7: **Else if** (waiting time > T_{V1} && don't receive random	21: **If**(the peer's response time >)
number that send by Peer)	22: the CP lost creation right
9: Send message for requesting random number	23: **End If**
10: **Else if** (waiting time > T_{V2} && don't receive	24: **End if**
the Peer's random number	25: **End for**
11: The Peer removed from the VP set	26: The Peer which is selected creates a complete
12: the number of VP = the number of CP -1	block
13: **End if**	27: Send to other Peers

Data consistency strategy for dynamic VP set. When a new VP set creates, if VENT just finishes creating a validation block, the new VP set will directly create the next validation block. Else, VENT will be forced to stop. For the micro block headers which have not been saved in validation block, the peer who sends them also do not receive the feedback information. So if peers once find VP set changed, then re-send peer micro block headers which do not have the feedback to VENT.

5   Experimental Evaluations

In this section, we evaluate EBCM with 1000-node experiments on an emulated network. The experiment implemented all EBCM elements that are significant. We take 2 s as a time slice, and the threshold value in the experiment is given in Table 1. We compare EBCM with Bitcoin in two sets of experiments, throughput and latency.

Table 1. The threshold value

Threshold	T_M	T_{V1}	T_{V2}	The size of micro block	The data entries of leader block and validation block	N_V
Value	2 s	5 s	10 s	1 MB	200	350

Figure 3 indicates the transaction latency of EBCM and bitcoin, EBCM is not more than 2 s that users can bear. Figure 4 shows throughput of transactions, EBCM can reach 100 thousands per second. The throughput of Tmall is about 120000 per second on November 11, 2015 which is the largest trading day of e-commerce in China. So we hold the opinion that EBCM can satisfy e-commerce requirement of performance. Through the statistical data we know the creation time of validation block is about 2 s, and the throughput of micro blocks can reach to 10000.

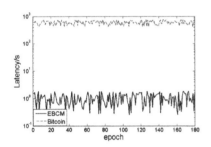

Fig. 3.   Transaction latency   **Fig. 4.**   Throughput of transactions

Through experiment, we can come to the conclusion that EBCM can satisfy the requirement of e-commerce. And under the same assumptions, EBCM has better performance than bitcoin.

6   Conclusion

This paper has been proposed EBCM which is suitable for e-commerce. EBCM can build a safe, credible, public, autonomous e-commerce transaction network to solve low credibility of transactions. It integrates e-commerce trading center as peer, which is convenient to the supervision department to carry out the audit. In the future, we will do more work about the storage mechanism of transactions and blocks, the no-sql retrieval mechanism, and a new mechanism to guarantee the data consistent.

Acknowledgment. This work is partially supported y SFC o.61572295; the Innovation Method Fund of China No. 2015IM010200; SDNSFC No.ZR2014FM031; the Science and Technology Development Plan Project of Shandong Province No. 2015GGX101015; the Shandong Province Independent Innovation Major Special Project No. 2015ZDXX0201B03.

References

1. Adelola, T., Dawson, R., et al.: Privacy and data protection in e-commerce in developing nations: evaluation of different data protection approaches (2015)
2. Nakamoto, S.: Bitcoin: a peer-to-peer electronic cash system. Consulted (2009)
3. Eyal, I., Gencer, A.E., Sirer, E.G., Renesse, R.V.: Bitcoin-NG: a scalable blockchain protocol (2015). http://arxiv.org/abs/1510.02037
4. King, S., Nadal, S.: PPCoin: Peer-to-Peer Crypto-Currency with Proof-of-Stake
5. Schuh, F., Larimer, D., BitShares 2.0: General Overview (2015)
6. Sompolinsky, Y., Zohar, A.: Secure high-rate transaction processing in bitcoin. In: Böhme, R., Okamoto, T. (eds.) FC 2015. LNCS, vol. 8975, pp. 507–527. Springer, Heidelberg (2015). doi: 10.1007/978-3-662-47854-7_32
7. Lewenberg, Y., Sompolinsky, Y., Zohar, A.: Inclusive block chain protocols. In: Böhme, R., Okamoto, T. (eds.) FC 2015. LNCS, vol. 8975, pp. 528–547. Springer, Heidelberg (2015). doi: 10.1007/978-3-662-47854-7_33
8. Luu, L., Narayanan, V., Baweja, K., Zheng, C., Gilbert, S., Saxena, P.: SCP: a computationally-scalable Byzantine consensus protocol for blockchains. Cryptology ePrint Archive, Report 2015/1168

Security Testing of Software on Embedded Devices Using x86 Platform

Yesheng Zhi[✉], Yuanyuan Zhang, Juanru Li, and Dawu Gu

Lab of Cryptology and Computer Security,
Shanghai Jiao Tong University, Shanghai, China
zleaves0818@gmail.com

Abstract. Security testing of software on embedded devices is often impeded for lacking advanced program analysis tools. The main obstacle is that state-of-the-art tools do not support the instruction set of common architectures of embedded device (e.g., MIPS). It requires either developing new program analysis tool aiming to architecture or introducing many manual efforts to help security testing. However, re-implementing a program analysis tool needs considerable amount of time and is generally a repetitive task. To address this issue efficiently, our observation is that most programs on embedded devices are compiled from source code of high level languages, and it is feasible to compile the same source code to different platforms. Therefore, it is also expected to directly translate the compiled executable to support another platform. This paper presents a binary translation based security testing approach for software on embedded devices. Our approach first translates a MIPS executable to an x86 executable leveraging the LLVM-IR, then reuses existing x86 program analysis tools to help employ in-depth security testing. This approach is not only efficient for it reuses existing tools and utilizes the x86 platform with higher performance to conduct security analysis and testing, but also more flexible for it can test code fragment with different levels of granularity (e.g., a function or an entire program). Our evaluation on frequently used data transformation algorithms and utilities illustrates the accuracy and efficiency of the proposed approach.

Keywords: Security testing · Binary translation · Embedded device · Binary analysis

1 Introduction

Security and privacy is considered as a significant requirement in embedded systems, especially considering that most of them are provided to system networks, private networks, or the Internet. However, the specialization of embedded system often comes with one or more inherent characteristics [9,10], which make

Partially supported by Major program of Shanghai Science and Technology Commission (Grant No: 15511103002).

security analysis and testing on embedded systems significantly stricter than on traditional commodity systems.

One way to employ security analysis is to leverage hardware debugging interface. This way requires dedicated hardwares and extreme resource requirements, therefore it can not be widely used in off-the-shelf embedded devices. To address, another way is leveraging dynamic binary translation (e.g., QEMU [4], Avatar [13]) to simulate and execute the binary program on PC system. The main drawback of dynamic binary translation is the large overhead of runtime translation and runtime optimization. Furthermore, for short-running programs, especially for interactive applications that are common on mobile devices, start-up time and response time are critical to their performances.

Consider that most state-of-the-art researches only focus on the x86 instruction set, and implement mature security tools. However, a embedded system usually uses specific instruction set architectures (ISAs), e.g., MIPS, etc. We implement an framework, BABELFISH, to reuse these well-developed testing tools for x86 architecture. By using mature security tools we can give a more efficient and accuracy analysis. Meantime, our work can apply more complex analysis and optimizations without large overheads, unlike dynamic translation. In our approach, we leverage a translator to lift MIPS binary to IA-32 architecture. In order to guarantee the accurate testing results, a fine-translated code should be provided by the binary translator. This code is evaluated from two aspects, code correctness and runtime efficiency:

(1) *Code Correctness:* The most important point is that the testing results provided by our framework should be consistent with those generated by testing tools working on MIPS binary directly. To ensure the code correctness, a good translator should translate 100% of the code if desired. Meanwhile, the translator should recover the correct control flow.

(2) *Runtime Efficiency:* We would like to provide optimized translated code that can perform similar with the native code. Unlike existing static binary translator, we make an improvement on translating register operations to improve efficiency of translated code.

2   System Design

We design BABELFISH, a framework to support security testing of MIPS binary (as presented in Fig. 1). The input of our framework is a stripped MIPS binary (without any symbol information and debug information). BABELFISH first translates the MIPS binary code to LLVM-IRs [1] statically.

Our approach provides two levels of security testing: the whole binary and specific functions in binary. Dealing with the whole binary, the translator will translate all necessary functions in MIPS binary. If we want to focus on testing some specified functions in MIPS binary, the translator of our framework also supports to translate part of functions in MIPS binary. The translator will only translate specified functions and all invoked functions according to call graph by static analysis.

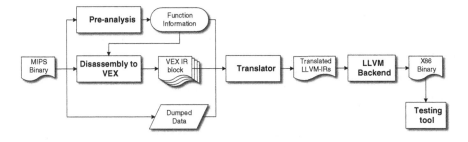

Fig. 1. Overview of BABELFISH

The module of LLVM-IRs, outputted by the translator, consists of all translated functions and global array variables of relocated data. This module will be compiled by LLVM backend into an executable binary or an object file. The x86 executable binary can be passed to testing tools of x86 binary for completing required security testing, like fuzzing, symbolic execution, taint analysis, etc. The object file can be linked into a test program for following security testing as well.

2.1   Challenge

Indirect Branch. During binary translating, translating branch instructions, especially indirect branch instructions, is the key to preserve the accuracy of recovered control flow. Unlike direct branch, it is difficult to find the destination address of an indirect branch until runtime. The control flow targets are dynamically calculated based on some immediate values in assembly instructions, jump tables and other references stored in data section. Combined with previous research [6], we first analyse the procedure of the indirect branch target calculation, and give a much accurate set of branch targets. With the set of branch targets, BABELFISH implements indirect branch using the LLVM *switch* instruction, depending on a mapping relation between target addresses of the indirect branch and corresponding destination addresses in the translated code.

Data Relocation. The data stored in data section is also an important portion in binary. The data will be dumped from data sections, and stored in arrays as global variables. While storing the data into the array, we must solve the relocatable problem. According to the research by Wang et al. [12], an immediate value can be a reference only if this value locates at the address space allocated for the binary. Here, We filter out references among all immediate values in data sections based on their target address. This simple filter is sufficient to identify concrete memory address. The immediate value as an operand in statements should be filtered as well. Once a reference is found during translating, it will be instantly replaced by the corresponding IR.

2.2 Binary Translating

The assembly-level binary translator first gives a pre-analysis on MIPS binary, utilizing an IDA script to export the information of function boundaries automatically. We also obtain the dynamic relocation entries of the file through objdump for dealing with the dynamic-link function calling.

With the pre-analysis results, we start to translate functions into LLVM-IRs individually. In order to facilitate translating a function call in LLVM-IR, we give a uniform form of translated function according to the most commonly used calling convention for 32-bit MIPS, the O32 ABI [2]:

Example of a Translated Function Described in C

```
uint32_t tranlated_func(const uint32_t args) {
// declare a array for the emulated stack frame
1:   uint8_t stack[64];
// load arguments storing in array args
2:   uint32_t arg0 = *(uint32_t *)args;
3:   uint32_t arg1 = *(uint32_t *)(args + 4);
...
// store callee's arguments to the stack array
4:   *(uint32_t *)stack = call_arg0;
5:   *(uint32_t *)(stack + 4) = call_arg1;
...
// call callee_func with the base address of stack
// as its only parameter
6:   uint32_t callee_ret = callee_func((uint32_t)stack);
...
}
```

At the beginning of each translated function, an array is allocated to complete translating the operation on stack frame with the same length of stack frame, and the translator loads the arguments from the address of array as the translated function's parameter (line 2–3). The length of stack frame is recorded to distinguish operations on the arguments of target function in assembly code. Subsequently, the translator follow the BFS ordering of function's control flow graph, and translated instructions in each basic blocks. Assembly code sequences in a basic block are firstly translated into VEX-IR representation, and then VEX-IR statements are translated into LLVM-IRs. VEX-IR abstracts binary code into a representation in a unified way, and lists all assembly side-effects, which allows for syntax-directed analysis.

During translating, we define the data type as *integer* or *pointer* type. What's more, the pointer variable is only used when we create it or we need to load/store the value from it, by leveraging the *ptrtoint* and *inttoptr* instruction in LLVM-IR. Once the translator get a pointer variable (e.g., like a memory reference or a return value of some system call), it convert its type to the integer without change its value using *ptrtoint* instruction. When we need to do load/store operation, we transfer the integer to a pointer, and then load the data that the pointer refers to, or store the data in where the pointer refers to. Having such transformation makes it convenient to do the other instruction translations, for their operands are always integer ones.

BABELFISH sets shadow registers and shadow stack memory for each block to record the data's IR representation, data type, and the data value if it is a immediate value. Data information is real-timely updated during translating. The value stored in register may succeeds from previous blocks. Especially when a register succeeds from two or more blocks, we need to add a *phi* instruction to define its value at the beginning of this block. The *phi* instruction takes a list of [⟨*value*⟩, ⟨*block_label*⟩] pairs as arguments, which is based on the data flow.

3   Evaluation

We evaluate BABELFISH with respect to its efficiency, the performance of translated code, and its capability to support program testing.

3.1   Experiments Setup

We tested BABELFISH with code fragments about typical data transformation algorithms including cryptographic algorithm (AES, DES, RC4), hash algorithm (MD5,SHA1), compress algorithm (Huffman) and sort algorithm (Quick Sort, Bubble Sort). Besides, to understand the ability of translating a complete executable, we study our translator's performance on *gzip* in detail. All programs to be translated are compiled by GCC 4.6.3 for MIPS32 architecture in little-endian, with the default configuration and optimization level -O2. We successfully translated all listed functions to LLVM-IRs. Then we lift translated IR to x86 assembly code using Clang 3.4. Finally, the translated x86 code is compared with the natively-compiled x86 executable binary, compiled by Clang 3.4 with -O2 optimization level, for the performance evaluation. The experiments are conducted on a machine with Intel Core i5-2320 @3 GHz running Ubuntu 14.04.

3.2   Translating Efficiency

Here, we only consider the time consumed by BABELFISH to translate MIPS code to LLVM-IRs. Processing time for each binary code is presented in Table 1. As expected, it takes more time to process larger functions. On average, BABELFISH spends 0.137 s per function.

For *gzip*, there are 19 K instructions and totally 154 functions, and it takes nearly 25 s to translate the whole MIPS binary to LLVM-IRs.

3.3   Translating Quality

The quality of translated code generated by BABELFISH is evaluated from two aspects: efficiency and correctness.

Table 1. Characteristics of translating functions

Algorithm	#Functions	#MIPS Insts	#IR Insts	Translation time (s)	x86 Insts Expansion
AES	4	1370	2492	0.707	17%
DES	2	2059	2775	0.653	4%
RC4	2	585	1435	0.375	64%
MD5	3	1198	1511	0.465	9.8%
SHA1	3	2063	2384	0.626	−12%
Huffman coding	4	191	392	0.197	15%
Quick Sort	2	62	159	0.084	11%
Bubble Sort	1	22	66	0.044	−19%
Total	21	7550	11214	3.154	7%

Correctness. We verify the correctness of BABELFISH by executing x86 binaries involving the translated functions with test input to verify the functionality. Semantic preservation is of significance to validity of testing the translated binary. We use the test cases provided by OpenSSL to check functionality of cryptographic functions and hash functions. As for Huffman coding and sort functions, we develop input by ourselves to verify the major functionality. All testing binaries pass the functionality tests without any error output.

Efficiency. The efficiency of translated code manifests from two aspect: size expansion and the execution time.

Comparing the number of IR instructions with that of MIPS instructions, the average expansion is 48% (shown in Table 1), considering with extra instructions to convert temporary variable between pointer type and integer type as well as the *phi* instructions. However, the size of x86 assembly code compiled from translated IR is only 7% bigger than that native-compiled version.

Next, we examine the execution time of the translated code. We conduct the executing of source MIPS binaries on QEMU [4] and the translated code on host x86 machine directly. Figure 2 shows the normalized execution time of testing source MIPS binary and x86 test binary compared to its corresponding native-compiled version. Test binaries on x86 have almost the same execution time with the corresponding version compiled from source code. The translated code is of runtime efficiency.

Similarly, we compare the translated *gzip* binary executable with the native-compiled version. On one hand, the translated binary is 2.7 times larger than the native-compiled one, while the *.text* section of the translated binary is 1.5 times the size of that in the native-compiled version. Consider that the data in *.bss* and *.sbss* sections were dumped from source binary and then were initialized to 0 during translation, whose size is around 322 kbyte. These data are stored in *.data* section of output binary. As *.bss* and *.sbss* sections are not calculated

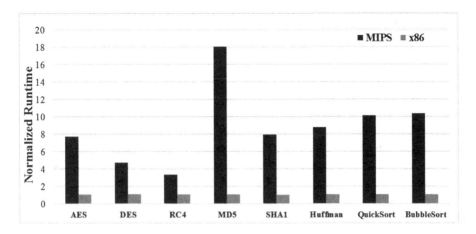

Fig. 2. Normalized execution time of source MIPS binary on QEMU and x86 translated binary compared to their natively-compiled version.

into the binary file size, the file expansion is acceptable. On the other hand, the translated executable roughly imposes 4% performance overhead compared with natively-compiled executable. The result shows that without any source code information, we can achieve a translated CPU intensive program using our framework, and such compiled binary have almost the same execution performance with the native-compiled version. This capability is convenient for testing a MIPS program by lifting it to an x86 version.

4   Related Work

Most security analysis and testing tools, mainly used for binary instrumentation, rewriting, and debugging, are based on same-ISA translators. Avater [13] is a framework to support dynamic security analysis of embedded devices' firmwares based on S2E [5], and it orchestrates the communication between an emulator and a target physical device. PROSPECT [8] can provide an arbitrary analysis environments, and enable dynamic code analysis of embedded binary code inside the environments.

A static translator translates programs offline and can apply more extensive (and potentially whole program) optimizations. Bansal et al. [3] propose an efficient binary translation approach using superoptimization techniques. DisIRer [7] uses machine descriptions of GCC in reverse to translate x86 instruction sequences into GCC's low-level Register Transfer Language (RTL). LLBT [11] is the effort relied on the LLVM infrastructure as well, but it translates ARM binaries into LLVM IRs.

5   Conclusion

Since the lack of security testing tool in MIPS and the inconvenience of dynamic emulation, we want to make use of the well-designed tools for x86 executable. Therefore, we propose BABELFISH, a framework that translates the input MIPS binary code to LLVM-IR statically, then uses LLVM compiler mapping the IR code into IA-32. Subsequently, we can make all possible security testings of it. We have developed a prototype version and evaluated it with several MIPS binaries. Our experiments show that the translated binary code almost have the same performance with those compiled from source code. The quality of translated code is convenient for security testing.

References

1. The llvm compiler infrastructure. http://www.lllvm.org
2. MIPS32 Architecture For Programmers Volume II: The MIPS32 Instruction Set (2001)
3. Bansal, S., Aiken, A.: Binary translation using peephole superoptimizers. In: Proceedings of the 8th USENIX Conference on Operating Systems Design and Implementation, pp. 177–192. USENIX Association (2008)
4. Bellard, F.: Qemu, a fast and portable dynamic translator. In: USENIX Annual Technical Conference, FREENIX Track, pp. 41–46 (2005)
5. Chipounov, V., Kuznetsov, V., Candea, G.: The S2E platform: design, implementation, and applications. ACM Trans. Comput. Syst. (TOCS) **30**(1), 2 (2012)
6. Fu, Y., Lin, Z., Brumley, D.: Automatically deriving pointer reference expressions from binary code for memory dump analysis. In: Proceedings of the 2015 10th Joint Meeting on Foundations of Software Engineering, pp. 614–624. ACM (2015)
7. Hwang, Y.-S., Lin, T.-Y., Chang, R.-G.: Disirer: converting a retargetable compiler into a multiplatform binary translator. ACM Trans. Archit. Code Optim. (TACO) **7**(4), 18 (2010)
8. Kammerstetter, M., Platzer, C., Kastner, W.: Prospect: peripheral proxying supported embedded code testing. In: Proceedings of the 9th ACM Symposium on Information, Computer and Communications Security, pp. 329–340. ACM (2014)
9. Parameswaran, S., Wolf, T.: Embedded systems security–an overview. Des. Autom. Embed. Syst. **12**(3), 173–183 (2008)
10. Serpanos, D.N., Voyiatzis, A.G.: Security challenges in embedded systems. ACM Trans. Embed. Comput. Syst. (TECS) **12**(1s), 66 (2013)
11. Shen, B.-Y., Chen, J.-Y., Hsu, W.-C., Yang, W.: LLBT: an LLVM-based static binary translator. In: Proceedings of the 2012 International Conference on Compilers, Architectures and Synthesis for Embedded Systems, pp. 51–60. ACM (2012)
12. Wang, S., Wang, P., Wu, D.: Reassembleable disassembling. In: 24th USENIX Security Symposium (USENIX Security 15), pp. 627–642 (2015)
13. Zaddach, J., Bruno, L., Francillon, L., Balzarotti, L.: Avatar: a framework to support dynamic security analysis of embedded systems' firmwares. In: NDSS (2014)

DRIS: Direct Reciprocity Based Image Score Enhances Performance in Collaborate Computing System

Kun Lu$^{(\boxtimes)}$, Shiyu Wang, and Qilong Zhen

School of Software, Dalian University of Technology,
Dalian 116620, Liaoning, China
lukun@dlut.edu.cn

Abstract. The key issue in collaborate computing systems is to induce agents work together towards a common task. Indirect reciprocity is a widely used method to promote cooperation. Image score is a classic indirect reciprocity mechanism which provided an insight on promoting cooperation. However, intuitively, people trust their own feelings more than other's opinions. Thus, in this paper, we introduce direct reciprocity into image score: when granting a service, a player should consider their own interaction histories in priority and consider image score if they have no interactions before. Extensive simulation results show that our proposed model can more effectively promote cooperation than classic image score under both complete and incomplete information.

Keywords: Direct reciprocity · Indirect reciprocity · Evolutionary game · Collaborative computing

1 Introduction

Cooperation is ubiquitous and plays a significant role in nature, human society and economy [1]. In collaborative computing system, such as distributed computing systems, P2P systems, etc., agents need to work together towards a common goal [2]. Without cooperation, the systems will eventually collapse. Thus, designing mechanisms to promote cooperation becomes a critical issue.

Direct and indirect reciprocity are two important mechanisms to promote cooperation [3].

The theory of direct reciprocity is first proposed by Trivers in 1970s [4]. In direct reciprocity mechanisms [5], each agent a records transaction histories with another agent b. If b cooperated with a in the last transaction, then a cooperates with b in this transaction. The famous competition held by Axelord further proved that direct reciprocity could promote cooperation [6]. However, direct reciprocity is a weak mechanism. It relies on repeated interactions between two individuals.

Indirect reciprocity mechanism [7,8] is also called reputation-based mechanism. It considers an individual's overall performance in a population [9].

© ICST Institute for Computer Sciences, Social Informatics and Telecommunications Engineering 2017
S. Wang and A. Zhou (Eds.): CollaborateCom 2016, LNICST 201, pp. 505–513, 2017.
DOI: 10.1007/978-3-319-59288-6_48

There is a trusted entity to help record each agent's reputation, which reflects how trusted an agent is. Agents with higher reputation have greater chances to be cooperated by other agents in following transactions. Image score [10] is a classic model for indirect reciprocity. In this model, image score is such an overall reputation value. Individuals consider recipient's image score before granting a service.

However, in real world interactions, people not only consider direct transaction histories, but also listen to other peoples' opinions. Thus, the combination of direct and indirect reciprocity is an interesting field.

In recent years, the combining of direct and indirect reciprocity draws lots of attention [11–16]. Gilbert Roberts [11] established a framework in which each individual uses one either direct indirect reciprocity and individuals evolve. It showed that direct reciprocity performs better when there were fewer individuals and more interactions. Meanwhile, indirect reciprocity alleviates the problem of lacking of interaction histories. Although, this paper gave an insight on combining direct and indirect reciprocity, it still didn't provide a complete simulation or theoretic model to clearly show how to combine these two mechanisms.

In our previous work [16], we proposed a hybrid trust model based on Eigen-Trust. In this model, recipient utilizes a two-phase reference method to take both indirect reputation and direct trust of a file provider into consideration before downloading. However, indirect reputation and direct trust work in different stages respectively.

In this paper, we propose a novel mechanism, which combines direct and indirect reciprocity in the same phase. Specifically, when an agent a gets a request from another agent b, a first considers b's direct transaction histories: if b granted a service to a before, then a grants a service to b in this transaction. Otherwise, agent a grants a service to b according to agent b's image score.

The contributions of this paper are as follows:

(1) A novel model combining direct and indirect reciprocity is proposed to promote cooperation.
(2) The decision making process is first considering direct transaction histories and indirect reciprocity information comes late, which helps to reduce accidental injuries to cooperative agents.
(3) Extensive simulations show that our proposed model promotes cooperation much more effectively than image score under both complete and incomplete information.

The rest of paper is organized as follows. In Sect. 2, we introduce our model in detail, including image score and our proposed model: DRIS. In Sect. 3, simulation results and some brief discussions are presented. In Sect. 4, we conclude this paper.

2 Model

2.1 Transaction Game

In this paper, we consider a collaborative system which provides resource provision services. In one transaction, one agent sends a request to a potential service provider, then the provider decides whether to grant a service or not. Thus, we abstract this process of transaction into a donor game.

A donor game is between two agents. One agent i plays as a service recipient and the other agent j plays as a donor. As shown in Table 1, if donor j grants a service, then the recipient i gets a payoff p and donor bears a cost c. Otherwise both players get a *zero* payoff. In donor game, it requires that $p > c$.

Table 1. Payoff matrix

	Donor	
	C	D
Recipient	$(p, -c)$	(0.0)

2.2 CIS: Classic Image Score

In image score, each agent i is assigned a strategy $S_i \in S$, where S is an available strategy set, $S = \{-5, -4, -3, -2, -1, 0, 1, 2, 3, 4, 5, 6\}$ and $S_i = -5$ represents fully cooperation, $S_i = 6$ represents fully defection. Each agent i has an image score $R_i \in R$, which reflects agent i's reputation. The set R is a set of available image score values and $R = \{-5, -4, -3, -2, -1, 0, 1, 2, 3, 4, 5\}$.

We consider a well-mixed population where each pair of agents can interact with each other. In one single game, a donor j gets a request from recipient i. The donor j first compares its strategy S_j with the recipient i's image score R_i, and donor j grants recipient i a service if $S_j \leq R_i$. If the donor j grants a service, its image score $R_j = R_j + 1$, otherwise, $R_j = R_j - 1$.

2.3 DRIS: Image Score with Direct Reciprocity

In DIRS, each agent i records direct transaction information towards agent j, DR_{ij}. In one single game (as shown in Fig. 1), donor j first checks its direct reciprocity DR_{ji}, if $DR_{ji} > 0$, which means i helped j before, then donor j fully cooperates with i; if $DR_{ji} < -2$, which means i defected on j more than twice, then donor j defects; otherwise, donor j considers its strategy S_j, i's image score R_i and the direct reciprocity DR_{ji}. If $S_j \leq R_i + DR_{ji}$, donor j cooperates, Otherwise, donor j defects. If donor j grants a service, then its image score $R_j = R_j + 1$ and $DR_{ij} = DR_{ij} + 1$; otherwise, its image score $R_j = R_j - 1$ and $DR_{ij} = DR_{ij} - 1$.

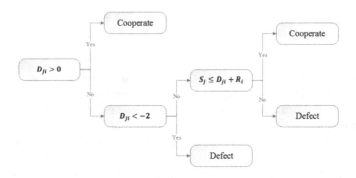

Fig. 1. Decision making of DRIS

To analyze the effect of direct reciprocity on image score, we consider two scenarios: (1) complete information and (2) incomplete information.

Complete information refers that one game can be seen by any other agents in the population. Thus, player i's image score R_i is shared a global variable and can be updated by all the agents in the population.

Different from complete information, incomplete information assumes that interactions between two agents are observed by only some of the agents in the population which are called observers. If no observer exists, image score is equal to direct reciprocity; if the proportion of observers equals to 1, then the model is equivalent to complete information. In each single game, observers are chosen randomly. Only observers and the recipient can update their perceptions of the donor j's image score.

2.4   Implementation of CIS and DRIS

The implementations are follow discrete time steps. As shown in Algorithm 1, the implementations are divided into $Tmax$ generations. In each generation, m games are played. After each game, information is updated. After each generation, agents reproduce their offspring with probability ρ_s. As shown in (1), the probability of agents with strategy s reproduces offspring (ρ_s) is proportional to its payoff P_s (see Table 2) over the total payoff of the system. Mutation refers to that some agents may change their strategies with a probability MR rather than its parent's strategy.

$$\rho_s = \frac{P_s}{\sum_{j \in S} P_j} \tag{1}$$

The implementation under incomplete information is shown in Algorithm 2. The main differences are in observer selection and information update. The observers are chosen randomly and only observers and the two agents in this transaction update their information.

Algorithm 1. Implementation under complete information

1: **for** *Generation* = 1 to *Tmax* **do**
2:   **for** *steps* = 1 to *m* **do**
3:     (a_j,a_i)= Random-choose()
4:     Game(a_j,a_i)
5:     Information-update(a_j,a_i)
6:   **end for**
7:   Statistic-payoff()
8:   Evolve()
9:   Mutation(MR)
10: **end for**

Algorithm 2. Implementation for incomplete information

1: **for** *Generation* = 1 to *Tmax* **do**
2:   **for** *steps* = 1 to *m* **do**
3:     (a_j,a_i)= Random-choose()
4:     Random-choose-observers()
5:     Game(a_j,a_i)
6:     Information-update($a_j,a_i,a_{o_1},\ldots,a_{o_n}$)
7:   **end for**
8:   Statistic-payoff()
9:   Evolve()
10:   Mutation(MR)
11: **end for**

Table 2. Definition of notations

Notation	Definition	Notation	Definition
$Tmax$	The number of evolution generation	m	The number of interactions
N	The number of individuals	n	The number of observers
c	Donor's cost in one game	p	Recipient's pay-off in one game
MR	Mutation rate	P_s	The total payoff of strategy s
ρ_s	The probability of reproducing offspring		

3   Simulation Results and Analysis

We perform simulations in a well-mixed population with N agents. In each simulation, we mainly consider the effectiveness of the mechanisms from three aspects: distribution of strategies, the average strategy and the average payoff of all players. Each of the results is derived from the average result out of 10^5 times of simulations.

3.1   Complete Information

We first consider the scenario under complete information. In Fig. 2, each value represents the probability of the strategy being the evolutionary stable strategy (ESS). As shown in Fig. 2(a)–(d), without mutation, no matter how large the total number of transactions is, our proposed model (DRIS) has similar performance as classic image score model (CIS). However, as shown in Fig. 2(e)–(f), when we consider mutation in this system, our DRIS performs better that CIS on promoting cooperation: the proportion of cooperative agents is larger than that in CIS.

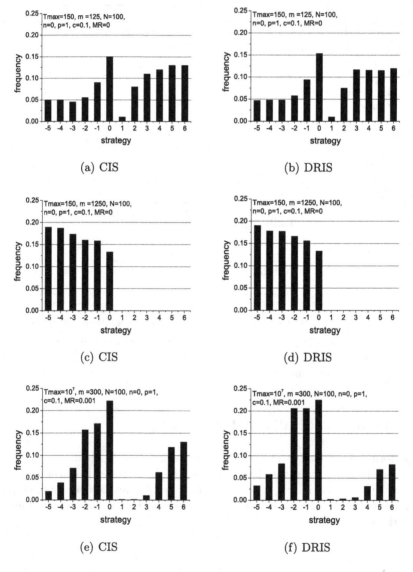

Fig. 2. Strategy frequency distribution at stable status under complete information

Under complete information, all of the transactions are visible. In this case, direct reciprocity is almost equivalent to indirect reciprocity, and the information is enough for CIS working. Thus, we get similar results. However, when mutation exists, direct reciprocity can resist the defective strategies generated by mutation and DRIS works a little better.

From another perspective, the average strategy dynamics is shown in Fig. 3. The average strategy is more frequently below 0 in DRIS (see Fig. 3(b)), which means our model is more effective on promoting cooperation.

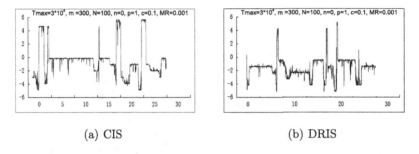

(a) CIS   (b) DRIS

Fig. 3. The average strategy dynamics under complete information

From the perspective of system benefit, we compare the dynamics of system average payoff. As shown in Fig. 4, our model can always have greater benefits than the classic model. Thus, our model is more effective on getting the system more profitable.

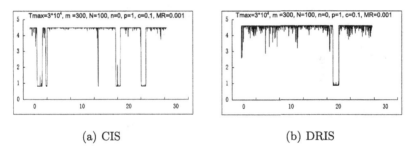

(a) CIS   (b) DRIS

Fig. 4. The average payoff with complete information

3.2   Incomplete Information

In this section, we present the effectiveness of our model under incomplete information. The major simulation results are similar to that under complete information. Thus, in this section we present the influence of observer proportion on promoting cooperation under incomplete information. As shown in Fig. 5, as the proportion of observer increases, the situation is more similar to complete information, thus, the probabilities of cooperation being ESS increases. Still, our model is always better than classic model.

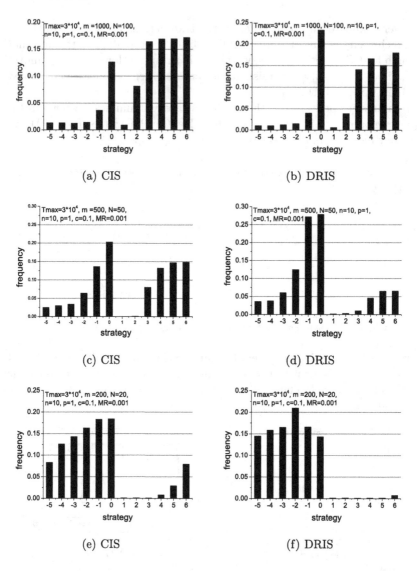

Fig. 5. Final strategy frequency distribution with incomplete information

Under incomplete information, image score is not accurate as the transactions are observed by only a few agents. Thus, direct reciprocity information is more feasible. It optimises the reputation and effectively improves cooperation among agents. Therefore, our proposed DRIS performs better than CIS.

4   Conclusion

In this paper, we present a novel model which introduces direct reciprocity into image score. Not only image score is considered when granting a service, but also direct reciprocity information. Simulation results show that under both complete information and incomplete information, our model is always better than the classic model on promoting cooperation and gaining system overall benefit.

Acknowledgment. This paper is supported by the National Science Foundation of China under grant No. 61272173, 61403059, 61572095.

References

1. Rand, D.G., Nowak, M.A.: Human cooperation. Trends Cogn. Sci. **17**(8), 413–425 (2013)
2. Lv, Y., Moscibroda, T.: Incentive networks. In: AAAI, pp. 1270–1276, January 2015
3. Nowak, M.A.: Five rules for the evolution of cooperation. Science **314**(5805), 1560–1563 (2006)
4. Trivers, R.L.: The evolution of reciprocal altruism. Q. Rev. Biol. **46**, 35–57 (1971)
5. Nowak, M.A., Sigmund, K.: Tit for tat in heterogeneous populations. Nature **355**(6357), 250–253 (1992)
6. Axelrod, R.M.: The Evolution of Cooperation. Basic Books, New York (2006)
7. Nowak, M.A., Sigmund, K.: Evolution of indirect reciprocity. Nature **437**(7063), 1291–1298 (2005)
8. Ghang, W., Nowak, M.A.: Indirect reciprocity with optional interactions. J. Theor. Biol. **365**, 1–11 (2015)
9. Alexander, R.D.: The Biology of Moral Systems. Transaction Publishers, Piscataway (1987)
10. Nowak, M.A., Sigmund, K.: Evolution of indirect reciprocity by image scoring. Nature **393**(6685), 573–577 (1998)
11. Roberts, G.: Evolution of direct and indirect reciprocity. Proc. Roy. Soc. Lond. B Biol. Sci. **275**(1631), 173–179 (2008)
12. Herne, K., Lappalainen, O., Kestil-Kekkonen, E.: Experimental comparison of direct, general, and indirect reciprocity. J. Socio-Econ. **45**, 38–46 (2013)
13. Molleman, L., van den Broek, E., Egas, M.: Personal experience and reputation interact in human decisions to help reciprocally. Proc. R. Soc. B **280**(1757), 20123044 (2013). The Royal Society
14. Phelps, S.: Emergence of social networks via direct and indirect reciprocity. Auton. Agent. Multi-Agent Syst. **27**(3), 355–374 (2013)
15. Balafoutas, L., Nikiforakis, N., Rockenbach, B.: Direct and indirect punishment among strangers in the field. Proc. Natl. Acad. Sci. **111**(45), 15924–15927 (2014)
16. Lu, K., Wang, J., Xie, L., Zhen, Q., Li, M.: An EigenTrust-based hybrid trust model in P2P file sharing networks. Procedia Comput. Sci. **94**, 366–371 (2016)

Research on Ant Colony Clustering Algorithm Based on HADOOP Platform

Zhihao Wang[1(✉)], Yonghua Huo[1], Junfang Wang[1], Kang Zhao[2], and Yang Yang[2]

[1] Science and Technology on Information Transmission and Dissemination in Communication Networks Laboratory, China Electronics Technology Group Corporation 54th Research Institute, Shijiazhuang, China
{cetc540016,jfwang2015}@sina.com,
tsdhyh2005@163.com
[2] State Key Laboratory of Networking and Switching Technology, Beijing University of Posts and Telecommunications, Beijing, China
489273711@qq.com, echo_lzjf@163.com

Abstract. Due to in the early period of the ant colony clustering algorithm convergence speed is very slow, this paper proposes a hybrid clustering algorithm based on ant colony clustering and MMK-means algorithm, which uses MMK-means algorithm to process the data, followed by ant colony clustering to finish clustering. Apart from that, this paper improves the ant colony clustering algorithm that makes ants using the best matching position, data object placement selecting and so on. We realize the algorithm in Hadoop platform, which can effectively reduce the time costs of clustering.

Keywords: Cluster · Hybrid algorithm · K-means · Ant colony algorithm

1 Introduction

Cluster analysis is a popular research branch of data mining. Clustering is the process that sets up the physical or abstract objects to similar objects composed of multiple classes or clusters. Clustering algorithms are applicable to the centralized data for clustering, while the actual data is distributed across different sites [1]. Due to the limit of transmission speed and safety factors, it is difficult to centralize the data in all sites to a central site. Besides, a large amount of data can result in a significant decrease on clustering efficiency.

Hadoop from the Apache open source community is an open source infrastructure software platform based on distributed system infrastructure which makes large-scale distributed computing and parallel processing widely used in cloud computing [2]. We propose a hybrid algorithm based on ant colony clustering and MMK-means

This work was supported by Open Subject Funds of Science and Technology on Information Transmission and Dissemination in Communication Networks Laboratory (ITD-U15002/KX15 2600011). NSFC(61401033,61372108,61272515). National Science and Technology Pillar Program Project (2015BAI11B01).

© ICST Institute for Computer Sciences, Social Informatics and Telecommunications Engineering 2017
S. Wang and A. Zhou (Eds.): CollaborateCom 2016, LNICST 201, pp. 514–520, 2017.
DOI: 10.1007/978-3-319-59288-6_49

algorithm. This hybrid algorithm overcomes the shortcoming that ant colony clustering algorithm has slow convergence speed. In addition, we improve the ant colony clustering mechanisms that ants using the best matching position, data object placement selecting and so on.

The rest of this paper is organized as follows: In the second section, the related works are introduced; the method proposed in this paper is introduced in the third section; the fourth section is the analysis and comparison of the performance of several methods. The fifth section is the summary.

2 Related Work

K-means algorithm has the advantages that it has small computational efforts and fast convergence speed and it is suitable for large data processing [3, 4]. But this approach has obvious shortcomings. We need to determine in advance the number of initial cluster centers and clusters. It is greatly influenced by subjective factors. Besides, clustering results have poor stability and are prone to local optima.

MMK-means algorithm makes use of data sampling technique to take samples from the mass of data (This way can reduce the computational cost). MMK-means algorithm uses the largest and minimum distance algorithm to calculate the number of clusters that K-means algorithm requires and the initial cluster centers [5]. Then MMK-means algorithm makes use of K-means algorithm to cluster. It is clear that the result of MMK-means is better than K-means.

Ant colony algorithm is a novel bionic algorithm based on artificial swarm intelligence, which is inspired by the collective behavior of social insects. For real ants, they have two important types of behavior: foraging and clustering. The algorithms of ant colony optimization (ACO) have their origins in the ant foraging behavior [6–8]. They were proposed by Marco Dorigo and are useful in solving discrete optimization problems.

3 The Parallel Design of the Hybrid Clustering Algorithm

Each grid places a data object and each ant moves randomly in the grid. The ant calculates the neighborhood similarity $f(i)$, then decides the probability of picking up or dropping data object [8], the lower the probability to pick up when degree of similarity is higher, the greater the probability to drop.

$$f(i) = \begin{cases} \frac{1}{\delta^2} \sum_{j \in L} (1 - \frac{\delta(i,j)}{\alpha}) & \text{if } f(i) > 0 \\ 0 & \text{otherwise} \end{cases} \qquad (1)$$

The neighborhood similarity $f(i)$ represents the average similarity of data i that the ants to pick up or drop with all the data objects in the visual radius r. $\delta(i,j)$ represents the distance between the data objects i and j. $\alpha \in [0, 1]$ is the similarity adjustment coefficient; δ^2 is the size of neighborhood area L. Ant is in the center of the neighborhood, and neighborhood visual radius can be estimated according to $(\delta-1)/2$.

If ants carry a data object at present, algorithm calculates the probability of ant put down the data P_d.

$$P_d = \begin{cases} 2f(i) & f(i) < k_d \\ 1 & f(i) \geq k_d \end{cases} \qquad (2)$$

The ant compares P_d with the random probability P_r, if $P_d > P_r$, the ant puts down current carrying data and mark status to "un-carry" at the same time. Then the ant randomly selects a free data object, or the ant move to other random location. If ants do not carry a data object at present, algorithm calculates the probability of ant pick up the data P_p according to the following formula.

$$P_p(i) = \left(\frac{k_p}{k_p + f(i)} \right)^2 \qquad (3)$$

The ant compares P_p with the random probability P_r, if $P_p > P_r$, the ant picks up data in the current location and mark status to "carry" at the same time. Then the ant moves to other random location, or let the ant randomly select a free data object.

Algorithm iterates until achieve the maximum number of iterations.

Here, we change the way that the ants always jump to the best matching position to the way that ant have different approaches in different stages. Improved algorithm commands ant move towards the direction of best matching position at the early stage. At the late stage ant makes a direct jump to the best match position. The ant needs to calculate the drop probability P_d when it moves to the new position. If $P_d > P_r$, the ant drops carrying data with placement policy. Or else, it means that short-term memory is not valid, the ant moves to another location randomly. The ant should update its short-term memory when it success drops data.

When the ant put down a data object, if the ant find a suitable location to place s, but s was already occupied by other data objects, the ant colony clustering algorithm's solution is that the ant moves randomly to another location, but this solution has great blindness, slow convergence speed, and cannot effectively use the available information. When the ant wants to put down an object, this suggests that the data ant carried is similar enough with other data objects within a visual radius.

Improved steps for data object strategies are as follows: The ant searches for empty positions whose distance from the current position is 1, if there is an empty position then the ant drop the data object carried in this empty position. Otherwise ant searches for empty positions whose distance from the current position is 2, followed by recursion, until the distance reaches the visible radius. If there's still no empty position when the search radius reaches the visible radius, the ant moves to another position randomly, this can prevent the ant cannot put data object down in cases when the ant cannot find a proper empty position in the long iterative process. We make the rule that when the times that an ant fails putting down a data object reach the threshold we set, the ant finds the best matching position and drops a data object in the best matching position or best matching position's surroundings.

Improved ant colony clustering algorithm based on MapReduce framework [7] is shown in Fig. 1.

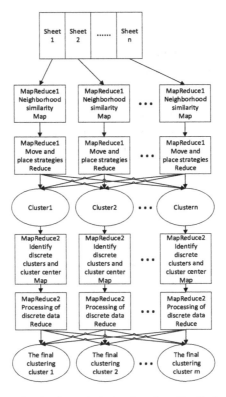

Fig. 1. Improved ant colony clustering based on MapReduce framework

(1) The original data set is divided into several pieces and distributed to each node. Map function of the MapReduce1 tasks is assigned to each node. Map function is responsible for mapping the data points in this node onto a two-dimensional grid randomly. Each Reduce function can be viewed as an ant, and responsible for the calculation of neighborhood similarity with Canberra distance. According to the number of iterations Reduce function make ants have variable movement speed (decreases in a random way), and along with the iteration ants' visual radius is increased gradually. If the case consistent with the "pick up principles" ant picks up data objects.

(2) When reaching the maximum number of iterations the algorithm enters MapReduce2 to deal with the clustering results. The clustering cluster is assigned to each node, the Map function in the MapReduce2 is responsible for comparing the number of data objects with threshold, if the number of data objects is greater than or equal to threshold, the cluster is identified as the correct cluster, if the number of data objects is less than the threshold, the cluster is identified as discrete cluster.

The algorithm calculates the center of all correct clustering clusters. Reduce function is responsible for calculating the distance of discrete data objects and the clustering center. If the distance conforms to the requirements of the threshold, the ant merge the data into the best match cluster, or mark the data as discrete data object.

(3) At last, algorithm output the final clustering results.

The hybrid clustering algorithm is shown in the Fig. 2. We first use of MMK-means algorithm's fast convergence characteristics to preprocess data. This section includes data sampling, using the maximum minimum distance method to select the cluster centers in the extracted data and merging adjacent center to obtain the initial cluster centers for K-means algorithm. After K- means algorithm clusters roughly by using the initial clustering center and clustering cluster number. At last, the algorithm uses improved ant colony clustering algorithm to cluster.

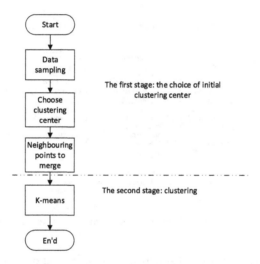

Fig. 2. The hybrid clustering based on MMK-means and ant colony clustering

4 Experiment and Analysis

Simulation data set's each property is in accordance with normal distribution. Dimension property is two-dimensional. Data set consists of five classes, and data for each class are in line with the Gaussian distribution. There are 1000 data objects in total. The simulation experiments in this article use the following parameter settings, and we take 30 experiments with the data set:

$P_p = 0.1$, $P_d = 0.1$, $\alpha = 0.1$, $N = 100$, short-term memory capacity of ant $N_{memory} = 20$, the number of ant $N_{ant} = 10$.

Figure 3 shows the clustering result after using improved ant colony clustering algorithm. The number of discrete points is significantly less than that generated by traditional ant colony clustering algorithm, due to the introduction of the discrete data processing strategy. Figure 4 shows the clustering result using the hybrid clustering algorithm based on MMK-means algorithm and ant colony clustering algorithm. The clustering effect is similar with that generated by improved ant colony clustering algorithm, because they use the same principle of clustering.

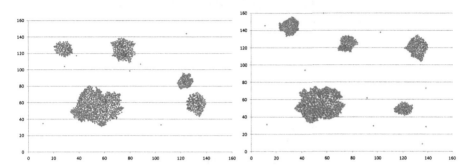

Fig. 3. The clustering result after using improved ant colony clustering algorithm

Fig. 4. The clustering result after using the hybrid clustering algorithm

F-measure is also known as F-score, the most common evaluation criteria in the field of information retrieval [1, 2]. Figure 5 shows the F-measure value of the five algorithms described in this article. The F-measure value of the hybrid clustering is superior to that of the improved ant colony clustering. The high-to-low order of accuracy of the clustering effect reflected by F-measure values is ant colony clustering, MMK-means and K-means. Improved clustering is better than ant colony clustering, mainly because the improved algorithm has adaptive characteristics.

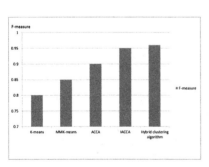

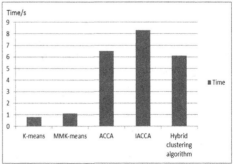

Fig. 5. F-measure of various clustering algorithms

Fig. 6. Time performance comparison of various clustering algorithms

Figure 6 shows the time performance comparison of various clustering algorithms. The time performance of the hybrid clustering is better than that of the improved ant colony clustering algorithm (IACCA) with decreasing by 26.2%. By sacrificing some time cost, it improves the effectiveness of clustering. MMK-means decreases the time performance by 50.8% than K-means, which is due to that MMK-means needs to calculate the additional parameters that the K-means algorithm needs. The hybrid clustering algorithm improves the time performance by 5.7% than the basic ant colony clustering algorithm (ACCA) and improves the time performance by 25.6% than IACCA. So the hybrid clustering algorithm can improve the convergence speed.

5 Conclusion

The proposed parallel design of MMK-means algorithm runs in parallel on Hadoop platform. Improved ant colony clustering algorithm and its parallel design effectively improve the clustering effect and the time cost. Finally, the mixed clustering algorithm accelerates the convergence speed and improves the clustering effect compared with ant colony clustering algorithm.

References

1. Wei, X.: Clustering algorithm based on the combination of genetic algorithm and ant colony algorithm. In: International Conference on Innovative Computing & Cloud Computing, pp. 45–49. ACM (2011)
2. Kenidra, B., Meshoul, S.: A data-clustering approach based on artificial ant colonies with control of emergence. In: Soft Computing and Pattern Recognition, pp. 430–435. IEEE (2014)
3. Asbern, A., Asha, P.: Performance evaluation of association mining in Hadoop single node cluster with big data. In: International Conference on Circuit, Power and Computing Technologies. IEEE (2015)
4. Jiang, H., Zhang, G., Cai, J.: An improved ant colony clustering algorithm based on lf algorithm. In: 2015 IEEE 12th International Conference on e-Business Engineering (ICEBE), pp. 194–197. IEEE Computer Society (2015)
5. Yu, H., Wang, D.: Mass log data processing and mining based on Hadoop and cloud computing. In: International Conference on Computer Science & Education, pp. 197–202 (2012)
6. Zhou, A., Wang, S., Sun, Q., et al.: Dynamic virtual resource renting method for maximizing the profits of a cloud service provider in a dynamic pricing model. In: International Conference on Parallel and Distributed Systems, pp. 944–945 (2013)
7. Wang, S., Zhou, A., Hsu, C.H., et al.: Provision of data-intensive services through energy- and QoS-aware virtual machine placement in national cloud data centers. IEEE Trans. Emerg. Top. Comput. 4(2), 1 (2015)
8. Mao, L., Shen, M.M.: An improved ant colony clustering algorithm based on dynamic neighborhood. In: IEEE International Conference on Intelligent Computing and Intelligent Systems, pp. 730–734 (2010)

Recommendflow: Use Topic Model to Automatically Recommend Stack Overflow Q&A in IDE

Sun Fumin[(✉)], Wang Xu, Sun Hailong, and Liu Xudong

Beihang University, Beijing, China
{sunfumin,wangxu,sunhl,liuxd}@act.buaa.edu.cn

Abstract. Developers often look information in the web during software development and maintenance. That means they spend time to formulate query, retrieve documents and process the results from many sources of information. Stack Overflow, one of the most popular question and answer sites and the most important information sources for developers, has become one of the most important information sources for developers. In this paper, we proposed a new approach that use LDA model and Q&A meta-information to automatically generate query from code context and recommend the retrieval Q&A to developers. We implemented the approach in Recommendflow, an Eclipse plugin. We considered one existing recommendation model as baseline and conducted an experiment to compare our approach with baseline. Our experiment on the test data set shows that LDA-based model outperforms existing Stack Overflow recommendation model.

Keywords: Crowd knowledge · Software development · Q&A · Topic model · Recommend system

1 Introduction

With the explosive development of software technology, developers face new software or programming issues more and more often. Developers always need knowledge beyond that they have already processed [1]. Stack Overflow is one of the most popular and important ways to look for information on the Internet [2].

However, retrieving information in internet forces developers switching between IDE and the web browsers, that is really time-consuming [3]. To solve this problem, some scholars have already proposed studies that integrate Stack Overflow into IDE which can help developers work efficiently. *Seahawk* [4], an eclipse plugin proposed by Ponzanelli et al. [6] in 2013, offers a way to retrieve and recommend Stack Overflow posts within IDE. Rahman et al. [5] propose an eclipse plugin, *SurfClipse*, that can retrieve Stack Overflow posts according to exceptions that are selected from console view or error log by developers. All the studies mentioned above just get the meta information in Stack Overflow (eg. votes, user reputation and posts content). We use LDA model [7], a suit of

© ICST Institute for Computer Sciences, Social Informatics and Telecommunications Engineering 2017
S. Wang and A. Zhou (Eds.): CollaborateCom 2016, LNICST 201, pp. 521–526, 2017.
DOI: 10.1007/978-3-319-59288-6_50

machine learning algorithms aim to discover latent topic structure in collections of documents.

The contribution of the paper are the following points. First we proposed LDA-based query generation model. We discuss query generation tasks and present LDA-based query generation model in Sect. 2. Second we proposed LDA-based ranking model and combine LDA-based Ranking with Meta-information ranking in Sect. 3. We implement this approach in Recommendflow, an Eclipse plugin, which is detailed in Sect. 4. Then we collected a test data set and conducted our experiment on the test data set in Sect. 5. Finally, Sect. 6 concludes and discusses possible direction for future work.

2   Query Generation

Our query generation model is motivated by the information retrieval ranking. In information retrieval, the basic approach for ranking query results is the query likelihood model where each document is scored by the probability of the model generating a query:

$$P(Q|D) = \prod_{q \in Q} P(q|D) \tag{1}$$

where d is a document, Q is the query and q is a query term in Q. $P(q|D)$ is the probability of the document model generating a term. The score shows how much a document matches the query. However, in query generation model there is not a given query. If all possible generated queries of the document are computed, we can easily generate one or Top N best query as follow:

$$P(Q|D) = Q = \arg\max_{Q \in \Omega} P(Q|D) = \arg\max_{Q \in \Omega} \prod_{i=1}^{L} P(q_i|D) \tag{2}$$

Note that since query has a fixed length, we just need to compute all $P(q|D)$ and then get Top L query terms to maximize the $P(Q|D)$. In this section, we introduce two methods of computing $P(q|D)$.

In LDA, when we get the posterior estimates of θ and φ, we can compute the probability of a term generating in a document as:

$$P(q|D, \hat{\theta}, \hat{\varphi}) = \sum_{z=1}^{K} P(q|z, \hat{\varphi}) P(z|\hat{\theta}, D) \tag{3}$$

where $\hat{\theta}$ and $\hat{\varphi}$ are the posterior estimates of θ. Blei et al.[9] used a variational Bayes approximation of the posterior distribution. There are alternative inference techniques: expectation propagation and Gibbs Sampling. We use Gibbs Sampling technique in this paper, so we can get $P(q|D)$ as follow:

$$p(q|D) = \sum_{z=1}^{K} \frac{c_{v,z}^{-} + \beta}{c_z + V\beta} \frac{c_{i,k}^{-} + \alpha}{L_i + K\alpha} \tag{4}$$

where $c_{v,z}^{-}$ is the number of instances of term q_i assigned to topic z except for the current word, with hyper-parameters α and β. $c_{i,k}^{-}$ is the number of terms in ith document assigned to topic z except for the current word, c_z is the total number of words assigned to topic z and L_i is the length of the ith document.

3   Ranking

As mentioned before, in information retrieval, scores between query and documents is used to sort results. In this paper we compute the score between code context and document instead of the score between query and document, because the query is generated from code context. We introduce two method of computing score of Stack Overflow posts, S_D.

As we mentioned in Sect. 2, the posterior estimates of θ and φ can be used to compute $P(t|D,\theta)$, the probability of document D generating the topic t. Thus we can get a probability topic vector for every document. And with the posterior estimates, LDA model can infer topic structure in developer's code context. We use *Cosine Similarity* to measure the similarity between the topic vector of Stack Overflow posts and the topic vector of developer's code context. Finally we define the S_D as:

$$S_D = \frac{\sum_{t=1}^{K} P(z|D,\varphi) \cdot P(z|D',\varphi')}{\sqrt{\sum_{i}^{K} P(z|D,\varphi)^2} \cdot \sqrt{\sum_{i}^{K} P(z|D',\varphi')}} \tag{5}$$

where D is the Stack Overflow post, D' is code context. LDA treat the Q&A as a vector of words which may ignore meta-information such as votes, user reputation and so on. So we combine LDA and meta-information. Note that if consider similarity between two topic vectors as a feature, we can combine LDA-based Model with meta information. We update the LDA-based Ranking model as:

$$S_D = \lambda \frac{\sum_{t=1}^{K} P(z|D,\varphi) \cdot P(z|D',\varphi')}{\sqrt{\sum_{i}^{K} P(z|D,\varphi)^2} \cdot \sqrt{\sum_{i}^{K} P(z|D',\varphi')}} + (1-\lambda) \sum_{i=1}^{n} w_i \cdot s_i \tag{6}$$

There is some meta information in Stack Overflow from which we can extract features as follow:

Question Votes: Every user can give every question a positive vote or a negative vote. It reflects the quality of the question.

Accepted Answer Votes: The accepted answer votes is normalized like the question votes. It reflects the quality of the accepted answer.

Questioner Reputation: Every user on Stack Overflow community has a reputation. It is a rough measurement of how much the community trusts the user.

Answerer Reputation: The reputation of user whose answer is accepted in
the question.

Content Similarity: The similarity between retrieved content of Stack Overflow posts and developer's code context. We first split the contents to words
then removing stop words and apply Porter Stemming. Finally we compute
similarity of two word vectors.

API method Similarity: It's similar with content similarity but compute similarity of API method word vector which extract from content and code context.

4   Recommendflow

Figure 1 show the architecture of *Recommendflow*. It is based on client-server
model which consists of two major components - client (Eclipse plugin) and
server (web service server). They communicate through Hyper Text Transfer
Protocol and send files in json format to each other.

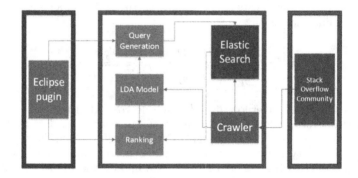

Fig. 1. Architecture.

To initiate, crawler crawled all Stack Over flow data (eg. question&answer
posts, user data) and processed them. Server added the processed data to elastic
search and trained LDA model on these data. Once developers change their
source code, the plugin sends code context to server side where LDA model
infers latent topics structure of it and query generation service formulates query
with the inferred structure. Then the server calls a new search through Elastic
Search. After computed score and sorted in *Ranking Service*, the retrieved posts
will be sent to plugin. To ensure our data are up to date, the server crawls Stack
Overflow and retrains LDA model regularly.

As we introduced before, *Recommenflow* both automatically recommends
Stack Overflow posts and offers search service. If developers formulate their query
by themselves, the server just skips over generating query step and retrieves
documents directly. Figure 2 represents *Recommendflow* user interface.

Fig. 2. Recommendflow User Interface.

5   Experiment

To evaluate our approach, we conducted our experiments on the test data set which is collected by ourselves. The test data set consisted of some codes and related Q&A. All related Q&A conducted a Q&A set. We processed each code and recommend Q&A from the Q&A set and record if the recommended is related to the code. We considered recommending model in [6] as baseline and compared our approach and baseline. The experiment result is presented in Fig. 3.

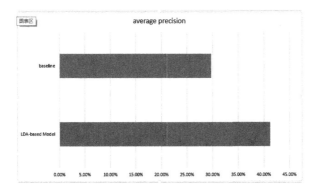

Fig. 3. Experiment result of the test data set in average precision.

6   Conclusion and Future Work

We have proposed a new approach to automatically generate query from code context and rank retrieval results, implemented it in a tool named Recommendflow and evaluated the method in the test data set. Our approach is based on

LDA model and experiment results on the test data set demonstrate that the LDA-based method outperforms the baseline.

We also have a plan to optimize our system and offer it to programmer community for free.

References

1. Ko, A.J., DeLine, R., Venolia G.: Information needs in collocated software development teams. In: Proceedings of the 29th International Conference on Software Engineering. IEEE Computer Society (2007)
2. Subramanian, S., Inozemtseva, L., Holmes, R.: Live API documentation. In: Proceedings of the 36th International Conference on Software Engineering. ACM (2014)
3. Brandt, J., Guo, P.J., Lewenstein, J., et al.: Two studies of opportunistic programming: interleaving web foraging, learning, and writing code. In: Proceedings of the SIGCHI Conference on Human Factors in Computing Systems. ACM (2009)
4. Ponzanelli, L., Bacchelli, A., Seahawk, L.M.: Stack overflow in the IDE. In: Proceedings of the 2013 International Conference on Software Engineering. IEEE Press (2013)
5. Rahman, M.M., Surfclipse, R.C.K.: Context-aware meta-search in the IDE. In: 2014 IEEE International Conference on Software Maintenance and Evolution (2014)
6. Ponzanelli, L., Bavota, G., Di Penta, M., et al.: Mining stackoverflow to turn the IDE into a self-confident programming prompter. In: Proceedings of the 11th Working Conference on Mining Software Repositories. ACM (2014)
7. Blei, D.M., Ng, A.Y., Jordan, M.I.: Latent Dirichlet allocation. J. Mach. Learn. Res. **3**, 993–1022 (2003)

CrowdEV: Crowdsourcing Software Design and Development

Duan Wei[✉]

Beihang University, Beijing, China
duanwei@act.buaa.edu.cn

Abstract. The Internet based software is growing very fast with the soaring of the Internet, traditional approaches, which specify requirement offline and develop in isolated teams, are no longer the best approach. Especially after the web 2.0 and the crowdsourcing came up, it has shown some very promising qualities in speeding up the software development. Taking advantage of this, we present a novel software developing approach, which specify requirement by online crowdsourcing with expert supervision and develop using micro-task based crowdsourcing. To verify the feasibility of our approach, we established an online platform CrowdEV and ran a user study on that, which resulted in a successful development of a SNS software within campus in 5 days, comparing with an open-source project that took 17 days for similar functions.

Keywords: Requirement engineering · Crowdsourcing · Micro-tasks · Software development

1 Introduction

After so many years since it's come to being, the traditional software development has created some very mature methodology and models, these approaches, however, are all within the domain of developing software with very small groups together, thus is very hard to meet the fast-growing need of modern software.

Based on this, we came up with a micro-task based crowdsourcing approach with expert supervision to speed up the development. Our key insight lies mainly in two aspects, the collaborative requirement specification and developing software using micro-task in a massive parallel way.

2 Related Work

Considering the specification and refinement of the software requirement, Patrick Finnegan [4] took the way of having the open-source groups participated the development of the commercial software, yet cannot guarantee the time and quality of software; Wang Hao [1] analyzed the spatial-temporal clustering characteristics of the workers on the Internet that share the same or similar skills and specialities, and optimized the traditional requirement specification process.

© ICST Institute for Computer Sciences, Social Informatics and Telecommunications Engineering 2017
S. Wang and A. Zhou (Eds.): CollaborateCom 2016, LNICST 201, pp. 527–532, 2017.
DOI: 10.1007/978-3-319-59288-6_51

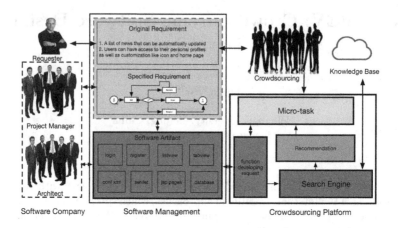

Fig. 1. The overall of the workflow.

In the field of crowdsourcing software development based on micro-tasks, many approaches aim at the decomposition of the project and the generation of the micro-tasks, for example, Little, Greg [7] analyzed the existing crowdsourcing algorithms and developed a script that can automatically decompose the tasks into a bunch of micro-tasks and publish them on the MTurk, CrowdForge [2] took the approach of Map Reduce and managed to have the workers into the process of the task decomposition. CrowdCode [6] however, took a dynamic way of generating micro-tasks to meet the changing need during the development.

3   Design

The key insight of our approach is that requesters can use CrowdEV to collaboratively specify and optimize the requirement of the software product by working with the online crowd as well as the expert project manager, and we have implemented a crowdsourcing software developing approach based on micro-tasks with code recommending to help multiple developers to finish the developing process in a highly parallel way thus to greatly decrease the time from the requesters' original idea to a highly usable software product into the market.

3.1   Workflow Overall

Our approach consists of 4 roles, Requester, Project Manager, Architect and Worker, the Project Manager(PM) and Architect are platform experts, using Product Requirement Document (PRD) and Prototype, these 4 roles will translate the original idea from Requester to final software product. To support communication and parallel development, we also provide 3 kinds of Tasks, which are Requirement Enrich Task (RET), Module Develop Task (MDT) and Function Develop Task (FDT). As is shown in Fig. 1.

From the graph we can see the whole process consists of two main parts, the collaborative requirement specification in which the requirement is defined and edited by requester and project manager and enriched by online worker, and the micro-task based software developing where modules of different granularity are decomposed, developed and assembled by architect and online worker.

3.2   Collaborative Requirement Specification

Traditional approaches use offline methods like focus group, questionnaires or one-to-one investigation, unlike those, we developed an online approach. After the Requester publishes the original ideas about the software product onto the platform in plain natural language, the PM will analyze and abstract software requirements from the description and format them into a formal PRD, which consists of two parts, the Feature and Scenario, the Feature part is organized as a tree structure, each represents an RET task, while every scenario also stand for one. The Crowd can only add new comments or new sub-requirement to the existing ones, the PM will choose from all the replies after the task is closed and return the result to the Requester.

3.3   Micro-task Based Crowdsourcing Software Development

Our approach implemented a task decomposing and designing mechanism that keeps evolving, as we all know, the requirement of the software is very hard to get fully specified before the development of the software, so is the design of the software, new problems and new requests often show up during the software development, taking reference from the Evolution Model for software development, we decomposed the responsibility to design the particular software architecture into the design of some core functional modules and iteratively decomposed it into the design of multiple minor artifacts of the software, during the designing process, new request may come up, developers can edit and expand their design by publishing new MDT or FDT.

When a worker is dealing with a FDT, to accelerate the development and lower the threshold for taking the task, we also get some similar code from github.com with an embed search engine as some reference for the worker.

Moreover, unlike typical micro-tasks which are independent and needs little human labor, the micro-tasks in software development are usually interdependent and requires communication and coordination during the development process. To deal with the problem, we also allow Worker to publish new FDT to help with his own task. The whole process is shown in Fig. 2.

3.4   Implementation

CrowdEV can be divided into two parts based on its function. The whole system is built mainly as a website, with an Android client being auxiliary. Using Android client, the worker can browse all the available micro-tasks and check

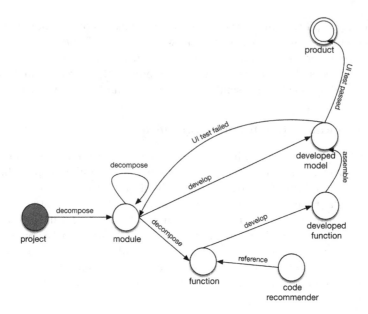

Fig. 2. Workflow of the crowdsourcing software development

out the micro-tasks he already accepted after signing in the system, the worker can also take part in the software requirement refining phase and publish their own enriching opinion, he can also agree or disagree with other workers' opinions using the client.

The platform provides a model for the software product, which capsulate the original request, the complete requirement data, the software prototype and the related micro-tasks with their answers. The platform also provides access to all those data for the requester of the project.

4   User Study

To verify the feasibility of our platform, we recruited 5 undergraduate students from our school as platform worker by email and contacts, these students all major in computer science, all took the Android developing related courses, all have at lease half a year of experience in Android developing, and all with the basic ability to write the simple JUNIT test cases, also, we recruited 4 post-graduate students who also major in computer science, yet with more experience in Android developing with an average of around 2 years, they are later going to be responsible for the decomposing of the MDT. At the same time, we hired one professional project manager as the expert manager of the platform and a experienced developer as the registered Architect on our platform from outside the campus.

Also to verify the advantage of faster development, we found an open-source project on Github.com which took the 9 participants 17 days to finish the core functions of the Android SNS project. We first analyze the function of the project and played as the Requester and publish the function on the platform, the PM, after communicating with us and the Crowd, finished the prototype in half a day, the Architect took another day and decomposed the project into a batch of MDT.

5 Result

The development of the whole project took 5 days. And in total, 11 participants (9 Workers, 1 Project Manager, 1 Architect) has finished the design and implementation of a software project which consists of 1044 lines of code by publishing 3 micro-tasks and got 7 submissions in software requirement specification and by generating 70 micro-tasks during development process. Though number of participants and user incentive may vary between two projects, this experiment does show some advantage in speeding up the software development.

The key insight of our approach lies in 3 aspects: first, the collaborative requirement specification finished by Requester, PM and Crowd can speed up the specification and lower the barrier of communication; second, the micro-task based software development, by developing software in a massive parallel way, can significantly speed up the development process comparing to some other crowdsourcing ways; finally, the function recommend and pseudo-call replacement can solve the interdependence among different tasks on some level (Table 1).

Table 1. Statistics about the experiment

Project	Requirement	Module	Task
IM	User account management	login and register	task 1–7
		user homepage	task 8–21
	Publish News Feed	news publish activity including UI	task 22–45
	Browse News Feed	news list activity including UI	task 46–58
		news detail activity including UI	task 59–70

6 Discussion

Our experiment created a minor yet fully usable software in only 2 days with 8 students and 2 professionals in total. Which shows the promising ability for crowdsourcing to speed up the software development.

One key insight of our approach is the crowdsourcing workflow with expert supervision, which showed great efficiency in speeding up the software development. In fact, getting expert involved into the crowdsourcing process is generally popular and often interpreted as golden test in current crowdsourcing markets [3,5,8].

Meanwhile, our platform has revealed some problems. The first one is the imbalance of the workload, the design of the core data structure, the architect still has a heavy burden in designing and assembling the product, which could be a bottle-neck for the time control of the whole project process. Also, our platform only support Android development, which is a bit limited scenario.

References

1. Wang, H., Wang, Y., Wang, J.: A participant recruitment framework for crowd-sourcing based software requirement acquisition. In: 2014 IEEE 9th International Conference on Global Software Engineering, pp. 65–73 IEEE (2014)
2. Kittur, A., Smus, B., Khamkar, S., et al.: Crowdforge: Crowdsourcing complex work. In: Proceedings of the 24th Annual ACM Symposium on User Interface Software and Technology, pp. 43–52 ACM (2011)
3. Sarasua, C., Simperl, E., Noy, N.F.: CROWDMAP: Crowdsourcing ontology alignment with microtasks. In: Cudré-Mauroux, P., Heflin, J., Sirin, E., Tudorache, T., Euzenat, J., Hauswirth, M., Parreira, J.X., Hendler, J., Schreiber, G., Bernstein, A., Blomqvist, E. (eds.) ISWC 2012. LNCS, vol. 7649, pp. 525–541. Springer, Heidelberg (2012). doi:10.1007/978-3-642-35176-1_33
4. Naparat, D., Finnegan, P.: Crowdsourcing Software Requirements and Development: A Mechanism-based Exploration of ?Opensourcing?[J] (2013)
5. Retelny, D., Robaszkiewicz, S., To, A., et al.: Expert crowdsourcing with flash teams. In: Proceedings of the 27th Annual ACM Symposium on User Interface Software and Technology, pp. 75–85. ACM (2014)
6. LaToza, T.D., Towne, W.B., Adriano, C.M., et al.: Microtask programming: Building software with a crowd. In: Proceedings of the 27th Annual ACM Symposium on User Interface Software and Technology, pp. 43–54. ACM (2014)
7. Little, G., Chilton, L.B., Goldman, M., et al.: TurKit: Human computation algorithms on mechanical turk. In: Proceedings of the 23nd Annual ACM Symposium on User Interface Software and Technology, pp. 57–66. ACM (2010)
8. Stol, K.J., Fitzgerald, B.: Two's company, three's a crowd: A case study of crowd-sourcing software development. In: Proceedings of the 36th International Conference on Software Engineering, pp. 187–198. ACM (2014)

Cloud Computing-based Enterprise XBRL Cross-Platform Collaborated Management

Liwen Zhang[1,2](✉)

[1] BeiJing JiaoTong University, Beijing, China
Zhlwen3721@bjtu.edu.cn
[2] Henan University of Economics and Law, Zhengzhou, China

Abstract. EXtensible Business Reporting Language (XBRL) is expected to develop into the global data standard for business financial reporting with the potential to change the way that accounting data collaborate processing. The improvement of interactivity of the Internet financial report relies on its data presentation standard. This paper attempts to take advantage of cloud computing technology to conduct comprehensive integration of the enterprise information systems according to XBRL classification criterion, and generate XBRL standard instance documents that will be stored in the cloud computing-based enterprise information data cloud. By employing XBRL processing technology, it is able to realize cross-platform XBRL system processing and offer references for the listed companies to realize XBRL cross-platform collaborated data management.

Keywords: XBRL · Collaborated · Cloud computing

1 Introduction

The rapid development of computer network and information technology gives rise to the innovation of the Internet financial report. XBRL makes it possible to realize financial information disclosure which is impossible under the traditional reporting mode. The development of XBRL innovatively transforms the traditional form of accounting reports of listed companies and leads the Internet financial report to develop in depth and breadth. It has become the actual demand for XBRL to enhance the resource integration and use ratio of XBRL report platforms, improve the quality of XBRL Internet financial report and focus on the data co-processing capability of cross-platform accounting information systems. A high-quality information network service platform for listed companies is the foundation for production of high-quality XBRL Internet financial data. The improvement of interactivity of the Internet financial report relies on its data presentation standard. It is very difficult for the traditional enterprise financial information output systems to realize cross-platform collaborated data processing. The differences in interaction among different financial information platforms result in the difficulties in effective utilization and prompt extracting of various financial information and non-financial information. This paper attempts to take advantage of cloud computing technology to conduct comprehensive integration of the enterprise information systems according to XBRL classification criterion, and generate

S. Wang and A. Zhou (Eds.): CollaborateCom 2016, LNICST 201, pp. 533–539, 2017.
DOI: 10.1007/978-3-319-59288-6_52

XBRL standard instance documents that will be stored in the cloud computing-based enterprise information resource pool. By employing XBRL processing technology, it is able to realize cross-platform XBRL system processing and offer references for the listed companies to realize XBRL cross-platform collaborated data management.

2 Technical Analysis for Cloud Computing-based XBRL Cross-Platform Collaborated Management

Designed on the paper-based accounting information, the traditional online accounting information system is the informatized processing of paper-based accounting data. Such preliminary forms of online financial reports only realize presentation of the written content in the traditional paper reports onto the electronic pages, which does not fundamentally improve the accounting information quality or realize capital market value gains. It is still not possible to effectively retrieve the financial information published in such formats or visually obtain the comparison between different indexes. The content and format are fixed. It can only receive information passively instead of customizing personalized financial reports. Traditional financial reports cannot now satisfy the stakeholders' demand in space and time for personalized information. The contradiction between the traditional financial information supply and the demand for personalized financial information and supervision becomes growingly prominent. The information supply and demand in the current capital market are far from reaching the Pareto Optimality. In order to resolve these issues fundamentally and realize free exchange of financial information, there shall be a unified technical standard for financial data.

2.1 Application of Cloud Computing-based XBRL Cross-Platform Collaborated Management

Cloud computing is a network-based, configurable sharing computing resource pool, and also a convenient model for access per demand. Its advantages include low cost and strong sharing capability. Cloud computing has been applied widely now. Through application of cloud computing technology, China generalized the XBRL classification criterion in 2009, and China Securities Regulatory Commission, Shanghai Stock Exchange and Shenzhen Stock Exchange stored XBRL instance documents in the relevant cloud computing accounting data resource pool. Financial information users of listed companies can extract relevant accounting data from the resource pool in the cloud service platform through employing XBRL technology. The data resources in the accounting information resource pool are highly shared. In addition, it is able to realize seamless provision of accounting information and generation of corresponding financial reports with the help of XBRL technology. This report mode works in this way: as the enterprise's financial data is stored in the dynamic data resource pool of the cloud platform, once any user needs to search any financial information, the system will adopt XBRL standard naming to encapsulate financial data and send it to the client in the form of hypertext; then, the client may check information and trace the information source by a browser or other APP.

2.2   Architecture of Cloud Computing-based XBRL Cross-Platform Collaborated Management

The bottom layer of the cloud computing-based accounting information platform for listed companies is the infrastructure composed of hardware and the operating system. On the layer above the bottom layer are various software systems and the management platform, including the deployed various information system management software, virtualized components, cloud computing management system and various virtual machines. Another layer above is XBRL basic data that can be either XBRL standard instance documents directly stored in the cloud platform resource pool or real-time extracted Web Service data provided by the enterprise. The top layer of the architecture is the application software service center made up of software provided by various software developers, as well as the data center. It is the core of the cloud computing, including the application center of financial software and various management software, program integration center and data storage & inquiry center. This kind of architecture, on the one hand, reflects the privacy and security of enterprise accounting data, and, on the other hand, better ensures users of enterprise accounting data to take advantage of XBRL technology in searching the required data and tracing the data sources, finally realizing high level of data sharing.

2.3   Technical Conditions for Development of XBRL Cross-Platform Collaborated Management by Enterprises

XBRL technical framework comprises three parts, namely, XBRL technical specifications, XBRL classification criterion and XBRL instance documents. In recent years, with the rapid development of cloud computing theory and technology, it becomes simple and convenient to realize network information management, and also provides a good data processing platform for the accounting information system and XBRL co-processing of listed companies. Through the data platform of the accounting information system cloud platform supplier, enterprises store the instance documents of accounting data in the accounting information resource pool according to the XBRL classification criterion. By integrating the data in the accounting data resource pool with the help of XBRL software, all kinds of accounting and financial information are offered to various financial data users.

3   Application of Cloud Computing-based Enterprise XBRL Cross-Platform Collaborated Management

Traditional online financial reports are only represented in the electronic form of paper-based financial reports. They are outdated, frequently swapping data, poor in information mining and data collaboration. In addition, they cannot be designed according to the individual demand of users, and data cannot be effectively traced. In contrast, concerning the cloud computing-based XBRL Internet financial reports, according to the global XBRL standard and regional requirements, XBRL instance documents are stored in the resource pool in a real-time way, so as to realize collaborated management of enterprise accounting data and XBRL.

3.1   Idea of XBRL Cross-Platform Collaborated Management

Different business systems may provide different XBRL presentation forms, realize supply as per demand and enhance cross-trade, cross-sector repeated availability of data information. The existing national XBRL classification criteria include XBRL Global Ledger (XBRL GL) and XBRL Financial Report (XBRL FR). XBRL FR is applied in the corporate financial report to be published to the public, while XBRL GL is used in the corporate accounting process. XBRL GL can present all information in each account and ledger, including both financial information and non-financial information. By using XBRL GL, enterprises can compile cross-platform data information through cloud computing technology, and formulate XBRL data standard form of documents. As XBRL GL classification criterion standardizes the various transaction data of enterprises, information demanders can mine data downward and extract the original data of economic businesses. By employing XBRL GL at the business level, information demanders can precisely extract the matter information of enterprises. XBRL GL can also store the data of the enterprise supply chain system, e-commerce system and other public management platforms in the relevant instance document resource pool according to XBRL classification criterion, so as to realize real-time processing of economic data generated during the production process. Users of statements can utilize XBRL technology to check, track and compile statements on the instance documents in the corporate information resources according to their information demand. Thus, the collaborated management and real-time reporting of various information resources are realized. XBRL can realize cross-platform data transmission and exchange, which is beneficial to share information. The design of XBRL cross-platform collaborated management is shown in Fig. 1.

3.2   Cloud Computing-based Enterprise XBRL Cross-Platform Collaborated Management

(1) Collaborated management of XBRL and enterprise accounting information system

According to statistics, more than 70% of enterprise information comes from accounting data. In the future, the co-processing of XBRL and accounting information system is inevitable. With the development and perfection of cloud accounting technology, enterprises will store the data of accounting information system as standard document formats in the accounting information sharing resource pool. And users of accounting statements can check and timely know the financial situations of enterprises through XBRL software generally designed by software developers. XBRL has unparalleled advantages in improving the information quality characteristics of accounting statements. Relevant normative studies and empirical studies indicate that XBRL financial reports can evidently improve the reliability, interactivity, real-time performance,

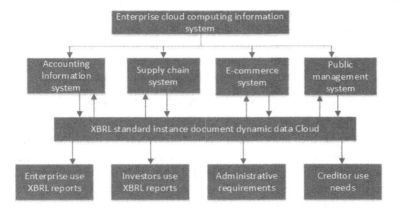

Fig. 1. XBRL cross-platform collaborated management design

comparability and understandability of accounting information. The idea of co-processing of XRBL and accounting information system transforms the previous management ideas of the accounting information system, and elevates the user satis-faction for statements, realizing balanced benefits among them. Therefore, XRBL technology is the technical guarantee for global and regional accounting inform-atization.

(2) Collaborated management of XBRL and enterprise supply chain system

The enterprise supply chain system reflects the production and commodity circulation process through controlling the product value-added process and distribution channel process. It starts from the origin of product production and ends at the consumers. Enterprises share demand information, inventory, production plan, sales plan and delivery plan by VLC for reflecting the supply chain process and realizing collaborative forecasting. This kind of collaborated management can reflect the optimized configu-ration process of production capacity in a systematic way, timely master the status of commodity circulation, effectively improve the capital turnover, and systematically analyze the liquidity and profitability of the enterprise in the future. It can also make accurate prediction of the capabilities of the external suppliers and dealers. The com-modity purchase information, inventory information and production information in the supply chain system can effectively reflect the operational capability of the enterprise. Through the single standard and planning of XBRL, enterprises can generate instance documents based on the real-time data from the supply chain, and store them in the dynamic resource pool. By employing XBRL technology, we can realize collaborated management of XRBL and the supply chain system. It is of practical significance for users of statements to timely know the configuration status of enterprise resources and capital turnover efficiency.

(3) Collaborated management of XBRL and e-commerce platform

The data of e-commerce transactions are normally dynamic data. Through the co-processing of XBRL and e-commerce, the dynamic profitability of the enterprise can be more timely represented. Based on the records of the transaction platform, e-commerce platform uses XBRL technology to convert transaction data to standard XBRL dynamic instance documents, and publish the dynamic instance documents of transactions to the dynamic electronic preparation information resource pool, thus improving the dynamic decision-making ability of the users of statements.

(4) Collaborated management of XBRL and other organizations

The subjects that use XBRL not only involve the providers of financial reports and business reports, but also involve their receivers and users, including listed companies, investors, accounting firms, regulatory organizations and other stakeholders. The enterprise operations must meet the demand for sustainable development. In addition to considering the state of operation, the responsibilities undertaken by enterprises for the social and natural environment should also be examined comprehensively, including environmental protection, public benefit and business reputation. Then, the corresponding instance documents will be generated. Through the collaborated management of XBRL and other organizations, investors can understand the relationships between enterprises and the government, as well as between various associations and the market; the information users can understand the financial information and non-financial information of enterprises as a whole.

4 Conclusion

In this paper, we investigate how the core value of XBRL to improve the financial information quality of listed companies. The purpose of XBRL collaborated management is to make the demanders of accounting information timely obtain real-time, dynamic original data, and allow the users of financial reports to track the information sources. XBRL provides technical support for the accounting information reports of enterprises. The idea of collaborated management expands the classification criteria of XBRL. Through the collaborated management of XBRL and other systems, we can realize better data exchange between financial systems and other management systems, integrate information resources, analyze the micro-economic activities of enterprises and support the decisions related to operational management. The cross-platform collaborative application of the cloud computing-based XBRL technology at the business level will play a positive role in comprehensive elevation of the accounting information quality of listed companies, the competitive edges of enterprise in the market and enterprise informatization.

References

1. Doolin, B., Troshani, I.: Organizational adoption of XBRL. Electron. Markets 17(3), 188–199 (2007)
2. Blind, K., Gauch, S.: Trends in ICT standards: the relationship between European standardisation bodies and standards consortia. Telecommun. Policy 32(7), 503–513 (2008)

3. Blind, K.: Factors influencing the lifetime of telecommunication and information technology standards: results of an explorative analysis of the PERINORM database. Int. J. IT Stan. Standard. Res. **5**(1), 1 (2007)
4. Bovee, M., et al.: Financial reporting and auditing agent with net knowledge (FRAANK) and eXtensible business reporting language (XBRL). J. Inf. Syst. **19**(1), 19–41 (2005)
5. Bonsón, E., Cortijo, V., Escobar, T.: Towards the global adoption of XBRL using international financial reporting standards. Int. J. Account. Inform. Syst. **10**(1), 46–60 (2009)
6. Hodge, F., Kennedy, D., Maines, L.A.: Does search-facilitating technology improve the transparency of financial reporting? Account. Rev. **79**(3), 687–703 (2004)
7. Kim, J., Lim, W.J., No, W.G.: The effect of first wave mandatory XBRL reporting across the financial information environment. J. Inf. Syst. **26**(1), 127–153 (2012)
8. Kim, J., Lim, W.J., No, W.G.: The effect of first wave mandatory XBRL reporting across the financial information environment. J. Inf. Syst. **26**(1), 127–153 (2013)
9. Liu, C., Luo, X., Teo, H.H.: The impact of XBRL adoption in PR China. Decis. Support Syst. **59**, 242–249 (2014)
10. Lin, Z.J., Liu, M.: The impact of corporate governance on auditor choice: evidence from China. J. Int. Account. Auditing Taxation **18**(1), 44–59 (2009)
11. Rao, Y., Guo, K., Hou, J.: XBRL taxonomy extensions in China. Int. J. Account. Inf. Manage. **21**(2), 133–147 (2013)

Alleviating Data Sparsity in Web Service QoS Prediction by Capturing Region Context Influence

Zhen Chen[1]([✉]), Limin Shen[1]([✉]), Dianlong You[1], Feng Li[2], and Chuan Ma[1]

[1] School of Information Science and Engineering, Yanshan University,
Qinhuangdao 066004, China
ysucz0815@163.com, {shenllmm,youdianlong}@sina.com
[2] School of Computer Science and Engineering, Northeastern University,
Shenyang 110000, China
{ysu_lifeng,tianyi_mc}@126.com

Abstract. With the advent of service computing paradigm, Web service QoS prediction has become a necessity to support high quality service recommendation and reliable Web-based system building. However, the inherent data sparsity issue and potentially strong but inconspicuous relation between users or Web services and their neighborhoods under the context of region information are overlooked in previous studies. In this paper, we propose a unified matrix factorization model by capturing the influences of region contexts from both user and service sides in an integrated way. Different from previous researches, our approach capitalizes on the advantages of latent feature and neighborhood approaches systematically so as to achieve accurate QoS prediction. Experimental results have shown the proposed approach outperforms its competitive methods with respect to accuracy efficiently, thereby demonstrating the positive effect that incorporation of explicit region context can have on alleviating the concerned data sparsity issue.

Keywords: Web service · QoS prediction · Data sparsity · Region context

1 Introduction

Web services are software systems designed to support interoperable machine-to-machine interaction over a network [1]. Due to the advantages of dynamic binding, loosely coupling and across platform, it facilitates the delivery of business applications as Web services are accessible to anyone, anytime, at any location and using any platform. Additionally, Web services give benefits to both users and providers in such a way that users get what they expect for their paid electronic solutions [2], while providers can concentrate on the core competencies of their business without devoting too many precious people to develop the specific functions [3].

© ICST Institute for Computer Sciences, Social Informatics and Telecommunications Engineering 2017
S. Wang and A. Zhou (Eds.): CollaborateCom 2016, LNICST 201, pp. 540–556, 2017.
DOI: 10.1007/978-3-319-59288-6_53

With the increasing amount and wide application of Web services, it becomes very challenging for users to find appropriate Web services with equivalent functionality [4]. For example, the number of available identification card inquiring services in Baidu API Store[1] is up to 30, as of May 2016. The wealth of Web services brings about a problem rather than a solution because users are drowning into the sea of service selection. Quality of service (QoS), characterizing the no-functional attributes of Web services, such as response time and throughput, is then introduced to solve this challenge by differentiating the performance differences of Web services [5]. However, it is often required to predict QoS values of Web services due the following facts: (1) the number of available Web services is large and is still growing, and a user has accessed a few Web services and the vast majority of QoS values are unknown, a problem known as *data sparsity*; (2) QoS data is related to the specific situation, users in different region areas might have dramatically different QoS experiences; (3) Testing all candidate Web services is not practical in application, because it is very time and resource consuming and some Web services need to be paid for a function call.

To tackle the problem of Web service QoS prediction, researchers have devised a number of collaborative filtering (CF) based methods, which could be divided into two main categories: neighborhood-based and model-based methods. Neighborhood-based methods exploit similar neighbors' ratings directly to make prediction. Shao et al. first introduce CF to make Web service QoS prediction [6]. They make similarity mining and prediction from users' neighborhood. Zheng et al. propose a hybrid QoS prediction method by combining user-based and service-based CF methods [7]. Wu et al. adopts a similar fusion method by designing an adjusted-cosine-based similarity to remove the impact of QoS scale [8]. Although neighborhood-based methods are intuitive and easy to be implemented, they suffer from the unavoidable data sparsity issue in CF method, and this will cause a major performance degradation when there are new users and services added to the system, a problem known as *cold-start*. Moreover, users can be neighbors only when they have co-invoked some services, while this is not always true because users in the same local region may also have positive correlations. These impede the generalization of neighborhood-based methods in real scenario.

Different from neighborhood-based method making prediction directly from similar neighbors, model-based methods exploit the known QoS ratings to infer users' and services' latent features that characterize the behavior of user invoking service. Matrix factorization (MF) is one of the most successful implementation techniques of latent feature model. In [9], the authors improve prediction accuracy by extending MF with user similar neighbors. Yin et al. believe users inside a local neighborhood share similar invocation experiences, and they extend MF with a location-based regulation term and make prediction with a combination of pre-processing results of classic MF and extended MF [10]. These methods improve prediction performance by considering user side neighborhood only, while ignoring the role of neighborhood from service side. Moreover, the inherent *data sparsity* and *cold start* issues remain fully unaddressed.

---

[1] http://apistore.baidu.com/.

Recently, researchers have introduced location information to improve QoS prediction accuracy further. Tang et al. exploit location information for neighbor selection in their neighborhood-based CF prediction method [11]. E et al. propose a similar method with [11] and improve neighbor selection method by calculating the geographical distance with user latitude and longitude information [12]. Besides location factor, Yu et al. in [13] introduce time factor to improve Web service QoS prediction. Region context is inherently existed in user-service rating system. In this paper, the main motivation for exploiting region context in Web service QoS prediction stems from the observations that the ideas we are exposed to and the choices we make are significantly influenced by our region neighborhoods. Different from previous researches, we study the benefit of region context and propose a **RE**gion context-aware **M**atrix **F**actorization (REMF) approach, which not only integrates the cooperation ideas behind collaborative filtering but also exploits region contexts of users and services to capture the local preferences and as well as alleviates the data sparsity problem to a large extent.

Our main contributions are summarized as follows.

(1) The insights that users and services are positively correlated under the context of region information are observed based on real-world dataset analysis.
(2) REMF was proposed specifically to model user and service region context influences, producing accurate predictions and alleviating data sparsity issue.
(3) Comprehensive evaluations using real-world dataset demonstrate the effectiveness and efficiency of REMF.

The remainder of this paper is organized as follows: Sect. 2 defines our problem formally and analyzes the underlying correlations between users or services and their neighbors under the context of region information. Section 3 introduces the details of our proposed approach. Section 4 presents experimental results and Sect. 5 concludes the work.

2   Problem Statement and Observations

2.1   Problem Statement

We first introduce the notations used in this paper. Let $U = \{u_1, u_2, ..., u_m\}$ and $S = \{s_1, s_2, ..., s_n\}$ denote the sets of users and Web services, respectively, where m is the number of users and n is the number of Web services. First, users invoked Web services on the Internet through standard protocols, such as XML, SOAP and WSDL. Second, if user u used service s and $r_{u,s}$ is the observed QoS rating, otherwise we use *null* denotes the unknown rating from u to s. Third, u submits the observed rating $r_{u,s}$ to the universal description, discovery and integration system, thus m users will contribute an $m \times n$ user-service QoS rating matrix $R = \{r_{u,s}\}_{m \times n}$. As we discussed before, there is a large number of Web services on the Internet, and most users would have accessed only a small fraction of the large universe of available Web services. Consequently, the matrix R is very sparse, and the limited available QoS data will degrade the prediction accuracy and hinder the application of Web service recommendation.

Different from QoS ratings which are explicitly contributed by users, region information is implicitly existed in every rating-based system. Let $URC = \{LonLat_u, AS_u, Country_u\}$ and $SRC = \{Provider_s, AS_s, Country_s\}$ denote the region contexts of user and service, respectively, where $LonLat_u, AS_u, Country_u$ be a set of users in the same longitude and latitude($LonLat$), autonomous system[2] (AS) and country, respectively; $Provider_s, AS_s, Country_s$ be a set of services belonging to the same provider, autonomous system and country, respectively. Figure 1 shows the elements relation of region contexts URC and SRC: $LonLat_u \subseteq AS_u \subseteq Country_u$, $Provider_s \subseteq AS_s \subseteq Country_s$.

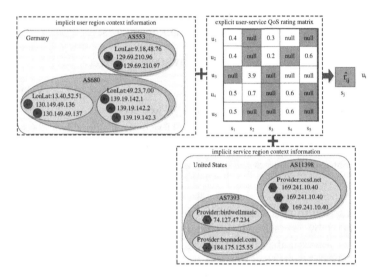

Fig. 1. Leveraging explicit QoS ratings and implicit region context for Web service QoS prediction

It is nature to assume that users with smaller region, such as in Fig. 1 u_1 and u_2 are in the same $LonLat$, will have a more similar QoS experiences on the Web services they co-invoked. This is true because users in the same $LonLat$ share the same network facilities. Moreover, services with smaller region, such as s_1 and s_2 belong to the same service provider, will give a more similar QoS performances to users as they share the same server load. Therefore, we argue that region context contains complementary information and motivates us to capture the significant influence of region context to support more accurate QoS prediction.

With the notations and motivations above, our problem can be stated as: given the known QoS ratings in R and the implicit region contexts including user region context URC and service region context SRC. We aim to predict

---

[2] An autonomous system (AS) is a collection of connected Internet protocol routing prefixes under the control of one or more network operators on behalf of a single administrative entity or domain that presents a common.

the unknown QoS values by using the explicit known QoS ratings in R and implicit user and service region contexts $\{URC, SRC\}$.

2.2 Observations

We collect publicly available real-world dataset WSDream for this study [14]. It contains 1,974,675 response time records collected by 339 users from 31 countries on 5,825 web services from 74 countries. Country information are collected in the dataset, while user *LonLat* and *AS* information, service *Provider* and *AS* information are not available, so we adopted an IP2Location[3] service to identify these missing region information for the purpose of prediction. Some statistics of WSDream dataset are shown in Table 1, where *AS* information of 938 Web services are not identified due to the failure of 817 $WSDLs$ to IP address conversion and 121 IPs are not recorded in the known ASs.

Table 1. Statistics of WSDream dataset

User	Value	Web service	Value
Num. of users	339	Num. of web services	5,825
Num. of user *LonLats*	159	Num. of web service providers	2,699
Num. of user *ASs*	137	Num. of web service *ASs*	1,032
Num. of user Countries	31	Num. of web service countries	74

The motivation in this study is that users'/services' QoS ratings are similar to or influenced by users/services that they are regionally related to. In this subsection, we investigate the influences of region contexts via studying the correlation between users/services and their corresponding region neighborhood. Specifically, with user and service region contexts $\{URC, SRC\}$, we ask the two questions: (1) Are users/services have the abilities to cluster a specified number of region neighbors? (2) Are users/services within smaller region more similar in terms of their region neighbors' ratings?

To answer the first question, we first give the definition of region neighbor. Let LN_u, AN_u, CN_u and PN_s, AN_s, CN_s be the set of neighbors of user u and service s at their corresponding region contexts URC and SRC, where $LN_u = \{\forall v | v \in LonLat_u\}$, $ANu = \{\forall v | v \in AS_u \wedge v \notin LonLat_u\}$, $CN_u = \{\forall v | v \in Country_u \wedge u \notin AS_u\}$, and $PN_s = \{\forall t | t \in Provider_s\}$, $AN_s = \{\forall t | t \in AN_s \wedge t \notin Provider_s\}$, $CN_s = \{\forall t | t \in Country_s \wedge t \notin AN_s\}$. Based on the definitions, the region neighbors of user u_1 in Fig. 1 can be clustered as: $LN_{u_1} = \{u_2\}, AN_{u_1} = \{u_3, u_4, u_5\}, CN_{u_1} = \{u_6, u_7\}$.

We conduct statistical distribution of users and services with different number of region neighbors, and Fig. 2 plots the statistical results. It can be found that the larger region scope, the more possibility to cluster the specified number of region neighbors, such as in *Country* region, the proportion of users and services

---

[3] https://www.ip2location.com.

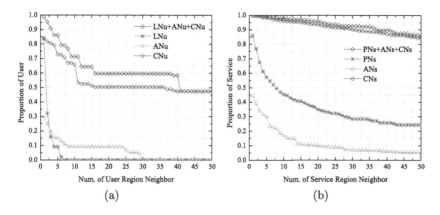

Fig. 2. Distribution of user and service with different number of region neighbors

having 30 neighbors is about 50% and 90% respectively, which is higher than the other region contexts. Moreover, by combining different region contexts, most users and services have the ability to obtain their region neighbors. Thus, the results from Fig. 2 suggest a positive answer with Observation 1 to the first question.

Observation 1. *Users and services have the abilities to obtain the specified number of region neighbors, and the larger region scope, the more likelihood of obtaining the specified number of region neighbors.*

For the second question, we want to investigate whether users and services are positively correlated with their region neighbors. In this work, we adopt the widely used Pearson Correlation Coefficient (PCC) similarity of users' and services' rating vector to measure their rating similarity [15]. With PCC, we calculate the similarity for each user/service and his region neighbors, and use the average PCC to evaluate correlation between them. For example, with the similarity $PCC(u,v)$ of user u and v, $v \in LN_u$, the average PCC of region neighbors is calculated as: $Avg.PCC(LN_u) = \frac{1}{|LN_u|} \sum_{v \in LN_u} PCC(u,v)$, which indicates the overall correlation of user u and his $LonLat$ region neighbors LN_u.

Since the distribution of users and services is decrease with the increasing of region neighbors. We vary the number of neighbor from 0 to 50 under different region contexts, and Fig. 3(a) and (b) plot the average PCC of users and services with different number of region neighbor, respectively. We observe that the average PCC of users/services and their region neighbors is 0.52 and 0.3, respectively, indicating that the QoS ratings of users and services are positively correlated with their region neighbors. Moreover, the smaller region scope, the higher average PCC. This suggests us that when modeling region context, we should give priority to more local region neighbors. With the above analysis, we have Observation 2.

Observation 2. *With smaller region scope, users' and services' rating are more correlated with their region neighbors, and vice versa.*

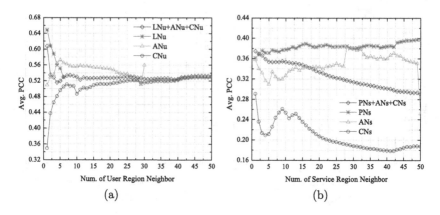

Fig. 3. Average of users and services PCC with different number of region neighbors

Positive observations to both questions provide the evidence of the significance of region contexts. With the verification of underlying relationship of region contexts and QoS ratings, we are ready study how to exploit the region context to alleviate the concerned data sparsity challenge in QoS prediction.

3 Our Method

3.1 Baseline Predictor

Our previous research demonstrates that Web service QoS data exhibit large user and Web service effects [16]. Specifically, some users tend to perceive higher response time than others due to the poor network while some Web services tend to perform lower response time than others due to the less server load. Thus, in order to adjust the QoS data by accounting for these effects, we suggest a baseline predictor. It estimates an unknown rating $\hat{r}_{0u,s}$ and accounts for user and service effects as follow.

$$\hat{r}_{0u,s} = b_a + b_u + b_s \tag{1}$$

where b_a is the global average of all ratings in matrix R, b_u and b_s represent the observed biases of u and s from average, respectively. To estimate b_u and b_s, we can solve the following optimization problem.

$$\ell = min\frac{1}{2}\sum_{u=1}^{m}\sum_{s=1}^{n}I_{u,s}(r_{u,s} - \hat{r}_{0u,s})^2 + \frac{\lambda_1}{2}\|b_u\|_F^2 + \frac{\lambda_2}{2}\|b_s\|_F^2 \tag{2}$$

where $I_{u,s}$ plays as an indicator which is equal to 1 when u has interacted with s, and is equal to 0 otherwise. $\|\|_F^2$ denotes the Frobenius norm. The first term in Eq. (2) tries to adjust bu and bs close to the real rating, and the other two regularization terms are added to avoid the over-fitting problem. Considering these effects is effective to improve prediction accuracy in our later experiments.

3.2   Matrix Factorization

Before modeling region context, we adopt a state-of-the-art prediction method based Matrix Factorization (MF) as our basic model. The idea behind MF is that user QoS rating behaviors are influenced by a reduced latent features and it performs a low-rank MF on matrix R. Let $p_u \in \mathbb{R}^{d \times m}$ and $q_s \in \mathbb{R}^{d \times n}$ denotes user and service feature vector respectively, for the missing rating $\hat{r}_{1u,s} = p_u^T q_s$, low-rank MF strives to make $\hat{r}_{1u,s}$ as close as possible to the ground truth $r_{u,s}$ by minimizing the following objective function.

$$\ell = min \frac{1}{2} \sum_{u=1}^{m} \sum_{s=1}^{n} I_{u,s}(r_{u,s} - \hat{r}_{1u,s})^2 + \frac{\lambda_3}{2} \|p_u\|_F^2 + \frac{\lambda_4}{2} \|q_s\|_F^2 \qquad (3)$$

There are several advantages of MF method [17]. (1) data sparsity issue can be alleviated by factorizing the user-service rating matrix, it allows to obtain meaningful relations between pairs of users or services, even though these users have invoked different services, or these services were accessed by different users; (2) MF can be solved by a simple optimization problem and a local optimal solution can be found by an gradient based method; (3) MF is extensible and enables us to integrate other meaningful sources of side information, such as user and service region contexts in the following subsection.

3.3   Modeling User Region Context Influence

The region context of user perspective reveals the rating correlation of users and their region neighborhood. The observations in Subsect. 2.2 suggest that users are able to cluster a specified number of positively correlated region neighbors. With user region context, users with closer region scope are more likely to have similar QoS experiences. Specifically, the QoS experience of a user u is influenced by the region neighbors that are in the same region area. Thus, the feature vector of u can be defined as a combination of the feature vectors p_v to the region neighbors RN_u of u.

$$\hat{p}_u = |RN_u|^{-\frac{1}{2}} \sum_{v \in RN_u} p_v \quad \hat{r}_{2u,s} = \hat{p}_u^T q_s = (|RN_u|^{-\frac{1}{2}} \sum_{v \in RN_u} p_v)^T q_s \qquad (4)$$

The combination for $\hat{p}_u$ is based on the fact that similar users will capture similar latent features, consequently transferring the knowledge from user region neighbors. Equation (4) indicates how the user region context is modeled in MF, and region neighbor RN determines whom are used to build the model. Observation 2 shows that users in smaller region have more positive correlation with their neighbors, and the neighbor selection order is suggested as follows: $LonLat$, AS and $Country$. Thus, region neighbors RN_u of u can be clustered as:

$$RN(u) = \begin{cases} \{v|v \in K_l(LN_u)\} & if \; |LN_u| \geq UK \\ \{v|v \in LN_u + K_a(AN_u)\} & if \; |LN_u| \leq UK \wedge |PN_u| + |AN_u| \geq UK \\ \{v|v \in LN_u + AN_u + K_c(CN_u)\} & otherwise \end{cases}$$

$$(5)$$

where UK denotes the number of user u's region neighbors.

3.4 Modeling Service Region Context Influence

The service side region context reveals the rating correlation of services and their region neighborhood. Previous observations also show that services' region context have a positive relationship with QoS ratings, so we adopt a similar method like the modeling of user context to capture the influence of service region context. Similarly, the feature vector of s can be defined as a combination of feature vectors q_t to the region neighbors RN_s of s.

$$\hat{q}_s = |RN_s|^{-\frac{1}{2}} \sum_{t \in RN_s} q_t \quad \hat{r}_{3u,s} = p_u^T \hat{q}_s = p_u^T (|RN_s|^{-\frac{1}{2}} \sum_{t \in RN_s} q_t) \tag{6}$$

The clustering method of region neighbors RN_s is suggested as follows:

$$RN(s) = \begin{cases} \{t | t \in K_p(PN_s)\} & if \ |PN_s| \geq SK \\ \{t | t \in PN_s + K_a(AN_s)\} & if \ |PN_s| \leq UK \wedge |PN_s| + |AN_s| \geq SK \\ \{t | t \in PN_s + AN_s + K_c(CN_s)\} & otherwise \end{cases} \tag{7}$$

where SK denotes the number of service s's region neighbors.

3.5 Ensemble Method

In the above subsections, we introduce our solutions to consider the bias effects and to model region contexts mathematically. With these solutions, we proposed an ensemble method REMF by leveraging bias information and region context systematically. The basic idea of REMF is that users/services with a same region context should have similar QoS experience/performance, and an unknown rating $\hat{r}_{u,s}$ can be predicted as a linear combination of ratings from the baseline predictor, MF and region neighbors aware methods.

$$\hat{r}_{u,s} = \alpha \hat{r}_{0u,s} + \beta \hat{r}_{1u,s} + \gamma \hat{r}_{2u,s} + \theta \hat{r}_{3u,s} \quad \alpha + \beta + \gamma + \theta = 1 \tag{8}$$

In Eq. (8), the first term is the bias effect, the second term is basic MF, and the last two terms are the influences of user and service region contexts. Here, we suggest a unified ensemble model REMF that improves prediction accuracy by capitalizing on the advantages of bias, neighborhood and latent feature methods. REMF is a post-processing method that user and service bias effects, region information and latent feature information are built systematically, rather than a simple combination of pre-processing factorization results. To factorize the assemble model, we aim to solve the following problem.

$$\ell = min \frac{1}{2} \sum_{u=1}^{m} \sum_{s=1}^{n} I_{u,s}(r_{u,s} - \hat{r}_{u,s})^2 + \frac{\lambda}{2}(|S_u|^{-\frac{1}{2}} \|b_u\|_F^2 + |U_s|^{-\frac{1}{2}} \|b_s\|_F^2 +$$
$$|S_u|^{-\frac{1}{2}} \|p_u\|_F^2 + |U_s|^{-\frac{1}{2}} \|q_s\|_F^2 + \sum_{v \in RN_u} |S_v|^{-\frac{1}{2}} \|p_v\|_F^2 + \sum_{t \in RN_s} |U_t|^{-\frac{1}{2}} \|q_t\|_F^2) \tag{9}$$

where S_u be a set of services invoked by user u, and U_s be a set of users who access service s. RN_u and RN_s be a set of region neighbors clustered by Eqs. (5) and (7), respectively.

The gradients of ℓ with respect to variables in set $Para =$ $\{b_u, b_s, p_u, q_s, RN_u, RN_s\}$ are:

$$\nabla b_u = -\alpha e_{u,s} + \lambda |S_u|^{-\frac{1}{2}} b_u \tag{10}$$

$$\nabla b_s = -\alpha e_{u,s} + \lambda |U_s|^{-\frac{1}{2}} b_s \tag{11}$$

$$\nabla p_u = -e_{u,s}(\beta q_s + \theta(|RN_s|^{-\frac{1}{2}} \sum_{t \in RN_s} q_t)) + \lambda |S_u|^{-\frac{1}{2}} p_u \tag{12}$$

$$\nabla q_s = -e_{u,s}(\beta p_u + \gamma(|RN_u|^{-\frac{1}{2}} \sum_{v \in RN_u} p_v)) + \lambda |U_s|^{-\frac{1}{2}} q_s \tag{13}$$

$$\forall v \in RN_u : \nabla p_v = -e_{u,s}\gamma |RN_u|^{-\frac{1}{2}} q_s + \lambda |S_v|^{-\frac{1}{2}} p_v \tag{14}$$

$$\forall t \in RN_s : \nabla q_t = -e_{u,s}\theta |RN_s|^{-\frac{1}{2}} p_u + \lambda |U_t|^{-\frac{1}{2}} q_t \tag{15}$$

where $e_{u,s} = r_{u,s} - \hat{r}_{u,s}$. An optimal solution of the objective function ℓ in Eq. (9) can be obtained by an stochastic gradient descent method, which iterates every non-*null* ratings in matrix R until convergence. The detailed algorithm is shown in Algorithm 1.

Algorithm 1. The proposed region context aware matrix factorization REMF

Input: rating matrix R, the region neighbor RN; parameters UK, SK, lr, d;

Output: user bias feature vector B_u, service bias feature vector B_s, user feature matrix U, service feature matrix S, user neighbor feature matrix UN, service neighbor feature matrix SN;

1: Initialize b_u, b_s, U, S, UN, SN randomly;
2: **while** not convergent **do**
3:    Calculate $\nabla b_u, \nabla b_s, \nabla p_u, \nabla q_s$;
4:    Update $b_u = b_u - lr\nabla b_u$;
5:    Update $b_s = b_s - lr\nabla b_s$;
6:    Update $p_u = p_u - lr\nabla p_u$;
7:    Update $q_s = q_s - lr\nabla q_s$;
8:    **for** each non-empty $v \in RN_u$ **do**
9:       calculate ∇p_v;
10:       Update $p_v = p_v - lr\nabla p_v$;
11:    **end for**
12:    **for** each non-empty $t \in RN_s$ **do**
13:       calculate ∇q_t;
14:       Update $q_t = q_t - lr\nabla q_t$;
15:    **end for**
16: **end while**

Algorithm 1 first initializes model parameters randomly. Then an iteration procedure is loaded for learning. Parameter lr is the learning rate that controls the speed of iteration. After learning all parameters, the unknown QoS ratings can be predicted with Eq. (8).

4   Experiments

In this section, we conduct experiments to answer the followings questions: (1) how does the proposed method REMF perform compared to the well-known predictors in both warm-start situation and cold-start situations? (2) how do the user region and service region contexts affect the prediction accuracy of REMF? (3) what is the impact of region neighborhood size? (4) how is the efficiency of REMF?

4.1   Experimental Settings

Publicly dataset WSDream is adopted and we choose response time QoS attribute to evaluate our proposed method, the region information are extracted by an IP2Location service. Some statistics of the dataset are presented in Table 1. In practical, the user-service QoS matrix R is very sparse, thus we choose $x\%$ ratings as the origin data to training the data and the remaining $1 - x\%$ as the testing data to predict. In the following experiment, x is conducted as 2.5, 5, 7.5, 10.

Two well-known metrics, Mean Absolute Error (MAE) and Root Mean Square Error (RMSE), are adopted to evaluate the prediction performance. The metric MAE is defined as:

$$MAE = \frac{1}{N} \sum |r_{u,s} - \hat{r}_{u,s}| \tag{16}$$

where N is the number of ratings in the testing set. RMSE is defined as:

$$RMSE = \sqrt{\frac{1}{N} \sum |r_{u,s} - \hat{r}_{u,s}|^2} \tag{17}$$

A smaller RMSE or MAE value means better performance. Note that previous work demonstrated that small improvement in RMSE or MAE terms can have a significant impact on the quality of the top-k recommendation [18].

We estimate the latent factors of REMF with Algorithm 1 and use a learned model for QoS prediction. We use training data to estimate REMF's parameters and select the one provide the optimal results. Table 2 presents the parameters used to make prediction.

4.2   Comparison of Different Predictor

In this section, we compare our REMF with various representative prediction methods as follows: GMEAN, UMEAN, IMEAN, UPCC, IPCC, WSRec [7], MF [15], NIMF [9] and Colbar [10]. GMEAN employs the global average to make

Table 2. Experimental parameter settings

λ	lt	α	β	γ	θ	UK	SK	Dimensionality d	Num. of iteration
0.02	0.012	0.1	0.3	0.3	0.3	10	20	11	17

prediction, which is equals to b_a in baseline predictor. UMEAN and IMEAN employ the mean QoS value of user and service as results respectively. UPCC, IPCC, WSRec are the neighborhood based CF, UPCC and IPCC use the similar neighbors of users and services to make collaborative prediction, respectively, and WSRec is the combination of them. MF conducts a basic matrix factorization on the QoS matrix, and NIMF extend MF by incorporating user neighborhood information, both of them can be realized through REMF by setting $\alpha = 0, \beta = 1, \gamma = 0, \theta = 0$ and $\alpha = 0, \beta = 0.5, \gamma = 0.5, \theta = 0$, respectively. Colbar integrates user location-aware neighbors in MF and make prediction by fusing the results of basic MF and Extended MF.

Tables 3 and 4 illustrates the compared results under $warm - start$ scenario (each user invokes at least one service, and each service has been accessed at least once) and $cold - start$ scenario (there exist 34 $cold - start$ users who do not invoke any services and 583 $cold - start$ services that do not accessed by

Table 3. Comparisons in warm-start scenario

Metric	MAE				RMSE			
Density	2.5%	5%	7.5%	10%	2.5%	5%	7.5%	10%
GMEAN	1.1099	1.0466	1.0258	1.0191	1.9758	1.9691	1.9676	1.9652
UMEAN	0.8686	0.8680	0.8703	0.8725	1.8565	1.8552	1.8527	1.8505
IMEAN	0.8666	0.7649	0.7245	0.7152	1.6680	1.5731	1.5487	1.5358
UPCC	0.7148	0.6948	0.6836	0.6712	1.5668	1.4966	1.4697	1.4209
IPCC	0.7180	0.7142	0.7074	0.6963	1.6059	1.5298	1.5032	1.4520
WSRec	0.7040	0.5999	0.5478	0.5265	1.5140	1.3618	1.3202	1.2925
MF	0.7389	0.6470	0.6358	0.5777	1.9502	1.6088	1.4379	1.3534
NIMF	0.6996	0.5584	0.5143	0.4953	1.5796	1.3523	1.2858	1.2415
Colbar	0.6720	0.5449	0.5136	0.4914	1.4790	1.3232	1.2691	1.2338
REMF	**0.6328**	**0.5320**	**0.5016**	**0.4805**	**1.4277**	**1.2812**	**1.2351**	**1.1995**

Table 4. Comparisons in cold-start scenario

Metric	MAE				RMSE			
Density	2.5%	5%	7.5%	10%	2.5%	5%	7.5%	10%
GMEAN	1.1071	1.0432	1.0424	1.0130	1.9752	1.9696	1.9648	1.9690
MF	0.7528	0.6824	0.6424	0.5977	1.7910	1.6770	1.5025	1.4912
REMF	**0.6645**	**0.5772**	**0.5374**	**0.5219**	**1.5851**	**1.4188**	**1.3650**	**1.3146**

any users), respectively. Observing from the above results we have the following observations: (1) REMF consistently obtains the lowest MAE and RMSE under all settings, especially compared with NIMF and Colbar, REMF obtains better results than them, this is because of the incorporating of service neighbors under region context. These demonstrate that exploiting region contexts can significantly improve prediction performance. (2) The accuracy of REMF is increased along with the increasing of matrix density. The major reason is that much more QoS rating data can afford more information on learning a more accurate model, which suggests us encouraging users to share their observed QoS rating to UDDI for better prediction. (3) In the pure $cold - start$ scenario, only GMEAN and MF methods can work, and the proposed REMF outperforms the compared methods. The average performance of REMF is reduced by 7.31% and 10.43% in terms of MAE and RMSE which is acceptable in practice.

With the above observations, we can answer the first question: by capturing the influence of region contexts, the proposed method is superior to other methods and alleviates the data-sparsity issue with better accuracy.

4.3 Impact of Assemble Weights

Assemble weights α, β, γ and θ are used to balance the effects of bias information, latent factor, user region context and service region context. To investigate the impact of these assemble weights, we train them with 6 combinations under different matrix densities and the results are shown in Table 5.

Table 5. Impact of assemble weights

Metric	MAE				RMSE			
Density	2.5%	5%	7.5%	10%	2.5%	5%	7.5%	10%
$\alpha = 1, \beta = 0, \gamma = 0, \theta = 0$	0.6693	0.6107	0.5519	0.5162	1.4654	1.3553	1.2904	1.2481
$\alpha = 0, \beta = 1, \gamma = 0, \theta = 0$	0.6934	0.6690	0.5904	0.5164	1.8603	1.5337	1.3812	1.2837
$\alpha = 0, \beta = 0, \gamma = 1, \theta = 0$	0.6904	0.6144	0.5790	0.5435	1.5930	1.4505	1.3807	1.3101
$\alpha = 0, \beta = 0, \gamma = 0, \theta = 1$	0.7668	0.6432	0.6059	0.5559	1.6747	1.3997	1.3581	1.2692
$\alpha = 0.25, \beta = 0.25, \gamma = 0.25, \theta = 0.25$	0.6192	0.5317	0.5006	0.4818	1.4241	1.2875	1.2383	1.1992
$\alpha = 0.1, \beta = 0.3, \gamma = 0.3, \theta = 0.3$	**0.6180**	**0.5309**	**0.4968**	**0.4767**	**1.4127**	**1.2775**	**1.2361**	**1.1960**

It is observed in Table 5 that the last 2 combinations have a relatively better performance compared with the first 4 combinations, which illustrates that users' and services' bias information and region context will all contribute positive influences to improve prediction performance. This shows the effectiveness of our assemble method and also explains why we choose $\alpha = 0.1, \beta = 0.3, \gamma = 0.3, \theta = 0.3$ in our experiment settings.

4.4   Impact of Neighborhood Size UK and SK

Parameters UK and SK determine the number of neighbors that will be used to transfer the knowledge from region contexts. When UK and SK are at near-zero values, REMF is thus degenerated to a basic MF model with biases. On the other hand, when UK and SK are set to be very large values, this indicates region contexts are fully considered in REMF. Table 6 shows the experimental results of REMF with different number of UK and SK.

Table 6. Impact of neighborhood size

Density	SK	MAE			RMSE			Time/Iteration (unit: s)		
		UK = 0	UK = 10	UK = 20	UK = 0	UK = 10	UK = 20	UK = 0	UK = 10	UK = 20
5%	0	*0.6648*	0.6343	0.6368	*0.5016*	0.4966	0.4954	*0.6300*	1.8171	2.7681
	10	0.6151	0.6176	0.6139	0.4934	0.4922	0.4916	2.0631	3.1700	4.1732
	20	0.6189	**0.6174**	0.6143	0.4934	**0.4921**	0.492	3.5102	**4.5630**	5.6463
	30	0.6160	0.6139	0.6139	0.4888	0.4892	0.4917	4.9072	5.9600	7.0034
10%	0	*1.6464*	1.5101	1.5055	*1.2444*	1.2331	1.2353	*1.3260*	3.6262	5.4513
	10	1.4187	1.4176	1.4121	1.2054	1.2033	1.2085	4.0842	6.3753	8.1864
	20	1.4196	**1.4127**	1.4096	1.2055	**1.2027**	1.2016	6.8393	**9.1235**	10.8000
	30	1.4148	1.4086	1.4100	1.2038	1.2021	1.2003	9.5575	11.8606	13.6727

From Table 6, we observe some interesting observations: (1) When UK = SK = 0 without considering region contexts, REMF have a relatively lager MAE and RMSE, and they decrease with the increase of UK and SK. This verifies that incorporating region context in REME can indeed contribute valuable information and improve performance. (2) When UK > 10 and SK > 20, varying UK and SK has little improvement on accuracy under different matrix density, and the accuracy even starts to fluctuate because too many neighbors may conclude lower correlated neighbors that will introduce noise and do harm for the performance. (3) More neighbors mean more computation time, the configuration, UK = 10, SK = 20, gives us an acceptable prediction accuracy and computation time, thus we set UK = 10, SK = 20 in the other experiments.

4.5   Efficiency Analysis

The theoretical time complexity of REMF is mainly based on the learning of $Para = \{b_u, b_s, p_u, q_s, RN_u, RN_s\}$, which is $O(d * |R| * K)$, where d is the number of latent feature, K is the max value of UK and SK, $K = max(UK, SK)$. Due to d and $K \ll |R|$, REMF is scalable and linear with respect to the number of observed QoS in matrix R. To evaluate the efficiency our proposed approach, we conduct experiments to study the average time per iteration in compared methods. The experiment results are shown in Table 7.

Table 7 shows that MF requires the least time in one iteration, NIMF and Colbor need about 2 s for each iteration when density is 10%, and our REMF

Table 7. Average time/iteration comparisons (unit: s)

Density	MF	NIMF	Colbor	REMF
5%	0.0630	1.0170	1.0930	4.4925
10%	0.1270	2.0351	2.1431	9.0148

obtains the largest computation time in one iteration. This because REMF integrates not only 10 user neighbors but also 20 service neighbors, while MF does not consider any neighbor information and NIMF and Colbor incorporate 10 user neighbors without considering service side information. The more neighbors mean the longer training time to learn these latent features. Note that experimental results show that there is higher predication accuracy of REMF than other methods in both warm-start and cold-start case. This shows a tradeoff between collaborative neighbors (accuracy) and efficiency.

Fortunately, Fig. 4 shows the performance of REMF with the number of iteration varying from 1 to 27. It is observed that both MAE and RMSE decrease with the increasing number of iteration, and arrives at a convergence when iteration number is about 17. The results reflect REMF have a fast convergence speed and good performance. It is worth noting in Table 7 when density = 10% the average time for one iteration is 9.0148 s, thus the overall leaning time of REMF is no more than 3 min. This indicates that REMF is applicable in practice.

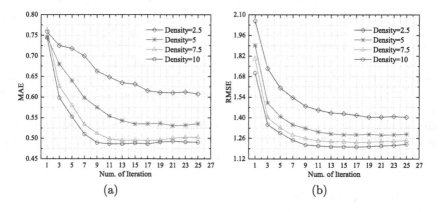

(a)   (b)

Fig. 4. Performance with different number of iteration

5   Conclusions and Future Work

This paper proposed a novel Web service QoS prediction approach by capturing region context influence, which makes contribution to alleviate the data sparsity issue with the following conclusions. (1) Publicly real-world Web service QoS data analysis shows that there exists a positive rating correlating between users/services and their region neighborhoods, which suggests that region context contains complementary information and provides necessary technical support for QoS prediction. (2) Our proposed method systematically integrates region contexts from both user and service sides into a unified model, which provides an effective solution for alleviating data sparsity issue and cold-start issue. (3) Comprehensive experimental results show that region context can efficiently and significantly improve the performance of Web service QoS prediction. For future research, we intend to further improve the proposed method by considering other relevant context such as social and time information.

Acknowledgements. This work is supported by National Natural Science Foundation of China (61272466, 61300193), Hebei Provincial Natural Science Foundation (F2016203290) and Colleges and Universities in Hebei Province Science and Technology Research Project (QN2016073).

References

1. Zhang, L., Zhang, J., Cai, H.: Services Computing. Springer & Tsinghua University Press, Beijing (2007)
2. Angelov, S., Grefen, P.: The business case for B2B e-contracting. In: Proceedings of the 6th International Conference on Electronic Commerce, pp. 31–40. ACM, New York (2004)
3. Moghaddam, M., Davis, J.G.: Service selection in web service composition: a comparative review of existing approaches. In: Bouguettaya, A., Sheng, Q.Z., Daniel, F. (eds.) Handbook on Web Services: Web Services Foundations, pp. 321–346. Springer, New York (2014)
4. Papazoglou, M.P., Traverso, P., Dustdar, S., Leymann, F.: Service-oriented computing: state of the art and research challenges. IEEE Comput. **40**(11), 38–45 (2007)
5. Ran, S.: A model for web services discovery with QoS. ACM SIGecomExchanges **4**(1), 1–10 (2003)
6. Shao, L., Zhang, J., Wei, Y.: Personalized QoS prediction for web service via collaborative filtering. In: Proceedings of IEEE Conference on Web Services, Salt Lake City, pp. 439–446. IEEE (2007)
7. Zheng, Z., Ma, H., Lyu, M.R.: QoS-aware web service recommendation by collaborative filtering. IEEE Trans. Serv. Comput. **4**(5), 140–152 (2011)
8. Wu, J., Chen, L., Feng, Y., Zheng, Z.: Predicting quality of service for selection by neighborhood-based collaborative filtering. IEEE Trans. Syst. Man Cybern. Syst. **43**(2), 428–439 (2013)
9. Zheng, Z., Ma, H., Lyu, M.R., King, I.: Collaborative web service QoS prediction via neighborhood integrated matrix factorization. IEEE Trans. Serv. Comput. **6**(3), 289–299 (2013)
10. Yin, J., Lo, W., Deng, S., Li, Y., Wu, Z., Xiong, N.: Colbar: a collaborative location-based regularization framework for QoS prediction. Inf. Sci. **265**, 68–84 (2014)
11. Tang, M., Jiang, Y., Liu, J., Liu, X.: Location-aware collaborative filtering for QoS-based service recommendation. In: Proceedings of the 19th International Conference on Web Services, Miami, pp. 202–209. IEEE (2012)
12. E, H., Tong, J., Song, M., Song, J.: QoS prediction algorithm used in location-aware hybrid web service. J. China Univ. Posts Telecommun. **22**(1), 42–49 (2015)

13. Yu, C., Huang, L.: A web service QoS prediction approach based on time- and location-aware collaborative filtering. SOCA **10**(2), 135–149 (2016)
14. Zheng, Z., Zhang, Y., Lyu, M.R.: Distributed QoS evaluation for real-world web services. In: Proceedings of the 8th International Conference on Web Services, Miami, pp. 83–90. IEEE (2010)
15. Benesty, J., Chen, J., Huang, Y.: Pearson correlation coefficient. In: Benesty, J., Chen, J., Huang, Y., Cohen, I. (eds.) Noise Reduction in Speech Processing, vol. 2(2), pp. 1–4. Springer, Heidelberg (2009)
16. Shen, L., Chen, Z., Li, F.: Service selection approach considering the uncertainty of QoS data. Comput. Integr. Manuf. Syst. **19**(10), 2652–2663 (2013)
17. Menon, A.K., Elkan, C.: Link prediction via matrix factorization. In: Gunopulos, D., Hofmann, T., Malerba, D., Vazirgiannis, M. (eds.) ECML PKDD 2011. LNCS, vol. 6912, pp. 437–452. Springer, Heidelberg (2011). doi:10.1007/978-3-642-23783-6_28
18. Koren, Y.: Factorization meets the neighborhood: a multifaceted collaborative filtering model. In: Proceedings of the 14th ACM SIGKDD, pp. 426–434. ACM, New York (2008)

A Participant Selection Method
for Crowdsensing Under an Incentive Mechanism

Wei Shen[1($\boxtimes$)], Shu Li[1], Jun Yang[1], Wanchun Dou[1], and Qiang Ni[2]

[1] State Key Laboratory for Novel Software Technology,
Nanjing University, Nanjing, China
shenwei0917@126.com, shuli@smail.nju.edu.cn, yangjun1210@163.com,
douwc@nju.edu.cn
[2] InfoLab21, School of Computing and Communications,
Lancaster University, Lancashire, UK
q.ni@lancaster.ac.uk

Abstract. With the rich set of embedded sensors installed in smartphones, a novel applications is emerged, i.e., Mobile Crowdsensing (MCS). Generally speaking, in a MCS application, each participant often gets equal reward. In some situations, this assumption is unfair for some valuable participants. With this observation, a novel framework is investigated in this paper with an incentive mechanism, instead of assuming that each participant should get equal reward. As a result, our method is validated by experiment enabled by real-life datasets.

Keywords: Mobile crowdsensing · Participant selection

1 Introduction

Nowadays, there is an increasing demand to retrieve the information of real-time air quality, noise level, speed of mobile network, etc. With this observation, Mobile Crowdsensing (MCS) is becoming a popular alternative technique to collect the time-sensitive and location-dependent information [5–7]. In a MCS application, a smart phone plays as a mobile sensor, which could display time-sensitive and location-sensitive information in a real-time way. In a MCS application, participant recruitment is a key issue. For achieving more and more information, participant should be attracted with a certain incentive mechanism. For example, in many MCS application, incentives are paid for attracting more and more volunteers to collect more and more information. On the other hand, a MCS application is often promoted with a certain budget. The total cost of a MCS system limited the scale of the participants. For example, in [9,10], some methods is presented, aiming at selecting a small number of participants to minimize the total cost in a MCS system. With these observations, we could find that it is a challenge to balance the budget and the scale of participants in a trade off way. Moreover, with certain budget, it is another challenge to set up an incentive mechanism. This incentive mechanism could lead the participants

© ICST Institute for Computer Sciences, Social Informatics and Telecommunications Engineering 2017
S. Wang and A. Zhou (Eds.): CollaborateCom 2016, LNICST 201, pp. 557–562, 2017.
DOI: 10.1007/978-3-319-59288-6_54

to cover all the area in an expected distributed way, which a MCS application system is interested. In view of this challenge, in this paper, a participant selection method is presented aims at trading off the relationship between the budget and the scale of participants in an expected distributed way. To the best of our knowledge, there is few works that consider these issues in a comprehensive way.

The rest of this paper is organized as follows. In Sect. 2, we present the system framework and define the problem. In Sect. 3, a two stage algorithm is designed to select participants. Section 4 experiment and evaluation are investigated. In Sect. 5, related works are discussed. Section 6 concludes the paper.

2   Problem Formulation and System Framework

2.1   System Model

Suppose that there is a continuous sensing task in our MCS system. In addition, there are a certain amount of participants which we denote $\mathbf{U}$ and their history trace information denoted by set $\mathbf{D}$ over a period of time. Our platform should divides this task into many sub-tasks, allocates each participant some sub-tasks and fairly give each participant rewards. After the completion of a sensing task, the smartphone returns the sensing data back to the platform which then manipulates the data and at last, forward the information to users. For a sub-task allocated to a participant, he may fail to complete. Therefore, we would allocate a sub-task to many participants to insure a low fail probability in a sensing area which we call it Probabilistic Coverage Constraint.

Before formally defining the problem of the sensing task allocation, we first introduce some notations defined as followed.

Definition 1 (Sensing Task). *In our MCS system, we divide our sensing task into N sensing area during T sensing circle, which we denote a sub-task in $j-th$ sensing area during $k-th$ sensing circle as H_{jk}.*

Definition 2 (Probabilistic Coverage Constraint (PCC)). *In our system, we would allocate a sub-task in a H_{jk} to some participants. For obtaining accurate information in it, we need control a maximum fail probability C_{jk} which all selected participants fail to complete this task. Therefore, in a H_{jk}, we need satisfy the constraint*

$$1 - \prod_{i=1}^{|S|}(1 - P_{i,j,k}) \geq C_{jk} \tag{1}$$

where $P_{i,j,k}$ is the probability the i-th participant fail to complete sensing task in H_{jk}.

Definition 3 (Adjoint Set). *If a sensing area of a H_{jk} is adjacent to another one $H_{\hat{j}\hat{k}}$, we call they are adjoint denoted as $\simeq$. Hence, a set $\mathbf{A}_j, \{H_{\hat{j}\hat{k}}|H_{jk} \simeq H_{\hat{j}\hat{k}}\}$, is a adjoint set of H_{jk}.*

2.2   Participants Selection Problem Formulation

In our system, we need to select a number of participants denoted by set **S** to help us complete a continuous task. A participant's incentive is consisted of base fees and additional fees which is related to the sub-tasks they complete. Hence, the total incentives in MCS system are

$$F = \sum_{i=1}^{|S|} f + \sum_{i=1}^{|S|} \sum_{j=1}^{N} \sum_{k=1}^{T} v_{jk} \cdot w_{ijk} \qquad (2)$$

where w_{ijk} denote whether the i-th participant upload the information in j-th sensing area during t-th sensing circle.

Our MCS system would minimize the total incentives F while satisfying the Probabilistic Coverage Constraint in each sensing area during all sensing circles. The problem is to find **S** as a subset of **U**, with the objective to

$$\min_{S} E(F), \ s.t. \ Cov_{jk}(|S|) \leq C_{jk} \qquad (3)$$

where $0 \leq j \leq N, 0 \leq k \leq T$ and $Cov_{jk}(|S|)$ is a probability that the participants in **S** complete the sub-task in H_{jk}.

3   Two Stage Algorithm

Participants' selection problem under incentive mechanism is NP-Hard. Because when we set $v_i = 0$, the problem is reduced to the participants' selection problem which has been proved to be NP-hard. In the next section, we use a two-stage algorithm to solve it.

3.1   Two-Stage Approximation Algorithm

Brute-Force Stage. In this stage, we enumerate all $\mathcal{O}(kn_k)$ possible subsets of objects that have up to k objects. Although the combinatorial number is easy to be calculated, the enumeration of a set is not easy. The steps of our algorithm is specified as following. We use a boolean array B to represent the enumeration of all sets. If the i-th value in B is 1, it represents that the $i-$th element in **U** is in this set. (1) We first set the first k elements as 1 in B and meanwhile record it in List L where we store the final enumeration. (2) Then, we find the first 10 sequence in position p in B and transform it to 10. (3) After that, we shift each 1 to right position before position p. Meanwhile, we would store each transformation into L. We repeat these option (2) and (3) till the right k position in B is all 1.

Algorithm 1. Parallel Greedy Stage

Input: L $Prodc_{jk}$
Output: List P_S
1: Initialize Array Q with equation (13) and decreasing it.
2: $P_S = L$.
3: Divide L to $L_1, L_2, ..., L_p$.
4: Do with each L_p on parallel
5: **for** $u = 0$ to $L_p.length$ **do**
6:     **for** $i = 0$ to $Q.length$ **do**
7:         Ergodic each sensing area H_{jk}
8:         $cov_{jk} = Prodc_{jk} * (1 - Q[i].P_{i,j,k})$;
9:         **if** $cov_{jk} > 1$ **then** $flag = 1$;
10:        **end if**
11:        **if** $flag == 0$ **then** $P_S \leftarrow i$;
12:        **end if**
13:    **end for**
14: **end for**

Parallel Greedy Stage. For each subset recruited by the brute-force stage, we use the greedy algorithm to fill up the rest of the "knapsack". In this stage, we design a quality function to help us select the participants.

$$Q(i) = \sum_{j=1}^{N} \sum_{k=1}^{T} \frac{(1 - P_{i,j,k})}{(1 - C_{jk})} * F_i \qquad (4)$$

where $\frac{1-P_{i,j,k}}{1-C_{jk}}$ stands for the ratio that a object occupies the knapsack. Therefore, $Q(i)$ stands for ratio of profit to size or profit density in our algorithm. To each subset calculated in stage 1, we can apply our greedy stage to fill up them on parallel. Therefore, we divide the List L into p sub-lists, $L_1, L_2, ..., L_p$ and respectively run on p physic machines or cores. In Algorithm 1, we specify the procedure of the greedy stage.

4   Evaluation

We evaluate the performance of our algorithms using real-life data traces and experiments. The dataset we used in evaluation is the GeoLife GPS Trajectory dataset, which was collected in (Microsoft Research Asia) Geolife project by 182 users in a period of over three years.

Table 1 specifies the performance comparison between TSA and baseline methods with different F and $E(V_{ij})$. It is easy to find that TSA always selects participants which are paid lower total incentives than other three methods. Although the number of participants selected by TSA is not always lowest in these four methods, the total incentives is lowest. When F is lower than $E(V_{ij})$, the number of participants TSA selects is not least int the four methods. When F is bigger than $E(V_{ij})$, TSA could select the least participant than other three

Table 1. The Performance Comparison between TSA and baseline methods with different F and $E(V_{ij})$

(a) $F = 0$, $E(V_{ij}) = 50$	Number	Cost	(b) $F = 100$, $E(V_{ij}) = 50$	Number	Cost
TSA	125	308.26	TSA	122	12208.70
MaxMin	182	312.29	MaxMin	182	18512.23
MaxCov	120	309.73	MaxCov	120	12309.73
MaxCom	131	310.72	MaxCom	131	136504.57

methods. It is good property that TSA could also solve the original participants selection problem with assumption that each participant should be paid equal as long as we set $E(V_{ij}) = 0$.

In summary, it can be concluded that TSA is better than other three baseline methods. In despite of the slightly long running time, the overall performance of the TSA is pretty good.

5   Related Work

Participant Selection Problem in MCS. In [8], Reddy *et al.* first study the research challenge of participant recruitment in participatory sensing, they propose a coverage-based recruitment strategy to select a predefined number of participants so as to maximize the spatial coverage. More recently, Zhang D propose a novel participants selection framework for mobile crowdsensing, which operate on top of energy-efficient Piggyback Crowdsensing and minimizes incentive payments by selecting a small number of participants while still satisfying PCC.

Incentive Mechanism in MCS. Incentive mechanism is an important research direction [1, 2]. Existing crowdsensing applications and systems lack good incentive mechanisms that can attract more user participation. Game theory has widely been used in incentive mechanism design in MCS systems, which is try to capture and tackle usrs' strategic behaviors. In addition, there are also some studies on designing recruitment/incentive mechanisms for participatory sensing [3, 4].

6   Conclusion

In this paper, we present a novel participant selection framework supporting Mobile Crowdsensing system development. In a MCS, each participant need complete some tasks that the system allocate and accordingly get rewards. Instead of assuming each participant get the same rewards in an MCS, we introduce a incentive mechanisms to evaluate each participant's incentives and then select suitable participants to minimize the total cost in an MCS. Our method is promoted by PG game theory. Experiments validated our method, and in the future, some real Mobile Crowdsensing system will be used to validate our method in a pervasive way.

Acknowledgment. This paper is partially supported by the National Science Foundation of China under Grant No. 91318301 and No. 61672276, the Key Research and Development Project of Jiangsu Province under Grant No. BE2015154, BE2016120, the Collaborative Innovation Center of Novel Software Technology, Nanjing University and the EU FP7 CROWN project under grant number PIRSES-GA-2013-610524.

References

1. Faltings, B., Li, J.J., Jurca, R.: Incentive mechanisms for community sensing. IEEE Trans. Comput. **63**, 115–128 (2014)
2. Fan, Y., Sun, H., Liu, X.: Poster: TRIM: a truthful incentive mechanism for dynamic and heterogeneous tasks in mobile crowdsensing. In: Proceedings of International Conference on Mobile Computing and NETWORKING (2015)
3. Lee, J.S., Hoh, B.: Dynamic pricing incentive for participatory sensing. Trans. Pervasive Mobile Comput. **6**, 693–708 (2010)
4. Lee, J.S., Hoh, B.: Sell your experiences: a market mechanism based incentive for participatory sensing. In: Proceedings of IEEE International Conference on Pervasive Computing and Communications (2010)
5. Lu, Y., Xiang, S., Wu, W., Wu, H.: A queue analytics system for taxi service using mobile crowd sensing. In: Proceedings of the 2015 ACM International Joint Conference on Pervasive and Ubiquitous Computing (2015)
6. Luo, C., Wu, F., Sun, J., Chen, C.W.: Compressive data gathering for large-scale wireless sensor networks. In: Proceedings of International Conference on Mobile Computing and Networking (2009)
7. Man, H.C., Southwell, R., Hou, F., Huang, J.: Distributed time-sensitive task selection in mobile crowdsensing. Transaction on Computer Science (2015)
8. Reddy, S., Estrin, D.: Recruitment framework for participatory sensing data collections. In: Proceedings of Pervasive (2010)
9. Zhang, D., Xiong, H., Wang, L., Chen, G.: CrowdRecruiter: selecting participants for piggyback crowdsensing under probabilistic coverage constraint. In: Proceedings of ACM International Joint Conference on Pervasive and Ubiquitous Computing (2014)
10. Zhao, Q., Zhu, Y., Zhu, H., Cao, J.: Fair energy-efficient sensing task allocation in participatory sensing with smartphones. In: Proceeding of International Conference on Computer (2014)

A Cluster-Based Cooperative Data Transmission in VANETs

Qi Fu[⊠], Anhua Chen, Yunxia Jiang, and Mingdong Tang

School of Computer Science and Engineering, Hunan University of Science and Technology,
Xiangtan, China
jackiefq@163.com, {ahchen,yunxia}@hnust.edu.cn,
tangmingdong@gmail.com

Abstract. Vehicular Ad hoc Networks (VANETs) is designed to have the capability to communicate directly with other vehicles or indirectly using the existing infrastructure. Due to the high-speed mobility of the vehicles, it is a challenging issue to route the messages to their final destination. In this paper, we discuss three relationship of velocity, mobility, relative distance, then a combined Quality of Service (QoS) metric based on them is proposed to meet the clustering requirement. Thereafter, a QoS-aware clustering protocol consisting of cluster head election and multipoints relay selection algorithms is proposed for Vehicle-to-Vehicle (V2V) communication and implemented with ns-2 simulator. Simulation results have confirmed the analysis and expected performance in terms of cluster head duration, packet delivery ratio, etc.

Keywords: Vehicular Ad hoc Networks · Quality of Service · Cluster · Mobility

1 Introduction

VANETs [1] is characterized by a very high mobility that would shorten the network lifetime and cause link failures due to the disconnections of mobile vehicles. Hence, maintaining the stability is a challenging task. Clustering is expected to be one of the most efficient solutions for this issue. In a clustering scheme, vehicle nodes may be assigned a different roles or status, such as cluster-head (CH), cluster-gateway (CG) or cluster-member (CM) [2]. The CH serves as a local coordinator for the creation and maintenance of the cluster, which is responsible for intra-cluster transmission arrangement, data forwarding etc. The CG normally can access neighboring clusters and forward the information with inter-cluster links. The CM usually is an ordinary non-CH node without any inter-cluster links. However, due to the characteristics of VANETs such as high speed, variable density of the nodes, the existing clustering schemes used for conventional MANETs may not be suitable for VANETs.

For efficient vehicle communication, many approaches are designed to form a stable cluster among the vehicles based upon position, destination, density and mobility of the node, QoS requirements, etc. For instance, [3] proposed a position-based and cross-layer-based clustering algorithm using hierarchical and geographical data collection and dissemination mechanism. However, this scheme incurs more communication

© ICST Institute for Computer Sciences, Social Informatics and Telecommunications Engineering 2017
S. Wang and A. Zhou (Eds.): CollaborateCom 2016, LNICST 201, pp. 563–568, 2017.
DOI: 10.1007/978-3-319-59288-6_55

overheads, the infrastructure information is needed. [4] proposed a utility-based clustering scheme. A status message used by utility is periodically sent by all the neighbouring vehicles to form their own CH. However it still applies many fixed parameters in utility, which fails to adapt to dynamics traffic and cluster reorganization. [5] proposed Broadcasting based Distributed Algorithm (BDA) to stabilize the existing clusters. However, all nodes attempt to re-evaluate their conditions by computing utility values at the same time which may cause traffic overhead. [6] proposed a beacon-based clustering model in which the clusters are formed based upon mobility metric and the signal power. However, it does not consider the losses in the wireless channel and the effects of multipath fading. [7] proposed a distributed clustering scheme based on force directed algorithms. According to the current state of the node, each node takes decisions to form and maintain stable clusters. [8] proposed a passive clustering aided protocol, which assesses the suitability of nodes using a multi-metric election strategy. [9] proposed a classical Optimized Link State Routing (OLSR). The basic idea is to elect a CH for each group of neighbor nodes, then the CHs select a set of specialized nodes, named Multi-Points Relay (MPRs), to reduce the overhead of flooding messages by minimizing the duplicate transmissions within the same zone.

2   The CQOLSR Protocol

In this paper, CQOLSR, a QoS-based clustering protocol for V2V communication is proposed and based on several new QoS metrics including the vehicle speed ratio, the rest distance ratio, the average relative mobility and their combined metric. The clustering scheme relies on the cluster-head election and the MPRs selection algorithm based on the stated QoS metrics. In the following, we present the details of the QoS metric and algorithms.

2.1   The QoS Metric

Before discussing the new metric, we suppose that the driving speed and the travelled distance of a vehicle can be obtained with help of the Global Positioning System (GPS) deployed in vehicles. Meanwhile we give the notations description firstly shown in Table 1, and several formulas are also defined based on these symbols.

We introduce three different parameters namely the *speedRatio* (velocity difference ratio), *restDRatio* (rest distance ratio) and *avgRM* (average relative mobility). The *speedRatio* is the velocity ratio of vehicle, which ensures the convergent velocity for cluster forming and MRP elections. Hence, its performance will contribute in prolonging the lifetime of the clusters and reducing the link failures. The *restDRatio* is the ratio of rest distance towards the destination, which is ensured to group the vehicles and to elect considerable CHs/MPRs with convergent residual distance. Hence, its performance will contribute in maintaining the stability of the clusters. The *avgRM* is a parameter for a vehicle to choose stable target vehicles within one/two-hop neighbors to form a cluster or to be a CH/MPR. This parameter is based on the relative mobility mentioned in [10], which can be calculated based on the hello packet delay on each vehicle. The specific calculation formulas of these parameters are given below where the variable i & j belongs to the set of V_n, $currXY(i)$ is the current coordinates of the vehicle i, the others are shown in Table 1.

$$speedRatio_i = \left(\left|V_{avg}(i) - V_{ran}(i)\right|\right) \Big/ (maxVelocity - minVelocity) \tag{1}$$

$$restDRatio_i = \sqrt{(curXY(i) - D_{xy}^j)^2} \Big/ D_{ij} \tag{2}$$

$$avgRM_i = \sum\nolimits_{i,i\neq j}^{j} 10 log_{10} \frac{PktDelay_{i,j}^{now}}{PktDelay_{i,j}^{old}} \Big/ NB_i^j \tag{3}$$

Table 1. Notations for formulas and algorithms

Symbol	Significance
V_n	A set of vehicles
$D_{tra}(i)$	The travelled distance of the i vehicle in V_n by now
$V_{ran}(i)$	The random velocity between $minVelocity$ and $maxVelocity$
$V_{avg}(i)$	The average velocity of the i vehicle in V_n by now
$minVelocity$	The minimum velocity limit
$maxVelocity$	The maximum velocity limit
D_{ij}	The distance between vehicle i and vehicle j, $i \neq j$
D_{xy}^j	The coordinates (x,y) value of the destination vehicle j
V_i^j	The destination vehicle j of the i vehicle in V_n
NB_i^j	The neighbor number of vehicle i within one or two hops
LB_i^j	The neighbor list of vehicle i with QoS values
$PktDelay_{i,j}$	The transport delays of two continuous messages, $i \neq j$
$avgRM_i$	The average relative mobility between vehicle i

Based on the above parameters, we introduce a combined QoS metric **QoS_i**, listed below to estimate the ability of a vehicle i to be a CHs or CGs(MPRs). In (4), the parameter **QC_i** is the residual capacity of queue of the vehicle i.

$$QoS_i = QC_i \times NB_i^j \times \frac{restDRatio_i}{speedRatio_i} \times avgRM_i \tag{4}$$

2.2 The CH and MPR Election Algorithm

In this section, we present a QoS-based CH election algorithm with two intervals namely *HelloDuration* and *CHDuration*. In the *HelloDuration*, the nodes broadcast *qHelloPkt* packet with their QoS values within one or two-hops away to build their own neighbor list and update the QoS values in the list. In the *CHDuration*, by locally broadcasting a special Clustering-HELLO packet (*cHelloPkt*), each node votes for its neighbor to elect the optimal CH which has the local maximal QoS metric value. Once the election procedure is done, the elected node acknowledges to act as a CH by broadcasting an ACK and Topology Control (TC) packet within 2-hops away. The pseudo-code is like this.

```
function CQOLSR_CH_Election{
  if(isHelloDuration()){
    foreach vehicle i,j ∈ Vₙ{

      if(isNull(LBᵢʲ)) send(qHelloPkt)
      else  collectAndUpdate(qHelloPkt,QoSᵢ) }
  if(isCHDuartion()){
    foreach vehicle i,j ∈ Vₙ {
      Broadcast(qHelloPkt);

      Seek(φ); //φ ∈ NBᵢʲ ∪{i} && QoS(φ)= max{QoS( NBᵢʲ ), QoSᵢ}
    }
    voteFor φ (cHelloPkt); updateMPRs(i, φ)}
  else {
    elect vehicle i to be the cluster head φ }

  foreach φ ∈ Vₙ {

    broadcast(ACK,TC) within NBᵢʲ }
}
```

When φ is elected, it need to select a set of optimal MPR nodes to interconnect the clusters and to form a connected network. The MPR selection algorithm uses *cgHelloPkt* packet to collect the path information through the network. The algorithm works as follows. In the forwarding phase, the source cluster head of message originator broadcast *cgHelloPkt* within 2-hops neighbors. Each intermediate node receiving this packet updates the *cgHelloPkt* with updated QoS values and forwards it to the destination cluster head. Meanwhile, the *cgHelloPkt* packet records each list of the visited node for tracing back the route later. In the backward phase, the intermediate nodes extract the QoS value from *cgHelloPkt*, compute the end-to-end delay and the combined QoS value, then calculate the reliability of each path between source and destination CH. Thereafter, we can get the ratio of reliability of all available paths and choose the optimal path with a maximum reliability ratio to be the data route. Afterwards, it selects the nodes belonging to the path having the maximum reliability ratio and located within the scope of its cluster as MPRs. Next, it sends back the *cgHelloPkt* packet until reaching the source cluster head.

3   Performance

The proposed protocol CQOLSR is implemented in NS-2. A simulation scene of 1000×1000 m is used to simulate a set of nodes varying from 30 to 100. Transmission range is [100, 200] m, the velocity is [10, 35] m/s. We present a comparison between CQOLSR, QOLSR and OLSR. The latter approaches ignore some important metrics like mobility while the former uses a combined QoS metric to build the QoS function to form stable clusters and mobile communication.

As shown in Fig. 1, the CH duration decreases with increasing vehicle speed, because the CHs cannot maintain a relatively stable QoS conditions to its neighbor vehicles for a specific period. CH duration is moderately reduced in CQOLSR than in others because of the consideration of the relative mobility with their neighbors to enhance the robustness of velocity. Meanwhile, the factor of vehicle transmission range also influences the stability and duration. This has a great effect on connection between cluster members and efficiently reduces the changing number of cluster nodes' state. Therefore, it is beneficial to cluster stability that increasing transmission range.

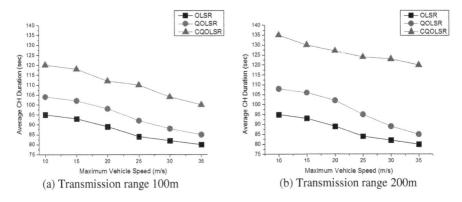

(a) Transmission range 100m   (b) Transmission range 200m

Fig. 1. Average CH duration vs. transmission range vs. maximum vehicle speed.

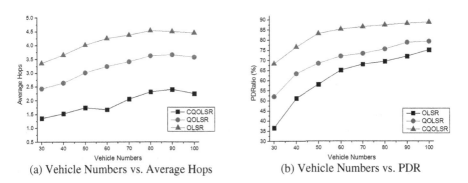

(a) Vehicle Numbers vs. Average Hops   (b) Vehicle Numbers vs. PDR

Fig. 2. Vehicle numbers vs. Average hops & PDR

As shown in Fig. 2, the average hops and Packet Deliver Ratio (PDR) are separately compared with node density. In CQOLSR, the optimal path to dada transmission is chosen according to the highest QoS value and the highest reliability ratio. This improvement is earned by considering the route time while calculating the reliability ratio value used to select the MPRs. The results prove that the CQOLSR gives higher PDR and less number of hops compared to other approaches.

4 Conclusion

In this paper, we proposed CQOLSR protocol for V2V data transmission. The protocol is composed of two components: the QoS-based CH election and the multi-hop MPR selection algorithms. To ensure the stability of clusters, we add the velocity, mobility and relative distance that represent the mobility metrics to the combined QoS metric. Simulation results prove that our protocol is able to extend the network lifetime, increase the packet delivery ratio and decrease the path length. However, we will have a lot of work to do. We don't optimize the MPR recovery algorithm able to select alternatives and keep the network connected in case of link failures, and don't consider the misbehaving node after clusters are formed. We will take them into consideration in the future work.

Acknowledgement. This work is supported by the National Science Foundation, under grant No. 61572186.

References

1. Allouche, Y., Segal, M.: Cluster-based beaconing process for VANET. Veh. Commun. **2**, 80–94 (2015)
2. Bali, R.S., Kumar, N., Rodrigues, J.J.P.C.: Clustering in vehicular ad hoc networks: taxonomy, challenges and solutions. Veh. Commun. **1**, 134–152 (2014)
3. Wang, Z., Liu, L., Zhou, M., Ansari, N.: A position based clustering technique for ad hoc intervehicle communication. IEEE Trans. Syst. Man Cybern. Part C Appl. Rev. **38**(2), 201–208 (2008)
4. Fan, W., Shi, Y., Chen, S., Zou, L.: A mobility metric based dynamic clustering algorithm (DCA) for VANETs. In: International Conference on Communication Technology and Application, Beijing, pp. 752–756 (2011)
5. Almalag, M.S., Weigle, M.C.: Using traffic flow for cluster formation in vehicular ad-hoc networks. In: Proceedings of the 35th IEEE Conference on Local Computer Networks, Denver, CO, pp. 631–636 (2010)
6. Little, T., Agarwal, A.: An information propagation scheme for VANETS, In: IEEE Proceedings of the 8th International Conference on Intelligent Transportation Systems, pp. 155–160 (2005)
7. Maglaras, L.A., Katsaros, D.: Distributed clustering in vehicular networks. In: IEEE Proceedings of the 8th International Conference on Wireless and Mobile Computing, Networking and Communications, Barcelona, pp. 593–599 (2012)
8. Wang, S., Lin, Y.: PassCAR: a passive clustering aided routing protocol for vehicular ad hoc networks. Comput. Commun. **36**, 170–179 (2013)
9. Clausen, T., Jacquet, P., Muhlethaler, P., Laouiti, A., Qayyum, A., Viennot, L.: Optimized link state routing protocol for ad hoc networks. In: Proceedings of the Multi Topic Conference (International), pp. 62–68 (2002). (RFC Editor)
10. Zhang, Z., Boukerche, A., Pazzi, R.: A novel multi-hop clustering scheme for vehicular ad-hoc networks. In: Proceedings of the ACM, Paris, France, pp. 19–26 (2011)

Accurate Text Classification via Maximum Entropy Model

Baoping Zou[(⊠)]

State Grid Info-Telecom Great Power Science and Technology Co.,
Ltd., Beijing, China
hello_grid80@sina.com

Abstract. Text classification and the research of classification algorithms or models play an important part in the research area of big data, which is among the hottest in our daily life contemporarily. The final target of task of text classification is to choose which is the correct class label that a given text input should belong to. In this paper, we try to propose a more accurate text classification approach by making full use of the principle of maximum entropy model. We conduct a series of experiments of our approach based on a real-world text dataset, which can be downloaded for public research use. The experimental results demonstrate that our proposed approach is very efficient for the task of text classification.

Keywords: Text classification · Maximum entropy model · Big data

1 Introduction

Text classification and the research of classification algorithms or models play an important part in the research area of big data, which is among the hottest in our daily life contemporarily. Nowdays text classification is a necessity for everyone because of the very large amount of text documents that we have to cope with every day and its ever going increasing speed. Against this background, there has been several text classification models to be proposed to solve this problem. In general, text classification models can be divided into two, namely topic-based and genre-based classification models. The former topic-based text categorization classifies text documents according to the topics of the text [1]. Texts can be many genres, which can be represented by a set of words with different weights, for example, scientific articles, news reports, and movie reviews, which is familiar to everybody now. While previous works on the latter genre classification found that this task has some different aspects, large or small, from the former topic-based categorization [2].

As we all know, typically most datasets that we have used for topic classification research are collected on purpose from the web sites such as newsgroups, forums, bulletin boards, email lists or broadcast. Apparently, they come in multi-sources, as a result consequently come with different formats, different sets of vocabularies. And even documents of the same genre have different writing styles. That is to say, the data are nine times out of ten heterogeneous.

S. Wang and A. Zhou (Eds.): CollaborateCom 2016, LNICST 201, pp. 569–576, 2017.
DOI: 10.1007/978-3-319-59288-6_56

As we have described before, intuitively the task of text classification is to classify a given document into a predefined category. An example of the predefined category set may be political, entertainment, sports, finances, and science. More formally, if we let letter d_i represent a document of the entire set of documents D and $\{c_1, c_2, \cdots, c_n\}$ represent the set of all categories, then the target of text classification task is to assign one category c_j to a document d_i. As is done in every supervised machine learning task, an initial training dataset is needed to get the parameters of the model. A document may be assigned to more than one category, but in this paper we only consider assigning a single category to each document. For example, a document may belong to entertainment, and at the same time belong to science too. But we should note that the probability that a document belongs to different categories may be always different.

Maximum entropy model is a general technique that always be used to compute the probability distributions from all sorts of data. The overriding inherent principle in maximum entropy is that when nothing is known, the probability distribution (i.e. the values of the probabilities) should be as uniform as possible, which meets the constraints of maximal entropy from which the model has its name. Labeled training data is used efficiently to derive a set of constraints, i.e. model parameters for the model that characterize the class-specific expectations for the wanted probability distributions. Constraints are represented as expected values of features, which can be any real-valued function of an example. The improved iterative scaling algorithm (IIS) is always used to find the maximum entropy distribution that is most consistent with the former given constraints. While in our text classification scenario, we use maximum entropy to estimate the conditional distribution of the class label of a given a document. A document is represented by a set of word count features with different weights. The labeled training data is used to compute the expected values of the word counts based on a class-by-class basis. The former mentioned Improved iterative scaling is used to find a text classifier of an exponential form that is in line with the constraints from the labeled training data.

Our experimental results demonstrate that maximum entropy principle is a technique that warrants further investigation for the task of text classification, and the proposed maximum entropy model is efficient for this work. On one real data set we used, for example, the maximum entropy model reduces the mean classification error by more or less 40% in comparison to the popular naive Bayes. While on another data sets we used, however, the basic maximum entropy model does not perform as well as naive Bayes. Here, there is apparent evidence that basic maximum entropy suffers from overfitting and poor feature selection, which has a bad influence on the accuracy. When a normal prior is added to the basic maximum entropy model, the classification performance is improved apparently in these cases. Overall, the maximum entropy model we used has a better performance than naive Bayes on two of three data sets. Many research direction of the maximum entropy model for further investigation still exist, which may improve performance even further in the future. These works include more efficient and effective feature selection methods, applying bigrams and phrases as features, and adjusting the appropriate prior knowledge based on the sparsity attributes of the used datasets.

This following of this paper proceeds as follows. Section 2 demonstrate the general framework of the maximum entropy model for computing the conditional probability and distributions. Then, the specific application of maximum entropy to the task of text classification is further discussed in Sect. 3. Related works about the task of text classification and how to apply maximum entropy into it are presented in Sect. 3.1. Experimental results on real datasets are presented in Sect. 3.2. Finally, Sect. 4 discusses our plans for future work.

2 Maximum Entropy Model

The motivating idea behind the maximum entropy principle lies in the fact that one should prefer the most uniform model parameters that also meet every given constraints [3], by which the entropy of the model is largest and this principle got its name the maximum entropy principle. For example, let us consider a four-way text classification task where we are told only that on average 30% of documents with the word children in them are in the school class. Intuitively, when we are given a document with children in it, we would say it has a 30% probability of being a school document, and a 23.3% probability for each of the other three classes. If a document does not have children we would compute the uniform class distribution, 35% each. This model is exactly the maximum entropy model that conforms to our known constraints. Computing the model is easy in this example, but when there are many constraints to meet, rigorous techniques are needed to find the only optimal solution.

In its most general formulation, the maximum entropy principle can be used to compute any probability distribution. In this work, we are more interested in text classification; thus we limit our further discussion to learning more accurate conditional distributions from the labeled training data. Specifically, we learn by the labeled training data by the maximum entropy model that the conditional distributions of the class label given a document.

2.1 Constraints and Features

In maximum entropy we use the labeled training data to set constraints on the conditional distribution. Each constraint expresses a characteristic of the training data that should also be demonstrated in the learned distribution and model parameters. We can make any selected real-valued function with two kinds of parameters, namely the document and the class, be a feature $f_i(d, c)$. Maximum entropy gives us the power to restrict the model distribution to have the same expected value for this feature as seen in the training data D, i.e. the prior knowledge and parameters. Thus, we get that the learned conditional distribution and trained parameters $P(c|d)$ must have the following property:

$$\frac{1}{|D|} \sum_{d \in D} f_i(d, c(d)) = \sum_d P(d) \sum_c P(c|d) f_i(d, c). \tag{1}$$

In practice, the document distribution $P(d)$ is unknown by us, and in fact we do not have to be interested in modeling it. Thus, we make use of our training data without the class labels, as an approximation estimation to the document distribution, and write down the following constraint:

$$\frac{1}{|D|}\sum_{d\in D} f_i(d, c(d)) = \frac{1}{|D|}\sum_{d\in D}\sum_c f_i(d, c). \tag{2}$$

Thus, when we use the maximum entropy model, the first step is to identify a set of feature functions that will come into role for the task of text classification process. Then, for each selected feature, measure its expected value over the training data and take it as a constraint for the model distribution.

2.2   Parametric Form

When constraints are estimated in this way, it is guaranteed that a unique distribution exists which will deduce the maximum value of the distribution entropy. Moreover, it can be proved that the distribution is always of the exponential form like this:

$$P(c|d) = \frac{1}{Z(d)}\exp\left(\sum_i w_i f_i(d, c)\right), \tag{3}$$

where each $f_i(d, c)$ is a feature, λ_i is a parameter to be estimated and $Z(d)$ is simply the normalizing factor to ensure a proper probability:

$$Z(d) = \sum_c \exp(\sum_i w_i f_i(d, c)). \tag{4}$$

When the constraints are computed from the labeled training data, the solution to the maximum entropy problem is equivalent to the solution to a dual maximum likelihood problem for models of the same exponential form. Additionally, it is guaranteed that the likelihood surface of the objective function is convex, which ensures a single global maximum and no local maxima. This suggests that this problem has a possible approach for finding one and only one maximum entropy solution. The steps are by the following: 1. First guess any initial exponential distribution of the correct form as a starting point; 2. then, perform the hill climbing algorithm or quasi-Newton algorithm in the potential likelihood space; 3. Iterate step 1 and 2 until the solution not changed. As there is no local maxima, the iteration will converge to the only maximum likelihood solution, which will also be the global maximum entropy solution.

Algorithm 1: BFGS algorithm for maximum entropy model learning

---

Input: feature function $f_1, f_2, \cdots, f_n$; empirical distribution $\tilde{P}(x, y)$,target function $f(w)$,gradient vector
    $g(w) = \nabla f(w)$,required precision parameter ϵ;

Output: optimal parameter vector w^*;

1 Initialize parameter vector $w^{(0)}$, get B_0 as positive definite matrix, set $k = 0$;

2 compute $g_k = g(w^{(k)})$;

3 if $\|g_k\| \leq \epsilon$ then

4 | stop and get $w^* = w^{(k)}$;

5 else

6 | continue;

7 by equation $B_k p_k = -g_k$, compute p_k;

8 one dimensional searching, get λ_k satisfying

$$f(w^{(k)} + \lambda_k p_k) = min_{\lambda \geq 0} f(w^{(k)} + \lambda p_k)$$

;

9 set $w^{(k+1)} = w^{(k)} + \lambda_k p_k$;

10 compute $g_{k+1} = g(w^{(k+1)})$;

11 if $\|g_k\| \leq \epsilon$ then

12 | stop and have $w^* = w^{(k+1)}$;

13 else

14

$$B_{k+1} = B_k + \frac{y_k y_k^T}{y_k^T \delta_k} - \frac{B_k \delta_k \delta_k^T B_k}{\delta_k^T B_k \delta_k}$$

, where,

$$y_k = g_{k+1} - g_k, \delta_k = w_{k+1} - w_k$$

;

15 $k = k + 1$, go to Line 7;

16 final ;

17 return w^*;

2.3　Parameter Learning

In [4], a number of algorithms for computing the parameters of maximum entropy models, which includes gradient ascent, iterative scaling, conjugate gradient, and variable metric methods. Surprisingly, the standardly used iterative scaling algorithms perform quite poorly in comparison to the others in practical scences. While for almost all of the test problems, a quasi-Newton algorithm such as BFGS, outperforms the other candidates for optimizing. As a result, in this paper, we use the quasi-Newton algorithm to train the parameters of the maximum entropy model.

For a maximum entropy model, we have

$$P_w(c|x) = \frac{\exp(\sum_{i=1}^{n} w_i f_i(d, c))}{\sum_c \exp(\sum_{i=1}^{n} w_i f_i(d, c))} \tag{5}$$

With simple mathematic manipulations, we get the objective function by the following

$$\min_{w \in R^n} f(w) = \sum_d \tilde{P}(d) \log \sum_c \exp(\sum_{i=1}^n w_i f_i(d,c)) - \sum_{d,c} \tilde{P}(d,c) \sum_{i=1}^n w_i f_i(d,c) \quad (6)$$

Then we can get the gradient vector as follows:

$$g(w) = (\frac{\partial f(w)}{\partial w_1}, \frac{\partial f(w)}{\partial w_2}, \cdots, \frac{\partial f(w)}{\partial w_n})^T, \quad (7)$$

where

$$\frac{\partial f(w)}{\partial w_i} = \sum_{d,c} \tilde{P}(d) P_w(c|d) f_i(d,c) - E_{\tilde{P}}(f_i), \ i = 1, 2, \cdots, n \quad (8)$$

The corresponding quasi-Newton algorithm is shown in Algorithm 1.

3   Experiment

In this section, we conduct extensive experiments on a real-world dataset. First we list the baseline models, then we introduce the dataset, at last, we demonstrate the experimental results.

3.1   Baseline Algorithm and Dataset

We compared the maximum entropy model with a number of baseline classification models. The baseline models and their basic information are as follows:

(1) kNN (k-nearest neighbors; here, k = 10). In kNN, an item is classified by a majority vote of its neighbors.
(2) LRC (Logistic Regression Classifier). LRC measures the relationship between a class label and features by estimating probabilities using a logistic function.
(3) NB (Naïve Bayes). NB applies Bayes' theorem by assuming independence among features.
(4) L-SVM (Linear-form support vector machine). L-SVM is a support vector machine with a linear-form kernel function.

For kNN, LRC and NB, we employed scikit-learn, whereas for L-SVM, we chose Weka. All models were used with default settings and parameters. It is worth noting that the implementation of L-SVM in Weka derives from LIBSVM, a well-known library for support vector machines.

We downloaded a real dataset, namely the Reuters-21578 dataset, from David Lewis' page[1]. And we applied the standard train/test split to get the training dataset and

---

[1] http://www.daviddlewis.com/resources/testcollections/reuters21578/.

test dataset. These documents all firstly appeared on the Reuters newswire in 1987, and then were manually classified by personnel from Reuters Ltd.

For the fact that the class distribution values for these documents is very skewed, two sub-collections are usually taken into account for text categorization tasks.

3.2 Experimental Results

Table 1 shows the comparison results between the maximum entropy model and the baseline models. We can see that the maximum entropy model performs better than the baseline models. The extensive use of many mature models from state-of-the-art machine learning packages as baseline guarantees a comprehensive experimental comparison.

Table 1. Comparison between the maximum entropy model and baseline models.

Models	Accuracy	F1-measure
Maximum Entropy Model	**0.78**	**0.81**
kNN	0.64	0.76
LRC	0.65	0.68
NB	0.69...	0.63
L-SVM	0.73...	0.77

4 Conclusion

In this paper, we investigate how to apply the maximum entropy model into text classification, and find that maximum entropy model give a more accurate classification results than baseline models. Firstly, we try to propose a more accurate text classification approach by making use of maximum entropy model. Then we conduct a series of experiments of our approach based on a real-world text dataset. At last the experimental results demonstrate that our proposed approach is very effective and efficient for text classification task. In the future, we will focus on how to apply the maximum entropy model for QoS measurement [5–7].

References

1. Yang, Y.: An evaluation of statistical approaches to text categorization. Inf. Retrieval **1**(1–2), 69–90 (1999)
2. Kessler, B., Numberg, G., Schütze, H.: Automatic detection of text genre. In: Proceedings of the 35th Annual Meeting of the Association for Computational Linguistics and Eighth Conference of the European Chapter of the Association for Computational Linguistics, pp. 32–38. Association for Computational Linguistics (1997)
3. Berger, A.L., Pietra, V.J.D., Pietra, S.A.D.: A maximum entropy approach to natural language processing. Computational Linguistics **22**(1), 39–71 (1996)

4. Malouf, R.: A comparison of algorithms for maximum entropy parameter estimation. In: Proceedings of the 6th Conference on Natural Language Learning, vol. 20, pp. 1–7. Association for Computational Linguistics, August 2002

5. Wang, S.G., Sun, Q.B., Yang, F.C.: Towards web service selection based on QoS estimation. Int. J. Web Grid Serv. **6**(4), 424–443 (2010)

6. Ma, Y., Wang, S., Hung, P.C.K., Hsu, C.-H., Sun, Q., Yang, F.: A highly accurate prediction algorithm for unknown web service QoS value. IEEE Trans. Serv. Comput. **99**, 1–10 (2015). doi:10.1109/TSC.2015.2407877. http://ieeexplore.ieee.org/xpls/abs_all.jsp?arnumber=7051279&tag=1

7. Wang, S., Ma, Y., Cheng, B., Yang, F., Chang, R.N.: Multi-dimensional QoS prediction for service recommendations. IEEE Trans. Serv. Comput. (2016). doi:10.1109/TSC.2016.2584058. https://www.computer.org/csdl/trans/sc/preprint/07498681.pdf

Back-Propagation Neural Network for QoS Prediction in Industrial Internets

Hong Chen[✉]

State Grid Info-Telecom Great Power Science and Technology Co., Ltd., Beijing, China
hongchengrid@sina.com

Abstract. As it is well known that QoS play an important role in industrial Internets. However, existing prediction methods failed in obtaining accurate QoS prediction results. Hence, in this paper, we proposed a high accurate approach for QoS prediction for industrial Internets. The key idea of this approach is to adopt back-propagation neural network to predict the QoS data. We implement our approach and experiment it based on a real-world QoS dataset. The experimental results show that our proposed approach can perform accurate QoS prediction results.

Keywords: Web service · QoS · BP neural network · Industrial internet

1 Introduction

With the rapid development of industrial Internet and the quick growth of the service number, service users have to face the massive candidate services which are functionally identical but different in non-functional properties. Due to the huge number of candidate services, service user cannot try all services to select the best one. So, how to choose the best service to satisfy the quality requirement of users is a significant concern for successfully building service-oriented applications [1]. As it is well known that quality of services (QoS) plays an important role in industrial Internets, it becomes a differentiating aspect for functionally equivalent services. Recently, many scholars argue that the QoS values of service cannot be easily acquired from the service provider or the third-party organizations. Therefore, it becomes a significant challenge to acquire the QoS value accurately.

In recent years, extensive research work have been conducted on QoS value prediction. Among them, collaborative filtering techniques are widely used. The main idea is to identify similar users and collect their useful QoS information to the active user. These approaches are based on the hypothesis that all user's value are trustworthy and the evaluation criteria are unified. In reality, some user's QoS values can be untrustworthy and the evaluation criteria may be diversified in industrial Internet [2]. So, many of the existing approaches failed in obtaining accurate QoS prediction results.

In this paper, we proposed a highly accurate approach for QoS prediction for industrial Internets. The key idea of this approach is to adopt back-propagation (BP) neural network to predict the QoS data. Through experiments based on the real dataset, our

© ICST Institute for Computer Sciences, Social Informatics and Telecommunications Engineering 2017
S. Wang and A. Zhou (Eds.): CollaborateCom 2016, LNICST 201, pp. 577–582, 2017.
DOI: 10.1007/978-3-319-59288-6_57

approach achieves good performance in terms of prediction accuracy. The remainder of this paper is organized as follows: In the next section we provide a detailed overview of the related works. Section 3 illustrates our prediction approach based on BP neural network. Section 4 presents experimental results. Finally, conclusions are provided in Sect. 5.

2   Related Work

The study on QoS plays an important role in Service-Oriented Computing domain. Thanks to the development of industrial Internet, many QoS-based issue have been discussed in recent literatures, covering the topic of service selection [3, 4], service composition [5, 6] and service recommendation [7–9].

From the aspect of supporting QoS-based service selection and composition in industrial Internet environments, researchers employ various forecasting technologies for Web services QoS prediction. Lo et al. [3] proposes an extended Matrix Factorization (EMF) framework with relational regularization to make missing QoS values prediction in service selection. In [4], the authors propose a Web service selection approach based on QoS estimation. Their aim is to perform accurate QoS estimation and alleviate the deviations between requiring and receiving QoS in Web service selection.

Recently, many QoS-based recommendation approaches have been put forward. For example, Kuang et al. [7] proposed a personalized service recommendation mechanism based on context-aware QoS prediction. In [8], the authors accomplish the QoS prediction by using fuzzy clustering method with calculating the users' similarity. In [9], the authors propose a novel landmark-based QoS prediction framework and then present two clustering-based prediction algorithms for Web services.

In addition, there are a number of studies about QoS value prediction [10] and QoS ranking prediction [11–16]. However, existing prediction methods failed in obtaining accurate QoS prediction results. In this paper, we proposed a highly accurate approach for QoS prediction for industrial Internets.

3   Our QoS Prediction Approach

In order to obtain higher prediction accuracy, we consider to employ the performance of web service to predict the QoS value. The value of QoS can be determined by multiple service attributes, and different service attributes correspond to different QoS values. Hence, QoS prediction is essentially a problem of multi-target recognition. BP neural network is one of the most popular methods for multi-target recognition. So, we employ BP neural network to predict the QoS value. The specific approach is described as follows.

3.1   BP Neural Network

The BP neural network algorithm is a multi-layer feed forward network trained by error back propagation algorithm. It is one of the most widely applied neural network models.

BP neural network can be used to learn and store a large number of input-output model mapping relations, and there is no requirement to disclose in advance the mathematical equation that describes these mapping relations. Its learning rule employs the steepest descent method in which the back propagation is used to achieve the minimum error sum of square by regulating the weight value and threshold value of the network.

The application of the standard BP network model is converted to a mathematical optimization problem. BP learning algorithm is a global optimization approach, which has a good generalization ability and resilient fault tolerance. The BP neural network has been an important tool to investigate prediction problems due to robust learning ability.

3.2   Constructing Prediction Model

The web service in the industrial Internet may have many attributes, such as response time, availability, throughput, and so on. These attributes jointly determine the value of QoS. Hence, we can determine the mapping relationship between the service attributes and QoS value. Based on this, we design the prediction model as described in Fig. 1. The BP neural network consists of three layers, the input layer, the hidden layer and the output layer.

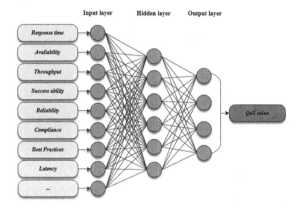

Fig. 1.   QoS prediction model based on BP neural network

The input layer contains n nodes, and each node represent an attribute of a service. The output layer contains q nodes, representing q kinds of QoS values, respectively. We can obtain the relevant parameters of BP neural network by the training data, so as to complete the prediction of QoS value. Hence, the core problem of prediction is transformed into the model training problem.

3.3 QoS Value Prediction

In order to predict the QoS value accurately, we first need to train the BP neural network model to get the appropriate parameters. Then, we can predict the QoS values by the trained BP neural network model.

When the BP network is constructed, we can determine the number of weights and bias based the number of input layer, output layer and hidden layer. The input-output problem is transformed into a non-linear mathematical optimization problem. The optimization goal is to find a set of weights and bias to make the global sum of the absolute error between the desired output and the predicted output reach to the lowest point. So we define the fitness function as follows:

$$F = \frac{1}{2m} \sum_{k=1}^{m} \sum_{o=1}^{q} (d_o(k) - y_o(k))^2,$$

where m is the number of samples, q is the number of output layer, $d_o(k)$ and $y_o(k)$ are the desired output and the predicted output of the k-th sample for the node o in BP network.

The BP neural network employs the steepest-descent method to solve the optimal problems, in which back propagation is used to achieve the minimum error sum of the square by regulating the weight value and a threshold value for the network. After training, the prediction model was set up. The QoS value for any unknown service can be obtained through the trained prediction model.

4   Experimental Study

In order to verify the performance of our approach, we implement our approach and experiment it based on a real-world QoS dataset.

4.1 Experimental Setup

We implemented experiments employing matlab 8.3 on IBM server with Inter Xeon E5-2670 eight-core 2.60 GHz CPU and 32 G RAM. Publicly available Quality of web services dataset (QWS) [17] is used for QoS prediction employing BP neural network model. Services in QWS dataset have four QoS values: (1) platinum (high quality); (2) gold; (3) silver and (4) bronze (low quality). The QoS prediction is based on the overall quality rating provided by WsRF. In the experiment, services are divided into two parts. One is the training data, and the other is the test data.

4.2   Metrics

In our experiment, Mean Absolute Error (MAE) and Root Mean Square Error (RMSE) metrics are used to evaluate the accuracy of prediction. MAE is defined as: $MAE = \frac{1}{N} \sum_i |R_i - \hat{R}_i|$, And RMSE is defined as: $RMSE = \sqrt{\frac{1}{N} \sum_i (R_i - \hat{R}_i)}$, where R_i denotes the QoS of service i, $\hat{R}_i$ represent the predicted QoS value of service i, and N is the number of all predicted values.

4.3   Comparison and Performance

In order to observe the performance of our approach, the Item Mean (IMean), the Naïve Bayes (NB) algorithm, the k-nearest neighbor (KNN) algorithm are chosen for comparative analysis. According to the dataset, we set the input layer number $n = 9$, the hidden layer number $p = 6$ and the output layer number $q = 4$.

Figure 2 shows the MAE and RMSE of the different methods. Obviously, our proposed BP neural network approach is the best both in MAE and RMSE, 0.373 and 0.594 respectively. And the corresponding prediction accuracy is the best. Hence, we can conclude that it is a promising way to improve the accuracy of QoS prediction.

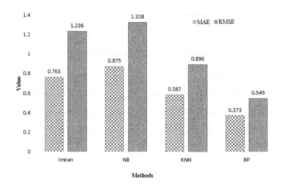

Fig. 2.   MAE and RMSE of different methods

5   Conclusion

In this paper, we propose a BP neural network model to improve the QoS prediction accuracy. The mapping relationship between service attributes and QoS value is employed, and modeled by BP neural network. Experimental results demonstrate that our approach can obviously improve the QoS prediction accuracy. In the future work, we will take the context information into consideration to improve the QoS prediction accuracy.

References

1. Zheng, Z., Zhang, Y., Lyu, M.R.: Distributed QoS evaluation for real-world web services. In: Proceedings of the 8th IEEE International Conference on Web Services, pp. 83–90 (2010)
2. Wang, S., Zheng, Z., Wu, Z., Lyu, M.R., Yang, F.: Reputation measurement and malicious feedback rating prevention in web service recommendation systems. IEEE Trans. Serv. Comput. **8**(5), 755–767 (2015)
3. Lo, W., Yin, J., Deng, S., Li, Y., Wu, Z.: An extended matrix factorization approach for QoS prediction in service selection. In: Proceedings of the 9th IEEE International Conference on Service computing, pp. 162–169 (2012)
4. Wang, S., Sun, Q., Yang, F.: Towards web service selection based on QoS estimation. Int. J. Web Grid Serv. **6**(4), 424–443 (2010)
5. Wang, X., Zhu, J., Shen, Y.: Network-aware QoS prediction for service composition using geolocation. IEEE Trans. Serv. Comput. **8**(4), 630–643 (2015)
6. Wang, S., Zhu, X., Yang, F.: Efficient QoS management for QoS-aware web service composition. Int. J. Web Grid Serv. **10**(1), 1–23 (2014)
7. Kuang, L., Xia, Y., Mao, Y.: Personalized services recommendation based on context-aware QoS prediction. In: Proceedings of the 19th IEEE International Conference on Web Services, pp. 400–406 (2012)
8. Zhang, M., Liu, X., Zhang, R., Sun, H.: A web service recommendation approach based on QoS prediction using fuzzy clustering. In: Proceedings of the 9th IEEE International Conference on Services Computing, pp. 138–145 (2012)
9. Zhu, J., Kang, Y., Zheng, Z., Lyu, M.R.: A clustering-based QoS prediction approach for Web service recommendation. In: Proceedings of the 15th IEEE International Symposium on Object/Component/Service-Oriented Real-Time Distributed Computing Workshops, pp. 93–98 (2012)
10. Wang, S., Sun, Q., Zou, H., Yang, F.: Particle swarm optimization with skyline operator for fast cloud-based web service composition. Mobile Netw. Appl. **18**(1), 116–121 (2013)
11. Wang, S., Liu, Z., Sun, Q., Zou, H., Yang, F.: Towards an accurate evaluation of quality of cloud service in service-oriented cloud computing. J. Intell. Manuf. **25**(2), 283–291 (2014)
12. Wang, S., Ma, Y., Cheng, B., Yang, F., Chang, R.N.: Multi-dimensional QoS prediction for service recommendations. IEEE Transaction on Services Computing (2016). doi:10.1109/TSC.2016.2584058
13. Wang, S., Huang, L., Hsu, C.-H., Yang, F.: Collaboration reputation for trustworthy Web service selection in social networks. J. Comput. Syst. Sci. **82**(1), 130–143 (2016)
14. Wang, S., Zheng, Z., Zhengping, W., Yang, F.: Context-aware mobile service adaptation via a co-evolution eXtended classifier system in mobile network environments. Mob. Inf. Syst. **10**(2), 197–215 (2014)
15. Wang, S., Hsu, C.-H., Liang, Z., Sun, Q., Yang, F.: Multi-user web service selection based on multi-QoS prediction. Inf. Syst. Front. **16**(1), 143–152 (2014)
16. Wang, S.G., Zheng, Z.B., Sun, Q.B., Zou, H., Yang, F.C.: Reliable web service selection via QoS uncertainty computing. Int. J. Web Grid Serv. **7**(4), 410–426 (2011)
17. Al-Masri, E., Mahmoud, Q.H.: Investigating web services on the world wide web. In: Proceedings of the 17th International Conference on World Wide Web, pp. 795–804 (2008)

AndroidProtect: Android Apps Security Analysis System

Tong Zhang[1(✉)], Tao Li[1,2], Hao Wang[1], and Zhijie Xiao[1]

[1] School of Computer Science and Technology, Wuhan University of Science and Technology, Wuhan 430065, Hubei, China
{ztl996816,1593487967,544247884}@qq.com,
litaowust@163.com
[2] Hubei Province Key Laboratory of Intelligent Information Processing and Real-Time Industrial System, Wuhan 430065, Hubei, China

Abstract. Android Apps market is the largest in the world. There are some features about Android Apps: massive, diverse, uncertain behaviors and permissions. That makes detecting malicious Apps very difficult. In this paper, a two layers model based on static analysis and dynamic analysis is proposed to solve it. We name the model AndroidProtect. We can use AndroidProtect to calculate feature value of massive Apps, monitor behavior of target Apps. The first layer identifies the dangerous Apps, The second layer analyzes their behavior. The experimental results show that in the case of similar static feature value, the dynamic analysis can fix deviation, and we can get more accurate assessment.

Keywords: App security · Android permissions · Background traffic

1 Introduction

To solve the security problem of Android Apps, We must face several challenges:

i. Huge number Apps: According to Tencent Mobile Security Lab [1], Number of Android virus package in the first half of 2014 is 2.06 times than 2012. The user who infected reached 89 million. And the App Stores Growth Accelerates releases that in 2014, Google play store has 1 million and 430 thousands Apps [2]. In China, 360 safe market has 117872 Apps [3].

ii. Android permissions: Because Android is an open system [4], In order to bring a better user experience, Google provide developers more than one hundred system permissions. For Android 4.4, there are 146 permissions [5]. Different features need different permissions, Reasonableness of permission applying needs assessment.

iii. Behavior of Apps: Due to different code logic, we can't determine when Apps use their permissions. Dynamic behavior is uncertainly problem for us, because we don't know the reasonableness of the calling.

© ICST Institute for Computer Sciences, Social Informatics and Telecommunications Engineering 2017
S. Wang and A. Zhou (Eds.): CollaborateCom 2016, LNICST 201, pp. 583–594, 2017.
DOI: 10.1007/978-3-319-59288-6_58

Currently some methods are proposed to solve this problem:

Shuke Zeng [6] proposes formal assessment method of static analysis. This method identify the port of privacy data first, then monitor the path that may be exploited by malicious Apps. This method can work fine with single App, but for massive Apps this may play a minor role.

Zhongyuan Qin [7] uses signature matching and decompiling to detect malicious Apps behavior change. Based on small files, Generating API signature, Method signature, Class signatures, APK signature. Then matching those against sample library, locate the malicious code. This method is based on matching the sample library. For increasing the number of Apps, this method works not well.

Guojun Peng [8] starts with malicious apps detecting, explains the process of system API, introduce determination method based on feature value and heuristic. This method is finger on single App. And it is difficult when face on massive Apps.

For the limitations of these methods, Hao Wang [9] proposed static permission detect method based on population. This paper is based on it, proposed the two layers model which is the AndroidProtect. Comprehensive permissions static detection and dynamic behavior analysis, detecting massive and permission uncertainty Apps. The first layer can analyze massive Apps' permissions and filter malicious Apps. The second layer dynamic detects background traffic for these results.

Through experiments, we crawl 1950 Apps from 360 market. The number of potentially dangerous is 385. The number of dangerous Apps is 37. We select 10 of dangerous Apps to monitor background traffic. The background traffic is regularly. Verify the accuracy of the feature value.

2 Model Architecture

We have established the following two layers model based on population and similarity calculation. The model includes 6 modules (Fig. 1):

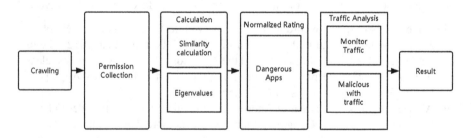

Fig. 1. Model architecture

   i. APP Crawling
  ii. Permission Collection
 iii. Permission Calculation
 iv. Normalized Rating
  v. Traffic Analysis
 vi. Result Store

Analysis process can be divided into the following steps:

Step 1: Using crawling to download target Apps with keywords from Apps market.

Step 2: Collecting Apps' permissions in each population.

Step 3: Calculating the character value of each population. Make the value as a baseline, analyze each App in this population. According to sensitivity of each permission, we score them. And using them to do calculation of Euclidean distance. According to the result, we can know the distribution of Apps' malicious value. Then we can divide the Apps that has dangerous tendency.

Step 4: For the dangerous Apps, we need to further analyze their behavior. User can't impact App's background traffic. So we can record the background traffic, to find the App's sensitive behavior.

Step 5: For the dangerous Apps again, we establish a coordinate system. The x-axis is malicious value. The y-axis is background traffic. After we put points in system, we can divide the dangerous Apps with their distance from origin to point.

2.1   APP Crawling

Using python write crawler, download Apps with keywords search from 360 App market. Since we crawl Apps randomly in market, the result is universal. And it can reflect distribution of Apps in market.

2.2   Permission Collection

We use the ADB tools and the Linux shell script to install APK in test machine. Apps are from the first module. After we finish the installing, we run the program to collect Apps' permissions. Then we save the permissions and the package name to database.

2.3   Permission Calculation

After we get the information of permissions, we should calculate the minimum of permissions and malicious value.

Minimum of permissions: We get permissions of each App in one population, then we find Intersection of them. The intersection is the minimum of permissions. One population has one minimum of permissions.

Malicious value: We assign Apps' permissions by their sensitivity. Different App has different permissions. We regard minimum of permissions as the baseline. Using Euclidean distance to calculate App's malicious value. This malicious value is about the static permissions.

2.4   Normalized Rating

When we get the malicious value from the above. We should sort them and rate them. We can know what Apps are dangerous.

Sorting: According to malicious values of population, we sort the list of Apps.
Mapping: After sorting, we should map the malicious to the [0–1] space. So we can do a divided by the value of the mapped. We are currently divided them into five rates. If the normalized value is closer to 1, the App's permissions are more sensitive, and the App is more dangerous. If the normalized value is closer to 0, the App's permissions are more common, and the App is less dangerous.

2.5   Traffic Analysis

Traffic analysis includes background traffic statistics and malicious value mixed traffic calculation.

Background traffic statistics: The background traffic is an important part of App security. Traffic is a real-time feature in one App. When period is enough, we can find the traffic law. This is effective but waste time. So we can't monitor all of Apps. So we choose the dangerous Apps which is found above.
Malicious value mixed traffic calculation: We established a coordinate System. The x-axis is malicious value, the y-axis is traffic. Point is the App. We calculate the Euclidean distance from point to origin. Then we can know the malicious value with background traffic.

2.6   Result Store

When we finish the analysis above, we should store the result and the sample of Apps. In the future, we will fix it and update it. After one population working, we can analyze another population.

3   Case Study

We have an example to illustrate the process of the model. The sample is "Camera Wizard", one of the Camera population.

We collect permissions of all Apps include "Camera Wizard". We find the App can download from Internet, read contact, access location and read message.

Then we calculate the minimum of permissions, then we use it to calculate malicious values of each Apps include "Camera Wizard". The malicious value of "Camera Wizard" is 351.99 We sort the values and mapped them to [0, 1] space. And we find "Camera Wizard" is in [0.8, 1]. So it's dangerous.

We monitor background traffic of "Camera Wizard". In 24 h, there is 210.4 kb. Then we use malicious value and background traffic to calculate Euclidean distance from point to origin. The result is 337.089.

4 Model

4.1 Model Definition

Permissions of App: *PermissionsApp = {Pi | Pi ∈ permissions of Android}*. It presents the permissions of App is all from Android.

Permissions storage structure: *PermissionMartix = {pij | i = 1, 2, ..., m; j = 1, 2, ..., n}*. In PermissionMatrix, if App i has a permission j, pij = 1. if not, pij = 0.

Individual of App: *I = (Permissions, Traffic)*. It presents the App information: Permissions and Traffic. Permissions and Traffic can be null.

The minimum set of permissions: *MinPermission = Permissions1 ∩ Permissions2 ∩ ... ∩ Permissionsi*. It is the insert of each App's permissions.

The max of permissions: *MaxPermission = Permissions1 ∪ Permissions2 ∪ ... ∪ Permissionsi*.

Non-essential set of permissions: *nPermission = Permissionapp − MinPermission*. It represents individual differences.

Population of App: *P = (Class, MaxPermissions, MinPermissions)*. Class is the name of Population. MaxPermissions stores all information of each App permissions, and MinPermission is the minimum set of permissions in this class. MinPermission is also called population characteristics.

Population operation: *∃P′ = (A0, A1, A2), P = (B0, B1, B2), if A0 = B0, P′ + P = (A0, A1 + A2, A2 ∩ B2)*. The operation shows how population is operated.

The malicious value: *D = (Permissions, MinPermissions)*. The malicious value of App is affected by the App's permissions and Popualtion's MinPermissions of App.

The malicious value with traffic: *DT = (D, Traffic)*. Each App has a malicious value. We fix the value with the traffic.

Normalization Method Value: *E = f(D)*. E is the value from the D using Normalization Method.

4.2 Model Algorithm

4.2.1 The Minimum Set of Permissions Search Algorithm

Input: Permissions of Apps in one Population.

Output: The minimum set of permissions in one Population.

a) Definition the MinPermissions.

   MinPermissions = Android.Permissions;

b) Travels all Apps in Population.

   For App in Population;

c) Calculate the intersection of MinPermissions and Appi.

   MinPermissions = MinPermissions ∩ App.Permissions;

d) Return the MinPermissions.

The minimum set of permissions in Population is the intersection of all Apps' permission in Population. The algorithm traverse App's permissions in Population. The time complexity is O(n).

4.2.2 Dynamic Evolution Algorithm

Input: The additional Population P', the old set of Population P.

Output: The Population P updated.

a) Traverse current Population Pi in P.

b) Compare Pi with P'

   i.   If P'.Class== Pi.Class Update the old Pi.

        Pi.MaxPermissions = Pi.MaxPermissions + P'.MaxPermissions;

        Pi.MinPermission = Pi.MinPermission + P'.MinPermission;

        Return P;

   ii. Else add P' into P.

        P. ADD (P');

        Return P;

Dynamic evolution algorithm is used to update the Population information when the market get update. When the market update new Population P', we will travels in set of Population. If there is a Pi and Pi.Class == P'.Class, we will update the Populations. If P' isn't in Populations, we will add it into those. So the time complexity is O(1) in best case, and the time complexity is O(n) in the worst case.

4.2.3   Individual Differences Algorithm

We use Euclidean distance to calculate App's malicious value. This malicious value is about the static permissions. We can know that there is more difference between App's permissions and MinPermissions, more dangerous the App is. So we use the algorithm:

$$D = \sqrt{\sum_{i=1}^{n}(X_i + Y_i)^2} \tag{1}$$

We propose the improved algorithm based on Euclidean distance to calculate the malicious value. We have developed the following rules.

Permissions is one App applying. MinPermissions is calculated from Population. nPermissions is calculated from Permission and MinPermission. The nPermissions is the Apps differences between each other.

$$Di = \sqrt{nPermissions} = \sqrt{\sum_{i=1}^{n}p_i^2}(p_i \in nPermissions) \tag{2}$$

We calculate malicious value by similarity calculation. We can find the differences of Apps' permissions. And Di presents the malicious value.

4.2.4   Rating System

We use Normalization Method to make malicious statistics. The Di is mapped into [0, 1]. Then we divide the results to 5 rates.

Sort the Di: We will sort the malicious values from big to small. We can know the Dmax and Dmin.

Normalization:

$$E_i = \frac{D_i}{D_{max} - D_{min}} \tag{3}$$

After the normalization, we can divide these Apps into 5 rates. The Ei is closer to 1, the Di is more dangerous. The Ei is closer to 0, the Di is less dangerous.

4.2.5   Malicious Value with Traffic

We established a coordinate System. The x-axis is malicious value, the y-axis is traffic. We calculate the distance from origin to point. That's the malicious value with traffic.

$$App_i = (D_i, Traffic_i) \tag{4}$$

$$DT_i = \sqrt{D_i^2 + Traffic_i^2} \tag{5}$$

We can use this algorithm to fix the malicious value. Because of the addition of the traffic, we can know the App's behavior.

5 Experimental Evaluation

Based on the two layers model, we have four experiments to evaluate the model. We crawl 1950 Apps for three Population include flashlight, reader and camera. All Apps are from 360 market. On Android 4.1.2, we install all Apps with ADB and collect their permission. Linux is the Ubuntu 14.04.

Experiment 1: Part privacy permissions diagram (Fig. 2).

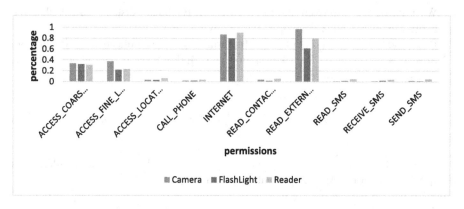

Fig. 2. Privacy permissions diagram in 3 population

From the diagram, we can know the proportion of privacy permission is similar in three Population. The INTERNET permission is the most, it's 90.5% in reader, 86.9% in camera, 79.7% in flashlight. The second is READ_EXTERNAL_STORAGE, it is 96.9%, it's 80.0% in reader and it is 61.5% in flashlight. We can see that the Android Apps' main permissions are Internet, read the external storage. Also, some Apps read CONTACT. The proportion of reader is 6.04%, camera is 3.97%, and flashlight is 1.93%. We can infer that these App has a great threat to user privacy.

Experiment 2: Normalized diagram (Fig. 3).

The data in this diagram presents that Population normalized value has a steady trend. Though the permissions is different in each Population, the value is similar. From 1 to 0.7, slope is large. From 0.7 to 0.3, slope is gentle. From 0.3 to 0, the slope is large again. This descript that most of Apps between 0.3 and 0.7. A small part is dangerous, and another small part is security. The results also proved our hypothesis, the evil Apps is not most (Fig. 4).

According to App normalized level, we rate them. From rate 5 to rate 1, it's more dangerous. Rate 1 is more danger than others. We can find it is similar to the normal distribution. Rate 3 has the most Apps. The dangerous Apps are less than the security Apps (Table 1).

There are parts of malicious Apps. They may have threat for users. We can see form information. The number of download is big, we sure that a great number of users are under privacy threat.

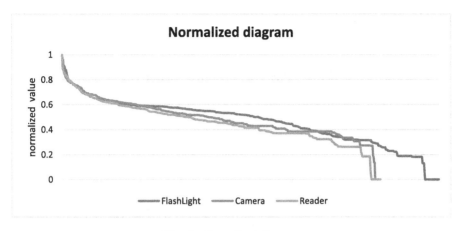

Fig. 3. Normalized diagram

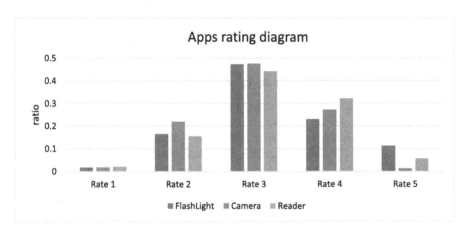

Fig. 4. App rating diagram

Table 1. Malicious Apps table

Package name	Downloads	Rate	Permissions analysis
com.kingnez.umasou.app	210000	Rate 1	Position, make calls, access contacts
com.chaozh.iReaderFree	60490000	Rate 1	Send and receive SMS, access contacts
com.iyd.reader.ReadingJoy	1340000	Rate 1	Send and receive SMS, access contacts, install App
com.sskj.flashlight	5000000	Rate 1	Receive SMS, location
com.kukukk.kfkdroid	870000	Rate 1	Download, make calls, location

Experiment 3: Background analysis (Fig. 5).

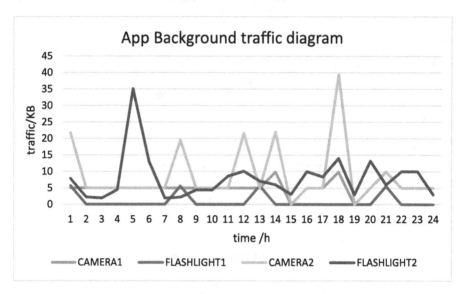

Fig. 5. App Background traffic diagram

From the diagram, we can find there is closely related between time and background traffic. Camera1 generates background traffic every hour, traffic volume in hour is always 5 kb or 10 kb. Flashlight1 generates traffic in 3 or 4 h, the volume is always 5 kb. Camera2 generates traffic every hour, 5 kb or 20 kb, in 18 pm, it is 40 kb. Flashlight2 generates traffic without law, but it is the largest 35 kb in 5 am. Most of the Apps are generates traffic regularly. The volume is similar. So we can infer that the Apps download or upload the same thing.

Experiment 4: Malicious with traffic

For the Apps with similar malicious, we should divide them by background traffic. This is the coordinate system (Fig. 6).

These points are A(319.26, 128.4), B(337.23, 24), C(300.87, 7.3), D(312.65, 2.5), E (320.9, 84.4), F(351.99, 210.4), G(313.69, 123.4), H(372.83, 185.5), I(384.55, 115.4), J(337.60, 7.2).

We can find that they have similar malicious value, but have different traffic. We can divide them with background traffic. Then we calculate the distance from point to origin (Fig. 7).

We can find that malicious value for static permissions is not comprehensive. We can add traffic to fix the result. Before we add the traffic, I is the most dangerous. After, the most dangerous is the H. We use this distance can divide the dangerous Apps.

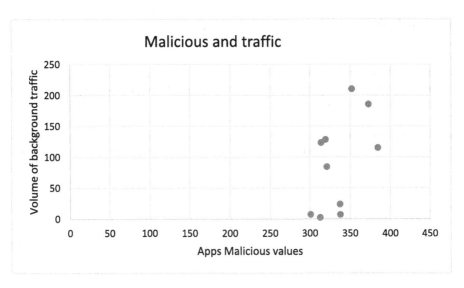

Fig. 6. Malicious and traffic

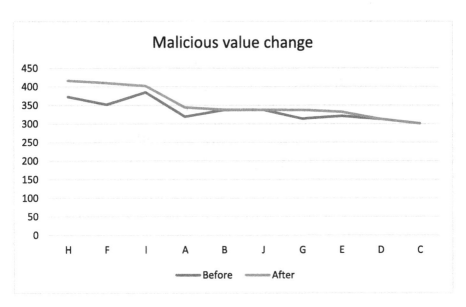

Fig. 7. Malicious value change

6   Conclusion

The experimental results show that in the case of similar static feature value, the dynamic analysis can fix deviation, and we can get more accurate assessment. But we also need improve our algorithm. We try to increase the number of populations. We have a lot of work to do.

Acknowledgement. Authors are partially supported by Colleges and Universities in Hubei Provincial College Students' Innovative Entrepreneurial Training Program (No. 201510488006).

References

1. Mobile Security Situation Android system in the first half 2014, 22 July 2014. http://m.qq.com/security_lab/news_detail_259.html
2. App Stores Growth Accelerates in 2014, 13 January 2015. http://blog.appfigures.com/app-stores-growth-accelerates-in-2014
3. Safe market, 31 May 2016. http://zhushou.360.cn/
4. Android Open Source Project, 31 May 2016. https://source.android.com/
5. Manifest.permission, 31 May 2016. https://developer.android.com/reference/android/Manifest.permission.html
6. Zeng, S.: Research on investigation of privacy protection in android operating system based on Static analysis. University of Science and Technology of China (2014)
7. Qin, Z., Wang, Z., Wu, F., et al.: Android malware detection based on multi-level signature matching. Appl. Res. Comput. **33**(3), 891–895 (2016)
8. Peng, G., Li, J., Sun, R., et al.: Android malware detection research and development. J. Wuhan Univ. (Nat. Sci. Ed.) **61**(1), 21–33 (2015)
9. Wang, H., Li, T., Zhang, T., Wang, J.: Android apps security evaluation system in the cloud. In: Guo, S., Liao, X., Liu, F., Zhu, Y. (eds.) CollaborateCom 2015. LNICSSITE, vol. 163, pp. 151–160. Springer, Cham (2016). doi:10.1007/978-3-319-28910-6_14

Improvement of Decision Tree ID3 Algorithm

Lin Zhu$^{(\boxtimes)}$ and Yang Yang

Beijing University of Posts and Telecommunications, Beijing, China
zlzl.zl@163.com, yyang@bupt.edu.cn

Abstract. This paper describes the basic concepts of the ID3 algorithm and its principles as well as the construction process. Because ID3 algorithm tends to select values for more attributes shortcomings, we introduce threshold, properties information gain rate and parameters to compensate for the lack of ID3 properties selected standard. Based on the above two points to achieve new property selection standard, the original ID3 algorithm is improved. Through the experiment, the improvements of the improved algorithm were compared. Experiment results show that the improved algorithm is effective.

Keywords: ID3 algorithm · Information gain · Information gain rate · Classification property

1 Introduction

With the rapid development of computer technology and network technology, amount of data information is also invaluable in multiples of growth. The purpose of data mining technology is how to effectively find potentially useful knowledge from these data. Data mining is a field of study and gradually developed at the end of the 1980s. It is from a lot of, incomplete, noisy, fuzzy actual application data. We extracted that people do not know in advance but is potentially useful information and knowledge in them.

2 ID3 Algorithm

ID3 algorithm is a typical decision tree learning algorithm. Its core is the tree nodes at all levels, with the information gain attribute selection method as a standard to help determine the appropriate property to generate each node. So you can choose when having the highest information gain attribute as an attribute of the current node to use subset of samples obtained by the division of the property, the minimum information required to classify.

This work was supported by Open Subject Funds of Science and Technology on Information Transmission and Dissemination in Communication Networks Laboratory (ITD-U15002/KX152600011). NSFC (61401033, 61372108, 61272515). National Science and Technology Pillar Program Project (2015BAI11B01).

© ICST Institute for Computer Sciences, Social Informatics and Telecommunications Engineering 2017
S. Wang and A. Zhou (Eds.): CollaborateCom 2016, LNICST 201, pp. 595–600, 2017.
DOI: 10.1007/978-3-319-59288-6_59

Suppose the training set size m, the set $S = A_1 * A_2 * \ldots * A_n$ is finite-dimensional vector space, and each vector space is $n_1, n_2, \ldots n_n$ dimensional subspace respectively.

Suppose $s_1, s_2, \ldots s_r$ is a subset of a vector space S. Its size is $m_1, m_2, \ldots m_r$, and $m = m_1 + m_2 + \ldots + m_r$. Then a decision tree to correctly determine Expectation needs:

$$I(S, m) = -\sum\nolimits_{i=1}^{n} \frac{m_i}{m} \log_2 \frac{m_i}{m} \qquad m = m_1 + m_2 + \ldots + m_r \tag{1}$$

If Property A_k is the root, the information entropy is:

$$E(I(A_k, m)) = \sum_{i=1}^{m} \frac{m_i}{m} I(A_k, m) \tag{2}$$

The information gain:

$$Gain(A_k) = I(S, m) - E(I(A_k, m)) \tag{3}$$

By selecting the maximum information gain attributes extension test attributes diffusion principle ID3 classification, choose each calculated maximum information gain attributes as a new node in the tree, and each attribute value of the property to build branch, according to this thinking divide training data sample set.

While ID3 is a typical decision tree classification algorithm, but there are still shortcomings: Since the ID3 algorithm is to choose the maximum entropy as an attribute selection standard, therefore, it will be more inclined to attribute more value, but not the property more value is optimal properties.

3 The Improved Algorithm

ID3 algorithm selects the maximum entropy as property standards, will be more inclined to more value property, but the property more value is not optimal properties. In this paper, ID3 algorithm for multi-valued attribute bias problems to improve, through the decision tree information gain rate, using the classification tree to determine the parameter values and re-establish the decision tree, thereby improving the value of the multi-algorithm bias problem.

Based on ID3 algorithm, we introduce the concept of information gain rate, using information gain rate instead of information gain attributes as selection standard, the formula of which the rate of information gain:

$$GainRate(A_k) = \frac{Gain(A_k)}{I(S, m)} \tag{4}$$

But the rate of information gain may be the case over compensation is approximately zero, thus introducing bias threshold r. For set S, there are n attributes, attribute bias threshold value of r is typically the average of all the attribute information entropy:

$$r = \frac{1}{n}\sum\nolimits_1^n E(I(A_k, m)) \tag{5}$$

Information gain ratio generated a decision tree, which effectively solve the multi-valued attribute bias problem. Meanwhile, the importance of property refers to all the properties of the importance of information gain contribution comparative results. The value can be defined as a subset of the properties A branch share Instances A proportion, by comparison to distinguish between information entropy gain contribution calculated to select the optimal properties. Importance of the role is to distinguish between different information attributes importance or dependence. The value can be defined as a subset of A proportion shares Instances A proportion, by comparison to distinguish between information entropy gain contribution calculated to select the optimal properties.

Thus, for the classification of different properties have different degrees of importance. Introducing parameter indicates the degree of importance, in order to increase the degree of importance of important properties, the improvement of information entropy formula:

$$E(I(A_k, m)) = \sum\nolimits_{i=1}^m \left(\frac{m_i}{m} + \alpha\right) I(A_k, m) \tag{6}$$

The resulting tree root attribute value is the proportion of first generation of a decision tree yes/no, non-root attribute value is 0.

Thus, the resulting decision tree to determine a parameter value, and by generating a decision tree again raised the importance of important attributes. Through a combination of both methods to make up for the shortcomings of traditional ID3 algorithm.

The improved algorithm steps:

(1) Calculate the Expectation information and information entropy of each attribute.
(2) For the set S, there are n attributes. R usually tend to the threshold value is the average of all the attribute information entropy.
(3) Computing the root attribute information gain.
(4) The information entropy of each attribute and the threshold value r are compared. If the entropy value is lower than the threshold r, we select the gain ratio standard; if higher than the threshold r, we select the information gain standard.
(5) Create node recursively until you've selected all properties.
(6) Determine the impact factor and parameter values.
(7) Replace the formula (3) is calculated using the formula of information entropy improved, decision trees again.

4 Analysis of Results

To further demonstrate the effectiveness of the algorithm can be used to provide data sets UCI comparison test.

The Fig. 1 is the original ID3 algorithm and improved algorithm comparison in accuracy and time in different amount of samples in different data sets.

Seen from Fig. 1, as data collection increases, the accuracy of the algorithm increases. The improved accuracy of the algorithms has greatly improved than the original ID3 algorithm. Seen from Fig. 2, when dealing with the same amount of records, the improved algorithm consumes more time than the original ID3 algorithm. In this paper, the improved algorithm sacrifices some time in exchange for a substantial increase accuracy. Time consuming optimization is still needed to continue the research work.

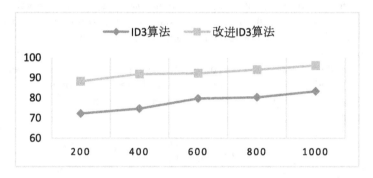

Fig. 1. Different sample sizes algorithm accuracy comparison

Figures 3 and 4 are in different data sets, the original ID3 algorithm and improved ID3 algorithm comparison results in terms of accuracy and computational time. We can see in this paper accuracy of the improved algorithm is significantly better than the accuracy of the original ID3 algorithm, but in the time-consuming slightly larger than the original ID3 algorithm. Thus, less time-consuming exchange for accuracy significantly improved, overall improved algorithm is better than the original ID3 algorithm.

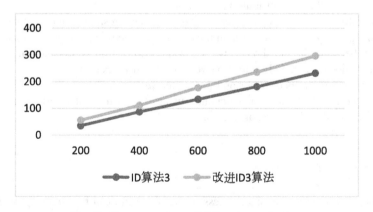

Fig. 2. The comparison of different sample sizes

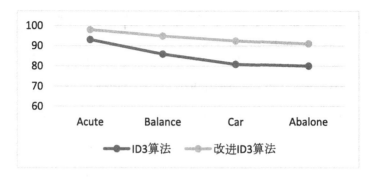

Fig. 3. The comparison of the accuracy level for different data

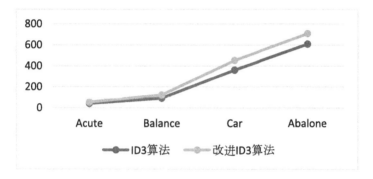

Fig. 4. Algorithm time under different sets of data comparison

5 Conclusion

ID3 algorithm is a decision tree algorithm, the most typical method, a large number of scholars have studied and analyzed. This paper describes the ID3 algorithm and its improved algorithm. First, we describe the basic principles of ID3 algorithm. The biggest shortcoming that is multi-valued attribute bias problem for this algorithm, by introducing information gain rate and parameters, to a certain extent overcome this major drawback. Experimental results show that: the new algorithm overcomes the disadvantages of ID3 algorithm tends to properties of more value than ID3 algorithm and has better classification performance on classification accuracy.

References

1. Wang, Y., Xuegang, H.: Decision tree ID3 algorithm research. J. Anhui Univ. (Nat. Sci. Edn.) **03**, 71–75 (2002)
2. Wang, X., Jiang, Y.: Analysis and improvement of decision tree ID3 algorithm. Comput. Eng. Des. **09**, 3069–3072 + 3076 (2011)

3. Liu, Q.: Improvement of Decision Tree ID3 Algorithm. Harbin Engineering University (2009)
4. Huang, Y., Fan, T., Wang, Y.: Decision tree ID3 algorithm improved algorithm. Comput. Knowl. Technol. **01**, 96–98 (2012)
5. Wang, S.: Decision tree ID3 algorithm and implementation. J. Qiqihar Univ. (Nat. Sci. Edn.) **03**, 64–68 (2012)
6. Wang, S.: ID3 decision tree algorithm analysis and improvement. J. Yichun Univ. **04**, 7–9 (2012)
7. Huang, Y., Fan, T.: Analysis and optimization decision tree ID3 algorithm. Comput. Eng. Des. **08**, 3089–3093 (2012)
8. Wang, M.: Data Mining Algorithm Optimization Research and Application. Anhui University (2014)
9. Wang, B.: Research and Application of Decision Tree Algorithm. Donghua University (2008)

A Method on Chinese Thesauri

Fu Chen[1(✉)], Xi Liu[1], Yuemei Xu[1], Miaohua Xu[2], and Guangjun Shi[3]

[1] Department of Computer Science and Technology, Beijing Foreign Studies University,
Beijing, China
chenfu@servst.com
[2] Hebei Surveying and Mapping Institute, Heibei, China
[3] Computer Network Information Center, Chinese Academy of Science, Beijing, China

Abstract. In recent years, text analysis has become increasingly heated in many fields. And now, majority methods of text analysis are using Word2vec, Naïve Bayes or so on to classify the large number of texts. But for the text itself, not all samples are useful for some high-requirement researches and only use one keywords to get the related sample is definitely not enough. In this paper, we provide a novel model of second text filtering with Chinese Thesauri. It includes roughly 5 steps: sample collecting, thesauri establishment, word-segment algorithm, word-frequency statistics and the calculation of text relevance. Its main purpose is making the sample texts more accurate with the keywords which are input by the user and avoiding the needless time and space waste.

Keywords: Chinese thesauri · Text analysis · Semantic distance

1 Introduction

In every kind of language, the relation of word to word is obviously not totally isolated. And this is also the basic of all those algorithms of calculating semantic distance in order to classify a text into a kind of assay. In this report, we will build a tree of all Chinese thesauri. And we will use this tree to find the thesauri of the keyword which is given by the user. In the meantime, every word will be attached with a weight to show its similarity or correlation with the user's key words, and the value will be used in the later filter procedure.

After the calculating of the weight of every thesaurus, the next step is to statistics the number of the keyword and thesauri in each assay. And compared with the text analysis of English assays, Chinese assays seems more difficult because the word in Chinese is not segmented by blank space and only have a punctuation after an integrated sentence or sense-group. So, before all the text analysis of Chinese assays, they should be word segmented. Only after the word segmented can Chinese assay be used to statistics the word that you want to count. Then, use the number and weight to calculate the correlation value with the keyword that user input earlier. And considering the sum of words if different from assay to assay, the correlation will be divided by the sum of words. And in order to make the comparison more obviously, we choose to use the thousandth to express the assay's correlation. At last, the correlation value can be a

© ICST Institute for Computer Sciences, Social Informatics and Telecommunications Engineering 2017
S. Wang and A. Zhou (Eds.): CollaborateCom 2016, LNICST 201, pp. 601–608, 2017.
DOI: 10.1007/978-3-319-59288-6_60

criterion of the second text filter. It can be very useful to get rid of the texts those are not up to the user's standard.

We choose a specific word Confucianism as the keywords which are supposed to be input by the users. First, we set a levels –tree based on the keywords' thesauri. Second, we calculate the thesauri' correlation value preparing for the latter calculation. This procedure is based on the shortest path of two nodes in a tree. Then we collect ten texts from Internet as our sample. And deal them with word-segment algorithm and word-frequency statistics. Finally, we use the value of words' correlation value, word frequency and the total number of word related with every sample text to gain the ulti-mate degree of correlation between each sample and the keywords. Figure 1. Shows the process diagram of our study.

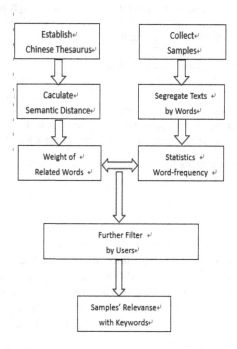

Fig. 1. The process diagram of our study

The remainder of this paper is structured as follow. In Sect. 2, we review and discuss the related work. Section 3 describes the establishment of the level-tree of Chinese thesauri and the algorithm of correlation value calculating between two words which is based on that level-tree. Section 4 shows the process of word-segment algorithm and word-frequency statistics in Chinese text. Section 5 is about the calculation of the rele-vance between the text and keywords. At last, we will talk about conclusion and future work in Sect. 6.

2   Paper Preparation

This section discusses related work on two key aspects of the article. Firstly, Subsect. 2.1 presents the origin and construction of Chinese Thesauri. Then, Subsect. 2.2 introduces the algorithm of text similarity computation.

2.1   Origin and Construction of Chinese Thesauri

A thesauri is a set of items (phrases or words) plus a set of relations between these items. And it can be divided to two types, manual and automatic. And in this paper, we will use the manual thesauri. There are two kinds of manual thesauri. The first are general-purpose and word-based thesauri like Roget's and WordNet. Those thesauri contain sense relations like antonym and synonym but are rarely used in IR systems. The second are IR-oriented and phrase-based thesauri like INSPEC, LCSH(Library of Congress Subject Headings), and MeSH(Medical Subject Headings). Those manual thesauri usually contain relations between thesaurus items such as BT(Broader Term), NT(Narrow Term), UF(Used For), and RT(Related To), and can be either general or specific, depending on the needs of thesaurus builders. This type of manual thesauri is widely used in commercial systems [1]. Thus, we chose the second kind of manual thesauri. But because of the expense, we only construct a part of the whole thesauri and just used for our experiment. Whenever the reader wants to use the algorithm in this paper, you can just construct your own thesauri as long as it can satisfy the requirement.

2.2   Algorithm of Text Similarity Computation

Displayed equations or formulas are centered and set on a separate line (with an extra line or halfline space above and below). Displayed expressions should be numbered for reference. The numbers should be consecutive within each section or within the contribution, with numbers enclosed in parentheses and set on the right margin.

For text-based semantic similarity, perhaps the most widely used approaches are the approximations obtained through query expansion, as performed in information retrieval (Voorhees 1993), or the latent semantic analysis method (Landauer, Foltz, & Laham 1998) that measures the similarity of texts by exploiting second-order word relations automatically acquired from large text collections [1]. In this paper, we choose to use the Chinese Thesauri to evaluate the text relevance with the keywords which is input by users. And it can be regarded as the second step after the calculating of word-frequency of the related words in texts and this step will be very useful to filter the samples more accurate.

3   Establishment of Chinese Thesauri

Thesauri in Chinese means the related words and alternative words of a keywords. And in the structure of level-tree, the parents node and brothers node can also shows special relations of two words. So, we try to classify all the Chinese words into a huge level-tree. The principle of the structure is the inclusion relation and the coordinative relation. And the shortest path between two nodes is obviously an important character of the tree. In the field of text analysis, the shortest path can be used to calculate the correlation of two words, which is also used in this paper.

3.1 Establish the Level-Tree

In order to make the theory more easy-to-understand, we choose a keywords to start our experiment as an example. The keywords we chose is "Confucianism" and it is of course that the user can chose any else words as long as he need. And in order to establish the thesauri level-tree, we add some related words like "Confucius", "Analects"(The Analects of Confucius) and so on. Figure 2. Shows the level-tree, which is a part of the integrated Chinese thesauri, used in the example experience in this paper.

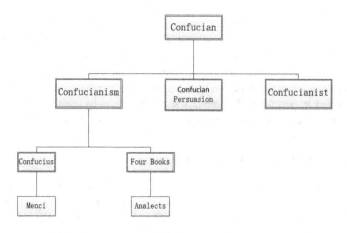

Fig. 2. The thesauri level-tree of our experience

After the establishment of the thesauri tree, we will use it to gain the correlation value of each related word. And based on the structure of level-tree, we choose to apply the Dijkstra algorithm to realize the process of traversing all the nodes, and get the shortest path between every related words and the keywords. Considering the principle of easy-to-understand and practical, we choose a simple formula as following show to calculate the semantic distance of the related words and the keywords:

$$Dist(C_i) = 1/(2^{L_i}) \tag{1}$$

The C_i represent the related words. L_i means the length of the shortest path of the related words and the keywords. $Dist(C_i)$ shows the degree of the relation of word C_i and the keywords. We definite the weight of the keywords "Confucianism" is 1, and any other words' weight will be based on the semantic distance between it and the keywords. Using this formula, we arrive at the conclusion that the correlation of "Confucian", "Confucius", "Four Books" is 0.5 and for "Confucian Persuasion", "Confucianist",

"Menci", "Analects", the value is 0.25. And the weights of those related words are showed in Fig. 3.

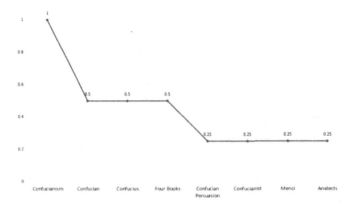

Fig. 3. The weights of related words

4 Word-Segment Algorithm and Word-Frequency Statistics

Differ from English text, the words in Chinese text don't have the blanks to divided from each other. It even ever made some trouble in the development of the text analysis in China. But not very long after the emerge of that problem, Jie-Ba algorithm was came up with. And in our experiment, we also choose to use it in order to divide the words in Chinese text. The Jie-Ba algorithm is based on the trie tree, which is a famous prefix tree. It includes more than 20,000 words, approximately cover the all common words that may be used in our ordinary life. And all these words are collected in a txt file. It is similar with the verb collocations in English, presenting the correlation between words and words like Fig. 4 shows.

And according to the trie tree, we are able to distinguish the divide method of the sample. Once the word matched and have no word longer than it can match, a blank will be added. And text will be segregated word by word. Jie-Ba algorithm provides three modes named full mode, default and search mode. Full mode can scan all the letters that can become a word, its speed is quick but can't solve the problem of ambiguity. The default mode is trying to segregate the text most accurately, so it is suitable for text analysis and we choose this mode for those reasons. As you can see by its name, the search mode fits the search engine and under this mode, text will be default segregated and long words will be cut again for a second time.

Fig. 4. The verb collocations in English

After word-segment, the text is divided word by word and segregated by blanks. So, it offers the condition of word-frequency and we don't need to worry about take the wrong match of words. And we use the same dictionary which is used by Jie-Ba algorithm to calculate the word-frequency in each sample text. It is easy to realize because it just need some cycles to match the words, gain the final data and output the result.

5   Calculation of Text Relevance

Provided the related words' weight and word frequency, the last step is to count the text relevance with the keywords. And we choose to use the following formula:

$$R(\text{Assayk}) = \left\{ \sum_{i=1}^{n} [Dist(Ci) * Nk, i] \right\} / MK \tag{2}$$

In the formula, Assayk represent the text. 'n' means the number of keywords and related words. Ci is the NO.i word, N(k,i) means the sum of word Ci in Assayk. And Mk is the sum number of word in Assayk. After calculation, we arrive at the conclusion of following data, which is showed in Figs. 5 and 6:

R(text1)=21.09‰

R(text2)=0.89‰

R(text3)=14.97‰

R(text4)=16.59‰

R(text5)=36.52‰

R(text6)=17.94‰

R(text7)=4.56‰

R(text8)=22.94‰

R(text9)=10.30‰

R(text10)=17.16‰

Fig. 5. Text relevance of samples

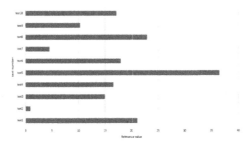

Fig. 6. Histogram of text relevance

And as the figure shows, every text is attached with its own value of the relevance between it and user's keyword. Using those data, we can offer the users a second select chance, limiting the relevance value of those texts that he gain from input the keywords in search engine only. And this step can further filter the samples to attain different users demand and class the texts, which contain the keyword, by the text relevance. It will be used in many high requirements research, because the texts is no more just texts but hold a relevance with the keywords in different degree.

6   Conclusion and Future Work

This paper presents a novel model to secondly filter the texts those are collected by input the keywords on the Internet. It is based on the Chinese Thesauri and related to the establishment of thesauri, word-segment algorithm, word-frequency statistics and the calculation of text relevance. Through the experiment, we validate the effectiveness and accuracy of our method. Using the Chinese Thesauri, we limit the relevance of all the samples, which can avoid the waste of analyzing the useless texts and make the samples attain the higher quality after the second filter.

Future word will include a number of aspects. Firstly, the existing thesaurus needs an more accurate standard and cover larger scale. It requires a more professional knowledge of linguistics and graph theory. Secondly, the language is always in the proceeding of change. At the same time, the Chinese Thesauri will also be changing. So, we need to continually update the structure of our thesauri into a more scientific framework. Finally, in order to make this model be used by not only the technical scholar but also the layman, we are supposed to get the entire algorithm into software. After this step, it will only require the user input the keywords and smallest relevance of the texts and keywords. Then, sample collecting, thesauri establishment, word-segment algorithm, word-frequency statistics and the calculation of text relevance will all be done automatically. It will largely enhance the features of using-friendly and efficient.

Acknowledgements. The research was supported in part by the National Science Foundation of China under No.61672104, 61170209, 61502038,U1509214;Program for New Century Excellent Talents in University No.NCET-13-0676. Key Program of BFSU 2011 Collaborative Innovation Center No.BFSU2011-ZD04.

References

1. Jing, Y., Crof, W.B.: An Association Thesauri for Information Retrieval (1994)
2. Mihalcea, R., Corley, C.: Corpus-based and Knowledge-based Measures of Text Semantic Similarity (2006)
3. Tausczik, Y.R., Pennebaker, J.W.: The Psychological Meaning of Words: LIWC and Computerized Text Analysis Methods (2010)
4. Scott, S., Matwin, S.: Text Classification Using WordNet Hypernyms (1998)
5. Roberts, C.W.: Text Analysis for the Social Sciences: Methods for Drawing Statistical Inferences from Texts and Transcript. Lawrence Erlbaum Associates, Mahwah (1997)
6. Lacity, M.C., Janson, M.A.: Understanding qualitative data: a framework of text analysis methods. J. Manage. Inf. Syst. **11**(2), 137–155 (1994)
7. Stone, P.J.: Thematic text analysis: new agendas for analyzing text content. In: Roberts, C. (ed.) Text Analysis for the Social Sciences. Lawrence Erlbaum Associates, Mahwah (1997)
8. Lehnert, W., Sundheim, B.: A Performance Evaluation of Text-Analysis Technologies. www.aaai.org
9. Soergel, D.: Indexing languages and thesauri: construction and maintenance (1974). www.dsoergel.com
10. Wang, Y.-C., Vandendorpe, J., Evens, M.: Relational thesauri in information retrieval. J. Am. Soc. Inf. Sci. **36**(1), 15–27 (1985). America
11. Larsen, H.L., Yager, R.R.: The use of fuzzy relational thesauri for classificatory problem solving in information retrieval and expert systems. IEEE Trans. Syst. Man Cybern. **23**(1), 31–41 (2002)
12. Budanitsky, A., Hirst, G.: Semantic distance in WordNet: an experimental, application-oriented evaluation of five measures (2001)

Formal Modelling and Analysis of TCP for Nodes Communication with ROS

Xiaojuan Li[1]([⊠]), Yanyan Huo[1], Yong Guan[1], Rui Wang[1], and Jie Zhang[2]

[1] Beijing Key Laboratory of Light Industrial Robot and Safety Verification, College of Information Engineering, Capital Normal University, Beijing 100048, China
Lixj66@gmail.com
[2] College of Information Science and Technology, Beijing University of Chemical Technology, Beijing 100029, China

Abstract. TCP (transportation control protocol) is widely used for supporting communications between robotic nodes with ROS (robotic operation system) for critical-task implementation. The probability of bit errors and lost packets is much higher for moving nodes under WLAN. So it is essential to analyze the performance and the reliability of the communication processes for nodes with ROS. It is built that the communication model of nodes for TCP in ROS by MDP(Markov Decision Process) and the reliability of that is analyzed in this paper. The Specifications of the TCP for nodes communication is formalized into the objective properties by PCTL(Probabilistic Computation Tree Logic), and the satisfiability of the properties is verified by the probabilistic model checker. The results can help the designers to make better strategies for the communication process over TCP in ROS of robotic nodes.

Keywords: Node network communication · Probabilistic model checking · Markov decision process

1 Introduction

With the increasingly development of robotic technology, many new applications are deployed in distributed nodes with ROS for cooperative tasks. The correctness and reliability of communication among nodes is getting more important in critical-task system. The transportation of commands and data among nodes with ROS is based on TCP(transport control protocol), which plays an important role for the communication reliability of nodes. Some work have been made on reliability analysis of TCP in WLAN. A adaptable TCP segment size scheme is proposed to improve the TCP communication performance in wireless environment [1]. Data link layer and sub-section connection is developed for improving the performance of TCP protocol in wireless network [3]. A reliability sorting algorithm is put forward for TCP data packet for the limited covert channel in [4]. These references basically use simulation, emulation or other traditional verification methods to analysis or improve the optimized methods for the reliability of TCP communication protocol.

© ICST Institute for Computer Sciences, Social Informatics and Telecommunications Engineering 2017
S. Wang and A. Zhou (Eds.): CollaborateCom 2016, LNICST 201, pp. 609–614, 2017.
DOI: 10.1007/978-3-319-59288-6_61

Formal method is based on strictly mathematical reasoning to analyze or check the correctness of design and implementation, which can be an automatic checking for a finite status system. Model checking can provide automatic checking whether a system abstraction model satisfy the properties, which are formalized from the specifications of design. A colored Petri net model for the TCP's connection is used to verify the correct of the communication protocol [7]. The verification and analysis for SpaceWire [8] communication protocol at the exchange level by model checking. The real-time properties of the session level of nodes with ROS [9] is verified by Uppaal. The Probabilistic model checking combines probability analysis and general model checking method technology, and it is a useful for the description of non-deterministic stochastic systems. The paper focuses on the analysis and verification of the reliability of the TCP transportation for nodes with ROS by probabilistic model checking (Table 1).

Table 1. Symbolic representation of the node1.

Symbol	Function
idle	Initial state, no request for connection
request	Sends the request signal
req_num	The number of sending request
ack1_num	The number of backtrack from the node2
ack2_num	The response number from node1 to node2
RECEIVE_NUM	The upper limit of receive message
SEND_NUM	The upper limit of send message
P	The rate of package lost

2   Formal Modelling of Nodes Communication Based on TCP

The operation communication between ROS nodes is controlled by a main node running as roscore, which is responsible for monitoring and management the all functional nodes' communication. All of the nodes must register in the ROS Master node while they start, and all nodes can communicate with each other after authorized by the master node. XML-RPC communication protocol is the calling mechanism of the communication between ROS nodes' communication, which is based on TCP protocol, and by adding the port on the transport layer, it can be represented corresponding application layer communication. In order to analysis and verify the performance of the nodes' communication protocol, this paper builds formal model and gives probabilistic analysis for the connection set up and sending or receiving message of the nodes.

The Markov Decision Process model for the connection and communication between node1 and node2 is built for the verification. The node1 model is shown in Fig. 1, While establishing the models for node1 and node2, the action translates from initial state "idle" to send-request state "request". After sending a request, the node1 will wait for confirmation information from the node2. If the node1 receives the confirmation from the node2, it will send a signal to the node2 again, if the node2 successfully receives the confirmation signal, then the connection was established successfully. Conversely, if the node1 does not receive confirmation signal from the node2 within the prescribed time limit, the node1 will keeping sending a signal to the node2 until it receives confirmation signal from the node2 or it reaches maximum retransmission limit. In order to make modelling and analysis the problem of establishing connection and sending message between node1 and node2, the paper extends the model by adding the sending data into the model after the connection is established successfully.

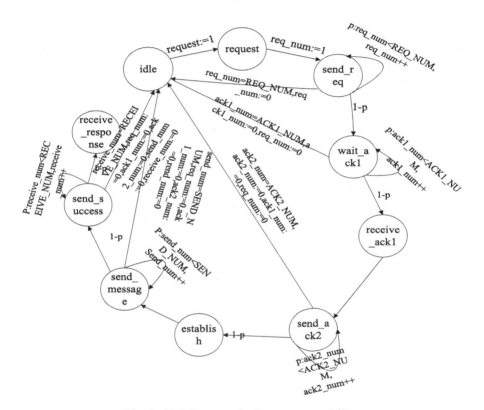

Fig. 1. Node1 communication process modelling

In the similar way, the model of the node2, which is receiver side, also describes the process of the three-way-handshake connection and data transmission. When a connection is requested from the node1 to the node2, the state of the node2 will change, and it will transfer from the initial state "idle" to the "wait-req" state. After receiving the request signal, the node2 turns into the "receive-req" state. Then after sending the confirmation signal to the node1 successfully, the node2 will be to "send Send-ack1" state, if the progress is successful, the node2 will transfer to receive "reveive-ack2" state, and wait for the acknowledgement signal from the node1, if it successfully receives the confirmation signal from the node1, it will move to "establish" state.

Next, the node1 and the node2 will send data each other. When the node2 receives the request from the node1 successfully, the node2 sends the corresponding service [15] to the node1, if the node1 receives the response message from the node2, then the transition have been completed successfully, During the period, the lost package may made the failure transmission between the node1 and the node2, it is taken into account in the formal models by adding the probability to the MDP models in the paper.

3   Verification and Probability Analysis

Critical properties for the nodes communication, which is translated into PCTL formula, is extracted from the design specification. Based on the formal models of the nodes that we have set up aboved, the properties are automatically verified by PRISM model checker and further be analyzed.

In the model of node1, c = 0, 1, 2, 3, 4, 5, 6, 7, 8, 9 respectively represent the node1 is at idle, request, send- req, wait-ack, receive-ack1, send-ack2, establish, send-message, send-success, receive-response state; and the node2 state s = 0, 1, 2, 3, 4, 5, 6, 7 respectively represent the node2 is at idle, wait-req, receive-req, send-ack1, receive-ack2, establish, receive-message, response-success state.

Property 1. The maximum probability under different package lost?
Pmax=?
[Fc=9&req_num=1&ack1_num=1&ack2_num=1&send_num=1&receive_num=1]

In Fig. 2, the horizontal axis represents the rate of the package lost in the wireless network, the vertical axis represents the maximum probability of the connection established and sending data successfully between the node1 and the node2. As Fig. 2 is shown, when the error probability is 0.05, the maximum probability of sending the correct data is less than 75%, the results is very important for optimizing the network in the design phase.

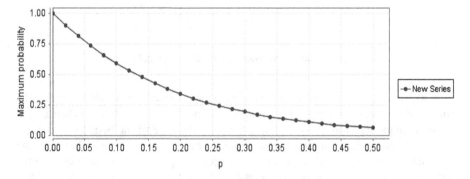

Fig. 2. The maximum probability under different package lost

Property 2. The maximum probability of the sending data successfully under different retransmission?

The maximum probability for first and second transferring successful is respectively expressed as following:

Pmax=?[F s=7&req_num=1&ack1_num=1&ack2_num=1&send_num=1]

Pmax=?[Fs=7&req_num=1&ack1_num=1&ack2_num=1&(send_num=2| send_num=1)]

The result shows that the maximum probability with first transferring is 0.6587, and the maximum probability is 0.7246 for second try shown in Fig. 3, which coincides with the experiment result, and it verified that the probability changes with the number of retransmission, and they are positive correlation. The results of the analysis lay a foundation to the future research or application about the communication nodes with ROS.

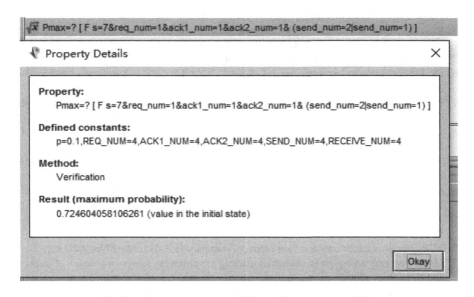

Fig. 3. The maximum probability under twice transmision

4   Conclusion

We builds the formal model and analysis the communication protocol in the wireless network for the nodes with ROS, and extracts some critical properties for analyze and checking. the reliability of the TCP between nodes with ROS is analyzed under different link error probability by probabilistic model checking, which provides useful strategies for designer, and is helpful for avoiding bug at design phrase.

Acknowledgement. The authors thank Beijing Key Laboratory of Electronic System Reliability Technology, Beijing Engineering Research Center of Highly Reliable Embedded System, Beijing Advanced Innovation Center for Imaging Technology, Beijing Collaborative Innovation Center of Mathematics and Information Science for their support. This work was supported by the National Natural Science Foundation of China (61373034, 61303014, 61472468, 61572331), the Project of Beijing Municipal Science & Technology Commission(Z141100002014001).

References

1. Huang, Z.: The real-time operating system development and implemen- tation for industrial robot controller. School of Mechanical Engineering & Automation, Beijing University of Aeronautics, Beijing (2013)
2. Han, H.: Improvement for wireless TCP based on bit error rate monitoring. J. Comput. Appl. **31**(10), 2657–2659 (2011)
3. Li, M., Zhang, Y., Xiang, D.: Improvement mechanism of transmission control protocol in wireless network. Comput. Eng. **42**(1), 103–108 (2016)
4. Wei, S., Yang, W., Shen, Y.: A secret communication method based on reliable packet ordering. J. Chin. Comput. Syst. **37**(1), 124–128 (2016)
5. Wang, Z.: Survey of model checking. Comput. Sci. **40**(6A), 1–14 (2013)
6. PRISM-probabilistic symbolic model checker [EB/OL] (2011). http://www.prismmodel checker.org/
7. Li, F.: Formal description and verification of TCP protocol based on colored Petri nets. Mod. Comput. **309**(6), 49–52 (2009)
8. Li, Y., Li, X., Guan, Y.: Formal modeling and probabilistic analysis of SpaceWire protocol. J. Chin. Comput. Syst. **34**(9), 25–29 (2013)
9. Wang, Y., Wang, R., Guan, Y.: Formal verification of node to node communication in RGMP-ROS hybrid operating system. J. Chin. Comput. Syst. **36**(10), 2379–2383 (2015)
10. Parker, D.A.: Implementation of Symbolic Model Checking for Probabilistic Systems. University of Birmingham (2002)
11. Su, K., Luo, X., Lu, G.: Symbolic model checking for CTL. Chin. J. Comput. **28**(11), 1798–1806 (2005)
12. TCP three-way-handshake and four recovery summary [EB/OL]. http://blog.csdn.net
13. Li, Z.: Research on design of intelligent gateway in substation. Jiangsu university of science and technology (2007)
14. Liu, Y.: Research on reliability design and test method of device driver. University of Electronic Science and technology (2014)
15. Wu, Y.: Design of P2P instant messaging software based on XMPP protocol. Electronic information technology and instruments of Zhejiang University, Hangzhou (2007)

On Demand Resource Scheduler Based on Estimating Progress of Jobs in Hadoop

Liangzhang Chen, Jie Xu, Kai Li, Zhonghao Lu, Qi Qi$^{(\boxtimes)}$,
and Jingyu Wang

State Key Laboratory of Networking and Switching Technology,
Beijing University of Posts and Telecommunications,
Beijing 100876, People's Republic of China
{luzhonghao,xujie,qiqi,wangjingyu}@ebupt.com

Abstract. In order to meet the need of setting deadline for Hadoop MapReduce job and improve resource utilization of Hadoop cluster, a resource scheduler based on collecting the running information of tasks is proposed. According to the information of resource usage, the progress of job, the deadline of job, and the handling time of job, we estimate the resource demand of jobs, and then schedule these jobs according to their resource demand. Meanwhile, a method to judge whether the resource of cluster can meet the deadline of all the jobs in cluster is proposed. When the jobs will miss the deadline under the allocated resources, scheduler applies to cloud platform for extra resources. Experimental results show the on demand resource scheduler can increase the utilization of resource in Hadoop cluster and approximately ensure the deadline of jobs.

Keywords: Hadoop · On demand · Scheduler · Job with deadline

1 Introduction

The Cloud Computing provides a virtualization of hardware and software resource pool to a variety of service for users in the network platform which makes it possible to store and compute the huge amounts of data.

At present, many cloud platforms provide data computing services, one of the most commonly used is the Hadoop [1] which is an open source project under the Apache organization. Hadoop is a distributed parallel programming framework for huge data processing and data-analysis. It can be deployed in the cloud platform resource pool and mainly focus on the huge amounts of data storage and computing.

But it is essential to use a resource manager to coordinate and schedule the Hadoop cluster resources. Yet Another Resource Negotiator (Yarn) is commonly used as a resource manager. There are three kinds of schedulers, simple First-In-First-Out (FIFO) Scheduler, Capacity Scheduler [2] and Hadoop Fair Scheduler (HFS) [3], which can only schedule resource based on the strategy of "FIFO" in each queue and be unaware of the Running information of jobs in Hadoop.

As users always setting deadline for Hadoop MapReduce job, it requires the scheduler has the ability to allocate resource according to the job's deadline. But now all the schedulers for Hadoop cannot allocate resource in terms of the job deadline. In

© ICST Institute for Computer Sciences, Social Informatics and Telecommunications Engineering 2017
S. Wang and A. Zhou (Eds.): CollaborateCom 2016, LNICST 201, pp. 615–626, 2017.
DOI: 10.1007/978-3-319-59288-6_62

this paper, we propose an on demand scheduler for Hadoop MapReduce job with deadline. For a given MapReduce job with deadline, the scheduler tries its best to allocate enough resources to meet the deadline of job. Meanwhile, this new kind of scheduler can judge whether the resource of cluster can meet the deadline of all the jobs in cluster. If not, the scheduler should request resources from Cloud platform to make all the jobs in cluster finished before deadline. This paper makes the following contributions.

A strategy to estimate the progress of Hadoop MapReduce job is proposed, which is the basis of on demand scheduling and resource judging strategy. The strategy uses the information of map tasks, shuffle, reduce tasks.

A concept of on demand resource scheduling is included, which describes the demand for resource. The resource demand is related to the deadline of job, the progress of job and the used resources of job.

An algorithm to judge whether the resources of cluster can meet the deadline of all the jobs in cluster is presented. This algorithm uses the information of resource demand, deadline, cluster resources and so on. In this algorithm, we also introduce the concept of work. When this algorithm judges cluster resource is not enough, it requests resources from Cloud platform.

The rest of paper is organized as follows. Section 2 reviews the related work. Section 3 gives details on the model of on demand resource scheduler. Section 4 shows the experimental results. Section 5 concludes the paper.

2 Related Work

In recent years, many researchers attempt to improve resource utilization of Hadoop cluster.

Polo *et al.* [4] introduce a new task scheduler that dynamically collects the performance data of MapReduce jobs and adjusts the resource allocation accordingly. But they only focus on the map phase and have no control over the reduce phase. Jockey [5] is designed for single job to maximize its economic utility. So Jockey is effective at guaranteeing job latency and minimizing the impact on the data parallel clusters. But it lacks scheduling mechanism among multiple jobs. A. Verma [6] proposes a framework, called ARIA, to estimate and allocate appropriate number of map and reduce slots for MapReduce applications so that they can meet their required deadlines. However, all of these studies only support resource inference and allocation and give no consideration to overtime budget and energy cost.

Gunho Lee *et al.* [7] present a architecture to allocate resources to a data analytical cluster in the cloud, and a scheduling scheme that uses progress share as a new fairness metric to fit the heterogeneous environment. In their resource allocation strategy, they actually divided nodes into two pools to reduce the cost brought by fluctuating resource demands of data analytical workloads. In our work, we also propose a multi-layer node model to reduce the cost of scale process and increase the flexibility of the cluster maintained by the datacenter. However, we propose an auto-scaling algorithm to automatically adjust each node layer instead of using only static threshold and single indicator which may cause fluctuation.

Wei Zhang *et al.* [8] refine the scheduler of virtualization layer to minimize interference on high priority interactive services. Toomas *et al.* [9] also propose a method named auto-scaling in Hadoop clusters, but their auto-scaling is only based on the workload of the Hadoop cluster which won't apply to various services environments. There are also efforts to study heterogeneous clusters in [10, 11]. These authors address the poor performance of MapReduce on heterogeneous clusters and propose a heterogeneous aware scheduling scheme. Although their work improves the performance of heterogeneous cloud environments, the auto-scaling algorithm in our paper pays more attention to the heterogeneous resource demands rather than complex physical environments.

Dachen Zhang [12] designs a model to meet the deadline of all jobs with limited resources, while we focus on how to provide resources for urgent jobs that will meet the deadline in a short time.

3 Model Description

In this section, we introduce the details of on demand resource scheduler. The scheduler consists of three functions which includes estimating progress of MapReduce jobs, scheduling resources and judging whether the resources of cluster are enough. Figure 1 shows the whole process.

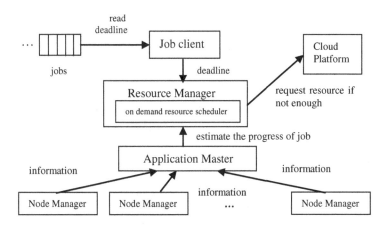

Fig. 1. The process of on demand resource scheduler

We can see that the Job Client read the deadline firstly, and then send it to the Resource Manager. Application Master collects the running information of Node Manager and sends it to Resource Manager. Resource Manager schedules the resource according to the strategy we propose, and judges whether cluster resource is enough. If cluster resource is not enough, it requests resource from the cloud platform.

3.1   Estimate Progress of MapReduce Job

We analyze the execution of the Hadoop MapReduce job firstly. According to the framework of Hadoop, MapReduce job is divided into many map tasks and reduce tasks, these tasks can be done on different nodes in cluster concurrently. In these tasks, map tasks focus on processing the split of original data and put the intermediate results on local nodes. These intermediate results will be transformed to the corresponding reduce tasks after the process of shuffle. Finally, reduce tasks produce the final result. In sum, the progress of a job consists of three parts, map, reduce and shuffle. Fig. 2 shows the specific execution of the Hadoop MapReduce job.

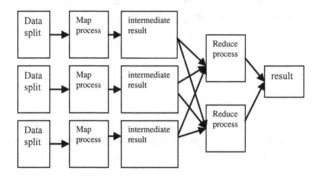

Fig. 2. The specific execution of the Hadoop

We use a linear Eq. (1) to fit the progress of MapReduce job.

$$p = \alpha p_{map} + \beta p_{red} + \gamma p_{sf} \tag{1}$$

Where p is the progress of job, p_{map} is the progress of all map tasks, p_{red} is the progress of all reduce tasks, p_{sf} is the progress of shuffle and α, β, γ are parameters.

Naturally, we need to estimate the handling time of each map task and the handling time of each reduce task in order to get the progress of general Map task and the progress of general Reduce task.

The handling time of map task and reduce task can be estimated by computing the average handling time of corresponding completed tasks. We can figure out the progress of map task at a cluster node over Eq. (2) when the nodes don't have failure. And if the node or job fails, the corresponding value is equal to 0.

$$p_{mapi} = \frac{t_{mapruni}}{t_{mapave}} \tag{2}$$

Where p_{mapi} is the progress of i-th map task, $t_{mapruni}$ is the time of the i-th map task has run for. t_{mapave} is the average time that completed map task used. The progress of a reduce task at a cluster node can be estimated by Eq. (3). Similarly, if the node or job fails, the corresponding value is equal to 0.

$$p_{redi} = \frac{t_{redruni}}{t_{redave}} \tag{3}$$

Where p_{redi} is the progress of i-th reduce task, $t_{redruni}$ is the time of the i-th reduce task has run for, t_{redave} is the average time that completed reduce task used.

The average progress of all map tasks can be estimated by Eq. (4).

$$p_{map} = \frac{\sum_{i=1}^{n} p_{mapi}}{n} \tag{4}$$

Where p_{map} is the average progress of all map tasks, p_{mapi} is the progress of i-th map task. n is the number of map tasks in cluster.

The average progress of all reduce tasks can be estimated by Eq. (5).

$$p_{red} = \frac{\sum_{i=1}^{m} p_{redi}}{m} \tag{5}$$

Where p_{red} is the average progress of all reduce tasks, p_{redi} is the progress of i-th reduce task and m is the number of reduce tasks in cluster.

The time of shuffle is the period of time from the end of map task to the start of reduce task. In this period, the data is transmitted from map task to reduce task. So we can approximately think that the start of a reduce task means that a process of shuffle has been finished. So the execution progress of shuffle can be estimated by Eq. (6).

$$p_{sf} = \frac{n_{redrun}}{n_{redtot}} \tag{6}$$

Where p_{sf} is the progress of shuffle, n_{redrun} is the number of reduce tasks has been launched and n_{redtot} is the number of all reduce tasks in cluster.

After many tests for this mathematical model, we can get optimized parameters. That is $\alpha = 0.45, \beta = 0.45, \gamma = 0.1$. Because the size of data that map task need to process is equal to the reduce task, so α is equal to β. It should be noted that these values are obtained with wordcount jobs. So the specific values may not be suitable for other types of job.

3.2 Strategy of Scheduler

At present, several existing schedulers are all based on the strategy of "FIFO". These strategies can't assign resource to the job which has urgent need for resource in time, but only assign resource based on the order of jobs in the queue. If a scheduler can assign resource reasonably with the information of running job, it is as far as possible to ensure that all jobs in cluster can be finished in its deadline.

We can simplify the problem. When the scheduler allocates resource, it allocates resource to the job with highest resource demand. The resource demand is an abstract concept. It describes the extent of demand for resource. The resource demand is related to the deadline of job, the progress of job and the used resources of job. The shorter job's deadline is, the higher the resource demand of job is. The less resource job has used, the higher the resource demand of job is. The smaller progress of job is, the higher the resource demand of job is.

In order to use specific value to describe resource demand, we need to make the following assumptions and analysis. We regard the resource that a map task or a reduce task uses as a unit resource. Because the running speed of job which has two child tasks is two times as fast as the job which has only one child task and each child task has equal resource, the running speed of job is proportional to the numbers of unit resource. On the premise of this conclusion, we have the following analysis: we set the unit running speed of job is s, the number of unit resource the job has is m, the handling time of job is t_1 and the progress of job is p. We can get Eq. (7).

$$smt_1 = p \tag{7}$$

The job can exactly be finished at the deadline t2, if the job can get n unit resource at present. We can get Eq. (8).

$$s(m+n)(t_2 - t_1) = 1 - p \tag{8}$$

We can get Eq. (9) according to the Eq. (7).

$$s = \frac{p}{mt_1} \tag{9}$$

We can get Eq. (10) according to the Eqs. (8) and (9).

$$n = \frac{(1-p)mt_1}{p(t_2 - t_1)} - m \tag{10}$$

We define the resource demand R is the number of unit resource n divided by the rest of the time to job's deadline t2–t1. We can get Eq. (11).

$$R = \frac{n}{t_2 - t_1} = \frac{(1-p)mt_1}{p(t_2 - t_1)^2} - \frac{m}{t_2 - t_1} \tag{11}$$

3.3   Design Algorithm to Judge Whether the Resource of Cluster Are Enough

The resources of cluster may not meet the deadline of all the jobs in cluster. We need to design an algorithm to judge whether we should request resources from cloud platform.

The algorithm that judges whether the resources of cluster are enough is related to many factors. For example, the size of cluster resource, the number of jobs in cluster, the size of data in each job, the deadline of each job, the current progress of each job, the size of resource each job has used and so on.

In order to analysis this problem, we can see a simple example first. We assume that there are three jobs in cluster. The current number of unit resource that the first job has used is 0, there is 1 unit time from current time to the first job's deadline. The first job can exactly be finished in deadline if first job gets 2 unit resource at present. The current number of unit resource that the second job has used is 0, there are 2 unit times from current time to the second job's deadline. The second job can exactly be finished in deadline if second job gets 2 unit resource at present. The current number of unit resource that the third job has used is 0, there are 3 unit times from current time to the third job's deadline. The third job can exactly be finished in deadline if third job gets 1 unit resource at present. There are three unit resource in cluster at present. Fig. 3 shows the problem. The length of rectangle is the deadline of job, the width of rectangle is resource that job should get at present, the area of rectangle is total remain work of job.

To judge whether the cluster resources can meet the deadline of the three applications, we introduce a concept of work firstly. We define a work for the progress of

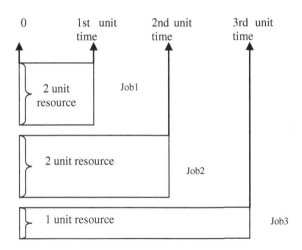

Fig. 3. Describe of the example

job which runs for a unit time using a unit resource. Because work is proportional to the running time, we set the value of work equal to the product of the size of resource and the length of running time. In the beginning, we can assign 2 unit resource to the first job and assign 1 unit resource to the second job. The first job will be finished and the second job will finish $1*1 = 1$work at the point of first unit time. At this time, we assign 2 unit resource which the first job frees to the second job. when coming at the point of second unit time, the second job has finished $1*1 + 3*1 = 4$work equal to the total work of the second job $2*2 = 4$, so the second job can exactly be finished at its deadline. At this time, we assign 3 unit resource which the second job frees to the third job. when coming at the point of third unit time, the third job has finished $3*1 = 3$work equal to the total work of the third job $1*3 = 3$, so the third job can also exactly be finished at its deadline. Through the above analysis, we can see that the cluster resources can exactly meet the deadline of three jobs in cluster.

Then we make a general analysis. The number of jobs in cluster is n and we sort the n jobs in ascending order of deadline. The i-th job can exactly be finished in deadline, if it get $m_1[i]$ unit resource at present. The i-th job has used $m_2[i]$ unit resource at present. There are $t[i]$ unit time from current time to the deadline of the i-th job, the remain unit resource in cluster is R_m unit resource at present. Based on the rule of Eq. (12), we do n times to judge. If n times of judgement all meet the Eq. (12), the cluster resources are enough to meet the deadline of all jobs in cluster. On the contrary, it should require resource for the cloud platform.

$$\sum_{i=1}^{k} m_1[i] * t[i] \leq R_m * t[k] + \sum_{i=1}^{k} m_2[i] * (t[k] - t[i])(1 \leq k \leq n) \qquad (12)$$

4 Experiment and Result

In this section, we evaluate on demand resource scheduler performance using word-count jobs in Hadoop 2.6. The whole cluster is deployed in a physical server, and nodes are virtual machines (VM).

First is whether cluster can request resources from cloud platform. Simply, we count the number of VMs as a symbol of requesting resources. Each VM is representative for requesting resources once. We take two experiments to verify the relationship between the size of resource scheduler requires and the size of job's data, the deadline of job. The first experiment is to make the job's deadline always equal to 2 min and increase the size of job's data. The second experiment is to make the size of job's data always equal to 16 G and increase the deadline of job. The Figs. 4 and 5 show the results. From the two forms, we can see that the more the size of job's data is, the more resource the scheduler requires. The shorter job's deadline is, the more resource the scheduler requires.

Second is about deadline and on demand resource scheduler is called as Adaptive Scheduler. We test the improvement on the job with deadline. We use two schedulers, Adaptive Scheduler is scheduled to meet deadline at utmost, and Capacity Scheduler follows the rule of FIFO. The whole cluster of this experiment has 5 child nodes, each node has 2 G memory and 2.2 MHz. 18 jobs with different deadline are submitted to the cluster. We set 2 min as the deadline for the former 14 jobs while the rest is 3 min. Actual time the job used and job's deadline are recorded and displayed in Figs. 6, 7, 8 and 9. In Fig. 6, we can see the time cost between Adaptive Scheduler and Capacity Scheduler. It is obvious that the time cost can be reduced 30% at least in most jobs. As shown in Figs. 7 and 8, Adaptive Scheduler is better than Capacity Scheduler. There are almost 28% jobs which can be finished before its deadline. But all jobs in Capacity Scheduler are finished after the deadline.

Because the deadline is not the same, we use data normalization to the time cost based on deadline. We compare the degree of improvement using Adaptive Scheduler

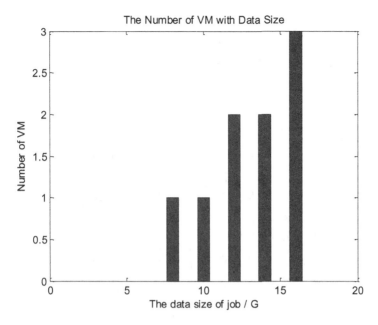

Fig. 4. The number of VM with data size

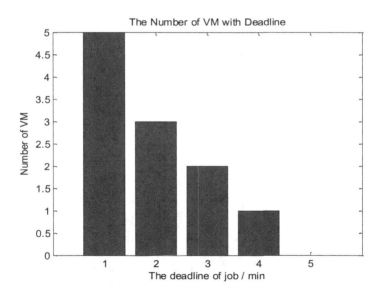

Fig. 5. The number of VM with deadline

and Capacity Scheduler. The ratio of deviation to deadline are showed in Fig. 9, where a positive number represents the actual time job used is less than job's deadline in vertical axis. The deviation of Adaptive Scheduler is less than 1, and all jobs can be finished before double deadline. The out part of the deadline is from requiring

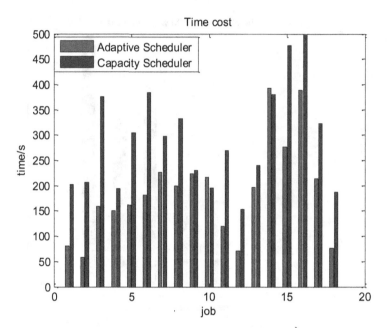

Fig. 6. Time cost of scheduler

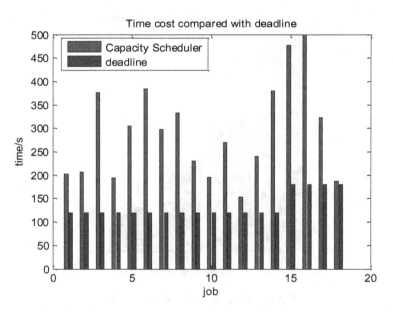

Fig. 7. Time cost compared with deadline of capacity scheduler

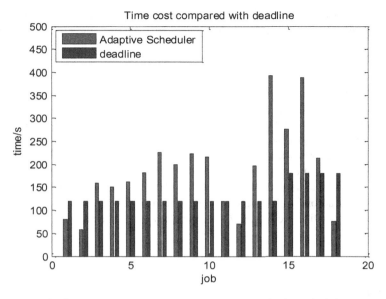

Fig. 8. Time cost compared with deadline of adaptive scheduler

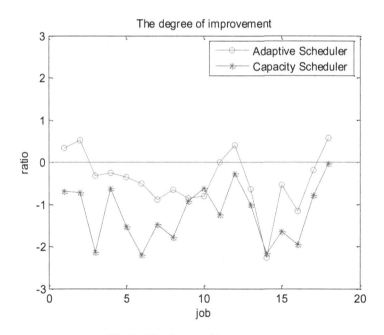

Fig. 9. The degree of improvement

resources which needs time. Therefore some jobs cannot be finished in its deadline. While Capacity Scheduler is more than double time, even up to threefold time or higher without time of requiring resources.

5 Conclusion

In this paper, we come up with on demand resource scheduler, which is aware of jobs' deadline and tries to guarantee the deadline by requesting resources from cloud platform. And results show the scheduler is useful for jobs with deadline. Even the model is not perfect, there must be altered to a more perfect model to make jobs meet the deadline. As more users submit jobs with its deadline, cloud platform still allocates fixed resources according to users' requirement. This mode can not match deadline with the amount of fixed resources. On demand resource scheduler can give a solution to this problem.

References

1. ApacheHadoop. http://hadoop.apache.org/
2. Capacity Scheduler. http://hadoop.apache.org/docs/r0.20.205.0/fairscheduler.html
3. Fair Scheduler. http://hadoop.apache.org/docs/r0.20.205.0/fairscheduler.html
4. Polo, J., Carrera, D., Becerra, Y., et al.: Performance-driven task co-scheduling for MapReduce environments. In: Network Operations and Management Symposium, pp. 373–380. IEEE (2010)
5. Ferguson, A.D., Bodik, P., Kandula, S., et al.: Jockey: guaranteed job latency in data parallel clusters. In: Eurosys Proceedings of the European Conference on Computer Systems, pp. 99–112 (2012)
6. Verma, A., Cherkasova, L., Campbell, R.H., et al.: ARIA: automatic resource inference and allocation for MapReduce environments. In: International Conference on Autonomic Computing (2011)
7. Lee, G., Chun, B., Katz, H., et al.: Heterogeneity-aware resource allocation and scheduling in the cloud. In: Cloud Computing (2011)
8. Zhang, W., Rajasekaran, S., Wood, T., et al.: MIMP: Deadline and interference aware scheduling of hadoop virtual machines. In: Cluster Computing and the Grid (2014)
9. Romer, T.: Autoscaling Hadoop Clusters. Master's thesis of University of Tartu faculty of mathematics and computer science (2010)
10. Rao, B.T., Sridevi, N.V., Reddy, V.K., et al.: Performance issues of heterogeneous Hadoop clusters in cloud computing. Comput. Sci. (2012)
11. Ahmad, F., Chakradhar, S.T., Raghunathan, A., et al.: Tarazu: optimizing MapReduce on heterogeneous clusters. ACM Sigarch Comput. Archit. News **40**(1), 61–74 (2012)
12. Cheng, D., Rao, J., Jiang, C.J., et al.: Resource and deadline-aware job scheduling in dynamic hadoop clusters, pp. 956–965 (2015)

Investigation on the Optimization for Storage Space in Register-Spilling

Guohui Li, Yonghua Hu[(⊠)], Yaqiong Qiu, and Wenti Huang

School of Computer Science and Engineering,
Hunan University of Science and Technology, Xiangtan 411201, China
hyhyt@126.com

Abstract. In order to make full use of the memory resources of computers, especially embedded systems, the multiplexing of storage space in register spilling is investigated and the corresponding method is presented in this paper. This method is based on the graph coloring register allocation method and on the basic principle of greedy algorithm. In this method, the register allocation candidates to be spilled, which do not conflict with each other, will be spilled to the same memory unit. Thus, in register spilling, less memory is needed and more load/store instructions using immediate values can be used. The effectiveness of the method is verified. Besides, the method is suitable for architectures with both scalar and vector operands.

Keywords: Register allocation · Spilling · Storage space · Compiling optimization

1 Introduction

In compiling, register allocation is an important optimization technology. The main conventional methods of register allocation can be classified into two main classes: linear scan register allocation [1] and graph-coloring [2]. There are also some other register allocation methods such as studying optimal spilling in the light of SSA [3], heuristic allocation method [4], allocation of repair strategies [5], layered allocation [6], etc. The graph-coloring method, which is a highly effective global register allocation method [7, 8], was proposed by Chaitin in 1981. The coloring process must ensure that the adjacent nodes have different colors. The number of colors that an interference graph needs in coloring is called as its register pressure, and the treatment modifying code in order to make the graph colorable is called "reducing register pressure".

Spilling symbolic registers [9–12] is a method for reducing register pressure. Its basic idea is to split the lifetime of a register allocation candidate into two or more lifetimes, i.e., dividing the live range of a symbolic register into two or more parts. Physical registers will get the gap time between live ranges of divided candidates. This process is helpful to reduce register pressure [13, 14]. The basic method of register-spilling is to spill candidates to memory. In conventional register-spilling

© ICST Institute for Computer Sciences, Social Informatics and Telecommunications Engineering 2017
S. Wang and A. Zhou (Eds.): CollaborateCom 2016, LNICST 201, pp. 627–633, 2017.
DOI: 10.1007/978-3-319-59288-6_63

algorithm [15, 16], each pending spilling candidate needs a storage unit, indicating that the storage space needed is directly proportional to the number of candidates to be spilled. This paper is devoted to the study of reducing the storage space for spilling in register allocation through storage units multiplexing. An algorithm that is based on the graph coloring register allocation method will be presented to realize this optimization. Not only will this algorithm not impact the register spilling result, but also it can greatly reduce the storage units needed in register spilling and thus improve the utilization of memory.

2   Optimization Algorithm

In order to optimize the storing of register allocation candidates (called webs in what follows) to be spilled, we define the following quantities to analyze the code:

(1) *NDimMtx* is an N-dimensional matrix template class, where *N* can be 1 or 2 for the problem considered in this paper.
(2) *AdjacentListRecord* is a data structure containing the needed information of an adjacent list record.
(3) *ApInstn* is code instruction object.
(4) *def* and *use* are definition object and use object, respectively.
(5) *DU* and *UD* are definition-use-chain and use-definition-chain, respectively.
(6) *spillWebs* is a set of webs to spilled (a web is made up of DUs), and *spillWebList* is the corresponding list form of *spillWebs*.
(7) *spillWebAdjList* is the adjacency list for the webs to be spilled.

The top-level process of our optimization method has the following main steps:

(1) First *Judge_NeedRegistersSpilling()* determines whether the register allocation needs spilling. If yes, the following steps should be executed.
(2) Next, *Find_SpillWebs()* function finds out all the webs to be spilled, and generates *spillWebs* and *spillWebList*.
(3) Next, *Get_SpillWebsConflictShip()* function analyzes the active ranges of the webs in *spillWebs*, judges whether they are overlapping.
(4) Then, *Assign_StorageSpaceToSpillWebs()* assigns storage units for each elements of *spillWebs*: it assigns the same storage spaces to the webs that don't conflict with each other, and assigns different storage spaces to those conflict with each other.
(5) At last, *Gen_SpillCode()* generates spilling and restore codes.

At the beginning of the optimization, the algorithm set the initial offset of the available storage space for spilling to *baseOffset*, a global static variable. Then, for each following register spilling process, the value of *baseOffset* will be equal to the address of the maximum offset determined by its previous register spilling process. The algorithm of the top-level structure of our method is as follows:

```
Procedure Optimise_SpillStorageSpace(spillWebs,
spillWebList, baseOffset, offset)
    spillWebList: a list of spillWebs
    baseOffset: global static variable
    begin
      baseOffset := available storage space start offset
      spill: Boolean
    spill := Judge_NeedRegistersSpilling( )
      if spill then
        Find_SpillWebs( )
        Get_SpillWebsConflictShip( )
        Assign_StorgeSpaceToSpillWebs()
        Gen_SpillCode( )
      fi
end  || Optimise_SpillStorageSpce
```

We assume that optimistic heuristic method is used to prune the interference graph. To describe whether a node in an interference graph result should be spilled, we set a Boolean value for each node as a flag to mark this status. We traverse the webs whose spilling flags are true and put them into *spillWebs* and *spillWebList*. As for the conflict relation among the webs to be spilled, it can be obtained directly from the existing adjacent matrix and adjacent list and is stored in the *spillWebAdjList* object corresponding to *spillWebs*.

In the process of register spilling, the address of the storage units assigned to the webs in *spillWebList* increases from the base address for spilling. For each web w, the algorithm traverses the storage units starting from the base address until it finds a unit whose corresponding web is not conflict with w. When the algorithm finds out such a storage unit, it assigns this storage unit to the web w and ends the traversing process. It should be noted that some architectures have both scalar and vector operands, and hence there will be scalar and vector webs in *spillWebList*. In our algorithm, we assume that the increment of traversing storage units for a scalar web is a, while that for a vector web is $m*a$, both m and a being integer.

The corresponding algorithm is as follows:

```
procedure Assign_StorgeSpaceToSpillWebs(spillWebList)
begin
  i, j, minUnusedOffset: integer
  a: size of a storage unit
  oneSpillWeb: spillWeb
  offsetUseByNeighbors: map<uint, bool>
  pInstn: instruction
  map<uint, bool>::iterator it
  for i := 1 to n do
     for (it =
spillWebAdjList[spillWebList[i]].adjNodes.begin();
         it !=
spillWebAdjList[spillWebList[i]].adjNodes.end();
         ++ it) do
         oneSpillWeb := (*it).first
         for
(spillWebAdjList[oneSpillWeb].storageUnits.ToHead();
            spillWebAdjList[oneSpillWeb].
storageUnits.CurNotNull()
            spillWebAdjList[oneSpillWeb].
storageUnits.ToNext()) do
            offsetUseByNeighbors[spillWebAdjList[oneSpill
Web].storageUnits.Cur()]=true
         od
     od
     minUnusedOffset := baseOffset
     while(1) do
         if
(offsetUseByNeighbors.count(offsetUseByNeighbors) < 1)
            spillWebAdjList[spillWebList[i]].storageUnits
.AddTail(minUnusedOffset)
            break
         fi
         if (pInstn is scalar)
           minUnusedOffset = minUnusedOffset + a
         else (pInstn is vector)
           minUnusedOffset = minUnusedOffset + m*a
         fi
     od
  od
  baseOffset := max(minUnusedOffset)
end || Assign_StorgeSpaceToSpillWebs
```

After all the webs in *spillWebs* being assigned storage units, the algorithm inserts corresponding spills and restores for them. This treatment is the same as that used in conventional graph coloring method, so we don't repeat it in this paper.

3   Verification

To show the effectiveness of our method, we demonstrate the using of the method in an example (see the left side of Fig. 1) by comparing with the conventional storage assigning method. We assume that the aim architecture has 4 general purpose registers, i.e., *R0*, *R1*, *R2*, and *R3*, and has a register *AR3* as the base address register for register spilling. In Fig. 1, the arrows are live ranges corresponding to the variables, and *a* stands for the size of a storage unit. The result intermediate codes after the first register spilling pass are shown in the right part of Fig. 1.

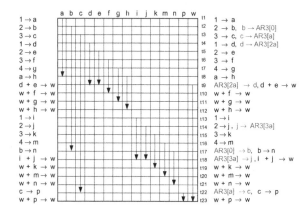

Fig. 1.   Schematic diagram of the first pass of register spilling for source codes.

The following physical register assigning process will find out that the assignment is not successful. Then a second register allocation pass with register spilling is needed, where *f* and *m* will be further spilled. The final allocation result is shown in the right part of Fig. 2. As a comparison, the allocation result based on the conventional storage unit assignment method for webs to be spilled is shown in the left part of Fig. 2.

According to this example, it is easy to see from Fig. 2 that 4 storage units is needed by our method but 6 storage units is needed by the conventional method. Of Course, it should be noted that the optimization effect of our method will be different for different codes because it depends on the conflict relations among register allocation candidates.

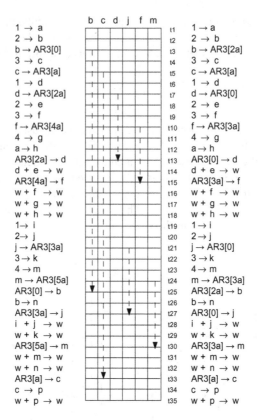

Fig. 2. Comparison diagram for the result code that the spilled data storing optimization is used and that the spilled data storing optimization is not used.

4 Conclusion

In this paper, an optimization method of storage space optimization in register spilling is presented. This method is based on graph coloring register allocation method and consists of several main steps, such as identifying the register allocation candidates to be spilled, analyzing the conflict relation among these candidates, assigning storage units to these candidates, etc. It is demonstrated by an example that the method can reduce the storage units needed in register spilling, and that the correctness of graph coloring register allocation will not be affected. Consequently, more load/store instructions that directly access memory can be used in register spilling, and thus reducing the pressure on offset registers.

Acknowledgment. This work was supported by National Natural Science Foundation of China (Grant No. 61308001) and graduate student innovation fund project (Grant Nos.S140027 and CX2015B537).

References

1. Poletto, M.: Linear scan register allocation. ACM Trans. Program. Lang. Syst. **21**, 895–913 (1999)
2. Briggs, P., Cooper, K., Kennedy, K., Torczon, L.: Coloring heuristics for register allocation. ACM SIGPLAN Not. **39**, 275–284 (1989)
3. Colombet, Q., Brandner, F., Darte, A.: Studying optimal spilling in the light of SSA. In: 14th International Conference on Compilers, Architectures and Synthesis for Embedded Systems, Taipei, pp. 25–34 (2011)
4. Tavares, A., Colombet, Q., Bigonha, M.: Decoupled graph-coloring register allocation with hierarchical aliasing. In: Proceedings of the 14th International Workshop on Software and Compilers for Embedded Systems, Goar, Germany, pp. 1–10 (2011)
5. Colombet, Q., Boissinot, B., Brisk, P.: Graph-coloring and tree scan register allocation using repairing. In: 14th International Conference on Compilers, Architectures and Synthesis for Embedded Systems, Taipei, pp. 45–54 (2011)
6. Diouf, B., Cohen, A., Rastello, F.: A polynomial spilling heuristic: layered allocation. R. Research Report, Project-Teams Parkas and Compsys (2012)
7. Chaitin, G., Auslander, M., Chandra, A.: Register allocation via coloring. J. Comput. Lang. **6**, 47–57 (1981)
8. Carole, D.-G., Hugues, F., Eli, G., Leslie, L.: Adaptive register allocation with a linear number of registers. In: 27th International Symposium, DISC 2013, Jerusalem, Israel, 14–18 October (2013)
9. Steven, S.: Advanced Compiler Design and Implementation. Elsevier Science, Amsterdam (1997). M. USA
10. Salgado, M., Ragel, R.G.: Register spilling for specific application domains in ASIPs. In: 7th International Conference on Information and Automation for Sustainability. IEEE (2014)
11. Wu, C., Lu, C., Lee, J.: Register spilling via transformed interference equations for PAC DSP architecture. Concurrency Comput. Pract. Experience **26**, 779–799 (2014)
12. Pfenning, F., Simmons, R.: Lecture Notes on Register Allocation Optimizations (2015). http://www.cs.cmu.edu/~rjsimmon/15411-f15/lec/17-regopt.pdf
13. Yin, M., Steve, C., Rong, G.: Low-cost register-pressure prediction for scalar replacement using pseudo-schedules. In: 2004 International Conference on Parallel Processing, 0190-3918/04 (2004)
14. Shobaki, G., Shawabkeh, M., Rmaileh, N.: Preallocation instruction scheduling with register pressure minimization using a combinatorial optimization approach. ACM Trans. Archit. Code Optim. **10**, 14 (2013)
15. Philipp. K., Frankfurt, M.: Bytewise register allocation. In: 18th International Workshop on Software and Compilers for Embedded Systems, New York (2015). 978-1-4503-3593-5
16. Gaow, Z., Han, L., Pang, J.: Research on SIMD auto-vectorization compiling optimization. J. Softw. **26**, 1265–1284 (2015)

An Improvement Direction for the Simple Random Walk Sampling: Adding Multi-homed Nodes and Reducing Inner Binate Nodes

Bo Jiao$^{(\boxtimes)}$, Ronghua Guo, Yican Jin, Xuejun Yuan, Zhe Han,
and Fei Huang

Luoyang Electronic Equipment Test Center, Luoyang 471003, China
bjluoyang@hotmail.com

Abstract. Graph sampling is an important technology for the network visualization. In this paper, we use the normalized Laplacian spectrum to evaluate diverse biased sampling algorithms on Internet topologies, and numerically find that the simple random walk (SRW) sampling performs much better than other sampling algorithms (e.g., breadth first search, forest fire and random jump). Moreover, we analyze the deficiency of the SRW using the physical meaning of the normalized Laplacian spectrum on the size-independent Internet structure. Finally, we indicate that more multi-homed nodes should be added and more inner binate nodes should be reduced for better performance of the SRW sampling graphs on the normalized Laplacian spectrum which is a powerful tool for the study of size-independent structure embedded in evolving systems.

Keywords: Simple random walk · Normalized laplacian spectrum · Single-homed and multi-homed networks · Graph sampling

1 Introduction

The autonomous system level Internet topology evolves over time which induces that the network size (i.e., the node number) of the realistic Internet is very large. To more clearly realize the network visualization, we may need a sampling graph that has much smaller size and captures plenty of size-independent structures similar to the original large realistic network. There are two types of sampling algorithms: unbiased approach [1] and biased approach [2, 3, 4]. The unbiased approach strives to mathematically demonstrate that the sampling probability of each node is uniform, and is commonly applied when we can not observe all nodes of the original network (e.g., due to call limit of online social networks). On the other hand, the biased approach is biased towards high-degree nodes that will be sampled with higher probabilities, and has been widely evaluated using the performance comparison of graph metrics between the sampling and original networks. Leskovec et al. [2] used the Kolmogorov-Smirnov D-statistic to compare diverse biased sampling algorithms. Also, Xu et al. [3] used the

---

B. Jiao–The research field of Dr. Bo Jiao includes evolving network and spectral graph theory.

degree distribution and the clustering coefficient to derive an optimum solution in a hybrid biased sampling framework. However, these works focused on general scale-free networks. In other words, they have not considered the unique structure embedded in the Internet topology and can not be applied for the detailed analysis of the Internet sampling technology. In this paper, we apply diverse biased sampling algorithms in Internet topologies and evaluate them using the normalized Laplacian spectrum since our recent works [5, 6, 7, 8, 9] have demonstrated that the spectrum represents fruitful physical meanings for the unique size-independent structure of the Internet topology.

2 Background

2.1 Biased Sampling Algorithms

These algorithms can be classified into two categories: graph traversal and random walk. For connected Internet topologies, each node in the graph traversal is visited exactly once; examples include Breath First Search (BFS) and Forest Fire (FF). Whereas each node in the random walk can be revisited many times; examples include Simple Random Walk (SRW) and Random Jump (RJ).

The BFS is a classic graph traversal algorithm that starts from a randomly selected seed in the original network and progressively explores all neighbors [4]. At each new iteration of the BFS, the earliest explored but not-yet-visited node is selected next. Consequently, the BFS discovers first the nodes closest to the seed.

The FF is a randomized version of the BFS [4]. For every neighbor v of the current node, the FF decides explore v with probability p. When $p = 1$, the FF reduces to the BFS. It is possible that the FF dies out before it covers nodes with the expected number. Thus, we revive the FF from a random node already in the sample.

The SRW's walker starts from a randomly selected seed in the original network [2]. At each new iteration of the SRW, if the walker currently stays at node v, it randomly moves to a neighbor of node v with probability $1/d_v$ where d_v denotes the degree (i.e., the number of neighbors) of node v.

The RJ is similar to the SRW [3]. The only difference is that at each new iteration, with probability $c = 0.15$ (the value commonly used in literature), the RJ randomly jumps to any node in the original network and re-starts the random walk.

2.2 Normalized Laplacian Spectrum

Let $G = (V,E)$ denote an undirected and simple graph where V and E are respectively node set and edge set, d_v denote the degree of node v in G, D denote the diagonal degree matrix of G, and $A = (a_{ij})$ denote the adjacency matrix where $a_{ij} = 1$ if $(v_i,v_j) \in E$ and $a_{ij} = 0$ otherwise. Then, the normalized Laplacian matrix of G is $L(G) = D^{-1/2}(D\text{-}A)D^{-1/2}$ [11], and the normalized Laplacian spectrum of G includes all eigenvalues of $L(G)$: $0 = y_1 \leq y_2 \leq \ldots \leq y_n \leq 2$ where n denotes the node number of G. The WSD is a metric defined as $\sum_{i=1,2,\ldots,n}(1 - y_i)^N$ [11] where 4 is the best selection of N [8], and the ME1 quantifies the number of the eigenvalue 1. Thus, we can determine that the spectrum can be described by two weakly-related spectral metrics (i.e., the ME1 and the WSD).

If G represents the Internet topology, we demonstrated that the ME1 reflects the node classification of G [5, 9]. Specifically, node set V can be classified into three subsets [10]: $P(G) = \{v \in V \mid d_v = 1\}$ called pendants, $Q(G) = \{v \in V \mid \exists\ w, (v, w) \in E,$ $w \in P(G)\}$ called quasi-pendants, and $R(G) = V \backslash (Q(G) \cup P(G))$. Let $Inner(G) = (V_I,$ $E_I)$ denote the subgraph of G induced by $R(G)$, and $d_I(v)$ denote the degree of node v in $Inner(G)$. Then, node set V_I (i.e., $R(G)$) can be further classified into six subsets [5]: $PI = \{v \in V_I \mid d_I(v) = 1 \wedge \forall (v, w) \in E_I, d_I(w) > 1\}$ called inner pendants, $QI = \{v \in V_I \mid \exists\ w, (v,w) \in E_I, w \in PI\}$ called inner quasi-pendants, $RI = \{v \in V_I \mid d_I(v) \geq 2 \wedge \forall (v,w) \in E_I, w \in QI\}$ called inner restricted nodes, $BI = \{v \in V_I \mid d_I(v) = 1 \wedge \forall (v,w) \in E_I,$ $d_I(w) = 1\}$ called inner binate nodes, $II = \{v \in V_I \mid d_I(v) = 0\}$ called inner isolated nodes and $OI = V_I \backslash (PI \cup QI \cup RI \cup BI \cup II)$ call-ed inner noise nodes. Additionally, we demonstrated that the ME1 is approximately equal to the periphery number minus the core number where $P(G)$, PI, RI, II and half of BI compose the periphery, $Q(G)$, QI and another half of BI compose the core, and OI is the system noise [9]. Also, we demonstrated that the WSD monotonically decreases as the network is transformed from singe-homed to multi-homed [9].

3   Real-World Data

We extract 24 real-world Internet graphs from AS-Caida dataset [12]. These graphs were explored from Jan 2004 to Nov 2007. We use these graphs to analyze sampling algorithms since they have stable performances of the ME1 and the WSD, as shown in Fig. 1. The network sizes of these graphs span the range from 16,301 to 26,475.

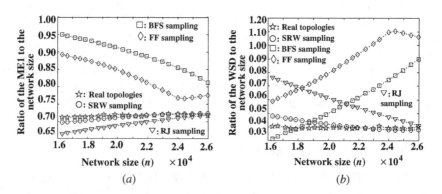

Fig. 1. Comparisons of the WE1 and the WSD on real-world and sampling graphs. (*a*) ME1/*n* vs. *n*. (*b*) WSD/*n* vs. *n*. The FF has $p = 0.7$ which is a good selection for $p \in \{0.5, 0.55, \ldots,$ 0.90\}.

For each biased sampling algorithm, the largest real-world graph having 26,475 nodes is selected as the original network, and the network sizes of a sequence of sampling graphs are set to fall in the range from 16,301 to 25,988 which are consistent with those of the top 23 smallest real-world Internet graphs. For a certain network size of sampling graphs, each sampling algorithm runs ten times and the corresponding statistic is the average over ten realizations.

4   Comparison of ME1 and WSD on Sampling Algorithms

As shown in Fig. 1, the SRW performs much more stable on the normalized Laplacian spectrum compared to other biased sampling algorithms, and its corresponding curves are much closer to those of the real-world dataset. To subtly analyze the SRW, we compare the SRW with one mutation of the SRW, called Random Walk Flying Back (RWFB). The only difference between the SRW and the RWFB is that at each new iteration, with a probability c, the RWFB flies back to the original seed selected by the SRW and restarts the random walk [2]. As shown in Fig. 2, when $c = 0.1$, the RWFB performs much better than the SRW. The comparison between the SRW and the RWFB will be used to explore the improvement direction of this type of algorithms.

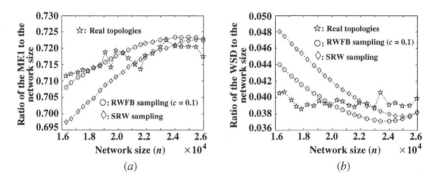

Fig. 2. Comparisons of the WE1 and the WSD on real-world and random walk sampling graphs. (a) ME1/n vs. n. (b) WSD/n vs. n.

5   Analysis for the Numerical Results

According to Sect. 2.2, for the Internet topology, node classification is an important feature reflected by the normalized Laplacian spectrum. Because the Internet topology has plenty of nodes with degree one, the pendant set $P(G)$ and the inner noise node set OI are respectively related to the largest and the smallest cardinalities. Thus, we analyze the two node set features of diverse sampling algorithms. The BFS is a graph traversal algorithm that constructs tree-like sampling graphs since each node is exactly visited once for this type of algorithms. Breath first principle induces small depths (where depth is defined as the maximum distance between root and leaves) of the tree-like sampling graphs. As is well known, trees with small depths have an extremely large number of pendants (i.e., leaves with degree one). Additionally, this situation will lead to extremely small cardinalities of other node sets. Although the FF is a randomized version, its many performances remain similar to the BFS. Thus, for the BFS and the FF, their pendant numbers are extremely larger than that of the real-world dataset, and their inner noise node numbers are approximately equal to zero. The RJ is a hybrid algorithm of the SRW and the Random Node (RN) samplings. The SRW is biased towards high-degree nodes while the RN uniformly samples each node. Thus, the small-degree node number of the hybrid algorithm RJ is larger than that of the SRW. Note that the pendant set is an important component of small-degree nodes, which explains why the pendant number of the RJ is obviously larger than that of the real-world dataset. Therefore, the bad performances on node classification of the BFS, the FF and the RJ are critical reasons for the best performance of the SRW on the normalized Laplacian spectrum, as shown in Fig. 1.

According to Sect. 2.2, the Internet topology can be divided into eight node classifications. Specifically, pendant set $P(G)$, inner isolated node set II, quasi-pendant set Q (G) and inner binate node set BI occupy the vast majority of the Internet nodes [9]. As shown in Fig. 3, we exhibit the evolving features of the four node sets on real-world and two random walk sampling graphs. Next, we will analyze the physical meaning embedded in Fig. 3 and investigate the improvement direction of the random walk sampling. Based on Fig. 3, for the RWFB, its pendant number, quasi-pendant number and inner binate node number are decreased and its inner isolated node number is increased in contrast to those of the SRW. The physical interpretation of these phenomena is presented in Fig. 4. In Fig. 4(a), each periphery node is attached to only one core node so these periphery nodes are single-homed. With the increasing of the links between periphery and core nodes, increasingly more nodes are transformed from single-homed to multi-homed, as shown in Fig. 4(b). As is well known, multi-homed nodes have better fault tolerance. Due to the rich club phenomenon, extremely few core nodes attract the majority of periphery nodes to connect with them. As shown in Fig. 4(b), inner binate nodes are generated by the small-degree core nodes which are connected with only one periphery node. If we remove the links between two inner binate nodes, in contrast to Fig. 4(a), all of the pendants, quasi-pendants and inner binate nodes will be reduced, and the inner isolated nodes will be added, as shown in Fig. 4(c). Thus, Fig. 4 explains why more added multi-homed nodes and more reduced inner binate nodes of the RWFB sampling graphs compared to those of the SRW induce the phenomenon shown in Fig. 3. The ME1 quantities the periphery number minus the core number [9], so the ME1 of Fig. 4(c) is obviously larger than that of Fig. 4(a) which verifies the phenomenon of Fig. 2(a). With the transformation from single-homed to multi-homed networks, the WSD monotonically decreases in general [9], so the WSD of Fig. 4(c) is commonly smaller than that of Fig. 4(a), which verifies the phenomenon of Fig. 2(b). Therefore, we can determine that adding multi-homed nodes and reducing inner binate nodes are the key reasons for the better performance of the RWFB in Fig. 2.

Although the RWFB performs better than the SRW on the normalized Laplacian spectrum, its stability of the evolving process on the spectrum is still unsatisfactory. Specially, as shown in Fig. 3, with the increasing of the size reduction ratio of the sampling graphs, the curves of the RWFB are father and father away from those of the real-world dataset. Additionally, the time complexity of the RWFB is very high since

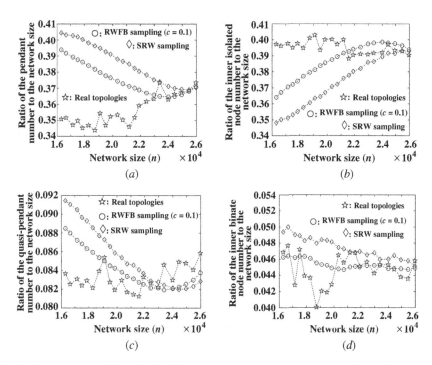

Fig. 3. Comparisons of the node classification on real-world and random walk sampling graphs. (*a*) pendant number/*n* vs. *n*. (*b*) inner isolated node number/*n* vs. *n*. (*c*) quasi-pendant number/*n* vs. *n*. (*d*) Inner binate node number/*n* vs. *n*.

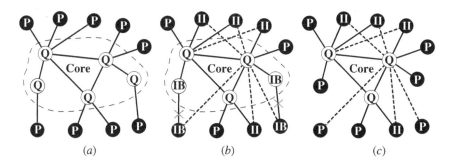

Fig. 4. Physical meaning embedded in Fig. 3. (*a*) A network with abundant single-homed nodes. (*b*) more multi-homed nodes are added. (*c*) More inner binate nodes are reduced. Note that white and black nodes respectively compose the core and periphery of the Internet, and P, Q, II and IB respectively denote pendant, quasi-pendant, inner isolated node and inner binate node.

flying back to the seed extremely increases the average visiting time of each node in the original network. However, based on the physical interpretation of Fig. 4, we can determine that adding multi-homed nodes and reducing inner binate nodes are valuable improvement directions for the simple random walk sampling algorithms.

Although only realistic autonomous system level Internet topologies with snapshots from Jan 2004 to Nov 2007 are analyzed in this paper, our recent studies [5, 9] verified that the physical meanings of the ME1 and the WSD hold for plenty of Internet evolving topologies. Specially, the core and periphery of the Internet (associated with the ME1) respectively are composed of the transit and stub nodes, which is consistent with the classical transit-stub model of the Internet [13]. Moreover, the transformation from single-homed to multi-homed (indicated by the WSD) reflects the Internet's requirement for better fault tolerance. Also, realistic Internet topologies derived from different data sources (e.g., AS-733, Oregon and AS-Caida) [12] keep plenty of similar size-independent structures [8]. Therefore, the derived results of this paper can be applied to more general cases of the Internet topology.

6   Conclusion

The normalized Laplacian spectrum is critical for evaluating graph sampling algorithms applied in the Internet visualization. In this paper, we use the spectrum to investigate the advantages and deficiencies of the SRW samplings and observe that the SRW and its mutation perform much better than other biased samplings. Additionally, based on the physical interpretation for the better performance of the RWFB, we indicate that adding multi-homed nodes and reducing inner binate nodes are important improvement directions for this type of SRW algorithms. In the future work, according to the improvement directions, we will design another mutation of the SRW which has better performance on the spectrum and higher runtime efficiency.

Acknowledgments. We would like to thank the anonymous reviewers for their comments that helped improve this paper. This paper is supported by the National Natural Science Foundation of China with Grant Nos. 61402485 and 61303061.

References

1. Lee, C.H., Xu, X., Eun, D.Y.: Beyond random walk and metropolis-hastings samplers: why you should not backtrack for unbiased graph sampling. ACM SIGMETRICS Perform. Eval. Rev. **40**, 319–330 (2012)
2. Leskovec, J., Faloutsos, C.: Sampling from large graphs. In: The 12th ACM SIGKDD International Conference on Knowledge Discovery and Data Mining, pp. 631–636 (2006)
3. Xu, X., Lee, C.H.: A general framework of hybrid graph sampling for complex network analysis. In: 2014 Proceedings IEEE INFOCOM, pp. 2795–2803 (2014)
4. Kurant, M., Markopoulou, A., Thiran, P.: Towards unbiased BFS sampling. IEEE J. Sel. Areas Commun. **29**, 1799–1809 (2011)
5. Jiao, B., Zhou, Y., Du, J., et al.: Study on the stability of the topology interactive growth mechanism using graph spectra. IET Commun. **8**, 2845–2857 (2014)
6. Jiao, B., Nie, Y., Shi, J., et al.: Scaling of weighted spectral distribution in deterministic scale-free networks. Phys. A Stat. Mech. Appl. **451**, 632–645 (2016)

7. Jiao, B., Shi, J., Wu, X., et al.: Correlation between weighted spectral distribution and average path length in evolving networks. Chaos Interdisc. J. Nonlinear Sci. **26**, 023110 (2016)
8. Jiao, B., Nie, Y., Shi, J., et al.: Accurately and quickly calculating the weighted spectral distribution. Telecommun. Syst. **62**, 231–243 (2016)
9. Jiao, B., Shi, J.: Graph perturbations and corresponding spectral changes in internet topologies. Comput. Commun. **76**, 77–86 (2016)
10. Vukadinović, D., Huang, P., Erlebach, T.: On the spectrum and structure of internet topology graphs. In: Unger, H., Böhme, T., Mikler, A. (eds.) IICS 2002. LNCS, vol. 2346, pp. 83–95. Springer, Heidelberg (2002). doi:10.1007/3-540-48080-3_8
11. Fay, D., Haddadi, H., Thomason, A., et al.: Weighted spectral distribution for internet topology analysis: theory and applications. IEEE/ACM Trans. Networking **18**, 164–176 (2010)
12. Leskovec, J.: Stanford Large Network Dataset Collection. http://snap.stanford.edu/data/
13. Calvert, K., Doar, M., Zegura, E.: Modeling internet topology. IEEE Trans. Commun. **35**, 160–163 (1997)

Detecting False Information
of Social Network in Big Data

Yi Xu[1(✉)], Furong Li[1], Jianyi Liu[1], Ru Zhang[1], Yuangang Yao[2],
and Dongfang Zhang[3]

[1] Information Security Center, Beijing University
of Posts and Telecommunications, Beijing, China
{xuyi0511, ronger19930711, liujy, zhangru}@bupt.edu.cn
[2] China Information Technology Security Evaluation Center, Beijing, China
yaoyg@itsec.gov.cn
[3] First Research Institute of the Ministry of Public Security of PRC,
Beijing, China
40319005@qq.com

Abstract. With the rapid development of social network, the information announced by this platform attracts more and more attention, because of the great harm brought by the false information, researching the false information detection of social network has great significance. This paper presents a model of social network false information detection, which firstly converting the information announced by social network into a three-dimensional vector, then comparing this vector with the three-dimensional vector converted by Internet events and calculating the similarity between social network and Internet, detecting the consistency of social network event and Internet event afterwards, finally gathering statistics and analyzing then we can get the similarity between social network event and Internet event, according to this, we can judge that the social network information is false or not.

Keywords: Social network · Information · Similarity · False · Detection

1 Introduction

At present, with the rapid growth of data volume, we enter the era of Big Data. While Big Data brings us extremely rich information, followed by this is a large number of false or outdated data, greatly reducing the application value of Big Data. The so-called "false information" is information that it is not authentic and maybe cause negative influence. Especially social network in Big Data, because announcing information by social network is open, anonymous, convenient and the spread of information is extensive and rapid, the problem of false information become more and more serious. For example, on April 24, 2013, hackers stole the Twitter of AP announced that the White House has been attacked by bomb attack, result in the Dow Jones Industrial Average Index plunged in a short time [1]. On March 2016, in microblog some say that somebody infect H7N9 because eating chicken, this led to people's panic for pandemic virus. This information may fool the cyber citizens, more seriously maybe cause social

© ICST Institute for Computer Sciences, Social Informatics and Telecommunications Engineering 2017
S. Wang and A. Zhou (Eds.): CollaborateCom 2016, LNICST 201, pp. 642–651, 2017.
DOI: 10.1007/978-3-319-59288-6_65

unrest [2]. It follows that it is important that detecting false information to prevent the spread of false information.

At the moment, the research of social network false information detection has been attracting more and more attention, domestic and international scholars have achieved some research result in this aspect. Akritidis et al. [3] presents two mechanisms: BP-Index Mechanism and BI-Index Mechanism. BP-Index Mechanism in charge of assessing amount of blogs that users announced; BI-Index Mechanism judges bloggers' influence according to the number of links and comment in a certain time. Combining the two mechanisms to evaluate whether the bloggers are recently influential or recently productive. Zolfaghar and Aghaie [4] presents a method to forecast users' trust issues with Machine Learning, this paper considers that social credibility can divided into five aspects: relationship credibility, honor credibility, knowledge credibility, similarity credibility and individuation credibility, maps these five aspects into the characteristic sets consist of context, behavior and feature information of credibility network topological structure. However, this paper doesn't analyze forecast of users' trust issues in dynamic state. Calais et al. [5] proposes a real-time emotion analysis method based on transfer learning strategy, this method acquires users' prejudice to information in social network and sets this prejudice as the essential attribute of users' behaviors to translate into textual features, so that structure emotion classification model to realize emotion analysis. Castillo et al. [6] proposes a method of automatically assessing Twitter information credibility aim at social network typical representative Twitter. The paper analyzes text content to judge information credibility by means of users' emotion and opinion on the information. However, this method depends on manual work, its efficiency is low in the practical application. Qiao et al. [7] presents a trust calculating algorithm based on the social network users' context. This method divides the user trust into two parts: generated by familiarity and similarity among the different social network users. This paper also provides the specific computing method. In the research of information credibility, there are a few typical system can help user judge network information credibility from several angles, mainly include: WISDOM, reframeit.com, Honto Search, Blekko.com, etc. [8].

On the problem of social network false information detection, scholars have obtained some achievement from different view, however, the achievement is little and scattered so that there is no systematic theory, we still have lots of problems to solve. This paper presents a model of social network false information detection, comparing the social network event with Internet event, calculating the similarity between the two, then detecting their consistency, according to this, we can judge that the social network information is false or not. This paper also provides specific computational formula about these process. Comparing with the common false information detection methods, this paper follows the point of view in information itself instead of users, and compares social network information with Internet information, it can guarantee the information detection is authentic and authoritative. In this paper, the Sect. 2 presents the model of social network false information detection and explains every module of this model; the Sect. 3 designs contrast experiments to prove that the model in this paper is feasible; at last, makes summary of work and outlooks the future work.

2   Detecting False Information of Social Network

This paper firstly extracts social network information keywords to be query items put into Google, screens the Internet information from web pages return by Google; then based on webpages screen, extracting the webpages event, this paper converts the information into a three-dimensional vector $\vec{E}(e,\ t,\ p)$, in this vector, E represents event vector, e represents event name, t represents time, p represents place, so that we can get the three-dimensional vector $\vec{E}_i(e_i, t_i, p_i)$ converted by social network events and $\vec{E}_j(e_j, t_j, p_j)$ converted by Internet events; calculating the similarity between this two vector; detecting the emotional tendency consistency of social network event and Internet event; after gathering statistics and analyzing we can get the similarity between social network event and Internet event, according to this, we can get the result that the social network information is false or not. The model as shown in Fig. 1.

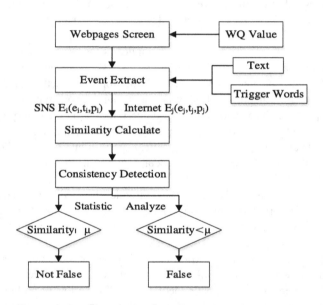

Fig. 1. The model of social network false information detection

2.1   Internet Information Screen

In order to screening the Internet information, this paper firstly extracts social network information keywords to be query items put into Google, aim at web pages return by Google, we screen the webpages by website quality value.

At present, the methods describing website quality are those used often: PageRank and Alexa. PageRank describes importance degree of website [9]. Alexa embodies popularity degree of website [10]. This paper comprehends PageRank and Alexa to rank the webpages, the definition of Website Quality Value as follows:

$$WQ(A) = \alpha \cdot PageRank(A) + \beta \cdot [1 - \frac{Alexa(A)}{10000}] \tag{1}$$

In this formula, A represents the website we need to calculate, 10000 is the quantity of Chinese website list which Alexa published, α, β ($0 \le \alpha, \beta \le 1 \&\& \alpha + \beta = 1$) is the weight of PageRank and Alexa.

2.2 Event Extract

In the social network information and Internet information, all of the events can be constituted of three elements, event name, time and place, this paper converts the information into a three-dimensional vector $\overrightarrow{E}(e, t, p)$, in this vector, E represents event vector, e represents event name, t represents time, p represents place.

This paper based on website screen, extracts the webpages return by Google. The format of the web information in webpages mostly is HTML. So we present a method based on Chinese text density to extract main body. Firstly, taking out HTML tags from webpages and reserving blank position, the left is text denoted by Ltext totals L lines. Dividing pieces turn down with k spacing from the first line denoted by $Block_i$, counting the total number of characters $SChar_i$ and the number of Chinese characters $CChar_i$ in the $Block_i$, the density of Chinese characters denoted by Den_i as shown in formula 2.

$$Den_i = \frac{CChar_i}{SChar_i} \tag{2}$$

The text is divided into L-k pieces, we draw the distribution image using [1, L-k] as horizontal axis and Den_i as vertical axis. There inevitably are a large number of Chinese characters in the main body of webpages, it lead to sudden rise of Chinese characters density. What we need to do is confirm the point of sudden rise and sudden fall to delimit a region with high Chinese characters density, the text in this region is the main body of webpages.

After obtaining the main body of webpages, this paper search the sentences which contain trigger words. The so-called "trigger word" is a word that describes the status of one event, it represents the event occurred so that it can commendably deciding the type of event, such as "happen" and "outbreak" [11]. In the natural language processing, the context field is from −8 to +9 apart from Core Words can contain more than 85% amount of information [12], we call this field effective range of event sentences. Because the sentence between two nearest periods from trigger word mostly in this effective range, so this paper put the sentence between two nearest periods from trigger word as the Internet event sentence. Aim at event sentences, using the method of matching rule to extract event information, based on the ICTCLAS, this paper defines the matching rule "\{ }/t" to extract time information. Similarly, defining the matching rule "\{ }/ns" or "\{ }/nsf" to extract place information. The process of extracting the event three-dimensional vector as follows:

Step 1: Segmenting the text and traversing the words, then searching the words whether belong to trigger words dictionary or not. If not, searching go on. If yes, putting the sentence between two nearest periods from trigger word as the event sentence.

Step 2: Using the method of matching rule to extract time information denoted by t in the event sentence; extract place information denoted by p; taking out t and p, the rest of the sentence is so called as event name denoted by e.

Step 3: Using the three extract elements to constituting the event three-dimensional vector $\vec{E}(e,t,p)$.

2.3   Similarity Calculate

In accordance with the event three-dimensional vector $\vec{E}(e,t,p)$, we compare social network event vector $\vec{E}_i(e_i,t_i,p_i)$ with webpages extract event vector $\vec{E}_j(e_j,t_j,p_j)$. The formula that how to calculate similarity value as follows:

$$Sim(\vec{E}_i, \vec{E}_j) = \cos(\vec{E}_i, \vec{E}_j) = \frac{\vec{E}_i \cdot \vec{E}_j}{|\vec{E}_i| \cdot |\vec{E}_j|} \quad (3)$$

Taking into consideration that there are lots of Chinese words in the similarity calculating proposed by this paper and the semantic information similarity these two key factors, this paper uses the method of calculating similarity based on HowNet Semantic Information. Using this method to obtain the event name similarity, time similarity and place similarity. The sentence similarity can translate into word similarity. In the HowNet, the word is expressed by one or more concepts and the concept is explained by primitive. So calculating word similarity can translate into calculating primitive similarity. In this paper, supposing two sentences are expressed as s_1 and s_2, they respectively include two words w_1 and w_2, the two words respectively include two concepts c_1 and c_2, this two concepts respectively include two primitive p_1 and p_2. Therefore, calculating similarity between s_1 and s_2 can translate into calculating similarity between p_1 and p_2. In the HowNet, the formula that how to calculate similarity between two primitive as follows:

$$Sim(p_1,p_2) = \frac{\delta}{d+\delta} \quad (4)$$

In this formula, p_1 and p_2 represent two primitive, d represents the distance between p_1 and p_2 in primitive gradation system, δ is an adjustable parameter [13].

In the HowNet, words are divided into notional words and function words, the similarity between notional words and function words is 0. Calculating function words similarity just need to calculate the primitive similarity. The function words concepts are mainly represented by four parts of primitive: $Sim_1(p_1,p_2)$, $Sim_2(p_1,p_2)$,

$Sim_3(p_1, p_2)$, $Sim_4(p_1, p_2)$, they represent four kinds of primitive, so the formula of calculating similarity between notional words as follows:

$$Sim(c_1, c_2) = \sum_{i=1}^{4} \lambda_i \prod_{j=1}^{i} Sim_j(p_1, p_2) \qquad (5)$$

In this formula, $\lambda_i(1 \leq i \leq 4)$ is an adjustable parameter and $\lambda_1 + \lambda_2 + \lambda_3 + = 1$, $\lambda_1 \geq \lambda_2 \geq \lambda_3 \geq \lambda_4$, it reflects the impact to ensemble similarity of sim_1 to sim_4 is decreasing.

Supposing two words w_1 and w_2, w_1 has m concepts: c_{11}, c_{12} ... c_{1m}, w_2 has n concepts: c_{21}, c_{22} ... c_{2n}, defining the similarity between w_1 and w_2 is:

$$Sim(w_1, w_2) = \max_{\substack{i = 1,2...m \\ j = 1,2...n}} Sim(c_{1i}, c_{2j}) \qquad (6)$$

Supposing two sentences $s_1(w_{11}, w_{12}...w_{1m})$, $s_2(w_{21}, w_{22}...w_{2n})$, w_{1i} and w_{2j} respectively represent the word contained within s_1 and s_2, so the formula that how to calculate similarity between sentences s_1 and s_2 as follows:

$$Sim(s_1, s_2) = \frac{\sum_{i=1}^{m} \max[\sum_{j=1}^{n} sim(w_{1i}, w_{2j})]}{m} \qquad (7)$$

The process of calculating similarity between social network event and Internet event as follows:

Step 1: After extracting the social network event vector $\vec{E}_i(e_i, t_i, p_i)$ and Internet event vector $\vec{E}_j(e_j, t_j, p_j)$, aim at the e_i and e_j, t_i and t_j, p_i and p_j, calculating event name similarity $SimE(e)$, time similarity $SimT(t)$, place similarity $SimP(p)$ by formula 7.

Step 2: Setting μ as the threshold value of judging the information is false or not, if $Sim(\vec{E}_i, \vec{E}_j)$ less than μ, it can be say that the event is false. Taking into consideration that if any one of event name, time and place differ greatly, it will heavily affect the authenticity of event. So that this paper stipulates that whichever the three values less than μ, we say that $Sim(\vec{E}_i, \vec{E}_j) = 0$. If $SimE(e)$, $SimT(t)$ and $SimP(p)$ are all not less than μ, commanding $\vec{E}_i(e_i, t_i, p_i)$ is the unit vector $(1, 1, 1)$ and $\vec{E}_j(e_j, t_j, p_j)$ is $\vec{E}_i(SimE(e_i, e_j), SimT(t_i, t_j), SimP(p_i, p_j))$. Using formula 3 can get the similarity between these two events; on the contrary, $Sim(i, j) = 0$.

2.4 Consistency Detection

After receiving the result of the similarity between social network information and Internet information, detecting the consistency of social network information and Internet information, detecting whether these two event information express same semantic information or not, mean to detect the emotional tendency in the two events is consistent or not.

At present, the method of calculating similarity not consider that oriented words may affect the sentences information, for example, "I very like Chinese football team" and "I very dislike Chinese football team", the similarity between two sentences will cause error comparing with the fact using the present similarity algorithm. Therefore, this paper detects the consistency of emotional tendency in the event information.

Acquiring the emotional tendency of sentence mainly through analyzing the commendation or derogation of the words, firstly segmenting the sentences and traversing the words, then extracting the adversative and appraisable words refer to the Antisense Primitive Dictionary and Adversative Words Dictionary so that judge the emotional tendency of the sentences. The specific computational process as follows:

Step 1: Segmenting sentences and traversing the words. Searching for the adversative words, if find that mark the sentences before the adversative words as 1 and mark the sentences after the adversative words as 2, giving up the sentence 1 and analyzing the sentence 2; if not find that analyze the whole sentences.

Step 2: Searching for the appraisable words and commanding the emotional tendency value of the sentences is 0, if find the commendatory words, mark the value +1; if find the derogatory words, mark the value −1;

Step 3: Working out the emotional tendency value of the social network sentences and Internet sentences denoted by Jud, comparing the social network sentences Jud with the Internet sentences Jud, if properties of positive and negative in social network sentences and Internet sentences are consistent, the emotional tendency of two sentences can be considered is consistent, whereas is not consistent;

Step 4: The Internet sentences can be considered as passing the consistency detection which emotional tendency is consistent with social network sentences, retaining the similarity between two events; if the sentences which emotional tendency is not consistent with social network sentences, they can be thought that not pass the consistency detection and the social network information is considered as false information, the similarity between two events is 0.

2.5   Statistics and Conclusion

This paper chooses the top n webpages return by Google ranked by WQ Value to analyze, it means that choose the top n webpages respectively denoted by $\vec{E}_1, \vec{E}_2, \vec{E}_3 \ldots$ $\vec{E}_j \ldots \vec{E}_n$. Comparing the similarity between social network event vector $\vec{E}_i(e_i, t_i, p_i)$ and Internet event vector $\vec{E}_j(e_j, t_j, p_j)$ according to Sects. 2.3 and 2.4 can obtain the similarity value $Sim(\vec{E}_i, \vec{E}_j)$ denoted by $Sim(i, j)$, sum to $Sim(i, 1), Sim(i, 2) \cdots Sim(i, j) \cdots Sim(i, n)$ n similarity data. The formula that how to calculate similarity between social network event i and Internet events as follows:

$$Sim(i) = \sum_{j=1}^{n} \frac{WQ(j)}{\sum_{j=1}^{n} WQ(j)} Sim(i, j) \tag{8}$$

If $Sim(i) < \mu$, the social network event i is false;
If $Sim(i) \geq \mu$, the social network event i is not false.

3 Experiment and Analysis

In order to verify the effect of the social network false information detection method propose by this paper, we design contrast experiments to compare the method propose by this paper with pre-existing methods and use the events announced by social network which have already taken place. This experiment mainly adopts the following performance indexes to measure system performance so as to objectively measure the performance of false information detection method:

Precision: $$P = \frac{The\ number\ of\ correctly\ detect\ false\ information}{The\ number\ of\ the\ test\ information} \times 100\% \quad (9)$$

Recall: $$R = \frac{The\ number\ of\ correctly\ detect\ false\ information}{The\ number\ of\ the\ actual\ false\ information} \times 100\% \quad (10)$$

F - Measure: $$F = \frac{2PR}{P+R} \times 100\% \quad (11)$$

This paper selects the Sina microblog hot events data set as the experimental data set, on the basis of refuting rumors by Sina official, chooses top 100 web pages return by Google as the Internet comparative information. Outside the false information detection method (denoted by Method 1) that this paper propose, at present, the common false information detection methods mainly include: Judging the information authenticity by calculating credibility of users (denoted by Method 2); Carlos Castillo proposes the method of automatically assessing social network popular theme information credibility through users' emotion and opinion on the information (denoted by Method 3). Comparing with these two methods, the experiment result as shown in Table 1.

Table 1. The experiment result of different false information detection methods

Method	Precision	Recall	F-Measure
1	88.33%	93.33%	90.76%
2	69.01%	70.04%	69.52%
3	86.10%	86.00%	86.05%

From the contrastive experiment data as shown in Table 1, the precision and recall of the method this paper proposed has a certain degree of increase comparing with pre-existing methods. Comparing with Method 2, this paper follows the point of view in information itself instead of users, this mainly considers about that the high-credibility users are hard to avoid announcing some unsupported information follow the trend, the credibility of users can not strictly correspond to the authenticity of information they announced. Comparing with Method 3, this paper compares social network information with Internet information to guarantee the contrastive information is authentic and authoritative, it makes the method this paper proposed has more practicability.

In order to verify significance of consistency detection to increase false information detection property propose by this paper, we design contrast experiments to compare conducting consistency detection with not conducting consistency detection, the comparison result as shown in Fig. 2.

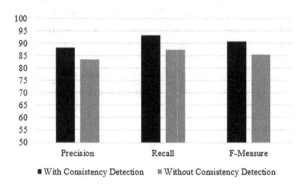

Fig. 2. Comparison of with or without consistency detection

From the contrastive experiment data as shown in Fig. 2, judging the emotional tendency of sentences and detecting the emotional tendency in the events is consistent or not can increase properties such as precision of false information detection. Thus it can be seen that the consistency detection module in the model proposed by this paper has great significance. This paper synthesizes advantage of pre-existing methods and presents a model of social network false information detection so that improves validity of false information detection, as a consequence, this paper has a certain feasibility.

4 Conclusions

With the rapid development of social network, announcing information by social network is open, anonymous, convenient and the spread of information is extensive and rapid, the information announced by this platform attracts more and more attention, because of the great harm brought by the false information, researching the false information detection of social network has great significance. This paper presents a model of social network false information detection, converting the information announced by social network into a three-dimensional vector, comparing this vector with the three-dimensional vector converted by Internet events, calculating the similarity between social network and Internet, detecting the consistency of social network event and Internet event, gathering statistics and analyzing then we can get the similarity between social network event and Internet event, according to this, we can judge that the social network information is false or not. This paper describes the essential flow and particular process of the model in detail, and conducts experiments with authentic social network data to verify whether the method this paper proposed is reasonable and effective or not. However, the method how to detect the information that can't searched out by Google is lacking, it need to be resolved in the later studies.

Acknowledgments. The author thanks the editor and reviewers for their suggestions to improve the quality of paper. This work was supported by the National Key Research and Development Program of China under Grant 2016YFB0800404 and NSF of China (U1536118) and NSF of China (U1433105).

References

1. Sina Technology. The Twitter of AP is attacked: announcing the false information that Obama has been attacked, 24 April 2013. http://www.ahwang.cn/zbah/20160319/1503617. shtml
2. Anhui Network: Somebody infect H7N9 because eating chicken in Huainan? Official: It is false information, 19 March 2016. http://tech.sina.com.cn/i/2013-04-24/08198273255.shtml
3. Akritidis, L., Katsaros, D., Bozanis, P.: Identifying the productive and influential bloggers in a community. IEEE Trans. Syst. Man Cybern. **41**(5), 759–764 (2011)
4. Zolfaghar, K., Aghaie, A.: A syntactical approach for interpersonal trust prediction in social web applications: combining contextual and structural data. Knowl.-Based Syst. **26**, 93–102 (2012)
5. Calais, G.P.H., Adriano, V., Wagner, M., Virgílio, A.: From bias to opinion: a transfer-learning approach to real-time sentiment analysis. In: Proceedings of the 17th ACM SIGKDD International Conference on Knowledge Discovery and Data Mining, pp. 150–158. ACM, CA (2011)
6. Castillo, C., Mendoza, M., Poblete, B.: Information credibility on twitter. In: Proceedings of the International Conference on World Wide Web (WWW), pp. 675–684 (2011)
7. Qiao, X.Q., Yang, C., Li, X.F., et al.: A trust calculating algorithm based on social networking service users' context. Jisuanji Xuebao Chin. J. Comput. **34**(12), 2403–2413 (2011)
8. Liu, T.: The problem of Internet information reliability, 01 December 2012. http://caai.cn/contents/49/102.html
9. Page, L., Brin, S., Motwani, R., et al.: The PageRank citation ranking: bringing order to the web (1999)
10. Sites, T.: Alexa Rank. The top, 500
11. Chen, Z., Ji, H.: Language specific issue and feature exploration in Chinese event extraction. In: Proceedings of the HLT-NAACL 2009, pp. 209–212. Omnipress, Madison (2009)
12. Lu, S., Bai, S.: Quantitative analysis of context field in natural language processing. Chin. J. Comput. Chin. Ed. **24**(7), 742–747 (2001)
13. Liu, Q., Li, S.: Word similarity computing based on How-Net. Comput. Linguist. Chin. Lang. Process. **7**(2), 59–76 (2002)

Security and Privacy in Collaborative System: Workshop on Multivariate Big Data Collaborations in Meteorology and Its Interdisciplines

Image Location Algorithm
by Histogram Matching

Xiaoqiang Zhang[1(✉)] and Junzhang Gao[2]

[1] School of Information and Electrical Engineering, China University of Mining
and Technology, Xuzhou 221116, Jiangsu, China
grayqiang@163.com
[2] Guangzhou ZLGMCU Development CO., LTD., Guangzhou 510000, China

Abstract. Image location affects the accuracy of image recognition. To improve accuracy and efficiency of the object location, the histogram matching method is designed, and a new common image location algorithm based on histogram matching is proposed. The algorithm uses the statistical characteristics of the histogram and determines the object location in the sequence image by calculating the histogram correlation between the object image and the pixel block of the image sequence. To verify the feasibility of the new algorithm, this paper locates the bird position in the sequence image of Flappy Bird (a popular mobile game) with the new algorithm. Experimental results show that the object in sequence images with the same size or almost the same size (such as direction variation), the algorithm is efficient and accurate. By testing 100 sequence images, the recognition rate of the new algorithm is 100%.

Keywords: Image location · Image recognition · Mobile game · Flappy Bird · Automatic operation

1 Introduction

With the rapid development of the computer vision and pattern recognition technology, how to quickly and accurately locate and identify the objects in a digital image becomes very important. Image location is the most important part of the image recognition technology. The result of image location can directly affect the accuracy of image recognition. At present, image location technology has been widely used in military cruise [1], oil leak detection [2], vehicle management [3–5], video surveillance [6] and medical diagnosis [7, 8] and other fields.

To protect the copyright of the digital image works and prevent the illegal attacker's malicious damage, Refs. [9–11] use the image watermarking technology to locate the image tampered area. To identify the vehicle license plate and realize the intelligent traffic management, Jianguo, et al. [5] proposed a vehicle license plate location algorithm based on the three-value image. In this algorithm, the color image is converted to the three-value gray image, and then using the color consistency among of characters in the vehicle license plate, the vehicle license plate is located by the character space line. For the implementation of maritime cruise monitoring, Lv, et al. [1] proposed a maritime target location algorithm based on the aerial image.

© ICST Institute for Computer Sciences, Social Informatics and Telecommunications Engineering 2017
S. Wang and A. Zhou (Eds.): CollaborateCom 2016, LNICST 201, pp. 655–664, 2017.
DOI: 10.1007/978-3-319-59288-6_66

By establishing the relationship between the pixels of the aerial image and the object marked points in three-dimension space, this algorithm establishes the geometric model of the center of the video camera, the image pixel and the sea target. For the realization of apple picking automation, Li, et al. [12] proposed a ripe apple location algorithm. This algorithm is mainly based on the three-point determination method of the circle, and the image removing noise technology. However, these existing algorithms are located for the specific object. To the best of our knowledge, few common image location algorithm has been proposed at present.

To improve the accuracy and efficiency of image location technology, a new common image location algorithm based on histogram matching is proposed in this paper. Experimental results show that the new algorithm is efficient and accurate.

The organization structure of this rest paper is as follows. Section 2 designs the histogram matching method; Sect. 3 designs an image location algorithm based on histogram matching; In Sect. 4 tests the new image location algorithm on Flappy Bird (a mobile game) and analyzes the algorithm performance; the conclusion and outlook are drawn in Sect. 5.

2   Histogram Matching Method

The image histogram indicates the statistical characteristics between each gray level and the occurrence frequency in a digital image [13]. Gray image histogram is used to count the occurrence frequency of 256 gray levels including 0, 1, 2, $\cdots$, 255 in the gray image. The histogram of Lena's gray image in Fig. 1 is as shown in Fig. 2.

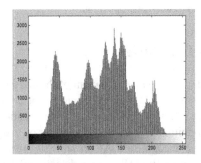

Fig. 1. Lena   **Fig. 2.** Lena's histogram

The histogram has the following three properties.

(1) If two images are exactly the same, then their corresponding histograms are exactly the same;
(2) If two images are similar, then their corresponding histograms are also similar;
(3) Two images arc different, but their corresponding histograms may be the same. However, the probability of this case is very low. If the image size is $m \times n$, then the occurrence probability of this case is $\left(\frac{1}{m \times n}\right)^{256} \approx 0$.

Using the above properties, this paper determines whether the two images are the same or not by making a comparison on their histograms. To achieve the purposes of image location, the histogram matching method is designed. For example, to locate the girl's head in Fig. 3 (called the location image), the specific steps are as follows.

 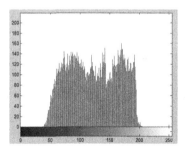

Fig. 3. Girl   **Fig. 4.** Girl's head   **Fig. 5.** Girl head's histogram

Step 1: Drawing the histogram of the object image

The histogram of Fig. 4 is as shown in Fig. 5.

Step 2: Drawing the histogram of the pixel block in the location image

Select a pixel block with the same size of the object image from the location image. The selected two pixel blocks are as shown in Fig. 6. The histogram of the pixel block 1 (i.e., the left selected area) is as shown in Fig. 7. The histogram of the pixel block 2 (i.e., the right selected area) is as shown in Fig. 8.

Fig. 6. Selected pixel blocks   **Fig. 7.** Pixel block 1's histogram

Step 3: Calculating the correlation of two histograms

Suppose two images are $A_{m \times n}$ and $B_{m \times n}$ respectively, and the correlation of their histograms is defined by

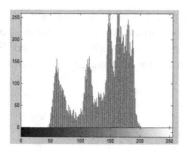

Fig. 8. Pixel block 2's histogram

$$r = \frac{1}{m \times n} \sum_{i=0}^{255} |a_i - b_i|, \tag{1}$$

where a_i is the pixel number of the i th gray level in $A_{m \times n}$, and b_i is the pixel number of the i th gray level in $B_{m \times n}$. Therefore, if $A_{m \times n}$ and $B_{m \times n}$ are exactly the same, then $r = 0$. Conversely, if $A_{m \times n}$ and $B_{m \times n}$ are different, then the value of r is larger and $r \leq 1$.

Using Eq. (1), the correlation between two histograms can be computed, which correspond to Fig. 4 and the selected pixel block 1 (or 2) is $r_1 = 0$ (or $r_2 = 0.5646$). Therefore, the selected pixel block 1 is the position of the girl's head in Fig. 3.

3   Algorithm Design

To locate the same object in sequence images, this paper proposes a new common image location algorithm based on histogram matching. The specific steps are as follows.

Step 1: Producing the object image

Choose an image $I_{m \times n}$ from sequence images, and then save the object pixel block in $I_{m \times n}$ as a separate image file, which is called the object image and denoted by $O_{s \times t}$.

Step 2: Drawing the histogram of the object image

Count the pixel number of each gray level in $O_{s \times t}$, and then draw the histogram H_o of $O_{s \times t}$.

Step 3: Locating the object in the first image of sequence images

Locate the object in the first image of sequence images. The specific steps are as follows.

Step 3.1: Selecting pixel blocks for the location.

Choose t continuous pixel columns including the object image in the first image $\{k, k+1, \cdots, k+t-1\}$, where k is an integer and $0 \leq k \leq n-t+1$. From the chosen t pixel columns, we segment the pixel blocks B_i with the size of $s \times t$ line by line from the t th row to the m th row, $i = 1, 2, \cdots, m-s+1$.

Step 3.2: Drawing the histograms of selected pixel blocks

Draw the histogram H_i of B_i, $i = 1, 2, \cdots, m-s+1$.

Step 3.3: Calculating the correlation between two histograms

Using Eq. (1), calculate the histogram correlation r_{oi} between H_o and H_i, $i = 1, 2, \cdots, m-s+1$.

Step 3.4: Locating the object

Select the minimum value r_{min} in the set $\{r_{oi}\}$, i.e.,

$$r_{min} = \min\{r_{oi}\}. \tag{2}$$

The pixel block B_{min} which corresponds to r_{min} is the object position in the first image.

Step 4: Locating the object in the subsequent images of sequence images

The video playback standard requires 25 frames per second. Therefore, the object displacement in two adjacent images of sequence images is very small. When select the location pixel area, we enlarge the boundary of B_{min} with p adjacent pixels. The other steps are the same to Steps 3.2, 3.3 and 3.4.

4 Verification Experiment and Algorithm Analysis

Flappy Bird is a simple but a little difficult mobile game developed by a Vietnamese named Dong Nguyen. The game was online on May 24, 2013, and it was very popular in February 2014. However, it was removed from Apple and Google App Store by developer himself in April 2014. The game officially returned to App Store in August 2014 [14]. In this game, players must control a fat bird through different water pipes which are viewed as obstacles. Game players generally believe that the game is easy to learn, but it is a little difficult to get a high score. Therefore, how to achieve the automatic operation of this game attracts researchers and game players' attention.

4.1 Verification Experiment

Image location is the core technology to realize the automatic operation of this game. For Flappy Bird, the bird location becomes very meaningful. By analyzing the characteristics of game images, we adopt the image location algorithm based on histogram matching to realize the bird location. The experiment object is the gray image of the game image. The experiment target is to locate the bird in sequence images. The process of the bird location is described in detail as follows.

Step 1: Producing the bird image

Randomly choose a game image as shown in Fig. 9, whose size is 600×400. Let the gray image of Fig. 9 be $I_{600 \times 400}$, which is as shown in Fig. 10. Saved the pixel block of the bird in Fig. 10 as a single image, which is called the bird image and denoted by $O_{32 \times 46}$, as shown in Fig. 11.

Fig. 9. Game image   **Fig. 10.** Gray game image   **Fig. 11.** Bird image

Step 2: Drawing the histogram of the bird image

The histogram of the bird image H_o is as shown in Fig. 12.

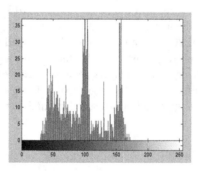

Fig. 12. Histogram of the bird image

Step 3: Locating the bird in the first image of sequence images

The first gray game image of Flappy Bird is as shown in Fig. 13. To locate the bird, the specific steps are as follows.

Step 3.1: Selecting pixel blocks for the location

Choose 46 continuous pixel columns including the bird image in the first image $\{94, 95, \cdots, 139\}$, which is marked with the dark gray color in Fig. 14. From the selected 46 pixel columns, we segment the pixel blocks B_i with the size of 32×46 line by line from the 32nd row to the 600th row, $i = 1, 2, \cdots, 569$.

Step 3.2: Drawing the histograms of selected pixel blocks

Draw the histogram H_i of B_i, $i = 1, 2, \cdots, 569$.

Step 3.3: Calculating the correlation between two histograms

Using Eq. (1), calculating the histogram correlation r_{oi} between H_o and H_i, $i = 1, 2, \cdots, 569$.

Step 3.4: Locating the bird

Select the minimum value $r_{\min} = 0$ in the set $\{r_{oi}\}$, which corresponds to the pixel block $B_{\min} = [94, 298, 32, 46]$ in Fig. 13, where $(94, 298)$ is the coordinate value of the upper-left corner pixel of $B_{\min}$, 32×46 is the size of $B_{\min}$. The location result is as shown in Fig. 15.

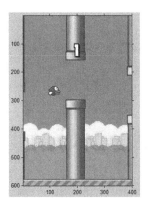 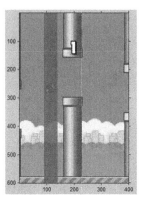 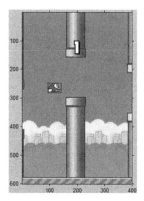

Fig. 13. The first game image

Fig. 14. The first marked game image

Fig. 15. Location result of the first game image

Step 4: Locating the bird in subsequent images of sequence images

By analyzing many game images of Flappy Bird, we can get the following features.

(1) The bird doesn't move in the left and right directions in essence, and only moves in the up and down directions. However, the water pipes move in the left and right directions;

(2) For two adjacent game images, the bird only moves a very short distance.

Considering these features, we enlarge the up and down borders of B_{min} with $p = 50$ adjacent pixels as the selected location pixel area. Therefore, the selected location pixel area is $[94, 298, 32 + 100, 46] = [44, 298, 132, 46]$, where $(44, 298)$ is the coordinate value of the upper-left corner pixel of the selected location pixel area, 132×46 is the size of the selected location pixel area. The other steps are the same to Steps 3.2, 3.3 and 3.4.

4.2   Algorithm Analysis

(1) Location accuracy analysis

By testing 100 continuous game images of Flappy Bird, the accuracy rate for the bird location is 100%. The location result of the second game image is as shown in Fig. 16. The location result of the 100th game image is as shown in Fig. 17. Figures 16 and 17 show that the location results are very correct.

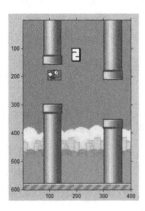

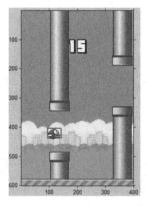

Fig. 16. Location result of the second game image

Fig. 17. Location result of the 100th game image

(2) Algorithm efficiency analysis

The algorithm efficiency is an important index to reflects whether an algorithm is practical or not. Meanwhile, the high execution efficiency is required for sequence images. Experimental result show that the execution time for bird location in the first game image is 0.3048 s, and the execution time for the bird location in the subsequent images is 0.05765 s on average. In all, the efficiency of our proposed algorithm is fast to satisfy the requirement of sequence images.

5 Conclusion and Outlook

Firstly, by studying the properties of image histogram, this paper design a histogram matching method; secondly, a new common image location algorithm based on histogram matching is proposed; finally, the bird of Flappy Bird is located with the new algorithm. Experimental results show that our proposed algorithm is feasible and efficient. Meanwhile, the location accuracy is desirable. By testing the new algorithm on 100 sequence images, the accuracy rate is 100%.

Our future work is as follows.

(1) Analyze the features of water pipes in Flappy Bird, and try to design a water pipe location algorithm;
(2) On the bases of the bird location algorithm and water pipe location algorithm, we will combine with the software and hardware to really realize the automation of Flappy Bird.

Acknowledgements. The research work of this paper is supported by the National Natural Science Foundation of China (61501465) and the Fundamental Research Funds for the Central Universities (2015QNA68).

References

1. Lv, Y., Lan, P.: Sea target positioning algorithm using aerial image. J. Shanghai Marit. Univ. **32**(4), 28–31 (2011). (in Chinese)
2. Suresh, G., Melsheimer, C., Koerber, J.-H., et al.: Automatic estimation of oil seep locations in synthetic aperture radar images. IEEE Trans. Geosci. Remote Sens. **53**(8), 4218–4230 (2015)
3. Liu, W.B., Wang, T.: Anti-noise car license plate location algorithm based on mathematical morphology edge detection. In: International Conference on Advances in Materials Science and Information Technologies in Industry. Xi'an, China, 11–12 January 2014
4. Hu, H.P., Bai, Y.P.: A kind of car license plate location based on color feature and mathematical morphology. In: International Conference on Structures and Building Materials. Guizhou, China, 09–10 March 2013
5. An, H., Jiang, J., Qi, M., Liu, H.: License plate location algorithm based on three-valued image. J. Electron. Measur. Instrum. **16**(1), 68–71 (2012). (in Chinese)
6. Ruffell, J., Innes, J., Bishop, C., et al.: Using pest monitoring data to inform the location and intensity of invasive-species control in New Zealand. Biol. Cons. **191**(11), 640–649 (2015)
7. Moon, W.K.: Location of triple-negative breast cancers: comparison with estrogen receptor-positive breast cancers on MR imaging. In: IMPAKT Breast Cancer Conference. Brussels, BELGIUM, 07–09 May 2015

8. Kim, W.H., Han, W., Chang, J.M., et al.: Location of triple-negative breast cancers: comparison with estrogen receptor-positive breast cancers on MR imaging. PLoS ONE **10** (1), e0116344 (2015)
9. Ouda, A.H., El-Sakka, M.R.: Correlation watermark for image authentication and alternation locations detection. In: 4th Conference on Mathematics of Image and Data Coding, Compression, and Encryption, San Diego, CA, 30–31 July 2001
10. Wu, F., Rui, G.S.: A digital image watermarking technique with detecting the location of any image interpolation. In: 6th International Symposium on Test and Measurement, Dalian, China, 01–04 June 2005
11. Lim, J., Lee, H., Lee, S., Kim, J.: Invertible watermarking algorithm with detecting locations of malicious manipulation for biometric image authentication. In: Zhang, D., Jain, A.K. (eds.) ICB 2006. LNCS, vol. 3832, pp. 763–769. Springer, Heidelberg (2005). doi:10.1007/11608288_102
12. Li, H., Liu, Q.: Study on technology of location of apples. J. Agric. Mech. Res. **105**(2), 54–57 (2016). (in Chinese)
13. Zhang, X., Wang, X., Cheng, Y.: Image encryption based on a genetic algorithm and a chaotic system. IEICE Trans. Commun. **E98-B**(5), 824–833 (2015)
14. Baidu Baike. Flappy bird, 4 May 2013. (in Chinese). http://baike.baidu.com/link?url=PCwedUn_N-oRCR7CeworTEptqi5mljHcTqitO6LY0Evr0OHTlK-svcCCcha-ng0nr9gGaN YmDAIPLO-XrMOyzK

Generate Integrated Land Cover Product for Regional Climate Model by Fusing Different Land Cover Products

Hao Gao[1(✉)], Gensuo Jia[2], and Yu Fu[3]

[1] National Satellite Meteorological Center, China Meteorological Administration,
Beijing 100081, China
gaohao@cma.gov.cn
[2] Key Laboratory of Regional Climate-Environment for Temperate East Asia,
Institute of Atmospheric Physics, Chinese Academy of Sciences, Beijing 100029, China
jiong@tea.ac.cn
[3] Climate Change Research Center, Chinese Academy of Sciences, Beijing 100029, China
fuyu@mail.iap.ac.cn

Abstract. Land cover and its change play an important role as a critical variables in global change studies and environment sciences. With many satellite-derived land cover products have become available at global and regional scales, it is possible to improve the quality of the product by integrating existing ones. In this paper, we propose a methodology to generate integrated land cover product for regional climate model over China. The integration rules were established based on the accuracies information from the ground truth. The accuracy of the integrated product was greatly improved, with overall accuracy of 68.7%, and class-specific accuracy ranging from 25.7% to 91.2%. Additionally, the spatial patterns of the land cover over China were well captured, and good agreement with the Landsat-based classification was achieved. Further, our results implicates the quality of the land cover products for integration are significant critical in our approach, the accuracy of the integrated land cover product is dependant on accuracy of the original products used for integration, especially of the local products. This integrated product could potentially improve the performance of regional climate models by providing better estimates of key land surface parameters over the region.

Keywords: Land cover · Satellite · Integration · Fusion · China

1 Introduction

Land use/cover change is considered as a critical variable in global change studies and environment science, which represents the influence of human activity and environment change and drives the biosphere-atmosphere interaction [1]. Land cover classification

Funded by: National Key Research and Development Program of China (Grant No. 2016YFA0600303), and the National Natural Science Foundation of China (Grant No. 41571425).

provides vital baseline information on the biophysical features of the Earth's surface, which plays an important role in regional to global scale Earth models, because land cover information is required to provide the initial conditions for parameterizing land surface processes [2]. Changes in land cover may also lead to significant consequences in environmental quality, climate change, and ecosystem health [3].

Currently, a number of global and regional scales land cover products have been developed from satellite data for various scientific and management needs [4–8]. They were widely used in a range of scientific studies including ecosystem, environment, climate change, and sustainable development. Although some progresses have been made for improving spatial parameterization, the quality of land cover products are still considered as a major bootle-neck that compromise the performance of regional models [9, 10]. Previous evaluation and inter-comparison of the land cover products showed obvious discrepancies and uncertainties existed among different land cover products, because of the differences in input data, spatial coverage, classifier algorithm, spatial resolution, classification schemes, and acquisition period of satellite data [11–13]. A more reliable and consistent land cover product are particularly important and essential for various applications.

Several international organizations have fostered land cover harmonization and strategies for interoperability and synergy among existing land cover products [14]. Recently, there were some attempts for end users to develop reliable land cover data by integrating different products based on fuzzy agreement scoring [15], Dempster-Shafer evidential reasoning [8], the majority rules [16], and synergistic approach [17, 18]. Despite of insufficient reference data available for thoroughly validating, the integrated products were considered more accurate than the originals. Though there are still some uncertainties with these methods, mainly because the existed products were produced using different input data, classifier algorithm, spatial resolution and classification schemes, developing integrated products from multi-satellite data is a reasonable alternative approach for land cover quality improvement in short-term.

The objective of this paper is to assess the overall and class-specific accuracy of the existing satellite-derived land cover products based on the validation points over China, and to develop a new framework for generating an integrated land cover product with IGBP classification scheme for regional climate model, according to specific fusion rules established in terms of accuracies of the various satellite-derived land cover products. A key focus is on assessing the accuracy improvement of the new integrated land cover products.

2   Data and Method

2.1   Land Cover Products

In this study, the 2001 MODIS Collection 51 global land cover product (MC51 hereafter) at 500-m spatial resolution with IGBP classification scheme, Global Land Cover 2000 (GLC2000) at 1-km spatial resolution with the Land Cover Classification System (LCCS), and some regional scale land cover products, such as the National Land Cover Datasets (NLCD) at 1-km spatial resolution, the Environment and Ecological Science

Data Center for Western China (WESTDC) land cover at 1-km spatial resolution with IGBP classification scheme were selected for integration.

2.2   Validation Points

A specific effort was made to establish validation points from multiple sources, including field investigation, coordinated enhanced observation project in arid and semi-arid China, Asia Fluxnet sites, Chinese Ecosystem Research Network (CERN) sites, Taiwan long term Ecological Research Network (TERN), Terrestrial Ecosystem Monitoring Sites (TEMS), and Degree Confluence Project (DCP). All the land cover categories of the validation points were interpreted according to the IGBP classification scheme. Finally, 1254 validation points were selected throughout China for subsequent validation efforts.

2.3   Evaluating Accuracy of the Land Cover Products

Most of the land cover products are validated, and their overall accuracy and class-specific accuracy are reported [5, 19]. Because different validation database and methods were used, the reported accuracy measures are not comparable and may not be considered as truly robust quantitative estimates. Here, all the land cover products for integration were evaluated using confusion matrix based on the validation points, the overall accuracy and class-specific accuracies were calculated and served as the foundation for integration. The integrated products were also evaluated against the validation points. Moreover, three subsets were selected for examining the spatial pattern of integrated product against the classification map interpreted from the Lansat TM, and for quantitative analyzing the each land cover class.

2.4   Land Cover Product Integration

Our integration approach was based on an idea that the more agreement of same land cover class among the products, the higher probability or likelihood that the specific land cover class exists at that pixel [15–17]. The process of integration was divided into two phases. First, all land cover products were assessed with the validation points, and each land cover categories were ranked based on the accuracy of the land cover categories before integration (Table 1). Then, each land cover categories was integrated based on rank value. The integrated process for each land cover categories based on rank value was illustrated in Fig. 1a. Land cover product #1 (LC#1) had the highest accuracy of the specific land cover categories evaluated by ground truth, and followed by LC#2, LC#3 and LC#4. The black pixels indicate that specific land cover category exist in each product. If all 4 products agree on the specific land cover categories exist in the pixel, a value of 1 is assigned for this pixel. A value of 2 was assigned to the pixel where the LC#1, LC#2 and LC#3 agree the specific land cover categories but LC#4 does not. There are 15 possible rank value with 4 land cover products, which was shown in Table 1. Finally, 17-class integrated layer, which were generated in the second phase, were integrated for the final land cover integration based on the value of rank assigned to each of pixels (Fig. 1b). A specific land cover category was assigned to a pixel if that category has the highest priority.

Table 1. The datasets ranking for integrating four land cover products.

Rank value	Land Cover#1	Land Cover#2	Land Cover#3	Land Cover#4
1	+	+	+	+
2	+	+	+	−
3	+	+	−	+
4	+	−	+	+
5	−	+	+	+
6	+	+	−	−
7	+	−	+	−
8	+	−	−	+
9	−	+	+	−
10	−	+	−	+
11	−	−	+	+
12	+	−	−	−
13	−	+	−	−
14	−	−	+	−
15	−	−	−	+

Land Cover#1 has the highest accuracy of the specific land cover category, followed by Land Cover#2, #2 and #4. The symbol "+" indicates the presence of the specific land cover category at the pixel and "−" indicates absence.

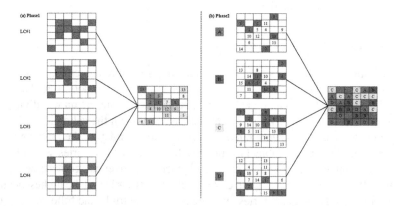

Fig. 1. Multi-satellite product integration based on rank value. (a) Integration of each land cover categories; The black pixels indicate that specific land cover category exist in each product, LC#1 has the highest accuracy assessed with the validation points followed by LC#2, LC#3 and LC#4. The numbers in pixels are the rank value which means the priority for integration, the smaller of the number, the higher priority for integration. (b) Final land cover product integration. A, B, C and D are the integrated land cover categories with the rank value generated from the Phase 1, and the numbers in the pixels indicate the priority of the specific land cover category.

Table 2. The overall and class-specific accuracy of the land cover products for integration

Land cover class	Accuracy (%)			
	MC51 2000	WESTDC	GLC2000	NLCD2000
0. Water	64.0	80.0	54.0	48.0
1. Evergreen needleleaf forest	33.3	35.9	38.5	/
2. Evergreen broadleaf forest	35.0	20.0	45.0	/
3. Deciduous needleleaf forest	22.7	18.2	31.8	/
4. Deciduous broadleaf forest	25.9	22.2	59.3	/
5. Mixed forest	46.8	25.5	21.3	/
6. Closed shrublands	19.6	30.4	16.1	30.0
7. Open shrublands	35.3	26.5	14.7	/
8. Woody savannas	41.2	44.1	14.7	/
9. Savannas	19.2	38.5	0.0	/
10. Grasslands	67.6	80.3	57.6	72.3
11. Permanent wetlands	16.1	32.3	19.4	19.4
12. Croplands	60.3	77.6	53.0	70.6
13. Urban and built-up	65.6	78.5	15.1	39.8
14. Cropland/natural vegetation mosaic	25.4	19.7	0.0	/
15. Snow and ice	44.4	55.6	50.0	61.1
16. Barren or sparsely vegetated	78.8	75.4	68.6	63.6
Overall	53.7	61.7	41.9	60.9

3   Results

3.1   Accuracy of the Land Cover Products

The overall and class-specific accuracy of land cover products used for integration were validated by validation points (Table 2). The overall accuracy of the MC51 2001, GLC2000, WESTDC, and NLCD 2000 are 53.7%, 41.9%, 61.7%, and 60.9%, respectively in China, which are remarkably lower than global area-weighted accuracy. The class-specific accuracies varied significantly. As expected, the accuracies of water, grasslands, croplands, snow and ice, and barren or sparsely vegetated were generally greater than the other categories. By contrast, the accuracies of remaining land cover categories were much lower, and varied significantly among products. Generally, the accuracies of forests in GLC2000 were much greater than in others. Other high accuracy cases include closed shrublands in WESTDC and NLCD 2000, open shrublands in MC51 2001 and WESTDC, permanent wetlands and urban and built-up in WESTDC, and snow and ice in NLCD 2000. Clearly, each land cover product has its advantages and limitations with specific land cover categories, which provided great opportunity and possibility for us to improve the quality of land cover data or integrate a new dataset that contained the advantages of each dataset based on the identified uncertain areas.

3.2   Comparison Between the MC51 and Integrated Land Cover Product

An integrated land cover product were created based on multi-satellite land cover products (Fig. 2). Remarkable differences were found between the MC51 products and integrated product. The major difference was found on the Tibetan Plateau, Inner Mongolia, Loess Plateau, and the edge area of barren area of northwest China, where grasslands replaced the open shrublands and barren or sparsely vegetated. Integrated product demonstrated similar land cover classification as previous results [8, 20], and similar to the 1:1000000 scale China vegetation map. Meanwhile, more oases in the desert are identified in integrated product. It seems to be reliably mapped, grasslands were clearly underestimated by MODIS, due to the presence of mixed classes such as Natural/cropland vegetation, and also the different definition of the grassland.

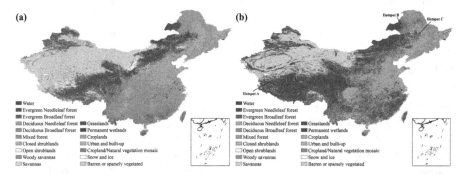

Fig. 2. Overview of the MODIS land cover products and integrated product. (a) MC51 2001; (b) Integrated land cover product for 2001.

Main plant functional types, and spatial pattern of forests in China are captured in the integrated product. Evergreen needleleaf forest are located in the south China and the edge area of Tibetan Plateau; Evergreen Broadleaf forest are mainly dominant in south China; Deciduous needleleaf forest are mainly placed in the Daxing'an Mountains of northwest China; Deciduous broadleaf forest are located in major mountain ranges in northwest and north China. By contrast with MC51 product, we found that much mixed forest are replaced by different forest types. The main patterns of forest in China are better captured by our integrated product, which are much similar to the China vegetation map. Such achievements are mainly contributed by GLC2000, due to its high accuracy of the forest types, which were produced by the regional and local experts. MODIS clearly overestimated the areas of mixed forest in China. Indeed, it is very difficult to distinguish classes with similar spectro-temporal-texture signals, especially for mapping continuum into discreted forest categories.

In addition, more inland water and permanent wetlands are presented in Sanjiang Plain, the largest wetland in China; and more inland water and permanent wetlands are identified in the flood plains of the Yellow River and Yangtze River. Meanwhile, more permanent wetlands are captured on the Tibetan Plateau, which are consistent with local studies [20, 21]. Further, more pixels were categorized into cropland on the Loess Plateau, and edge of the Mongolia plateau. All these characteristics are better captured in our product, indicated by greater agreements with local products and validation points. Indeed, the classes with much higher accuracy in local land cover products are well represented in the integrated product. Local land cover product played an important role in the integration process, and their contribution are significant. The quality of the participant land cover products are critical in our integration method, because their classification confidence could transferred to the integrated product, and affected the quality of the final product.

3.3   Accuracy of the Integrated Land Cover Product

The integrated land cover product for 2001 were also validated with validation points (Table 3). The overall accuracy of the integrated product were 68.7%, a 15.0% increase from original MC51 product. The class-specific accuracies differed significantly, ranging from 25.7% (cropland/natural vegetation mosaic) to 91.2% (grasslands). Generally, the accuracy of most categories was significantly increased in integrated product. However, the accuracy of mixed forest, open shrubland, woody savannas, and barren or sparsely vegetated were decreased. The grassland has the greatest increase of accuracy (23.6%), followed by permanent wetlands (22.6%), deciduous broadleaf forest (22.2%), water (18%), croplands (17.9%), savannas (15.4%), deciduous needleleaf forest (13.7%), closed shrublands (12.5%), snow and ice (11.7%), and evergreen broadleaf forest (10.0%). In addition, the percentage area of forests, grassland, built-up in integrated products generally have high agreements with the statistical yearbook, the forest inventory data (1999–2003), and the 1:1000000 scale China vegetation map. It is very interesting to see that major improvements of accuracy were achieved in classes with high accuracy in the local land cover product, such as water, closed shrubland, grassland, permanent wetlands, croplands, urban and built-up, snow and ice. Obviously, the local land cover product with high accuracy play an important role in the integration procedure. On the other hand, some land cover classes still have low accuracy, such as open scrublands, woody savannas, savannas, cropland/natural vegetation mosaic, and mixed forests. These classes may be easily confused due to the spectral similarity. For woody savannas, and savannas, only one classification scheme was used for MODIS product, and their accuracies are much lower than others. Discrepancy of the accuracy among the individual categories largely resulted from the significant difference of participant products, highly supports from local land cover products are significantly important for our integration method.

Table 3. The overall and class-specific accuracy of the integrated product validated by validation points

Land cover class	Accuracy (%)
0. Water	82.0
1. Evergreen needleleaf forest	34.8
2. Evergreen broadleaf forest	45.0
3. Deciduous needleleaf forest	36.4
4. Deciduous broadleaf forest	48.1
5. Mixed forest	31.5
6. Closed shrublands	32.1
7. Open shrublands	30.5
8. Woody savannas	26.5
9. Savannas	34.6
10. Grasslands	91.2
11. Permanent wetlands	38.7
12. Croplands	78.2
13. Urban and built-up	67.7
14. Cropland/natural vegetation mosaic	25.7
15. Snow and ice	55.6
16. Barren or sparsely vegetated	78.3
Overall	68.7

3.4   Detail Comparison of the Products in Subsets

Three local subsets were selected for comparing with 1:1000000 scale China vegetation map, and classification products based on the Landsat-7 satellite data to further evaluate the integrated product (Fig. 3). Generally, the land cover pattern of the integrated products in each subset appears similar to the China vegetation map and Landsat-7 classification. The integrated product was validated against the Landsat-7 classification. The accuracy of the integrated product was 53.4%, 52.8%, and 55.3% for region A, B and C, respectively, which have improved by about 8.2% to 24.8%. For region A in the Tibetan Plateau, the distribution pattern of the land cover classes in integrated product presented good agreement with Landsat-based classification and national vegetation map. The MC51 products apparently underestimated grassland. For region B in the boundary area of the Daxin'anling Mountains, the MC51 products significantly overestimated croplands, and the transition zone were also not clear. The extent of the cropland in integrated product is accordant with the reality, and forest types were also classified at high accuracy. For region C in the Sanjiang plain, MC51 product underestimated water, permanent wetlands, and overestimated the grassland. But in integrated product, they agreed with reference data well. Overall, our integrated product achieved greater overall accuracy than MC51 product. But, some land cover classes were more or less overestimated in some regions. It is interesting where the grassland or wetlands was overestimated in local product, they were also overestimated in integrated product. Apparently, the accuracy of the participant products also can affect the quality of the integrated product.

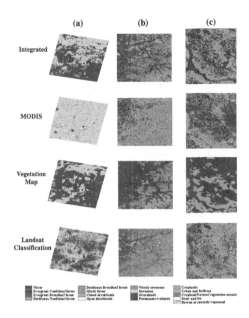

Fig. 3. Comparison of the three local subsets among four land cover map. (a) Subset A in the Tibetan Plateau of northwest China; (b) Subset B in the Daxin'anling Mountain of northeast China; (c) Subset C in the Sanjiang plain of northeast China.

4 Discussion and Conclusion

A method based on the accuracy of multi-satellite land cover products was proposed and applied to integrate a land cover product for 2001 over China. The accuracy of the MODIS, GLC2000, WESTDC, and NLCD2000 land cover products were validated with validation points to establish integration rules. Generally, the distribution patterns of the land cover in integrated product were captured reliably. The overall accuracy of the integrated product was 68.7%, a major improvement compared to the original MC51 product. Most of the class-specific accuracy in integrated product increased. Additionally, the distribution patterns of the land cover in our integrated product showed good agreement with Landsat-based classification and 1:1000000 scale national vegetation map. The quality of the land cover products for integration are critical in our integration method, the accuracy of the integrated product is dependant on the accuracy of participant land cover products for integration. Local land cover products played an important role in the integration process, their contribution are significant. Major improvement of classification accuracy was found in classes that are supported by the local products.

The integration rules in our study are established in terms of the accuracy validated by the ground truth, which are more objective and credible, but some limitations still need to be considered. First, in the preprocessing process, the LCCS classification schemes used in the GLC2000 product was translated to IGBP classification scheme according to recommended relationship. Meanwhile, the different spatial resolution with the products were resampled to the same spatial resolution, which may have introduced additional uncertainty. Second, the accuracy of participant land cover products need to be further validated as additional reference data become available. Our results implicate high accuracy of the participant products could bring great improvement of the quality of the integrated product. Finally, the integrated product also need to be further rigorous validated against ground truth. With high quality land cover products become available in the future, we also expect to improve methods to produce more accurate and up-to-date land cover products for climate modeling.

Acknowledgments. The study was supported by the National Key Research and Development Program of China (Grant No. 2016YFA0600303). We thank the Land Processes Distributed Active Archive Center (LP DAAC), the Joint Research Centre (JRC) of Global Vegetation Monitoring Units, the Data Sharing Infrastructure of Earth System Science, and the Environmental & Ecological Science Data Center for West China, National Natural Science Foundation of China for their helpful response to our inquiry on satellite product.

References

1. Turner, B.L., Lambin, E.F., Reenberg, A.: The emergence of land change science for global environmental change and sustainability. Proc. Natl. Acad. Sci. **104**, 20666–20671 (2007)
2. Bonan, G.B., Levis, S., Kergoat, L., Oleson, K.W.: Landscapes as patches of plant functional types: an integrating concept for climate and ecosystem models. Global Biogeochem. Cycles **16**, 1021 (2002)
3. Feddema, J.J., Oleson, K.W., Bonan, G.B., et al.: The importance of land-cover change in simulating future climates. Science **310**, 1674–1678 (2005)
4. Bartholomé, E., Belward, A.S.: GLC2000: a new approach to global land cover mapping from earth observation data. Inter. J. Remote Sens. **26**, 1959–1977 (2005)
5. Friedl, M.A., Sulla-Menashe, D., Tan, B., et al.: Modis collection 5 global land cover: algorithm refinements and characterization of new datasets. Remote Sens. Environ. **114**, 168–182 (2010)
6. GLOBCOVER 2009: Products Description and Validation Report. http://ionia1.esrin.esa.int/docs/GLOBCOVER2009_Validation_Report_2.2.pdf
7. Liu, J., Liu, M., Deng, X., Zhuang, D., Zhang, Z., Luo, D.: The land use and land cover change database and its relative studies in China. J. Geog. Sci. **12**, 275–282 (2002)
8. Ran, Y.H., Li, X., Lu, L., Li, Z.Y.: Large-scale land cover mapping with the integration of multi-source information based on the Dempster-Shafer theory. Int. J. Geogr. Inf. Sci. **26**, 169–191 (2012)
9. Ge, J., Qi, J., Lofgren, B.M., et al.: Impacts of land use/cover classification accuracy on regional climate simulations. J. Geophys. Res. **112**, D05107 (2007)
10. Sertel, E., Robock, A., Ormeci, C.: Impacts of land cover data quality on regional climate simulations. Int. J. Climatol. **30**, 1942–1953 (2010)
11. McCallum, I., Obersteiner, M., Nilsson, S., Shvidenko, A.: A spatial comparison of four satellite derived 1 km global land cover datasets. Int. J. Appl. Earth Obs. Geoinf. **8**, 246–255 (2006)
12. Herold, M., Mayaux, P., Woodcock, C.E., et al.: Some challenges in global land cover mapping: an assessment of agreement and accuracy in existing 1 km datasets. Remote Sens. Environ. **112**, 2538–2556 (2008)

13. Kaptué, T.A.T., Roujean, J.L., De Jong, S.M.: Comparison and relative quality assessment of the GLC2000, GLOBCOVER, MODIS and ECOCLIMAP land cover data sets at the African continental scale. Int. J. Appl. Earth Obs. Geoinf. **13**, 207–219 (2011)
14. Herold, M., Woodcock, C.E., Gregorio, A.D., et al.: A joint initiative for harmonization and validation of land cover datasets. IEEE Trans. Geosci. Remote Sens. **44**, 1719–1727 (2006)
15. Jung, M., Henkel, K., Herold, M., Churkina, G.: Exploiting synergies of global land cover products for carbon cycle modeling. Remote Sens. Environ. **101**, 534–553 (2006)
16. Kinoshita, T., Iwao, K., Yamagata, Y.: Creation of a global land cover and a probability map through a new map integration method. Int. J. Appl. Earth Obs. Geoinf. **28**, 70–77 (2014)
17. Fritz, S., You, L., Bun, A., et al.: Cropland for sub-Saharan Africa: a synergistic approach using five land cover data sets. Geophys. Res. Lett. **38**, L04404 (2011)
18. Pérez-Hoyos, A., García-Haro, F.J., San-Miguel-Ayanz, J.: A methodology to generate a synergetic land-cover map by fusion of different land-cover products. Int. J. Appl. Earth Obs. Geoinf. **19**, 72–87 (2012)
19. Mayaux, P.: Validation of the global land cover 2000 map. IEEE Trans. Geosci. Remote Sens. **44**, 1728–1739 (2006)
20. Zhang, Z., Wang, X., Zhao, X., et al.: A 2010 update of National Land Use/Cover Database of China at 1:100000 scale using medium spatial resolution satellite images. Remote Sens. Environ. **149**, 142–154 (2014)
21. Zhang, S.: An introduction of wetland science database in China. Sci. Geogr. Sin. **22**, 188–189 (2002)

Security and Privacy in Collaborative System: Workshop on Social Network Analysis

A Novel Social Search Model Based on Clustering Friends in LBSNs

Yang Sun, Jiuxin Cao[(✉)], Tao Zhou, and Shuai Xu

Jiangsu Provincial Key Laboratory of Network and Information Security,
School of Computer Science and Engineering, Southeast University, Nanjing, China
{sunyang,jx.cao,zhoutao,xushuai}@seu.edu.cn

Abstract. With the development of online social networks (OSNs), OSNs have become an indispensable part in people's life. People tend to search information through OSNs rather than traditional search engines. Especially with the appearance of location-based social networks (LBSNs), social search in LBSNs is increasingly important in the burgeoning mobile trend. This paper proposes a novel social search model, harnesses users' social relationship and location features provided by LBSNs to design a ranking algorithm that takes three kinds of ranking scores into account comprehensively: Social Score (scores based on social influence), Searching Score (scores based on professional relevance) and Spatial Score (scores based on distance), finally produces high-quality searching results. Once receiving users' query, the social search engine aims to return a list of ranking POIs (points of interests) that satisfies users. The dataset is extracted from Foursquare, a real-world LBSN. The experiment results show that the ranking algorithm can benefit the social search model in LBSNs evidently.

Keywords: LBSNs · Social search model · Social Score · Searching Score · Spatial Score

1 Introduction

In the past few years, with the rapid development in the mobile field, location-based social network services such as Foursquare and Yelp, have seen increasing popularity, attracting millions of users. Supported by the capabilities of portable devices like smart phones, the location-aware technology like GPS and Wi-Fi, people can easily share their locations, comments and other information with other users. The LBSN [1] services not only help users to strengthen their social connections, but also provide useful searching information.

Information retrieval and knowledge discovery are the main purposes of the web search. Because of the fast and updated information available on the web, users usually rely on search engines to obtain the information. Searching is always considered as an individual activity [2] in traditional social engines like Google, however, with the popularity of OSNs, people are pursuing personalized searching and mass collaboration. Social search [3] could meet people's needs, which makes users find out right people (friends, other similar users or domain experts) quickly and accurately to answer

© ICST Institute for Computer Sciences, Social Informatics and Telecommunications Engineering 2017
S. Wang and A. Zhou (Eds.): CollaborateCom 2016, LNICST 201, pp. 679–689, 2017.
DOI: 10.1007/978-3-319-59288-6_68

questions. Recently, Facebook has partnered with Bing and introduced a social search engine called "Graph Search" [4] that associates the results with friends' suggestions.

Applying social search on the LBSNs is an appealing trend. When users search a nearest POI with friends visiting experiences provided by LBSNs, in addition to the traditional social information, exploiting useful location information could make searching results more accurate. For example, if a user wants to search a suitable restaurant for dinner, however, he does not be familiar with the surrounding restaurants, then all the restaurants are candidates and it is better to pick a restaurant which is near the place and has received high evaluations from his friends. On the one hand, the searching results are high-quality. The picked restaurants are both short-distance and high-evaluation, which is better than the traditional social search that only considers social relation; on the other hand, the social search engine provides believable results to users. Users are more inclined to believe and choose POIs once showing friends' experience or evaluations.

Considering such problems, in this paper, we propose a social search model and design a novel ranking algorithm. The dataset is extracted from Foursquare that is a heterogeneous network, and the data is quite sparse. Sparse data could largely influence the accuracy of results. To enhance the data density, we creatively cluster user's friends in the research of social search. Based on clustering friends, the ranking algorithm creatively considers Social Score, Searching Score and Spatial Score comprehensively. Social Score means social influence, social features include not only the traditional social relationship but also location features; Searching Score means professional relevance, which measures the similarity between the query and POIs; Spatial Score is the distance between the locations of users and POIs, the shorter distance means the better score.

The contributions of this paper can be summarized as follows:

1. To enhance the data density and reduce the influence of the sparse data, as far as we know, it is the first time to apply clustering users' friends in the research of social search in LBSNs;
2. To get high-quality ranking results and consider the distance factor in reality, in addition to the traditional Social Score, we take Searching Score and Spatial Score into account in the research of social search.

The rest of this paper is organized as follows. Section 2 reviews related work on social search in OSNs and LBSNs. Then an overview of the social search model is introduced in Sect. 3. The details of the ranking algorithm is presented in Sect. 4. Section 5 describes the validation of our model. Finally, we conclude this paper and state several directions for future work in Sect. 6.

2   Related Work

With the increasing popularity of social networking platforms, social search is attracting significant number of interests in the research field since traditional search engines do not always provide high-quality searching results. However, social search is personalized, so there are different social search engines and social search algorithms [5], a lot of works are done based on different start points.

Some researches concentrate on the problem of designing social search engine. HeyStaks [6, 7] is an Irish social search engine, it applies the recommended technology on Google, Bing and Yahoo based on users' interests and reputation, then returns searching results from Twitter and OSNs. M. R. Bouadjenek, H. Hacid and M. Bouzeghoub [8] introduce a social search engine called LAICOS, which includes social information and personal services. On the one hand, it can provide personalized social document representations; on the other hand, users can use its personalized social query expansion framework to expand searching process. Horowitz and Kamvar [9] design a large-scale social search engine called Aardvark. They use an intimacy metric between users and connect users with specific questions to find the user who is most likely to be able to answer the question. The intimacy is set based on many features, including vocabulary match, profile similarity, social connection and so on.

Some other researches focus on the problem of improving social algorithms. D. Sharma et al. [10] present a self-adapting social search algorithm based on proximity, similarity and interaction. Bao et al. [11] explore the use of social annotations, they propose SocialPageRank to measure the page popularity based on its annotations and SocialSimRank for the similarity between social annotations and web queries. Guo Liang et al. [12] present two ranking algorithms: topic relevance rank (TRR) evaluates users' professional score on the relevant topics; social relation rank (SRR) captures the social relation strength between users.

However, there are quite few researches on social search in LBSNs. Hu et al. [13] define friends-based k nearest neighbors (F-KNN) query, which aims at finding objects near the query location as well as receiving high evaluation from user's friends. But they pay main attention to increasing the searching speed, so they design a F-Quadtree index, and do not perform well on the searching accuracy based on social features. Yuan et al. [14] propose a KNN search on road networks by incorporating social influence, but they do not perform well on the speed of the computation of the social influence over large road and social networks. In contrast to the above works, our research aims to design a good social search model that provides accurate results quickly.

3 The Social Search Model

The social search model is shown in Fig. 1. Vertically, like traditional search engines, the whole architecture is divided into two parts: offline crawler and online searching. Horizontally, there are three main parts: Social Score, Searching Score and Spatial Score. The different functions of these components are described below.

Database. Database maintains the data basis of the social search architecture. The dataset is crawled and extracted from Foursquare, the data types include user's ID and relation; POIs' information that users need to search, including POIs' name, ID, category, description, latitude and longitude; check-ins' ID; timezone.

Searching Score. In this part, we design a search engine based on Lucene [15]. The core of search engine is Inverted Index [16]. We build an Inverted Index based on POIs' information. Then by calculating the similarity scores between user's query and the

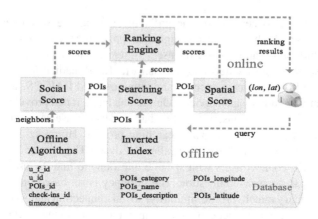

Fig. 1. This is the figure displaying the model of social search

"document" in the index, the alternative POIs' names are picked out and sent to the Social Score and Spatial Score. The similarity scores are sent to Ranking Engine.

Social Score. This part provides offline algorithms, which are updated K-means and updated KNN, the purpose of the updated K-Means is to cluster users' friends to enhance the data density; the purpose of updated KNN is to find out some friends that are most similar with users. Users are always more inclined to believe the most similar friends [17]. Then we extract some social features including friends' activity and evaluation on the alternative POIs to calculate social scores that are sent to the Ranking Engine.

Spatial Score. Users are more inclined to visit short-distance POIs, so the distance between the locations of users and alternative POIs could be transformed as scores that are sent to the Ranking Engine.

Ranking Engine. This part produces the final alternative POIs' ranking results. We assign proper weight coefficients to the three kinds of ranking scores according to their own importance, the sum of three weight coefficients is 1. The final results are returned to users.

4   The Ranking Algorithm

The ranking algorithm of the social search in this paper is to take Searching Score, Social Score and Spatial Score into account comprehensively. Each kind of score has a different weight coefficient according to their own importance. The whole process is that users input a query like "Starbucks coffee", the ranking result is a list of POIs' names about Starbucks and coffee, the aim in our research is fast speed and accurate results. The detailed description of the algorithm is given below.

4.1 Searching Score

Searching Score means professional relevance. In this part, we first design a search engine, the purpose is that when users input a query, the ranking result is some alternative POIs according to the ranking scores of similarity. Then the searching scores are sent to Ranking Engine and the alternative POIs are sent to Social Score and Spatial Score. This part is divided into offline Inverted Index and online searching.

Offline Inverted Index. Inverted index is the core of search engine. In traditional search engines, the forward index is the "document" and the backward index is the "term". Similarly, based on our dataset, we take POIs' name, category, description as the "document" and POIs' name as the "term" to build a Inverted Index.

Online Searching. Apache Lucene is a free and open-source information retrieval software library, the search engine in this paper is designed based on it. The process is as follows. When users input a query - "Starbucks coffee", the tokenizer in the Lucene divides the phrase into "Starbucks" and "coffee". Then the similarity algorithm in Lucene is used to calculate similarity scores between the query and the "document", the scores are sorted in descending order and we pick out the searched POIs' names as the candidates. In the similarity algorithm, to improve professional relevance, we give POIs' name the highest weight, then POIs' category, finally POIs' description. The candidates are sent to Social Score and Spatial Score. The similarity scores are sent to Ranking Engine.

4.2 Social Score

Social Score means social influence. In this part, offline algorithms are used to pick out the user's some most similar friends (10, 20, 30, ...); online we extract some social features from these friends such as activity, evaluation on the alternative POIs. The purpose is to make sure that the most similar friends produce the highest-quality social scores.

Offline Algorithms. As mentioned above, social search is to find out the right people to answer questions [18]. Friends are the right people, so we use updated KNN algorithm to find out some most similar friends. Before that, to reduce the bad influence of sparse data, we use updated K-means algorithm to cluster friends to improve the data density. Because of so many data, K-means algorithm has good clustering effect among the clustering algorithms. "Check-ins" is an unique location-based data type from the Foursquare. When a user goes to a POI and feels good, he would click the "Check-In" tag, which means he has gone there once, the more "check-ins" means the higher evaluation on the POI.

We use updated K-means algorithm, the similarity metric is the vector, not the distance, so compared with Euclidean Distance, Cosine Similarity [19] is better to measure the similarity between friends. If two friends have more "check-ins" on the same POI, they are more similar. The similarity formula is given below.

$$sim(f_{i_1}, f_{i_2}) = \frac{\sum\limits_{l_j \in L} c_{f_{i_1}, l_j} c_{f_{i_2}, l_j}}{\sqrt{\sum\limits_{l_j \in L} c_{f_{i_1}, l_j}^2} \sqrt{\sum\limits_{l_j \in L} c_{f_{i_2}, l_j}^2}} \tag{1}$$

Where c_{f_i, l_j} means the number of "check-ins" a friend visited a POI; L means all the POIs.

K-means requires a certain number of clustering -k, after many experiments, we find that when k is 3, the clustering effect is best.

Algorithm 1. Updated K-means

Input: k =3, data={ f_i , l_j , c_{f_i,l_j} };

Output: $matrix(k,n)$, $matrix(m,k)$;

1.Select a friend randomly as an initial clustering center in each cluster of k ;

2.For $i=1:m$ {

3.   Calculate similarity scores between f_i and clustering center k ;

4.   Pick out the highest similarity score;

5.   If(the highest score > threshold){

6. f_i belongs to the cluster;

7.   }

8.}

9.In each cluster, take the average number of all the friends' check-ins as the clustering center, recalculate every clustering center;

10.Until the clustering centers remain stable.

We get $matrix(k, n)$ and $matrix(m, k)$. n is the number of POIs and m is the number of user's friends. $matrix(k, n)$ means clustering centers' evaluation on POIs. $matrix(m, k)$ means the similarity between friends and clustering centers.

Algorithm 2. Updated KNN

Input: $matrix(k,n)$, $matrix(m,k)$, the user's "check-ins";

Output: the user's h nearest neighbors;

1.Calculate the similarity between the user and k clustering centers and get $1 \times k$ vector, $(v_1, v_2, ..., v_k)$;

2.Calculate Euclidean Distance between the vector and $matrix(m,k)$;

3.Take h friends that get smallest distance as the user's nearest neighbors.

And the Euclidean Distance formula is given below.

$$dis(u,f_i) = \sqrt{\sum_{j=1}^{k} (sim(u, k_j) - sim(f_i, k_j))^2} \qquad (2)$$

Therefore, when the user inputs a query, the h friends could produce social influence on alternative POIs for the user.

Online Social Features. We have got alternative POIs and h nearest neighbors, then we need suitable social features to show social influence based on the "check-ins". There are two such social features: activity and evaluation.

Friends' activity can be measured by the number of "check-ins". A user's friend who has more check-ins is more active in the district, so the POIs he recommends are more believable. The activity formula is given below.

$$act(f_i) = \sum_{l_j \in L} C_{f_i, l_j} \qquad (3)$$

Where $act(f_i)$ is the number of check-ins of f_i on all the POIs in the district.

Friends' evaluation on alternative POIs can be also measured by the number of check-ins, a friend who has more check-ins on a POI means that he often goes there, so the evaluation is high. The evaluation formula is given below.

$$eva(f_i, l_j) = c_{f_i, l_j}, l_j \in CL \qquad (4)$$

Where CL means the alternative POIs.

So the social influence formula is given below.

$$social(l_j) = \sum_{i=1,j=1}^{h,x} eva(f_i, l_j) * act(f_i) \tag{5}$$

Where x is the number of candidate POIs.

4.3 Spatial Score

Users are more inclined to go to short-distance POIs, so distance is an important factor that influences ranking results. We need to calculate the distance between the locations of users and each candidate POI, the distance formula is given below.

$$dis(l_1, l_2) = R * \arccos(\sin(lat_1) * \sin(lat_2) * \cos(lon_1 - lon_2) + \cos(lat_1)\cos(lat_2)) * PI/180 \tag{6}$$

Where R is the radius of the Earth.

4.4 Ranking Engine

We have got three kinds of scores: Social Score, Searching Score and Spatial Score. To produce the final ranking result, we assign three different weight coefficients to them. The ranking formula is given below.

$$r(u, l_j) = \alpha * query(l_j) + \beta * social(l_j) + (1 - \alpha - \beta) * dis(l_j)$$
$$(\alpha + \beta) \in [0, 1]l_j \in CL \tag{7}$$

In this paper, β is the highest, α is the second, $(1 - \alpha - \beta)$ is the smallest. Because we study the social search in LBSNs, the social coefficient should be the highest to emphasize social influence. Then compared Searching Score with Spatial Score, the professional relevance is more importance. After many experiments, when $\alpha = 0.3$, $\beta = 0.61 - \alpha - \beta = 0.1$, the F1-measure in Sect. 5 has the best result, which means the best effectiveness. To calculate simply and accurately, we do normalization on the three kinds of scores.

5   Evaluation

We perform a set of experiments on the real-world data to validate our proposed algorithm. The dataset is sampled from Foursquare, a popular LBSN across the world. We select the dataset in the New York by matching the timezone, there are 413,989 check-ins, 4,741 users, 56,868 POIs and 128892 social links. The data sparsity is 1.07%.

Evaluating the search results is a great challenge since relevance judgments can only be assessed by the searchers themselves, especially in the social search context. We divide all the users into the training set and the test set by 10-fold cross-validation, then we selected a group of volunteers from the tested users randomly to help us initiate 500 queries and manually judge the Top-10, 20, 30 searching results obtained from four methods: traditional KNN search, which does not contain clustering friends, Searching

Score and Spatial Score (Method1); traditional KNN search based on clustering friends, which does not contain Searching Score and Spatial Score (Method2); KNN search based on clustering friends, which does not contain Spatial Score (Method3); the ranking algorithm in this paper (Method4). We use Method1 as the baseline.

For the purpose of evaluation, we use precision, recall and F1-Measure [20] as the effectiveness metric (Top-N ranking POIs, N = 10, 20, 30). The comparison results are presented in Figs. 2, 3 and 4. We can see that, our ranking algorithm (Method4) is better than other three methods. Method2 is better than Method1, which means that improving data density by clustering users' friends is effective, and friends are the right people in the research of social search. Method3 is better than Method2, which means that professional relevance (Searching Score) is also an important factor in enhancing the accuracy of searching results. And our ranking algorithm is the best, which means taking Social Score, Searching Score and Spatial Score into account comprehensively is suitable to be applied in the social search in LBSNs.

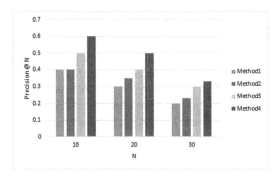

Fig. 2. This is the figure displaying the Precision of Top-N (N = 10, 20, 30)

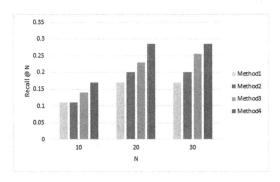

Fig. 3. This is the figure displaying the Recall of Top-N (N = 10, 20, 30)

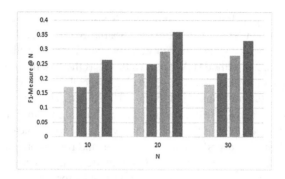

Fig. 4. This is the figure displaying the F1-Measure of Top-N (N = 10, 20, 30)

6   Conclusion and Future Work

In this paper, we propose a social search model for LBSNs. To produce high-quality searching results quickly, a novel ranking algorithm that considers Social Score, Searching Score and Spatial Score comprehensively is proposed. Meanwhile, to solve the problem of sparse data from heterogeneous networks, considering the offline and online mechanism of traditional search engines, we creatively enhance the density by clustering users' friends off the line, which reduces the influence on the accuracy while online searching. We have performed experiment on the real-world data collected from a popular LBSN across the world. The experiment results demonstrate the effectiveness of our ranking algorithm.

In fact, there are still a lot of optimizable opportunities to explore in our work. Firstly, we can get other data types, in addition to the "check-ins", users would write comments on the POIs that they have visited, although compared with the "check-ins", the data of comments is much sparser, which still produces some influence on social part. Secondly, semantic analysis could be used in calculating the similarity between the query and the "document" in the Inverted Index to improve the accuracy. Thirdly, how to run the ranking algorithm at a low time and memory cost are worth further analyzing for future research.

Acknowledgments. This work is supported by National Natural Science Foundation of China (61272531, 61202449, 61272054, 61370207, 61370208, 61300024, 61320106007 and 61472081), China high technology 863 program (2013AA013503), Jiangsu Technology Planning Program (SBY2014021039-10), Jiangsu Provincial Key Laboratory of Network and Information Security under Grant No. BM2003201 and Key Laboratory of Computer Network and Information Integration of Ministry of Education of China under Grant No. 93k-9.

References

1. Andris, C.: LBSN data and the social butterfly effect (vision paper). In: Proceedings of the 8th ACM SIGSPATIAL International Workshop on Location-Based Social Networks. ACM (2015)
2. Irfan, R., et al.: Survey on social networking services. IET Netw. **2**(4), 224–234 (2013)
3. Freyne, J., Smyth, B.: An experiment in social search. In: Bra, P.M.E., Nejdl, W. (eds.) AH 2004. LNCS, vol. 3137, pp. 95–103. Springer, Heidelberg (2004). doi:10.1007/978-3-540-27780-4_13
4. Khan, Z.C., Mashiane, T.: An analysis of Facebook's graph search. In: Information Security for South Africa (ISSA). IEEE (2014)
5. Evans, B.M., Chi, E.H.: Towards a model of understanding social search. In: Proceedings of the 2008 ACM Conference on Computer Supported Cooperative Work. ACM (2008)
6. Smyth, B., Briggs, P., Coyle, M., O'Mahony, M.: Google shared. A case-study in social search. In: Houben, G.-J., McCalla, G., Pianesi, F., Zancanaro, M. (eds.) UMAP 2009. LNCS, vol. 5535, pp. 283–294. Springer, Heidelberg (2009). doi:10.1007/978-3-642-02247-0_27
7. McNally, K., O'Mahony, M.P., Coyle, M., Briggs, P., Smyth, B.: A case study of collaboration and reputation in social web search. ACM Trans. Intell. Syst. Technol. (TIST) **3**(1), 4 (2011)
8. Bouadjenek, M.R., Hacid, H., Bouzeghoub, M.: LAICOS: an open source platform for personalized social web search. In: Proceedings of the 19th ACM SIGKDD International Conference on Knowledge Discovery and Data Mining, pp. 1446–1449. ACM (2013)
9. Horowitz, D., Kamvar, S.D.: The anatomy of a large-scale social search engine. In: Proceedings of the 19th International Conference on World Wide Web, pp. 431–440. ACM (2010)
10. Sharma, D., Alam, A.K.Z., Dasgupta, P., Saha, D.: A ranking algorithm for online social network search. In: Proceedings of the 6th ACM India Computing Convention, p. 17. ACM (2013)
11. Bao, S., Xue, G., Wu, X., Yu, Y., Fei, B., Su, Z.: Optimizing web search using social annotations. In: Proceedings of the 16th International Conference on World Wide Web, pp. 501–510. ACM (2007)
12. Guo, L., Que, X., Cui, Y., Wang, W., Cheng, S.: A hybrid social search model based on the user's online social networks. In: 2012 IEEE 2nd International Conference on Cloud Computing and Intelligent Systems (CCIS), vol. 2, pp. 553–558. IEEE (2012)
13. Hu, H., Feng, J., Liu, S., Zhu, X.: Social-Aware KNN search in location-based social networks. In: Li, F., Li, G., Hwang, S., Yao, B., Zhang, Z. (eds.) WAIM 2014. LNCS, vol. 8485, pp. 242–254. Springer, Cham (2014). doi:10.1007/978-3-319-08010-9_27
14. Yuan, Y., Lian, X., Chen, L., Sun, Y., Wang, G.: RS k NN: k NN search on road networks by incorporating social influence. IEEE Trans. Knowl. Data Eng. **28**(6), 1575–1588 (2016)
15. Hatcher, E., Gospodnetic, O.: Lucene in action (2004)
16. Inverted Index. https://en.wikipedia.org/wiki/Inverted_index
17. Liu, F., Lee, H.J.: Use of social network information to enhance collaborative filtering performance. Expert Syst. Appl. **37**(7), 4772–4778 (2010)
18. Chi, E.H.: Information seeking can be social. Computer **3**, 42–46 (2009)
19. Ye, M., et al.: Exploiting geographical influence for collaborative point-of-interest recommendation. In: Proceedings of the 34th International ACM SIGIR Conference on Research and Development in Information Retrieval. ACM (2011)
20. Precision, Recall, F1-measure. https://en.wikipedia.org/wiki/Precision_and_recall

Services Computing for Big Data: Challenges and Opportunities

Gang Huang[✉]

Key Lab of High-Confidence Software Technologies, MoE, China, Peking University,
No.5, Yiheyuan Road, Haidian District, Beijing 100871, China
hg@pku.edu.cn

Abstract. In the era of Big Data, data becomes a type of resource like the material and energy. However, a huge volume of deep data resides in the billions of information islands whose data cannot be open to the third parties easily and naturally. In this keynote, we discuss why and how Services Computing can be the silver bullet to the grand challenge of opening and sharing such deep data.

Keywords: Big data · Services computing · Client-Cloud Convergence

1   Information Island Crisis in the Era of Big Data

In the era of big data, data becomes a type of resource like the material and energy. There are many types and sources of data while the main body is in the billions of IT systems connected by the Internet. The well known data in the Internet is the surface data from the World Wide Web, which is information centric, and can be retrieved by standard web crawlers or search engines such as Google, Baidu, Bing, etc. Till June 2016, it is reported that there have been 4.5+ million web sites with 200+ billion web pages. However, such surface data accounts for very small portion of all data that resides on the Web, because so much data can be fetched only in a "service-oriented" way. Such data is stored deeply in enterprise information systems, desktop applications, mobile apps and embedded systems. These systems use some private technologies and do not follow the standard web technologies. As a result, they cannot be accessed via crawlers.

Indeed, deep data is the core competitive advantage of big data. However, collecting deep data is quite challenging because of the information islands, which cannot open their internal data, functions and workflows in an intuitive and easy way.

Opening the information islands raises various challenging issues. Typically, a Web system consists of three tiers, back-end DB, application logic that can be hosted by middleware, and the front-end applications. Considering the type of front-end, there can be three types, i.e., Client/Server, Browser/Server, and App/Server. To collect the deep data and enable the connection between information islands, various specific or ad-hoc solutions for different levels and scenarios have been proposed. Typical technologies include DB exporter/importer,

© ICST Institute for Computer Sciences, Social Informatics and Telecommunications Engineering 2017
S. Wang and A. Zhou (Eds.): CollaborateCom 2016, LNICST 201, pp. 690–696, 2017.
DOI: 10.1007/978-3-319-59288-6_69

crawler, refactoring, package interception on network, and so on. However, these solutions are quite ad-hoc, and heavily depend on the application infrastructure, e.g., hardware, OS, security policies. As a result, they are of high difficulty, risk, and cost, but error-prone and difficult-to-generalize.

2 Services Computing: The Silver Bullet for Opening Information Island

Given the urgent requirements of collecting deep data, it calls for promising and feasible solutions to address the information island crisis. Essentially, connecting the information islands indicates the deep and on-demand resource sharing. In the US NSF "Grand-Challenge" Project (2008–2012), tens of professors from Stanford, UC Berkeley, and so on, proposed the programmable open mobile Internet (POMI). McKeown *et al.* proposed the concept of *"Software-Defined Network"* along with software APIs to decompose the management of network hardware and connect isolated hardware and share network resources [1], and finally promotes the emergence and popularity of SDN as well as its related huge industry. Such a success exactly brings "silver bullet" to open the hardware islands of computer networks.

However, compared to the hardware, opening the software islands is more complex. Google In-App search can search some app contents only when those apps implement some pre-defined interfaces, but such manually re-engineered approach is infeasible to the millions of apps in Google Play today. Besides the pre-defined interfaces approach, Apple iOS spotlight can search the data preloaded by apps but such cached data is always out-of-time and partial if the apps are seldom opened by the user. Still in the POMI project, Klemmer *et al.* [2] proposed *"Design Pattern Mining"* to open and share dynamic Web data. More specifically, they create APIs and make record-and-replay to recover the structure as well as the associated data.

Indeed, these preceding work has made the preliminary efforts to open information islands. Essentially, we can infer that such an **API-based** solution can be a promising way, **which is the core of services computing**. Services computing is one of the most important computing paradigms for the Internet computing environment. From software system perspective, services computing aims to build software application systems by connecting various independently developed services, or more specifically, APIs, and thus enables the dynamic and flexible adaptation to the emergent requirements.

Indeed, services computing faces a long-term debates of the unsuccessful and unexpected adoption of Web services technologies such as SOAP, WSDL, and UDDI. However, services computing itself is not limited to the underlying technologies and platforms, but provides a programing paradigm to establish the ubiquitous and pervasive fabric and realize the interoperability between isolated "building blocks" [3].

3   Our Research Practice: Client-Cloud Convergence

We position services computing as a "Silver Bullet" to open the information islands. In the past ten years, our research group in Peking University, has made a systematic solution in this direction. Due to page limit, we then summarize the efforts as follows.

3.1   Deep Control of Web Pages

The first effort of our silver bullet is to control the web pages for opening information islands. To this end, we choose the services mashups as the target application. Services mashups essentially integrate data from multiple sources such as web pages and web services. To enable services mashup, the first research question is that very few services mashup components can be found on the Internet. In our opinion, the web pages can provide a large amount of "deep" data, but without APIs.

To open the web pages, we try to encapsulate any web page as a web mashup component which can expose any data from a web page. We propose the service component model that can parse a web page and extract any data from the page [4]. By our service component model, we can open any data from a web page and release it as an API (service interface actually). Based on such a model, we further implement a browser-based runtime to enable the flexible interaction between every single "componentized" web pages.

3.2   Deep Control of Web Browser

The second part of our silver bullet is that we control the web browser for opening information islands. Web browser plays as the runtime infrastructure of web pages, and thus controls the behavior of web pages such as requesting data from servers, parsing the data, and rendering them on visualized UI. To further support the web pages that do not well comply with our service component model, we choose to control the web browser, which is the runtime of web pages, and enable data extraction. We make an in-depth study of the popular Chrome web browser (10 + Million LoC) and perform model checking of its runtime behavior for understanding the whole browser-based services mashups. More specifically, we redefine the security mechanisms of standard web, i.e., sand-box and single-origin, so that they can interact with each other. It should be noted that, such a solution essentially plays as the similar role of HTML5 *postmessage()*, but our idea was drawn three years earlier.

3.3   Deep Control of Browser/Server Interaction

We then control the interaction between web browser and web server for opening information islands. In practice, it is well known that loading web pages is quite slow, and the situation becomes even worse for services mashups. We then focus on whether standard Browser/Server interactions unfit services mashup. To this end, we find the imperfectness of current web cache, and redefine the cache mechanism with fine-grained service interfaces as well as the underlying browser facility, so that developers can easily control the cache strategies of HTTP and HTML. In this way, the cache performance can be improved with 58% [5].

Additionally, rich services mashups not only suffer from slow page load, but further cannot work well on mobile devices such as smartphones. For example, Chess games, 3D Graphics, RPGs related mashups have severely poor user experiences. Hence, we control and save web-page-based services mashups with less computing resources and energy. To this end, we propose the first approach to leveraging the cloud-side resources and making the H5 programs offloading from mobile browser to cloud. We use very advanced techniques to analyze the constraints of JavaScript programs, partition the code, and offload those computation-intensive code to cloud. With our approach, we gain 49x page load time improvement and 92% energy saving [6].

3.4 Client-Cloud Convergence

These preceding efforts, indeed, provide the preliminary foundations to enable the opening and sharing data from isolated information islands. To further synthesize these results, we propose a vision, namely Client-Cloud-Convergence [7], which means any part of data, computation, control flow, and even user interaction can be on demand distributed, executed and collaborated in any devices and clouds.

We extend the classical Model-View-Controller programming model with a new Service element so that the Browser/Server applications, the Client/Server applications and the mobile App/Server applications can be smoothly transformed to service oriented applications. We name such a systematic support as SM@RT, which is not limited to web systems. For example, we re-implement the SM@RT approach in Java systems. This model helps to automatically analyze the Java bytecode and offload the computation-intensive code to the cloud, re-direct the Java invocation, and finally reduce the execution time and battery energy consumption of the Android apps drastically [8].

3.5 Summary

In a short summary, our 10 years research makes substantial breakthrough of opening the deep data of all C/S, B/S, and A/S in current networked software architecture, as illustrated in Fig. 1. The core idea is to automatically analyze the executable code (rather than source code) and runtime data of legacy systems, and then automatically generate a Service-Model-View-Controller (SMVC) model instance which is causally connected with the running legacy system. The causal connection means any runtime change of the legacy system will immediately lead to the corresponding change in the SMVC model, and vice versa. The SMVC model instance exposes a set of Application Programming Interfaces to

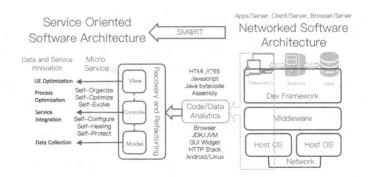

Fig. 1. Technical architecture for Client-Cloud Convergence

the third parties, so that the data, function and workflow of the legacy systems can be read and written in an open and real-time manner.

4   Our Industrial Practice: The YanCloud System

Beyond the academia results, we also develop our commercial system, called Yan-Cloud for Data-as-a-Service, as illustrated in Fig. 2, and gain various successful applications in real-world industrial practices.

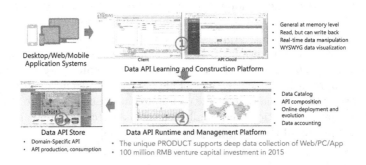

Fig. 2. YanCloud for data as a service

More specifically, the YanCloud consists of three major parts. The first is the Data API Learning and Construction Platform, which can generate data access interfaces of the given Desktop/Web/Mobile Application Systems. The second is Data API Runtime and Management Platform, which hosts and executes the SMVC model instance. The third is Data API Store, which is similar with mobile App Store but the App is "de-assembled" to APIs. With YanCloud DaaS, one can generate, deploy, operate, manage, buy, or sell APIs of any legacy systems.

In the past one year, YanCloud DaaS has been successfully applied in more than 500 systems covering e-Government, Smart City, education, finance, power-grid in 23 provinces across China. Compared to the traditional data collection solutions of our partners, including Digital China and other Top 100 software companies in China, YanCloud improves the engineering efficiency by 100 times while saves the labor cost by 90% on average. Since more and more deep data can be collected by YanCloud, we build up an API store for sharing and crowdsourcing of data, algorithms, applications and stakeholders, so that the entrepreneur based on big data becomes possible. In particular, we recently focus on a killer application of YanCloud DaaS, enabling emergent cooperation among mobile APPs. Recall that, YanCloud can open the data, functions and workflows of mobile apps. As a result, we can search and use the data and functions internal of mobile apps. We can also sense the user behavior of a mobile app and then recommend the data and functions of the other apps. In other words, the data and functions of a mobile app can cooperate with those of other mobile apps in an emergent fashion.

5   Future Outlook

Compared to the Web, the wide adoption of mobile apps have created much larger opportunities and challenges for opening the isolated information islands. The inter-organization deep-data sharing in Demand-Side Platform allows the data related to the advertisement to bid among mobile apps. Much more data can be shared through APIs in a situational way, which brings the phenomenon of API economy. For example, everyday there are billions of API requests of Google and Facebook, rather than their mobile apps. Obviously, compared to the manner of sharing the data as a static data set, sharing the data via APIs will be the best-of-the-breed. We believe the API economy will be one of the most important business models of big data.

However, in the context of API-economy and big data, services computing plays as fundamental "fabric". The era has changed, but some essences stay. We still need services description, discovery, invocation, and composition, but calls for entirely new technologies. We shall focus more on API economy by services computing, e.g., API generation and specification, API management, API operation, and API composition for situational requirements. In that sense, services computing will play a very important role in API economy and has unique values to the era of big data.

Acknowledgments. This work was supported by the High-Tech Research and Development Program of China under Grant No.2015AA01A203, and National Natural Science Foundation of China under Grant No.61421091, 61370020, 61528201. The author would like to thank colleagues from the System Research Lab in the Institute of Software, Peking University, and the supports from "Peking University-Digit China" Collaborative Innovation Center.

References

1. Martn, C., Michael, J.F., Justin, P., Jianying, L., Natasha, G., Nick, M., Scott, S.: Rethinking enterprise network control. IEEE/ACM Trans. Netw. **17**(4), 1270–1283 (2009)
2. Ranjitha K., Arvind S., Csar T., Maxine L., Salman A., Scott R. K., Jerry O.T.: Webzeitgeist: Design Mining the Web. In: 2013 ACM SIGCHI Conference on Human Factors in Computing Systems, pp. 3083–3092. ACM, New York (2013)
3. Qiao, X.Q., Chen, J.L., Tan, W., Schahram, D.: Service provisioning in content-centric networking: challenges, opportunities, and promising directions. IEEE Internet Comput. **20**(2), 26–33 (2016)
4. Liu, X.Z., Huang, G., Zhao, Q., Mei, H., Blake, M.B.: iMashup: a Mashup-based framework for service composition. Sci. China Inf. Sci. **57**(1), 1–20 (2014)
5. Liu, X.Z., Ma, Y., Liu, Y.X., Xie, T., Huang, G.: Demystifying the imperfect client-side cache performance of mobile web browsing. IEEE Trans. Mob. Comput. **15**(9), 2206–2220 (2016)
6. Wang, X.D., Liu, X.Z., Zhang, Y., Huang, G.: Migration and execution of JavaScript applications between mobile devices and cloud. In: Conference on Systems. Programming, and Applications: Software for Humanity, pp. 83–84. ACM, New York (2012)
7. Huang, G., Liu, X.Z., Ma, Y., Lu, X., Zhang, Y., Xiong, Y.F.: Programming situational mobile web applications with cloud-mobile convergence: an internetware-oriented approach. IEEE Trans. Serv. Comput. (to appear)
8. Zhang, Y., Huang, G., Liu, X.Z., Zhang, W., Mei, H., Yang, S.X.: Refactoring android Java code for on-demand computation offloading. In: 27th Annual ACM SIGPLAN Conference on Object-Oriented Programming, Systems, Languages, and Applications, pp. 233–248. ACM, New York (2012)

Author Index